西 潮

蔣夢麟 著

TIDES FROM THE WEST

A

CHINESE AUTOBIOGRAPHY

BY

CHIANG MONLIN

商務印書館

西潮　TIDES FROM THE WEST: A CHINESE AUTOBIOGRAPHY

作　　者：蔣夢麟

譯　　者：蔣夢麟

責任編輯：何阿三

封面設計：黃鑫浩

出　　版：商務印書館（香港）有限公司

　　　　　香港筲箕灣耀興道 3 號東 廣場 8 樓

　　　　　http://www.commercialpress.com.hk

發　　行：香港聯合書刊物流有限公司

　　　　　香港新界大埔汀麗路 36 號中華商務印刷大廈 3 字樓

印　　刷：美雅印刷製本有限公司

　　　　　九龍觀塘榮業街 6 號海濱工業大廈 4 樓 A

版　　次：2020 年 6 月第 1 版第 1 次印刷

　　　　　© 2020 商務印書館（香港）有限公司

　　　　　ISBN 978 962 07 5852 2

　　　　　Printed in Hong Kong

目錄

CONTENTS

序

　　這是一本充滿了智慧的書。這裏面所包含晶瑩的智慧，不只是從學問的研究得來，更是從生活的體驗得來。

　　讀這本書好像是泛舟在時間的洪流之中，一重一重世間的層巒疊嶂、激湍奔濤，都在我們民族和個人的生命中經過。而且這段時間乃是歷史上一個極不平凡時代的新序幕，舉凡人類中各個集團的衝突，乃至東西文化的蕩磨，都集中在這風雲際會。

　　時代的轉變愈快，被人們忽略的史實愈多。若當時的人不予以記載，則後起的人更無從知道，無從了解。這種忽略和遺忘都是人類很大的損失，因為在不斷的歷史的過程中間，以往的經驗，正是後來的教訓。

　　了解這種意義，才能認識蔣夢麟先生這本書所蘊藏的價值。他生長在這極不平凡時代已經過了 70 年。他從中國學究的私塾到西洋自由的學府；從古老的農村社會到近代的都市文明；從身經滿清專制的皇朝到接受革命思想的洗禮；他多年生活在廣大的外國人羣裏面；更不斷生活在廣大中國人羣尤其是知識青年羣眾裏面。他置身於中西文化思想交流的漩渦，同時也看遍了覆雨翻雲、滄海桑田的世局。經過了七十年華，正是他智慧結晶的時候，到此時而寫他富有哲學內涵和人生風趣的回憶，其所反映的決不是他的一生，而是他一生所經歷的時代。

《西潮》這本書裏面每一片段都含有對於社會和人生的透視。古人所謂「小中見大」正可於此中求之。其將東西文化相提並論之處，尤其可以發人深省。著者好舉平凡的故事，間雜以微妙而不傷人的諷刺，真使我們感受到一股敦厚淳樸的風味。這種風味在當今是不容易嚐到的了。至於其中的妙語妙喻，不斷的流露，正像珍珠泉的泉水，有如粒粒的明珠，連串的噴了上來。

這本書最難達到的境界，就是著者講這個極不平凡時代的事實，而以極平易近人的口吻寫出來，這正像孟鄰先生做人處世的態度。若不是具備高度文化的修養，真是望塵莫及的。我何敢序孟鄰先生的大著，只能引王荊公兩句詩以形容他的寫作和生平。詩云：「看似平常最奇絕，成如容易卻艱難。」

羅家倫

1959 年 12 月 6 日

PREFACE

This volume will try to tell the story of what has happened in China during the last hundred years, from the cession of Hong Kong in 1842 to the blitzkrieg of Pearl Harbor in 1941, with emphasis on the latter half of that period. A century is a long time, but of China's more than four thousand years of history it is but a small fraction, less than one fortieth. Yet the change China has gone through in that brief span is unprecedented in her long life. And now more rapid changes on a still larger scale are about to take place.

Since the first exchange of gunfire at Marco Polo Bridge the attention of the world has been drawn to China. The heroic resistance at Shanghai, Taierchuan, and Changsha has evoked sympathy and admiration in the hearts of millions of China's friends throughout the world. The part China is destined to play in the affairs of nations will be of great interest to the world in the period before us. She has been appraised somewhat too high by her well-wishers and somewhat too low by those who do not know her. In either case the interest is there and the fact remains that she has fought almost singlehanded, for eight long, suffering years, a strong enemy sustained by religious-patriotic fanaticism, superior weapons, and efficient organization.

Neither by her friends nor by her own efforts could China be lifted overnight to the level of modern industrialized democracies; nor could she be exterminated by her enemies in a few years or even a few centuries. In the time ahead of us she will become a focus of attention for the world, since future peace—at least one of the major factors of peace—will depend much on a prosperous and strong China.

How is this great country to be made prosperous and strong? The problem must be solved by herself alone. Effective co-operation of friendly Powers will accelerate her success, but she alone must bear the responsibility of making herself worthy to be a leading partner of peace in the world.

China is a nation neither of angels nor of incompetents; she is a nation of common mortals with feelings, ideas, love and hate, hopes and despair, beauty and ugliness, accomplishments and failings, virtues and vices. It is hoped that the world will not expect from her people more than it does from other ordinary human beings. She has no panacea for all her troubles, nor any magic box by aid of which she can transform herself at will into what she desires to be. Whatever success she has achieved has been paid for with sweat in time of peace and with blood in time of war.

To the question "What is the trouble with China?" the author can only answer that there are a number of troubles waiting for solution in that vast country of teeming millions, more than she will be able to solve in any limited span of time. Some were created by enemies who tried to conquer her, others by herself during the time of metamorphosis; still others have been imposed on her by force of circumstance or as legacies of the past. Some of the more difficult problems have been solved or partially solved during recent years before the war; many others remain to be dealt with in due course of time.

Looking back over the last fifty years which he has personally experienced—over the past hundred years with which he is familiar, and even farther, down the long reaches of China's history which he has been taught—the author has traced to the best of his knowledge the threads of a number of problems, some lying deep in her past, others arising from the rapid changes which caught her unprepared. He has tried to tell, within the limits of discretion, what has happened in China, especially during the last fifty years. For those friends who desire to co-operate with her, with a view to solving some of the difficult problems of a more enduring peace, this moderate volume may be helpful in giving an insight into the life and problems of the Chinese people. For co-operation cannot possibly proceed without mutual understanding. To understand what is actually the background—the mental, emotional, and moral constitution—of the country, is essential for a lasting co-operation.

With the above ideas in mind the author has described ordinary happenings in some detail so as to acquaint the reader in some measure of intimacy with the mental, emotional, and moral make-up of the Chinese people as revealed through their life in peace and war. As small things often reflect major developments in a country, it is hoped that some sense of the meaning of greater events may be gathered from these apparent trifles of daily life.

Chiang Mon-lin
Chongqing, 1943

作者序

　　《西潮》裏所談的是中國過去 100 年間所發生的故事，從 1842 年香港割讓起到 1941 年珍珠港事變止，尤其着重後 50 年間的事。一個世紀是相當長的一段時間，但是在 4,000 多年的中國歷史裏，卻只是短暫的一個片段，幾乎不到四十分之一。不過中國在這段短短的時間內所經歷的變遷，在她悠久的生命史上卻是空前的，而且更大規模的變化還正在醞釀中。

　　自從蘆溝橋的槍聲劃破長空，中國的局勢已經引起全世界人士的注意。國軍在淞滬、台兒莊以及長沙的英勇戰績，已經贏得全球中國友人的同情與欽敬。在未來的歲月中，中國勢將在國際舞台上擔任眾所矚目的角色。這些年來，愛護中國的人士未免把她估計得太高，不了解中國的人士則又把她估計得太低。無論是估計過高或過低，對中國的關切是一致的；而她幾乎孤立無援地苦戰八年之久，也是無可否認的事實。在這漫長痛苦的八年中，她與具有優越的武器、嚴密的組織以及宗教的愛國狂熱的強敵相週旋，愈戰愈奮，始終不屈。

　　不論是本身的努力，或者友邦的援助，都不能使中國在旦夕之間達到現代工業化民主國家的水準；但是她的敵人也不可能在幾年之內，甚至幾百年之內，滅亡她。在未來的歲月中，中國將是舉世人士注意力的焦點，因為未來的和平與中國之能否臻於富強是息息相關的。

中國怎樣才能臻於富強呢？這個問題必須由她自己單獨來解決。友邦的密切合作固然可以加速她的成功，但是她必須獨立擔負起使自己成為世界和平支柱的責任。

中國既不是一個天神般萬能的國家，也不是一個低能的毫無作為的國家。她是一羣有感情、有思想的凡人結合而成的國家。他們有愛、有恨；有美、有醜；有善、有惡；有成就、有失敗；有時充滿希望，有時陷於絕望。他們只是一羣平平常常的人，世界人士不能對他們有分外的要求和期望。中國沒有解決一切困難的萬應靈丹，也沒有隨心所欲脫胎換骨的魔術。如果她已經有所成就的話，那也是平時以汗，戰時以血換來的。

如果有人問：「中國的問題究竟在哪裏？」作者只能答覆：中國正有無數的問題等待 4 億 5,000 萬人民去解決，而且不是任何短時間內所能解決。有些問題是企圖征服她的敵人造成的，有些則是蛻變過程中她本身所製造的；另有一些問題是客觀環境引起的，也有一些問題則是歷史的包袱，有一些比較困難的問題已經在戰前幾年內解決，或者局部解決，更有許多問題則尚待分別緩急，逐一解決。

回顧作者身經目睹過去的 50 年，以及作者所熟悉過去的 100 年，甚至追溯到作者所研習過的中國的悠久歷史，作者已經就其所知探求出若干問題的線索，有些問題深深植根於過去，有些則由急劇的變化所引起。作者已經力求平直客觀地陳述中國過去所發生的變遷，尤其是過去 50 年內所發生的事情。對於願意與中國合作，共同解決妨礙持久和平的若干問題的國際友人，本書或可提供一點資料，幫助他們了解中國人民的生活與問題。合作是勉強不來的，必須彼此相互了解，然後才能合作。欲謀持久的合作，必須先對一國的真實背景有所了解，包括心理、情感以及道德等各方面。

因此，作者對於日常瑣事也往往不厭其詳地加以描寫，希望藉此使讀者對中國人民在戰時與平時所反映的心理、情感和道德等，能有比較親切的認識，日常瑣事往往可以反映一個國家的重大變遷，希望讀者多少能從作者所記述的身邊瑣事中，發現重大史實的意義。

蔣夢麟

1943 年於重慶

前言：邊城昆明

炸彈像冰雹一樣從天空掉下，在我們周圍爆炸，處身在這樣的一次世界大動亂中，我們不禁要問：這些可怕的事情究竟為甚麼會發生呢？

過去幾十年內世界上所發生的事情自然不是從天上掉下來的。任何事情都有它的起因。本書的大部分內容是二次大戰將結束時在昆明寫的，當我們暫時忘掉現實環境而陷入沉思時，我常常發現一件事情如何導致另一件事情，以及相伴而生的政治、社會變化。昆明是滇緬公路的終點，俯瞰着平靜的昆明湖，城中到處是敵機轟炸後的斷垣殘壁，很像龐貝古城的遺跡。我在這邊城裏冥想過去的一切，生平所經歷的事情像夢境一樣一幕一幕地展現在眼前；於是我撿出紙筆，記下了過去半世紀中我親眼目睹的祖國生活中的急劇變化。

當我開始寫《西潮》的故事時，載運軍火的卡車正從緬甸源源駛抵昆明，以「飛虎隊」聞名於世的美國志願航空隊戰鬥機在我們頭上軋軋掠過。成百上千發國難財的商人和以「帶黃魚」起家的卡車司機徜徉街頭，口袋裏裝滿了鈔票。物價則一日三跳，有如脫韁的野馬。

一位英國朋友對西南聯大的一位教授說，我們應該在戰事初起時就好好控制物價。這位教授帶點幽默地回答說：「是呀！等下一次戰爭時，我們大概就不會這樣笨了。」這位教授說：如果他有資本，他或許早已學一位古希臘哲學家的榜樣了。據說那位希臘哲學家預料橄欖將欠收而囤積了一大批橄欖。後來橄欖果然收成不好，這位哲學家也就發了大財。可惜我們的教授既沒有資本，也沒有那種未卜先知的本領，而且他的愛國心也不容許他幹損人利己的勾當。

珍珠港事變以後，同盟國節節失利。香港、馬來聯邦和新加坡相繼陷落，敵軍繼續向緬甸推進。中國趕派軍隊馳援印緬戰區，經激戰後撤至緬北的叢林澤地，有時還不得不靠香蕉樹根充飢。尤其使他們寢食難安的是從樹上落到他們身上的水蛭，這些吸血鬼鑽到你的皮下，不動聲色地吸走了你的血液。你如果想用力把它拉出來，它就老實不客氣連肉帶血銜走一口。對付這些吸血鬼最好的辦法是在它們身上擦鹽，但是在叢林裏卻又找不到鹽。在這種環境下，唯一的辦法是用手死勁去拍，拍得它們放口為止。

成千成萬的緬甸華僑沿着滇緬公路撤退回中國。敵機沿途轟炸他們，用機槍掃射他們，三千男女老幼就這樣慘死在途中。難民像潮水一樣沿滇緬公路湧入昆明。街頭擁滿了家破人亡的苦難人民，許多公共建築被指定為臨時收容所。經過兩三個月以後，他們才逐漸疏散到鄰近省份，許多人則直接回到福建和廣東老家。

8萬左右的農民以及男女老幼，胼手胝足建築成功的滇緬公路現在已經因另一端被切斷而告癱瘓。一度曾為國際交通孔道的昆明現在也成為孤城，旅客只有坐飛機才能去印度。25萬人加工趕築的滇緬鐵路，原來預定12個月內完成，但是部分築成以後也因戰局逆轉而中止了。中國已與世界各地隔絕，敵人從三方包圍着她，只有涓涓滴滴的外來補給靠越過世界駝峰的空運在維持着。中國就在這種孤立無援的窘境中堅持到底，寸土必爭，直到戰事結束為止。

我們且把近代歷史暫時擱在一邊，讓我們回顧一下過去，看看能否從歷史中找出一點教訓。

（原載《傳記文學》第十七卷第六期）

PROLOGUE: FRONTIER CITY

During a world upheaval with bombs dropping from the sky and bursting all around, one is apt to wonder what caused these terrible things to happen.

What has happened in the world in the last decade is not something that merely dropped from the sky. Events have their causes. In the last years of the war, as I cast my mental view beyond the horizons of Kunming, where most of this volume was written, I saw how one event had led to another, with consequent social and political changes. Musing over the past in that scenic city on the Burma Road overlooking tranquil, historic Kunming Lake, with bomb-shattered houses standing around me like the remnants of Pompeii, the scenes of what had happened during my lifetime unfolded themselves like a dream clearly and vividly before me; and I set pen to paper to put down what I had seen with my own eyes during the last half century of rapid change in the life of my country.

As I began to write we were in the midst of heavy munitions traffic coming in by truck from Burma. The fighting planes of the American Volunteer Group known as the "Flying Tigers" droned over our heads. War profiteers and truck drivers roamed the streets by hundreds and thousands with their pockets full of bank notes, while the price of commodities soared sky-high.

A British friend remarked to a professor of our university that we ought to have controlled prices at the beginning of the war. "Well," said the professor with a tinge of humor, "we will know better in the next war." He went on to remark that if he had had the capital he might have followed the example of the Greek philosopher who cornered olives in ancient Greece in anticipation of a poor olive crop. When the crop failed, he was rich. But the professor had no capital and too little of that sort of foresight, and in addition, too much of patriotism in his way.

After Pearl Harbor came waves of bad news of the Allies. Hong Kong, the Malay States, and Singapore fell one after the other. The enemy headed for Burma. China rushed troops there; they retreated, after a stubborn resistance, through the mountains and swamps of Upper Burma, living on banana roots. They were greatly annoyed by the leeches that dropped on their heads from trees, suckers that hooked onto you and drank your blood. If you tried to tear one off, it carried away in its mouth a piece of your flesh. The best way of getting rid of these nasty parasites was to rub salt on them, but salt there was none. The next best way, in the circumstances, was to slap at them until they gave you up.

Chinese nationals in Burma left by tens of thousands, and made their way back to China by the Burma Road. Enemy planes bombed and machine-gunned them. Three thousand people, men and women, young and old, died on the way. A torrent of refugees flowed along the road into Kunming.Streets were crowded with thousands of distressed people and public buildings were set aside for their temporary lodging. After two or three months they gradually melted into the neighboring provinces; many went back to their native provinces of Fukien and Kwangtung.

The Burma Road, built in eight months by the hands of some eighty thousand farmers, men, women, and children, was now cut at the other end and rendered useless. Kunming, once on the high-way of international traffic, was now an isolated city, and only by air could one travel to India. The Yunnan-Burma Railway, under construction by 250,000 men, was to be finished within twelve months; it was partially built, then suspended. China was cut off from the world, with the enemy on three sides and only the faintest trickle of supplies remaining. In this isolation she held out, fighting for her national existence every inch of the way, until the end of the war.

Let us forget recent history for the moment and look back to the past to see what we can learn from it. ◉

第一部

滿清末年

第一章
西風東漸

差不多 2000 年以前，幾位東方的智者，循着天空一顆巨星的指示，追尋到一個新宗教的誕生地。這個宗教便是基督教。基督教後來在西方國家的生活中佔着極其重要的地位。基督教以和平仁愛為宗旨，要求教徒們遇到「有人掌摑你的右頰時，你就把左頰也湊過去。」基督教的教徒經過不斷的磨難和挫折，不顧羅馬猛獅的威脅和異教徒的摧殘迫害，逆來順受，終於在羅馬帝國各民族之間傳播開來了。幾百年之後，它以同樣堅忍的精神慢慢地流傳到中國。

景教徒在唐朝 (618—905) 時來到中國，唐室君主曾為他們建造了景教寺，但是景教徒的傳教成績卻很有限。再過了幾百年，在 17 世紀中葉，耶穌會教士帶着西方的天文學來到中國，終於得到明朝 (1368—1643) 皇帝的垂青。

在這同時，活力旺盛的西方民族，不但接受了新興的基督教，而且發展了科學，完成了許許多多的發明，為近代的工業革命奠立了基礎。科學和發明漸漸流傳到東方，先是涓涓滴滴地流注，接着匯為川流江濤，最後成為排山倒海的狂潮巨浪，氾濫整個東方，而且幾乎把中國沖塌了。

中國人與基督教或任何其他宗教一向沒有甚麼糾紛，不過到了 19 世紀中葉，基督教與以兵艦做靠山的商業行為結了夥，因而在中國人的心目中，這個宣揚愛人如己的宗教也就成為侵略者的工具了。人們發現一種宗教與武力形影不離時，對這種宗教的印象自然就不同了。而且中國人也實在無法不把基督教和武力脅迫相提並論。慢慢地人們產生了一種印象，認為如來佛是騎着白象到中國的，耶穌基督卻是騎在炮彈上飛過來的。

我們吃過炮彈的苦頭，因而也就對炮彈發生興趣。一旦我們學會製造炮彈，報仇雪恥的機會就來了。我們可以暫時不管這些炮彈是怎麼來的，因為對我們這些凡夫俗子而言，保全性命究竟比拯救靈魂來得重要。

歷史的發展真是離奇莫測。我們從研究炮彈而研究到機械發明；機械發明而導致政治改革；由於政治改革的需要，我們開始研究政治理論；政治理論又使我們再度接觸西方的哲學。在另一方面，我們從機械發明而發現科學，由科學進而了解科學方法和科學思想。一步一步地我們離炮彈越來越遠了，但是從另一角度來看，也可以說離炮彈越來越近了。

故事說來很長，但是都是在短短 100 年之內發生的，而且緊張熱烈的部分還不過五十年的樣子。我說 100 年，因為香港本來可以在 1942 年「慶祝」香港成為「英國領土」的 100 週年紀念，但是這也是歷史上偶然的一件事，英國的舊盟邦日本卻在前一年以閃擊戰的方式把香港搶走了。我提到香港，決不是有意挖舊瘡疤，而是因為香港在中國歐化的早期歷史上，恰恰是現成的紀念碑。大家都知道，香港這羣小島是中國在所謂「鴉片戰爭」中失敗以後在 1842 年割讓給英國的。這次戰爭的起因是中國繼禁止鴉片進口之後，又在廣州焚毀大批鴉片。鴉片是英國由印度輸出的主要貨物，於是英國就以炮彈回敬中國，中國被擊敗了。

1842 年的中英條約同時規定中國的五個沿海城市開放為商埠。這就是所謂「五口通商」。大批西方商品隨着潮湧而至。這五個商埠以差不多相似的距離散佈在比較繁盛的中國南半部，為中國造成了與外來勢力接觸的新邊疆。過去中國只有北方和西北那樣的內陸邊疆，現在中國的地圖起了變化，這轉變正是中國歷史的轉折點。

這五個商埠 —— 廣州、廈門、福州、寧波和上海 —— 由南向北互相銜接，成為西方貨品的集散地，舶來品由這五個口岸轉銷至中國最富的珠江流域和長江流域各地。

西方商人在兵艦支持之下像章魚一樣盤據着這些口岸，同時把觸鬚伸展到內地的富庶省份。中國本身對於這些滲透並不自覺，對於必然產生的後果更茫無所知。億萬人民依舊悠然自得地過着日子，像過去一樣過他們從搖籃到墳墓的生活，從沒有想到在現代化的工作上下工夫。一部分人則毫不經心地開始採用外國貨了，有的是為了實用，有的是為了享受，另一些人則純然為了好奇。

但是，西方列強的兵艦政策不但帶來了貨品和鴉片，同時也帶來了西方科學文化的種子。這在當時是看不出來的，但是後來這些種子終於發芽滋長，使中國厚蒙其利——這也是歷史上的一大諷刺。

這時候，日本也正以一日千里之勢向歐化的途程邁進，中國對此卻毫無所覺。半世紀以後，這個蕞爾島國突然在東海裏搖身一變，形成了一個碩大的怪物，並且在 1894 年出其不意地咬了東亞睡獅一大口。中國繼香港之後又丟了台灣。這隻東亞睡獅這時可真有點兒感到疼痛了，茫茫然揉着惺忪的睡眼，不知道究竟是甚麼擾了它的清夢？

我原先的計劃只是想寫下我對祖國的所見所感，但是當我讓這些心目中的景象一一展佈在紙上時，我所寫下的可就有點像自傳，有點像回憶錄，也有點像近代史。不管它像甚麼，它記錄了我心目中不可磨滅的景象，這些景象歷歷如繪地浮現在我的腦際，一如隔昨才發生的經歷。在急遽遞嬗的歷史中，我自覺只是時代巨輪上一顆小輪齒而已。🌀

第二章
鄉村生活

我出生在一個小村莊裏的小康之家。兄弟姊妹五人，我是最小的一個，三位哥哥，一位姊姊。我出生的前夕，我父親夢到一隻熊到家裏來，據說那是生男孩的徵兆。第二天，這個吉兆應驗了，託庇祖先在天之靈，我們家又添了一個兒子。

我大哥出生時，父親曾經夢到收到一束蘭花，因此我大哥就取名夢蘭。我二哥也以同樣的原因取名為夢桃。不用說，我自然取名為夢熊了。姊姊和三哥誕生時，父親卻沒有夢到甚麼。後來在我進浙江高等學堂時，為了先前的學校裏鬧了事，夢熊這個名字入了黑名單，於是就改為夢麟了。

我出生在戰亂頻仍的時代裏。我出生的那一年，英國從中國拿走了對緬甸的宗主權；出生的前一年恰恰是中法戰爭結束的一年，中國對越南的宗主權就在那一年讓渡給法國。中國把宗主權一再割讓，正是外國列強進一步侵略中國本土的序幕，因為中國之保有屬國，完全是拿它們當緩衝地帶，而不是為了剝削它們。中國從來不干涉這些邊緣國家的內政。

這情形很像一隻桔子，桔皮被剝去以後，微生物就開始往桔子內部侵蝕了。但是中國百姓卻懵然不覺，西南邊疆的戰爭隔得太遠了，它們不過是浩瀚的海洋上的一陣泡沫。鄉村裏的人更毫不關心，他們一向與外界隔絕，談狐說鬼的故事比這些軍國大事更能引起他們的興趣。但是中國的國防軍力的一部分卻就是從這些對戰爭不感興趣的鄉村徵募而來的。

我慢慢懂得一些人情世故之後，我注意到村裏的人講起太平天國革命的故事時，卻比談當前國家大事起勁多了。我們鄉間呼太平軍為長毛，因為他們蓄髮不剃頭。凡聽到有變亂的事，一概稱之為長毛造反。大約在我出生的 30 年前，我們村莊的一角曾經被太平軍破壞。一位木匠出身的蔣氏族長就參加過太平軍。人們說他當過長毛的，他自己也直認不諱。他告訴我們許多太平軍擄掠殺戮煮吃人肉的故事，許多還是他自己親身參加的。我看他的雙目發出一種怪光，我父親說，這是因為吃了人肉的緣故。我聽了這些恐怖的故事，常常為之毛骨悚然。這位族長說，太平軍裏每天要做禱告感謝天父天兄（上帝和耶穌）。有一天做禱告以後，想要討好一位老長毛，就說了幾句「天父夾天兄，長毛奪咸豐」一套吉利話。老長毛點頭稱許他。他抖了，就繼續念道：「天下打不通，仍舊還咸豐。」「媽」的一聲，刀光一閃，從他頭上掠過。從此以後，他不敢再和老長毛開玩笑了。

這樣關於長毛的故事，大家都歡喜講，歡喜聽。但是村裏的人只有偶然才提到近年來的國際戰爭，而且漠不關心。其間還有些怪誕不經的勝利，後來想起來可憐亦復可笑。事實上，中國軍隊固然在某些戰役上有過良好的表現，結果卻總是一敗塗地的。

現代發明的鋒芒還沒有到達鄉村，因而這些鄉村也就像五百年前一樣地保守、原始、寧靜。但是鄉下人卻並不閒，農人忙着耕耘、播種、收穫；漁人得在運河裏撒網捕魚；女人得紡織縫補；商人忙着買賣；工匠忙着製作精巧的成品；讀書人則高聲朗誦，默記四書五經，然後參加科舉。

中國有成千上萬這樣的村落，因為地形或氣候的關係，村莊大小和生活習慣可能稍有不同，但是使他們聚居一起的傳統、家族關係和行業卻大致相同。共同的文字、共同的生活理想、共同的文化和共同的科舉制度則使整個國家結為一體而成為大家所知道的中華帝國。（我們現在稱中華民國，在辛亥革命以前，歐美人稱我們為中華帝國。）

以上所說的那些成千成萬的村莊，加上大城市和商業中心，使全國所需要的糧食、貨品、學人、士兵，以及政府的大小官吏供應無缺。只要這些村鎮城市不接觸現代文明，中國就可以一直原封不動，如果中國能在通商口岸四周築起高牆，中國也可能再經幾百年而一成不變。但是西洋潮流卻不肯限於幾個通商口岸裏。這潮流先沖激着附近的地區，然後循着河道和公路向外伸展。五個商埠附近的，以及交通線附近的村鎮首先被沖倒。現代文明像是移植過來的樹木，很快地就在肥沃的中國土壤上發芽滋長，在短短五十年之內就深入中國內地了。

蔣村是散佈在錢塘江沿岸沖積平原上的許多村莊之一，村與村之間常是綿延一兩里的繁茂的稻田，錢塘江以風景優美聞名於世，上游有富春江的景色，江口有著名的錢塘江大潮。幾百年來，江水沿岸積留下肥沃的泥土，使兩岸逐步向杭州灣擴伸。居民就在江邊新生地上築起臨時的圍堤截留海水曬鹽。每年的鹽產量相當可觀，足以供應幾百萬人的需要。

經過若干年代以後，江岸再度向前伸展，原來曬鹽的地方鹽分漸漸消失淨盡，於是居民就在離江相當遠的地方築起堤防，保護漸趨乾燥的土地，準備在上面蓄草放牧。再過一段長時期以後，這塊土地上面就可以植棉或種桑了。要把這種土地改為稻田，也許要再過五十年。因為種稻需要大量的水，而挖池塘築圳渠來灌溉稻田是需要相當時間的，同時土地本身也需要相當時間才能慢慢變為沃土。

我童年時代的蔣村，離杭州灣約有20里之遙。圍繞着它的還有無數的村莊。大大小小，四面八方都有，往南一直到山麓，往北到海邊，往東往西則有較大的城鎮和都市，中間有旱道或河汊相通。蔣氏族譜告訴我們，我們的祖先是從徽州遷到奉化暫駐，又從奉化遷到餘姚。徽州是錢塘江的發源地，我們的祖先到餘姚來，可能就是為了開墾江邊新生地。在我幼年時，我們蔣氏家廟的前面還有古堤岸的遺跡，那家廟叫做「四勿祠」，奉祠宋朝當過御史的一位祖先，他是奉化人，名叫蔣峴。然而一般人卻慣叫「陟塘廟」，因為幾百年前，廟前橫着一條堤塘。

讀者或許要問：甚麼叫「四勿」呢？那就是《論語》裏的非禮勿視、非禮勿聽、非禮勿言、非禮勿動四句話。我們玩具店裏所看到的三隻猴子分別蒙起眼睛、耳朵、嘴巴，就是指這回事。至於為甚麼沒有第四隻猴子，因為那三隻猴子坐着不動，就可以代表了。但是我們那位御史公卻把這四勿改為「勿欺心、勿負主、勿求田、勿問舍」，人稱之為「四勿先生」。這些自古流傳下來的處世格言是很多的。我們利用一切可能的方法，諸如寺廟、戲院、家庭、玩具、格言、學校、歷史、故事等等，來灌輸道德觀念，使這些觀念成為日常生活中的習慣。以道德規範約束人民生活是中國社會得以穩定的理由之一。

幾千年以來，中國的人口從北方漸漸擴展到南方，先到長江流域，繼至珠江流域，最後到了西南山區。中華民族一再南遷的理由很多，南方土地肥沃、塞外好戰部落入侵，以及人口的自然繁殖都有關係，且從宋朝以後，黃河一再泛濫，更使人們想念江南樂土。我的祖先在早期就由北而南，由南而東，最後終於在杭州灣沿岸定居下來。

蔣姓的始祖是三千多年前受封的一位公子王孫。他的名字叫做百齡，是代周成王攝政的周公的第三個兒子。他在紀元前十二世紀末期被封在黃河流域下游的一塊小地方，他的封地叫做「蔣」，他的子孫也就以蔣為氏了。蔣是茭白古名。那塊封地之所以定名為蔣，可能是那一帶地方茭白生長得特別繁茂的緣故。

在三國時代，也就是公元第三世紀，我們的一位祖先曾在歷史上露了臉。他的名字叫蔣琬，住在長江流域南部的湘鄉，從蜀先主入蜀。諸葛亮稱他是社稷之才。這證明住在長江以南的蔣姓子孫，在第三世紀以前就從黃河流域南遷了。從我們的始祖起到現在，所有嫡系子孫的名字，在我們的族譜上都有紀錄可考。至於確實到甚麼程度，我卻不敢說，因為他們的生平事跡很少人知道，考證起來是很困難的。但相傳江南無二蔣，所以我們至少可以說一句：住在長江以南所有姓蔣的都是同宗同支的。究竟可以正確地追溯到多遠，我們可不知道了。不過我們確切知道：住在浙江省境的蔣姓子弟，都在徽州找到了共同的宗脈。

我在宗譜中從遷餘姚的始祖傳到我為第 17 世。蔣姓首先定居在我們村裏的是五百多年前來的，那是元朝末年的事。這五百多年之中，兩個朝代是外來民族建立的，一個是漢族自己的王朝，蔣姓一族曾經看到元朝的沒落、明朝和滿清的興衰，以及幾乎推翻滿清的太平天國。朝代更換了，蔣村卻依然故我，人們還是照常地過活、做工，最後入土長眠。

太平軍到了村子裏，村中曾經有幾所房子焚毀，留在村子裏的老弱有被活活燒死的，有一處大門口殘存的石階上留有紅斑，據傳說是某位老太婆在此燒死時所流的血。大多數的老百姓都逃到山裏躲起來，但是戰事一平定，大家又像蜜蜂回巢一樣回到村裏。在我童年時代，村裏還可以看到兵燹以後留下來的殘垣斷瓦。

村裏的人告訴我，滿洲人推翻明朝的消息，一直到新朝廷的聖旨到了村裏時，大家才知道。清帝聖旨到達村裏時，鄰村還正在演社戲呢！改朝換代以後，族人生活上的唯一改變是強迫留辮子，同時聖旨嚴禁男人再穿明朝式樣的衣服。大家敢怒不敢言，但是死後入殮時，男人還是穿明朝衣冠。因此我們族中流行着一句話：「男投（降）女不投，活投死不投。」就是説男人投降，女人卻不投降，活人投降，死人卻不投降。一些人一直維持這個辦法到1911 年清室覆亡、民國建立為止，中間經過 250 年之久。

我們村上只有 60 來戶人家，人口約 300 人，是個很小的村莊。它的三面環繞着河汉，南面是一條石板路，通往鄰近的村莊和城鎮。小河汊可以通到大河，再由大河可以到達杭州、蘇州和上海等大城市。

蔣村雖然小，水陸交通卻很便利。河汉上隨處是石橋，河的兩岸則滿是綠柳垂楊。河中盛產魚、蝦、鱔、鰻、龜、鱉。柳蔭之下，常有人悠閒地在垂釣。耕牛慢慢地踱着方步，繞着轉動牛車，把河水汲到水槽再送到田裏。冬天是連阡穿陌的麥穗，夏天是一片稻海，使人生四季長青之感，麥穗和稻穗隨着微風的吹拂，漾起一片漣漪，燕子就在綠波之上的藍空中穿梭翱翔。老鷹忽高忽低地繞村迴旋着，乘老母雞不備的時候就俯衝而下，攫走小雞。

這就是我童年時代的背景，也是我家族的環境。他們安定地在那裏生活了五百多年，他們很少碰到水災或旱災，在這漫長的幾百年中也不過遇上一兩次的變亂和戰爭。他們和平而滿足地生活在他們自己的世界裏，貧富之間也沒有太大的差別。富饒的稻穀、棉花、蠶絲、魚蝦、雞鴨、蔬菜使人民豐衣足食。

幾百年來，不論朝代如何更換，不論是太平盛世或戰禍頻仍，中國鄉村裏的道德、信仰和風俗習慣卻始終不變。鄉下人覺得這個世界已經很不錯，不必再求進步。生命本身也許很短暫，但是投胎轉世時可能有更大的幸福。人死以後，據說靈魂就離開肉體，轉投到初生的嬰兒身上。我自己就親眼看到過綁赴刑場處決的罪犯，對圍觀的羣眾高喊：「十八年之後又是一條好漢！」這是何等的達觀！

我們村子裏的人說：一個壞人或作孽多端的人，死後要轉世為窮人，或者變馬變豬，甚至靈魂支離割裂，變為蚊蠅小蟲。好人善士的靈魂轉世時則可以享更高的福祿。這些都是隨佛教而來的印度傳說而被中國道教所採用的。佛教本身，倒不大理會這些事。

善惡當然有公認的標準。「萬惡淫為首，百善孝為先。」孝道使中國家庭制度維繫不墮；貞操則使中國種族保持純淨。敬老憐貧、忠信篤敬也被認為是善行。重利盤剝、奸詐謊騙則列為罪行。斥責惡行時常罵人來生變豬變犬。

商業往來講究一諾千金。一般而論，大家都忠實可靠。欺詐的人必然受親朋戚友一致的唾棄。

婚姻是由媒妁之言、父母之命決定的。通例是男子二十而娶，女子十八而嫁。妻子死了，丈夫大概都要續弦，中上之家的女人如果死了丈夫，卻照例要守寡。守寡的可憐人算是最貞節的，死後皇帝還要給她們建貞節牌坊。這種牌坊在鄉間到處可以看見的。

村裏的事全由族長來處理，不待外界的干涉。祠堂就是衙門。「族長」不一定是老頭子，也可能是代表族中輩分最高一代的年輕人。族長們有責任監督敬先祭祖的禮儀遵奉不渝，族人中起了爭執時，他們還須負責加以評斷。沒有經過族長評理以前，任何人不許打官司。族長升堂審判叫做「開祠堂門」，全村的人都可以來參觀。祖宗牌位前面點起香燭，使得每個人都覺得祖先在天之靈就在冥冥之中監視似的，在祖先的面前，當事的兩邊不能有半句謊話。一般而論，說老實話的居多。

仲裁者力求做得公平。自然，村中的輿論也是重要的因素，還有，鄰村的輿論也得考慮。族長們如果評斷不公，就會玷污了祠堂的名譽。因此，爭執多半在祠堂裏得到公平的解決，大家用不到上衙門打官司。

實際上真需要「開祠堂門」來解決的事情並不多，因為大家認為「開祠堂門」是件大事，只有特別嚴重的案子才需要這樣做。一般的糾紛只是在祠堂前評個理就解決了。讀書人和士紳在地方上的權威很大。他們參加排難解紛，也參加制定村裏的規矩，他們還與鄰村的士紳成立組織，共同解決糾紛，照顧鄰近村莊的共同福利。

田賦由地主送到離村約二十里的縣庫去，糧吏從來不必到村裏來。老百姓根本不理會官府的存在，這就是所謂「天高皇帝遠」。

除了崇拜祖先之外，大家要信甚麼就信甚麼。上佛寺、拜神仙、供關公、祭土地，悉聽尊便。沒有宗教限制，也沒有宗教迫害。你信你的神，我拜我的佛，各不相涉，並且還有把各式各樣的神擠在一起大家來拜。這就是通常所稱的「道教」。如果基督徒肯讓基督與中國神並供在中國廟宇裏，我相信村裏人一定會像崇拜其他神佛一樣虔敬崇拜基督。

一般老百姓都是很老實的，人家說甚麼，他們就相信。迷信就是在這種背景下產生的，而且像滾雪球一樣越滾越大，幾百年積聚下來的迷信，當然是非常可觀的。我提到過村裏的人相信靈魂輪迴之說。這似乎與散鬼遊魂之說互相矛盾的。不過，凡關於鬼神的事，我們本來是不甚深究的，幾種矛盾的說法，可以同時平行。據說靈魂與鬼是兩回事。靈魂轉入輪迴，鬼則飄遊宇宙之間。偉人聖哲的鬼就成了神，永遠存在於冥冥之中，凡夫俗子的鬼則逐漸飄散消逝，最後化為烏有。鬼能夠隨心所欲，隨時隨地出現。它可以住在祠堂裏，也可以住在墳墓裏，高興怎麼樣就怎麼樣。我國不惜巨資建造富麗堂皇的墳墓和宮殿式的祠堂，大概和這些信仰不是沒有關係的。這種鬼話各地皆有，雖各有不同，但大體是一致的。

中國人對一切事物的看法都不脫人本位的色彩。如果鬼神與活人之間毫無關係或毫無接觸，那末大家就不會覺得鬼神有甚麼用處，或許根本就不會相信它們真的存在。寺廟祠堂裏固然有神佛的塑像，也有祖宗的靈牌，但是這些偶像或木主雖然令人望之生畏，卻不能走出神龕直接與生人交談，除非在夢中出現。人們需要更具體、更實際的表現，因此就有了巫婆、扶乩和解夢。

如果一個人懷念作古了的朋友或去世的親戚，他可以請一位巫婆把鬼魂召了來。當巫婆的多半是遠地來的女人。被召的鬼魂來時，巫婆的耳朵就會連續抽搐三次。普通人是不能控制耳朵的肌肉的，巫婆的耳朵能夠自己動，使得大家相信它的確有鬼神附體。她說話時，壓着喉嚨像貓叫，因此她講的話可以由聽的人隨意附會。如果巫婆在談話中摸清了對方的心思，她的話也就說得更清楚點，往往使聽的人心悅誠服。

真也好，假也好，這辦法至少使活着的親戚朋友心裏得點安慰。50 年前，我自己就曾經透過巫婆與我故世的母親談過話，那種驚心動魄的經驗至今還不能忘記。

扶乩可比較高級了，扶乩的人多半是有知識的。兩個人分執一根橫木條的兩端，木條的中央接着一根木棒，木棒就在沙盤裏寫字。神佛或者名人的鬼魂可以被請降壇，寫字賜教。扶乩可以預言未來，可以預言來年的收成，也可以預告饑荒，甚至和平或戰亂，幾乎甚麼問題都可以問。完全不會作詩的也能寫出詩來。寫的人也能寫出素昧平生的人的名字。懂一點心理學的人大概都能解釋，這是一種潛意識的作用。但是有好幾位外國留學的博士學士，到如今還是相信扶乩。有一位哈佛大學畢業生，於抗戰期間任鹽務某要職，扶乩報告預言，推測戰局，終被政府革職。

巫婆只能召致去世的親戚朋友的鬼魂，扶乩卻能召喚神佛。在做夢時，鬼魂和神佛都能自動地來託夢。我聽過許多關於做夢應驗的事，但是多半不記得了。我記得一個圓夢的例子是這樣的：我的一位曾叔祖到杭州去應鄉試，俗稱考舉人，他在考棚裏夢到一隻碩大無比的手伸進窗子。因為他從來沒有見過這樣大的手，這個夢就被解釋為他將獨佔鰲頭的徵兆。放榜時我的曾叔祖居然中試第一名，俗稱解元。

神佛、死去的親戚朋友或者精靈鬼怪可能由託夢提出希望、請求或者警告。一位死了的母親可能要求她兒子給她修茸墳墓。死了的父親可能向兒子討紙錢。死人下葬時總要燒點紙錢，以備陰間使用。

我們村裏發生過一件事，好幾年以後，大家談起來還是娓娓不倦。一位叫阿義的青年農夫預備用船載穀子進城市。那天早上，他坐在家裏發呆，人家問他為甚麼，他說前一晚他死去的母親來託夢，警告他不要走近水邊。他的游泳技術很高明，他猜不透這個夢究竟是甚麼意思。

黃昏時，他安然划着船回到家，用竹篙把船攏了岸。他對站在岸上的朋友開玩笑，說他自己的危險總算過去了，說罷還哈哈大笑。突然間他足下一滑就跌進河裏去了。掙扎了一陣子，他就沉入水底。朋友們趕緊潛水去救，但是到處找不到。半小時後他被拖上來了，但是已經手足冰冷，一命嗚呼。原來他跌入河中以後，手足就被水邊的一棵陳年老柳的盤根纏住了。

大家說他是被水鬼抓下去的，或許那是一隻以柳樹根作窩的水猴子。好幾個游泳技術很好的人都在那個地方淹死。村裏的人常常看到那個「水鬼」在月光下坐在附近的橋上賞月。它一看到有人走近就撲通一聲鑽到水裏去。

各式各樣無法解釋的現象都使迷信的雪球越滾越大，錯覺、幻象、夢魘、想像、巧合、謠言都是因素。時間更使迷信愈積愈多。

村中的醫藥當然也很原始。我們得走好幾里路才能在大鎮裏找到草藥醫生，俗稱「草頭郎中」。對於通常的病痛或者某些特殊的病症，中國藥是很有效的。但是對於許多嚴重的病症，草藥不但無效而且危險。

我自己曾經兩次病得奄奄一息，結果卻都給草藥救起了。有一次病了好幾個月，瘦得只剩皮包骨，結果是一位專精兒科的草藥醫生救了我的命。另一次我染了白喉，請了一位中國的喉科專家來醫治。他用一根細針在我喉頭附近刺了一遍，然後敷上一些白粉。我不知道那是甚麼東西，只覺得喉頭涼爽舒服，很像抽過一支薄荷煙的感覺。

喉頭是舒服一點了，病狀卻起了變化。我的扁桃腺腫得像鵝蛋那末大，兩頰鼓起像氣球，我甚至連流質的食物都無法下嚥。鼻子一直出血不止，最後連呼吸也感到困難了。正在奄奄一息的時候，我父親認為只有「死馬當作活馬醫」了。於是他就在古老的醫書裏翻尋秘方，結果真地找到一劑主治類似症候的方子。我吃了好幾服重藥。頭一劑藥就發生驗效，一兩個小時之後，病勢居然大有起色。第二天早晨我的扁桃腺腫消了許多，個把星期以後飲食也恢復正常。

我曾經親眼目睹跌斷的腿用老法子治好，傷風咳嗽、風濕和眼睛紅腫被草藥治好的例子更是多不勝舉。

中醫很早以前就發現可以從人體採取一種預防天花的「瘴苗」，他們用一種草藥塞到病嬰的鼻孔裏，再把這種草藥塞到正常兒童的鼻孔裏時，就可以引起一種比較溫和的病症。這樣「種了痘」的孩子自然不免有死亡，因此我父親寧願讓孩子按現代方法種牛痘。我們兄弟姊妹以及許多親戚的子弟都用現代方法種痘，而且從來沒有出過毛病。

我們村子裏的人不知道怎樣治療瘧疾。我們只好聽它自生自滅地流行幾個禮拜，甚至好幾個月。我們村子附近總算沒有發現惡性瘧疾，患了病的人雖然傷了元氣，倒還沒有人因此致命。後來傳教士和商人從上海帶來奎寧粉，叫做金雞納霜，吃了很有效，於是大家才發現了西藥的妙用。

村裏有些人相信神力可以治病。他們到寺廟裏焚香祝禱，然後在香爐裏取了一撮香灰作為治療百病的萬應靈丹。這是一種心理治療，在心理學應用得上的時候，也的確能醫好一些病。

我家的花園裏，每月有每月當令的花，陰曆正月是茶花，二月是杏花，三月桃花，四月薔薇，五月石榴，六月荷花，七月鳳仙，八月桂花，九月菊花，十月芙蓉，十一月水仙，十二月臘梅。每種花都有特別的花仙做代表。

最受歡迎的季節花是春天的桃花、夏天的荷花，秋天的桂花和菊花。季節到來時，村裏的人就成羣結隊出來賞花。

過年過節時，無論男女老幼都可以高興一陣子。最重要的年節，通常從十二月二十三日開始。灶神就在這一天上天報告這一家一年來的家庭瑣事。

中國人都相信多神主義的，在道教裏，眾神之主是玉皇大帝。據說玉皇大帝也有公卿大臣和州官吏卒，和中國的皇帝完全一樣。玉皇大帝派灶神監視家庭事務，因此灶神必須在年終歲尾提出報告。灶神是吃素的，因此在它啟程上天時，大家就預備素齋來祭送。灶神對好事壞事都要報告，因此大家一年到頭都謹言慎行。送灶神和迎灶神時都要設家宴、燒紙錢、放鞭炮。

除夕時，家家都大雞大肉地慶祝，叫做吃年夜飯。吃年夜飯時，家庭的每一個分子都得參加。如果有人遠行未歸，也得留個空座位給他。紅燭高燒到天明，多數的大人還得「守歲」，要坐到子夜以後才睡。第二天早晨，也就是正月初一早晨，一家人都參加拜天地。祭拜時自然又免不了點香燭、焚紙錢和放鞭炮。

新年的慶祝節目之一是燈節，從正月十三開始，一直到正月十八，十八以後年節也就算結束了。燈節時家家戶戶和大街小巷到處張燈結綵。花燈的式樣很多，馬、兔、蝴蝶、蜻蜓、螳螂、蟬、蓮花，應有盡有。我們常常到大城市去看迎燈賽會，街上總是人山人海。

五月裏的端午節和八月裏的中秋節也是重要的節日。端午節有龍舟比賽。慶祝中秋節卻比較安靜，也比較富於詩意 —— 吃過晚飯後我們就在月色下散步，欣賞團圓滿月中的玉兔在月桂下搗藥。

迎神賽會很普遍，普通有好幾百人參加，沿途圍觀的則有幾千人。這些場合通常總帶點宗教色彩，有時是一位神佛出巡各村莊。神像坐在一乘木雕的裝飾華麗的轎子裏，前面由旌旗華蓋、猛龍怪獸、吹鼓手、踩高蹺的人等等開道前導。

迎神行列經過時，掉獅舞龍就在各村的廣場上舉行。踩高蹺的人，在街頭扮演戲劇中的各種腳色。一面一面繡着龍虎獅子的巨幅旗幟，由十來個人扛着遊行，前前後後則由繩索圍起來。這樣的行列在曠野的大路上移動時，看來真好威風呀！這種舉大旗遊行的起源，據說是明代倭寇入侵時老百姓以此向他們示威的。

碰到過年過節，或者慶祝神佛生日，或者其他重要時節，活動的戲班子就到村莊上來表演。戲通常在下午三點鐘左右開始，一直演到第二天早晨，中間有一段休息的時間，以便大家吃晚飯。開演時總是鑼鼓喧天，告訴大家戲正在開始。演的戲多半是根據歷史故事編的，人民也就從戲裏學習歷史。每一齣戲都包括一點道德上的教訓，因此演戲可以同時達到三重目的：教授歷史、灌輸道德、供給娛樂。

女角是由男人扮演的，這是和莎士比亞時代的英國一樣。演員塗抹形形色色的臉譜象徵忠奸善惡。白鼻子代表奸詐、狡猾、卑鄙或小丑。在日常生活中我們也常常指這一類人為白鼻子。紅臉代表正直、忠耿等等，但是紅臉的人心地總是很厚道的。黑臉象徵鐵面無私。這種象徵性的臉譜一直到現在還被各地國劇所採用。

這就是我的童年的環境。這種環境已經很快地成為歷史陳跡。這個轉變首由外國品的輸入啟其端，繼由西方思想和兵艦的入侵加速其進程；終將由現代的科學、發明和工業化，完畢其全程。✿

第三章
童年教育

在我的童年時代，沒有學校，只有家塾。男孩子在家塾裏準備功課應付科舉或者學點實用的知識以便經商，女孩子不能和男孩子一道上學，要讀書就得另請先生，窮苦人家的子弟請不起先生，因此也就注定了當文盲的命運。

一位先生通常教數十位學生，都是分別教授的。家塾裏沒有黑板，也不分班級。先生從清晨到薄暮都端端正正地坐在那裏，學生們自然也就不敢亂蹦亂跳。那時候時鐘是很難見到的。家塾裏當然沒有鐘。冬天白晝比較短。天黑後我們就點起菜油燈，在昏暗的燈光下唸書，時間是靠日晷來計算的。碰到陰天或下雨，那就只好亂猜了。猜錯一兩個小時是常事，好在書是個別教授的，猜錯個把鐘頭也無所謂。

我在六歲時進家塾，一般小孩子差不多都在這個年歲「啟蒙」的。事實上我那時才五歲零一個月的樣子，因為照我家鄉的演算法，一個人生下來就算一歲了。家塾裏的書桌太高，我的椅子下面必須墊上一個木架子之後我才夠得上書桌，因此我坐到椅子上時，兩隻腳總是懸空的。

我最先唸的書叫《三字經》，每句三個字，而且是押韻的，因此小孩子記起來比較容易。事隔六十多年，我現在還能背出一大半，開頭幾句是：「人之初，性本善。性相近，習相遠。苟不教，性乃遷。」性善論是儒家人生哲學和教育原理的出發點，這種看法曾對18世紀的大光明時代的法國學派產生過重大的影響。

雖然我現在已經懂得甚麼叫「性本善」，在當時卻真莫名其妙。

我恨透了家塾裏的生活。有一天，我乘先生不注意我的時候，偷偷地爬下椅子，像一隻掙脫鎖鏈的小狗，一溜煙逃回家中，躲到母親的懷裏。母親自然很感意外，但是她只是慈祥地問我：「你怎麼跑回家來了，孩子？」

我答道：「家塾不好，先生不好，書本不好。」

「你不怕先生嗎？他也許會到家裏來找你呢！」母親笑着説。

「先生，我要殺了他！家塾，我要放把火燒了它！」我急着説。

母親並沒有把我送回家塾，那位先生也沒有找上門來。

第二天早上，奶媽喊醒了我，對我説了許多好話，總算把我勸回家塾。從童年時代起我就吃軟不吃硬。好好勸我，要我幹甚麼都行，高壓手段可沒有用。經過奶媽一陣委婉的勸諫，我終於自動地重新去上學了。

我帶着一張自備的竹椅子，家裏一位傭人跟着我到了家塾，把竹椅子放到木架上，使我剛好夠得着書桌。先生沒有出聲，裝作不知道我曾經逃過學，但是我注意到好幾位同學對着我裝鬼臉。我討厭他們，但是裝作沒有看見。我爬上椅子坐在那裏，兩隻腳卻懸空掛着，沒有休息的地方。我的課也上了，書卻仍舊是那本《三字經》。我高聲朗誦着不知所云的課文，一遍又一遍地唸得爛熟。等到太陽不偏不倚地照到我們的頭上時，我們知道那是正午了。先生讓我們回家吃午飯，吃過飯我馬上回到家塾繼續唸那課同樣的書，一直到日落西山才散學。

一日又一日地過去，課程卻一成不變。一本書唸完了之後，接着又是一本不知所云的書。接受訓練的只是記憶力和耐心。

唸書時先生要我們做到「三到」，那就是心到、眼到、口到。所謂心到就是注意力集中，不但讀書如此，做任何事情都得如此。眼到對學習中國文字特別重要，因為中國字的筆劃錯綜複雜，稍一不慎就可能讀別字。所謂口到就是把一段書高聲朗誦幾百遍，使得句子脫口而出，這樣可以減輕記憶力的負擔。先生警告我們，唸書不能取巧強記，因為勉強記住的字句很容易忘記。如果我們背書時有些疙瘩，先生就會要我們一遍又一遍地再唸，甚至唸上一兩百遍。碰上先生心情不好，腦袋上就會吃栗子。天黑放學時，常常有些學生頭皮上帶着幾個大疙瘩回家。

不管學生願意不願意，他們必須守規矩，而且要絕對服從。我們根本不知道甚麼叫禮拜天。每逢陰曆初一、十五，我們就有半天假。碰到節慶，倒也全天放假，例如端午節和中秋節。新年的假期比較長，從十二月二十一直到正月二十。

　　在家塾裏唸了幾年之後，我漸漸長大了，也記得不少的字。這時先生才開始把課文的意思解釋給我聽，因此唸起書來也不再像以前那樣吃力了。從四書五經裏，我開始慢慢了解做人的道理。按照儒家的理想，做人要先從修身着手，其次齊家，然後治國、平天下。其中深義到後來我才完全體會。

　　在最初幾年，家塾生活對我而言簡直像監獄，唯一的區別是：真正監獄裏的犯人沒有希望，而家塾的學生們都有着前程無限的憧憬。所有的學者名流、達官貴人不是都經過寒窗苦讀的煎熬嗎？

　　「吃得苦中苦，方為人上人。」

　　「天子重英豪，文章教爾曹。」

　　「萬般皆下品，惟有讀書高。」

　　「別人懷寶劍，我有筆如刀。」

　　這些成語驅策着我向學問之途邁進，正如初春空氣中的芳香吸引着一匹慵懶的馬兒步向碧綠的草原，否則我恐怕早已丟下書本跑到上海做生意去了。理想、希望和意志可說是決定一生榮枯的最重要的因素。教育如果不能啟發一個人的理想、希望和意志，單單強調學生的興趣，那是捨本逐末的辦法。只有以啟發理想為主、培養興趣為輔時，興趣才能成為教育上的一個重要因素。

　　在老式私塾裏死背古書似乎乏味又愚蠢，但是背古書倒也有背古書的好處。一個人到了成年時，常常可以從背的古書裏找到立身處事的指南針。在一個安定的社會裏，一切守舊成風，行為的準則也很少變化。因此我覺得我國的老式教學方法似乎已足以應付當時的實際需要。自然，像我家鄉的那個私塾當然是個極端的例子，那只有給小孩子添些無謂的苦難。我怕許多有前途的孩子，在未發現學問的重要以前就給嚇跑了。

在我的家塾裏，課程裏根本沒有運動或體育這個項目。小孩子們不許拔步飛跑，他們必須保持「體統」一步一步慢慢地走。吃過中飯以後，我們得馬上練字。我們簡直被磨得毫無朝氣。

話雖如此，小孩子還是能夠自行設法來滿足他們嬉戲的本能。如果先生不在，家塾可就是我們的天下了。有時候我們把書桌搬在一起，拼成一個戲台在上面演戲，椅子板凳就成了舞台上的道具。有時候我們就玩捉迷藏。有一次，我被蒙上眼睛當瞎子，剛巧先生回來了，其餘的孩子都偷偷地溜了，我輕而易舉地就抓到一個人——我的先生。當我發現闖了禍時，我簡直嚇昏了。到現在想起這件事尚有餘悸。

春天來時，放了學我們就去放風箏，風箏都是我們自己做的。風箏的形式不一，有的像蜈蚣，有的像蝴蝶。夜晚時，我們把一串燈籠隨着風箏送到天空，燈籠的數目通常是五個、七個或九個。比較小的孩子就玩小風箏，式樣通常是蜻蜓、燕子或老鷹。「燕子」風箏設計得最妙，通常是成對的，一根細竹片的兩端各紮一隻「燕子」，然後把竹片擺平在風箏繩子上。送上天空以後，一對對的「燕子」隨風擺動，活像比翼雙飛的真燕子。有一次，我還看到好幾隻真的燕子在一隻「燕子」風箏附近盤旋，大概是在找伴兒。

滿天星斗的夏夜，村子裏的小孩子們就捉螢火蟲玩兒。有些小孩子則寧願聽大人們講故事。講故事的大人，手中總是搖着一柄大蒲扇，一方面為了驅暑，一方面也是為了驅逐糾纏不清的蚊子。口中銜旱煙杆，旁邊放着小茶壺，慢條斯理地敘述歷史人物的故事、改朝換代的情形，以及村中的掌故。

大人告訴我們，大約 250 年前，清兵入關推翻了明朝，盜賊蜂起，天下大亂，但是我們村中卻安謐如恒。後來聖旨到了村裏，命令所有的男人按照滿洲韃子的髮式，剃去頭頂前面的頭髮，而在後腦勺上留起辮子。男子聽了如同晴天霹靂，女人們則急得哭了，剃頭匠奉派到村子裏強制執行，他們是奉旨行事，如果有人抗旨不肯剃頭，就有殺頭的危險。留頭究竟比留髮重要，二者既然不可兼得，大家也就只好乖乖地伸出脖子，任由剃頭匠剃髮編辮了。當然，後來大家看慣了，也就覺得無所謂，但是初次剃髮留辮子的時候，那樣子看起來一定是很滑稽的。……

從這位講故事的長者口中，我們總算學到了一點歷史，那是在家塾中學不到的。此外，我們還得到一點關於人類學的傳說。故事是這樣的：

幾萬年以前，我們的祖先也像猴子一樣長着尾巴。那時的人可說介於人與猿猴之間。人猿年歲長大以後，他的尾巴就漸漸變為黃色。人猿的尾巴共有十節，十節中如有九節變黃，他就知道自己快要死了。於是他就爬到窰洞裏深居簡出，結果就死在窰洞裏面。再經過幾千年以後，人的尾巴掉了，所以現在的人都沒有尾巴，但是尾巴的痕跡仍舊存在。不信，你可以順着背脊骨往下摸，尾巴根兒還是可以摸得到的。

下面是一則關於技擊的故事：

一位學徒在一家米店前賣米。在沒有生意的時候，這位學徒就抓着米粒玩兒，他一把一把地把米抓起來，然後又一把一把地把米擲回米筐裏。有一天，一位和尚來化米，那位學徒不但沒有拿米給和尚，反而抓了幾顆米擲到和尚臉上。想不到那幾顆米竟然顆顆深陷到和尚的皮肉裏面去了。和尚似乎不生氣，反而向那位學徒深深一鞠躬，雙手合什，唸了一聲「南無阿彌陀佛」就走了。

七天之後，一位拳師經過村裏，他看到米店學徒臉色蒼白，就問學徒究竟是怎麼回事。學徒把和尚化米的事說了，拳師聽了不禁搖頭歎息：「啊呀，你怎麼可得罪他呢？他是當今武林首屈一指的人物呀！他在向你鞠躬的時候，你已經受了致命的內傷，不出七七四十九天，你就活不成了！幸好我還有藥可以給你醫治，不過你要趕快躲開，永遠不要再撞上這位和尚。四十九天之後他還會再來的。趕快備口棺木，放幾塊磚頭在棺材裏，假裝你已經死了入殮待葬就是了。」

四十九天之後，和尚果然又來找學徒了。人們告訴他學徒已經死了。和尚歎口氣說：「可憐！可憐！」和尚要看看棺材，大家就帶他去看，他用手輕輕地把棺蓋從頭至尾撫摸一遍，唸了一聲「南無阿彌陀佛」就走了。和尚走了之後，大家打開棺蓋一看，裏面的磚頭已經全部粉碎。

小孩子們全都豎起耳朵聽這些故事，這些故事就是我們課外知識的主要來源之一。

我們家塾裏的先生，前前後後換了好幾個。其中之一是位心地仁厚然而土頭土腦的老學究。他的命運多舛，屢次參加府試都沒有考上秀才，最後只好死心塌地教私塾。他的臉團團如滿月，身材矮胖，一副銅框眼鏡老是低低地滑到鼻樑上，兩隻眼睛就打從眼鏡上面看人。他沒有留鬚，鼻子下面卻養着一撮蓬鬆的灰色鬍子。碰到喝蛋花湯的日子，他的鬍子上常常掛着幾片黃蛋花。他的故事多得說不盡，簡直是一部活的百科全書。但是他的文才很差，我想這或許就是他屢試不中的緣故。不過人很風趣，善於笑謔。他在有些事情上非常健忘，看過朋友回到家塾時，不是忘了雨傘，就是丟了扇子。老是這樣丟三落四究竟不是事，於是他就把他出門時必帶的東西開了個清單：煙管、雨傘、毛巾、扇。每當他告辭回家時，他就念一遍：「煙管、雨傘、毛巾、扇。」冬天不需要帶扇子的時候，他也照樣要按清單唸扇子。有時候他也記得根本沒有帶扇子出門，有時卻仍然到處找扇子，他的朋友和學生就在暗中竊笑。

我童年時的知識範圍，可以說只局限於四書五經，以及私塾先生和村中長輩所告訴我的事。我背得出不少的古書，也記得很多的故事，因此我的童年教育可以說主要的是記憶工作。幸而我生長在鄉村，可以從大自然獲得不少的知識和啟發。有一次，我注意到生長的皂莢樹上的甲蟲頭上長着鹿角一樣的角，這些角和枝上的刺長得一模一樣，人家告訴我，這些甲蟲是樹上長出來的，因此也就和母體長得很像。不過我總覺得有點相信不過。我心裏想，如果一棵樹真能生下甲蟲，那末甲蟲產下的卵也就應該可以作皂莢樹的種了。甲蟲卵既然種不出皂莢樹，那麼甲蟲的角和皂莢樹的刺這樣相像一定另有原因。後來我看到一隻鳥在皂莢樹上啄蟲吃，但是這隻鳥對於身旁長着鹿角的甲蟲卻視而不見。於是我恍然大悟，原來甲蟲的角是摹擬着刺而生的，目的是保護自己以免被鳥兒啄死。

河汉的兩岸長着許多柏樹，柏子可以榨油製蠟燭，因此柏樹的土名就叫蠟燭樹。冬天裏農夫們用稻草把樹幹裹起來，春天到了，就把稻草取下燒掉。一般人相信，這種辦法可以產生一種神秘的力量殺死寄生蟲。事實上這件事毫無神奇之處，只要我們在樹幹上紮上足夠的稻草，寄生蟲就只好在稻草上產卵，燒掉稻草等於毀掉蟲卵，寄生蟲也就無法繁殖了。

在我童年時代裏，這類對自然的粗淺研究的例子很多，舉了前面的兩個例子，我想也就夠了。

由此可見我的童年教育共有三個來源。第一是在私塾裏唸的古書，來自古書的知識，一方面是立身處世的指標，另一方面也成為後來研究現代社會科學的基礎。第二個知識來源是聽故事，這使我在欣賞現代文學方面奠立了基礎。第三個知識來源是對自然的粗淺研究，不過在這種粗淺研究的根基上卻可以移接現代科學的幼苗。如果我生長在草木稀少的大城市裏，那我勢將失去非常重要的自然訓練的機會，我的一生可能完全改觀。每一個小孩子所具備的感受力、觀察力、好奇心和理解力等等天賦，都可能被我童年所受的全憑記憶的傳統訓練所窒息。

我得承認，我並沒有像某些同學那樣用功讀書，因為我不喜歡死記，我願意觀察、觸摸、理解。我的先生們認為這是我的不幸、我的個性上的禍根。

我喜歡玩，喜歡聽故事。我喜歡打破砂鍋問到底，使大人感到討厭。我喜歡看着稻田裏的青蛙捉蚱蜢，或者鵝鴨在河裏戲水。我欣賞新篁解籜。我的先生認為這些癖好都是禍根。我自己也相信將來不會有出息。但是命運是不可捉摸的，我的這些禍根後來竟成為福因，而先生們認定的某些同學的福因結果都證明是禍根。那些好學生後來有的死於肺癆，有的成為書呆，在西化潮流橫掃中國時無法適應日新月異的環境而落伍了。🔖

第四章
家庭影響

　　童年時代和青春時代的可塑性最大，因而家庭影響往往有決定性的作用。這時期中所養成的習慣，不論好壞，將來都很難根除。大致說來，我所受到的家庭影響是良好而且健全的。

　　我的父親是位小地主，而且是上海當地幾家錢莊的股東。祖父留給父親的遺產相當可觀，同時父親生活儉樸，因此一家人一向用不着為銀錢操心。父親為人忠厚而慷慨，蔣村的人非常敬重他，同時也受到鄰村人士的普遍崇敬。他自奉儉約，對公益事業卻很慷慨，常常大量捐款給慈善機構。

　　他從來沒有說過一句存心騙人的話，因此與他交往的人全都信任他的話。他相信風水和算命。同時他又相信行善積德可以感召神明，使行善者添福增壽，因此前生注定的命運也可以因善行而改變。我父親的道德人品對我的影響的確很大，我唯一的遺憾是沒有好好學到父親的榜樣。

　　我的母親是位很有教養而且姿容美麗的女人。我童年時對她的印象已經有點模糊了。我記得她能夠彈七弦古琴，而且能夠撫琴幽歌。她最喜歡唱的一支歌，叫做「古琴引」，詞為：音音音，爾負心。真負心，辜負我，到如今。記得當年低低唱，千千斟，一曲值千金。如今放我枯牆陰，秋風芳草白雲深，斷橋流水過故人。淒淒切切，冷冷清清，淒淒切切，冷冷清清。

　　有人說：像我母親那樣青春美貌的婦人唱這樣悲切的歌，是不吉利的。

　　母親彈琴的書齋，屋後長着一棵幾丈高的大樟樹。離樟樹不遠的地方種着一排竹子，這排竹子也就成為我家的籬笆。竹叢的外面圍繞着一條小河。大樟樹的樹蔭下長着一棵紫荊花和一棵香團樹，但是這兩棵樹只能在大樟樹扶疏的枝葉之間爭取些微的陽光。母親坐在客廳裏，可以諦聽小鳥的囀唱，也可以聽到魚兒戲水的聲音。太陽下山時，平射過來的陽光穿過竹叢把竹影子投映在窗簾上，隨風飄動。書齋的牆上滿是名家書畫。她的嵌着白玉的古琴則安放在長長的紅木琴几上，琴几的四足則雕着鳳凰。

她去世以後，客廳的佈置一直保留了好幾年沒有變動。她的一張畫像高懸在牆的中央。但是母親已經不在了！她用過的古琴用一塊軟緞蓋着，仍舊放在紅木琴几上。我有時不禁要想像自己就是那個飲泣孤塚幽幽低訴的古琴。

我母親去世時還很年輕。我看到母親穿着華麗的繡花裙襖躺在棺裏，裙襖外面罩一個長長的紅綢披風，一直蓋到足踝，披風上綴着大紅的頭兜，只有她的臉露在外面，一顆很大的珍珠襯着紅頭兜在她額頭發出閃閃的亮光。

我的繼母是位治家很能幹的主婦，待人也很和氣，但不久也去世，此後父親也就不再續弦了。

我的祖父當過上海某銀莊的經理。太平天國時（1851—1864）祖父在上海舊城設了一個小錢攤，後來錢攤發展為小錢莊，進而成為頭等錢莊。這種錢莊是無限責任的機構，做些信用貸款的生意。墨西哥鷹洋傳到中國成為銀兩的輔幣以後，洋錢漸漸受到國人的歡迎。後來流通漸廣，假幣也跟着比例增加，但是錢莊裏的人只要在指尖上輕輕地把兩塊銀元敲敲，他們就能夠辨別哪個是真，哪個是假，我祖父的本領更使一般錢莊老闆佩服，他一眼就能看出哪個是真的，哪個是假。

不幸他在盛年時傷了一條腿，後來嚴重到必須切去，祖父也就因為血液中毒辭世。父親當時還只有12歲左右，祖父給他留下了7000兩銀子，在當時說起來，這已經是一筆相當大的遺產了。父親成了無告的孤兒，就歸他未來的丈人照顧。由於投資得當，調度謹慎，這筆財產逐漸增加，三十年之後，已經合到七萬兩銀子。

從上面這一點家庭歷史裏，讀者不難想像我的家庭一定在早年就已受到西方的影響。

父親很有點發明的頭腦。他喜歡自己設計，或者畫出圖樣來，然後指示木匠、鐵匠、銅匠、農夫或篾匠按照尺寸照樣打造。他自己設計過造房子，也實驗過養蠶、植桑、造槍（照着西方一種過時了的式樣），而且按着他的想像製造過許多別的東西。最後他想出一個打造「輪船」的聰明辦法，但是他的「輪船」卻是不利用蒸汽的。父親為了視察業務，常常需要到上海去。他先坐槳划的木船到寧波，然後從寧波乘輪船到上海。他常說：「坐木船從蔣村到寧波要花三天兩夜，但是坐輪船從寧波到上海，路雖然遠十倍，一夜之間就到了。」因此他就畫了一個藍圖，預備建造一艘具體而微的輪船。

木匠和造船匠都被找來了。木匠奉命製造水輪，造船匠則按照我父親的計劃造船，隔了一個月，船已經造得差不多。小「輪船」下水的那一天，許多人跑來參觀，大家看了這艘新奇的「輪船」都讚不絕口。「輪船」停靠在我家附近的小河裏，父親僱了兩位彪形大漢分執木柄的兩端來推動水輪。「輪船」慢慢開始在水中移動時，岸上圍觀的人不禁歡呼起來。不久這隻船的速度也逐漸增加。但是到了速度差不多和槳划的船相等時，水手們再怎樣出力，船的速度也不增加了。乘客們指手劃腳，巴不得能使船駛得快一點，有幾位甚至親自動手幫着轉水輪。但是這隻船似乎很頑固，始終保持原來的速度不增加。

父親把水輪修改了好幾次，希望使速度增加。但是一切努力終歸白費。更糟的是船行相當距離以後，水草慢慢纏到水輪上，而且愈積愈多，最後甚至連轉都轉不動了。父親歎口氣說：「唉！究竟還是造輪船的洋人有辦法。」

那條「輪船」最後改為普通槳划的船。但是船身太重，划也划不動。幾年之後，我們發現那條船已經棄置在岸上朽爛腐敗，船底長了厚厚的一層青苔。固然這次嘗試是失敗了，父親卻一直想再來試一下，後來有人告訴他瓦特和蒸汽機的故事，他才放棄了造船的雄心。他發現除了輪船的外表之外，還有更深奧的原理存在。從這時候起，他就一心一意要讓他的兒子受現代教育，希望他們將來能有一天學會洋人製造神奇東西的「秘訣」。

這個造輪船的故事也正是中國如何開始向西化的途程探索前進的實例。

不過，在人倫道德上父親卻一直不大贊成外國人的辦法。固然也認為「外國人倒也同我們中國人一樣地忠實、講理、勤勞」，但是除此之外，他並不覺得外國人有甚麼可取的地方。話雖如此，他卻也不反對他的孩子們學習外國人的生活方式和習慣。

我的先生卻反對我父親的看法。他說：「『奇技淫巧』是要傷風敗俗的。先聖以前不就是這樣說過嗎？」他認為只有樸素的生活才能保持高度的道德水準。我的舅父也持同樣的看法。他用一張紅紙寫下他的人生觀，又把紅紙貼在書桌近旁的牆上：「每日清晨一支香，謝天謝地謝三光。國有忠臣護社稷，家無逆子鬧爺娘，……但願處處田稻好，我雖貧時也不妨。」

我的舅父是位秀才，他總是攜帶着一根長長的旱煙杆，比普通的手杖還長。他經常用煙管的銅斗敲着磚地。他在老年時額頭也不顯皺紋，足見他心境寧靜，身體健康，而且心滿意足。他斯文有禮，我從來沒有看到他發脾氣。他說話很慢，但是很清楚，也從來不罵人。🌸

第五章
山雨欲來風滿樓

　　新年裏常常有些小販到村子裏賣畫片，有些畫的是國家大事，有的則是戲中情節。有一年新春假期裏，有一套新鮮的圖畫引起小孩子們的濃厚興趣。這套五彩圖畫繪的是 1894 年（甲午年）中日戰爭的故事。其中有一張畫的是渤海上的海戰場面，日本艦隊中的一艘軍艦已被幾罐裝滿火藥的大瓦罐擊中起火，軍艦正在下沉。圖中還畫着幾百個同樣的大瓦罐在海上漂浮。這種瓦罐，就是當時民間所通用的夜壺，夜間小便時使用的。另一幅畫中則畫着一羣帶了銬鏈的日本俘虜，有的則關在籠子裏。中國打了大勝仗了！自然，那只是紙上的勝仗，但是我們小孩子們卻深信不疑。後來我年紀大一點以後，我才知道我國實際上是被日本打敗了，而且割讓了台灣，我們的海軍被日本消滅，高麗也被日本搶走了。短短九年之內，中國已經相繼喪失了三個承認中國宗主權的外圍國，最先是越南，繼之是緬甸，現在又丟了高麗。

　　一個夏天的傍晚，一位臨時僱工氣喘如牛地從我父親的書房裏跑了出來。他說在書房裏聽到一陣叮噹的聲音，但是房裏找不到人影。他說那一定是鬼在作怪。後來一追究，原來是時鐘在報時。

　　從無可稽考的年代起，鄉下人一直利用刀片敲擊火石來取火，現在忽然有人從上海帶來了幾盒火柴。大人們對這種簡便的取火方法非常高興。小孩們也很開心，在黑暗的角落，手上火柴一擦，就可以發出螢火蟲一樣的光亮。火柴在當時叫「自來火」，因為一擦就着；也叫「洋火」，因為它是從外洋運進來的。

　　時鐘實際上並無必要，因為在鄉村裏，時間算得再准也沒有用處。早二三個鐘頭，遲二三個鐘頭又有甚麼關係？鄉下人計時間是以天和月做單位的，並不以分成小時來計算。火柴其實也是奢侈品——用刀片火石不也是一直過得很好嗎？至於煤油，那可又當別論了，煤油燈可以把黑夜照得如同白晝，這與菜油燈的昏暗燈光比起來真有天淵之別。

美孚洋行是把中國從「黑暗時代」導引到現代文明的執炬者。大家買火柴、時鐘是出於好奇，買煤油卻由於生活上的必要。但事情並不到此為止。煤油既然成為必需品，那末，取代信差的電報以及取代舢舨和帆船的輪船又何嘗不是必需品呢？依此類推，必需的東西也就愈來愈多。

很少人能夠在整體上發現細微末節的重要性。當我們毫不在意地玩着火柴或享受煤油燈的時候，誰也想不到是在玩火，這點星星之火終於使全中國烈焰燭天。火柴和煤油是火山爆發前的跡象，這個「火山」爆發以後，先是破壞了蔣村以及其他村莊的和平和安寧，最後終於震撼了全中國。

基督教傳教士曾在無意中把外國貨品介紹到中國內地。傳教士們不顧艱難險阻、瘴癘瘟疫甚至生命危險，遍歷窮鄉僻壤，去拯救不相信上帝的中國人的靈魂。他們足跡所至，隨身攜帶的煤油、洋布、鐘錶、肥皂等等也就到了內地。一般老百姓似乎對這些東西比對福音更感興趣。這些舶來品開拓了中國老百姓的眼界，同時也激起了國人對物質文明的向往。傳教士原來的目的是傳佈耶穌基督的福音，結果卻無意中為洋貨開拓了市場。

我不是說傳教士應對中國現代商業的成長負主要責任，但是他們至少在這方面擔任了一個角色，而且是重要的一角，因為他們深入到中國內地的每一角落。主角自然還是西方列強的商船和兵艦。基督教傳教士加上兵艦，終於逼使文弱的、以農為本的古老中國步上現代工商業的道路。

我曾經目睹買辦階級的成長以及士大夫階級的沒落。我自己也幾乎參加了士大夫的行列，但是最後總算偷偷地溜掉了。所謂買辦階級，就是本國商人和外國商人之間的中國人。外國商人把貨運到上海、天津等通商港埠，這些貨品再通過買辦，從大商埠轉銷到各城鎮村莊。買辦們在轉手之間就可以大筆地賺錢，因此吃這一行飯的人也就愈來愈多。事業心比較強、際遇比較好的人，紛紛加入直接間接買賣外國貨的新行業。有的人發大財，有的人則豐衣足食。際遇比較差的可就落了伍，有的依舊種田耕地，有的則守在舊行業裏謀生。田地的入息有限，舊行業在外國競爭之下又一落千丈，於是舊有的經濟制度很快地就開始崩潰了。結果是一大羣人無可避免地失了謀生糊口的機會。這些不幸的人，一方面嫉妒新興的暴發戶，一方面又不滿於舊日的行業，或者根本喪失了舊有的職業，結果就鋌而走險。曹娥江大潮正在沖激着水閘，象徵着即將破壞蔣村安寧的動亂正在奔騰澎湃。

一個秋天的下午，我正在田野裏追逐嬉戲，忽然聽到一陣緊急狂驟的鑼聲。敲鑼的人一面狂奔着，一面高喊堤塘已經沖塌了，洪水正向村中漫過來。我拼命跑回家裏，並把這消息告訴路上所碰到的一切人。

大家馬上忙作一團。我們趕快準備好船隻、木浴盆，以及所有可以浮得起來的東西，以便應付即將來臨的災難。有的人則決定爬到大樹上去暫避。第二天早晨，洪水已經沖進我家的大門，水頭像巨蟒一樣奔進院子。到了中午時，小孩已經坐上浴盆，在大廳裏划來划去了。

堤塘缺口終於用沙包堵住，曹娥江也不再氾濫了。洪水在我們村裏以及鄰近村莊停留約一星期，然後慢慢退到低地，最後隨江河入海，同時捲走了所有的稻作。

大約一星期以後，一隻大船在傍晚時分載着許多人向我們村莊划過來。這隻船在我家附近停下，船上的人也紛紛離船上岸。我們為防意外，趕緊閉起大門。他們用大石頭來搗大門，最後終於排闥而入。領頭的人身材魁偉，顯然孔武有力，辮子盤在頭頂上。他帶着一夥人走到天井裏，高喊：「我們肚子餓，我們要借糧。」其餘人也就跟着吶喊助威。他們搜索了穀倉，但是沒有馬上動手搬；他們要「借」。最後經過隔壁一位農人的調停，他們「借」走了幾擔穀子以後，就回船啟航了。這是隨後發生的一連串變亂的首次警號。

性質相近然而比較嚴重的事件，接二連三地在鄰村發生。開始時是「借」，隨後就變質為搶劫。搶劫事件像野火一樣到處蔓延，鄉間微薄的官兵武力根本無法加以阻遏。而且搶糧食不能處以極刑，但是在那種情勢下，恐怕只有極刑才能加以遏止，至少暫時不至如此猖獗。

「借糧」的事件一直延續至那年冬天。不久之後，殺人擄掠的暴行終於在孫莊首次發生。被害的孫君在上海有一爿生意興隆的木行。孫君的父親曾在上海承包「洋行」的營造工程而發了大財。

那是一個凜冽的冬夜，孫莊的人很早就躲到被窩去了。有人從窗子裏發現黑暗中有一隊火把正從大路上向孫莊移動。火把臨近孫莊時，大家聽到一陣槍聲。強盜來了！強盜衝開孫家的大門，搶走了孫家所有的金銀財帛 —— 名貴的羊裘皮襖、金銀器皿、珍珠寶石，無一幸免。他們並且擄走了孫君，把他綁在一根長竹竿的頂端，然後又把他壓到河底。第二天孫家的人拖起竹竿才發現他的屍體。

搶劫的風潮迅速蔓延到各村莊。幾百年來鄉村人們所享受的和平與安寧，一夜之間喪失殆盡。我們沒有一夜能夠安穩地睡。我父親從上海買來了手槍以及舊式的長槍。大家開始練習放槍，小孩子也不例外。我們拿鳥雀當活靶，因此連鳥雀都遭了殃。我們輪班睡覺，值班的人就負責守夜。一聽到犬吠，我們就向空放槍警告盜匪，自然有時是虛驚，有時卻的確把強盜嚇跑了。為了節省彈藥，我們常常在槍聲中夾帶些爆仗。

永遠這樣緊張下去究竟不是事。父親最後無可奈何地帶了一家大小搬到上海住下來。

我們搬家之前的兩年內，我曾在紹興繼續我的學業。我還在家塾裏唸書的時候，父親曾經問我將來願意做生意還是預備做官。我的兩位哥哥都已經決定步入仕途。父親要我決定之前，仔細考慮一番。

做官可以光宗耀祖，幾百年來，年輕人無不心嚮往之。自然我也很希望將來能做官。在另一方面，新近發財的人可以享受新穎奇巧的外國貨，這般人的生活也是一種強烈的引誘。名利之間的選擇，多少與一個人思想中所已灌輸進去的觀念和理想有點關聯。

我聽人家說，我們中國人分為士、農、工、商四個階級。雖然每一階級在整個社會裏都有特定的任務，士大夫都是統治階級，因此也是最尊榮的一級，依照亞里斯多德的主張，哲學家當為國王，所以我們可以說，哲人、學士如果做不到帝王，至少也應該是公卿、宰相。中國的貴族階級除極少數例外，都不是世襲的，而是由於本身努力達到的。俗語說：秀才是宰相的根苗。如果我去經商，那麼將來不就與功名無緣了嗎？

因此我決心續求學問。自然，我當時對學問的意義並不十分了解；我只覺得那是向上層社會爬的階梯。在我們村子裏，農、工、商三類人都不稀罕。種田的不必說了，商人也不少。好多人在上海做生意，從上海帶回來很多好玩的東西：小洋刀、哨子、皮球、洋娃娃、汽槍、手錶等等，多不勝舉。至於工匠，我們的一位族長就是木匠，他的兒子們也是的。一位遠房叔叔是銀匠，專門打造鄉村婦女裝飾的指環、手鐲、釵簪之類。至於讀書的人，那可不同了。凡是族人之中有功名的，家廟中都有一面金碧輝煌的匾額，舉人以上的家廟前面還有高高的旗杆，懸掛他們的旗幟。我還記得有一天縣太爺到鄰村查辦命案，他乘坐一頂四人扛抬的綠呢暖轎，紅纓帽上綴着一顆金頂，胸前掛着一串朝珠。四名轎夫每人戴着一頂尖錐形的黑帽，帽頂插着一根鵝毛。暖轎前面有一對銅鑼開道，縣太爺所經之處，老百姓就得肅靜回避。他是本縣的父母官，我們老百姓的生命財產都得聽他發落。他的權勢怎麼來的？讀書呀！

於是我知道了讀書人的地位，也知道做一名讀書人的好處。他可以一級一級地往上爬，甚至有一天當了大官，還可以在北京皇宮裏飲御賜香茗呢！像我這樣的一位鄉下孩子，足步向未逾越鄰近的村鎮，他希望讀書做官應是很自然的事。我幼稚的心靈裏，幻想着自己一天比一天神氣，功名步步高升，中了秀才再中了舉人，中了舉人再中進士，終於有一天當了很大很大的官，比那位縣知事要大得好多好多，身穿蟒袍，腰懸玉帶，紅纓帽上綴着大紅頂子，胸前掛着長長的朝珠，顯顯赫赫地回到故鄉，使村子裏的人看得目瞪口呆。這些美麗的憧憬，在我眼前一幕幕展開，我的前程多麼光明呀！只要我能用心熟讀經書就行了。

我的童年教育雖然枯燥乏味，卻也在我的思想裏模模糊糊地留下學問重於一切的印象。政府官吏都是經過科舉選拔的，但是只有有學問的人才有希望金榜題名。官吏受人敬重，是因為學問本身在中國普遍受人敬重的關係。

因此我最後決定努力向學，準備參加科舉考試。父親自然欣然同意，家塾的教育是不夠的，因此父親把我送到離村約 40 里的紹興府去進中西學堂，我的兩位哥哥則已先我一年入學。我們是乘條又小又窄的河船去的。小船的一邊是一柄長槳，是利用腳力來划的，另一邊則是一柄用手操縱的短槳，作用等於船舵。沿岸我們看到許多紀念烈女節婦的牌坊。沿岸相隔相當的距離就有一個比較熱鬧的市鎮。我們一大早動身，中途在一個大鎮過了一夜，第二天下午就到了府城。

顧名思義，中西學堂教的不但是我國舊學，而且有西洋學科。這在中國教育史上還是一種新嘗試。雖然先生解釋得很粗淺，我總算開始接觸西方知識了。在這以前，我對西洋的認識只限於進口的洋貨。現在我那充滿了神仙狐鬼的腦子，卻開始與思想上的舶來品接觸了。

我在中西學堂裏首先學到的一件不可思議的事是地圓學說。我一向認為地球是平的。後來先生又告訴我，閃電是陰電和陽電撞擊的結果，並不是電神的鏡子裏發出來的閃光；雷的成因也相同，並非雷神擊鼓所生。這簡直使我目瞪口呆。從基本物理學我又學到雨是怎樣形成的。巨龍在雲端張口噴水成雨的觀念只好放棄了。了解燃燒的原理以後，我更放棄了火神的觀念。過去為我們所崇拜的神佛，像是烈日照射下的雪人，一個接着一個溶化。這是我了解一點科學的開端，也是我思想中怪力亂神信仰的結束。我在鄉村裏曾經養成研究自然的習慣，我喜歡觀察，喜歡說理，雖然有時自己根本就不知道其中的深意。這種習慣在中西學堂裏得到繼續發展的機會。我還是像過去一樣強於理解而不善記憶，凡是合理的新觀念我都樂於接受，對記憶中的舊觀念則棄如敝屣。

中西學堂的課程大部分還是屬於文科方面的：中國文學、經書和歷史。記憶的工作相當多，記憶既非我之所長，我的考試成績也就經常在中等以下。我在學校中顯得庸庸碌碌，較之當時頭角崢嶸的若干學生，顯有遜色。教師們對我的評價如此，我自己也做如是觀。

校中外國語分為英文、日文、法文三組。我先選修英文，後來又加選日文。我的日文教師是中川先生，我從他那裏學到了正確的日文發音。英文是一位中國老師教的，他的英語發音錯得一塌糊塗，後來我千辛萬苦才算改正過來。他一開始就把我們導入歧途，連字母發音都咬不准。最可笑的是他竟把字母 z 唸成「烏才」。

1898 年，我在學校裏聽到一個消息，說是光緒皇帝聽了康有為和梁啟超的話，已經決定廢科舉，辦學校。這使老一輩的學人大驚失色。但是康、梁的維新運動有如曇花一現，不久慈禧太后再度垂簾聽政，康有為和梁啟超亡命日本。中國又回到老路子，我放假回到鄉村時，看到大街的牆上張貼着黃紙繕寫的聖旨，一面是漢文，一面是滿文，寫的是通緝康、梁的命令。看起來，維新運動就此壽終正寢了。這個維新運動，以後叫做戊戌政變，是中國近代思想史的一個轉折點。雖不為革命黨人所樂道，而歷史的事實卻不能因政見不同而抹殺的。我記得梁氏逝世的消息傳到南京以後，蔡孑民先生和我兩人曾在中央政治會議提請國民政府明令表揚其功勳。適值胡展堂先生為主席，一見提案，面孔漲得通紅，便開口大罵。於是我們自動把提案取消了事。

紹興的名勝古蹟很多，它原是古代越國的都城。越王勾踐在紀元前 494 年被以蘇州為京城的吳王夫差所擊敗。勾踐定下「二十年計劃」，臥薪嘗膽，生聚教訓，終於在紀元前 473 年擊敗驕奢淫逸的吳王夫差，復興越國。

勾踐臥薪嘗膽、雪恥復國的故事，差不多已經成為家喻戶曉的格言。這則歷史教訓使一切在公私事業上遭受挫折的人重新燃起希望，它說明了忍耐、勇氣、刻苦和詳密計劃的重要性。我在勾踐臥薪嘗膽的故址領受這個歷史教訓，自然印象特別深刻。

南宋（紀元 1127—1276）的高宗也曾在紹興駐節。當時金兵南侵，宋康王渡江南遷，京城也從開封遷到杭州，離紹興府城不遠，還有南宋皇帝的陵寢。

紹興師爺是全國皆知的。全國大小衙門，幾乎到處有紹興師爺插足，紹興老酒更是名震遐邇。紹興府更出過許多歷史上有名的學者、哲學家、詩人和書法家。紹興府包括八個縣，我的故鄉餘姚便是其中一縣。

紹興的風景也很有名，這裏有迂迴曲折的小溪、橋樑密佈的小河、奔騰湍急的大江、平滑如鏡的湖泊，以及蜿蜒起伏的丘陵，山光水色使學人哲士留連忘返。

我在紹興讀了兩年書，知識大增。我開始了解 1894 年中日戰爭的意義：日本戰勝我國是吸收了西洋學術的結果。光緒皇帝的維新運動是受了這次失敗的刺激。中國預備學敵人的榜樣，學校裏有日文課程就是這個道理。

在紹興的兩年學校生活結束以後，鄉村裏盜警頻仍，使我們無法再安居下去。於是父親帶了我們一家遷到上海。我的大哥已在搬家的前一年亡故。到了上海以後，我暫時進了一家天主教學校繼續唸英文，教我們英文的是一個法國神父。我心裏想，這位英文先生既然是外國人，發音一定很準確。他的發音與我過去那位中國先生確乎迥然不同，過去那位先生把「兄弟」唸成「布朗德」，現在的法國先生卻教我們唸「布拉達」。後來我才發現那不是英國音或美國音，而是法國音。不過我在這個天主教學校裏的時間不久。因為一時找不到合適的學校，父親就讓我二哥到一位美國太太那裏學英文，二哥又把學到的英文轉授給我，因此二哥就成為學英文的「掮客」了。我對這辦法很不滿意，但是父親認為這是很聰明的安排，因為這樣可以省錢。

上海在 1899 年前後還是個小城，居留的外國人也不過 3、4 千，但是這些洋人卻都趾高氣揚，自視甚高。市政倒辦得不錯，街道寬大清潔，有電燈，也有煤氣燈。我覺得洋人真了不起，他們居然懂得電的秘密。他們發明了蒸汽機，又能建造輪船。他們在我的心目中已經成為新的神，原先心目中的神佛在我接受科學知識之後已經煙消雲散了。但是有時候他們又像是魔鬼，因為他們不可一世的神氣以及巡捕手中的木棒使我害怕，外灘公園門口掛着一個牌子寫着：「犬與華人不得入內」。犬居華人之上，這就很夠人受的了。在我的心目中，外國人是半神半鬼的怪物，很像三頭六臂的千手觀音，三隻手分別拿着電燈、輪船、洋娃娃，另外三隻手分別拿着巡棍、手槍、鴉片。從某一邊看，他是天使；從另一邊看，他卻是魔鬼。

中國人對西方文明的看法總不出這兩個極端，印象因人而異，也因時而異。李鴻章看到西方文明醜惡猙獰的一面，因此決定建立海軍，以魔鬼之矛攻魔鬼之盾。光緒帝看到西方文明光明和善的一面，因此想建立新式的學校制度。慈禧太后和義和團看到可憎的一面，想用中國的陳舊武器驅逐魔鬼。麻煩的是這位怪物的黑暗面和光明面是不可分的。它有時像是佛法無邊的神，有時又像猙獰凶殘的魔鬼，但是它憑藉的力量是相同的。我們要就不接受西方文明，要接受就得好壞一齊收下。日本就是一個很好的榜樣。沒奈何，我們只好向我們過去的敵人學習了。

我們在上海住了將近兩年。有一天晚上，我們聽說慈禧太后已經命令各省總督把所有的外國人一齊殺光。於是我們連夜舉家遷離上海，那是1900年的事，也就是義和團戰爭的開始。義和團的人自稱能用符咒對付刀槍子彈，拳術也是訓練節目之一。因此，義和團有拳匪之稱。他們預備破壞一切外國製造的東西，同時殺死所有使用外國貨的人。他們要把運進這些可惡的外國貨而阻絕他們生路的洋人統統殺光。把這些害人的外國貨介紹到中國來的教會、學校、傳教士、基督徒都罪無可逭。用刀劍、法術把這些人殺光吧！放把火把外國人的財產統統燒光！

朝廷本身也想把康有為、梁啟超介紹進來的外國思想一掃而光，免得有人再搞甚麼維新運動。義和團要消滅物質的外國貨，而慈禧太后則想消滅精神上的外國貨。不論是物質上的或者精神上的，反正都是外國貨，都是外國人造的孽。殺呀！殺光外國人！工業革命開始時，英國人曾經搗毀了威脅他們生活的機器。義和團做得更徹底，他們要同時破壞血肉構成的「機器」。

南方的人對外國人的看法稍有不同，他們歡迎外國貨，他們不覺得外國貨是盜匪的起因，他們認為毛病在於清室的苛捐雜稅以及官吏的腐敗無能。

他們要革命。

北方的老百姓和朝廷，認為外國人杜絕了他們的生路，那是對的。但是他們想藉破壞血肉構成的「機器」來解決問題卻錯了。南方的人認為朝廷本身的腐敗是苦難唯一的原因，想不到更大的原因是洋貨進口。推理是錯了，但是展開革命的行動卻是對的。歷史似乎包括一連串的意外事件、不合邏輯的推理和意想不到的結果。歷史上的風雲人物似乎不過是命運之神擺佈的工具而已。

外國人咒罵中國的盜匪，殊不知盜匪正是他們自己的貨品所引起的。在我的童年時代裏，大家都害怕老虎、鬼怪和強盜，但是實際上並沒有真的老虎、鬼怪或強盜。我們只在圖畫書中看到這些東西。忽然之間，強盜在實際生活中出現了，好像是老虎沖進你的居室，也像是鬼怪在你背後緊追不捨。最後我們所懼怕的是強盜，老虎和鬼怪卻都被遺忘了。🔚

第六章
繼續就學

在我 15 歲的時候，父親又帶我回到故鄉。我們怕義和團之亂會蔓延到上海，因此就回到鄉下去住。在蔣村住了不久，鄉下土匪愈鬧愈凶，又遷到餘姚城裏，我在餘姚縣裏的一所學校裏唸英文和算術，另外還請了一位家庭教師教中文。

大概一年之後，我到了杭州。杭州是浙江的省會，也是我國蠶絲工業的中心和五大茶市之一。杭州的綢緞和龍井茶是全國聞名的。

「上有天堂，下有蘇杭」，杭州的風景更是盡人皆知。城東南有杭州灣的錢塘大潮；城西有平滑如鏡的西湖，湖邊山麓到處是古寺別墅。馬哥·孛羅遊記中就曾盛道杭州的風景。杭州是吳越和南宋的故都，南宋曾在這裏定都150 年之久，因此名勝古跡很多。墨人騷客更代有所出。湖濱的文瀾閣收藏有四庫全書及其他要籍，正是莘莘學子潛心研究的好去處。

我在這個文化城中瞎打瞎撞，進了一所非常落伍的學校。校長是位木匠出身的美國傳教士。我以為在這所教會學校裏，至少可以學好英文，事實上卻大謬不然。這位傳教士抱着一股宗教熱忱來到中國，在主持這所教會學校之前，曾經在我的故鄉紹興府傳過教。因為他只教《聖經》，我也摸不清他肚子裏究竟有多少學問。在我們學生的心目中，士、農、工、商，士為首，對木匠出身的人多少有點輕視。我的英文教師更是俗不可耐的人物。他入教不久，靈魂也許已經得救，但是那張嘴卻很能夠使他進拔舌地獄。我為了找位英文好教師，曾經一再轉學，結果總使我大失所望。

在這所教會學校裏，學生們每天早晨必須參加禮拜。我們唱的是中文讚美詩，有些頑皮的學生就把讚美詩改編為打油詩，結果在學校裏傳誦一時。雖然我也參加主日學校和每天早晨的禮拜，我心靈卻似緊閉雙扉的河蚌，嚴拒一切精神上的舶來品。我既然已經擺脫了神仙鬼怪這一套，自然不願再接受類似的東西。而且從那時起，我在宗教方面一直是個「不可知」論者，我認為與其求死後靈魂的永恆，不如在今世奠立不朽根基。這與儒家的基本觀念剛好符合。

校園之內唯一像樣的建築是禮拜堂和校長官舍。學生則住在鴿籠一樣的土房裏，上課有時在這些宿舍裏，有時在那間破破爛爛的飯廳裏。

大概是出於好奇吧，學生們常常喜歡到校長官舍附近去散步。校長不高興學生走進他的住宅，不速之客常常被攆出來。有一次，一位強悍的學生說甚麼也不肯走開，結果與一位路過的教員發生衝突。

圍觀的人漸聚漸多。那位學生說先生摑他的耳光，同時放聲大哭，希望引起羣眾的同情。這場紛擾遂即像野火一樣波及全校。學生會多數決議，要求校長立即開革那位打人的教員。校長斷然拒絕學生的要求，羣眾的情緒愈漲愈高。校長冷然告訴學生說：如果他們不喜歡這個學校，就請他們捲舖蓋。不到兩個小時，全體學生都跑光了。

我所受的教會學校教育就此結束。但我毫不後悔，我巴不得早一天離開這個學校。

或許有人要問：為甚麼這樣的事會突然發生呢？其實這不只是學生桀傲難馴的表現而已，那耳光不過是導火線。這類事件也絕不局限於這所小小的教會學校，學生反抗學校當局已經成為全國的普遍風氣。

一年以前，上海南洋公學首先發生學潮。一位學生放了一瓶墨水在教授的坐椅上，教授不注意一屁股坐了上去，弄得全身墨跡。教授盛怒之下報告了校長，接着幾個嫌疑較大的學生被開除。這引起了學生會和學校當局之間的衝突，學生會方面還有許多教授的支持。結果全體學生離開學校。

年輕的一代正在轉變，從馴服轉變為反抗。一般老百姓看到中國受列強的侵略，就怪清廷顢頇無能；受到國父革命理論薰陶和鼓勵的學生們則熱血沸騰，隨時隨地準備發作。首當其衝的就是學校當局。

浙江省立高等學堂接着起了風潮。起因是一位學生與來校視察巡撫的一名轎夫發生齟齬,結果全校罷課,學生集體離開學校。類似的事件相繼在其他學校發生,卒使許多學府弦歌中輟。學潮並且迅速蔓延到全國。

思想較新的人同情罷課的學生,斥責學校當局過於專制;思想守舊的人則同情學校當局,嚴詞譴責學生。不論是同情學生或者是同情學校當局的,似乎沒有人體會到這就是革命的前夕,從學生初鬧學潮開始,到1911年辛亥革命成功、中華民國誕生為止,其間不過短短8年而已。

這種反抗運動可說是新興的知識分子對一向控制中國的舊士大夫階級的反抗,不但是知識上的反抗,而且是社會的和政治的反抗。自從強調物競天擇、適者生存的進化論以及其他科學觀念輸入中國以後,年輕一代的思想已經起了急劇的變化。十八世紀的個人觀念與十九世紀的工業革命同時並臨:個人自由表現於對舊制度的反抗;工業革命則表現於使中國舊行業日趨式微的舶來品。中國的舊有制度正在崩潰,新的制度尚待建設。

全國普遍顯現擾攘不安。貧窮、饑饉、瘟疫、貪污、國際知識的貧乏以及外國侵略的壓力都是因素,青年學生不過是這場戰亂中的急先鋒而已,使全國學府遍燃烽火的,不是一隻無足輕重的墨水瓶,不是一個在教會學校裏被刮了耳光的學生,也不是一次學生與轎夫之間的齟齬而已。

我們離開那所教會學校以後,我們的學生會自行籌辦了一個學校,取名「改進學社」。這個名稱是當時著名的學者章炳麟給我們起的。這位一代大儒,穿了和服木屐,履聲郭橐,溢於堂外。他說,改進的意思是改良、進步。這當然是我們願意聽的。我們的妄想是,希望把這個學校辦得和牛津大學或者劍橋大學一樣,真是稚氣十足。但是不久我們就嘗到幻滅的滋味。不到半年,學生就漸漸散了,結果只剩下幾個被選擔任職務的學生。當這幾位職員發現再沒有選舉他們的羣眾時,他們也就另覓求學之所去了。

我自己進了浙江高等學堂。我原來的名字「夢熊」已經入了鬧事學生的黑名單,因此就改用「夢麟」註冊。我參加入學考試,幸被錄取。當時的高等學堂,正當罷課學潮之後重新改組,是一向有「學人之省」之稱的浙江省的最高學府。它的前身是求是書院。「求是」是前輩學者做學問的一貫態度。求是書院和紹興的中西學堂有很多相似的地方，課程中包括一些外國語和科學科目。後來新學科愈來愈見重要，所占時間也愈來愈多，求是書院終於發展為一種新式的學校，同時改名為浙江高等學堂。

這個學堂既然辦在省城，同時又由政府負擔經費，它自然而然地成為全省文化運動的中心。它的課程和中西學堂很相似，不過功課比較深，科目比較多，先生教得比較好，全憑記憶的工作比較少。它已粗具現代學校的規模。

我自從進了紹興的中西學堂以後，一直在黑暗中摸索。看到東邊有一點閃爍的亮光，我就摸到東邊；東邊亮光一閃而逝以後，我又連忙轉身撲向西邊。現在進了浙江高等學堂，眼前豁然開朗，對一切都可以看得比較真切了。我開始讀英文原版的世界史。開始時似乎很難了解外國人民的所作所為，正如一個人試圖了解羣眾行動時一樣困難。後來我才慢慢地了解西方文化的發展。自然那只是一種粗枝大葉而且模模糊糊的了解，但是這一點了解已經鼓起我對西洋史的興趣，同時奠定了進一步研究的基礎。

在浙江高等學堂裏所接觸的知識非常廣泛。從課本裏，從課外閱讀，以及師友的談話中，我對中國以及整個世界的知識日漸增長。我漸漸熟悉將近4000 年的中國歷史，同時對於歷代興衰的原因也有了相當的了解。這是我後來對西洋史從事比較研究的一個基礎。

近代史上值得研究的問題就更多：首先是 1894 年使台灣割讓於日本的中日戰爭，童年時代所看到的彩色圖畫曾使我對它產生錯誤的印象；其次是1898 年康有為和梁啟超的維新運動，那是我在中西學堂讀書時所發生的；再其次是 1900 年的義和團戰爭，我在上海時曾經聽到許多關於義和團的消息；然後是 1904 年的日俄戰爭，我在杭州唸書時正在進行。每一件事都有豐富的資料足供研究而且使人深省。

我們也可以用倒捲珠簾的方式來研究歷史：1885 年的中法戰爭使中國喪失了越南；太平天國始於 1851 年而終於 1864 年，其間還出現過戈登將軍和華德將軍的常勝軍；1840 年鴉片戰爭的結果使中國失去了香港；如果再往上追溯，明末清初有耶穌會教士來華傳教，元朝有馬哥・孛羅來華遊歷；再往上可以追溯到中國與羅馬帝國的關係。

梁啟超在東京出版的「新民叢報」是份綜合性的刊物，內容從短篇小說到形而上學，無所不包。其中有基本科學常識，有歷史，有政治論著，有自傳，有文學作品。梁氏簡潔的文筆深入淺出，能使人了解任何新穎或困難的問題。當時正需要介紹西方觀念到中國，梁氏深入淺出的才能尤其顯得重要。梁啟超的文筆簡明、有力、流暢，學生們讀來裨益非淺，我就是千千萬萬受其影響的學生之一。我認為這位偉大的學者，在介紹現代知識給年輕一代的工作上，其貢獻較同時代的任何人為大。他的「新民叢報」是當時每一位渴求新知識的青年的智慧源泉。

在政治上，他主張在清廷主持之下進行立憲維新。這時候，革命黨人也出版了許多刊物，宣傳孫中山先生的激烈思想。中山先生認為共和政體勝於君主立憲，同時他認為中國應由中國人自己來統治，而不應由腐敗無能的滿洲人來統治。浙籍學生在東京也出版了一個定名「浙江潮」的月刊。這個雜誌因為攻擊清廷過於激烈，以致與若干類似的雜誌同時被郵政當局禁止寄遞。但是日本政府卻同情中國留學生的革命運動，因此這些被禁的雜誌仍舊不斷地從日本流入上海租界。因此上海就成為革命思想的交易所，同情革命的人以及營求厚利者再從上海把革命書刊走私到其他城市。

浙江高等學堂本身就到處有宣傳革命的小冊子、雜誌和書籍，有的描寫清兵入關時的暴行，有的則描寫清廷的腐敗，有的則描寫清廷對滿人和漢人的不平等待遇。學生們如飢似渴地讀着這些書刊，幾乎沒有任何力量足以阻止他們。

事實上，清廷腐敗無能的實例，在校門之外就俯拾即是。杭州城牆之內就有一個滿洲人住的小城，裏面駐紮着監視漢人的「旗兵」。兩百多年前，政府特地劃出這個城中之城作為駐紮杭州的「旗兵」的營房。這些旗兵的子子孫孫一直就住在這裏，名義上仍舊是軍人。滿漢通婚原則上是禁止的，但是滿人如果願意娶漢人為妻是准許的，實際上這類婚姻很少就是了。太平軍圍城時，杭州的旗人全部被殺。內戰結束以後，原來駐紮湖北荊州的一部分旗兵移駐杭州，來填補空缺。這些從荊州來的旗人當時還有健在的，而且說的是湖北話。雖然他們多數已經去世，但是他們的子女仍舊住在那裏，而且說他們父輩所說的方言。道地杭州人很容易察覺這些旗人的湖北口音。但是從第三代開始，他們就說杭州的本地方言了。

當時的浙江高等學堂裏有十名旗人子弟。這幾位青年人對學校中的革命運動裝聾作啞，應付得很得當。其中一人原是蒙古人的後裔，他甚至告訴我，他也贊成革清朝的命，因為他雖然是「旗兵」，卻不是滿人。

這些所謂旗兵，實際上絕對不是兵；他們和老百姓毫無區別。他們在所謂「兵營」裏娶妻養子，對衝鋒陷陣的武事毫無所知。唯一的區別是他們有政府的俸餉而無所事事，他們過的是一種寄生生活，因之身體、智力和道德都日漸衰退。他們經常出入西湖湖濱的茶館，有的則按當時的習尚提着鳥籠到處遊蕩，一般老百姓都敬而遠之。如果有人得罪他們，就隨時有挨揍的危險。這些墮落、腐化、驕傲的活榜樣，在青年學生羣中普遍引起憎恨的鄙夷。他們所引起的反感，比起革命宣傳的效果只有過之而無不及。

我們從梁啟超獲得精神食糧，孫中山先生以及其他革命志士，則使我們的革命情緒不斷增漲。到了重要關頭，引發革命行動的就是這種情緒。後來時機成熟，理想和行動兼顧的孫中山先生終於決定性地戰勝主張君主立憲的新士大夫階級。

這就是浙江高等學堂的一般氣氛。其他學校的情形也大都如此。我對這一切活動都感興趣。我喜歡搜求消息，喜歡就所獲得的資料加以思考分析，同時也喜歡使自己感情奔放，參加行動。但是我常常適可而止。為求萬全，我仍舊準備參加科舉考試。除了革命，科舉似乎仍舊是參加政府工作的不二途徑，並且我覺得革命似乎遙遙無期，而且困難重重。我有時候非常膽小而怕羞，有時候卻又非常大膽而莽撞，因此我對自己的性格始終沒有自信。所以我的行動常常很謹慎，在採取確切的行動之前，喜歡先探索一下道路。尤其碰到岔路時，我總是考慮再三才能作決定。如果猶豫不決，我很可能呆坐道旁，想入非非。但是一旦作了決定，我必定堅持到底。我一生犯過許多錯誤，但沒有犯不可挽回的錯誤，所以沒有讓時代潮流把我捲走。🔵

第七章
參加郡試

郡試快到了。一天清早，我從杭州動身往紹興去，因為我們那一區的郡試是在紹興舉行。行李夫用一根扁擔挑起行李走出校門，我緊緊地跟在他的後面。扁擔的一端繫着一隻皮箱和一隻網籃，另一端是鋪蓋卷。走到校門口，碰到一位教師，他向我微微一笑，並祝我吉星高照。

穿過許多平坦的石板路，又穿過許多迂迴狹窄的小巷，我們終於到了錢塘江邊。渡船碼頭離岸約有一里路，我小心翼翼地踏上吱吱作響的木板通過一條便橋到達碼頭。渡船上有好幾把笨重的木槳，風向對時也偶然張起帆篷。船行很慢，同時是逆水行駛，所以整整花了兩個小時才渡過錢塘江。當時誰也想不到 30 年之後竟有一條鋼鐵大橋橫跨寬闊的江面，橋上還可以同時行駛火車和汽車。

上岸以後僱了一乘小轎。穿過綿亘數里的桑林，到達一個人煙稠密的市區，然後轉船續向紹興進發，船上乘客擠得像沙丁魚。我們只能直挺挺地平躺着睡，如果你縮一縮腿，原來放腿的地方馬上就會被人佔據；如果你想側轉身睡一下，你就別想再躺平。

在船上過了一夜，第二天早晨到達紹興。寄宿在一個製扇工匠的家裏，房間又小又暗，而且充滿了製扇用的某種植物油氣味。晚上就在菜油燈下讀書，但是燈光太暗，看小字很吃力。我們不敢用煤油燈，因為屋子裏到處是易燃的製扇材料，黑暗中摸索時還常要跌跤。

考試開始時，清晨四點左右大家就齊集在試院門前，聽候點名。那是一個初秋的早晨，天氣相當冷。幾千位考生擠在院子裏，每人頭上戴着一頂沒有頂子的紅纓帽，手裏提着一個燈籠、一隻考籃。大廳門口擺着一張長桌。

監考官就是紹興知府，昂然坐在長桌後面。他戴着藍色晶頂的紅纓帽，穿着深藍色的長袍，外罩黑馬褂，胸前垂着一串朝珠。那是他的全套官服。他提起朱筆順着名單，開始點名。他每點一個名，站在他旁邊的人就拖着長腔唱出考生的名字。考生聽到自己的名字以後，就高聲答應：「有！某某人保。」保的人也隨即唱名證明。監考官望一眼以後，如果認為並無舛錯，就用朱筆在考生名字上加上紅點。

考生點名後就可以進考棚了。他的帽子和衣服都得經過搜索，以防夾帶，任何寫了字的紙頭都要沒收。

考生魚貫進入考棚，找出自己的位置分別就座。座位都是事先編好號碼的。考卷上有寫好考生姓名的浮簽，繳卷時就撕去浮簽。考卷的一角另有彌封的號碼，錄取名單決定以後才開拆彌封，以免徇私舞弊。清末時，政府各部門無不百弊叢生。唯有科舉制度頗能保持獨立，不為外力所染。科舉功名之所以受人器重，大概就是這個緣故。

考試的題目不出四書五經的範圍，所以每個考生必須把四書五經背得爛熟。我在家塾裏以及後來在紹興中西學堂裏，已經在這方面下過苦功。題目寫在方形的燈籠罩子上，白罩子上寫着黑字，燈籠裏面點着蠟燭，因此從遠遠的地方就可以看得很清楚。提燈籠的人把燈籠擎得高高的，在考生座位之間的甬道上來回走好幾次，所以大家都不會看漏題目。

將近中午時，辦事人員開始核對考生的進度，每一份考卷的最末一行都蓋上印子。下午四點鐘左右，炮聲響了，那是收卷的第一次訊號。大門打開，吹鼓手也嗚嗚啦啦開始吹奏起來。考生繳了卷，在樂聲中慢慢走出大門，大門外親戚朋友正在焦急地等待着。繳了卷的人完全出來以後，大門又重新關上。第二次繳卷的訊號大約在一小時以後發出，同樣鳴炮奏樂。第三次下令收卷則在六點鐘左右，這一次可不再鳴炮奏樂。

考試以後，我們要等上十天、八天，才能知道考試結果。因此放榜以前我們可以大大地玩一陣。試院附近到處是書舖，我常碰到全省聞名的舉人徐錫麟，在書舖裏抽出書來看。我認識他，因為他曾在紹興中西學堂教算學。

想不到不出數年，他的心臟被挖出來，在安徽巡撫恩銘靈前致祭，因他為革命刺殺了恩銘。街頭巷尾還有象棋攤子，棋盤兩邊都寫着「觀棋不語真君子，落子無悔大丈夫」兩句俗語。街上有臨時的酒樓飯館，出售著名的紹興酒和價廉物美的菜肴。一毛錢買一壺酒。醉蚶、糟雞、家鄉肉，每盤也只要一毛。如肯費三四毛錢，保管你買得滿面春風，齒頰留香。城裏有流動的戲班子，高興的時候，我們還可以看看戲。

放榜的那一天，一大羣人擠在試院大門前一座高牆前面守候。放榜時鳴炮奏樂，儀式非常隆重。榜上寫的是錄取考生的號碼，而非姓名。號碼排成一圓圈，以免有先後次序的分別。

我發現自己的號碼也排入圓圈，列在牆上那張其大無比的長方形榜上，真是喜出望外。號碼是黑墨大字寫的，但是我還是不肯相信自己的眼睛，連揉了幾次眼，發現自己的號碼的的確確排在榜上的大圈圈內，這才放了心。連忙擠出人羣，回到寄宿的地方。在我往外擠的時候，看到另一位考生也正在往外跑。他打着一把傘，這把傘忽然被一根柵欄鈎住，他一拖，傘就向上翻成荷葉形。可是這位興奮過度的考生，似乎根本沒有注意他的傘翻向天了，還是匆匆忙忙往前跑。

幾天之後，舉行複試。複試要淘汰一部分人，所以初試錄取的還得捏一把汗。複試時運氣還算不錯。放榜時，發現自己的名字列在居中的某一行上。

第三次考試只是虛應故事而已。除了寫一篇文章以外，名義上我們還得默寫一段《聖諭廣訓》（皇帝訓諭士子的上諭）；但是我們每人都可以帶一冊進考場，而且老實不客氣地照抄一遍。這次考試由學政（俗稱學台）親自蒞場監考。試院大門口的兩旁樹着兩根旗竿，旗竿上飄着長達15尺的長幡，幡上寫的就是這位學台的官銜。記得他的官銜是：「禮部侍郎提督浙江全省學政……」

再過幾天之後，我一大早就被窗外一陣噹噹小鑼驚醒。原來是試差來報喜。我已經考取了附生，也就是平常所說的秀才。試差帶來一份捷報，那是一張大約六尺長，四尺寬的紅紙，上面用宋楷大字寫着：

「貴府相公某蒙禮部侍郎提督浙江全省學政某考試錄取餘姚縣學附生」所謂「縣學」只有一所空無所有的孔廟，由一位「教諭」主持，事實上這位「教諭」並不設帳講學，所謂「縣學」是有名無實的。按我們家庭經濟狀況，我須呈繳一百元的贄敬，拜見老師，不過經過討價還價，只繳了一半，也並沒有和老師見過面。

當討價還價正在進行的時候，父親惱怒了說，孔廟裏應該拜財神才是。旁邊一位老先生說，那是說不得的。從前有一位才子金聖歎，因為譏笑老師，說了一句「把孔子牌位取消，把財神抬進學宮」的話，奉旨殺了頭。臨刑前這位玩世不恭的才子歎道：「殺頭至痛也，聖歎於無意中得之，豈不快哉。」

郡試以後，又再度回到浙江高等學堂，接受新式教育。我離開紹興時，房東告訴我，一位同住在他店裏的考生憤憤不平地對他說，學台簡直瞎了眼，居然取了像我這樣目不識丁的人，其意若曰像他那樣滿腹經綸的人反而落第，真是豈有此理。我笑笑沒說甚麼，考試中本來不免有幸與不幸的！

回到學校以後，馬上又埋頭讀書，整天為代數、物理、動物學和歷史等功課而忙碌，課餘之暇，又如飢似渴地閱讀革命書刊，並與同學討論當時的政治問題。郡試的那段日子和浙江高等學堂的生活恍若隔世。靜定的、霧樣迷濛的中世紀生活，似乎在一夜之間就轉變為洶湧的革命時代的漩渦。我像是做了一場大夢。

兩個月以後，寒假到了。奉父親之命回到鄉間，接受親戚朋友的道賀。那時我是十九歲，至親們都希望我有遠大的前程，如果祖墳的風水好，很可能一步一步由秀才而舉人，由舉人而進士，光大門楣，榮及鄉里，甚至使祖先在天之靈也感到欣慰。二哥已早我幾年考取了秀才，那時正在北京大學（京師大學堂）讀書。當時的學生們聽說京師大學四個字，沒有不肅然起敬的。想不到 15 年之後我竟為時會所迫承乏了北京大學的校長職務。回想起來，真令人覺得命運不可捉摸。

在紹興時曾經收到一份捷報，不久，試差又用一份同樣以紅紙寫的捷報，敲着銅鑼分向我家鄉的親戚家屬報喜。開筵慶祝的那一天，穿起藍綢衫，戴了一頂銀雀頂的紅纓帽。好幾百親戚朋友，包括婦孺老少，齊來道賀，一連吃了兩天喜酒。大廳中張燈結綵，並有吹班奏樂助興。最高興的自然是父親，他希望他的兒子有一天能在朝中做到宰相，因為俗語說：「秀才為宰相之根苗」。至於我自己，簡直有點迷惘。兩個互相矛盾的勢力正在拉着，一個把我往舊世界拖，一個把我往新世界拖。我不知道怎麼辦。

在鄉間住了三個星期，學校重新開學，我又再度全神貫注地開始研究新學問。在浙江高等學堂再逗留了半年光景，到暑假快開始時，又離開了。滿腦子矛盾的思想，簡直使尚未成熟的心靈無法忍受，新與舊的衝突，立憲與革命的衝突，常常鬧得頭腦天旋地轉，有時覺得坐立不安，有時又默坐出神，出神時，會覺得自己忽然上衝霄漢，然後又驟然落地，結果在地上跌得粉碎，立刻被旋風吹散無蹤了。

我的近親當中曾經發現有人患精神病，我有時不禁懷疑自己是否也有點神經質的遺傳。父親和叔祖都説過，我小時候的思想行動本來就與常兒不同。我還記得有一天伯祖罵我，説我將來如不成君子必成流氓。雖然不大明白這話的意思，但是我心裏想，一定要做君子。

這個世界的確是個瘋狂的世界，難道我也真的發了瘋嗎？至少有一個問題在腦子裏還是很清楚的：那就是如何拯救祖國，免受列強的瓜分。革命正迅速地在全國青年學生羣中生根發展。投身革命運動的青年學生愈多，孫中山先生的影響也愈來愈廣。清室覆亡已經近在旦夕了。

我渴望找個更理想、更西化的學校。因為這時候已經看得清楚：不論立憲維新或者革命，西化的潮流已經無法抗拒。有一天早晨，無意中闖進禁止學生入內的走廊，碰到了學監。他問有甚麼事，我只好臨時扯了個謊，説母親生病，寫信來要我回家。

「哦！那太不幸了。你還是趕快回家吧！」學監很同情地説。

回到宿舍，收拾起行李，當天上午就離開學校，乘小火輪沿運河到了上海。參加上海南洋公學的入學考試，結果幸被錄取。那是 1904 年的事。為爭取滿洲控制權的日俄戰爭正在激烈進行。✿

第八章
西化運動

　　雖然新舊之爭仍在方興未艾，立憲與革命孰長孰短亦無定論，中國這時已經無可置疑地踏上西化之路了。日本對帝俄的勝利，更使中國的西化運動獲得新的鼓勵，這時聚集東京的中國留學生已近五萬人，東京已經成為新知識的中心。國內方面，政府也已經開始一連串的革新運動，教育、軍事、警政都已根據日本的藍圖採取新制度。許多人相信：經過日本同化修正的西方制度和組織，要比純粹的西洋制度更能適合中國的國情，因此他們主張通過日本接受西洋文化。但是也有一班人認為：既然我們必須接受西洋文明，何不直接向西洋學習？

　　我是主張直接向西方學習的，雖然許多留學日本的朋友來信辯難，我卻始終堅持自己的看法。進了南洋公學，就是想給自己打點基礎，以便到美國留學。這裏一切西洋學科的課本都是英文的，剛好合了我的心意。

　　南洋公學開辦時，採納了美國傳教士福開森博士的許多意見。南洋公學是交通大學的前身，交通大學附近的福開森路，就是為紀念這位美國傳教士而命名的。南洋公學的預科，一切按照美國的中學學制辦理，因此南洋公學可說是升入美國大學的最好階梯。學校裏有好幾位講授現代學科的美國人。在校兩年，在英文閱讀方面已經沒有多大困難，不過講卻始終講不好。學校教的英文並不根據語音學原理，我的舌頭又太硬，始終跟不上。

　　課程方面分為兩類，一類是中國舊學，一類是西洋學科。我在兩方面的成績都還過得去，有一次還同時僥倖獲得兩類考試的榮譽獎。因此蒙校長召見，謬承獎勉。

　　校舍是根據西洋設計而建築的，主要建築的中心有一座鐘樓，數里之外就可以望見。有一排房子的前面是一個足球場，常年綠草如茵，而且打掃得很整齊。學校當局鼓勵學生玩足球和棒球，學生們對一般的運動也都很感興趣。

我生來體弱，進了南洋公學以後，開始體會到要有高深的學問，必須先有強健的體魄。除了每日的體操和輕度的運動之外，還給自己定了一套鍛煉身體的辦法。每天六點鐘光景，練習半小時的啞鈴，晚間就寢前再練一刻鐘。繼續不斷地練了三年，此後身體一直很好，而且心情也總是很愉快。

包括德、智、體三要素的斯賓塞爾教育原則這時已經介紹到中國。為了發展德育，就溫習了四書，同時開始研究宋明的哲學家以及歷代中外偉人的傳記，希望借此學習他們的榜樣，碰到認為足資借鑒的言行時，就把它們摘錄在日記本上。然後仔細加以思考，試着照樣去做，同時注意其成績。這些成績也記載在日記上，以備進一步的考核。

每當發現對某些問題的中西見解非常相似、甚至完全相同時，我總有難以形容的喜悅。如果中西賢哲都持同一見解，那末照着做自然就不會錯了。當發現歧見時，就加以研究，設法找出其中的原因。這樣就不知不覺地做了一項東西道德行為標準的比較研究。這種研究工作最重要的結果是學到了如何在道德觀念中區別重要的與不重要的，以及基本的與浮面的東西。

從此以後，對於如何立身處世開始有了比較肯定、比較確切、也比較自信的見解，因為道德觀念是指導行為的準繩。

我開始了解東西方的整體性，同時也更深切地體會到宋儒陸象山所說的「東海有聖人出焉，此心同，此理同。西海有聖人出焉，此心同，此理同」的名言。同時開始體會到紊亂中的統一，因為我發現基本道理原極有限，了解這些基本道理之間的異同矛盾正可以互相發明，互相印證。使我感到頭暈眼花的只是細微末節的紛擾而已。孟子和陸象山告訴我們，做學問要抓住要點而捨棄細節，要完全憑我們的理智辨別是非。於是我開始發展以理解為基礎的判斷能力，不再依賴傳統的信仰。這是思想上的一次大解放，像是脫下一身緊繃繃的衫褲那樣舒服而自由。

但是，理解力也不能憑空生存。想得太多，結果除失望外一無成就，這樣是犯了孔子所說的「思而不學」的毛病。當然，導向正確思想的途徑還是從思想本身開始，然後從經驗中學習如何思想。你不可能教導一個根本不用腦筋的人如何去思想。後來我留美時讀到杜威的「我們如何思想」，使我的信念更為加強。

儒家說，正心誠意是修身的出發點，修身則是治國、平天下的根基。因此，我想，救國必先救己。於是決心努力讀書、思考，努力鍛鍊身體，努力敦品勵行。我想，這就是修身的正確途徑了，有了良好的身心修養，將來才能為國服務。

在南洋公學讀書的時候，清廷終於在 1905 年採取了教育改革的重要步驟，毅然宣佈廢止科舉。年輕一代迷戀過去的大門從此關閉。廢科舉的詔書是日本戰勝帝俄所促成的。代替科舉的是抄襲自日本的一套新教育制度。日本的教育制度是模仿西方的。追本溯源，中國的新教育制度仍舊來自西方。中國現在總算不折不扣地踏上西化的途程了。

在這以前，上海曾經是我國革命分子文化運動的中心。中國的知識分子和革命領袖，躲在上海公共租界和法租界，可以享受言論自由和出版自由。政治犯和激烈分子在租界裏討論，發表他們的見解，思想自由而且蓬勃一時，情形足與希臘的城邦媲美。

我自己除了在南洋公學接受課本知識之外，也參加了各式各樣的活動，但是學習的性質居多，談不到積極工作。到禮拜六和禮拜天時，常常到福州路的奇芳茶館去坐坐。那時候，上海所有的學生都喜歡到「奇芳」去吃茶，同時參加熱烈的討論。茶館裏有一位叫「野雞大王」的，每日在那裏兜售新書，他那副樣子，去過「奇芳」的人沒有一個會忘記。他穿着一身破爛的西裝，頭上戴着一頂灰色的滿是油垢的鴨舌頭帽。他專門販賣革命書刊給學生，他的貨色當中還包括一本叫「性學新論」的小冊子，據他解釋，那只是用來吸引讀者的。誰也不知道他的名字。吳稚暉先生說，他知道他是誰，並告訴了我他的名字，我卻忘記了。我們也不曉得他住在甚麼地方。任何革命書刊都可以從他那裏買得到。這些書，因租界當局應中國政府之請，在名義上是禁止販賣的。

科舉廢止的同一年，孫中山先生在東京組織同盟會，參加的學生有好幾百人，中山先生被選為主席。這一年也就是日本和俄國簽訂《朴茨茅斯條約》，結束日俄戰爭的一年。日本在擊敗西方列強之一的俄國以後，正蠢蠢欲動，預備侵略中國。十年之後，日本向中國提出著名的二十一條要求，16年以後，發動 9・18 瀋陽事變，最後終於在民國 26 年與中國發生全面戰爭。

當時，上海正在熱烈展開抵制美貨運動，抗議美國國會通過排華法案。學生和商人聯合挨戶勸告中國商店店主不要售賣美國貨。店主亟於賣掉被抵制的貨品，只好削價脫售，有許多顧客倒也樂於從後門把貨色買走。羣眾大會中，大家爭着發表激烈演說，反對排華法案。有一次會中，一位慷慨激昂的演說者捶胸頓足，結果把鞋跟頓掉了。鞋跟飛到聽眾頭上，引得哄堂大笑。

翌年也發生一件重要的事情。江浙兩省的紳士同上海的學生和商人聯合起來反對英國人投資建築蘇杭甬鐵路。示威的方式包括羣眾大會、發通電、街頭演說等等，同時開始招股準備用本國資金建築這條鐵路，路線要改為由上海經杭州到寧波。以上海代替蘇州的理由很奇怪，說蘇州是個內陸城市，鐵路不經過蘇州，可以使蘇州免受外國的影響。英國人對路線讓步了，鐵路也在第二年動工興建。

那幾年裏，全國各校的學生倒是都能與學校當局相安無事，一方面是因為他們對校外活動的興趣提高，另一方面是因為他們對於給學校當局找些無謂的麻煩已經感到厭倦。不過，他們卻把注意力轉移到為他們做飯的廚子身上去了。當時上海學生的伙食費是每月六塊錢；在內地，只要三塊錢。因此飯菜不會好到哪裏去。但是學生對伙食很不滿意，不是埋怨米太粗糙，就是埋怨菜蔬質地太差，因此常常要求加菜 —— 通常是加炒蛋，因為炒蛋最方便。當時雞蛋也很便宜，一塊錢可以買 5、60 個。有時候，學生們就砸碎碗碟出氣，甚至把廚子揍一頓。幾乎沒有一個學校沒有「飯廳風潮」。

1907 年，安徽省城安慶發生了一次曇花一現的革命。革命領袖是徐錫麟，我們在前面曾提起他過。他是安徽省警務督辦，曾在紹興中西學堂教過書，我們在前面也曾經提及。（中西學堂就是我最初接觸西方學問的地方，我在那裏學到地球是圓的。）他中過舉人，在中西學堂教過幾年書以後，又到日本留學。他回國後向朋友借了五萬塊錢，捐了道台的缺，後來被派到安慶。他控制了警察以後，親手槍殺安徽巡撫，並在安慶發動革命。他同兩名親信帶了警校學生及警察部隊佔領軍械庫，在庫門口架起大炮據守。但是他們因缺乏軍事訓練，無法使用大炮，結果被官兵沖入，徐錫麟當場被捕。他的兩位親信，一名叫陳伯平的陣亡了，一位叫馬子夷的事後被捕。

馬子夷是我在浙江高等學堂的同學，他和陳伯平從日本赴安慶時，曾在上海逗留一個時期。兩個人幾乎每天都來看我，大談革命運動。他們認為革命是救中國的唯一途徑，還約我同他們一道去安慶。但是一位當錢莊經理的堂兄勸我先到日本去一趟。那年暑假，就和一位朋友去東京，順便參觀一個展覽會。我們離滬赴日的前夕，馬子夷、陳伯平和我三個人在一枝香酒樓聚餐話別。第二天我去日本，他們也搭長江輪船赴安慶。想不到一枝香酒樓一別竟成永訣。

初次乘大洋輪船，樣樣覺得新奇。抽水馬桶其妙無比。日本茶房禮貌周到。第二天早晨，我們到達長崎，優美的風景給我很深的印象。下午經過馬關，就是李鴻章在 1895 年與日本簽訂「馬關條約」的地方。我們在神戶上岸，從神戶乘火車到東京，在新橋車站落車。一位在東京讀書的朋友領我們到小石川 23 番君代館住下。東京的街道當時還沒有鋪石子，更沒有柏油，那天又下雨，結果滿地泥濘。

我到上野公園的展覽會參觀了好幾十趟，對日本的工業發展印象很深。在一個展覽戰利品的戰跡博物館裏，看到中日戰爭中俘獲的中國軍旗、軍服和武器，簡直使我慚愧得無地自容。夜間整個公園被幾萬盞電燈照耀得如同白晝，興高采烈的日本人提着燈籠在公園中遊行，高呼萬歲。兩年前，他們陶醉於對俄的勝利，至今猶狂喜不已。我孤零零地站在一個假山頂上望着遊行的隊伍，觸景生情，不禁泫然涕下。

到日本後約一星期，君代館的下女在清晨拿了一份日文報紙來，我從報上獲悉徐錫麟在安慶起義失敗的消息。如果我不來日本而跟那兩位朋友去安慶，恐怕我不會今日在此講「西潮」的故事了。

我對日本的一般印象非常良好。整個國家像個大花園，人民衣飾整飭，城市清潔。他們內心或許很驕傲，對生客卻很有禮貌。強迫教育使國民的一般水準遠較中國為高，這或許就是使日本成為世界強國的秘密所在。這是我在日本停留一月後帶回來的印象。後來赴美國學教育學，也受這些感想的指示。但是國家興衰事情並不如此簡單，讓我等機會再談罷。

不久以後，又開始為學校功課而忙碌。第二年暑假，跑到杭州參加浙江省官費留美考試，結果未被錄取。於是向父親拿到幾千塊錢，預備到加利福尼亞州深造。⑯

第二部

留美時期

第九章
負笈西行

我拿出一部分錢，買了衣帽雜物和一張往三藩市的頭等船票，其餘的錢就以兩塊墨西哥鷹洋對一元美金的比例兌取美鈔。上船前，找了一家理髮店剪去辮子。理髮匠舉起利剪，抓住我的辮子時，我簡直有上斷頭台的感覺，全身汗毛直豎。咔嚓兩聲，辮子剪斷了，我的腦袋也像是隨着剪聲落了地。理髮匠用紙把辮子包好還給我。上船後，我把這包辮子丟入大海，讓它隨波逐浪而去。

我拿到醫生證明書和護照之後，到上海的美國總領事館請求簽證，按照移民條例第六節規定，申請以學生身份赴美。簽證後買好船票，搭乘美國郵船公司的輪船往三藩市。那時是 1908 年 8 月底。同船有 10 來位中國同學。郵船啟碇，慢慢駛離祖國海岸，我的早年生活也就此告一段落。在上船前，我曾經練了好幾個星期的秋千，所以在 24 天的航程中，一直沒有暈船。

這隻郵船比我前一年赴神戶時所搭的那艘日本輪船遠為寬大豪華。船上最使我驚奇的事是跳舞。我生長在男女授受不親的社會裏，初次看到男女相偎相依、婆娑起舞的情形，覺得非常不順眼。旁觀了幾次之後，我才慢慢開始欣賞跳舞的優美。

船到三藩市，一位港口醫生上船來檢查健康，對中國學生的眼睛檢查得特別仔細，唯恐有人患砂眼。

我上岸時第一個印象是移民局官員和警察所反映的國家權力。美國這個共和政體的國家，她的人民似乎比君主專制的中國人民更少個人自由，這簡直弄得我莫名其妙。我們在中國時，天高皇帝遠，一向很少感受國家權力的拘束。

我們在三藩市逗留了幾個鐘頭，還到唐人街轉了一趟。我和另一位也預備進加州大學的同學，由加大中國同學會主席領路到了卜技利。晚飯在夏德克路的天光餐館吃，每人付兩角五分錢，吃的有湯、紅燒牛肉、一塊蘋果餅和一杯咖啡。我租了班克洛夫路的柯爾太太的一間房子。柯爾太太已有相當年紀，但是很健談，對中國學生很關切。她吩咐我出門以前必定要關燈；洗東西以後必定要關好自來水龍頭；花生殼決不能丟到抽水馬桶裏；銀錢決不能隨便丟在桌子上；出門時不必鎖門；如果我願意鎖門，就把鑰匙留下藏在地毯下面。她說：「如果你需要甚麼，你只管告訴我就是了。我很了解客居異國的心情。你就拿我的家當自己的家好了，不必客氣。」隨後她向我道了晚安才走。

到卜技利時，加大秋季班已經開學，因此我只好等到春季再說。我請了加大的一位女同學給我補習英文，學費每小時五毛錢。這段時間內，我把全部精力花在英文上。每天早晨必讀「三藩市紀事報」，另外還訂了一份「展望」週刊，作為精讀的資料。《韋氏大學字典》一直不離手，碰到稍有疑問的字就打開字典來查，四個月下來，居然字彙大增，讀報紙、雜誌也不覺得吃力了。

初到美國時，就英文而論，我簡直是半盲、半聾、半啞。如果我希望能在學校裏跟得上功課，這些障礙必須先行克服。頭一重障礙，經過四個月的不斷努力，總算大致克服了，完全克服它也不過是時間問題而已。第二重障礙要靠多聽人家談話和教授講課才能慢慢克服。教授講課還算比較容易懂，因為教授們的演講，思想有系統，語調比較慢，發音也清晰。普通談話的範圍比較廣泛，而且包括一連串互不銜接而且五花八門的觀念，要抓住談話的線索頗不容易。到劇院去聽話劇對白，其難易則介於演講與談話之間。

最困難的是克服開不得口的難關。主要的原因是我在中國時一開始就走錯了路。錯誤的習慣已經根深蒂固，必須花很長的時間才能矯正過來。其次是我根本不懂語音學的方法，單憑模仿，不一定能得到準確的發音。因為口中發出的聲音與耳朵聽到的聲音之間，以及耳朵與口舌之間，究竟還有很大的差別。耳朵不一定能夠抓住正確的音調，口舌也不一定能夠遵照耳朵的指示發出正確的聲音。此外，加利福尼亞這個地方對中國人並不太親熱，難得使人不生身處異地、萬事小心的感覺。我更特別敏感，不敢貿然與美國人廝混，別人想接近我時，我也很怕羞。許多可貴的社會關係都因此斷絕了。語言只有多與人接觸才能進步，我既然這樣固步自封，這方面的進步自然慢之又慢。後來我進了加大，這種口語上的缺陷，嚴重地影響了我在課內課外參加討論的機會。有人問我問題時，我常常是臉一紅，頭一低，不知如何回答。教授們總算特別客氣，從來不勉強我回答任何問題。也許他們了解我處境的窘困，也許是他們知道我是外國人，所以特別加以原諒。無論如何，他們知道，我雖然噤若寒蟬，對功課仍舊很用心，因為我的考試成績多半列在乙等以上。

日月如梭，不久聖誕節就到了。聖誕前夕，我獨自在一家餐館裏吃晚餐。菜比初到三藩市那一天好得多，花的錢，不必說，也非那次可比。飯後上街閒遊，碰到沒有拉起窗簾的人家，我就從窗戶眺望他們歡欣團聚的情形。每戶人家差不多都有滿飾小電燈或蠟燭的聖誕樹。

大除夕，我和幾位中國同學從卜技利渡海到三藩市。從渡輪上可以遠遠地看到對岸的鐘樓裝飾着幾千盞電燈。上岸後，發現三藩市到處人山人海。碼頭上候船室裏的自動鋼琴震耳欲聾。這些鋼琴只要投下一枚鎳幣就能自動彈奏。我隨着人潮慢慢地在大街上閒逛，耳朵裏滿是小喇叭和小鼗鼓的嘈音，玩喇叭和鼗鼓的人特別喜歡湊着漂亮的太太小姐們的耳朵開玩笑，這些太太小姐們雖然耳朵吃了苦頭，但仍然覺得這些玩笑是一種恭維，因此總是和顏悅色地報以一笑。空中到處飄揚着五彩紙條，有的甚至纏到人們的頸上。碎花紙像彩色的雪花飛落在人們的頭上。我轉到唐人街，發現成羣結隊的人在欣賞東方色彩的櫥窗裝飾。噼噼啪啪的鞭炮聲，使人覺得像在中國過新年。

午夜鐘聲一響，大家一面提高嗓門大喊「新年快樂！」一面亂撳汽車喇叭或者大搖響鈴。五光十色的紙條片更是漫天飛舞。這是我在美國所過的第一個新年。美國人的和善和天真好玩使我留下深刻的印象。在他們的歡笑嬉遊中可以看出美國的確是個年輕的民族。

那晚回家時已經很遲，身體雖然疲倦，精神卻很輕鬆，上牀後一直睡到第二天日上三竿起身。早飯後，我在卜技利的住宅區打了個轉。住宅多半沿着徐緩的山坡建築，四周則圍繞着花畦和草地。玫瑰花在加州溫和的冬天裏到處盛開着，卜技利四季如春，通常長空蔚藍不見朵雲，很像雲南的昆明、台灣的台南，而溫度較低。

新年之後，我興奮地等待着加大第二個學期在二月間開學。心中滿懷希望，我對語言的學習也加倍努力。快開學時，我以上海南洋公學的學分申請入學，結果獲準進入農學院，以中文學分抵補了拉丁文的學分。

我過去的準備工作偏重文科方面，結果轉到農科，我的動機應該在這裏解釋一下。我轉農科並非像有些青年學生聽天由命那樣的隨便，而是經過深思熟慮才慎重決定的。我想，中國既然以農立國，那末只有改進農業，才能使最大多數的中國人得到幸福和溫飽。同時我幼時在以耕作為主的鄉村裏生長，對花草樹木和鳥獸蟲魚本來就有濃厚的興趣。為國家，為私人，農業都似乎是最合適的學科。此外我還有一個次要的考慮，我在孩提時代身體一向羸弱，我想如果能在田野裏多接觸新鮮空氣，對我身體一定大有裨益。

第一學期選的功課是植物學、動物學、生理衛生、英文、德文和體育。除了體育是每週 6 小時以外，其餘每科都是三小時。我按照指示到大學路一家書店買教科書。我想買植物學教科書時，說了半天店員還是聽不懂，後來我只好用手指指書架上那本書，他才恍然大悟。原來植物學這個名詞的英文字（botany）重音應放在第一音節，我卻把重音唸在第二音節上去了。經過店員重複一遍這個字的讀音以後，我才發現自己的錯誤。買了書以後心裏很高興，既買到書，同時又學會一個英文字的正確發音，真是一舉兩得。後來教授要我們到植物園（botanical garden）去研究某種草木，我因為不知道植物園在哪裏，只好向管清潔的校工打聽。念到植物園的植物這個英文字時，我自作聰明把重音唸在第一音節上，我心裏想，「植物學」這個英文字的重音既然在第一音節上，舉一反三，「植物園」中「植物」一字的重音自然也應該在第一音節上了。結果弄得那位工友瞠目不知所答。我只好重複了一遍，工友揣摩了一會之後才恍然大悟。原來是我舉一反三的辦法出了毛病，「植物 (的)」這個字的重音卻應該在第二音節上。

可惜當時我還沒有學會任何美國的俚語村言，否則恐怕「他 × 的」一類粗話早已脫口而出了。英文重音的捉摸不定曾經使許多學英文的人傷透腦筋。固然重音也有規則可循，但是每條規則總有許多例外，以致例外的反而成了規則。因此每個字都得個別處理，要花很大工夫才能慢慢學會每個字的正確發音。

植物學和動物學引起我很大的興趣。植物學教授在講解顯微鏡用法時曾說過笑話：「你們不要以為從顯微鏡裏可以看到大如巨象的蒼蠅。事實上，你們恐怕連半隻蒼蠅腿都看不到呢！」

我在中國讀書時，課餘之暇常常喜歡研究鳥獸蟲魚的生活情形，尤其在私塾時代，一天到晚死背枯燥乏味的古書，這種膚淺的自然研究正可調節一下單調的生活，因而也就慢慢培養了觀察自然的興趣。早年的即興觀察和目前對動植物學的興趣，有一個共通的出發點 —— 好奇，最大的差別在於使用的工具。顯微鏡是眼睛的引伸，可以使人看到肉眼無法辨別的細微物體。使用顯微鏡的結果，使人發現多如繁星的細菌。望遠鏡是眼睛的另一種引伸，利用望遠鏡可以觀察無窮無數的繁星。我渴望到黎克天文台去見識見識世界上最大的一具望遠鏡，但是始終因故不克遂願。後來花了二毛五分錢，從街頭的一架望遠鏡去眺望行星，發現銀色的土星帶着耀目的星環，在蔚藍的天空中冉冉移動，與學校裏天體掛圖上所看到的一模一樣。當時的經驗真是又驚又喜。

在農學院讀了半年，一位朋友勸我放棄農科之類的實用科學，另選一門社會科學。他認為農科固然重要，但是還有別的學科對中國更重要。他說，除非我們能參酌西方國家的近代發展來解決政治問題和社會問題，那末農業問題也就無法解決。其次，如果不改修社會科學，我的眼光可能就局限於實用科學的小圈子，無法了解農業以外的重大問題。

我曾經研究過中國史，也研究過西洋史的概略，對各時代各國國力消長的情形有相當的了解，因此對於這位朋友的忠告頗能領略。他的話使我一再考慮，因為我已再度面臨三岔路口，遲早總得有個決定。我曾經提到，碰到足以影響一生的重要關頭，我從不輕率作任何決定。

一天清早，我正預備到農場看擠牛奶的情形，路上碰到一羣蹦蹦跳跳的小孩子去上學。我忽然想起：我在這裏研究如何培育動物和植物，為甚麼不研究研究如何培育人才呢？農場不去了，一直跑上卜技利的山頭，坐在一棵古橡樹下，凝望着旭日照耀下的三藩市和金門港口的美景。腦子裏思潮起伏，細數着中國歷代興衰的前因後果。忽然之間，眼前恍惚有一羣天真爛漫的小孩，像凌波仙子一樣從海灣的波濤中湧出，要求我給他們讀書的學校，於是我毅然決定轉到社會科學學院，選教育為主科。

從山頭跑回學校時已近晌午，我直跑到註冊組去找蘇頓先生，請求從農學院轉到社會科學學院。經過一番詰難和辯解，轉院總算成功了。從 1909 年秋天起，我開始選修邏輯學、倫理學、心理學和英國史，我的大學生涯也從此步入正途。

歲月平靜而愉快地過去，時間之沙積聚的結果，我的知識也在大學的學術氣氛下逐漸增長。

從邏輯學裏我學到思維是有一定的方法的。換一句話說，我們必須根據邏輯方法來思考。觀察對於歸納推理非常重要，因此我希望訓練自己的觀察能力。我開始觀察校園之內，以及大學附近所接觸到的許許多多事物。母牛為甚麼要裝鈴？尤加利樹的葉子為甚麼垂直地掛着？加州的罌粟花為甚麼都是黃的？

有一天早晨，我沿着卜技利的山坡散步時，發現一條水管正在汩汩流水。水從哪裏來的呢？沿着水管找，終於找到了水源，我的心中也充滿了童稚的喜悅。這時我已到了相當高的山頭，我很想知道山嶺那一邊究竟有些甚麼。翻過一山又一山，發現這些小山簡直多不勝數。越爬越高，而且離住處也越來越遠。最後只好放棄初衷，沿着一條小路回家。歸途上發現許多農家，還有許多清澈的小溪和幽靜的樹林。

這種漫無選擇的觀察，結果自然只有失望。最後我終於發現，觀察必須有固定的對象和確切的目的，不能聽憑興之所至亂觀亂察。天文學家觀察星球，植物學家則觀察草木的生長。後來我又發現另外一種稱為實驗的受控制的觀察，科學發現就是由實驗而來的。

唸倫理學時，我學到道德原則與行為規律的區別。道德原則可以告訴我們，為甚麼若干公認的規律切合某階段文化的需要；行為規律只要求大家遵守，不必追究規律背後的原則問題，也不必追究這些規律與現代社會的關係。

在中國，人們的生活是受公認的行為規律所規範的。追究這些行為規律背後的道德原則時，我的腦海裏馬上起了洶湧的波瀾。一向被認為最終真理的舊有道德基礎，像遭遇地震一樣開始搖搖欲墜。同時，赫利・奧佛斯屈裏特 (Harry Overstreet) 教授也給了我很大的啟示。傳統的教授通常只知道信仰公認的真理，同時希望他的學生們如此做。奧佛斯屈裏特教授的思想卻特別敏銳，因此促使我探測道德原則的基石上的每一裂縫。我們上倫理學課，總有一場熱烈的討論。我平常不敢參加這些討論，一方面由於我英語會話能力不夠，另一方面是由於自卑感而來的怕羞心理。因為 1909 年前後是中國現代史上最黑暗的時期，而且我們對中國的前途也很少自信。雖然不參加討論，聽得卻很用心，很像一隻聰明伶俐的小狗豎起耳朵聽它主人說話，意思是懂了，嘴巴卻不能講。

我們必須讀的參考書包括柏拉圖、亞里斯多德、約翰福音和奧裏留士等。念了柏拉圖和亞里斯多德之後，使我對希臘人窮根究底的頭腦留有深刻的印象。我覺得四書富於道德的色彩，希臘哲學家卻洋溢着敏銳的智慧。這印象使我後來研究希臘史，並且做了一次古代希臘思想和中國古代思想的比較研究。研究希臘哲學家的結果，同時使我了解希臘思想在現代歐洲文明中所占的重要地位，以及希臘文被認為自由教育不可缺少的一部分的原因。

讀了約翰福音之後，我開始了解耶穌所宣揚的愛的意義。如果撇開基督教的教條和教會不談，這種「愛敵如己」的哲學，實在是最高的理想。如果一個人真能愛敵如己，那末世界上也就不會再有敵人了。

「你們能夠做到愛你們的敵人嗎？」教授向全班發問，沒有人回答。

「我不能夠，」那隻一直尖起耳朵諦聽的狗吠了。

「不能夠？」教授微笑着反問。

我引述了孔子所說的「以直報怨，以德報德」作答。教授聽了以後插嘴說：「這也很有道理啊，是不是？」同學們沒有人回答。下課後一位年輕的美國男同學過來拍拍我的肩膀說：「愛敵如己！吹牛，是不是？」

奧裏留士的言論很像宋朝哲學家。他沉思默想的結果，發現理智是一切行為的準則。如果把他的著述譯為中文，並把他與宋儒相提並論，很可能使人真偽莫辨。

對於歐美的東西，我總喜歡用中國的尺度來衡量。這就是從已知到未知的辦法。根據過去的經驗，利用過去的經驗獲得新經驗也就是獲得新知識的正途。譬如說，如果一個小孩從來沒有見過飛機，我們可以解釋給他聽，飛機像一隻飛鳥，也像一隻長着翅膀的船，他就會了解飛機是怎麼回事。如果一個小孩根本沒有見過鳥或船，使他了解飛機可就不容易了。一個中國學生如果要了解西方文明，也只能根據他對本國文化的了解。他對本國文化的了解愈深，對西方文化的了解愈易，根據這種推理，我覺得自己在國內求學時，常常為讀經史子集而深夜不眠，這種苦功總沒有白費，我現在之所以能夠吸收、消化西洋思想，完全是這些苦功的結果。我想，我今後的工作就是找出中國究竟缺少些甚麼，然後向西方吸收所需要的東西。心裏有了這些觀念以後，我漸漸增加了自信，減少了羞怯，同時前途也顯得更為光明。

我對學問的興趣很廣泛，選讀的功課包括上古史、英國史、哲學史、政治學，甚至譯為英文的俄國文學。托爾斯泰的作品更是愛不釋手，尤其是《安娜‧卡列尼娜》和《戰爭與和平》。我參加過許多著名學者和政治家的公開演講會，聽過桑太耶那、泰戈爾、大衛、斯坦、約登、威爾遜（當時是普林斯頓校長）以及其他學者的演講。對科學、文學、藝術、政治和哲學我全有興趣。也聽過塔虎脱和羅斯福的演説。羅斯福在加大希臘劇場演説時，曾經説過：「我攫取了巴拿馬運河，國會要辯論，讓它辯論就是了。」他演説時的強調語氣和典型姿勢，至今猶歷歷可憶。

中國的傳統教育似乎很褊狹，但是在這種教育的範圍之內也包羅萬象。有如百科全書，這種表面褊狹的教育，事實上恰是廣泛知識的基礎。我對知識的興趣很廣泛，可能就是傳統思想訓練的結果。中國古書包括各方面的知識，例如歷史、哲學、文學、政治經濟、政府制度、軍事、外交等等。事實上絕不褊狹。古書之外，學生們還接受農業、灌溉、天文、數學等實用科學的知識。可見中國的傳統學者絕非褊狹的專家，相反地，他具備學問的廣泛基礎。除此之外，虛心追求真理是儒家學者的一貫目標，不過，他們的知識只限於書本上的學問，這也許是他們欠缺的地方。在某一意義上説，書本知識可能是褊狹的。

幼時曾經讀過一本押韻的書，書名《幼學瓊林》，裏面包括的問題非常廣泛，從天文地理到草木蟲魚無所不包，中間還夾雜着城市、商業、耕作、遊記、發明、哲學、政治等等題材。押韻的書容易背誦，到現在為止，我仍舊能夠背出那本書的大部分。

卜技利的小山上有長滿青苔的橡樹和芳香撲鼻的尤加利樹；田野裏到處是黃色的罌粟花；私人花園裏紅玫瑰在溫煦的加州太陽下盛放着。這裏正是美國西部黃金世界，本地子弟的理想園地。我萬幸得享母校的愛護和培育，使我這個來自東方古國的遊子得以發育成長，衷心銘感，無以言宣。

加州氣候冬暖夏涼，四季如春，我在這裏的四年生活確是輕鬆愉快。加州少雨，因此戶外活動很少受影響。冬天雖然有陣雨，也只是使山上的青草變得更綠，或者使花園中的玫瑰花洗滌得更嬌豔。除了冬天陣雨之外，幾乎沒有任何惡劣的氣候影響希臘劇場的演出，劇場四周圍繞着密茂的尤加利樹。莎翁名劇、希臘悲劇、星期演奏會和公開演講會都在露天舉行。離劇場不遠是運動場，校際比賽和田徑賽就在那裏舉行。青年運動員都竭其全力為他們的母校爭取榮譽。美育、體育和智育齊頭並進。這就是古希臘格言所稱「健全的心寓於健全的身」──這就是古希臘格言的實踐。

在校園的中心矗立着一座鐘樓，睥睨着周圍的建築。通到大學路的大門口有一重大門，叫「賽色門」，門上有許多栩栩如生的浮雕裸像。這些裸像引起許多女學生的家長抗議。我的倫理學教授說：「讓女學生們多看一些男人的裸體像，可以糾正她們忸怩作態的習慣。」老圖書館（後來拆除改建為陀氏圖書館）的閱覽室裏就有維納斯以及其他希臘女神裸體的塑像。但是男學生的家長從未有過批評。我初次看到這些希臘裸體人像時，心裏也有點疑惑，為甚麼學校當局竟把這些「猥褻」的東西擺在智慧的源泉。後來，我猜想他們大概是要灌輸「完美的思想寓於完美的身體」的觀念。在希臘人看起來，美麗、健康和智慧是三位一體而不可分割的。

橡樹叢中那次「仲夏夜之夢」的演出，真是美的極致。青春、愛情、美麗、歡愉全在這次可喜的演出中活生生地表現出來了。

學校附近有許多以希臘字母做代表的兄弟會和姊妹會。聽說兄弟會和姊妹會的會員們歡聚一堂，生活非常愉快。我一直沒有機會去作客。後來有人約我到某兄弟會去作客，但是附帶一個條件──我必須投票選舉這個兄弟會的會員出任班主席和其他職員。事先，他們曾經把全班同學列一名單，碰到可能選舉他們的對頭人，他們就說這個「要不得！」同時在名字上打上叉。

我到那個兄弟會時，備受殷勤招待，令人沒齒難忘。第二天舉行投票，為了確保中國人一諾千金的名譽，我自然照單圈選不誤，同時我也很高興能在這次競選中結交了好幾位朋友。

選舉之後不久，學校裏有一次營火會。究竟慶祝甚麼卻記不清楚了。融融的火光照耀着這班青年的快樂面龐。男男女女齊聲高歌。每一支歌結束時，必定有一陣吶喊。木柴的爆裂聲，女孩子吃吃的笑聲和男孩子的呼喊聲，至今猶在耳際縈繞。我忽然在火光燭照下邂逅一位曾經受我一票之賜的同學。使我大出意外的是這位同學竟對我視若路人，過去的那份親熱勁兒不知哪裏去了！人情冷暖，大概就是如此吧！他對我的熱情，我已經以「神聖的一票」來報答，有債還債，現在這筆賬已經結清，誰也不欠誰的。從此以後，我再也不拿選舉交換招待，同時在學校選舉中從此沒有再投票。

在「北樓」的地下室裏，有一間同學經營的「合作社」，合作社的門口掛着一塊牌子，上面寫着：「我們相信上帝，其餘人等，一律現錢交易。」合作社裏最興隆的生意是五分錢一個的熱狗，味道不錯。

學校裏最難忘的人是哲學館的一位老工友，我的先生同學們也許已經忘記他，至少我始終忘不了。他個子高而瘦削，行動循規蹈矩。灰色的長眉毛幾乎蓋到眼睛，很像一隻北京叭兒狗，眼睛深陷在眼眶裏。從眉毛下面，人們可以發現他的眼睛閃爍着友善而熱情的光輝。我和這位老工友一見如故，下課以後，或者星期天有空，我常常到地下室去拜訪他，他從加州大學還是一個小規模的學校時開始，就一直住在那地下室裏。

他當過兵，曾在內戰期間在聯邦軍隊麾下參加許多戰役。他生活在回憶中，喜歡講童年和內戰的故事。我從他那裏獲悉早年美國的情形。這些情形離現在將近百年，許多情形與當時中國差不多，某些方面甚至還更糟。他告訴我，他幼年時美國流通好幾種貨幣：英鎊、法郎，還有荷蘭盾。現代衛生設備在他看起來一文不值。有一次他指着一卷草紙對我說：「現代的人雖然有這些衛生東西，還不是年紀輕輕就死了。我們當時可沒有甚麼衛生設備，也沒有你們所謂的現代醫藥。你看我，我年紀這麼大，身體多健康！」他直起腰板，挺起胸脯，像一位立正的士兵，讓我欣賞他的精神體魄。

西點軍校在他看起來也是笑話，「你以為他們能打仗呀？那才笑話！他們全靠幾套制服撐場面，遊行時他們穿得倒真整齊。但是說到打仗——差遠了！我可以教教他們。有一次作戰時，我單槍匹馬就把一隊叛軍殺得精光，如果他們想學習如何打仗，還是讓他們來找我吧！」

雖然內戰已經結束那末多年，他對參加南部同盟的人卻始終恨之入骨。他說，有一次戰役結束之後，他發現一位敵人受傷躺在地上，他正預備去救助。「你曉得這傢伙怎麼着？他一槍就向我射過來！」他瞪着兩隻眼睛狠狠地望着我，好像我就是那個不知好歹的傢伙似的。我説：「那你怎麽辦？」「我一槍就把這畜生當場解決了。」他回答説。

　　這位軍人出身的老工友，對我而論，是加州大學不可分的一部分，他自己也如此看法，因為他曾經親見加大的發育成長。▣

第十章
美國華埠

我到美國第一年的十月底以前，中國發生了重大的變故，光緒皇帝和慈禧太后相繼去世。關於這件事，在美國的中國學生隊裏有兩種不同的傳說：一説慈禧太后先去世，她的親信怕光緒皇帝重掌政權，於是謀殺光緒皇帝以絕後患。另一説法是慈禧太后臨死前派了一名太監到囚禁光緒的瀛台，告訴病弱的光緒帝說：「老佛爺」希望他服用她送去的藥，光緒帝自然了解太后的用意，就把藥吞服了，不久毒發身亡。慈禧太后駕崩以前，已經接到光緒帝服毒死亡的報告，於是發下聖旨，宣佈光緒之死，並由光緒的小侄子溥儀繼承皇位。

不論這些説法的真確性如何，在卜技利的中國學生一致認為「老太婆」（這是大家私底下給慈禧太后的渾號）一死，中國必定有一場大亂。後來事實證明確是如此。溥儀登基以後，他的父親載淳出任攝政王。皇帝是個小孩子，攝政王對政務也毫無經驗，因此清廷的威信一落千丈，三年以後，辛亥革命成功，清室終於被推翻。

我早在 1909 年參加「大同日報」擔任主筆。這報是孫中山先生在三藩市的革命機關報。那一年的一個秋天晚上，我與「大同日報」的另一個編輯，以後在國內大名鼎鼎的劉麻哥成禺，初次晉謁孫先生。他住在唐人街附近的史多克頓街的一家旅館裏。我進門的時候，因為心情緊張，一顆心怦怦直跳。孫先生在他的房間裏很客氣地接見我們。房間很小，一張床，幾張椅子，還有一張小書桌。靠窗的地方有個小小的洗臉盆，窗簾是拉上的。

劉麻哥把我介紹給這位中國革命運動的領袖。孫先生似乎有一種不可抗拒的引力，任何人如果有機會和他談話，馬上會完全信賴他。他的天庭飽滿，眉毛濃黑，一望而知是位智慧極高、意念堅強的人物。他的澄澈而和善的眼睛顯示了他的坦率和熱情。他的緊閉的嘴唇和堅定的下巴，則顯示出他是個勇敢果斷的人。他的肌肉堅實，身體強壯，予人鎮定沉着的印象。談話時他的論據清楚而有力，即使你不同意他的看法，也會覺得他的觀點無可批駁。除非你有意打斷話頭，他總是娓娓不倦地向你發揮他的理論。他說話很慢，但是句句清楚，使人覺得他的話無不出於至誠。他也能很安詳地聽別人講話，但是很快就抓住人家的談話要點。

後來我發現他對各種書都有濃厚的興趣，不論是中文書，或者英文書。他把可能節省下來的錢全部用來買書。他讀書不快，但是記憶力卻非常驚人。孫先生博覽羣書，所以對中西文化的發展有清晰的了解。

他喜歡聽笑話，雖然他自己很少說，每次聽到有趣的笑話時總是大笑不止。

他喜歡魚類和蔬菜，很少吃肉類食物。喜歡中菜，不大喜歡西菜。他常說：「中國菜是全世界最好的菜。」

孫先生是位真正的民主主義者，他曾在三藩市唐人街的街頭演說。頭頂飄揚着國民黨的黨旗，他就站在人行道上向圍集他四周的人演說。孫先生非常了解一般人的心理，總是盡量選用通俗平易的詞句來表達他的思想。他會故意地問：「甚麼叫革命？」「革命就是打倒滿洲佬。」聽眾很容易明白他的意思，因此就跟着喊打倒滿洲佬。接着他就用極淺近的話解釋，為甚麼必須打倒滿洲佬，推翻滿清建立共和以後他的計劃怎麼樣，老百姓在新政府下可以享受甚麼好處等等。

在開始講話以前，他總先估量一下他的聽眾，然後選擇適當的題目，臨時決定適當的講話的方式，然後再滔滔不絕地發表他的意見。他能自始至終把握聽眾的注意力。他也隨時願意發表演說，因為他有驚人的演說天才。

孫中山先生對人性有深切的了解，對於祖國和人民有熱烈的愛，對於建立新中國所需要的東西有深邃的見解。這一切的一切，使他在新中國的發展過程中成為無可置辯的領袖。他常常到南部各州、東部各州去旅行，有時又到歐洲，但是經常要回到三藩市來，每次回到三藩市，我和劉麻哥就去看他。

1911 年 10 月 8 日，大概晚上 8 點鐘左右，孫先生穿着一件深色的大衣和一頂常禮帽，到了「大同日報」的編輯部。他似乎很快樂，但是很鎮靜。他平靜地告訴我們，據他從某方面得到的消息，一切似乎很順利，計劃在武漢起義的一羣人已經完成部署，隨時可以採取行動。兩天以後，消息傳至三藩市，武昌已經爆發革命了。這就是辛亥年 10 月 10 日的武漢革命，接着滿清政府被推翻，這一天也成為中華民國的國慶日。

在孫先生的指導之下，我和劉麻哥為「大同日報」連續寫了三年的社論。開始時我們兩人輪流隔日撰寫。我們一方面在加大讀書，一方面為報紙寫社論，常常開夜車到深夜，趕寫第二天早上見報的文章。大學的功課絕不輕鬆，我們，尤其是我，深感這種額外工作負擔之重。成功以後，劉麻哥回國了，我只好獨立承擔每日社論的重任。我雖然深深關切祖國的前途，但是這種身不由己的經常寫作，終於扼殺了我一切寫作的興趣。我一直在無休無止的壓力下工作，而且倉促成文，作品的素質日見低落，而且養成散漫而匆促的思想習慣，用字也無暇推敲。有時思想阻滯，如同阻塞了的水管裏的水滴，但是筆頭的字還是像一羣漫無目的的流浪者湧到紙上。我對於這些不速之客實在生氣，但是我還是由他們去了，因為他們至少可以填滿空白。

最初擔任這份工作時，對於寫作的確非常有興趣，字斟句酌，務求至當。這情形很像選擇適當的錢幣，使它能投進自動售貨機的放錢口。如果你匆匆忙忙希望把一大把錢幣同時擠進放錢口，機器自然就阻塞了，多餘的錢怎麼也放不進去，結果就散落一地。一個人不得不在匆忙中寫文章，情形就是這樣，結果是毫無意義的一大堆文字浪費了篇幅。

1912 年畢業後，我終於放棄了這份工作，心裏感到很輕鬆。從此以後我一直怕寫文章，很像美國小學生怕用拉丁文作文一樣。工作如果成為苦差，並且必須在匆忙中完成，這種工作絕無好成績。這樣養成的壞習慣後來很難矯正。

在我四年的大學時期裏，約有五萬華僑集中在西海岸的各城市，包括薩克拉孟多、三藩市、屋崙、聖多謝、洛杉磯等，另外還有零星的小羣華僑和個人散佈在較小的城鎮和鄉村。華僑集中的區域就叫唐人街或中國城，也稱華埠。三藩市的華埠是美洲各城中最大的一個，共有華僑兩萬餘人。主要的街道原來叫杜邦街，後來改稱葛蘭德路，究竟為甚麼改，我不知道。葛蘭德路很繁華。東方古董舖、普通稱為「雜碎館」的中國飯館、算命測字的攤子、假借俱樂部名義的賭場、供奉中國神佛的廟宇等等，吸引了無數的遊客和尋歡作樂的人。有一個年輕美麗的美國人告訴我，她曾在一家東方古董舖中看到一件非常稀奇的東西 —— 一尊坐在一朵蓮花座上的大佛；她還在一家中國飯館吃過鳥巢（燕窩）、魚翅和雜碎。她對這一切感到新奇萬分，説得手舞足蹈。她的妹妹們都睜着眼睛、張着嘴巴聽她。「真的啊！」她的老祖母從眼鏡上面望着她，兩隻手則仍舊不停地織着毛線。

「你用筷子怎麼喝湯呢？」一位小妹妹滿腹狐疑地問。

「正像你用麥管吸汽水一樣吸湯呀！小妹妹。」我代為回答，引得大家大笑。

也有許多華僑開洗衣店。他們一天到晚忙着漿洗衣服，常常忙到深夜。許多美國家庭喜歡把衣服送到中國洗衣店洗，因為手洗不像機器那樣容易損壞衣服。這些來自「天朝」的子孫，節衣縮食省下有限的一點錢，把省下的錢裝在袋裏藏在牀下。但是他們卻慷慨地捐錢給孫中山先生的革命運動，或者把錢寄回廣東，扶養他們的家人或親戚，同時使他們的故鄉變為富足。

廣東是中國最富的省份，一方面是廣東人在香港以及其他地方經商發財的關係，另一方面也是因為各地華僑把積蓄匯回廣東的緣故。華僑遍佈於馬來西亞、印尼、菲律賓及南美、北美各地。各地的華僑多半是從廣東或福建來的。

上千萬的華僑生活在外國，他們在外國辛勤工作從不剝削別人，相反地，他們的勞力卻常常受到剝削。他們除父母所賜的血肉之軀外，別無資本。他們像一羣蜜蜂，辛勤工作，節衣縮食，忍氣吞聲，把花蜜從遙遠的花朵運送到在中國的蜂房。他們得不到任何政治力量的支持，他們也沒有攜帶槍炮到外國來。他們幫着居留地的人民築路、開礦、種植樹木，以一天辛勞的工作換回幾個美金或先令。不錯，有些人，尤其是在新加坡和印尼，的確發了財，住着皇宮樣的大廈和別墅，生活得像印度的土大王，另一些人也躋入中產階級，買田置產，但是富有的和小康的究竟還是少數。大多數的華僑必須辛勤工作，而且只有辛勤工作才能糊口或稍有積蓄。

在美國的華僑，沒有很富的，也沒有很窮的。多數都是老實可靠、辛勤工作的人。幾乎所有的人都寄一點錢回廣東。他們的生活方式主要是中國式的。你如果乘一隻船沿薩克拉孟多江航行，你可以看到兩岸散佈着一些華僑城鎮和村落，店舖門前掛着大字書寫的中文招牌如「長途糧食」、「道地藥材」等類。你可能以為自己是在沿着長江或運河航行呢。

有一天，我曾經在薩克拉孟多江沿岸的一處中國城上岸，訪一位蘆筍園的主人。這位主人叫丁山，是孫中山先生的朋友，他拿鮮嫩的蘆筍招待我，非常肥美多汁，後來一吃到蘆筍，我總要想起他。他還有一間製造蘆筍的罐頭廠，所製的罐頭借用美國商標出售。因此我常常想，美國的某些蘆筍罐頭，可能就是華僑種植和裝罐的。他賺錢的辦法的確好，而且很巧妙。他為工人開設了許多娛樂場所，他說，工人們辛苦了一天，必須有散散心的地方；如果他不開辦娛樂場所，工人們就會找到他的鄰居所開的娛樂場所去。他的用意是「肥水不流外人田」。結果到他娛樂場所來玩的人，都貢獻了一點「肥水」，他的財產也就愈來愈多了。

在美國以及世界各地的華僑，真不愧為炎黃裔冑。男子留着辮子，女人甚至還纏足。在三藩市的華僑街頭，可以發現賣卦算命的攤子。有一位算命先生告訴一位來算命的白人說：「好運道，快快的，大發財。」旁邊一位黑人也想算算命，算命先生把同樣的話重複一遍，黑人大為得意。如果這位算命先生說到此地為止，自然太平無事，但是他偏偏要畫蛇添足，對黑人說：「快快地，不再黑，像他——」同時用手指着那位白人。黑人氣得一腳踢翻算命攤子，阿諛過分成為侮辱，此即一例。

華僑還有許多雜貨店，出售鹹魚、鰻鯗、蛇肉、醬油、魚翅、燕窩、乾鮑以及其他從廣州或香港運到美國的貨色。有一次，我到一家雜貨舖想買一些東西。但是我的廣東話太蹩腳，沒法使店員明白我要買的東西。只好拿一張紙把它寫下來，旁邊站着一位老太婆只曉得中國有許多不同的方言，卻不曉得中國只有一種共同的文字，看了我寫的文字大為驚奇，她問店裏的人：這位唐人既然不能講唐話（她指廣東話），為甚麼他能寫唐字呢？許多好奇的人圍住我看，有一位稍稍懂點普通話的人問道：「你到廣州省城去過沒有？」我回答說：「沒有。」「那末你過去在那裏買東西呢？」「上海。」我笑着夾起一瓶醬油和一包貨物走了。

唐人街的學校仍舊保持舊式的課程。學生們要高聲朗誦古書，和我小時候的情形一模一樣。離唐人街不遠的美國學校對它們毫無影響。

這是辛亥革命以前的情形。革命以後，唐人街開始起了變化，因為中國本身也在變化，而且是急劇的變化，短短幾年之內，算命賣卦的不見了。辮子的數目也迅速減少，終至完全絕跡。青年女子停止纏足，學校制度改革了，採用了新式的課程；送到附近美國學校上學的孩子逐漸增加。唐人街雖然想抗拒美國鄰居的影響，但是祖國有了改革，而且在生活方式上有了改變以後，這些忠貞的炎黃裔冑也終於亦步亦趨了。⬛

第十一章
紐約生活

　　時間一年一年地過去，我的知識學問隨之增長，同時自信心也加強了。民國元年，即 1912 年，我以教育為主科，歷史與哲學為兩附科，畢業於加大教育學系，並承學校贈給名譽獎，旋赴紐約入哥倫比亞大學研究院續學。

　　我在哥大學到如何以科學方法應用於社會現象，而且體會到科學研究的精神。我在哥大遇到許多誨人不倦的教授，我從他們得到許多啟示，他們的教導更使我終生銘感。我想在這裏特別提一筆其中一位後來與北京大學發生密切關係的教授。他就是約翰・杜威博士。他是胡適博士和我在哥倫比亞大學時的業師，後來又曾在北京大學擔任過兩年的客座教授。他的著作、演講以及在華期間與我國思想界的交往，曾經對我國的教育理論與實踐發生重大的影響。他的實驗哲學與中國人講求實際的心理不謀而合。但是他警告我們說：「一件事若過於注重實用，就反為不切實用。」

　　我不預備詳談在哥大的那幾年生活，總之，在那幾年裏獲益很大。我對美國生活和美國語言已感習慣，而且可以隨時隨地從所接觸的事物汲取知識而無事倍功半之苦。

　　紐約給我印象較深的事物是它的摩天大樓、川流不息的地道車和高架電車、高樓屋頂上的炫目的霓虹燈廣告；劇場、影院、夜總會、旅館、飯店；出售高貴商品的第五街、生活浪漫不拘的格林威治村、東區的貧民窟等等。

　　在社會生活方面，新英格蘭人、愛爾蘭人、波蘭人、義大利人、希臘人、猶太人等各族雜處，和睦如鄰，此外還有幾千名華僑聚居在唐人街附近。當時在這個大都會裏的中國菜館就有五百家之多。紐約市密集的人口中龍蛇混雜，包括政客、流氓、學者、藝術家、工業家、金融鉅子、百萬富翁、貧民窟的貧民以及各色人等，但是基本上這些人都是美國的產物。有人說：「你一走進紐約，就等於離開了美國。」事實上大謬不然。只有美國這樣的國家才能產生這樣高度工業化的大都市，也只有美國才能出現這種相容並蓄的大熔爐。種族摩擦的事可說絕無僅有。一個人只要不太逾越法律的範圍，就可以在紐約為所欲為。只要他不太違背習俗，誰也不會干涉他的私人行動。只要能夠找到聽眾，誰都可以評論古今，臧否時政。

法律範圍之內的自由，理智領域之內的思想自由和言論自由在紐約發揮得淋漓盡致，大規模的工商業，國際性的銀行業務，發明、機械和資源的極度利用，處處顯示美國主義的精神和實例。在紐約，我們可以發現整個美國主義的縮影。我們很可能為這個縮影的眩目的外表所迷惑而忽視美國主義的正常狀態，這種正常狀態在美國其餘各地都顯而易見。

暑假裏我常常到紐約州東北部的阿地隆台克山區去避暑。有一年暑假，我和幾位中國朋友到彩虹湖去，在湖中叢山中的一個小島上露營。白天時我們就到附近的小湖去划船垂釣。釣魚的成績很不錯，常常滿載而歸，而且包括十斤以上的梭魚。我們露營的小島上，到處是又肥又大的青蛙，我幼時在我們鄉下就曾學會捉蛙，想不到到了美國之後居然有機會大顯身手。一根釣竿，一根細繩，一枚用大小適度的針屈曲而成的釣鈎，再加一塊紅布就是釣蛙的全副道具了。這些臨時裝備成績驚人，我們常常在一小時之內就捉到二十多隻青蛙，足夠我們大嚼兩餐。彩虹湖附近的居民從未吃過田雞，他們很佩服我們的捉蛙技術，但是他們的心裏一定在想：「這些野蠻的中國人真古怪！」

晚上我們常常參加附近居民的倉中舞會，隨着主人彈奏的提琴曲子婆娑起舞。我還依稀記得他們所唱的一支歌，大意是：

所有的戶樞都長了銹，

門窗也都歪斜傾倒，

屋頂遮不住日曬雨漏，

我的唯一的朋友，

是灌木叢後面的，

一隻黃色的小狗。

這支歌反映山區孤村生活的孤獨和寂寞，但是對城市居民而言，它卻刻劃了一種寧靜迷人的生活。

我們有時也深入到枝葉蔽天的原始森林裏。山徑兩旁的杜松發散着芬芳的氣息。我們採擷了這些芳香的常綠枝葉來裝枕頭，把大自然帶回錦衾之中，陣陣發散的芳香更使我們的夢鄉充滿了溫馨。

有時我們也會在濃密的樹林中迷途。那時我們就只好循着火車汽笛的聲音，找到鐵路軌道以後才能回來。經過幾次教訓以後，我們進森林時就帶指南針了。

在鄉下住了一段時間之後，重新回到城市，的確另有一番愉悅之感。從鄉村回到城市，城市會顯得特別清新可喜；從城市到了鄉村，鄉村卻又顯得特別迷人。原因就是環境的改變和鮮明的對照。外國人到中國時，常常迷戀於悠閒的中國生活和它的湖光山色；而中國人到了異國時卻又常常留戀外國的都市生活。因此我們常常發現許多歐美人士對中國的東西比中國人自己更喜愛。在另一方面，也有許多中國人對歐美的東西比西洋人自己更喜愛。這就是環境改換和先後對照的關係，改換和對照可以破除單調而使心神清新。但是事物的本身價值並不因心理狀態的改變而有所不同。

我在紐約求學的一段時期裏，中日關係突起變化，以致兩國以後勢成水火。日本經過約 50 年的維新之後，於 1894 年一擊而敗中國，聲威漸震。中國人以德報怨，並未因戰敗而懷恨在心。這次戰釁反而意外地引起中國人對日本的欽仰和感激 —— 欽仰日本在短短 50 年內所完成的重大革新，感激日本喚醒中國對自己前途的樂觀。甲午之戰可説燃起了中國人心中的希望。戰後一段時期中國曾力求追隨日本而發奮圖強。

每年到日本留學的學生數以千計。中國在軍事、警務、教育各方面都採取了新制度，而由留日返國的學生主其事。中國開始從日本發現西方文明的重要。日俄戰爭更使中國的革新運動獲得新動力 —— 日本已成為中國人心中的偶像了。

中國通過她的東鄰逐漸吸收了西方文明，但是中國不久發現，日本值得效法的東西還是從歐美學習而來的。更巧的是美國退還了八國聯軍之後的庚子賠款，中國利用庚款選派了更多的留美學生。在過去，中國學生也有以官費或自費到歐美留學的，但是人數很少，現在從西洋回國的留學生人數逐漸增加，而且開始掌握政府、工商業以及教育界的若干重要位置。傳教士，尤其是美國的傳教士，通過教會學校幫助中國教育了年輕的一代。因此，中國與日本的文化關係開始逐漸疏遠，中國人心目中的日本偶像也漸行萎縮，但是日本人卻並未意識到這種轉變。

日本利用第一次世界大戰的機會，在民國 4 年即 1915 年突然向袁世凱政府提出著名二十一條要求，如果中國接受這些要求，勢將成為日本的保護國。日本之所以突然提出二十一條，是因為西方列強在戰事進行中自顧不暇，同時帝俄軍事力量急劇衰退，以致遠東均勢破壞。中國既受東鄰日本的逼迫，乃不得不求助於西方國家，中日兩國從此分道揚鑣，此後數十年間的國際政治也因而改觀。如果日本具有遠大的眼光，能在中國的苦難時期協助中國，那末中日兩國也許一直和睦相處，而第二次世界大戰的情形也就完全不同了。

駐華盛頓的中國大使館經政府授意把二十一條要求的內容泄漏了，那時我正在紐約讀書。這消息使西方各國首都大為震驚。抵制日貨運動像野火一樣在中國各地迅速蔓延以示抗議，但是日本軍艦已經結集在中國的重要口岸，同時日本在南滿和山東的軍隊也已經動員。民國 4 年即 1915 年 5 月 7 日，也就是日本提出二十一條要求之後四個月，日本向袁世凱提出最後通牒，袁世凱終於在兩天之後接受二十一條要求。

後來情勢演變，這些要求終於化為烏有，但是中國對日本的欽慕和感激卻由此轉變為恐懼和猜疑。從此以後，不論日本說甚麼，中國總是滿腹懷疑，不敢置信；不論日本做甚麼，中國總是懷着恐懼的心情加以警戒。日本越表示親善，中國越覺得她居心叵測。

我們的東鄰質問我們：「你們為甚麼不像我們愛你們一樣地愛我們？」

我們回答說：「你們正在用刺刀談戀愛，我們又怎麼能愛你們？」

9．18 事變前幾年，一位日本將官有一天問我：「中國為甚麼要挑撥西方列強與日本作對？」

「為保持均勢，以免中國被你們併吞。」我很坦白地回答。

「日本併吞中國！我們怎麼會呢？這簡直是笑話。」

「一點也不笑話，將軍。上次大戰時列強自顧不暇，日本不是曾經乘機向中國提出二十一條要求嗎？如果這些要求條條實現，日本不是就可以鯨吞中國嗎？」

「哦，哦——？」這位將軍像是吃驚不小的樣子。

「一點不錯。」我直截了當地回答。🔷

第三部

民國初年

第十二章
急劇變化

　　我在民國 6 年即 1917 年 6 月間離美返國，美國正為有史以來第一次參加歐戰而忙着動員。離美前夕，心情相當複雜，那晚睡在哥倫比亞大學的赫特萊樓，思潮起伏，一夜不曾闔眼。時間慢慢消逝，終於東方發白。初夏的曙光從窗外爬藤的夾縫漏進房裏。清晨的空氣顯得特別溫柔，薔薇花瓣上滿積着晶瑩的露珠。附近圖書館前石階上的聖母銅像，似乎懷着沉重的心情在向我微笑道別，祝她撫育的義子一帆風順。我站在窗前佇望着 5 年來朝夕相伴的景物，不禁熱淚盈眶。難道我就這樣丟下我的朋友，永遠離開這智慧的源泉嗎？但是學成回國是我的責任，因為我已享受了留美的特權。那天下午我在中央車站搭火車離開紐約前往俄亥俄州的一個城市。火車慢慢移動離開車站時，我不住地回頭望着揮手送別的美國朋友，直到無法再看到這些青年男女朋友的影子時才坐下。

　　一位朋友陪我到俄亥俄州去看他的朋友。男主人有事進城去了，由漂亮的女主人招待我們。主人家裏沒有男孩，只有一位掌上明珠。這位黑髮女郎明媚動人，長着一張鵝蛋臉，而且熱情洋溢，真是人見人愛。

　　我們在那裏住了兩星期，正是大家忙着登記應召入伍的時候，第一批新兵正在集合出發，隊伍浩浩蕩蕩經過大街，開往營地受訓。街道兩旁人山人海，母親們、愛人們、朋友們紛紛向出征的勇士道別，有的擁吻不捨，有的淚流滿面，就是旁觀的人也為之鼻酸。

　　作客期間，我們曾經數度在月明之夜划船遊湖。湖上遍佈着滿長金色和銀色水仙花的小嶼。螢火蟲像流星樣在夜空中閃爍。魚兒在月色下跳躍戲水。女孩子們則齊聲歡唱。我還記得一支她們喜歡唱的歌：

六月的空氣溫暖而清新

你為甚麼不肯打開你的瓣兒？

難道你怕會有人

悄悄地偷走你的心？

青蛙們也嘶着粗野的歌喉隨聲和唱，女孩子唱了一支又接着一支，直到晚風帶來寒意，大家才意識到夜色已深。於是我們棄舟登岸，在斜瀉而下的月色中踏着遍沾露珠的草地回家。

時間在不知不覺間飛逝，兩個禮拜的愉快生活旋告結束。我向朋友們道別，搭了一輛火車去三藩市。郵船慢慢離開金門海口時，我站在甲板上望着東方，心裏念念不忘在紐約的朋友們。再會吧，朋友們！再會吧，美國！

回到上海時還是夏天。離開 9 年，上海已經變了。許多街道比以前寬闊，也比以前平坦。租界範圍之外也已經鋪築了許多新路。百貨公司、高等旅館、屋頂花園、遊樂場、跳舞場都比以前多了好幾倍。上海已經追上紐約的風氣了。

離開祖國的幾年之內，上海的學校也增加了好幾倍；但是除了少數例外，所有學校的經費都是由私人或中國政府負擔的。少數例外的學校是多年以前公共租界當局興辦的。自從這些落伍的學校在幾十年前創立以來，租界當局的收入我想至少已經增加百倍。但還是讓中國人永遠無知無識罷 ——這樣，控制和剝削都比較方便。

年輕女孩子已剪短頭髮，而且穿起高齊膝蓋的短裙，哦！對不起，我說錯了，我的意思是指她們穿了僅到膝蓋的旗袍，當時流行的式樣就是如此。當時中國摩登女子的這種衣服是相當有道理的，從肩到膝，平直無華，料子多半是綢緞，長短隨時尚而定。這原是滿洲旗人的長袍，於清朝進關時男子被迫而穿着的，滿清覆亡以後也被漢家女子採用，因此稱為「旗」袍。

到處可以看到穿着高跟鞋的青年婦女。當你聽到人行道高跟皮鞋的急驟的篤篤聲時，你就知道年輕的一代與她們的母親已經大不相同了。過去的羞怯之態已不復存在。也許是穿着新式鞋子的結果，她們的身體發育也比以前健美了。從前女人是纏足的。天足運動是中國改革運動的一部分，開始於日俄戰爭前後，但是在辛亥革命成功以前進展始終很慢。我想高跟鞋可能是促使天足運動迅速成功的原因，因為女人們看到別人穿起高跟鞋婀娜多姿，自然就不願意再把她們女兒的足硬擠到繡花鞋裏了。

男子已經剪掉辮子，但是仍舊沒有捨棄長衫，因為大家已經忘記了長衫本來就是旗袍。穿着長衫而沒有辮子，看起來似乎很滑稽。但是不久之後，我也像大家一樣穿起長衫來了，因為無論革命與不革命，旗袍究竟比較方便而且舒服。誰也不能抵抗既方便又舒服的誘惑，這是人情之常。

也有一些人仍舊留着辮子，尤其是老年人。他們看不出剪辮子有甚麼好處。辮子已經在中國人頭上養了兩百多年，就讓它再留幾百年也無所謂。任何運動中總不免有死硬派的。

在美國時，我喜歡用中國的尺度來衡量美國的東西。現在回國以後，我把辦法剛剛顛倒過來，喜歡用美國的尺度來衡量中國的東西，有時更可能用一種混合的尺度，一種不中不西、亦中亦西的尺度，或者遊移於兩者之間。

我可憐黃包車夫，他們為了幾個銅板，跑得氣喘吁吁，汗流浹背，尤其在夏天，烈日炙灼着他們的背脊，更是慘不忍睹。我的美國尺度告訴我，這太不人道。有時我碰到一些野獸似的外國人簡直拿黃包車夫當狗一樣踢罵——其實我說「當狗一樣踢罵」是不對的，我在美國就從來沒有看見一個人踢罵過狗。看到這種情形，我真是熱血沸騰，很想打抱不平，把這些衣冠禽獸踢回一頓。但是一想到支持他們的治外法權時，我只好壓抑了滿腔氣憤。我想起了「小不忍則亂大謀」的古訓。「懦夫！」我的美國尺度在譏笑我。「忍耐！」祖先的中國尺度又在勸慰我。大家還是少坐黃包車，多乘公共汽車和電車罷！但是這些可憐的黃包車夫又將何以為生？回到鄉下種田嗎？不可能，他們本來就是農村的剩餘勞力。擺在他們面前的只有三條路：身強力壯的去當強盜，身體弱的去當小偷，身體更弱的去當乞丐。那末怎麼辦？還是讓他們拖黃包車罷！兜了半天圈子，結果還是老地方。

那末就發展工業，讓他們去做工吧。但是沒有一個穩定的政府，工業又無法發展。農村裏農夫過剩，只要軍閥們肯出錢，或者肯讓他們到處擄掠，這些過剩的農夫隨時可以應募當兵，在這種情形下，欲求政府穩定勢不可得。因此發展工業的路還是走不通。

租界公園門口的告示牌已經有了改進，「犬與華人不得入內」的禁條已經修改為「只准高等華人入內」。甚至一向趾高氣揚的洋人，也開始發現有些值得尊重的東西，正在中國抬頭。

關於上海的事，暫時談到此地為止。

上海這個華東大海港和商業中心，現在已經與向有人間天堂之稱的蘇州和杭州由鐵道互相銜接。由上海到蘇州的鐵路再往西通到南京，在下關渡長江與津浦鐵路銜接，往北直通天津和當時的首都北京。上海往南的鐵路止於杭州，尚未通到寧波。

我的家鄉離寧波不遠。寧波雖是五口通商的五口之一，但是始終未發展為重要的商埠，因為上海迅速發展為世界大商埠之一，使寧波黯然無光。寧波與上海之間有三家輪船公司的船隻每夜對開一次；兩家是英國公司，第三家就是招商局。許多年前我父親曾經拿這些輪船作藍本，打造沒有鍋爐而使用手轉木輪的「輪船」，結果無法行駛。我從上海經寧波還鄉，與我哥哥搭的就是這種輪船的二等艙。

事隔 20 年，乘客的生活無多大改變。過道和甲板上乘客擠得像沙丁魚，一伸腳就可能踩到別人。我們為了占住艙位，下午五點鐘左右就上了船。小販成羣結隊上船叫賣，家常雜物，應有盡有，多半還是舶來品。水果販提了香蕉、蘋果和梨子上船售賣。我和哥哥還因此辯論了一場。哥哥要買部分腐敗的水果，因為比較便宜。「不行，」我說，「買水果的錢固然省了，看醫生的錢卻多了。」

「哈，哈——我吃爛梨子、爛蘋果已經好幾年，」他說，「爛的味道反而好。我從來沒有吃出過毛病。」他隨手撿起一個又大又紅，然而爛了一部分的蘋果，咬掉爛的一部分，其餘的全部吞落肚，我聳聳肩膀，他仰天大笑。

天亮前我們經過寧波港口的鎮海炮台。1885 年中法戰爭時鎮海炮台曾經發炮轟死一位法軍的海軍上將。

天亮了，碼頭上的喧嚷聲震耳欲聾。腳夫們一擁上船拼命搶奪行李。一個不留神，你的東西就會不翼而飛。我和哥哥好容易在人叢中擠下跳板，緊緊地釘在行李夫的背後，唯恐他們提了我們的東西溜之大吉。

寧波幾乎與 9 年前一模一樣。空氣中充塞着鹹魚的氣味。我對這種氣味頗能安之若素，因我從小就經常吃鹹魚。寧波是個魚市，而且離寧波不遠的地方就盛產食鹽。我們跟着行李夫到了車站，發現一列火車正準備升火開往我的家鄉餘姚。沿鐵道我看到綿互數里的稻田，稻波蕩漾，稻花在秋晨的陽光下發光，整齊的稻田在車窗前移動，像是一幅廣袤無邊的巨畫。清晨的空氣中洋溢着稻香，呵，這就是我的家鄉！

火車進餘姚車站時，我的一顆心興奮得怦怦直跳。我們越過一座幾百年前建造的大石橋，橋下退落的潮水正順着江流急瀉而下。從橋洞裏還可以看到釣翁們在江邊垂釣。這橋名曰武勝橋，意指英武常勝。因為四百年前當地居民為保衛餘姚縣城，曾與自日本海入侵的倭寇屢次在橋頭堡作戰。這些倭寇大家都認為就是日本人。

我們跑進院子時，秋陽高照，已是晌午時分。父親站在大廳前的石階上，兩鬢斑白，微露老態，但是身體顯然很好，精神也很旺健。他的慈祥眼睛和含笑的雙唇洋溢着慈父的深情。我兄弟兩人恭恭敬敬地向他老人家行了三鞠躬禮。舊式的叩頭禮在某些人之間已經隨着清朝的覆亡而成為歷史陳跡了。

父親已經剪掉辮子，但是仍然穿着舊式布鞋。他說話不多；在這種場合，沉默勝似千言萬語。我們隨即進入大廳。直背的椅子靠牆很對稱地排列着，顯見他的生活方式仍然很少改變。正牆上懸着鑲嵌貝殼的對聯，右聯是「海闊憑魚躍」，左聯是「天空任鳥飛」。對聯的中間是一幅墨竹，竹葉似乎受秋風吹拂，都傾向一邊。這一切很可以顯示一種滿足的，安靜的，而且安定的生活。

大廳後面有一個小院子，長方形的大盤子裏堆砌着山景，因此使高牆的院子裏平添山水之勝。小寺小塔高踞假山之上，四周則圍繞着似乎已歷數百年的小樹。山坳裏散坐着小小的猴子，母猴的身旁則偎依着更小的小猴，這些微小的假猴顯得如此玲瓏可愛，我真希望它們能夠變成活猴一樣大小而跳進我的懷裏。小寺小塔之外還有一個小涼亭，亭邊長着一叢篁竹。假池子裏則有喋喋的金魚和探鬐覓食的小蝦。這一切的一切，都使人有置身自然之感。

劉老丈聽說我回家了，當天下午就來看我。在我童年時代，劉老丈曾經講許多故事給我們聽，小孩子們都很喜歡他。那天下午，他講了許多有趣的故事。他告訴我，老百姓們聽到革命成功的消息時歡喜得甚麼似的。城裏的人一夜之間就把辮子剪光了。年輕人買了西裝，穿起來很像一羣猴子。他又告訴我，短裙與短髮如何在後來侵入縣城。革命以後，他那留了七十多年的辮子居然也剪掉了，可見他對革命和民國仍然是很贊成的，起先他有點想不通，沒有皇帝坐龍庭，這個世界還成甚麼樣子？但是過了一段時期以後，他才相信民國的總統，照樣可以保持天下太平。他說，反正天高皇帝遠，地方治安本來就靠地方官府來維持。民國以來，地方官府居然做得還不錯。

他說，50年前太平軍侵入縣城時，許多腦袋連辮子一起落了地，現在我們雖然丟掉辮子，腦袋總還存在。他一邊說，一邊用他皮包骨的手指摸着腦袋，樣子非常滑稽，因此引得大家都笑了。那天晚飯吃得比較早，飯後他告辭回家，暮色蒼茫中不留神在庭前石階上滑了一跤，幸虧旁邊有人趕緊抓住他的肩膀，攙住他沒有跌傷。他搖搖頭自己開自己的玩笑說：「三千年前姜太公八十遇文王，我劉太公八十要見閻王了。」說罷哈哈大笑，興高采烈地回家去了。

幾天之後消息傳來，劉太公真地見閻王去了。對我而言，我失去了一位童年時代的老朋友，而且再也聽不到這位風趣的老人給我講故事了。

15年前左右，姊姊和我創辦的一所學校現在已經改為縣立女子學校。大概有100名左右的女孩子正在讀書。她們在操場上追逐嬉笑，蕩鞦韆蕩得半天高。新生一代的女性正在成長。她們用風琴彈奏「史華尼河」和「迪伯拉萊」等西洋歌曲，流行的中國歌更是聲聞戶外。

我在家裏住了一星期左右，隨後就到鄉下去看看蔣村的老朋友。童年時代的小孩子現在都已成人長大，當時的成年人現在已經是鬢髮斑白的老人。至於當年的老人，現在多已經入土長眠，只有極少數歷經村中滄桑的老人還健在。

村莊的情形倒不像我想像中的那樣糟。早年的盜匪之災已經斂跡，因為老百姓現在已經能夠適應新興的行業，而且許多人已經到上海謀生去了。上海自工商業發展以後，已經可以容納不少人。任何變革正像分娩一樣，總是有痛苦的。但是在分娩以後，產婦隨即恢復正常，而且因為添了小寶寶而沾沾自喜。中國一度厭惡的變革現在已經根深蒂固，無法動搖，而且愈變愈厲，中國也就身不由己地不斷往前邁進 —— 至於究竟往哪裏跑，或者為甚麼往前跑，億萬百姓卻了無所知。

我的大伯母已經臥病好幾個月，看到我回家非常高興，吩咐我坐到她的床邊，還伸出顫巍巍的手來撫摸我的手，她告訴我過去 16 年中誰生了兒子，誰結了婚，誰故世。她說世界變了，簡直變得面目全非。女人已經不再紡紗織布，因為洋布又好又便宜。她們已經沒有多少事可以做，因此有些就與鄰居吵架消磨光陰，有些則去唸經拜菩薩。年輕的一代都上學堂了。有些女孩則編織髮網和網線餐巾銷售到美國去，入息不錯。很多男孩子跑到上海工廠或機械公司當學徒，他們就了新行業，賺錢比以前多。現在村子裏種田的人很缺乏，但是強盜卻也絕跡了。天下大概從此太平無事，夜裏聽到犬吠，大家也不再像十年前那樣提心吊膽。

但是她發現進過學校的青年男女有些事實在要不得。他們說拜菩薩是迷信，又說向祖先燒紙錢是愚蠢的事。他們認為根本沒有灶神。廟宇裏的菩薩塑像在他們看來不過是泥塑木雕。他們認為應該把這些佛像一齊丟到河裏，以便破除迷信。他們說男女應該平等。女孩子說她們有權自行選擇丈夫、離婚或者丈夫死了以後有權再嫁，又說舊日纏足是殘酷而不人道的辦法，說外國藥丸比中國藥草好得多。他們說根本沒有鬼，也沒有靈魂輪迴這回事。人死了之後除了留下一堆化學元素的化合物之外甚麼也沒有了。他們說唯一不朽的東西就是為人民、為國家服務。

一隻肥肥的黑貓跳上床，在她枕旁咪咪直叫。她有氣無力地問我：「美國也有貓嗎?」我說是的。再一看,她已經睡熟了。我輕輕地走出房間,黑貓則仍在她枕旁呼嚕作響,並且伸出軟綿綿的爪子去碰碰老太太的臉頰。

我和大伯母談話時,我的姪女一直在旁邊聽着。我走出房間以後,她也趕緊追了出來。她向我伸伸舌頭,很淘氣地對我說:「婆婆太老了,看不慣這種變化。」一個月之後,這位老太太終於離開這個瘋狂的不斷在變的世界。

接着我去拜望三叔母,她的年歲也不小了,身體卻很健旺。我的三叔父有很多田地,而且養了許多雞、鴨、鵝和豬。三叔母告訴我一個悲慘的故事。我的一位童年時代的朋友在上海,做黃金投機生意,蝕了很多錢,結果失了業,回到村裏賦閒。一年前他吞鴉片自殺,他的寡婦和子女弄得一貧如洗,其中一位孩子就在皂莢樹下小河中捉蝦時淹死了。

三叔母捉住一隻又肥又大的閹雞,而且親自下廚。雞燒得很鮮美,雞之外還有魚有蝦。

三叔父告訴我,上一年大家開始用肥田粉種白菜,結果白菜大得非常,許多人認為這種大得出奇的白菜一定有毒,紛紛把白菜拔起來丟掉。但三叔父卻不肯丟,而且廉價從別人那裏買來醃起來。醃好的鹹菜香脆可口,這位老人真夠精明。

小時候曾經抱過我的一位老太婆也從村子裏來看我。她已經九十多歲,耳朵已經半聾,卻從她的村子走了四里多路來看我。她仔仔細細地把我從頭到腳端詳一番,看我並無異樣才安了心。她說,這位大孩子從前又瘦又小,而且很頑皮。他曾經在他哥哥的膝頭咬了一口,留下紫色的齒印,結果自己號啕大哭,怪哥哥的膝蓋碰痛了他的牙齒。

「你記不記得那兩位兄弟在父死之後分家的事?」她問我。兩兄弟每人分到他們父親的房子的一個邊廂,又在大廳的正中樹了一片竹牆,把大廳平分為二。一位兄弟在他的那一半廳子裏養了一頭牛,另一位兄弟氣不過,就把他的半邊廳子改為豬欄來報復。他們父親留下一條船,結果也被鋸為兩半。這兩位缺德兄弟真該天誅地滅!後來祝融光顧,他們的房子燒得精光。老天爺是有眼的!

他們把那塊地基賣掉了。一位在上海做生意的富商後來在這塊地上建了一座大洋房。洋房完工時，她曾經進去參觀，轉彎抹角的走廊、樓梯和玻璃門，弄得她頭昏眼花，進去以後簡直出不來。她試過沙發和彈簧床，一坐就深陷不起，真是嚇了一大跳。最使她驚奇的是屋主人從上海買來的一架機器。輪子一轉，全屋子的燈泡都亮了，黑夜竟同白晝一樣亮。

　　管機器的是她鄰居的兒子。他是在上海學會開機器的。她做夢也想不到這位笨頭笨腦的孩子居然能夠撥弄那樣複雜的一件機器。她離得遠遠地看着飛轉的輪子，唯恐被捲進去碾成肉漿。

　　她還注意到另一件怪事：廚房裏沒有灶神。這一家人而且不拜祖先。廚房裏沒有灶神，她倒不大在乎，但是一個家庭怎麼可以沒有祖宗牌位？據說屋主人相信一種不拜其他神佛的教。她可不願意信這個教，因為她喜歡到所有的廟宇去跑跑，高興拜哪位菩薩就拜哪位。她倒也願意拜拜屋主人相信的那位「菩薩」。因為上一年夏天她發瘧疾時，那個「廟」裏的先生曾經給她金雞納霜丸，結果把她的病治好了。但是她希望也能向別的菩薩跪下來叩頭，求它們消災賜福。

　　她說她窮得常常無以為炊，餓肚子是常事。我父親已經每月給她一點米救濟她，但是她的小孫女死了父母，現在靠她過活，因此吃了她一部分糧食。我拿出一張二十元的鈔票塞在她手裏。她高高興興地走了，嘴裏咕嚕着：「從小時候起，我就知道這孩子心腸好，心腸好。」

　　有一天傍晚，我去祭掃母親的墳墓，墳前點起一對蠟燭和一束香。沒有風，香煙裊裊地升起。我不知不覺地跪倒地上叩了幾個頭，童年的記憶復活了，一切恍如隔昨。我似乎覺得自己仍然是個小孩子，像兒時一樣地向母親致敬，我希望母親的魂魄能夠張着雙臂歡迎我，撫慰我。我希望能夠爬到她懷裏，聽她甜美的催眠曲。我的一切思想和情感都回復到童年時代。母親去世時我才七歲，因此我對母愛的經驗並不多，也許想像中的母親比真實的母親更溫柔、更親密。至少，死去的母親不會打你，你頑皮，她也不會發脾氣。

　　從村子裏到火車站，大約有三里路，中間是一片稻田。車站建在一個平靜的湖泊岸旁，這個湖叫牟山湖，土名西湖，是一個灌溉好幾萬畝田的蓄水庫。湖的三面環山，山上盛產楊梅和竹筍。我步行至車站以後就搭了一列火車到曹娥江邊。鐵路橋梁還沒有完成，因為從德國訂的材料因第一次世界大戰影響遲遲未能到達，所以靠渡船渡江。通往杭州的鐵路工程也因缺乏材料停頓了。從此到杭州的一大段空隙由輪船來銜接。多數旅客都願意乘輪船，因為櫓船太慢，大家不願乘坐，所以舊式小船的生意非常清淡。

傍晚時到達錢塘江邊，再由小火輪渡過錢塘江，只花 20 分鐘。我中學時代的櫓搖的渡船已經不見了。

日落前我到了杭州，住進一家俯瞰西湖的旅館。太陽正落到雷峰塔背後，天上斜映着一片彩霞。一邊是尖削的保塔在夕陽餘暉中矗立山頂，它的正對面，短矮的雷峰塔襯着蔥翠的山色蹲踞在西湖另一邊的山坳裏。玲瓏的遊船點綴着粼粼起皺的湖面。魚兒戲水，倦鳥歸巢，暮靄像一層輕紗，慢慢地籠罩了湖濱山麓的叢林別墅。只有縷縷炊煙飄散在夜空。我感到無比的寧靜。時代雖然進步了，西湖卻嫵媚依舊。

但是許多事情已經有了變化。我的冥想不久就被高跟鞋的篤篤聲給粉碎了，一羣穿着短裙，剪短了頭髮的摩登少女正踏着細碎的步子在湖濱散步。湖濱路在我中學時代原是旗下營的所在。辛亥革命鏟平了旗下營，後來一個新市區終於在這廢墟上建立起來，街道寬闊，但是兩旁的半西式的建築卻並不美觀。飯館、戲院、酒店、茶樓已經取代古老的旗下營而紛紛出現，同時還建了湖濱公園，以便招徠週末從上海乘火車來的遊客。杭州已經成為觀光的中心了。

我在十多年前讀過書的浙江高等學堂已經停辦，原址現已改為省長公署的辦公廳。從前宮殿式的撫台衙門已在革命期間被焚，在市中心留下一片長滿野草閒花的長方形大空地。

革命波及杭州時不曾流半滴血。新軍的將領會商之後黑夜中在杭州街頭佈下幾尊輕型火炮，結果未發一槍一彈就逼得撫台投降。新軍放了把火焚毀撫台衙門，算是革命的象徵，火光照得全城通紅。旗下營則據守他們的小城作勢抵抗，後來經過談判，革命軍承諾不傷害旗下營的任何人，清兵終於投降。旗人領袖桂翰香代表旗下營接受條件。但桂本人卻被他的私人仇敵藉口他陰謀叛亂抓去槍斃了。新當選的都督湯壽潛是位有名的文人，對於這件卑鄙的事非常氣憤，鬧着要辭職。但是這件事總算沒有鬧僵，後來湯壽潛被召至南京，在臨時大總統孫中山先生之下擔任交通部長。

旗下新市區的東北已經建了 500 間平房，安置舊日旗兵的家屬。有些旗人已經與漢人熔於一爐而離開了他們的安置區。幾年之後，全體旗人都失去蹤跡，一度養尊處優的統治者已經與過去的被統治者匯為一流了。旗人從此成為歷史上的名詞，他們的生活情景雖然始終迴旋在我的記憶裏，但是有關他們的故事已經漸漸成為民間傳說。至於清朝的崛起與沒落，且讓史家去記述罷！

從前的文人雅士喜歡到古色古香的茶館去，一面靜靜地品茗，一面憑窗欣賞湖光山色，現在這些茶館已經為不可抵禦的現代文明所取代，只有一兩家殘留的老茶館使人發懷古之幽情，這種古趣盎然的茶館當然還有人去，泡上一杯龍井，披閱唐宋詩詞。這樣可以使人重新回到快樂的舊日子。

我曾經提到杭州是蠶絲工業的中心。若干工廠已經採用紡織機器，但是許多小規模的工廠仍舊使用手織機。一所工業專科學校已經成立，裏面就有紡織的課程。受過化學工程教育的畢業生在城市開辦了幾家小工廠，裝了電動的機器。杭州已經有電燈、電話，它似乎已經到了工業化的前夕了。

我大約逗留了一個星期，重遊了許多少年時代常去的名勝古跡。離商業中心較遠的地方，我發現舊式生活受現代文明的影響也較少。在山區或窮鄉僻壤，舊日淳樸的生活依然令人迷戀。參天古木和幽篁修竹所環繞的寺廟仍然像幾百年以前一樣的清幽安靜。和尚們的生活很少變化，仍舊和過去一樣誦佛唸經。鄉下人還是和他們的祖先一樣種茶植桑，外國貨固然也偶然發現，但是數量微不足道。不過，現代文明的前鋒已經到達，學校裏已經採用現代課本。在現代教育的影響下，雖然生活方式未曾改變，新生一代的心理卻正在轉變。播在年輕人心中的新思想的種子，遲早是會發芽苗長的。🜂

第十三章
軍閥割據

　　年輕時我注意到文官總比武官高些。朝廷命官紅纓帽的頂子分幾種不同的顏色。階級最高的是紅頂子，其次是粉紅的，再其次是深藍的、翠藍的和白色的，最後是金黃的也就是最低的一級。我常常看到戴粉紅頂子的武官向階級比較低的藍頂子文官叩頭，心裏覺得很奇怪。據說歷朝皇帝深恐武官擅權跋扈，所以特意讓文官控制武官。歷史告訴我們，國家一旦受軍閥控制，必定要形成割據的局面。晚唐的歷史就是最好的教訓，俗語說：「好鐵不打釘，好男不當兵。」因此大家都瞧不起軍人。記得鄉村有一位品行不端的人去當兵，在他告假返鄉時，大家把他看做瘟神似的，都遠遠地避開他。我們有個牢不可破的觀念，認為當兵的都是壞人，可鄙、可怕而且可憎。

　　在另一方面，國家的武力如果一蹶不振，碰到外來侵略就毫無能力抵抗了。宋朝亡於蒙古人，明朝亡於滿洲韃靼，情形就是如此。前臨深淵，後是魔鬼，我們究將何去何從？

　　最要緊的是救中國——北方由陸路來的和東南由海道來的強敵都得應付。那末，怎麼辦？趕快建立一支裝備現代武器的現代化軍隊吧！士兵必須訓練有素，而且精忠報國。我們怎麼可以瞧不起軍人呢？他們是保衛國土的英雄，是中國的救星，有了他們，中國才可以免受西方列強的分割。鄙視他們，千萬不可以——我們必須提高軍人的地位，尊敬他們，甚至崇拜他們。不然誰又肯當兵？

　　大家的心理開始轉變了。窮則變，變則通：我們建立了一支現代化的軍隊，裝備外國武器，穿着新式制服，而且還有軍樂隊。我見過這樣的一隊現代軍隊的行軍陣容，洋鼓洋號前導，精神飽滿，步伐整齊，令人肅然起敬。

我看得出神，恍惚自己已經成人長大，正在行列中邁步前進——向勝利進軍，我站在靜靜圍觀的羣眾中，心裏喜不自勝。這是我首次看到現代的軍隊。是的，我們必須尊敬士兵和軍官。從此以後，只有好男才配當兵。我們必須依賴他們恢復中國過去的光榮。從前的舊式軍隊中，士兵穿着馬甲，佩着弓箭，或者背着歐洲國家廢棄不用賣給中國的舊槍。與今天的現代軍隊比起來真是差得太遠了！

我在杭州浙江高等學堂讀書時，一位高等學堂的老學生剛從日本士官學校回來探望師友。他穿着嶄新的軍服，腰旁佩着長劍，劍鞘閃閃發光。這就是中國軍隊的未來將領，我們無不懷着欽敬的心情熱烈地歡迎他。

許多這樣的未來將領正從日本回國，受命組織新軍。幾年之內新軍部隊漸次建立，駐在國內各軍略要地。中國已經武裝起來保衛她自己了。

不久辛亥革命爆發，革命軍的訓練也許不及政府軍那樣精良，但是革命的將領和士兵卻充滿着愛國熱情，隨時準備為國犧牲。革命號角一響，政府新軍相繼向孫中山先生投誠。短短幾個月之內，統治了中國幾百年的滿清帝室就像秋風掃落葉般消逝了。全國人民歡欣鼓舞，中國已經獲得新生，前途光明燦爛。滿清政府訓練新軍，結果自速滅亡，讓他們去自怨自艾吧！讓我們為這些受過現代訓練的將領的優越表現歡呼！

但是勝利的狂歡不久就成為過去。慶祝的燭光終於化為黑煙而熄滅。新軍將領們對滿清反目無情，對革命更無所愛。他們已經嘗到權勢的滋味，絕不肯輕易放棄；而且食髓知味，渴望攫取更大更高的權勢，結果你搶我奪，自相殘殺起來。

孫中山先生已經在民國元年即 1912 年回國。革命軍和滿清政府談判結果。宣統皇帝決定退位，民國接着成立。革命軍同意讓小溥儀仍舊住在紫禁城裏。革命人士準備草擬憲法，成立參議會，選舉總統，不久臨時參議會選舉孫中山先生為中華民國臨時大總統。

中山先生不久辭職，讓位給袁世凱。後來新選的國會選舉袁世凱為總統，不過，那多少是威脅利誘的結果。於是政權又再度落到反動分子的手裏去了。袁世凱原來是清朝的官吏，負責訓練新軍，他一度失寵於清廷，革命爆發後被召回北京。

孫先生認為他對國家所能提供的貢獻，最重要的還是建築鐵路，因此他甘願主持國有鐵道而讓袁世凱統治國家。但是孫先生不久就覺醒了。袁世凱上台時，他很清楚他的實力在於他所控制的軍隊。他把國會看做一個惹人討厭卻又無可避免的東西，不過他想，只要他能夠控制軍隊，國會除了給他一點小麻煩外，絕對奈何他不得。這位國家的新元首在強大的軍隊支持之下，竟然篡竊了許多並不屬於總統的權力。他隨時威脅恐嚇異己，甚至不惜採取卑鄙的暗殺手段。在政治上，他很懂得「分而治之」的那一套，竭力在中山先生的國民黨內部製造摩擦。他更進一步鼓勵成立許多小政黨，企圖削弱國民黨的勢力。

他接着採取步驟來削除國民黨的武力。他首先暗殺國民黨的政治領袖宋教仁，接着下令解除南方各省所有國民黨將領督軍職務，企圖激起各省的反抗，然後加以武力掃蕩。孫中山先生想發動二次革命而沒有成功。這時候袁世凱差不多已經以武力控制全國，於是藉口這次「叛變」，預備取消國會中國民黨籍議員的資格。南方被他鎮壓住以後，他的野心愈來愈大，亟欲攫取更大的權力和尊榮。民國4年他正預備自立為皇帝時，各省紛紛通電反對，因此被逼放棄皇帝夢，旋即憂傷而死。

民國6年（1917年），孫中山先生在廣州建立根據地，希望在那裏成立一支軍隊的核心，發動新革命而推翻軍閥，不料在民國11年（1922年）反被廣州軍閥陳炯明所推翻。不過翌年孫先生終於在廣州成立新政府，國民革命運動聲勢得以重振。但這僅是一個開端。自從野心勃勃而不擇手段的袁世凱死了以後，中國一直四分五裂，各省之間內戰頻仍，政局擾攘達12年之久，直到民國17年（1928年）蔣總司令北伐成功，國家才重歸統一。

中華民國成立以後，16年來中國一直掌握在軍閥手裏。內戰一次接着一次發生。這些內戰多半還是外國勢力慫恿和支持的。內戰的結果，國力損耗，民生凋敝，並且為日本侵略鋪了路。革命前途似乎黑暗一片。內戰中獲勝的軍閥趾高氣揚，野心愈來愈大，不斷爭取更大的權力。被擊敗的軍閥則夾起尾巴躲在天津和上海的租界裏待機再起，機會一來就重啟戰釁，使人民又增加一場災禍。

　　一度被鄙視、後來受尊重的軍人，現在又再度被人鄙視了。🔚

第十四章
知識分子的覺醒

我從杭州到上海以後就進當時最大的書局商務印書館當編輯，同時兼了江蘇省教育會的一名理事，膳宿就由教育會供給。但是年輕人幹不慣磨桌子的生活，一年之後我就辭職了。與商務印書館之間的銀錢往來也在翌年清結。

我與幾位朋友在國立北京大學和江蘇省教育會贊助下開始發行「新教育」月刊，由我任主編。雜誌創辦後6個月就銷到1萬份。它的主要目標是「養成健全之個人，創造進化的社會」。

那時正是歐戰後不久，自由與民主正風靡全世界，威爾遜主義已引起中國有識之士的注意。中國青年正浸淫於戰後由歐美湧至的新思想。報紙與雜誌均以巨大篇幅報道國際新聞和近代發展。中國已經開始追上世界的新思潮了。

「新青年」正在鼓吹德先生與賽先生（即民主與科學），以求中國新生。這本思想激進的雜誌原為幾年前陳獨秀所創辦，後來由北京大學的一羣教授共同編輯。「新青年」在介紹新思想時，自然而然對舊信仰和舊傳統展開激烈的攻擊。有些投稿人甚至高喊「打倒孔家店」！這些激烈的言論固然招致一般讀者的強烈反感，但是全國青年卻已普遍沾染知識革命的情緒。

孫中山先生於民國7年移居上海。我們前面已經談過新誕生的民國的坎坷命運，而且一部分正受着割據各省的軍閥統治。中山先生的國民黨，最強大的據點是南方和上海。民國6年（1917年），國民黨成立新政府對抗北京政府，以求維護革命人士所致力的原則，並進而推廣於全國。當時廣州的南方政府是由總裁控制的。若干參加分子的政治見解非常膚淺，孫先生無法同意，乃離粵北上定居滬瀆，從事中國實業計劃的研究。

他的目光遠超乎當時的政治紛爭之外，他的實業計劃如果順利實現，可以解除人民貧困，促使國家富強，並使中國躋於現代工業化國家之林。根據中山先生的計劃，中國的工業建設分為食衣住行四大類。這些都是人民生活所必需的，孫先生就根據這些因素計劃中國的工業建設。

他設計了貫串中國廣大領土內所有重要商業路線和軍運路線的鐵路網和公路網；他定下發展中國商埠和海港計劃；他也定下疏浚河流、水利建設、荒地開墾等的計劃大綱。他又設計了發展天然資源和建設輕重工業的藍圖。他鑒於中國森林砍伐過度，又定下在華中華北造林的計劃。

他對工業發展規定了兩個原則：(一) 凡是可以由私人經營的就歸私人經營；(二) 私人能力所不及或可能造成壟斷的則歸國家經營。政府有責鼓勵私人企業，並以法律保護之。苛捐雜稅必須廢除，幣制必須改善並予於統一。官方干涉和障礙必須清除，交通必須發展以利商品的流通。

鐵道、公路、疏浚河流、水利、墾荒、商埠、海港等都規定由國家主持。政府並須在山西省建立大規模的煤鐵工廠。歡迎外國資本，並將僱用外國專家。

孫中山先生是中國第一位有過現代科學訓練的政治家。他的科學知識和精確的計算實在驚人。為了計劃中國的工業發展，他親自繪製地圖和表格，並收集資料，詳加核對。實業計劃中所包括的河床和港灣的深度和層次等細節他無不了若指掌。有一次我給他一張導淮委員會的淮河水利圖，他馬上把它在地板上展開，非常認真地加以研究。後來我發現這幅水利圖在他書房的壁上掛著。

在他仔細研究工業建設的有關問題和解決辦法以後，他就用英文寫下來。打字工作全部歸孫夫人負責，校閱原稿的工作則由余日章和我負責。一切資料數位都詳予核對，如果有甚麼建議，孫先生無不樂予考慮。凡是孫先生所計劃的工作，無論是政治的、哲學的、科學的或其他，他都以極大的熱忱去進行。他虛懷若谷，對於任何建議和批評都樂於接受。

因為他的眼光和計劃超越了他的時代，許多與他同時代的人常常覺得他的計劃不切實際，常常引用「知之非艱，行之唯艱」的傳統觀念來答覆他。他對這些人的短視常常感到困擾。當他在 40 年前宣導革命運動時，他就曾遭遇到同樣的障礙。後來他寫了一篇叫「心理建設」的文章，提倡知難行易的學說。中西思想重點不同的地方其中之一就是中國人重應用，而西洋人重理知。中國人重實際，所以常常過分強調實踐過程中的困難，有時是實在的困難，有時只是想像的，以致忽視實際問題背後的原理原則。凡是經常接觸抽象原則和理論的人，或者熟悉如何由問題中找出基本原則的人，都不難了解中山先生的立論。在另一方面，凡是慣常注重近功實利而不耐深思熟慮的人，可就不容易了解中山先生的主張了。在清室式微的日子裏，中國並不缺乏銳意改革的人，但是真能洞燭病根，且能策定治本計劃的人卻很少。孫先生深知西方文化的發展過程，同時對中國的發展前途具有遠大的眼光，因此他深感超越近功近利的原理原則的重要，他知道只有高瞻遠矚的知識才能徹底了解問題的本質。

只要我們把握這種基本的知識，實踐起來就不會有不可解除的困難了。真正的困難在於發見基本的道理。事實上，不但真知灼見的事情，必能便利地推行，而在許多地方，即使所知不深，亦能推行無阻。例如水泥匠和木匠，只要他們照着建築師的吩咐去做，即使他們不懂得建築學，也照樣能執行複雜的建築藍圖。醫藥方面的情況更明顯，診斷常常比用藥困難，醫科學生知道得很清楚，在研究醫學之前，他必須對生理學和解剖學先有相當的了解，而在研究生理學和解剖學之前則又得先研究物理與化學等普通科學。每一種科學都是許多為學問而學問的人們經過幾百年繼續不斷研究所積累的結果。由此可見醫學的基礎知識之獲得比行醫遠為艱難。

與孫先生同時代的人只求近功，不肯研究中國實際問題的癥結所在，希望不必根據歷史、社會學、心理學、科學等所得的知識，就把事情辦好，更不願根據科學知識來訂定國家的建設計劃。因此他們誣衊孫先生的計劃是不切實際的空中樓閣。他們的「現實的」眼光根本看不到遠大的問題，更不知道他們自己的缺點就是無知和淺見，缺乏實際能力倒在其次。以實在而論，他們自己認為知道的東西，實只限於淺薄的個人經驗或不過根據一種常識的推斷。這樣的知識雖然容易獲得，但以此為實踐基礎反常常會遭受最後的失敗。

在西洋人看起來，這些或許只是理論與實踐，或者知識與行為的哲學論爭，似乎與中國的革命和建設不發生關係。但是中山先生卻把它看得很嚴重，認為心理建設是其他建設的基礎，不論是政治建設、實業建設或社會建設。有一天我和羅志希同杜威先生謁見孫先生談到知難行易問題，杜威教授對中山先生說：「過重實用，則反不切實用。沒有人在西方相信『知』是一件容易的事。」

「新教育」月刊，一方面受到思想界革命風氣的影響，一方面因為我個人受到中山先生的啟示，所以在教學法上主張自發自動，強調兒童的需要，擁護杜威教授在他的「民主與教育」中所提出的主張。在中國的教育原理方面，「新教育」擁護孟子的性善主張，因此認為教育就是使兒童的本性得到正常的發展。事實上孔子以後，中國教育的主流一直都遵循著性善的原則。不過年代一久，所謂人性中的「善」就慢慢地變為受古代傳統所規範的某些道德教條了。因此我們的主張在理論上似很新鮮，實踐起來卻可能離本來的原則很遠很遠。所謂「發展本性」在事實上可能變為只是遵守傳統教條，中國發生的實際情形正是如此。

自從盧梭、裴斯塔洛齊、福祿培，以及後來的杜威等人的學說被介紹至中國思想界以後，大家對孟子學說開始有了比較清晰的認識，中國兒童應該從不合現代需要的刻板的行為規律中解放出來。我們應該誘導兒童自行思想，協助他們根據他們本身的需要，而不是根據大人的需要，來解決他們自己的問題。我們應該啟發兒童對自然環境的興趣。根據兒童心理學的原則，兒童只能看做兒童；他不是一個小大人，不能單拿知識來填，更不應拿書本來填，教育應該幫助兒童在心智、身體和團體活動各方面成長。

這些就是指導「新教育」的思想原則。讀者不難覺察，這與當時國內的革命思想是恰好符合的。「新教育」月刊與北京大學師生間知識上的密切關係，終於使我在第二年跑進這個知識革命的大漩渦，擔任了教育學教授，並於校長蔡先生請假時代理校長。⑯

第十五章
北京大學和學生運動

　　如果你丟一塊石子在一池止水的中央，一圈又一圈的微波就會從中蕩漾開來，而且愈漾愈遠，愈漾愈大。北京曾為五朝京城，歷時一千餘年，因此成為保守勢力的中心，慈禧太后就在這裏的龍座上統治着全中國。光緒皇帝在 1898 年變法維新，結果有如曇花一現，所留下的唯一痕跡只是國立北京大學，當時稱為京師大學堂或直呼為大學堂，維新運動短暫的潮水已經消退而成為歷史陳跡，只留下一些貝殼，星散在這恬靜的古都裏，供人憑弔。但是在北京大學裏，卻結集着好些蘊蓄珍珠的活貝；由於命運之神的擺佈，北京大學終於在短短 30 年歷史之內對中國文化與思想提供了重大的貢獻。

　　在靜水中投下知識革命之石的是蔡孑民先生 (元培)。蔡先生在 1916 年 (民國 5 年) 出任北京大學校長，他是中國文化所孕育出來的著名學者，但是充滿了西洋學人的精神，尤其是古希臘文化的自由研究精神。他的「為學問而學問」的信仰，植根於對古希臘文化的透徹了解，這種信仰與中國「學以致用」的思想適成強烈的對照。蔡先生對學問的看法，基本上是與中山先生的看法一致的，不過孫先生的見解來自自然科學，蔡先生的見解則導源於希臘哲學。

　　這位著名的學者認為美的欣賞比宗教信仰更重要。這是希臘文化交融的一個耐人尋味的實例。蔡先生的思想中融合着中國學者對自然的傳統愛好和希臘人對美的敏感，結果產生對西洋雕塑和中國雕刻的愛好；他喜愛中國的山水畫，也喜愛西洋油畫；對中西建築和中西音樂都一樣喜歡。他對宗教的看法基本上是中國人的傳統見解；認為宗教不過是道德的一部分。他希望以愛美的習慣來提高青年的道德觀念。這也就是古語所謂「移風易俗莫大於樂」的傳統信念。高尚的道德基於七情調和，要做到七情調和則必須透過藝術和與音樂有密切關係的詩歌。

蔡先生崇信自然科學。他不但相信科學可以產生發明、機器，以及其他實益，他並且相信科學可以培養有系統的思想和研究的心理習慣，有了系統的思想和研究，才有定理定則的發現，定理定則則是一切真知灼見的基礎。

蔡先生年輕時鋒芒很露。他在紹興中西學堂當校長時，有一天晚上參加一個宴會，酒過三巡之後，他推杯而起，高聲批評康有為、梁啟超維新運動的不徹底，因為他們主張保存滿清皇室來領導維新。說到激烈時，他高舉右臂大喊道：「我蔡元培可不這樣。除非你推翻滿清，否則任何改革都不可能！」

蔡先生在早年寫過許多才華橫溢、見解精闢的文章，與當時四平八穩、言之無物的科舉八股適成強烈的對照。有一位浙江省老鄉人曾經告訴我，蔡元培寫過一篇怪文，一開頭就引用《禮記》裏的「飲食男女，人之大欲存焉」一句。繳卷時間到時，他就把這篇文章繳給考官。蔡先生就在這場鄉試裏中了舉人。後來他又考取進士，當時他不過三十歲左右，以後就成為翰林。

蔡先生晚年表現了中國文人的一切優點，同時虛懷若谷，樂於接受西洋觀念。他那從眼鏡上面望出來的兩隻眼睛，機警而沉着；他的語調雖然平板，但是從容、清晰、流利而懇摯。他從來不疾言厲色對人，但是在氣憤時，他的話也會變得非常快捷、嚴厲、扼要 —— 像法官宣判一樣的簡單明了，也像絨布下面冒出來的匕首那樣的尖銳。

他的身材矮小，但是行動沉穩。他讀書時，伸出纖細的手指迅速地翻着書頁，似乎是一目十行地讀，而且有過目不忘之稱。他對自然和藝術的愛好使他的心境平靜，思想崇高，趣味雅潔，態度懇切而平和，生活樸素而謙抑。他虛懷若谷，對於任何意見、批評或建議都欣然接納。

當時的總統黎元洪選派了這位傑出的學者出任北大校長。北大在蔡校長主持之下，開始一連串的重大改革。自古以來，中國的知識領域一直是由文學獨霸的，現在，北京大學卻使科學與文學分庭抗禮了。歷史、哲學和四書五經也要根據現代的科學方法來研究。為學問而學問的精神蓬勃一時。保守派、維新派和激進派都同樣有機會爭一日之短長。背後拖着長辮、心裏眷戀帝制的老先生與思想激進的新人物並坐討論，同席笑謔。教室裏，座談會上，社交場合裏，到處討論着知識、文化、家庭、社會關係和政治制度等等問題。

這情形很像中國先秦時代，或者古希臘蘇格拉底和亞里斯多德時代的重演。蔡先生就是中國的老哲人蘇格拉底，同時，如果不是全國到處有同情他的人，蔡先生也很可能遭遇蘇格拉底同樣的命運。在南方建有堅強根據地的國民黨黨員中，同情蔡先生的人尤其多。但是中國的和外國的保守人士卻一直指責北京大學鼓吹「三無主義」──無宗教、無政府、無家庭──與蘇格拉底被古希臘人指責戕害青年心靈的情形如出一轍。爭辯不足以消除這些毫無根據的猜疑，只有歷史才能證明它們的虛妄。歷史不是已經證明了蘇格拉底的清白無罪嗎？

我已經提到蔡先生提倡美學以替代宗教，提倡自由研究以追求真理。北大文學院院長陳仲甫（獨秀）則提倡賽先生和德先生，認為那是使中國現代化的兩種武器。自由研究導致思想自由；科學破壞了舊信仰，民主則確立了民權的主張。同時，哲學教授胡適之（適）那時正在進行文學革命，主張以白話文代替文言作表情達意的工具。白話比較接近中國的口語，因此比較易學，易懂。它是表達思想的比較良好也比較容易的工具。在過去知識原是士大夫階級的專利品，推行白話的目的就是普及知識。白話運動推行結果，全國各地產生了無數的青年作家。幾年之後，教育部並下令全國小學校一律採用白話為教學工具。

北大是北京知識沙漠上的綠洲。知識革命的種子在這塊小小的綠洲上很快地就發育滋長。三年之中，知識革命的風氣已經遍佈整個北京大學。

這裏讓我們追述一些往事。一個運動的發生，絕不是偶然的，必有其前因與後果。在知識活動的蓬勃氣氛下，一種思想上和道德上的不安迅即在學生之中發展開來。我曾經談過學生如何因細故而鬧學潮的情形，那主要是受了 18 世紀以自由、平等、博愛為口號的法國政治思想的影響，同時青年們認為中國的遲遲沒有進步，並且因而招致外國侵略應由清廷負其咎，因此掀起學潮表示反抗。

第一次學潮於 1902 年發生於上海南洋公學，即所謂罷學風潮。我在前篇已經講過。幾年之後，這種學生反抗運動終至變質而流為對付學校廚子的「飯廳風潮」。最後學校當局想出「請君入甕」的辦法，把伙食交由學生自己辦理。不過零星的風潮仍舊持續了 15、6 年之久。有一次「飯廳風潮」甚至導致慘劇。杭州的一所中學，學生與廚子發生糾紛，廚子憤而在飯裏下了毒藥，結果十多位學生中毒而死。我在慘案發生後去過這所中學，發現許多學生正在臥牀呻吟，另有十多具棺木停放在操場上，等待死者家屬前來認領葬殮。

表現於學潮的反抗情緒固然漸成過去，反抗力量卻轉移到革命思想上的發展，而且在學校之外獲得廣大的支持，終至發為政治革命而於 1911 年推翻滿清。

第二度的學生反抗運動突然在 1919 年（民國 8 年）5 月 4 日在北京爆發。此即所謂五四運動。事情經過是這樣的：消息從巴黎和會傳到中國，說歐戰中的戰勝國已經決定把山東半島上的青島送給日本。青島原是由中國租借給德國的海港，歐戰期間，日本從德國手中奪取青島。中國已經對德宣戰，戰後這塊租地自然毫無疑問地應該歸還中國。消息傳來，舉國騷然。北京學生在一羣北大學生領導下舉行示威，反對簽訂凡爾賽和約。三千學生舉行羣眾大會，並在街頭遊行示威，反對接受喪權辱國的條件，高喊「還我青島！」、「抵制日貨！」、「打倒賣國賊！」寫着同樣的標語的旗幟滿街飄揚。

當時的北京政府仍舊在軍人的掌握之下，僅有民主政體和議會政治的外表，在廣州的中山先生的國民黨以及其餘各地的擁護者，雖然努力設法維護辛亥革命所艱辛締造的民主政制，卻未着實效。北京政府的要員中有三位敢犯眾怒的親日分子。他們的政治立場是盡人皆知的。這三位親日分子——交通總長曹汝霖，駐日公使陸宗輿，和另一位要員章宗祥結果就成為學生憤恨的對象，羣眾蜂擁到曹宅，因為傳說那裏正在舉行秘密會議。學生破門而入，滿屋子搜索這三位「賣國賊」。曹汝霖和陸宗輿從後門溜走了；章宗祥則被羣眾抓到打傷。學生們以為已經把他打死了，於是一鬨而散，離去前把所有的東西砸得稀爛，並且在屋子裏放了一把火。

這時武裝警察和憲兵已經趕到，把屋子圍得水泄不通。他們逮捕了近60位學生帶往司令部，其餘的1千多名學生跟在後面不肯散，各人自承應對這次事件負責，要求入獄。結果全體被關到北京大學第三院（法學院），外面由憲警嚴密駐守。

有關這次遊行示威的消息，遭到嚴密的檢查與封鎖。但是有幾個學生終於蒙過政府的耳目，透過天津租界的一個外國機構發出一通電報。這電報就是5號上海各報新聞的唯一來源。

五號早晨報紙到達我手裏時，我正在吃早餐。各報的首頁都用大字標題刊登這條新聞，內容大致如下：

北京學生遊行示威反對簽訂凡爾賽和約。三親日要員曹汝霖、陸宗輿、章宗祥遭學生圍毆。曹汝霖住宅被焚，數千人於大隊憲警監視下拘留於北京大學第三院。羣眾領袖被捕，下落不明。

除此簡短新聞外，別無其他報道。

這消息震動了整個上海市。當天下午，公共團體如教育會、商會、職業工會等紛紛致電北京政府，要求把那三位大員撤職，同時釋放被捕或被扣的學生。第二天一整天，全上海都焦急地等待着政府的答覆，但是杳無消息。於是全市學生開始罷課，提出與各團體相同的要求，同時開始進行街頭演說。

第二天早晨，各校男女學生成羣結隊沿着南京路挨戶訪問，勸告店家罷市。各商店有的出於同情、有的出於懼怕，就把店門關起來了。許多人則仿照左鄰右舍的榜樣，也紛紛關門歇市。不到一個鐘頭，南京路上的所有店戶都關上了大門了，警察干涉無效。

罷市風聲迅即蔓延開來，到了中午時，全上海的店都關了。成千成萬的人在街頭聚談觀望，交通幾乎阻塞。租界巡捕束手無策。男女童子軍代替巡捕在街頭維持秩序，指揮交通。由剪了短髮的女童子軍來維持人潮洶湧的大街的秩序，在上海公共租界倒真是一件新鮮的事。中國人和外國人同樣覺得奇怪，為甚麼羣眾這麼樂意接受這些小孩子的指揮，而對巡捕們卻大發脾氣。

幾天之內，罷課成為全國性的風潮，上海附近各城市的商店和商業機構全都關了門。上海是長江流域下游的商業中心，這個大都市的心臟停止跳動以後，附近各城市也就隨着癱瘓，停止活動，倒不一定對學生表同情。

租界當局聽説自來水廠和電燈廠的僱員要參加罷工，大起驚慌。後來經過商會和學生代表的調停，這些人才算被勸住沒有罷工。各方壓力繼續了一個多星期，北京政府終於屈服，親日三官員辭職，全體學生釋放。

各地學生既然得到全國人士的同情與支持，不免因這次勝利而驕矜自喜。各學府與政府也從此無有寧日。北京學生獲得這次勝利以後，繼續煽動羣眾，攻擊政府的腐敗以及他們認為束縛青年思想的舊傳統。學生們因為得到全國輿情的支持，已經戰勝了政府。參加遊行示威，反對簽訂凡爾賽和約，是每一個中國人都願意做的事。學生們因為有較好的組織，比較敢言，比較衝動，顧慮比較少，所以打了頭陣，並且因此撥動了全國人民的心弦。

親日官員辭職，被捕學生釋放，上海和其他各地的全面罷課罷市風潮歇止以後，大家以為「五四」事件就此結束，至少暫時如此。但是北京大學本身卻成了問題。蔡校長顯然因為事情鬧大而感到意外，這時已經辭職而悄然離開北京，臨行在報上登了一個廣告引《白虎通》裏的幾句話說：「殺君馬者道旁兒，民亦勞止，汔可小休。」他先到天津，然後到上海，最後悄然到了杭州，住在一個朋友的家裏。住處就在著名的西湖旁邊，臨湖依山，環境非常優美，他希望能像傳統的文人雅士，就此息隱山林。雖然大家一再敦勸，他仍舊不肯回到北大。他説，他從來無意鼓勵學生鬧學潮，但是學生們示威遊行，反對接受凡爾賽和約有關山東問題的條款，那是出乎愛國熱情，實在無可厚非。至於北京大學，他認為今後將不易維持紀律，因為學生們很可能為勝利而陶醉。他們既然嘗到權力的滋味，以後他們的慾望恐怕難以滿足了。這就是他對學生運動的態度。有人說他隨時準備鼓勵學生鬧風潮，那是太歪曲事實了。

他最後同意由我前往北京大學代理他的職務。我因情勢所迫，只好勉強同意擔負起這副重擔，我於是在 7 月間偕學生會代表張國燾乘了火車，前赴北京。到了北京大學，初次遇見了當時北大學生，以後任台大校長的傅孟真（斯年），現在台灣任「國史館長」的羅志希（家倫）。兩位是北大「五四」的健將，不但善於謀略，而且各自舞着犀利的一支筆，好比公孫大娘舞劍似的，光芒四照。他們約好了好多同學，組織了一個新潮社，出版了一種雜誌，叫做「新潮」，向舊思想進攻。我現在寫「西潮」，實在自從「五四」以後，中國本土，已捲起了洶湧澎湃的新潮，而影響了中國將來的命運。然而「五四」之起因，實為第一次世界大戰後，歐洲帝國主義之崩潰，以及日本帝國主義的猖狂。所以畢竟還是與西潮有關。

我到校以後，學生團體開了一個歡迎大會。當時的演說中，有如下一段：

「……故諸君當以學問為莫大的任務。西洋文化先進國家到今日之地位，係累世文化積聚而成，非旦夕可幾。千百年來，經多少學問家累世不斷的勞苦工作而始成今日之文化。故救國之要道，在從事增進文化之基礎工作，而以自己的學問功夫為立腳點，此豈搖旗吶喊之運動所可幾？當法國之圍困德國時，有德國學者費希德在圍城中之大學講演，而作「致國民書」曰：『增進德國之文化，以救德國。』國人行之，遂樹普魯士敗法之基礎。故救國當謀文化之增進，而負此增進文化之責者，唯有青年學生。……」

暴風雨過去以後，烏雲漸散，霽日重現，蔡先生也于 9 月間重回北大復職視事。

北大再度改組，基礎益臻健全。新設總務處，由總務長處理校中庶務。原有處室也有所調整，使成為一個系統化的有機體，教務長負責教務。校中最高立法機構是評議會，會員由教授互選；教務長、總務長，以及各院院長為當然會員。評議會有權制訂各項規程，授予學位，並維持學生風紀。各行政委員會則負責行政工作。北大於是走上教授治校的道路。學術自由、教授治校，以及無畏地追求真理，成為治校的準則。學生自治會受到鼓勵，以實現民主精神。

此後 7 年中，雖然政治上狂風暴雨迭起，北大卻在有勇氣、有遠見的人士主持下，引滿帆篷，安穩前進。圖書館的藏書大量增加，實驗設備也大見改善。國際知名學者如杜威和羅素，相繼應邀來校擔任客座教授。

這兩位西方的哲學家，對中國的文化運動各有貢獻。杜威引導中國青年，根據個人和社會的需要，來研究教育和社會問題。無庸諱言的，以這樣的方式來考慮問題，自然要引起許多其他的問題。在當時變化比較遲鈍的中國實際社會中自然會產生許多糾紛。國民黨的一位領袖胡漢民先生有一次對我說，各校風潮迭起，就是受了杜威學說的影響。此可以代表一部分人士對於杜威影響的估計。他的學說使學生對社會問題發生興趣也是事實。這種情緒對後來的反軍閥運動卻有很大的貢獻。

羅素則使青年人開始對社會進化的原理發生興趣。研究這些進化的原理的結果，使青年人同時反對宗教和帝國主義。傳教士和英國使館都不歡迎羅素。他住在一個中國旅館裏，拒絕接見他本國使館的官員。我曾經聽到一位英國使館的官員表示，他們很後悔讓羅素先生來華訪問。羅素教授曾在北京染患嚴重的肺炎，醫生們一度認為已經無可救藥。他病愈後，我聽到一位女傳教士說：「他好了麼？那是很可惜的。」我轉告羅素先生，他聽了哈哈大笑。

第一次世界大戰後，中國的思想界，自由風氣非常濃厚，無論是研究社會問題或社會原理，總使慣於思索的人們難於安枕，使感情奔放的人們趨向行動。戰後歐洲的西洋思想就是在這種氣氛下介紹進來的。各式各樣的「主義」都在中國活躍一時。大體而論，知識分子大都循着西方民主途徑前進，但是其中也有一部分人受到 1917 年俄國革命的鼓勵而嚮往馬克思主義。「新青年」的主編陳獨秀辭去北大文學院院長的職務，成為中國共產運動的領袖。反對日本帝國主義的運動也促使知識分子普遍同情俄國革命。第三國際於 1923 年派越飛到北京與中國知識分子接觸。某晚,北京擷英飯店有一次歡迎越飛的宴會。蔡校長於席中致歡迎詞說:「俄國革命已經予中國的革命運動極大的鼓勵。」

俄國曾經一再宣佈,準備把北滿的中東鐵路歸還中國,並且希望中國能夠順利掃除軍閥,驅除侵略中國的帝國主義。蘇俄對中國的這番好意,受到所有知識分子以及一般老百姓的歡迎。這種表面上友好表示的後果之一,就是為蘇俄式的共產主義在中國鋪了一條路。

在這同時,許多留學歐美大學的傑出科學家也紛紛回國領導學生,從事科學研究。教員與學生都出了許多刊物。音樂協會、藝術協會、體育協會、圖書館協會紛紛成立,多如雨後春筍。教授李守常(大釗)並領導組織了一個馬克思主義研究會。當時北京報紙附欄,稱這研究會為「馬神廟某大學之牛克斯研究會」,不過作為嘲笑之對象而已。馬神廟者北京大學所在地也。此時北大已經敲開大門招收女生。北大是中國教育史上第一所給男女學生同等待遇的高等學府。教員和學生在學術自由和自由研究的空氣裏,工作得非常和諧而愉快。

北大所發生的影響非常深遠。北京古都靜水中所投下的每一顆知識之石,餘波都會到達全國的每一角落。甚至各地的中學也沿襲了北大的組織制度,提倡思想自由,開始招收女生。北大發起任何運動,進步的報紙、雜誌和政黨無不紛起回應。國民革命的勢力,就在這種氛圍中日漸擴展,同時中國共產黨也在這環境中漸具雛型。

軍閥之間的衝突正在這古都的附近間歇進行着。在這些時斷時續的戰事中,北京各城門有一次關閉幾達一星期之久。槍炮聲通常在薄暮時開始,一直持續到第二天早晨。有一次,我們曾經跑到北京飯店的屋頂去眺望炮火,那真叫做隔岸觀火,你可以欣賞夜空中交織的火網,但是絕無被火花灼傷的危險。炮彈拖着長長的火光,在空中飛馳,像是千萬條彩虹互相交織。隆隆的炮聲震得屋頂搖搖晃晃,像是遭到輕微的地震。從黃昏到清晨,炮火一直不停。我回家上牀時，根本不能把耳朵貼着枕頭睡，因為這樣炮聲顯得特別響亮。因此我只能仰天躺着睡，讓耳朵朝着天花板，同時注意到電燈罩子在微微搖晃。玻璃窗也嘎嘎作響。我有一隻德國種的狼犬，名叫狼兒，它被炮聲吵得無法再在地板上安睡，一直哼個不停。它的耳朵一貼到地板，它就驚跳起來，哼唧幾聲之後，它沖到房門旁，拼命在門上抓，它一定以為怪聲是我臥房的地板下面發出來的。第二天早上，我罵了它一頓，說它前一晚不該那麼搗亂。它似乎自知理屈，只用兩隻眼睛怯生生地望着我。早餐時我到處找不到狼兒，從此再不見它的蹤影。大概它跑出去想找塊安靜地，夜裏不會有惡作劇的魔鬼在地下大敲大擂，好讓它安安穩穩地睡覺。不過，我想它大概是很失望的。

有一天，我和一位朋友在圍城中沿着順城門大街散步。老百姓還是照常操作，毫無緊張的樣子。拉黃包車和坐黃包車的也與平常毫無異樣。我們從西單牌樓轉到西長安街，然後又轉到中央公園。皇宮前午門譙樓上的黃色琉璃瓦，在夕陽下映着澄碧的秋空閃閃發亮。我們在一顆古柏的濃蔭下選了一個地方坐下。這些古老的柏樹是幾百年前清朝的開國皇帝種植的。有的排成長列，有的圍成方形。空氣中充塞着柏樹的芳香，微風帶着這些醉人的香味吹拂着我們的面龐。我們圍坐在桌子旁，靜聽着鄰座酒客的議論。大家都在議論戰事，猜測着誰會勝利，誰將入據北京。誰勝誰敗，大家好像都不在乎。操心又怎麼樣？北京已經見過不少的戰事，飽經滄桑之後，北京還不是依然故我？沉默的午門譙樓就是見證。

「城門都關了，不知道我們能不能叫個魚吃吃。」我的朋友說。

堂倌拿了一條活生生的魚來問我們：「先生們喜歡怎麼個燒法？」

「一魚兩吃。一半醋溜，一半紅燒。」

魚燒好端上來了，有一碟似乎不大新鮮。

「這是怎麼回事？這一半是死魚呀！」我的朋友質問堂倌，堂倌鞠了一躬，只是嘻嘻地笑。

「哦，我知道了！這條魚一定是從城牆跳進來的。碰到地的一邊碰死了，另一邊卻仍然活着。」我代為解釋。堂倌再度跑過來時，我的朋友從桌上抓起一把空酒壺，翻過來給他看。「怎麼！你給我們一把空酒壺呀！」

「對不起，」堂倌笑嘻嘻地說，「酒燙跑了！」他馬上給我們重新拿了一壺。當然，兩壺酒都記在我們賬上。

我們在黃昏時回家。那天晚上，戰鬥停止了，我又想起狼兒。這一晚，它大概可以在城裏找個地方，安靜地睡一覺了。第二天早上，我們發現政府已經易手。皇宮依然無恙。老百姓照常過活。各城門大開，成千成萬的人從鄉下挑着蔬菜、肉類、雞蛋、魚蝦湧進北京城。小孩子們在戰場上撿起廢彈殼，以幾塊錢的代價在街頭出售。許多人拿這些炮彈殼制花瓶。

城外有些人家破人亡，我亦失掉了我的狼兒。

一般而論，在這些漫長痛苦的日子裏，因戰事而喪失的生命財產並不嚴重。使中國陷於癱瘓而成為鄰邦侵略之目標的，實為人心之動盪，交通之破壞，經濟之崩潰，以及國民安定生活之遭破壞。國家陷於四分五裂，全國性的建設計劃幾乎成為不可能。中國當務之急就是統一。

蔡校長赴歐旅行時，我又再度代理北大校長。這時我接到中山先生一封信，對北大的各種運動大加獎譽，最後並勉勵我「率領三千子弟，參加革命」。

孫先生可惜未能有生之年看到他的希望實現，不過短短數年之後，他的繼承人蔣總司令，率領革命軍從廣州北伐，所向披靡，先至長江流域，繼至黃河流域，終至底定北京。開始於北京，隨後遍及全國各階層的革命運動，已先為這次國民革命軍的新勝利奠定了心理的基礎。⓰

第十六章
擾攘不安的歲月

　　蔡校長和胡適之他們料得不錯，學生們在「五四」勝利之後，果然為成功之酒陶醉了。這不是蔡校長等的力量，或者國內的任何力量所能阻止的，因為不滿的情緒已經在中國的政治、社會和知識的土壤上長得根深蒂固。學校裏的學生竟然取代了學校當局聘請或解聘教員的權力。如果所求不遂，他們就罷課鬧事。教員如果考試嚴格或者贊成嚴格一點的紀律，學生就馬上罷課反對他們。他們要求學校津貼春假中的旅行費用，要求津貼學生活動的經費，要求免費發給講義。總之，他們向學校予取予求，但是從來不考慮對學校的義務。他們沉醉於權力，自私到極點。有人一提到「校規」他們就會瞪起眼睛，噘起嘴巴，咬牙切齒，隨時預備揍人。

　　有一次，北大的評議會通過一項辦法，規定學生必須繳講義費。這可威脅到他們的荷包了。數百學生馬上集合示威，反對此項規定。蔡校長趕到現場，告訴他們，必須服從學校規則。學生們卻把他的話當耳邊風。羣眾湧進教室和辦公室，要找主張這條「可惡的」規定的人算賬。蔡校長告訴他們，講義費的規定應由他單獨負責。

　　「你們這班懦夫！」他很氣憤地喊道，袖子高高地捲到肘子以上，兩隻拳頭不斷在空中搖晃。「有膽的就請站出來與我決鬥。如果你們那一個敢碰一碰教員，我就揍他。」

　　羣眾在他面前圍了個半圓形。蔡校長向他們逼進幾步，他們就往後退幾步，始終保持着相當的距離。這位平常馴如綿羊、靜如處子的學者，忽然之間變為正義之獅了。

　　羣眾漸漸散去，他也回到了辦公室。門外仍舊聚着 50 名左右的學生，要求取消講義費的規定。走廊上擠滿了好奇的圍觀者。事情成了僵局。後來教務長顧孟余先生答應考慮延期收費，才算把事情解決。所謂延期，自然是無限延攬。這就是當時全國所知的北大講義風潮。

鬧得最兇的人往往躲在人們背後高聲叫罵，我注意到這些搗亂分子之中有一位高個子青年，因為他個子太高，所以無法逃出別人的視線。我不認識他，後來被學校開除的一批人之中，也沒有他的名字。若干年之後，我發現他已經成為神氣十足的官兒，我一眼就認出他來。他的相貌決不會讓人認錯，他的叫罵聲仍舊縈迴在我的耳畔。他已經成為手腕圓滑的政客，而且是位手辣心黑的貪員，抗戰勝利後不久故世，留下一大堆造孽錢。

幾年之後，發生了一次反對我自己的風潮，因為我拒絕考慮他們的要求。一羣學生關起學校大門，把我關在辦公室。胡適之先生打電話給我，問我願不願意找警察來解圍，但是我謝絕了。大門關閉了近兩小時。那些下課後要回家的人在裏面吵着要出去，在門外準備來上課的人則吵着要進來。羣眾領袖無法應付他們自己同學的抗議，最後只好打開大門。我走出辦公室時，後面跟着一、二十人，隨跟隨罵着。我回過頭來時，發現有幾個學生緊釘在我背後。北大評議會決定開除我所能記得的以及後來查出的鬧事學生。

好幾年以後，我偶然經過昆明中央航空學校的校園。航空學校原來在杭州，戰時遷到昆明。忽然一位漂亮的青年軍官走到我面前，他向我行過軍禮告訴我，他就是被北京大學開除的一位學生。我馬上認出他那誠實的面孔和健美的體格。鬧學潮時緊迫在我背後所表現的那副醜惡的樣子已經完全轉變了，他的眼睛閃耀着快樂的光輝，唇邊蕩漾着笑意。這次邂逅使我們彼此都很高興。航空學校的校長後來告訴我，這位青年軍官是他們最優秀的飛行員和教官之一。

這些例子足以說明學生運動中包含各式各樣的分子。那些能對奮鬥的目標深信不疑，不論這些目標事實上是否正確，而且願意對他們的行為負責的人，結果總證明是好公民，而那些鬼頭鬼腦的傢伙，卻多半成為社會的不良分子。

學生們所選擇的攻擊目標，常常是政府無法解決或者未能圓滿解決的國際問題。因此，他們常能獲得國人的同情；他們的力量也就在此。中日之間的「事件」日漸增多以後，學生的示威遊行常常被日本人解釋為反日運動。糾紛的根源在於二十一條要求和凡爾賽和約所引起的山東問題。自從遠東均勢破壞以後，日本幾乎享有控制中國的特權。門戶開放政策已經取代瓜分中國的政策。但是門戶開放政策必須以均勢為基礎，均勢一旦破壞，中國只有兩條路可走──一條路是任由日本宰割，另一條路就是自我振作，隨時隨地與日本打個分明。

學生們決定奮起作戰，起先是遊行、示威、罷課和抵制日貨，接着就轉而攻擊北京政府，因為他們認為一切毛病都出在北京政府身上。他們發現沒有重要的國際問題或國內問題足資攻擊時，他們就與學校當局作對。原因在於青年心理上的不穩。一旦他們受到刺激而採取行動時，這種不穩的情緒就爆發了。想壓制這種澎湃的情緒是很困難的。

若干學生團體，包括青年共產黨員，開始把他們的注意力轉移到勞工運動以及工人的不穩情緒上。沿海商埠的工人正蠢蠢欲動。鐵路工人和工廠工人已開始騷動，而且蔓延各地。他們不久就與學生攜手，參加羣眾大會和遊行。勞工運動是不可輕侮的武器。在廣州的國民黨政府，曾以總罷工癱瘓香港，使這個英國殖民地在工商業上成為荒漠，歷時 18 月之久。

全國性的反英情緒是民國 14 年的上海「5．30 慘案」激起的。5 月 30 日那一天，一羣同情勞工運動的人在上海大馬路（南京路）遊行示威，公共租界當局竟然下令向羣眾開槍，好幾個人中彈身死，傷者更不計其數。工人、商人和學生在國民黨及共產黨領導之下，隨即發動全面罷工、罷市、罷課，上海再度變為死城。6 月 23 日，廣州的學生、工人、商人和軍人繼起回應，發動反英示威遊行。羣眾行近沙面租界時，駐防英軍又向羣眾開槍。於是香港各界亦開始罷工、罷市、罷課，使香港也變為死城。北京英國使館的華籍僱員，在學生煽動之下，也進行同情罷工，致使這批英國外交官員很久都沒有廚子和聽差侍候。

自從工人運動與學生運動彼此呼應以後，遊行示威者人數動以萬計，北京不時有各色人等參加的羣眾大會出現，街頭遊行行列常常長達數里，羣眾手搖旗幟，高呼口號，無不慷慨激昂。一位白俄看到這種情形時，不覺怵然心驚。他曾經在俄國看到不少這樣的集會，他說這是革命即將來臨的徵兆，因此他擔心是否能繼續在中國平安住下去。

　　學生們找不到遊行示威的機會時，曾經拿學校當局作為鬥爭的對象，工人的情形亦復如此。他們找不到示威的對象時，就把一股怨氣發洩在僱主的身上。不過，中央政府或地方政府對付罷工工人，可比對付學生簡單多了。他們有時用武力來彈壓罷工工人，有時就乾脆拿機關槍來掃射。

　　段祺瑞執政的政府顯然認為機關槍是對付一切羣眾行動的不二法門，因此，在一羣學生包圍執政府時，段執政就老實不客氣下令用機關槍掃射。我在事前曾經得到消息，說政府已經下令，學生如果包圍執政府，軍隊就開槍。因此我警告學生不可冒險，並設法阻止他們參加；但是他們已經在校內列隊集合，準備出發，結果不肯聽我的勸告。他們一到了執政府，子彈就像雨點一樣落到他們頭上了。

　　我在下午 4 點鐘左右得到發生慘劇的消息後馬上趕到出事地點。段執政官邸門前的廣場上，男女學生傷亡枕藉，連傷者與死者都難辨別。救護車來了以後，把所有留着一口氣的全部運走，最後留下 20 多具死屍，仍舊躺在地上。許多重傷的在送往醫院的途中死去，更有許多人則在手術台上斷了氣。我們向各醫院調查之後，發現死傷人數當在 100 以上。這個數目還不包括經包紮後即行回家的人在內。

　　段祺瑞政府的這種行動，引起全國普遍的抗議，段政府後來終於垮台，此為原因之一。

　　學生勢力這樣強大而且這樣囂張跋扈，除了我前面所談到的原因之外，另一原因是這些學生多半是當時統治階級的子女。學生的反抗運動，也可以說等於子女對父母的反抗。做父母的最感棘手的問題就是對付桀驁不馴的子女，尤其是這些子女的行為偏偏又受到鄰居們的支持。工人們的情形可就不同了；他們的父母或親戚，既不是政府大員，也不是社會聞人，因此他們命中注定要挨警察的皮鞭或軍隊的刺刀。只有在學生領導之下，或者與學生合作時，工人才能表現較大的力量。

學生運動在校內享有教師的同情，在校外又有國民黨員和共產黨員的支持，因此勢力更見強大。此外還牽涉到其他的政治勢力。故而情形愈來愈複雜，聲勢也愈來愈浩大。學生運動自從民國 8 年開始以來，背後一直有教員在支持。就是滿清時代的首次學潮，也是教員支持的。

後來教員也發生罷教事件，要求北京政府發放欠薪，情勢更趨複雜。北大以及其他 7 個國立大專學校的教員，一直不能按時領到薪水。他們常常兩、三個月才能領到半個月的薪俸。他們一罷課，通常可以從教育部擠出半個月至一個月的薪水。

有一次，好幾百位教員在大羣學生簇擁之下，佔據了整個教育部的辦公廳，要求發放欠薪。8 個國立學校的校長也到了教育部，擔任居間調停的工作。教員與學生聯合起來，強迫馬鄰翼教育次長和 8 位校長一齊前往總統府，要求發薪水。這位次長走到教育部門口時，藉口天在下雨，不肯繼續往外走。一位走在他旁邊的學生汪翰，馬上把自己的雨傘打開遞給他，並且很直率地說：「喏，這把雨傘你拿去！」於是這位次長只好無可奈何地繼續前進，後面跟着 8 位心裏同樣不怎麼樂意的校長。羣眾走近總統府時，憲兵、警察趕緊關起大門。教員與學生在門外吵着要進去。忽然大門打開了，大羣武裝憲警蜂擁而出，刺刀亂刺，槍把亂劈。上了年紀的教員和年輕的女學生紛紛跌到溝裏，有的滿身泥濘，有的一臉血跡，叫的叫，哭的哭，亂成一片。法政大學校長王家駒像死人一樣躺在地上。北大政治學教授李大釗挺身與士兵理論，責備他們毫無同情心，不該欺侮餓肚皮的窮教員。北大國文系教授馬敍倫額頭被打腫一大塊，鼻孔流血，對着憲兵大喊：「你們只會打自己中國人，你們為甚麼不去打日本人？」

這位馬教授後來被送到法國醫院診治，政府派了一位曾任省長的要員前往慰問並致歉意。坐在病榻旁的馬教授的老母說：

「這孩子是我的獨子，政府幾乎要他的命，請問這是甚麼道理？」

曾任省長的那位要員回答道：「老伯母請放心，小侄略知相法，我看這位老弟的相貌，紅光煥發，前途必有一步大運。老伯母福壽無疆，只管放心就是。至於這些無知士兵無法無天，政府至感抱歉。老伯母，小侄向您道歉。」

老太太居然被哄得安靜下來，病房裏其餘的人卻幾乎笑出聲來了。躺在醫院病床上的其他教員，也都因為這位要員的風趣而面露笑容。

這件事情總算這樣過去了。另有一次，教員們擁到財政部要求發放欠薪，部裏的人一個個從後門溜走，結果留下一所空房子。有一次學生們因為不滿政府應付某一強國的外交政策，衝進外交部打爛一面大鏡和好些精緻的座椅。學生、教員和工人聯合起來罷工罷課，反對北京政府和侵略中國權益的列強。多事的那幾年裏，差不多沒有一個月不發生一兩次風潮，不是罷課就是罷工。

在那時候當大學校長真是傷透腦筋。政府只有偶然發點經費，往往一欠就是一兩年。學生要求更多的行動自由，政府則要求維持秩序，嚴守紀律。出了事時，不論在校內校外，校長都得負責。發生遊行、示威或暴動時，大家馬上找到校長，不是要他阻止這一邊，就是要他幫助那一邊。每次電話鈴聲一響，他就嚇一跳。他日夜奔忙的唯一報酬，就是兩鬢迅速增加的白髮。

我講這些話，決不是開玩笑。我記下這些往事以後，又做了場惡夢，有時看到青年男女橫屍北京街頭，有時又看到憲兵包圍北京大學要求交出羣眾領袖。夢中驚醒之後，輾轉反側無法安枕，一閉上眼睛，一幕幕的悲劇就重新出現。

有一天，我和一位老教授在北京中央公園的柏樹下喝茶。這位老教授曾經說過一段話，頗足代表當時擾攘不安的情形。

「這裏鬧風潮，那裏鬧風潮，到處鬧風潮——昨天罷課，今天罷工，明天罷市，天天罷、罷、罷。校長先生，你預備怎麼辦？這情形究竟到哪一天才結束。有人說，新的精神已經誕生，但是我說，舊日安寧的精神倒真是死了！」

第四部

國家統一

第十七章
憲政的試驗

　　軍閥時代的一天晚上，俄國駐北京大使加拉罕舉行宴會，招待當地首要。出席宴會的約有 60 人。上菜上到烤乳豬時，席上一些客人，一面斜眼看看在座的國會議長、副議長，一面望着熱氣蒸騰的烤乳豬，不覺掩嘴而笑。這種吃吃的笑聲，迅即傳染到全體賓客，只有那位議長和那位副議長，板起面孔裝聾作啞。最後我看到有人向蘇俄大使咬耳朵，弄得這位大使也忍俊不止。

　　這裏頭有個典故。從前印尼的橡園主人和礦場老闆，常常以不法手段向中國招募工人。中國的勞工招募所，就把南洋說得天堂似的，花點錢把工人誘騙到南洋羣島，轉賣給當地的開發公司。這些被當做貨色出賣的可憐蟲就叫「豬仔」。他們有的是自甘賣身，有的根本糊裏糊塗就被當豬一樣賣掉了。

　　民國初年，國會的議員受賄舞弊，弄得聲名狼藉，普受鄙視，許多人就罵他們是「豬仔議員」，因為他們只看誰出價高，就把自己賣給誰。當然，絕大多數的議員是正直無私的，但是這些人毫無組織，因此也就無法制止其中的敗類。於是「豬仔」之名就普遍加在國會議員的頭上了，壞人營私結黨時，好人也必須團結一致，要不然，好人蒙冤不白，那是自作自受。有一次他們在萬牲園裏的豳風堂宴會，有人把豳字解作「豬積如山」，一時全城傳誦，此後議員們就不敢再在那裏請客了。

　　中國成文憲法的觀念是從美國介紹來的。美國的憲法是美國人民思想信仰的具體表現，而且是根據人民的生活發展而來的。中國的憲法只是抄襲外國的觀念，起草憲法的人隨意取捨，根本沒有考慮到中國人的生活習慣或思想觀念。

革命前的帝政時代末年，由紳士階級組成的省諮議局倒是成績斐然，因為他們的目標大致相同，而且紳士階級裏也不乏領袖人才。同時各省巡撫威望甚高，足以約束省諮議局。碰到重大問題時，諮議局裏很少發生政治糾紛。通過的議案大致都是為省民謀福利的，貪污舞弊絕無僅有。

民國元年，中山先生在南京任臨時大總統時，參政會頗有成為現代國會的跡象，因為參政員代表革命利益，而且有革命領袖在領導工作，孫先生擔任總統，眾望所歸，威望一時無兩。後來袁世凱繼任總統，國會裏可就有了糾紛了。革命領袖憎惡專制反動的袁世凱，袁也憎惡革命領袖。但因他掌握軍隊，不惜以武力恐嚇國會議員，為此後國會發展史上開了惡例。我不妨在這裏舉一個例子，藉以說明恐嚇手段對議會風氣所產生的惡劣影響。事情發生在選舉袁世凱為總統的時候，選舉時有攝影師在場拍照。當時室內照須用鎂光粉，點燃鎂光粉時會發出炫目的閃光和震耳的響聲。鎂光粉爆炸時，許多人以為是炸彈，紛紛奪路逃命。有一位議員躲到桌子底下，高喊：「我選舉的是袁世凱！」另外有些人則落掉鞋子，事情過去以後到處找鞋。這場戲終以彈劾國會秘書張公權為結束，說他不該讓攝影師以「炸彈」驚擾國會。

在袁世凱擔任總統期間，經常活動的五六個政黨之間糾紛迭起，派系之爭和意氣之爭非常激烈。這個被老百姓瞧不起的國會後來終於被袁世凱稱帝運動以及張勳復辟運動的潮流所捲走。不過兩次運動相繼失敗，國會亦告恢復。政治權力一部分操在各省督軍手裏，一部分操在有名無實的北京中央政府手裏。這時的北京政府，已經威信掃地，無力控制國會。北方軍閥曹錕賄選獲任總統之後，國會威信一落千丈，此後情勢演變，國會聲望更是每況愈下。

國會議員之中，許多是賄選而來。享譽國際、憤世嫉俗的學者辜鴻銘告訴我，有一次選舉時，曾有一位哥倫比亞大學畢業的陳博士，出八百大洋收買他的選票，他把錢收下了，跑到天津逛了一趟胡同，根本沒有去投票。

後來在北京飯店的一次國際性聚會上，辜鴻銘碰到這位賄選的人，他指着這人對大家操英語說：「這傢伙要拿八百塊錢買我，各位先生，你們看我辜鴻銘真的這麼賤嗎？」

若干不良分子就是這樣混進國會的，雖然這種人數目不多，但是已足以使國會顯得有點像拍賣場，誰出錢最高，就把議席賣給誰。

北京學生現在開始把他們的攻擊目標移到這個「腐敗之家」頭上了。有一天下午，好幾千男女學生包圍了國會，要求取消議程上若干有關教育的議案。結果學生與守衛警察發生衝突。若干學生氣憤之餘，竟在幾天之後從天津偷運來三顆炸彈準備去炸議會。這事被我們勸阻了，總算沒有見諸行動，炸彈也運出城外丟到河裏。幾個禮拜之後，一位漁夫撿到其中的一顆炸彈，他把炸彈提在手裏搖來搖去，希望弄清楚裏面究竟是甚麼東西。轟隆一聲，炸彈爆炸，炸得這位好奇的漁人血肉橫飛。警方認為這顆炸彈是革命時期投進河去的，因此根本未進行任何調查。

國會與學生之間的衝突仍然不斷發生。國會議員最先想確立人民代表的權威，學生們卻反唇以「豬仔」相譏。國會預備彈劾北大校長，學生就發動示威遊行，高舉畫着豬玀的旗幟，並且揚言要搗毀國會。國會自知本身有弱點，最後只好高懸免戰牌，不敢再捋學校與學生的虎須。憤世嫉俗的辜鴻銘既看不起學生，也看不起議員，他有一天對我說：「你相信民主，這實在是民狂。」

如果一個機關只是被公眾憎恨，它也許仍舊有存在的餘地，如果這個機關成為公眾冷諷熱嘲的對象，即使那是為了其中少數人的行為，多數人也會因此遭殃，而整個機關也就像沉船一樣難逃劫數了。中國憲政初期的國會，情形就是如此。後來有些軍閥抓住機會，乾脆把它一腳踢開。

我們可以從兩個不同的角度來看軍閥時代的憲政。一方面是軍閥以威脅利誘來破壞憲政，他們沒有領導民主團體的威信、原則或政策。袁世凱垮台以後，中央政府的權力已經名存實亡，實際權力操縱在互相殘殺的各省督軍手裏。他們根本不理甚麼叫法律，他們只曉得自己持有封建軍隊的武力。

中央政府既不能維持憲政原則，也不能確立治國政策，事實上這個政府已經無足輕重，不值得擁護也不值得反對。

在另一方面，國會裏的議員，很少有人關心國家利益。他們念念不忘的只是他們本省的或本地的利益，甚至只是本身的利益。他們對國家利益的觀念，本來就很模糊，因此對國家大事也就不可能有整套的指導原則或政策。除了地方事件或私人利益之外，既無組織，亦無領導。中國人愛好自由，但是對有組織的民主政治，也就是對憲政，卻無經驗，也不懂組織對民主的重要。中西國情不同，想使中國遵循西洋的憲政規模，無異趕東方之車，朝向西方的一顆星走着。憲政試驗的失敗，實在毫不足奇。

中山先生有鑒於此，所以在他的民主憲政計劃中，設計了訓政制度，作為過渡到憲政政府的跳板。依照他的計劃，先有軍政時期以達國家統一，接着是一個以黨領政的訓政時期，最後才過渡到正式的憲政時期。民國16年，北伐成功，國民黨在南京建立訓政政府，銳意革除國會的腐敗風氣。此後10年間，國民黨在蔣委員長領導下，剷除軍閥，統一全國。日本軍閥所導致的國難，使統一的局面更為加強。

國家統一是實行憲政的先決條件。孫中山先生已經制定建國的原則，只要政府與國會能有堅強的領導，人民與政府一致尊重法律，中國無疑地將在民主憲政的道路上大步邁進。⏻

第十八章
中山先生之逝世

出師未捷身先死，長使英雄淚滿襟。

此為杜甫詠諸葛武侯之句，宋宗澤元帥假以自挽者也。如果拿這兩句詩來描寫中山先生之死，真是再恰當沒有了。這位偉大的領袖，致力國民革命達 40 年之久，不幸在國家建設正需要他的時候，死神就把他攫走了。

民國 14 年（1925 年）春天，孫先生因為宵旰勤勞的結果，幾個月來身體一直不怎麼好。他在容許共產黨參加國民黨以後，更採取了進一步的行動。他鑒於中國仍舊陷於分裂，同時鑒於只有團結才能產生力量，乃毅然應北洋軍閥之邀，離粵北上，到北京討論統一國家的計劃。北上途中，他曾繞道訪問日本，希望說服日本朝野，使他們相信強大統一的中國是對日本有利的。到達天津時，他竟病倒了。我到天津謁見孫先生及夫人並報告北京政情後，不日返京。過了幾天，大家把他從天津護送到北京，我赴車站往迎。猛地裏從車上跳下來一位老友湖北劉麻哥，抓住了我的領口，喝道：「你好，你們養成那麼多的共產黨員禍國殃民。」我說：「麻哥，你胡說。」他笑道：「小心，共產黨都是壞東西啦。」先生到北京後病勢仍是很重，無法討論統一計劃，且一直臥牀不能起身。執政段祺瑞託稱足疾亦未往謁。北京協和醫院的醫師對先生的病均告束手，胡適之先生推薦了一位中醫陸仲安。但是孫先生不願服中藥。他說，他本身是醫生，他知道現代醫藥束手時，中醫的確有時也能治好疑難的病症。他說：「一隻沒有裝羅盤的船也可能到達目的地，而一隻裝了羅盤的船有時反而不能到達。但是我寧願利用科學儀器來航行。」朋友仍舊一再勸他吃點中藥，他不忍過於拂逆朋友的好意，最後終於同意了。但是這隻沒裝羅盤的船卻始終沒有到達彼岸。

孫先生自協和醫院移住顧少川（維鈞）寓。顧寓寬敞宏麗，建於 17 世紀，原為著名美人陳圓圓的故居。陳為明將吳三桂之妻，據說吳三桂為了從闖王李自成手中搶救陳圓圓，不惜叛明降清，並引清兵入關。

民國 14 年 3 月 12 日早晨，行轅顧問馬素打電話來通知我，孫先生已入彌留狀態。我連忙趕到他的臨時寓所。我進他臥室時，孫先生已經不能說話。在我到達前不久，他曾經說過：「和平、奮鬥、救中國。……」這就是他的最後遺囑了。大家退到客廳裏，面面相覷。「先生還有復原的希望嗎？」一個國民黨元老輕輕地問。大家都搖搖頭，欲言又止。

沉默愈來愈使人感到窒息，幾乎彼此的呼吸都清晰可聞。時間一分一秒無聲地過去，有些人倚在牆上，茫然望着天花板。有些人躺在沙發上，閉起眼睛沉思。也有幾個人躡手躡腳跑進孫先生臥室，然後又一聲不響地回到客廳。

忽然客廳裏的人都尖起耳朵，諦聽臥室內隱約傳來的一陣啜泣聲，隱約的哭聲接着轉為號啕痛哭 —— 這位偉大的領袖已經撒手逝世了。我們進入臥室時，我發現孫先生的容顏澄澈寧靜，像是在安睡。他的公子哲生先生坐在牀旁的一張小凳上，呆呆地瞪着兩隻眼，像是一個石頭人。孫夫人伏身牀上，埋頭在蓋被裏飲泣，哭聲悽楚，使人心碎。汪精衛站在牀頭號啕痛哭，同時拿着一條手帕擦眼淚。吳稚暉老先生背着雙手站在一邊，含淚而立。

覆蓋着國旗的中山先生的遺體舁出大廳時，鮑羅廷很感慨地對我說：如果孫先生能夠多活幾年，甚至幾個月，中國的局勢也許會完全改觀的。協和醫院檢驗結果，發現中山先生係死於肝癌。

孫先生的靈柩停放在中央公園的社稷壇，任人瞻仰遺容。一星期裏，每天至少有兩三萬人前來向他們的領袖致最後的敬意。出殯行列長達四五里，執紼在 10 萬人以上，包括從小學到大學的全部學生、教員、政府官員、商人、工人和農人。

靈柩暫停厝在離北京城約 15 里的西山碧雲寺石塔裏。石塔建於數百年前，略帶西藏風味，由白色大理石建成，塔尖是鍍金的青銅打造的。石塔高踞碧雲寺南方，四周古松圍繞，春風中松濤低吟，芬芳撲鼻。碧空澄澈，綠茵遍地，潺潺的溪水和碧雲寺的簷角的鈴聲相應和，交織成清輕的音樂。

畢生致力於科學和奮鬥的孫先生，現在終於在藝術與自然交織的優美環境中安息了。

中國的革命領袖已經安息，但是他所領導的國民黨內部卻開始有了糾紛。國民黨的一羣要員，借北來參加中山先生葬禮之便，就在西山他的臨時陵墓前集會。討論如何對付國民黨內勢力日漸膨大的共產黨。這就是以後所稱的西山會議派。在會議中有人哭着說：「先生呀，先生離我們去了，叛黨的共黨分子，要把我們的黨毀滅了。」於是跨黨的共產黨徒，和親共的一班小嘍囉，趕到孫先生的靈前，把會議打散了。從此以後，國民黨的正式黨員與跨黨的共產分子之間，裂痕日深一日。兩年以後，也就是民國 16 年 (1927) 國民革命軍佔領南京，國民黨發動清黨，共產黨徒終於被逐出黨。

按：羅家倫先生主編「國父年譜」738 頁對中山先生民國 14 年於北平治療情形，曾有刊載，誌錄如下：

18 日自協和醫院移居鐵獅子胡同行轅。是日，先生離協和醫院，乘醫院特備汽車，緩駛至鐵獅子胡同行轅。家屬及友好同志，多以為醫院既經宣告絕望，仍當不惜採取任何方法，以延長先生壽命。於是有推薦中醫陸仲安者；因陸曾醫治胡適博士，若由胡進言，先生或不峻拒。乃推李煜瀛 (石曾) 赴天津訪胡 (時胡適有事赴津)，告以來意，約其同歸。胡初以推薦醫生責任太重，有難色。後抵京見汪兆銘等，力言侍疾者均惶急萬狀，莫不以挽救先生生命為第一，且因先生平時對胡甚客氣，換一生人往說，或可採納。胡乃偕陸同往。胡先入臥室進言。先生語胡曰：「適之！你知道我是學西醫的人。」胡謂：「不妨一試，服藥與否再由先生決定。」語至此，孫夫人在牀邊急乘間言曰：「陸先生已在此，何妨看看。」語訖即握先生腕，先生點首，神情淒惋，蓋不欲重拂其意，乃伸手而以面移向內望。孫夫人即轉身往牀之內方坐下，目光與先生對視。🅑

第十九章
反軍閥運動

學生遊行罷課鬧了好幾年，加上軍閥互相殘殺，北京政府的力量終於一蹶不振，軍閥則像印度土大王一樣統治各省。在北京的中央政府首腦，無時不需要鄰近各省的支援，如果軍閥一翻臉，隨時可以長驅直入北京城。北京政府在各省的根基愈來愈脆弱，政權本身亦隨之搖搖欲墜。某一軍閥進入北京接收政權，另一軍閥馬上陰謀取而代之。當政的人如果遭遇民意的強烈反對，例如學生遊行示威，其他軍閥便利用機會從中取利。權謀、內戰、政變，各種政治力量縱橫捭闔的結果，北京政府隨時在更換主人。我在北京的最初 9 年之中，所看到的變遷實在太多了，留在記憶中的是一大堆亂糟糟的悲喜劇場面。我像是埃及沙漠中一座金字塔，淡淡遙望着行行列列來來往往的駝影，反映在斜陽籠罩着的浩浩平沙之上，駝鈴奏出哀怨的曲調，悠揚於晚紅之中。

北京政府的經濟狀況非常窘困，國庫應有的收入，都被各省軍閥扣留，用以維持他們的私人軍隊或徑入私人腰包。中央政府通常只能以極高的利息向銀行借一點錢，這一點錢之中的一部分，還得用於籠絡支持政府然而需索無饜的軍閥。我們前面已經提到教員薪水拖欠的情形。不但教員如此，就是政府官員和駐外使節的薪水，也往往一欠就是好幾個月，甚至好幾年。

「北京政府的前途究竟怎麼樣呢？」有一天，一位美國外交官這樣問我。

「它會像河灘失水的蚌，日趨乾涸，最後只剩下一個蚌殼。」我回答說。

情勢一年不如一年，終至老百姓對政府的最後一點敬意也消失了。學生幫同破壞了它的威信，軍閥們則把它整個埋葬在北京的塵土裏。數年後在美國遇見那位美國朋友，他問我是否忘了蚌殼的故事，我說沒有。

在那時候，廣州的國民革命運動則以一日千里之勢在發展，國民黨的革命運動一直享有大眾的支持，尤其是知識分子和學生，甚至連北洋軍閥中的一些開明分子也同情國民黨。一籃爛橘子裏，有時也能找出幾個好的來的。

中山先生雖然逝世了，國民黨的精神卻始終未沮喪。孫先生所建立的革命武力核心，繼續在蔣介石將軍為校長的黃埔軍校發展茁壯，短短幾年之內，蔣將軍的國民革命軍已經完成訓練，隨時可予北洋軍隊以致命的打擊。民國 16 即 1927 年，革命軍以雷霆萬鈞之勢長驅北伐，左翼直入華中而下漢口，右翼循閩浙沿海北上而達杭州，繼以鉗形攻勢會師南京。革命軍攻克南京後，遂以南京為國民政府首都。

國民革命軍開始北伐的那一年，北洋軍閥張宗昌亦於同時入據北京，這位聲名狼藉的軍閥，體健如牛，腦笨如豬，性暴如虎。他的利爪隨時會伸向他不喜歡的任何人，或者他垂涎的任何漂亮女人。我曾在一個治安委員會席上見過他幾面，當時我是這個委員會的委員之一。他那副尊容，真叫人望而生畏。京報編輯邵飄萍被槍斃的那天晚上，北京政府的前總理孫寶琦告訴我，我的名字已經上了黑名單，我感覺到魔爪的影子已經向我伸過來了。剛好王亮疇（寵惠）來訪，我不假思索，連忙跳上他的軍警不會盤查的紅牌汽車，直駛東交民巷使館界，在六國飯店辟室住下。第二天跑到美國使館向一位美國朋友開玩笑說：「我天天叫打倒帝國主義，現在卻投入帝國主義懷抱求保護了。」還有校長室秘書政治學教授李守常（大釗）、女生張挹蘭等六、七人先後逃入使館界舊東清鐵路辦事處躲避。他們後來被張作霖派兵捕去，處絞刑而死。我在六國飯店住了 3 個月，經常以寫字消遣。

同住在六國飯店的亦有幾個人，地質學教授，以後任中央研究院院長朱驪先（家驊）就是其中之一。好些朋友不時探望我們，但是在那裏關了 3 個月，即使那是一個豪華「監獄」，也有點吃不消。我們一直在設法逃出北京，後來局勢比較松弛一點時，就相繼溜出來了。我的一位朋友有一位年輕能幹的太太，我之能夠逃出北京，就是她一手策劃的。她冒充我的太太，同乘一輛古老的馬車陪送我到東車站，一路上居然逃過警察的耳目。陌生人望我一眼，都會使我心驚肉跳，雖然我在外表上仍舊竭力裝作若無其事的樣子。我擠在人潮中搭上一輛去天津的火車，然後從天津搭英國商船到上海。

在船上碰到朱騮先，他正預備轉道上海赴廣州，後來他出任廣州中山大學校長。我本人則由上海轉赴杭州。當時滬杭鐵路已告中斷，因此我只好繞道赴杭。這時何敬之將軍（應欽）所率領的國民革命軍尚未到達浙江，北京政府委派的浙江省長正準備起義反抗北洋政府向國民革命軍輸誠。我去拜訪他時，他向我透露了參加南方集團的計劃。他告訴我，他已經派了1000人沿鐵路進駐江蘇邊境，江浙之間的鐵路已告中斷。

我心裏想，他準是被別人的勝利陶醉了，否則他怎麼會企圖與實力強他十倍的敵人作戰呢？第二天早晨，我就離開杭州，繞道重回上海。幾星期以後，他的軍隊被北洋軍打得落花流水。北洋軍進杭州時，他被捕處決。

不久北洋軍閥命運逆轉，國民革命軍進佔杭州。我也再度回到西子湖畔。杭州人熱烈歡迎國民革命軍。這些現代裝備的軍隊勝利進軍杭州時，成千成萬的市民滿面笑容地列隊歡迎。我站在人叢中觀望，一顆心高興得怦怦亂跳。經過16年之後，一支現代化的中國軍隊的信譽又重新建立起來了。

大約一年之後，蔣總司令在民國17年即1928年完成部署，準備繼續北伐。他指揮的軍隊渡過長江，沿津浦路向北京推進。北伐軍抵達山東濟南府邊緣時，日本人唯恐中國統一，藉口保護在山東的權益和日本皇民的生命財產，竟由青島派兵沿膠濟路向濟南推進。他們的目的是製造「事件」，以破壞中國的統一計劃。所謂「事件」，自然就是中日之間公開衝突。日軍在濟南府殘殺山東交涉員及其僚屬，希望藉此激起中國的報復行動。

蔣總司令洞燭日人陰謀，深恐小不忍而亂大謀，決定暫避其鋒，把國民革命軍的前頭部隊調離山東，並以迅雷不及掩耳的手段渡過黃河，直逼北京。因而國民革命軍未遭阻撓，統一目標亦賴以實現。日本軍隊在山東終於撲了空。

國民革命軍到達後，北京隨即陷落，北京政府的紙老虎被南風一吹就倒了。

民國 16 年國民革命軍進杭州時，我被任為省政府委員兼教育廳長。我在政府中擔任工作的經驗也就在杭州開始了。杭州是浙江的省會，也是我青年時代讀書的地方。省政府由省政府委員會組成。國民政府在南京成立以前，所有省府委員以及主席都是由國民革命軍總司令蔣介石將軍委派的。

省府委員之中有五位分別兼任民政廳長、財政廳長、軍事廳長、建設廳長和教育廳長。省府委員會之上則有國民黨中央政治會議浙江分會，負責全省一般政策，政策決定後即下令省政府執行。會議主席由省主席張靜江先生擔任，由我任秘書長。這是我第一次擔任國民黨要職。後來省境情勢漸趨穩定，政分會遂告撤銷。

省政府和南京的國民政府一樣充滿着改革和建設的精神，中央政府的重大施政，我將在下一章加以敍述。省政府的建設計劃相當龐大，但是革命之後，此項計劃難免受經費支絀的限制。因此只能將工作集中在鋪築公路上面，幾年之內的確鋪了不少公路。省城本身也有許多道路經省政府指定拓寬或添建。兩年之後，杭州城內已經添築了許多寬闊的馬路。西湖沿岸和蘇堤也闢了馬路，直達西山各名勝，另有一條公路與上海銜接，招來了不少度週末的遊客。短短 3 年之內，杭州已經煥然一新了。市區之內，西湖之濱，以及湖邊山麓，新建洋房別墅像雨後春筍一樣出現，人口激增，商業也盛極一時。

各縣市也新建了許多電燈廠。若干鄉村裏還裝設了蒸汽幫浦灌溉稻田。因為浙江是絲織業中心，政府開始提倡科學養蠶法，以科學方法培育蠶種，然後轉售給養蠶的人。頭一年裏，科學蠶種曾經引起強烈的反對，因養蠶的人受了以傳統方法培育蠶種的人的影響，對於科學蠶種發生懷疑。但是事實勝於雄辯，第二年中，政府出產的新式蠶種已經供不應求了。

為了改善田租制度，政府舉辦全省耕地調查，工作繼續了好幾年。浙江省所採用的辦法，與共產黨對農地所採的激烈手段適成對照。浙江省採取一種比較溫和的「二五減租」辦法，也就是佃農付給地主的田租普遍減低百分之二十五。佃農通常以主要作物收穫的百分之五十付給地主田租，「二五減租」以後，佃農就只要付收成的百分之三七點五了。田租的租率已經維持了幾百年，計算方法各地互有差別，實行「二五減租」以後，有些地方的佃農得到很大的利益，在另一些地方，這個減租辦法卻在地主與佃農之間引起嚴重的糾紛。減租委員會所收受的訟案多如山積，全省各地普遍發生糾紛，減租辦法終於幾年之後放棄。推行減租最力的沈玄廬（定一）被暗殺，死因迄今未明。

不久之後，掃除文盲運動開始。經過 6、7 年時間，除了普通的小學之外，短期的民眾識字班增加了幾千個。

省內的教育制度進行一次新試驗。國立浙江大學成立，由我擔任校長。浙大不但主持高等教育，並且主管全省公立學校。教育廳取消，浙大校長則成為省府委員。另外兩省也繼起仿效，各自成立大學。經過兩年的試驗，另外幾省發生內部糾紛和政治爭執，整個制度終於在民國 18 年即 1929 年廢止，那時我任國民政府教育部長，所以培植這個制度和埋葬這個制度的都是我自己。

我在杭州整整住了一年，翌年膺任教育部長，同時兼任浙江大學校長，因此經常往返京杭之間。民國 18 年，我辭去浙大校長的兼職，在南京再住了一年，後以中央大學易長及勞動大學停辦兩事與元老們意見相左，被迫辭職。

我當時年壯氣盛，有決策，必貫徹到底，不肯通融，在我自以為勵精圖治，在人則等於一意孤行。我本世居越中，耳濡目染，頗知紹興師爺化大為小、化小為無的訣竅。今背道而馳，自然碰壁。武力革命難，政治革命更難，思想革命尤難，這是我所受的教訓。

在我辭職的前夜，吳稚暉先生突然來教育部，雙目炯炯有光，在南京當時電燈朦朧的深夜，看來似乎更覺明顯。他老先生問我中央、勞動兩校所犯何罪，並為兩校訟冤。據吳老先生的看法，部長是當朝大臣，應該多管國家大事，少管學校小事。最後用指向我一點，厲聲說道：「你真是無大臣之風。」

我恭恭敬敬地站起來回答説：「先生坐，何至於是，我知罪矣。」

第二天我就辭了職，不日離京，回北京大學去了。劉半農教授聞之，贈我圖章一方，文曰：「無大臣之風。」🐾

第二十章
國民黨之出掌政權

國民革命軍攻克北京以後，中國重歸統一，首都亦由北京遷至南京，北京則改為北平。

北京曾為遼、金、元、明、清五代的首都，歷時 1000 餘年。現在國都固然改定為南京，北平卻仍舊是文化和藝術的中心。中國知識階級除了本地方言之外所說的，以及廣播電台所採用和學校所教授的「官話」或「國語」就是以北京方言做基礎的。

國民政府從北方黃河流域遷都南方的長江流域，主要原因有二。第一個理由是革命精神已經彌漫長江流域，因此也是革命精神比較容易生根的肥沃土壤，黃河流域則是反動軍閥的根據地。第二個理由：長江流域是中國金融力量的中心，足以供應政府必需的經費。

在 1851 年至 1864 年之間，南京曾是太平天國的首都。太平軍潰敗以後，南京破壞殆盡，而且始終不曾恢復舊觀。城內的廢墟、麥田、菜圃、果園比蓋了房子的街道還多。街道狹窄，路面高低不平，而且骯髒不堪，電燈昏暗如菜油燈。差個專人送信往往比打電話還快。

這座雄踞揚子江邊的古城，在古時是文物教化的中心，尤其是在南朝時代，所謂南朝金粉是也。女人、醇酒、清歌、妙舞一直縈迴在歷代騷人墨客的記憶裏。秦淮河橫越城內，連接了盛長百合的湖泊。河上滿是金碧輝煌高懸彩燈的畫舫。秦淮河兩岸酒樓歌榭櫛比，雕樑畫棟，門口掛着竹簾子，妙曼的曲調和醉人的幽香從竹簾後一陣陣飄送出來，此所謂：

「此曲只應天上有，人間哪得幾回聞。」

這就是舊日京華。但是南京是戰略要地，國內每有重大戰事，南京必定要遭一場浩劫，每經一次戰禍，它的精華也就失去其大半。戰事結束，和平重臨，南京又會在廢墟上重建，恢復舊日的光輝。我所描寫的往昔金陵生活，就是根據歷史記載而來的。

不過，自從太平天國滅亡，劫後南京一直未曾恢復昔日的美麗。歷次重建似乎只是庸俗藝匠對於古本的臨摹，經過一再臨摹之後，原作的光彩漸漸消失，留下的只是俗不可耐的贗品。

秦淮河仍舊在南京城內流過，畫舫歌榭也依然存在。但是形式、素質和內容都遠非昔比了。風雅的生活已經隨滾滾江流沖走了。

國民革命軍進入南京以後，一種新精神隨之誕生 —— 一種改革和建設的精神。大家要拿現代科學來復興往昔的藝術。在這瘡痍滿目的廢墟上，一座柏油馬路四通八達的現代城市建立起來了。街道旁栽種了葱翠的樹木，供市民遊息的公園也先後開始設計和建立。自動電話、電燈和自來水也裝設了，停泊南京附近的美國兵艦的水上飛機則從空中測繪了一幅南京地圖，南京的新都市計劃就是根據這幅地圖設計的。國民政府成立了首都建設設計委員會，我以教育部長的身分成為該委員會的委員之一。這個設計委員會在一位美國建築師的協助下，辛勤工作了一年多。這位美國建築師對北京的中國宮殿式建築很有研究，委員會的目標是儘量保持中國建築的宏偉和華麗，同時兼有現代都市的便利和衛生設備。

陳舊傾圮的建築被拆除了，以便鋪築道路或重建新屋。商業日漸發達，現代戲院倍增，人口急速增加。秦淮河和湖泊一一加以疏浚，古刹和其他公共建築也都開始修葺。

政府建造了中央博物院，來陳列北平故宮博物院的一部分珍品，而且在南京城內朝天宮一座小山裏，造了一個不虞空襲的鋼骨水泥的地下室，來保藏貴重文物。因為中央博物院的董事們早已預料到日本不久即將發動對華侵略，南京當然是他們的攻擊目標。華北局勢惡化，長城戰雲密佈之時，故宮博物院的貴重寶藏即以數百輛火車運至南京，並且在南京失陷之前，全部轉運內地，保留於山洞石室之中。

交通部大樓和鐵道部大樓都是鋼骨水泥的建築，裏面有現代的照明、通風等設備。但是它們的建築圖樣卻是完全中式的，釉瓦、雕樑、畫棟、花窗，以及其他古色古香的裝潢。這兩幢雄偉的建築峙立在新都交通要道中山路的兩旁，成為配合現代需要的中國古代藝術的紀程碑。其他的建築也已設計好藍圖，後以戰事影響而告擱置。

中山陵位於城外紫金山之麓，上覆琉璃瓦，柱子全部是白色大理石。陵前有層層疊疊步步高升花崗岩的石階。山上栽種着從全國各地移來的不同林木。山坡上點綴着各種各樣的花木和果樹，山腳建造了一個運動場和游泳池。

政府在南京附近規劃了一個示範新村，由市府設計包括道路、下水道、電話、電燈、學校等的建設藍圖。幾年之內，私人新建房屋已到處矗立，房屋周圍都有廣大的空地，闢為東方式的花園。樹木蔥翠，花枝招展，小鳥啁啾，溪水低吟，古老的生活方式已為新生活所取代，科學與藝術，工作與娛樂，天工與人力，齊頭並進，相得益彰。

這就是實驗中的胚芽，大家希望它發展滋長，將來有一天可以推廣到全國的每一角落。這只是個平凡的開端，但是已經有了相當的成果，因為這個新村運動已經在數年之內推廣到許多大城市及其附近地區。如果持之以恆，而且經濟有進一步的發展，這些新村勢將使新中國的生活方式全面改觀。

我們無法奢望北京政府垮台之後，軍閥們隨之銷聲匿跡。他們的實力仍舊根深蒂固地盤據在各省。中國幅員遼闊，交通不便，兼以人心未定，凡此種種，無不使軍閥們蠢蠢欲動。時機一到，他們就企圖擴張勢力：他們像血液中的細菌一樣潛伏在各省，身體衰弱，就會乘機偷襲。蔣總司令從揮軍攻克北京到對日抗戰的前夕，十年間為統一國家，真是宵旰辛勞，席不暇暖。

羅馬帝國的將軍們曾以縱橫輻輳的道路鞏固其帝國，蔣總司令也深知開闢公路、鐵路和航空線的重要。他以南京為中心，建築了向各省輻射的公路、鐵路和航空線。國民政府成立以前，交通網的一部分業已存在。國民黨執政以後，就以原有的交通網為基礎，新建了許多支線和衛接線。邊遠城市則闢航空線以資聯繫。從新首都北飛可達北平、開封、西安和蘭州，南飛可達福州、廣州和昆明，西航則達漢口、重慶及成都。

連接漢口與廣州及香港對岸九龍的新鐵路也築成了。如果日本不在此時侵略東北，我們很可能在民國 20 年（1931 年）就可以從香港或上海乘火車直達巴黎。如果從上海出發，可搭直達車經南京、濟南到天津，從天津搭北寧路出長城到瀋陽，從瀋陽搭中國自建而與日人所有的南滿鐵路平行的長春鐵路到齊齊哈爾；從齊齊哈爾有鐵路支線與西伯利亞鐵路連接。中國統一努力的進展以及在東北自建鐵路，促使日人企圖一舉而占滿洲（即東三省），乃在民國 20 年（1931 年）9 月 18 日挑起「瀋陽事件」，亦即「9・18事變」。

滬杭甬鐵路錢塘江至曹娥江之間的一段缺口也填補起來了，但是鋪軌工作卻因戰事發生而停止。不過蘇州與杭州之間的蘇杭鐵道剛在戰事開始以前就鋪築完成了。另一條從杭州到江西的浙贛鐵路剛好在抗戰前完成，抗戰期間更西延至湖南境內，在株洲與粵漢路銜接。後來湘桂鐵路完成，再往西可以直達廣西的桂林。

公路的發展更為迅速。京杭國道是在我居留南京期間建成的，在這條公路正式開放以前，我曾經很榮幸地參加通車典禮。京杭國道穿越江浙兩省最富庶的地區。當車子沿太湖奔馳時，我們真想留下來小住幾天，坐在松樹之下，眺望着遠帆在夕陽餘暉中出沒。漁人們在湖邊撒網捕魚，漁網中跳躍着金鱗閃燦的鯉魚。太湖是我國五大湖之一，湖水灌溉了我國人口最密、文化最高的江浙兩省千萬畝肥沃的農田。

京杭國道同時經過一個盜匪如毛的區域，但是公路通車以後，盜匪隨之銷聲匿跡，因為現在如遇匪警，軍隊可以隨時趕到出事地點了。

建設進展之時，各地也不斷發生事故。有時缺乏現代道路的地區發生變亂，鐵路和公路常常需要以賽跑的姿態趕築到出事地點。抗戰前一年，福建省發生叛變，中央軍迅速沿新築成的浙贛鐵路及公路從杭州趕赴福建，變亂旋即敉平。鐵路公路愈多，叛亂與盜匪也愈會減少，各地間貨運賴以暢流更不必說了。

交通是現代化和改革的關鍵，也是發現國家未來發展機會的鑰匙。因此國民政府的建設計劃就從建築鐵道公路着手。交通建設也是確保國家統一之一法，如果有完善的道路可資利用，地方性變亂很容易就可以敉平。除此之外，交通愈便利愈發達，人民交往也愈頻繁，觀念交流也愈容易。偏僻地區的名勝風景，旦夕之間就成為學者、畫家、詩人和愛好自然者的徜徉之所了。

各省在國民政府影響之下也開始修築更多的道路。原有道路在國民黨執政以後很快就開始修補拓展。因之抗戰期間軍隊得以在各省之間暢通無阻。抗戰前一兩年，旅客可以從南京坐汽車直達昆明，換一句話說，可以從華東沿海直達西南邊城，也就是滇緬公路的起點。

在行政方面，政府正設法增加行政效率。政府設計了一種新式的檔案處理辦法並在各機關試行。公文程式也經過簡化。

文官考試制度重新恢復，但是見過清朝科舉制度的人也許會失望，因為考試錄取的人已經不再有從前那種煊赫的排場和榮耀。

新的法典也開始擬訂。婦女的地位提高到與男人一樣。過去只有兒子可以繼承父親的產業，現在女兒也享有同等的繼承權了。男女到達結婚年齡就可以享受婚姻自由。只要當事兩邊協議，就可構成合法的離婚。

學校課程統一，科學鐘點增加，體育普遍受重視。管理大學的法律也公佈了。中央研究院等機構先後成立，以進行科學、歷史、經濟學和工程等的高深研究。

厘金制度宣告廢止。對於這種苛擾的國內關卡制度，我們將在下章再加論列。政府財政基礎漸見鞏固，全國幣制統一，政府所屬的各銀行也加以改組。不久之後，銀元禁止流通，一律改用法幣，抗戰期間我們開始了解此一措施的重要，如果我們一直依賴笨重的銀子作交易的媒介，勢將無法進行長期抗戰，如果在抗戰期間才能進行幣制改革，也必定要引起嚴重的紊亂。

從民國 16 年（1927 年）定都南京開始，到民國 26 年（1937 年）蘆溝橋事變止，其間只有短短 10 年工夫讓國民政府從事建設。 10 年之間還有斷續的變亂和其他障礙阻滯改革和建設的進展，但在這短期間內，居然建築了 4千5百多公里的鐵路，而在過去 50 年內所建的鐵路也不過 1 萬 6 千公里而已。 10 年之內建築的公路超過 10 萬公里，新添電報線路則在 1 萬多公里以上。在這樣短的時間之內，自然各方面的建設成就都很有限，評斷成績時，不能不考慮到時間因素。

國民黨執政以後，與共產黨的鬥爭仍在繼續進行。共產黨雖然失去對城市的控制，他們在鄉村地區的勢力卻漸漸擴展，同時在農民之間積極展開工作。從民國 17 年（1928 年）到民國 23 年（1934 年）之間，農民暴動普遍及 18 行省內 200 餘縣，無數地主被「清算」，土地被分配給農民，手段之激烈與俄國革命初期無異。

共產黨的根據地是江西省，一共佔領了 59 縣，經過國民政府軍隊多次圍剿，共產黨終於撤退到西北邊陲，而在延安建立「陝甘寧邊政府」。他們為適應環境時放棄激烈手段，而採一種比較溫和的土地改革政策，實際上就是變相的國民黨土地減租政策。

這時候，蔣委員長在人民間的聲望隆極一時，因此許多軍閥或為輿情所迫，或受其精神感召，不得不承認他的國家領袖地位。

最顯著而且最富戲劇性的例子就是西安事變。當時蔣委員長出巡，先至洛陽，繼飛西安。他召集了許多軍政首長在西安會商國事並面授機宜。突然一件夢想不到的事發生了。夜深人靜之時，他的行館華清池附近槍聲忽起，武裝軍隊漸逼漸近，到處搜他的蹤跡。蔣委員長身經百戰，行動非常機警，終於突圍而出，不幸最後被發現而送交張學良將軍。蔣委員長曾經花了不少的心血培植張學良，這次事變實在出他的意料之外。不過在另一方面來說，西安事變卻也反映了人民希望國家統一以抵抗日本侵略的心情。

西安事變的消息廣播全國以後，老百姓無不憂心如焚，婦女小孩甚至泣不成聲。全國各方紛電西安，勸諫張學良三思而行。蔣夫人和宋子文先生不顧身入虎穴的危險，徑行飛往西安。張學良在全國輿情壓迫下，終於改變初衷，最後護送蔣委員長和蔣夫人安返洛陽。

蔣委員長在西安未有脫險消息以前，美國大使館的美軍陸戰隊營房裏曾舉行一次舞會，參加的有各使館人員，我也是來賓之一，一位塔斯社記者斯拉配克問我為甚麼不跳舞。我告訴他正為委員長的安全擔憂，所以無心跳舞，他很平靜地對我說：「你放心好了，他馬上就會出來。他決不會有甚麼意外。」我睜大了眼睛望着他說：「但願你的預言能成事實。」

第二天晚上快吃飯的時候，我的電話響了。「喂，這裏是中央社。蔣委員長已經安抵洛陽，並已轉飛南京。」這消息太好了，簡直不像真的，我幾乎不能相信自己的耳朵。我打電話給胡適之，他正在請客。我把消息告訴他以後，客人的歡呼聲從電話筒裏都清晰可聞。

號外最先送到東安市場的吉祥戲園，觀眾之間馬上掀起一片歡呼聲，弄得戲台上唱戲的人們莫名其妙。大約半小時之後，北平嚴冬夜晚的靜寂忽然被震耳的鞭爆聲衝破了，漆黑的夜空中到處飛舞着爆竹焰火的火星。

我有一位朋友當時正搭乘火車從南京到上海，火車駛近蘇州時，車中乘客被蘇州城內的一片爆竹聲弄得莫名其妙。到達車站時他們才得到這個好消息，乘客也都想放幾個鞭爆以發泄抑積已久的情緒，但是車站上買不到爆竹，於是車上的女學生們就放開喉嚨高唱起來了。

軍閥蹂躪國家達至 25 年之久，人民一直渴望能產生一位全國領袖來掃除這些統一的障礙。他們發現蔣委員長正是這樣的一位領袖。他遭遇到雙重的困難，他一方面要把那些作勢噬人的「虎狼」從各省的巢穴驅逐出去，一方面又須建立足夠的實力抵抗日本的侵略。但是輿論民心卻一致堅決支持他達成他的任務。🔊

中國生活面面觀

第二十一章
陋規制度

　　凡是親見清室覆亡的人都知道：滿清政府失敗的主要原因之一就是財政制度的腐敗。公務人員的薪水只是點綴品，實際上全靠陋規來維持。陋規是不公開的公家收支，為政府及社會所默認的。以現在用語來説，好像我們大家所稱的黑市。這種辦法削弱了公務人員的公德心，也使他們把不規則的收入看成理所當然的事。清廷對官吏的這種收入視若當然，常説「規矩如此」，竟把陋規變成規矩了。這些官吏對下屬營私舞弊也就開隻眼閉隻眼。如果拿一棵樹來比喻政府的話，這種陋規的毒汁可以説已經流遍樹上的每一枝葉，每一根芽。

　　政府只要求税收機關向國庫繳納定額的税款。主持税收的官吏可以利用各式各樣的藉口和理由，在正規賦税之外加征各種規費。這樣一來，如果有一兩銀子到了國庫，至少也另有一兩銀子成了陋規金。在滿清末年，「漏」入私人腰包的錢遠較繳入國庫的錢為多。清廷需用浩繁，只好一味向官吏需索。官吏向民間搜刮，結果官場陋規愈來愈多，人民負擔也愈來愈重。乾隆皇帝幾次下江南，開支浩大，都靠官吏孝敬、民間搜刮而來，清代在乾隆朝為極盛時代，而衰運亦在此時開始。

　　清代後期，徵税與捐官等方法均未能使清廷達到籌款的目的，因此不得不乞靈於借貸外債，而以讓渡鐵路建築權或礦產開採權為交換條件。這自然是飲鳩止渴的辦法。現在或許還有人記得清廷將四川省內鐵路收歸國有，以為轉讓築路權予外國公司之張本，結果觸發了辛亥革命的導火線。時遭光緒帝國喪，地方士紳披麻帶孝，頭頂「德宗景皇帝神位」，長跪於總督衙門之前，哭呼先帝，保佑四川，不使鐵路收歸國有，弄得政府啼笑皆非。

所謂陋規制度究竟是怎麼一種辦法呢？中國當時分為 22 行省，大約包括 2000 個縣。縣的行政首長是知縣，他不但掌管一縣的財政，同時還是一縣的司法官。他的薪水每月不過數兩銀子，簡直微不足道。因此他的一切費用都只能在陋規金上開支。如果上級官員經過他那一縣，他除了負責招待之外，還得供應旅途一切需要財物。對於上級官員的隨員也得送「禮」，所謂「禮」通常都是送的錢。

　　我的故鄉餘姚城外的姚江岸上有一座接官亭，這是各縣都有的。如果有上級官員過境，知縣就在亭裏迎候。大約 60 年前的一個下午，我發現亭子附近聚了一大堆人。我趕過去一看，原來是大家在觀望學台和他的隨行人員紛紛下船；有些上岸。這位學台正預備去寧波主持郡試。前一日，知縣已經從老百姓手中「抓」去好幾條大船，那條專為這位學台預備的船上裝了好幾隻加封條的箱子，至於箱子裏面裝些甚麼，自然只有經手的人才知道了。

　　我遙望着學台等一行換了船，學台踏上最華麗的一隻，隨後這隻載着官吏和陋規禮金的小型艦隊就揚帆順着退潮駛往寧波去了。那種氣派使我頓生「大丈夫當如是也」的感觸。我心裏說從今以後一定要用功讀書，以便將來有一天也當起學台享受封藏在箱子裏面的神秘禮物。

　　知縣還得經常給藩台的幕僚送禮，否則他就別想他們給他在藩台面前說好話；如果搞得不好，這些師爺們還可能在公事上吹毛求疵呢。各種禮金加起來，一個知縣為保宦海一帆風順所化的錢就很可觀了。同時人情世故也告訴他必須未雨綢繆，何況他還得養活一家大小以及跟隨他的一班人呢！

　　有靠山的候補知縣無不垂涎收入比較大的縣份。以我的故鄉餘姚縣而論，就我所能記憶的，沒有一個知縣在我們的縣裏任職 1 年以上。正常的任期是三年，一位知縣如果當上三年，大概可以搜刮到 10 萬元叮噹作響的銀洋。這在當時是很大的數目。因此藩台只派些代理知縣，任期通常一年。這樣一來，候補知縣們的分肥機會也就比較多了。

　　知縣任滿離職時，通常都得正式拜望藩台一次，藩台總要問一聲他的缺好不好。當時對於所補的職位叫做缺，也就是等於問他得到了多少陋規金，他的親朋戚友與他談話，也常常以同樣的問題做開場白，說「老兄你的缺想必很好罷」。

經手政府收支的官吏，官階愈高，「漏」入他私人腰包的數目也愈大。據說上海道台每年可以獲利 10 萬兩銀子。所以上海道的缺，是全國缺中最肥的。富庶省份的藩台、督撫以及北京有勢力的王公大臣，每年的收入也都很可觀。

連平定太平天國之亂的學者政治家曾國藩也贊成陋規制度。他曾在一封信裏為陋規制度辯護，認為要順利推行政務，就不得不如此；他說一個官吏的必要開支太大，而且還得贍養一家和親戚。咸豐、同治年間住在北京的名士李蒪客曾在日記裏抱怨總督張之洞送他的「禮」太輕。過了幾天日記裏又有一段記載，為：「午後至陶然亭，張之洞來，我避之。」可見張之洞從陋規金中提出來贈與李蒪客的禮太輕，結果就得罪了這位名士了。

在滿清時代，有前程的候補官員只要化很少的錢，甚至不必出錢，就會有僕從跟隨他們。這些僕從們也會含辛茹苦地追隨不捨，希望有朝一日他們的主人時來運轉，他們也就可以分享陋規了。如果真的吉星高照，主子和奴才就沆瀣一氣，大刮一筆。如果流年不利，官爵遲遲不能到手，僕從們也還株守不去，直至最後一線希望消滅時為止。一些倒楣的主人，受不住飢寒煎熬，只好投繯自盡，以求解脫。我在杭州讀書時，曾經聽說有一位賦閒多年的候補知縣，因為受不住債主催逼，結果在大除夕自縊了。

變相的陋規惡習甚至流佈於小康之家，廚子買菜時要揩油，僕人購買家用雜物時也要撈一筆。尤其在北平，僕人們來買東西時，商店照規矩會自動把價格提高一成，作為僕人們的傭金，這在北平通俗叫做「底子錢」。

這種變相的陋規之風甚至吹到外國而進入拿破崙的家裏。拿破崙有個中國廚子，服務周到而熱心。這位偉大的法國將軍臨死時記起他的忠僕，就吩咐他的左右說：「你們要好好地待他，因為他的國家將來是要成為世界最偉大的國家之一的。不過這位中國朋友很愛錢的，你們給他五百法郎罷！」自然，中國人並非個個如此。哥倫比亞大學的丁良（譯音）中國文學講座基金，就是為紀念一位中國洗衣工人而設的，基金的來源是他一生辛勤漿洗衣服的積蓄。丁良臨死時把一袋金子交給他的東家，託付他做一點有益於中國的事。這位東家就拿這筆錢，再加上他自己的一筆捐款，在哥大設置了中國文學講座，來紀念這位愛國的洗衣工人。

陋規之風更瀰漫了整個釐金制度，釐金制度像一個碩大無朋的章魚把它的觸鬚伸展到全國的每一條交通線上，吮吸着國內工商業的血液。釐金是在太平天國時期設置的，旨在籌措戰費以供應清廷士卒。太平軍雖然被平定，釐金卻始終未取消。

釐金方面的陋規大致是這樣的：凡是懂得如何敲詐老百姓的人都可以向政府經紀人出價投標，只要他出價高，譬如說一年 20 萬塊錢，他就可以獲得在某一關卡或若干關卡徵收釐金的權利。這些關卡通常設在官道上的貨物必經之地，得標的人就成為此一關卡的釐卡委員，受權向過往的貨物徵稅。如果他能在一年之內收到 30 萬塊錢，他把 20 萬繳交政府，其餘的錢就歸他本人及其合夥者所有。因此他規定大多數的貨物都得抽稅，以便充實他們的私囊。

有一次我看到一條裝西瓜的木船從關卡附近的一座橋下經過。這條船馬上被岸上伸下來的一根竹柄撓鈎攔住了，同時岸上跳下好幾位稽查，用鐵棒往西瓜堆裏亂戳亂擀。西瓜主人慌了手腳，哀求他們手下留情，同時答應他們，要繳多少稅收就繳多少稅。「稅」繳過以後，這位可憐的農夫才得繼續鼓棹前進。

小商人和農夫對釐金無不深惡痛絕，如果有機會，每一個人都願意把關卡砸個稀爛。有一次，一羣青年士子乘船去參加科舉，途經一處釐金關卡，卡上着令停船，他們根本不予理睬。稽查們扣住船隻，並且開始搜檢行李。這羣士子蜂擁上岸，衝進關卡，見物就砸，結果把關卡打得落花流水。只留下那面象徵朝廷權威，上面寫着「奉旨徵收釐金」的旗子低垂在空中，圍觀的羣眾以不勝欽慕的目光佇望着這些士子揚長而去。

辛亥革命以後，陋規制度逐漸被戢止，釐金制度亦於稍後廢止。官吏的薪俸也提高了。但是貪污案件還是屢見不鮮，僕役間的揩油風氣迄今未衰。有一位太太罵她的廚子揩油揩得太貪心，結果與廚子大吵其架。有人批評這廚子貪心得像條餓狼，他的答覆是：「如果一個人不貪心，他也就不會當廚子了。」

北京某大使館的廚子每買一個雞蛋，就向主人索價一毛，大使秘書的廚子為主人買蛋，卻只索價五分錢一隻。大使夫人問：「為甚麼我買雞蛋要比秘書太太多花錢呢？」她的廚子答道：「太太，大使的薪水要比秘書先生的高呀！」汽車主人也常常發現汽油箱「漏」油，原因就是司機「揩」油。不必要的修理，更使保養費大得驚人。

自從民國 16 年（1927 年）國民黨執政以來，中國一直在設法阻遏政府中的貪污風氣，並且規定了幾種對貪污舞弊的嚴厲罰則。但是陋規制度在清朝以前就已存在。數百年的積習，不是幾年之內，甚至 2、30 年之內所能完全革除的。自從現代財政制度建立，公家道德逐漸提高以後，中國已經革除了很多積弊。行政技術正與時俱進，相信她在不久的將來一定可以達到組織健全的現代國家的水準，徵收賦稅和控制財政的有效辦法也會漸次建立。不幸當時內亂外患並乘，致使功敗垂成。

我們中國人一向相信人之初性本善，認為邪惡的產生只是缺乏正當的教育而使善良的本性湮沒，中國社會風氣的敗壞導源於腐朽的財政制度，而非缺乏責任感。但是這種制度對社會風氣產生極大的不良影響，因此我們迄今仍蒙受其遺毒。

實際的例子已經指出，補救之道在於建立良好的制度，來接替腐敗的制度。單單廢止壞制度，還是不夠的。英國人為中國建立的關稅制度，一開始就擺脫了陋規的惡劣影響。海關僱員都經過良好的訓練，薪俸也相當優厚，退休之後還有充裕的養老金。徇情偏私的情形很少發生。中國為了保證償付外債而把國家重要收入的控制權交付給外國政府，這原是國家的奇恥大辱，而且嚴重威脅到主權的完整，但是因此而建立關稅制度卻是中國的意外收穫。

郵政也是根據西方制度建立的。創辦迄今，行政效率始終很高。就是在漫長的內戰時期，郵遞工作也從未中斷。抗戰期間，日軍佔領區與中國大後方之間，郵遞一直暢通無阻，郵差們常常穿越火線把郵件送達收件人手裏。

鹽務機構是另一實例。八年抗戰期間，人民的這種日用必需品始終供應無缺。

治黃河的河督衙門從前一向以陋規制度聞名於世；事實上著名的山東菜和河南菜就是這些食厭珍饈、腰纏萬貫的治黃老爺們光顧的結果。同樣地，揚州菜之所以出名，就是因為貪圖口福的揚州鹽商而來。

黃河水利委員會成立以後，改由受過現代訓練的工程師主持疏浚工作，陋規制度也就隨滾滾河水沖入黃海去了。老饕已隨陋規制度消失，只有烹飪藝術依舊存在。美食家至今對揚州菜讚不絕口，但是自從組織完善的現代鹽務制度建立以後，宣導揚州菜的鹽商已無法立足了。

這些成就可以說是依賴外國協助而來的。但是我要請問：這些成就究竟由於外國人的良好道德，還是由於他們介紹到中國來的良好制度呢？沒有健全的品德，這些制度固然無法實行，但是單憑外國人的道德難道就能收到預期的效果嗎？單憑少數高居要津的外國專家就能夠制止千千萬萬中國職員的不法行為嗎？海關、鹽務、郵政之所以成功，還是靠良好制度下的基層中國職員的通力合作。這就是孟子所謂：「徒善不足以為政，徒法不足以自行。」

中國的現代銀行制度和鐵道管理也是值得稱道的實例。一般而論，銀行與鐵路的行政效率都很高，而且沒有銀錢上的重大舞弊案件。

中國的現代大學除了實事求是的學術立場之外，也是經費從無私弊的又一實例。抗戰期間，因為物價高昂，教授生活非常清苦，但是他們始終辛苦工作，力求維持學術水準。絕大多數的學生，除了接受現代訓練之外，在教授和大學當局的良好影響之下，對於如何誠實而有效地運用公款，也自然養成正確的觀念和良好的習慣。

最重要的是對公款處理的態度已經起了根本的轉變，過去大家都默認甚至讚揚陋規制度，到了抗戰以前的幾年，有識之士不但討厭它而且隨時加以譏諷，這種風氣的轉變，再加採用現代方法，當時我們相信對於將來公共行政各方面的經費處理，必將發生重大良好的影響。

要消滅僕役、廚子和司機的揩油行為可難得多了。或許要經過5、60年之後才能提高這些人的經濟地位，在他們的經濟地位確切提高以前，我們無法奢望他們臨財不苟。如果真的到了那一天，也許我們已經不容易找到願意當家庭僕役的人了。抗戰時我在昆明居留的8年期間，我倒在我的傭人中碰到過一位男僕、一位女傭和一位司機從來沒有揩過油。✿

第二十二章
社會組織和社會進步

　　一般人都說中國的四萬萬人像一盤散沙，如果說中國的人是由許多自治的小單位構成的，倒更切近事實。中國的民主體制包括千千萬萬的這種單位，由幾千年來累積下來的共同的語言、共同的文化和共同的生活理想疏鬆地聯繫在一起。這些或大或小的單位是以家庭、行業和傳統為基礎而形成的。個人由這些共同的關係與各自治團體發生聯繫，因此團體內各分子的關係比對廣大的社會更為親切。他們對地方問題比對國家大事了解較深。這就是立憲國會失敗的癥結，也是老百姓聽憑軍閥統治的原因。我們在前面曾經一再提到「天高皇帝遠」的觀念，帝制時代的這種觀念就是上述心理狀態產生的。

　　個人如非因特殊事故與所屬社會破裂，永遠是小單位的一部分，但是各單位之間並無全國性的組織使其密切團結。這是中國國民生活中的優點，同時也是弱點。好處在於使中國生活民主，雖經數百年之戰亂以及異族之入侵而仍能屹立無恙，壞處在於中央政權軟弱無能，因而易遭異族侵凌。

　　中國人民生活中這些單位的存在是有它歷史的背景的。它們是幾千年歷史演變的結果。我們的祖先逐漸向人口比較稀少的地區遷移時，他們總是成羣結隊而行，在各地構成許多獨立的部落，這些部落後來便發展為自治的村莊或鄉鎮。廣大的中華帝國就是千百年來由這些聚族而居者向邊疆和平原拓殖而形成的。近年來由於研究中國各地方言的結果，我們已經追溯出這種發展的途徑。我們發現廣東話與唐朝的口語有密切的關係，因此我們可以推斷多數的廣東人是唐朝的後裔。遷到廣東較晚的移民又另行形成不同的部落，所說的方言也迥然不同，那就是我們所謂的客家話。客家話所顯示的語言特徵是屬於近世紀的。甚至長江流域各地方言之間的些微差別，也可以隱約顯示拓殖過程中的先後。

第 10 世紀，唐朝滅亡，中國北方普遍遭塞外入侵的異族蹂躪，因而也加速了中國人口的南遷。南方各省，尤其是廣東、湖北和浙江一帶，不易遭受外族的侵略，所受戰禍較輕，因此就成了中國文化的蓄水庫，並在過去六七十年內灌溉了新中國大塊的土地。

如果要使某一改革對國家統一與團結切實有效，這種改革必須直接使這些古老的區域單位在家庭制度上、行業上和傳統上發生某種程度的變化，反過來說，這些單位係共同的語言、文化和生活理想所維繫，那麼任何經由共同語言所產生的文化和理想的變化，也勢必影響這些社會集團的生活，並且進而影響國家的生活。

外國商品開始影響中國行業時，中國就開始變化了，維繫中國社會的三條繩索之一因而鬆散。這是受現代影響的最初改變，這種改變人們是不大知道的。以後現代思想經由書籍、報紙和學校制度等輸入中國，又鬆散了傳統這一條繩索。最後留下來的一條繩索 —— 家庭的聯繫，也終於不得不隨其他兩條繩索一起鬆散。

人們因探索新的有效的團結而引起各式各樣的紛亂。首先受到新思潮影響的是學生，首先鬧事的也是他們；新興工業的工人喪失了舊日行業的維繫力量，因此也就跟着學生一起滋生事端。軍閥之間的內戰，憲政的失敗，以及敗壞風氣的陋規制度，既未阻止舊有社會組織的瓦解，亦未阻滯社會的進步。軍閥所引起的禍患只是中國廣大的「社會之海」面上的泡沫。不論有沒有互相殘殺的軍閥，或者聲譽掃地的國會，或者敗壞風氣的陋規，海面底下的潛流仍在滾滾而進。軍閥、國會、陋規只是浮面上的禍患，那些自治單位本身仍然寧靜如恆，在道德方面也潔淨無瑕。

在悠久的歷史過程中，尤其在唐朝末年以後中國的國防一直很脆弱，因為侵略她的異族全部組織嚴密，隨時準備作戰，而中國的社會組織卻是升平世界的產物。國防部隊是由太平無事的社會中徵募來的，維持這些軍隊的中央政府也只是一個和平社會上層的空架子。

明室領導下的漢族之所以能推翻蒙古人所建立的元朝，並非由於漢人本身的軍事力量，而是由於蒙古人本身力量的衰竭。成吉思汗的子孫在歐亞兩大陸連年征戰之後，武力已消耗殆盡。中國在明成祖御宇期間，曾經組織成一支強大的軍隊，並且征服了滿洲的大部分；但是成祖駕崩以後，這支軍隊的實力也就日趨式微。驍勇善戰的滿洲人在關外崛起以後，明室對韃靼入侵簡直束手無策，結果沒有經過激烈戰鬥，明朝就亡在滿洲人手裏了。滿清入主中國 100 餘年以後，結果也染上了漢人的和平習氣，等到西方列強的兵艦來攻擊中國時，清室也是同樣束手無策。

日本研究歷史的結果，認為歷史是會重演的，因此就在 1894 年發動對中國大陸的攻擊。到那一年為止，日本的設想並沒有錯。但是自從中國學到西方的「訣竅」以後，中國的歷史演變途徑就開始轉向了。日本不是對這種轉變懵然無知，就是有意防患於未然。無論動機如何，日本終於在 30 年之後又向中國大陸發動了另一次戰爭。結果發現她的途程上障礙重重，使她大感意外。

日本遭遇的障礙就是中國的社會進步，日本已經看到高據中國社會之上的腐敗無能的北京帝制政府，這個政府的財政力量已經被陋規制度腐蝕殆盡；稍後日本又在水面上看到互相征戰的軍閥；但是她對過去 50 年間在中國的浩瀚海洋之中緩慢地、然而不斷地流動的潛流，卻茫然無知。

在過去，秘密幫會是全國組織的維繫力量。幫會弟兄生活於鄉村單位之外而聚集於大城市附近或通商孔道。他們的主要目的是互相保護，抵制壓迫，但是這種動機有時候會墮落為不法買賣。他們在內亂時可以表現相當大的力量，但是以之應付外國侵略卻無多大用處。他們缺乏現代思想，也不懂甚麼叫社會進步。

現在的情形可不同了，全國千千萬萬自治單位的邊緣，已經圍集了充滿國家觀念和愛國熱情的人，他們反對地域偏見和家族觀念。這些人像蜜蜂一樣繞着蜂巢喧嚷不休，最後就在蜂巢邊緣聚集起來。從蜂巢裏面溜出來參加巢外集團的個人愈來愈多。外面圍集的羣眾數量增加以後，他們開始闖進蜂巢，終至影響了整個社會的生活。同時他們開始把自己組織為全國性的社會，拿中國作為他們的共同蜂巢。

中國現代的全國性社團就是這樣形成的。輪船、公路、鐵路、航空等交通網的迅速擴展，更加速了社團發展的過程。教育會、商會、工會、科學團體、工程學會、政治學會等社團都紛紛成立全國性組織。所有政黨，包括國民黨以及意見與其相左的政黨，都鼓勵人民考慮全國性的問題。大專學校吸收了家庭的分子，而把他們塑造成國家的領袖。學校都在努力把國家民族觀念和愛國心灌輸到新生一代正在發育的心靈裏。

雖然內戰頻仍，各省的公立學校甚至在國家統一之前就已經增加了好幾倍。私人常常以創辦學校來表達他們的愛國忠忱。千千萬萬的小學畢業生，跑進本鄉本土的自治社會，把愛國觀念散佈到全國的每一角落。

中日正沿長城作戰時，我在內地旅行，途中看到一個孤單的小孩在扮軍人作遊戲。他把一棵樹當作假想敵，拿他的匕首猛刺這棵樹。然後他又想像敵人向他還擊，他裝出自衞的姿勢，接着躺倒在地上，閉起眼睛自言自語說：「我為國犧牲了！」顯然地他在想像自己為保衞國家而抵抗日本侵略。抗戰後期，我在後方邊荒地區看到一個小孩拿鏟子挖了一個小墳。墳挖成以後，他在墳上立了一個木牌，上書「漢奸」。那時少數重慶政要已經出亡投靠日本去了。有一次，一位礦冶工程師經過某山區，那裏離最近的學校也有好幾里路，他卻看到幾位小孩在他們村莊牆上書寫「三民主義萬歲！」這些例子可以顯示全國性的團結力量已經代地方性的維繫力量興起了。

小孩子們在新的教育制度影響之下，大家都能拿紙折飛機拋在空中滑翔。他們製造小小的抽水機，也能做玩具汽車。他們開始養成研究機械的習慣，這對國家的未來工業化運動也是個良好的基礎。

近年來輕工業的發展，從地方單位吸收了許多人，他們開始彼此聯繫，組成全國性的團體。廣播從空中給人民帶來許多新觀念。風俗習慣、迷信、方言、民歌、宗教、家庭工業、垂危的本地行業及苦難農民的經濟情況，都經過仔細調查，並且根據高等學府和學術團體所收集的資料很科學地加以研究。中國已開始從科學研究中了解她自己了。

50 年的動盪已經促使人們思索，他們的人生觀開始轉變了。他們希望在侵略威脅下從事有效的組織，以團結全國的力量，同時為國家的進步辛勤工作，期望能在混亂中創造安定。這種新生的社會意識和國家意識或許還不夠堅強，因為它還不能充分應付戰爭。但是這種意識可以產生堅忍不拔的意志來進行堅強的抵抗。從這一方面來看，社會意識和國家意識的力量是驚人的。⑯

第二十三章
迷人的北京

　　正像巴黎繼承了古羅馬帝國的精神，北京也繼承了中華帝國黃金時代的精神。巴黎是西方都市之都，北京則是東方的都市之都。如果你到過巴黎，你會覺得它不但是法國人的首都，而且是你自己的城市；同樣地，北京不僅是中國人的都市，也是全世界人士的都市。住在巴黎和北平的人都會說：「這是我的城市，我願意永遠住在這裏。」

　　我在北京住了 15 年，直到民國 26 年（1937 年）抗戰開始，才離開北京。回想過去的日子，甚至連北京飛揚的塵土都富於愉快的聯想。我懷念北京的塵土，希望有一天能再看看這些塵土。清晨旭日初升，陽光照射在紙窗上，窗外爬藤的陰影則在紙窗上隨風擺動。紅木書桌上，已在一夜之間鋪上一層薄薄的輕沙。拿起雞毛帚，輕輕地拂去桌上的塵土，你會感到一種難以形容的樂趣。然後你再拂去筆筒和硯台上的灰塵；筆筒刻着山水風景，你可以順便欣賞一番，硯台或許是幾百年來許多文人學士用過的，他們也像你一樣曾經小心翼翼地拂拭過它。乾隆間出窰的瓷器，周朝的銅器，4000 年前用於卜筮的商朝甲骨，也有待你仔細揩擦。還有靜靜地躺在書架上的線裝書，這些書是西方還不懂得印刷術以前印的。用你的手指碰一碰這些書的封面，你會發現飛揚的塵土已經一視同仁地光顧到這些古籍。

　　拂去案頭雜物上的灰塵，你會覺得已經圓滿地完成這一早晨的初步工作。陽光映耀，藤影搖曳的紙窗在向你微笑，纖塵不染的書桌以及案頭擺設的古董在向你點頭；於是你心滿意足地開始處理你這一天的工作。

　　這種古色古香的氣氛可以使你回想到孔夫子設帳授徒的春秋時代；或者景教徒初至中國的唐朝時代；或者耶穌會教士在明朝製造天文儀器的時

代；或是拿破崙長驅直入俄羅斯，迫得飲街燈燈油的時代；或者回想到成吉思汗派遣他的常勝軍直入多瑙河盆地，建立橫跨歐亞兩大洲的蒙古帝國，並且把北京定為他的一位兒子的京城。我們可以從北京正確地了解歷史，因為北京不僅像大自然一樣偉大，而且像歷史一樣悠久。它曾是五個朝代的京城，一代繼替一代興起，一代又接着一代滅亡，但是北京卻始終屹立無恙。

皇宮建築都是長方形的，而且很對稱地排得像一張安樂椅，中間有一個寬闊的長方形天井，天井中央擺着一隻青銅鍍金的大香爐，點了香，香煙就裊裊地升入天空。宮門前站着一排排的銅鹿，宮門口則有雄踞着的一對對石獅或銅獅把守。這種三面圍着雄偉建築的天井，數在 100 以上，星羅棋佈在紫禁城內，紫禁城的周圍是一座長方形的黃色城牆，城牆四角矗立着黃瓦的碉樓。北京皇城由元朝開始建造，明朝時曾予改建，清朝再予改良而成目前的形式。

碰到晴空澄碧、艷陽高照的日子，宮殿屋頂的黃色釉瓦就閃耀生輝。在暮靄四合或曙色初露之時，紫禁城的大門 —— 午門 —— 上的譙樓映着蒼茫的天色，很像半空中的碉堡。在萬里無雲的月夜，這些譙樓更像是月亮中的神仙官闕，可望而不可即。

民國成立以後，滿清的末朝皇帝溥儀暫時仍統治着北京的這個城中之城，少數殘留的清廷官吏還每隔半月覲見一次。這些官吏穿着舊日滿清官服聚集在紫禁城的後門聽候召見，仍執君臣之禮。民國 13 年（1924 年）馮玉祥入京，終於把溥儀逐出紫禁城。

政變後不久，我受命入故宮監督政府的一個委員會逐屋封閉各門。當時宮內還留有幾個太監，我從他們口中得到好些有關宮廷生活的知識，以及過去許多皇帝、皇后、王子、公主等等的趣聞軼事。

其中一則故事涉及一面從天花板一直垂到牆腳的大鏡子，據說慈禧太后喜歡坐在鏡子前面，看看她自己究竟多威嚴。有一天陝西撫台奉命入宮覲見，他進門後首先看到鏡子裏的太后，於是馬上跪倒對鏡中人大叩其頭。

「那末太后怎麼樣呢？我想她一定很生氣吧！」我說。

「哦，不，不！她笑了，而且很和藹地對他說：『你弄錯了，那是鏡子呀。』」

我遇到幾個曾經侍候過王子讀書的太監，但是這幾個太監竟然全都目不識丁。宮廷規矩禁止他們受教育，因此他們對於王子唸些甚麼始終毫無所知。

走廊上掛着許多鳥架，上面站着紅色、黃色以及藍色的鸚鵡，嘴裏說着公主們花了不少時間教它們的話，「請進！客來了。倒茶……」一隻藍色的鸚鵡這樣對我說，那只紅色的和那只黃色的跟着喊：「倒茶！倒茶！」這是我第一次看到藍色的鸚鵡。金魚在宮中的水池中追逐嬉戲，有白色的、黑色的、紅色的和金色的。其中有許多幾乎長達一尺，它們的潛望鏡一樣的眼睛朝天望着，它們的絲綢樣的尾巴好像幾柄相連的扇子在水中搖曳生姿。

溥儀住的宮殿看起來很俗氣，大廳中央擺着一張似乎很粗俗的長長的外國桌子，桌子四周放着幾張醜陋的椅子。桌子上擺着一對紅色的玻璃花瓶。這房間看起來倒很像美國鄉下的次等客棧，真想不到就是中國皇帝的居室。所有的精美傢俱和藝術珍品已經被棄置而收拾到後宮去了。通商口岸的粗俗的西方文明已經侵入到皇宮；對照之下，使人覺得沒有再比這更不調和的了。低級雜誌四散各處，新切開的半隻蘋果和一盒新打開的餅乾還放在桌子上。溥儀顯然因事起倉卒，匆匆出走，無暇收拾房間。

後來各宮啟封清點藝術珍藏時，奇珍拱璧之多實在驚人。其中有足以亂真的玉琢西瓜，有「雨過天青」色的瓷器，有經歷 3000 年滄桑的銅器，還有皇帝御用的玉璽。

唐、宋、元、明、清的歷代名畫，更是美不勝收。有些山水畫，描寫大自然的美麗和諧，使人神遊其中，樂而忘返；有些名家畫的鳥維妙維肖，躍然紙上；魚兒邀遊水中，栩栩如生；鵝嘶雞啼，如聞其聲；竹影扶疏，迎風搖曳；荷塘新葉，晨露欲滴；蘭蕙飄香，清芬可把。中國的名畫，不僅力求外貌的近似，而且要表現動態、聲音、色澤和特徵，希望啟發想像，甚至激發情感。換一句話說，就是要描摹事物的神韻。

這個委員會包括 100 多職員，兩年中翻箱倒篋，搜遍了皇宮的每一角落，把歷代帝王積聚下來的千萬件奇珍異寶一一登記點驗。有些倉庫密密層層滿是蜘蛛網，有些倉庫的灰塵幾乎可以淹沒足踝，顯見已經百年以上無人問津。有些古物已經好久沒有人碰過，究竟多少，誰也不知道。

最後故宮終於開放，同時故宮博物院成立，主持古物展覽事宜。一般民眾，尤其是年輕的一代，總算大開眼界，有機會欣賞幾百年來中國藝術豐富而偉大的成就。北京本來就是藝術中心，鑒賞家很多，藝術家也不少，故宮博物院開放以後，更使北京生色不少。過去深藏在皇宮後院的東西，現在大都可以欣賞了，過去只有皇室才能接觸的東西，現在已經公諸大眾。抗戰初期，政府就把故宮古物南運，由北平而南京而西南內地。戰後運回南京。復因戰亂而運至台灣。現在台中所陳列之古物，就是從北平故宮運來的。

科學是心智探究自然法則的表現，藝術則是心靈對自然實體所感所觸的表現。藝術是人生的一種表現，它使人生更豐富，更美滿；科學是心智活動的產物，旨在滿足知識上的慾望，結果就創造物質文明。在現代文明裏，藝術與科學必須攜手合作，才能使人生圓滿無缺。

紫禁城之西，有三個互相銜接的湖，叫南海、中海和北海，湖與湖之間的小溪上有似駝背形的石橋，沿湖遍植百年古木，湖裏盛開着荷花，環湖的山峰上矗立着金黃色琉璃瓦、朱紅柱子和雕樑畫棟的亭子。據說有一次在湖中捕到一條魚，魚身上還掛着一塊寫着明朝（1368—1643）永樂年間放生的金牌。

中海之中有個瀛台，那是一個周圍遍植荷花的小島，1898 年維新運動失敗後，光緒皇帝就被慈禧太后囚禁在瀛台，後來在 1909 年死在那裏。小島上建着許多庭院寬敞的宮殿。長着綠苔的古樹高高地俯蓋着設計複雜的宮殿上的黃瓦，各亭台之間有迂迴曲折的朱紅色的走廊互相連接。御花園中建有假山，洞穴怪石畢具，使人恍如置身深山之中。至於不幸的光緒皇帝是否在這美麗的監獄裏樂而忘憂，那恐怕只有光緒皇帝自己和跟隨他的人才知道了。在他被幽禁的寂寞的日子裏，他一直受着身心病痛的困擾，最後還是死神解脫了他的痛苦。

湖水原先是用石渠從西山轉引來的泉水。公路旁邊至今仍可發現部分殘留的管道。北京的下水道系統更是舊日的一項偉大的工程成就。用以排泄市內污水的地下溝渠很像現代地道車的隧道。到了清朝末期，所有這些下水道都淤塞了，但是每年檢查下水道一次的制度卻維持到清朝末年。早年時，檢查人員必須身入下水道，從這一頭查到那一頭，看看有沒有需要修補的地方。後來下水道垃圾淤塞，這些檢查人員就用一種非常巧妙的手段欺蒙他們的上司：兩個穿制服的檢查員在下水道的一端爬下去躲起來，另外兩個穿着同樣制服的檢查員則預先躲在另一端，檢查官騎馬到了出口處時，事先躲在那裏的檢查員也就爬出來了。這個例子也說明了這個下水道系統表面上雖然仍舊存在，但是它的精神卻因多年來陽奉陰違的結果而煙消雲散了。滿清末年，這類事情在政府各部門都有發生，所以清廷終於只剩下一個空架子，實在毫不足奇。

北京滿城都是樹木。私人住宅的寬敞的庭院和花園裏到處是枝葉扶疏、滿長青苔的參天古木。如果你站在煤山或其他高地眺望北京，整個城市簡直像是建在森林裏面。平行交叉的街道像是棋盤上縱橫的線條交織着北京的「林園」。根據由來已久的皇家規矩，北京城裏只許種樹，不准砍樹。年代一久，大家已經忘記了這規矩，卻在無形中養成愛護樹木的良好習慣 —— 這個例子說明了制度本身雖然已經被遺忘，但是制度的精神卻已深植人心。中國新生的秘密就在這裏。

在北京住過的人，很少人會忘記蔚藍天空下閃閃發光的宮殿和其他公共建築。頤和園和公園裏有幾百年前栽種的古松。有的成行成列，有的則圍成方形，空氣中充塞着松香。烹調精美的酒樓飯館隨時可以滿足老饕們的胃口。古董舖陳列着五光十色的古玩玉器，使鑒賞家目不暇接。公共圖書館和私人圖書館的書架上保存着幾千年來的智慧結晶。年代最久的是商朝（公元前1766—前1122）的甲骨，這些甲骨使我們對中國歷史上霧樣迷濛的時代開始有了概念。此外還有令人肅然起敬的天壇。它使我們體會到自然的偉大和人類精神的崇高。

現代的國立北京大學於 1898 年成立，直接繼承了國子監的傳統，在幾百年積累下來的文化氛圍中，北京大學的成立幾乎可以說只是昨天的事。北大不僅是原有文化的中心，而且是現代化智慧的源泉。學者、藝術家、音樂家、作家和科學家從各方彙集到北京，在這古城的和諧的氛圍中發展他們的心智，培育他們的心靈。古代的文物，現代思想的影響，以及對將來的希望，在這裏匯為一股智慧的巨流，全國青年就紛紛來此古城，暢飲這智慧的甘泉。🐚

第二十四章
杭州、南京、上海、北京

　　杭州富山水之勝，上海是洋貨的集散地，南京充滿了革命精神，北京則是歷代的帝都，也是藝術和悠閒之都。我出生在浙江省的一個小村裏，童年時生活在農夫工匠之間，與他們的孩子共同嬉戲。少年時代在杭州讀書，後來又在上海繼續求學。留美回國以後，因為工作的關係先住在上海，繼至北京、南京、杭州，最後又回到北京，一直到抗戰開始。

　　就地理來說，北京位於黃河流域的華北平原，離天津不遠。其餘三地則是長江流域的南方城市。杭州位於杭州灣口錢塘江之岸，與北京之間從前有運河可通。運河全長 2074 公里，橫越長江、黃河兩大河，至今仍有一部分可通舟楫。1 千 3 百多年前，隋煬帝動員全國人力，築此運河，河成而隋亡。唐皮日休有詩云：

　　「人道隋亡是此河，至今千里賴通波。

　　若無水殿龍舟事，共論禹功不較多。」

　　上海在杭州的東北，據黃浦江之岸。黃浦江位於長江口而入黃海，所謂黃海實際上是與太平洋不可分的一部分，僅僅名稱不同而已。南京離海較遠，位於滬杭兩地的西北，雄踞長江南岸。自南京沿長江東下可達揚州，運河即在此越江入江南，馬哥・孛羅曾在元朝揚州當過太守。北京、南京、上海、杭州四城之間現在均有鐵路互通，也可以說是太平洋沿岸的城市。

　　長江下游的江南都市，氣候大致差不多，春秋兩季的天氣尤其溫煦宜人。楊柳發芽就表示春天到了，遊春的人喜歡採摘新枝回家裝飾門戶，表示迎春。樹葉轉紅則表示秋天到了，夕陽紅葉曾給詩人帶來不少靈感。春天有一段雨季，雨水較多，其餘三季晴雨參半，夏天不太熱，冬天也不太冷。

土壤非常肥沃，主要農作物是稻，養蠶是普遍的家庭工業。魚、蝦、蟹、蚌、鰻、牛、羊、豬、蔬菜、水果遍地皆是，著名的揚州菜就是拿這些東西來做材料的。

上海是長江流域的金融中心。上海的繁榮應該歸功於外國人的工商活動，外國資本是上海經濟結構的基礎，外國商人和資本家因而成為上海的貴族階級，住在上海的人都得向這些洋人低頭。這些洋人有他們自己的生活圈子，許多外國人雖然在上海住了幾十年，中國對他們卻仍然是個「謎樣的地方」。他們住在富麗幽邃的花園洋房裏，有恭順的中國僕人們侍候着，生活得有如王公貴族。主人們靠剝削致富，僕人們則靠揩油分肥。他們的俱樂部拒絕華人參加，似乎沒有一個華人值得結識；他們的圖書館也沒有一本值得一讀的書。他們自大、無知、頑固，而且充滿種族歧視，就是對於他們自己國內的科學發明和藝術創造也不聞不問，對於正在中國或他們本國發展的新思想和潮流更無所知。他們唯一的目標就是賺錢。

地位僅僅次於這些洋人的是中國買辦，他們像洋主子一樣無知，也像洋主子一樣富足。中國商人非常尊敬外國銀行裏和洋行裏的買辦。買辦們張大嘴巴向洋主子討骨頭時，他們的同胞也就流着口水，不勝羨慕地大搖其尾巴。買辦階級很像煉金術士，可以點銅成銀，他們的洋主子則點銀成金。買辦們花了一部分銀子去討小老婆，他們的洋主子卻高明多了，只要在「女朋友」身上花點金子。

上海的第三等人物是商人。他們從買辦手中購買洋貨，賺了錢以後就匯錢回家買田置產。他們偶然回鄉探親時，自然而然觸動了鄉下人的「靈機」，因此到上海做生意的人也愈來愈多。

我所談的上海種種情形，多半是身經目睹的，絕無誇張之詞，因為我的許多親戚就是在上海做生意的，其中有些還是買辦。我對他們的生活思想知道得很清楚；同時，我認得不少住在上海的外國人，也聽過不少關於他們的故事。開明的外國人，尤其是我所熟悉的美國人，每當我們談起上海，總是緊蹙雙眉，搖頭歎息。

第四等人是工廠工人。他們是農村的過剩人口，因為在農村無法過活，結果放棄耕作而到上海來賺錢。他們是貧民窟的居民。

第五等人，也就是最低賤的一等人，是拉人力車的苦力。他們多半是來自江北的貧苦縣份。這些名為萬物之靈的動物，拖着人力車，像牛馬一樣滿街奔跑。這種又便宜又方便的交通工具使上海的活動川流不息，使上海商業動脈中的血液保持循環的，就是人力車苦力。

這五等人合在一起，就構成了一般人所說的「租界心理」，一種崇拜權勢、講究表面的心理。權勢包括財力、武力、治外法權等等，表面功夫則表現於繪畫、書法、歌唱、音樂，以及生活各方面的膚淺庸俗。我們通稱這種「租界心理」為「海派」，相對的作風則叫「京派」，也就是北京派。「京派」崇尚意義深刻的藝術，力求完美。上海是金融海洋，但是在知識上卻是一片沙漠。

上海人一天到晚都像螞蟻覓食一樣忙忙碌碌。他們聚斂愈多，也就愈受人敬重。在上海，無論中國文化或西洋文明都是糟糕透頂。中國人誤解西方文明，西洋人也誤解中國文化；中國人仇恨外國人，外國人也瞧中國人不起，誰都不能說誰沒有理由。但是他們有一個共通之點——同樣地沒有文化；也有一個共同的諒解——斂財。這兩種因素終使上海人和外國人成為金錢上的難兄難弟。「你刮我的錢，我揩你的油。」

沙漠之中還是有綠洲的，上海的可取之處也就在此。在本世紀的最初10年裏，治外法權曾使上海成為革命思想和革命書籍的避難所和交換處。進化論和民主思想的種子最初就散播在這些綠洲上，之後又隨風飄散到中國各文化中心。科學和民主的種子在其他各地發育滋長為合抱大樹，在上海卻始終高不盈尺。在民國10年到20年間，上海因受治外法權的庇護，軍閥無法染指，上海及其附近地區的工業曾有急速的發展。留學生回國掌握金融和工業大權以後，中國更開始利用管理和生產上的外國訣竅，不過這些訣竅多半是直接從歐美學來的，與上海的外國人關係較小。

北京的生活可就不同了。除了美麗的宮殿和宮內園苑之外，我們第一個印象是北京城內似乎只有兩個階級：拉人力車和被人力車拉的。但是你在北京住久了以後，你會發現被人力車拉的也分好幾個階級。不過要找出一個「上層」階級倒也不容易，大家和睦相處，所不同的只是職業而已。在過去，旗人出生以後就是貴族；但這些貴族現在已經與平民大眾融為一體。大家都生而平等，要出人頭地，就得靠自己努力。唯一的貴族階級是有學問的人——畫家、書法家、詩人、哲學家、歷史家、文學家以及近代的科學家和工程師。

一眼就能辨別真偽的藝術鑑賞家，製作各式各樣藝術品的工匠，腦中裝着活目錄的書商，替你篆刻圖章，使你儼然有名重百世之感的金石家，美化你的客廳臥室的地毯設計師，大家融融泄泄地生活在一起，有的陶醉於自己的鑑賞力，有的則以能為別人製造藝術品而自豪。鑑賞、技藝也是北京生活的特徵。

差不多每一個人都可以抽空以不同的方式來欣賞美麗的東西。你可以逛逛古老的書舖，與店主人聊上一陣，欣賞一番書架上的古籍和新書，神游於古今知識的寶庫之中，只要你有興致，你不妨在這裏消磨兩三個鐘頭，臨走時店夥會很客氣地請你再度光臨。除非你自己高興，你不一定要買。

如果你有興致，你可以跑進古董舖，欣賞書畫珠寶，包括貴重的真品和巧妙的贋品。無論你買不買，都會受到歡迎，但是等到你真的對這些東西發生興趣時，就是要你拿出留着吃晚飯的最後一塊錢，你也在所不惜了。

你也可以跑到戲園裏去，欣賞名伶唱戲。他們多半唱得無懈可擊，聲聲動人心弦。要不然你就跑到故宮博物院，去欣賞歷代天才所創造的藝術珍品，我在前面所提到的「京派」作風就是在這種永遠追求完美、追求更深遠的人生意義的氛圍下產生的。

如果你高興，你也可以跑到皇宮內苑所改的「中央公園」，坐在長滿青苔的古樹下品茗，或是坐在假山的古石上閒眺池中的白鵝戲水。在星期天，你可以騎驢，或者坐人力車，或者乘汽車到西山去憑弔名勝古跡，呼吸充塞着古松芳香的空氣。

尋求正當娛樂時，學者、藝術家、工匠、科學家和工程師一致欣賞古老的北京。工作時，他們各自在不同的行業上埋頭努力。科學家們在實驗室裏從事研究，希望對人類的知識寶庫提供貢獻；工程師拿起計算尺和繪圖儀器，設計未來建設的藍圖；學者們埋頭在書堆裏，希望從歷史教訓裏找尋未來的理想；工匠們在努力創造美麗的器皿；藝術家們從自然和歷史文物裏獲得靈感，用靈巧的手指把心目中的形象表達於畫紙或其他材料。

　　連年戰亂並沒有使北京受到多大的影響，政府雖然一再易手，這個可愛的古城仍然還是老樣子。我在前面曾經提到，國都遷移南京以後，北京已經改名為北平。但是在精神上，北平仍舊是北京，隨着國都的遷移，北京的一部分也轉到政府的新址，例如一部分學者和藝術家、建築式樣和藝術珍藏，但是北平的氣氛和情趣卻始終未變。鐵路和飛機使這兩個城市的血液彼此交流，結果兩蒙其利。

　　南京和北平不同，它是個必須從廢墟上重建的城市。新都裏充滿着拆除舊屋、建築新廈的精神。北京的人固然也憧憬着未來，他們卻始終浸淫於舊日的光輝裏，但是南京除了歷史記憶之外，並無足資依賴的過去，一切都得從頭做起。因此大家都在思考、計劃和工作，生活也跟着這些活動而顯得緊張。每個人都忙着開會和執行命令。空氣永遠是那麼緊張，北京的悠閒精神無法在南京發榮滋長。

　　街上行人熙來攘往，人力車夫爭先恐後，就是懶洋洋的驢子也受了急急忙忙的行人車輛的感染而加緊了腳步。每月都有新道路和新建築出現，到處在發展，而且是急速地發展。

　　甚至連娛樂都得花很大氣力去爭取。飯館只能在擁擠的角落裏供應飯菜，新店面尚未建築完工。人們在花園裏栽花種木，焦急地等待裏花木長大。你需要東西全得臨時設法。除非你不斷地積極工作，你就會落伍；你必須努力不懈，才能追上時代精神。經過 6、7 年的辛勤工作之後，南京終於成為嶄新而繁榮的都市了。舊日廢墟正在迅速地消失，思考、計劃和工作的精神不斷在發展，而且擴散到各省的其他城市，國家的前途也因而大放光明。

你為了追趕上世界的進步潮流，計劃或許很遠大，甚至已經跑在時代的前頭，但是實際行動勢必無法趕上你的思想。你可以栽花種木，但是你不能使它們在一夜之間長大成蔭；鐵路公路必須一尺一碼地鋪築，改革計劃也不能在旦夕之間實現。於是，你可能要問：我們又何必這樣惶惶不可終日呢？

當時有幾句流行的話，頗足代表一般人的感慨，這幾句話是：「議而不決，決而不辦，辦而不通。」當然，實際的情形並不至於如此之糟，但是有一件事情是無可置疑的：大家都覺得他們的工作成績不如理想。其實，這就是進步的精神。

杭州與前面所談的三個城市都有一點相像，但是與它們又都不同。在古文化上，杭州有點像北京，因為它是「學人之省」的首府，但是缺少北京的雄偉。杭州像上海一樣帶點商業色彩，但是色調比較清淡，同時因為沒有洋主子存在，故有表現個性的自由。在改革和建設的精神上，它有點像南京，但是氣魄較小。杭州究竟只是中國一省裏的城市，北京和南京卻是全國性的都市。

杭州最大的資產是西湖。西湖不但饒山水之勝，而且使人聯想到歷代文人雅士的風流韻事，但是杭州的缺點也就在此。因為杭州人把西湖視如拱璧，眼光也就局限於此；他們甚至自欺欺人地以為西湖比太平洋還偉大，並且足與天堂媲美。他們已經被「上有天堂，下有蘇杭」的俗諺所催眠而信以為真。他們想：且別管蘇州怎麼樣，杭州就在這裏，所以這裏也就是天堂。

自我來台灣以後，從經驗中證實，蘇杭確是天堂，因為既無地震，又無颱風。

杭州人的心目中只有西湖，你如果在這裏住得太久，你不免有沉醉於西湖的危險。此種情況，自古已然。昔人有詩為證云：

「山外青山樓外樓，西湖歌舞幾時休。

暖風吹得遊人醉，卻把杭州作汴州。」

但是，從南京傳播過來的改革和建設的精神終於把杭州從沉醉中喚醒了。揉揉眼睛以後，它漸漸看出浙江省未來發展的遠景以及它在重建中國的過程中所應擔負的任務。

北京也有它遼闊寧靜的一面。從城外西山之頂可以鳥瞰北京內外：永定河蜿蜒於廣漠的田野之間；向東可以看到城內的塔尖；向西可以看到橫跨永定河之上的蘆溝橋，它像一條沉睡的巨龍，不理會戰爭，也不理會和平，在這條年代久遠的長橋之下，挾着黃沙的河水日以繼夜地、經年累月地奔流着。

「永定」是「永遠安定」或者「永久和平」的意思。和平真能永維不墜嗎？國人存着這個希望，因此也就給這條河取了這麼個名字。但是我們並未努力保持和平，結果和平從我們手上溜走，隨着蘆溝橋下的河水奔騰而去。民國 26 年（1937 年）7 月 7 日，日本軍隊未經宣戰而發動了對蘆溝橋的攻擊，終使烽火燃遍了整個中國。為步步勝利所陶醉的日本，把在中國的戰火日積月累的貯蓄在魔盒裏滋長，終至民國 30 年（1941 年）12 月 7 日變為一道金光向珍珠港閃擊。🌸

第六部

抗戰時期

第二十五章
東北與朝鮮

民國 7 年（1918 年）夏天，也就是中日戰爭爆發前 19 年，我曾經和一位朋友到東北去過一趟。日本侵略中國是從東北開始的，我們且來看看民國初年時那裏的情形。

我們從上海搭火車到南京，在下關渡長江到浦口，再搭津浦鐵路火車到北京，自浦口北上，火車穿越廣漠的平原，一共走了兩天兩夜。這還是我第一次經過這一區域。飛揚的沙塵，乾旱的黃土，以及遍野的玉蜀黍，與江南潮濕的黑土，蜿蜒的溪澗，連綿的稻田和起伏的丘陵，適成強烈的對比。

我心裏想，北方與南方地理環境的不同，可能與兩地人民體魄和心理的差異有很大的關係。我的祖先幾百年來所居住的華東江浙兩省，曾在歷史上出過無數的學者、藝術家和政治家；但是我現在經過的蘇北和皖北卻似乎是全國最貧窮的地區，境內樹木砍伐殆盡，淮河更不時泛濫成災。

車離蘇北進入黃河流域的山東省境。山東是華北的沿海省份之一，人民個子高大，肌肉結實，生活勤勞，但是人煙過於稠密，省民不得不向外謀發展。最後我們到了北京，使我有機會初次瞻仰故都的公園、宮殿、博物院和花園。我們從北京循京奉鐵路續向瀋陽進展，途經長城的終點山海關。全球聞名的萬里長城，西起甘肅的嘉峪關，像一條巨龍蜿蜒而東，以迄於渤海岸的山海關，把中國本部與滿洲及蒙古隔為兩半。在火車穿越山海關以前，我們隨處可以聽到知了（蟬）在枝頭此唱彼和，喧鬧的情形與中國其他各地完全一樣。但一出山海關就不聞蟬聲了。原來知了只在長城以內生長、歌唱。

我們在夜色蒼茫中到達瀋陽，車站建在城內的日本租界裏。街頭到處是日本商店，很像日本的一座小城。日本勢力侵入滿洲已經是鐵的事實，除非中國與日本一決雌雄，否則這種情勢絕無法遏止。在歷史上，滿洲和蒙古一直是中國禍患之源。這兩個廣大區域裏的民族如匈奴、蒙古和韃靼，不時越過長城入侵，致令中原板蕩，民不聊生。日本人一旦盤據滿洲，勢將成為現代的韃靼。

我們拜訪了好幾位在當地軍閥張作霖手下做事的官員，從他們那裏聽到許多關於滿洲的情形。我們原來打算去看張作霖，但是被朋友勸住了。瀋陽是奉天省的省會，也是 300 年前滿洲人征服中國以前的京城。我們參觀了瀋陽附近的皇陵，清兵入關前的清室諸王就葬在那裏。

我們從瀋陽搭日本人經營的南滿鐵路到寬城子。寬城子就是我們現在所知道的長春市，民國 20 年 (1931 年) 9．18 事變後一度改名新京而成為偽滿洲國的首都。日本勢力侵入寬城子的跡象非常顯著，日本商店隨處可見。

鐵道兩旁是一望無際的麥田，繁茂的麥穗說明了長城之外這塊遼闊的處女地正是中國最富庶的地方，供應每年從山東、河北來的千萬移民，綽有餘裕。從中國搶走東北等於剝奪了她的生存空間，並使黃河流域的省份窒息而死。

寬城子是日人經營的南滿鐵路的終點，也是原由帝俄經營的中東鐵路的起點。中東鐵路公司承襲了沙皇政府的腐敗作風，由一羣貪污無能的白俄僱員在管理。買了票的乘客上車時還得爭奪座位，不買票坐霸王車的人反而大模大樣佔據着舒適的車廂。扒竊之風非常猖獗。有一位乘客，穿着皮鞋睡在臥車的上舖，早上醒來，發現一隻皮鞋已經不翼而飛。他眼睜睜地望着那隻失掉鞋子的腳，想不通鞋子被人脫走時他為甚麼毫無知覺。我也想不通，偷鞋子的賊光偷一隻鞋子究竟有甚麼用途。這件怪事發生以後，全體乘客都小心翼翼地守着自己的行李不敢離開。我的那位朋友為了保險起見，趕緊把攜帶的盧布塞到內衣口袋裏，晚上並且穿着長衫睡覺。第二天早上他的盧布仍然不翼而飛。回程經過哈爾濱車站時，我從車窗探身與中國海關的一位美國官員談話，我發覺有人摸我臀部的褲袋。我還來不及轉身，自己的盧布也不見了。

破敗的哈爾濱市是我國最北的國際都市，也是東方與西方的交會地，衣衫襤褸的中俄兩國的窮孩子在街頭一道玩耍，中俄通婚的事也屢見不鮮。小孩子們說着一種混雜的語言，一半中文，一半俄文。哈爾濱貧苦居民不分畛域地交往相處，對我倒是一件新鮮的事。在上海，頑固的洋人總是瞧不起比他們窮的中國人，把中國人看成瘟疫似的。這或許是因為很少赤貧的歐洲人到上海來住的緣故。但是最重要的原因，還是俄國多混血兒。韃靼與斯拉夫血統合流已經有相當的年代了。

從前平坦整潔的哈爾濱街道，已經多年未曾修整。我們所坐的馬車，在崎嶇的路面經過時，忽上忽下地顛簸震盪，我們必須經常緊緊抓住一點東西，才不致於跌出車外，舒服不舒服自然談不到了。下水道大部淤塞。一陣暴雨之後，街道便成澤國，積水深可沒脛。我們曾經碰到不少從南方來的人在這裏做生意。這城裏的商人們靠小麥、大豆和礦砂的投機居奇，全都利市百倍。他們只知道賺錢，可沒有時間理會這個俄國人發展起來的城市究竟殘破到甚麼程度。

我們隨後又到吉林省城吉林，當地優美的風景給我們很深的印象。吉林城建築在松花江北岸，爬上城內山頭的寺廟眺望江景，寬闊處有如湖泊，使我想起了杭州的西湖。江中盛產魚鮮，松花江的白魚是大家公認最為鮮美的一種魚。帝制時代，只有皇帝、后妃以及王公大臣才有吃到白魚的口福。北京郊外青龍橋在夏季有白魚市，因為慈禧太后常在頤和園駐蹕避暑。直到北伐以前，我們在青龍橋還可買到白魚。大家相信能夠延年益壽的人參也是吉林的特產，每年有大量的人參運入關內，銷售各省。

我們又到黑龍江的省會齊齊哈爾逗留了一個短時期，我們在那裏經歷了一次氣候由夏轉冬的急遽變化。我們發現綠葉在一夜之間枯萎，紛紛從枝頭飛墜。齊齊哈爾已經是中國境內最北的都市，除非搭乘連接西伯利亞鐵路的支線火車前往西伯利亞，我們已無法再往北前進。

回到哈爾濱以後，我們包了一隻汽船，沿平靜的松花江順流駛往富錦縣。舟行兩日一夜，沿途飽覽山光水色，曲折迂迴的江上不時出現原始森林遮掩着的島嶼，夜間月明如洗，北國夏夜的空氣更是清新涼爽。月亮倒映在河水裏，我們的船緩緩經過時，水面激起銀鱗似的微波。松花江本身也常常有山窮水盡疑無路的情境，江水似乎匯為湖泊，森林覆蓋得黑森森的山峰，常常在月色輝映中橫阻去路。但是當我們駛近山麓時，江流會或左或右忽然回轉，我們的船也繞山而過，河道再度向前平伸，江水繼續向天邊外滾滾奔流而去。

富錦縣是個農倉林立的城市。周圍幾百里內所出產的小麥和大豆都運集在這個邊城裏。冬天裏四周用冰磚築起城牆，以防止土匪「紅鬍子」的襲擊。入夏冰磚融化，因為夏天盜匪較少，防務也可以稍稍鬆弛。這裏每個人都帶着槍，也都知道如何放槍。這些邊陲省份的人民仍然保持着原始作風，充滿了戰鬥精神，未曾因古老文化的薰染而變得文弱，與長城以內的老大民族適成強烈的對比。抗戰前，中國空軍就曾從東北處女地的這羣強壯的人民中吸收了大批最優秀的鬥士。

我們的最終目的是羅匋縣和我們一位朋友的農場。羅匋縣在黑龍江與松花江匯合處三角地帶的尖端，黑龍江下游與松花江合流後叫混同江。我們從富錦改乘小船順流而下，於傍晚到達羅匋，當晚寄宿在一個孤零零的小茅屋裏，寬闊的磚炕的一部分已經睡着一位老太婆和一隻小貓，剩下的一角就用以安頓我們。泥地上睡着兩隻肥豬，它們似乎睡得很安穩，時而發出重濁的鼾聲。蚊子和臭蟲擾得我們整夜不能入睡。

天亮以前我們就起個大早望農場進發。一行四人騎着馬，魚貫穿越連綿數里的樹林和麥田。在我們到達目的地以前，太陽已經爬上樹梢。黑龍江彼岸俄羅斯境內的山嶺依稀可辨。馬蠅漸聚漸多，咬得我們坐騎血流如注。我騎的是一匹白馬，馬身上血流如汗，下垂如柳條。我們只有用馬尾鬃製的蠅拂盡力驅逐這些馬蠅。早上 6 點鐘光景，我們到達一個丹麥人經營的農場，據說一星期前曾有一夥紅鬍子光顧這裏。各處牆壁彈痕累累。

我們在 8 點鐘左右到達目的地。在最初幾年裏，這塊處女地上所經營的農場，每年種植的收益相當不錯，真正的問題在乎盜匪。幾個月以前，「小白龍」曾經帶着一夥人到農場來光顧一次，擄走大批的雞鴨牛羊。土匪們似乎對農場上的人相當友善，還用他們的破槍枝換走一批新槍。農場經理說：「無論如何，土匪並不如想像中的那麼壞。如果日本人控制東三省，那我們就真的完蛋了。」

羅甸縣是我們這次北行的終站，在滿洲大陸的南端，我們曾訪問過日本的租借地大連與旅順。大連是個商港，東北的大豆就是由這裏大量出口的。旅順港是個海軍基地，也是東北的門戶，1904 年日俄戰爭就為此而發。帝俄失敗以後，租借權也就轉入日人之手。從旅順和朝鮮開始而貫穿南滿的鐵路已使日本人控制了東三省的心臟和動脈。

我們在這海軍基地漫遊了一天，爬上許多山頭，希望能夠鳥瞰全港。夕陽銜山時我們終於在一處山頭上看到一個石碑，碑上刻着日本東鄉大將引金人的兩句詩云：

「擁兵百萬西湖上，立馬吳山第一峰。」

南宋曾在 1127 年建都杭州，吳山第一峰就在西湖之濱，金人則於 1276 年征服南宋。日俄戰爭以後，東鄉大將和他同胞的夢想就是步武金人的後塵。大約 30 年之後，這個夢想居然實現。繼攻陷上海之後，日軍終於進佔杭州，騎馬登上吳山第一峰。

朝鮮是日本帝國主義到達亞洲大陸的跳板。1894 年的中日戰爭就是因為朝鮮而引起的。為控制這個古老王國而起的中日戰爭是日本侵略亞洲大陸的開端，也為中國歷史揭開了新的一頁，接着而來的是中國的維新運動、革命、內戰、災禍、國恥以及西化運動和現代化運動。

我們在遊歷滿洲以後就轉往朝鮮。我們坐火車渡過鴨綠江到達仁川，由仁川續行到達朝鮮京城漢城。

日本的朝鮮總督就住在漢城。雄偉的西式總督府建在王宮的正前面，像是故意要侮辱朝鮮國王似的。國王已經不再存在，王宮卻仍留在那裏忍受被擠在總督府背後的侮辱。

王宮與北京的中國宮殿一模一樣，不過規模卻小得多，所以只能算是小型宮殿。據熟悉李朝掌故的韓人某君對我說：中國欽差來訪時，李王必須降階親迎；如奉上諭，李王尚須跪接聖旨。

王宮的後面有個中國式的亭，嬪妃們就在這亭子裏表演唐朝時的中國古代歌舞。在朝鮮和日本，古代的中國風俗習慣至今仍風行不衰。他們對中國字的發音，他們的風俗習慣、舞蹈、音樂和生活方式都可追溯到唐代的影響。當我站在那個亭子裏眺望着籠罩在煙霧裏的漢城小山時，我不禁神馳於唐朝（618—905）的輝煌時代，當時的中國文化有如麗日中天，光芒四射，遠及日本、朝鮮和越南等地，成了一個遠東文化圈。這個燦爛的文化的祖國已因歷經外族入侵而改變了她的風俗習慣和生活方式。19世紀時，日本在中國唐朝的文化基礎上吸收了西洋文明而創立了一種新的文化，終於併吞了朝鮮，而且食髓知味，正預備鯨吞她的恩師中國。但是日本倒也給了中國一個教訓：如何在古文化的基礎上建立一個富強的新中國。中國的一連串改革、革命、西化運動和現代化運動也就是這樣開始的。

在我思前想後的當兒，太陽已經從雲層後面探出頭來，漢城山頭的煙霧也很快消散了。引我到王宮去的是位精通漢學的韓國老學者，他一直默然站在我旁邊，這時才提醒我晚上的一個宴會。我們離開亭子後經過閔妃被刺的地方，據說閔妃因同情中國而遭日人暗殺。「我知道你心裏在想甚麼，」這位老學者對我說：「我國現在要振作也太晚了。我們的國王已經因沉湎聲色歌舞而貽誤國事。但是中國是有光明的前途的，中國是你的國家，也可以看作是我的祖國。我已經老了，老弟，你還年輕，你好好地為中國努力吧！」

我們到達中國總領事館時，晚餐已經準備好了。總領事館在從前是中國特使的官邸。中國、帝俄和日本競爭這位朝鮮小姐的四角戀愛期間，這座歷史性的大廈裏面究竟有過甚麼活動，恐怕只有參與其事的人才知道。歷史記載只給我們一個模糊的輪廓；私人記錄即使有，也迄今未發表。一切情形只能憑後人想像了。

漢城的生活正在迅速地日本化。日本的商場、銀行、店舖和飯館，佔據着大街鬧市。大企業的經理、政府官員、重要學府的教員全都是日本人，被征服者的生活習慣，正像他們的皇宮一樣，正在步步往後退縮。街頭不時可以碰到朝鮮人蹲踞在人行道上，嘴裏銜着長煙筒，吞雲吐霧，悠然自得；婦女們頭上頂着沉重的籃子，悠閒地在街上走過。幾處講授四書五經的老式學校已有無法維持之勢。我曾經去過這樣的一所學校，那裏有一位教經書的老先生，十多位學生則圍着他蹲踞在墊席上。朝鮮人和日本人仍舊保持着中國的古代方式，蹲踞在地板上。地板下面即使在夏天也用溫火烘着，墊席打掃得和牀鋪一樣清潔。學生們必須背誦中國經書，和我童年時的情形完全一樣。雖然他們採用同樣的課本，字句發音卻迥然不同。他們像中國的廣東和日本、越南一樣，中國字的發音和唐朝人的讀法相似或竟相同。

所有人都穿着棉絮布襪，夏季也不例外。我問他們這是甚麼道理，他們說是因為北方的土地太寒。但是他們身上卻都穿着非常涼爽的白色麻布長衫。

朝鮮人、日本人和越南人，都愛好中國的山水畫、書法和詩詞。但是這三個民族都保持着他們自己的特色。藝術方面如此，生活方面亦然。朝鮮和越南後來受明朝的影響較大；日本則為海洋所隔離，且明代與德川幕府，彼此均以鎖國為政策，故所受影響不多。此外，以海為家的日本人富於冒險精神，因此保持着古代中國的尚武精神；朝鮮人和越南人則深受明以後幾百年來中國崇尚文事的影響。授予中國文人莫大尊榮的科舉制度曾經傳入朝鮮和越南，卻止於日本大門之外。

朝鮮的年輕一代因受日本人控制下的現代學校的影響，對中國的態度已有急劇的轉變；在這些學校裏，日本天皇被奉為神明，日本人的優點被捧上天，中國人的缺點則被過分描寫。如果說朝鮮青年對日本的態度是仇恨，那麼對中國的態度就是鄙夷。年老的一代惋嘆充滿中國文化的黃金時代已成為過去，年輕的一代雖有少數人認為自己是大日本帝國的天皇子民，而大多數的青年卻仍仇視日本。🅜

第二十六章
戰雲密佈

我辭卸國民政府的教育部長以後，於民國 19 年（1930 年）10 月回到北京——這時已改稱北平。但北京大學校名以歷史關係名未改。旋奉當時任行政院長的蔣委員長之命，再度承乏北京大學校務。

學生遊行示威的次數已大見減少。國都遷往南方以後，政治活動的重心已跟着轉移，學生們示威反對的對象已經不多，只有日本的侵略偶然激發學生的示威行動。日本在東北發動侵略以後，此時已經向關內迅速擴展。

民國 20 年（1931 年）9 月 19 日早晨，我正坐在北大校長室裏辦公，忽然電話傳來前一天發生的驚人消息：日本人已經在瀋陽發動突擊，國軍為避免衝突，已撤出瀋陽。

我在前面曾經逐點指出日本侵華的來龍去脈，概括地說起來，發展過程約略如下：

1894 年（甲午）中日第一次戰爭以後，中國這位小姐開始崇拜日本英雄。她塗脂抹粉，希望能獲得意中人的垂青。但是她所崇拜的對像卻報以鄙夷的冷笑。記得小時候曾經作過一篇短文，呈給日文師中川先生請教。裏面提到「中日同文同種」的話，我的日文教師筆下絕對不留情隨筆批道：「不對！不對，中日兩國並非同種，你的國將被列強瓜分，可憐，可憐！」這個無情的反駁，像一把利劍刺進了我稚嫩的心靈，記得那天晚上，我不禁為國家的前途流淚。

中國固然無法獲得她意中人的愛情：但是她希望至少能與日本做個朋友。想不到日本竟出其不意地掏出匕首向她刺來，差一點就結束了她的性命。這就是大家所知道的「二十一條」的要求。從此以後，她才逐漸明白，她的意中人原來是個帶着武士道假面具的歹人。後來日本倒轉頭向她示愛，她也一直不肯理睬他了。因為這時候她已經知道得很清楚，他向她追求不過是為了她的豐厚粧奩——中國的天然資源而已。

接着來的是一幕謀財害命的慘劇。日本這個歹徒，把經濟「合作」的繩子套到她的脖子上，同時又要她相信那是一條珍珠項鍊，叫做東亞共榮圈。民國 20 年 9 月 18 日晚上，正當大家都沉睡的時候，他忽然把繩圈勒緊了。

她從夢中驚醒，馬上拔腳飛逃。但是套在她脖子上的共榮圈卻始終無法擺脫，她逃得愈遠，繩子就拖得愈長，而且繩子的另一端始終掌握在歹徒魔術師的手裏。她在驚駭之餘大呼救命。美國國務卿史汀生呼籲英國與美國聯合向日本提出嚴重抗議。西蒙爵士代表英國拒絕了。弄得史汀生孤掌難鳴，日本因而得以肆無忌憚地繼續推行既定政策。

對中國並不太熱心的一班朋友，在李頓爵士率領之下，懶洋洋地前來營救。他們訪問了犯罪的現場瀋陽，並且宣告日本有罪。瀋陽郵政當局的義籍局長樸萊第在他給李頓爵士的備忘錄裏明白指出：如果列強不在東北就地阻遏日本侵略，他相信不出三年，他的祖國義大利就要染指阿比西尼亞。那位樸局長把備忘錄交我讀了一遍並且自語道：「但是我人微言輕，誰又肯理會小小一位郵政局長的話呢？」

「對不起，小姐，」中國的朋友說：「我們除了宣佈對你的同情之外，實在無能為力了。」

同情是有了，援助卻毫無踪影。

幾個月以後，我因事回到南方。民國 21 年 (1932 年) 1 月 28 日下午，我前往上海車站，準備搭火車回北平。進車站後，發現情勢迥異平常，整個車站像荒涼的村落。一位原車站警衛是認識我的，他告訴我，已經沒有往外開的車子。「看樣子，日本人馬上要發動攻擊了。」他說，「你最好馬上離開這裏。恐怕這裏隨時要出事呢！」

那天夜裏，我突然被一陣炮聲驚醒，接着是一陣軋軋的機槍聲。我從牀上跳起來，隨着旅館裏的人跑到屋頂觀望。天空被車站附近射來的炮火映得通紅。日本侵略似乎已經追在我腳跟後面，從北方到了南方，我所住的10層高樓的旅館在租界以內，日本炮火不會打過來的。我同一班旅客都作隔岸觀火。隆隆的大炮聲、拍拍的機槍聲終宵不斷。第二天早晨，我再度爬上屋頂，發現商務印書館正在起火燃燒，心裏有說不出的難過。好幾架日本轟炸機在輪番轟炸商務印書館的房子。黑煙沖天，紙片漫天飛舞，有些碎紙片上還可以看到「商務印書館」的字樣。

日本已經展開對上海的攻擊。結果引起一場民國26年（1937年）以前最激烈的戰事，但是中國終於被迫接受條件，準許日本在上海駐兵。

從民國19年到26年的7年內，我一直把握着北大之舵，竭智盡能，希望把這學問之舟平穩渡過中日衝突中的驚濤駭浪。在許多朋友協助之下，尤其是胡適之、丁在君（文江）和傅孟真（斯年），北大幸能平穩前進，僅僅偶爾調整帆篷而已。

科學教學和學術研究的水準提高了。對中國歷史和文學的研究也在認真進行。教授們有充裕的時間從事研究，同時誘導學生集中精力追求學問，一度曾是革命活動和學生運動漩渦的北大，已經逐漸轉變為學術中心了。七年之中只有一次值得記錄的示威運動。當日軍迅速向長城推進時，京滬一帶的學生大聲疾呼，要求政府立即對日作戰。大規模的示威遊行不時在南京發生，北平的學生也亟欲參加此一救國運動。有一天，一大羣學生聚集東火車站，準備搭乘南下的火車。軍警當局不准他們上車，這班男女青年就日夜躺臥在鐵軌上，不讓火車出站。最後當局只好讓幾百名學生南下，與他們在南京的同志會師。

我們頭上的烏雲愈來愈密，此後幾年中我們為了爭取時間，只好小心翼翼地在淺水裏緩緩前進，不敢闖進急流，以免正面撞上日本侵華的浪潮。但是我們的謹慎是與懦怯不同的。每當日本的第五縱隊偽裝的學者來這「文化中心」（實際上他們卻把北大看成反日運動的中心）「拜訪」時，我們總是毫無保留地表示我們的態度。記得有一位日本學者曾經對北大教授們滔滔不絕地大談中日文化關係，結果我們告訴他，除了日本的軍事野心之外，我們可看不出中日之間有甚麼文化關係存在。「只要你們肯放棄武力侵略的野心，中日兩國自然就能攜手合作的。」

這些學者，包括地質學家、經濟學家、生物學家等等，不時來拜訪我們，希望爭取北大的「友誼」。他們一致埋怨我們的反日運動。我們告訴他們，我們不一定是反日，不過我們反對日本軍國主義卻是真的。但是他們一心一意要滅亡中國，除了中國完全投降，他們絕不會改變方針。

這時，駐屯東三省的日本關東軍正迅速向長城之內推進。國軍先沿長城浴血奮戰，繼在河北省北部步步抵抗，最後終於撤退到北平及其近郊。傷兵絡繹於途。各醫院到處人滿。北大教職員也發動設立了一所傷兵醫院，由內子陶曾主持院務，教職員太太和女學生充任職員和看護。因為這醫院的關係，我與作戰部隊有了較密切的接觸，同時，獲悉他們的心理狀態。他們認為作戰失利完全是由於缺乏現代武器，尤其是槍支，因而以血肉之軀築成的長城，終被敵人衝破了。

國軍以血肉築成長城抗禦敵人的彈雨火海，主要的憑藉就是這種不屈不撓的精神。這種精神使中國在漫長痛苦的 8 年之中愈戰愈勇，雖然千千萬萬的人受傷死亡，中國卻始終連哼都不哼一聲。我們雖然節節失利，卻終於贏得戰爭。

戰事正在沿長城進行時，當時的軍政部長何敬之（應欽）將軍曾親至北平指揮作戰。他和我都希望能達成停戰以換取時間。我訪晤英國大使藍浦生，探詢他有無出任調人之意。他說日本大使館的須磨先生曾經對他暗示，日本也希望停戰。藍浦生大使當即拍電報向倫敦請示，倫敦覆電同意由他出任調人。我們經由美國駐華大使詹森先生把這件事通知華盛頓。但是這個計劃終於胎死腹中，因為當時的外交部長羅鈞任（文幹）告訴在南京的英國大使館說，除了他本人之外，誰也無權與外國辦交涉。

不久日軍突破國軍沿長城佈置的防線，步步向北平逼近，北平軍民已開始準備撤退。

我當時因為割盲腸之後正躺在北京協和醫院，對外面的情形很隔膜。

有一天清早，我聽到日本飛機在頭上盤旋，直覺地感到情勢不妙。我得到主治醫生的許可，忍痛步行到何敬之將軍的寓所。他見我還留在北平城內，很感意外。他告訴我日軍馬上會發動攻擊，勸我快離開北平，於是我準備第二天就離開。第二天早晨，我的電話響了，是何將軍打來的：「我們已經談妥停戰，你不必走了。」我馬上打電話把這消息轉告胡適之。

「真的嗎？日本飛機還在我們頭上盤旋呢！」他說。

「何敬之將軍剛剛打電話來這樣說的。」我所能回答的也僅此而已。後來才知道黃膺白（郛）已代表中國在午夜簽訂塘沽協定，根據此項協定，日軍在佔領河北省北部以後，將暫時停止前進。

日軍佔領上述地區後，就在當地成立「自治政府」，並催促留在河北的國軍司令官與他們合作，在北平也成立一個「自治政府」。北平城內謠言滿天飛，說河北省境內的司令宋哲元將軍即將對日本人屈服。北大教授就在這緊急關頭發表宣言，聲明誓死反對華北的所謂「自治運動」。事實上，宋哲元將軍也並沒有答應日本人的要求。

一兩個月以後的一個下午，一個日本憲兵到北大來找我。「日本在東交民巷的駐防軍請你去一趟，談談他們希望了解並且需要你加以解釋的事情。」他這樣告訴我。我答應在一小時之內就去，這位日本兵也就告辭回去了。

我把這件事通知家裏的幾位朋友之後，在天黑以前單獨往東交民巷日本兵營。我走進河邊將軍的辦公室以後，聽到門鎖哧嚓一聲，顯然門已下了鎖。一位日本大佐站起來對我說：「請坐。」我坐下時，用眼睛掃了旁邊一眼，發現一位士官拔出手槍站在門口。

「我們司令請你到這裏來，希望知道你為甚麼要進行大規模的反日宣傳。」他一邊說，一邊遞過一支香煙來。

「你說甚麼？我進行反日宣傳？絕無其事！」我回答說，同時接過他的煙。

「那末，你有沒有在那個反對自治運動的宣言上簽字？」

「是的,我簽了名的。那是我們的內政問題,與反日運動毫無關係。」

「你寫過一本攻擊日本的書。」

「拿這本書出來給我看看!」

「那末你是日本的朋友嗎?」

「這話不一定對。我是日本人民的朋友,但是也是日本軍國主義的敵人,正像我是中國軍國主義的敵人一樣。」

「呃,你知道,關東軍對這件事有點小誤會。你願不願意到大連去與阪垣將軍談談?」這時電話鈴響了,大佐接了電話以後轉身對我說:「已經給你準備好專車。你願意今晚去大連嗎?」

「我不去。」

「不要怕,日本憲兵要陪你去的,他們可以保護你。」

「我不是怕,如果我真的怕,我也不會單獨到這裏來了。如果你們要強迫我去,那就請便吧 —— 我已經在你們掌握之中了。不過我勸你們不要強迫我。如果全世界人士,包括東京在內,知道日本軍隊綁架了北京大學的校長,那你們可就要成為笑柄了。」

他的臉色變了,好像我忽然成了一個棘手的問題。「你不要怕呀!」他心不在焉地說。

「怕嗎?不,不。中國聖人說過,要我們臨難毋苟免,我相信你也一定知道這句話。你是相信武士道的,武士道絕不會損害一個毫無能力的人。」我抽着煙,很平靜地對他說。

電話又響了,他再度轉身對我說:「好了,蔣校長,司令要我謝謝你這次的光臨。你或許願意改天再去大連 —— 你願意甚麼時候去都行。謝謝你。再見!」門鎖又是咔嚓一響。大佐幫我穿好大衣,陪我到汽車旁邊,還替我打開汽車門。這時夜色已經四合了。我獨自到日本兵營,也有朋友說我不應該去的,聽日本人來捕好了。他們敢麼?

第二天下午,宋哲元將軍派了一位少將來勸我離開北平,因為他怕自己無力保護我。我向他的代表致謝,不過告訴他,我將繼續留在北平負起我的責任。

不久以後，蔣委員長因陳辭修將軍北上之便，亦來代表慰問。

我繼續在北平住下來，而且居然平安無事。偶然也有些朝鮮浪人到北大來尋釁找岔，這些事曾經一一報告給我知道，但是我並未予以重視。不久日本人的策略開始轉變了。松室孝良將軍受命來北平擔任日軍的特別代表。他與我交了朋友，常常到我家裏來。他大罵那位日本將軍不該在東交民巷兵營折磨我。大概半年光景，我們私人之間一直保持非常友好的關係。他任期屆滿時，穿了全副武裝來向我辭行。他告訴我，他已奉命調往東北與西伯利亞交界的海拉爾去指揮一個騎兵師。他說戰雲愈來愈低，如果中國與日本真的發生衝突，那是很不幸的。「戰事一旦發生，」他說，「日軍勢將深入漢口。」

「是的，將軍，我同意你的看法。兩國之間不幸而發生公開衝突，很可能會引起國際糾紛，那時整個日本艦隊都可能葬身海底，日本帝國會縮小為太平洋地圖上的幾粒小黑點。」

他歎了一口氣：「那當然也可能。但是日本仍舊是獨立的國家，中國卻不免要被西方列強消滅了。」

「也可能如此。下次碰面時，希望我們不必為愚蠢的作為而抱頭痛哭。不管將來發生甚麼事情，將軍，希望我們永遠是朋友。」我們就這樣懷着沉重的心情分別了。戰事結束若干年後，我經過東京偕內子陶曾往訪，相對話舊，不禁感慨系之。

接替他的是今井將軍。他來拜訪我，我也曾去回拜。我們談得很坦白，和我跟松室孝良談話的情形大致相似。有一次，日本貴族院的兩位議員來訪，其中一位曾任台灣總督。四顧無人之後，他低聲問我，在東交民巷日本兵營拘留我的是誰。我告訴他是高橋。他搖頭說：

「豈有此理！」

這時候日本人已經明白，北大並無意於馬上發起反日運動，他們希望能與北大裏的主要教授建立友誼，而把北大拉到日本這一邊。雙方來往都很審慎，北大與日軍之間的緊張情勢至此已漸漸緩和了。

後來田代將軍來到天津擔任當地駐軍司令。日本以及其他列強，因條約規定有權在天津駐軍，田代特地跑到北平來，設宴招待中日雙方文武要員。田代在席間發表演說，鼓吹中日經濟合作，中國官員也曾有人繼起發言，但是措詞都相當含糊。我除了吃飯時偶爾說笑外，對於經濟合作問題始終不發一言。幾天之後，忽然南京來了密電，告訴我，日本大使館已經暗示外交部，說北大校長支持中日合作。

這就是日本人對付中國的手段。程式大概是：先來一套甜言蜜語，繼之挑撥陰謀，然後威脅恫嚇，接着又是甜言蜜語，最後施行閃電攻擊。先後次序可能有所改變，但是從來不離征服中國的基本方針。日本人在珍珠港事變以前對付美國的，也是這一套。⑱

第二十七章
抗戰初期

　　未改名北平以前的北京是文化活動和學生運動的中心，易名以後則變為中日衝突的中心。民國 26 年（1937 年）之初，北平附近事端迭起，戰事已如箭在弦上，不得不發。7 月 7 日的晚上，終於發生蘆溝橋事變。日軍在夜色掩護下發動攻擊，從蘆溝橋的彼端向北平近郊進襲，城內駐軍當即予以還擊。

　　戰神降臨北平時，我正在廬山。當時蔣委員長在這華中避暑勝地召集了一羣知識分子商討軍國大事，有一天午後，天空萬里無雲，樹影疏疏落落地點綴着綠油油的草地。蔣委員長曾經為他的客人準備了許多簡單雅潔的房子，我吃過午飯正在一幢單開間獨立的宿舍裏休息，一面眺望着窗外一棵枝葉扶疏的大樹，一面諦聽着枝頭知了的唱和。忽然「中央日報」程社長滄波來敲門，告訴我日軍在前一晚對蘆溝橋發動攻擊的消息，我從牀上跳起來追問詳情，但是他所知也很有限。

　　我們曾經討論可能的發展。因為我剛從北平來，他問我，根據我所知道的北平情況，對時局有何看法。我告訴他，以我對當地日軍司令官的印象以及他們的保守見解來判斷，這次事變似乎仍舊是地方性事件。日本的計劃似乎還是蠶食中國，一時恐怕尚無鯨吞的準備。但是蠶食的結果，日本很可能在數年之內即根深蒂固地盤據華北而無法撼其分毫，到那時候，長江流域也就危在旦夕了。日本已經以漸進的方式吞噬東北而進窺華北，將來華北對華中、華南的局勢亦復如是。同樣的方法，同樣的過程。這似乎就是日本對付中國的政策。

　　戰事斷斷續續相持了好幾天。12 天以後，北平城外的零星戰事仍在進行，蔣委員長在牯嶺對幾千名在廬山訓練團受訓的將領演說，認為日本即將對中國發動全面攻擊，呼籲大家準備不計代價保衛國家。他說：「全面戰爭一旦開始，我們必須隨時準備犧牲。……這次戰爭必將曠日持久，時間拖得愈長，我們的犧牲也就愈大。」

在這次演說裏，我初次聽見蔣委員長稱呼侵華的日軍為倭寇，並表示對日問題的堅決主張。倭寇這個名詞，在一般聽眾或不甚注意，但在明代長期遭倭寇蹂躪的寧波和紹興人，聽到這種稱呼，就會覺得事態嚴重。當時的聽眾之中有陳誠將軍、胡宗南將軍，以及其他後來在各區建立殊勳的許多將領。這次演說後不久，蔣委員長飛返南京，各將領亦分別返防。我和幾位朋友飛到南京，希望趕返北平，但是北上火車已全部停頓。

在此後的兩個星期內，戰事像洪水一樣泛濫北平附近。宋哲元將軍英勇奮戰，部下傷亡慘重。日軍司令田代對中國問題的看法一向很保守，我知道得很清楚，不幸田代忽然病倒，思想激進的少壯軍官遂得控制日本部隊。數日後田代去世。究竟是病故、自殺或被殺，雖然謠言滿天飛，誰也弄不清楚底細。宋哲元將軍仍舊希望把事件局部化，要求兼程北上的中央政府軍隊暫時停留在保定。結果中央部隊就在保定留下來了。

但是現由少壯軍人指揮的日本軍卻並未停止前進；宋哲元將軍的部隊四面八方受到攻擊。一位高級將領並在作戰時陣亡。宋將軍不得已撤出北平，日軍未經抵抗即進入故都。

日軍已經控制北平了，華北是否會像瀋陽陷落後的東北，遭逢同樣的命運呢？日本會不會在華北暫時停下來，在華北等上幾年，然後再以之為攻擊南方的基地呢？日本是不是已等得不耐煩，準備一舉攻下南方而圖一勞永逸呢？二者似乎均有可能。日本的漸進政策似乎對中國更危險。南京的高級官員以及各省的軍事領袖全都贊成全面抵抗侵略。結果全國上下，包括政府官員、軍事將領和平民百姓，萬眾一心，一致奮起應付空前的國難。

這時候，日本已開始派遣軍隊循海道開抵上海。中國也在同時派軍隊沿長江東下趕到滬瀆。在這小小的區域裏，已有好幾萬軍隊結集對峙着，戰事一觸即發。究竟那一方面先發第一槍都無關宏旨，不論是一位粗心大意的士兵無意中走火，或者是掌握大權者的決策。

日軍官兵大家都知道，製造瀋陽事變的負責將領如本莊繁和土肥原等均曾因功而獲得最高級的勳獎。一手製造蘆溝橋事變的人，無疑地也會獲得同樣的勳獎。誰又能怪渡海而來上海的日軍將領也想一顯身手呢？

我們在南京的人都知道，密佈在全國上空的烏雲勢將迸發為狂風暴雨。我離開南京循公路到杭州，在湖濱一位朋友的別墅裏住了幾天，我們沒有一天不擔心，在淞滬對壘的中日軍隊會發生衝突。我的朋友王文伯不時打長途電話到上海探問情況。8 月 12 日，上海方面的回答很短促：「沒有消息。明天 10 點鐘，10 點鐘，再見！」接着電話就掛斷了。

第二天早上 10 點鐘，歷史性的時刻終於來臨。濃煙上沖霄漢，雙方的轟炸機交互炸射對方陣地，全面戰爭已經開始了。從此不再有地方性的事件，也不再有蠶食的機會。日本要就一口吞下中國，要就完全放棄。但是吞下去倒也不容易，放棄嗎？她又捨不得。這局面注定是一場長期戰爭。

兩天以後，一個烏雲密佈的下午，我正坐在柳蔭下欣賞湖邊淺水中魚兒穿梭往返，城的這一邊隱隱傳來陣陣雷聲。有人打電話給我：「喂！你聽到沒有？」接着又是一陣雷聲。「是呀，在打雷。」

「不是 —— 敵人在轟炸我們的機場！」

7 架沒有戰鬥機掩護的木更津隊轟炸機已經從台灣松山機場飛到杭州。駐紮筧橋的中國戰鬥機當即升空攔擊，並當場擊落其 5 架，其餘 2 架奪路逃命，但是也在離杭州不遠處被迫降落，飛行員被俘。我到紹興專員公署去看一位俘虜，據他說，他們在台灣的指揮官曾經告訴他們，中國根本沒有戰鬥機。

第二天，日軍開始轟炸南京。戰事剛開始時，日本人在一個地方只丟一個炸彈，所以他們所有的炸彈都是分散的。這種轟炸方式所造成的損害遠較集中轟炸為小。一年之後，日軍與俄軍在偽滿與西伯利亞交界處的張高峰發生衝突，日本人才從俄國學到集中轟炸的戰術。

我的朋友王文伯是浙江省政府委員兼建設廳廳長。戰事開始以後，他的工作自然跟着緊張起來了。他調集了好幾百輛公路車，把軍火運給前方。有一次，大約20輛車子結隊駛往前方，結果這隊車輛誤入敵人後方而遭圍攻。其中的一位司機跳下車子躲在田野裏，後來借夜色掩護爬出敵人陣地回到杭州。幾天之後，他找了另外一輛卡車，又再度上前線擔任運輸工作去了。

難民從上海像潮水一樣湧到杭州。廟宇裏住滿了婦孺老幼。山區的小茅屋也成了衣裝入時摩登小姐的臨時香閨。她們還是像以前一樣談笑，似乎根本沒有發生過任何變故。我們中國人就有這點本領，即使身臨危難，也常能處之泰然。

我有一位朋友，本來是上海的棉紗大王，「8·13」戰事發生後，帶着他的子女逃到杭州，暫時住在山中的一所廟宇裏。他告訴我，他預備給他的家人蓋一幢房子。

「為甚麼？」我問他。

「上海作戰期間，我想在杭州住下來。」他説。

我真想不到他對這次戰爭有這樣的看法。我勸他最好還是遷到內地去，因為戰事必定要蔓延到杭州以及所有的沿海城市，甚至可能遠及華中的漢口。他聽到這些話，好像沒法相信似的。5年之後，我在重慶碰到他，他告訴我，他們一家人在戰火擴及杭州以前就離開西湖了。

與北方三個大學有關的人士正在南京商議學校內遷的計劃。大家有意把北平的北京大學、清華大學和天津的南開大學從北方撤退而在長沙成立聯合大學。胡適之從南京打電話給我，要我回到南京商量實施這個計劃的辦法。我經過考慮，勉強同意了這個計劃。

我曉得在戰事結束以前恐怕沒有機會再見到父親和我的老家。而且戰局前途很難逆料，因此我就向朋友借了一輛別克轎車駛回家鄉。這時父親年紀已經很大，看到我回家自然笑逐顏開。我離家重返南京時告訴父親説，中國將在火光血海中獲得新生。

「你這是甚麼意思？」他目不轉睛地望着我，雙目炯炯有光。

「事情是這樣的：這次戰爭將是一次長期戰爭，千千萬萬的房屋將化為灰燼，千千萬萬的百姓將死於非命。這就是我所説的火光血海，最後中國將獲得勝利。」

當我向父親告別時，我心裏有一個感覺，怕自己從此沒有機會再見我所敬愛的父親了。父親所施於我的實在太多了，但是我所報答他的卻又如此之少。後來我的家鄉遭到轟炸時，他遷到山中，以栽花養鳥自娛。戰事發生兩年以後的一個早上，他像平常一樣起得很早，他忽然感到有點頭暈，回到臥室，即告去世。享年80。他不過是戰爭的間接受害者之一。戰爭對老年人實在是很大的磨難。

我回南京逗留幾天之後就搭輪溯江而至漢口，碼頭附近沿江堆積着大批木箱，裏面裝着政府的檔案、中央大學圖書館的書籍和故宮博物院的古物（即現在台中之古物）。從南京至漢口途中，我們曾碰到滿載軍隊的船隻，順流東下增援上海。

我從漢口搭粵漢鐵路赴長沙，沿途碰到好幾批軍隊擠在敞篷車裏，由廣東、廣西向北開往漢口。這次戰爭現在的的確確是全國性的，不再像過去一樣是地方性的戰事了。士兵們的鬥志非常激昂，我問他們往哪裏去。

「打日本鬼！」他們異口同聲地説。⑯

第二十八章
戰時的長沙

　　長沙是個內陸城市。住在長沙的一段時期是我有生以來第一次遠離海洋。甚至在留美期間，我也一直住在沿海地區，先在加利福尼亞住了 4 年，後來又在紐約住了 5 年。住在內陸城市使我有乾燥之感，雖然長沙的氣候很潮濕，而且離洞庭湖也不遠。我心目中最理想的居所是大平原附近的山區，或者山區附近的平原，但是都不能離海太遠。離海過遠，我心目中的空間似乎就會被堅實的土地所充塞，覺得身心都不舒暢。

　　我到達長沙時，清華大學的梅貽琦校長已經先到那裏。在動亂時期主持一個大學本來就是頭痛的事，在戰時主持大學校務自然更難，尤其是要三個個性不同、歷史各異的大學共同生活，而且三校各有思想不同的教授們，各人有各人的意見。我一面為戰局擔憂，一面又為戰區裏或淪陷區裏的親戚朋友擔心，我的身體就有點支持不住了。「頭痛」不過是一種比喻的說法，但是真正的胃病可使我的精神和體力大受影響。雖然胃病時發，我仍勉強打起精神和梅校長共同負起責任來，幸靠同仁的和衷共濟，我們才把這條由混雜水手操縱的危舟渡過驚濤駭浪。

　　聯合大學在長沙成立以後，北大、清華、南開三校的學生都陸續來了。有的是從天津搭英國輪船先到香港，然後再搭飛機或粵漢鐵路火車來的，有的則由北平搭平漢鐵路火車先到漢口，然後轉粵漢鐵路到長沙。幾星期之內，大概就有 200 名教授和 1,000 多名學生齊集在長沙聖經學校了。聯合大學租了聖經學校為臨時校舍。書籍和實驗儀器則是在香港購置運來的，不到兩個月，聯大就粗具規模了。

　　因為在長沙城內找不到地方，我們就把文學院搬到佛教聖地南嶽衡山。

我曾經到南嶽去過兩次，留下許多不可磨滅的回憶。其中一次我和幾位朋友曾深入叢山之中暢遊 3 日，途中還曾經過一條山路，明朝末年一位流亡皇帝（永曆帝）在 3 百年前為逃避清兵追趕曾經走過這條山路。現在路旁還樹着一個紀念碑，碑上刻着所有追隨他的臣子的名字。在我們經過的一所寺廟裏，看見一棵松樹，據一位老僧說是永曆帝所手植的。說來奇怪，這棵松樹竟長得像一位佝僂的老翁，似乎是長途跋涉之後正在那裏休息。我們先後在同一的路上走過，而且暫駐在同一寺廟裏，為甚麼？同是為了由北方來的異族入侵。一千多年來，中國始終為外來侵略所苦。

第一夜我們住宿在方廣寺。明朝滅亡以後，一位著名的遺老即曾在方廣寺度其餘年。那天晚上夜空澄澈，團明月在山頭冉冉移動，我從來沒有看到過這樣低、這樣近的月亮，好像一伸手就可以觸到它這張笑臉。

第二夜我們住在接近南嶽極峰的一個寺院裏。山峰的頂端有清泉汩汩流出，泉旁有個火神廟。這個廟頗足代表中國通俗的想法，我們一向認為火旁邊隨時預備着水，因為水可以剋火。

第二天早晨，我們在這火神廟附近看到了日出奇觀，太陽從雲海裏冉冉升起，最先透過雲層發出紫色的光輝，接着發出金黃色、粉紅和藍色的光彩，最後浮出雲端，像一個金色的鴕鳥蛋躺臥在雪白的天鵝絨墊子上。忽然之間它分裂為四個金光燦爛的橘子，轉瞬之間卻又復合為一個大火球。接着的一段短暫時刻中，它似乎每秒鐘都在變換色彩，很像電影的彩色鏡頭在轉動。一會兒它又暫時停住不動了，四散發射着柔和的金光，最後又變為一個耀目大火球，使我們不得不轉移視線。雲海中的冰山不見了，平靜的雲浪也跟着消逝，只剩下一層輕霧籠罩着腳下的山谷。透過輕霧，我們看到縷縷炊煙正在煦和的旭日照耀下裊裊升起。

來南嶽朝山進香的人絡繹於途，有的香客還是從幾百里之外步行來的。男女老幼，貧賤富貴，都來向菩薩頂禮膜拜。

長沙是湖南的省會，湖南是著名的魚米之鄉，所產稻米養活了全省人口以外，還可以供應省外幾百萬人的食用。湘江裏最多的是魚、蝦、鱔、鰻和甲魚，省內所產橘子和柿子鮮紅豔麗。貧富咸宜的豆腐潔白勻淨如濃縮的牛奶。唯一的缺點是濕氣太重，一年之中雨天和陰天遠較晴天為多。

我每次坐飛機由長沙起飛時，總會想到海龍王的水晶宮。我的頭上有悠悠白雲，腳下則是輕紗樣的薄霧籠罩着全城，正像一層蛋白圍繞着蛋黃。再向上升更有一層雲擋住了陽光。在長沙天空飛行終逃不了層層遮蓋的雲。

湖南人的身體健壯，個性剛強，而且刻苦耐勞，他們尚武好鬥，一言不合就彼此罵起來，甚至動拳頭。公路車站上我們常常看到「不要開口罵人，不要動手打人」的標語。人力車夫在街上慢吞吞像散步，絕不肯拔步飛奔。如果你要他跑得快一點，他準會告訴你「你老下來拉吧 —— 我倒要看看你老怎麼個跑法」。湖南人的性子固然急，但行動卻不和脾氣相同，一個人脾氣的緩急和行動的快慢可見並不一致的，湖南人拉黃包車就是一個例子。

他們很爽直，也很真摯，但是脾氣固執，不容易受別人意見的影響。他們要就是你的朋友，要就是你的敵人，沒有折衷的餘地。他們是很出色的軍人，所以有「無湘不成軍」的說法。曾國藩在清同治 3 年（1864 年）擊敗太平軍，就是靠他的湘軍。現在的軍隊裏，差不多各單位都有湖南人，湖南是中國的斯巴達。

抗戰期間，日本人曾三度進犯長沙而連遭三次大敗。老百姓在槍林彈雨中協助國軍抗敵，傷亡慘重。

在長沙我們不斷有上海戰事的消息。國軍以血肉之軀抵禦日軍的火海和彈雨，使敵人無法越過國軍防線達 3 月之久。後來國軍為避免繼續作無謂的犧牲，終於撤出上海。敵軍接着包圍南京，首都人民開始全面撤退，千千萬萬的人沿公路湧至長沙。卡車、轎車成羣結隊到達，長沙忽然之間擠滿了難民。從南京撤出的政府部會，有的遷至長沙，有的則遷到漢口。

日軍不久進入南京，士兵獸性大發。許多婦女被輪姦殺死，無辜百姓在逃難時遭到日軍機槍任意掃射。日軍在南京的暴行，將在人類歷史上永遠留下不可磨滅的污點。

新年裏，日軍溯江進逼南昌。中國軍隊結集在漢口附近，日軍則似有進窺長沙模樣。湖南省會已隨時有受到敵人攻擊的危險。我飛到漢口，想探探政府對聯大續遷內地的意見。我先去看教育部陳立夫部長，他建議最好還是去看總司令本人。因此我就去謁見委員長了。他贊成把聯大再往西遷，我建議遷往昆明，因為那裏可以經滇越鐵路與海運銜接。他馬上表示同意，並且提議應先派人到昆明勘尋校址。

民國 27 年（1938 年）正月，就在準備搬遷中過去了。書籍和科學儀器都裝了箱，卡車和汽油也買了。2 月間，準備工作已經大致完成，我從長沙飛到香港，然後搭法國郵船到越南的海防。我從海防搭火車到法屬越南首府河內，再由河內乘滇越鐵路火車，經過叢山峻嶺而達昆明。🔴

日軍入侵前夕之越南與緬甸

　　我由長沙繞道越南赴昆明途中，發現越南也保留着許多古代中國的風俗習慣，正如 20 多年前我在朝鮮所發現的。越南人與朝鮮人一樣，穿着一種近似明朝服飾的衣服。他們唸中國字時，發音與唐代語言相像；鄉村、城市和行政區也採用中國地名，這些地名的讀音多少與唐代的讀音相似。亦可以說與廣東音相似。

　　越文是中文的一種變體，在一般用途上，法國人卻寧取一種拉丁化的越文。這種拉丁化文字在一般人學起來自然容易得多，但以此為表達高深思想之工具是不夠的。

　　越南國王保大在順化的宮殿很像過去朝鮮李王的宮室，但是與北京的紫禁城比起來，規模同樣地小得多了。事實上，越南皇宮很像明朝皇宮殘留的一枝，法國人一直保留着越南皇宮，拿它作活的博物館看待，日本人卻寧願把朝鮮國王送到日本，想把他改造為日本人。

　　有人告訴我，越南王的始祖葬在昆明某山頭，因為他本來是中國人。後來有一天下午，我曾經去找越南王陵寢的故址，結果沒有找到。

　　法國殖民地政府的所在地河內已經發展為現代化的法國城市，街道寬闊，公共建築巍然矗立。但是一般農民所住的鄉村卻骯髒破落，與河內相較，真有天淵之別。自由、平等、博愛，原來如此！殖民地政府是一種時代的倒置，也就是非常倒退的制度，總督們到殖民地來只是為了剝削榨取，對人民的福利漠不關心，這與現代的政治原理恰恰背道而馳。

　　不過，我想在這裏聲明一句：菲律賓的殖民地政府應該例外。美國人有一個理想──提高菲人的文化水準，美國在菲賓的殖民政府，在當地建立了一種足與美國學校媲美的學校制度。我曾在民國 20 年（1931 年）去過菲律賓，所到之處，學校都在傳授歷史、文學、科學和民主思想。美國正按照自己的模型，致力建設菲律賓為一民主共和國。菲律賓在歐美人殖民地制度下，獲得兩大貢獻。一是西班牙人留下來的天主教。二是美國人留下來的民主制度和言論自由。

英國的生存寄託在殖民地上，法國也得靠殖民地的資源維持生存。如果說英法對殖民地人民的福利還沒有完全漠視的話，那也只是為了養活母雞，好讓它多生一些蛋而已。英國人養雞生蛋的方法更是妙不可言，他們控制了主要的工業，而讓當地人民在餘留的行業上自覓生路。讓雞到田野裏自行尋覓穀粒小蟲充饑。雞能找到穀粒小蟲就心滿意足了，養雞的人則撿起晶瑩的雞蛋笑顏逐開。英國人從來不干涉殖民地人民的風俗或迷信思想，除了影響公共衛生的事情以外，當地人民可以自由自在地過活而不受干擾。因為公共衛生不但與被統治者有關，與統治者也有同樣的關係，傳染病或瘟疫是不認膚色人種的。道路修得寬敞平坦，而且保養得很好，因為治安和商業是要靠良好的道路來維持的。防禦力量只建立到足以鎮壓當地叛亂的程度，抵禦其他強國的攻擊則有賴大英帝國的威望。這種威望衰退時，殖民地就不免要受強鄰的覬覦了。香港和緬甸一度失陷就是這個道理，英國這樣珍惜她的威望，尤其是在遠東的威望，也是這個道理。

緬甸與雲南省的西南角接壤，珍珠港事變前約一年，我曾經奉命組織一個友好訪問團到緬甸，我參觀過煉油廠、鋸木廠和碾米廠，這些都是緬甸的主要工業，統由英國控制，其餘的行業則留歸緬甸人經營。被視為神聖的牛只閒蕩仰光街頭，警察從來不加干涉。到處是寺院，院內矗立着鍍金的寶塔，生活着普受統治者及被統治者尊崇的僧侶。緬甸人在英國統治之下自由過活，像一羣吃飽了小蟲穀粒的母雞悠然自得，至少，我看不出一點不滿的情緒，養的人則心滿意足地撿取他們的雞蛋。

但是總督們在祖國照耀出來的光明在殖民地裏卻不能完全隔絕。在印度，甘地的行動一直不受干擾，只有在緊急危難時才遭受監禁。像甘地的這種行動，在某些歐洲國家的殖民地裏或許早已受到陰毒的處置了。但是大不列顛究竟是自由之邦，自由的光輝不免要透過殖民地上空的雲層而惠及當地人民。各種跡象顯示，英國對殖民地正在採取一種比較開明的政策。我希望這些照射到海外殖民地的微光能擴大為強烈的自由火炬，引導殖民地人民向光明的前途邁進。

就文化形態而言，越南王國是屬於中國型的，緬甸則是印度型的。從前緬甸國王在曼達來的宮殿就是印度式的建築。城鎮的地名也看不出與中國有絲毫的淵源。越南人和中國人一樣，吃飯時用的是筷子；緬甸卻和印度人一樣用手指。但是越南和緬甸在過去曾一度尊重中國的宗主權，中國在兩國宗主權的喪失是中國覺醒的原因之一。

緬甸落入英人手中以後，緬甸的王室就逃到雲南，生活費用一直由雲南省政府供給，不過緬甸王的頭銜已經有名無實了。緬王的子孫後來進了中國學校，結果歸化為中國人。但是雲南騰沖一帶的人仍舊知道，這些緬甸王室後裔的祖先，曾經在曼達來皇宮的雀屏寶座上，統治過有鍍金寶塔和黃袍僧人的王國。🕉

第三十章

大學逃難

中日戰爭爆發以後，原來集中在沿海省份的大學紛紛遷往內地，除了我前面提到過的北大、清華、南開三所大學之外，接近戰區以及可能受戰爭影響的高等學府都逐漸向內地遷移，到抗戰快結束時，在內地重建的大學和獨立學院，數目當在 20 左右，學生總數約 1 萬 6,000 人。

這些學府四散在內地各省。有的借用廟宇祠堂，有的則借用當地學校的一部分校舍上課。公共建築找不到時，有的學校就租用私人宅院，也有些學校臨時搭了茅篷土屋。所有學校都已盡可能帶出來一部分圖書儀器，數量當然很有限，然而就是這一點點簡陋的設備也經常受到敵機故意而無情的轟炸。

許多學生是從淪陷區來的，父母對他們的接濟自然斷絕了；有些學生甚至與戰區裏的家庭完全音信不通。有些在淪陷區的家長，雖然明知子弟在內地讀書，遇到敵偽人員查問時，寧願把兒子報成死亡，以免招致無謂的麻煩。後來由政府撥了大筆經費來照顧這些無依無靠的學生。

因為日本侵略是從華北開始的，所以最先受到影響的大學自然是在平津區的學校。平津區陷敵以後，許多教員和學生知道在侵略者的刺刀下絕無精神自由的希望，結果紛紛追隨他們的學校向南或其他地方轉進。當時政府尚在南京，看到這種情形，便下令在後方成立兩個聯合大學，一個在長沙，另一個在西北的西安。西北聯大包含過去的兩個國立大學和兩個獨立學院。它後來從西安遷到漢中，因為校舍分散，結果多少又回復了原來各單位的傳統。

戰事蔓延其他各地以後，原來還能留在原地上課的大學也步我們的後塵內遷了。結果國立中央大學從南京搬到戰時首都重慶，浙江大學從杭州搬到貴州，中山大學從廣州搬到雲南。

我想詳細地敍述一下長沙臨時大學的情形，它是怎麼聯合起來的，後來又如何從長沙遷移到昆明。這故事也許可以說明一般大學播遷的情形。

我在前面已談到，長沙臨時大學是原在北平和天津的三所大學奉教育部之命聯合而成的。這三所大學就是國立北京大學、國立清華大學和私立南開大學。三所大學的校長成立校務委員會，教職員全部轉到臨時大學。民國 26 年 (1937 年) 00 月 1 日在長沙復課，註冊學生有從原來 3 個大學來的約 1,250 人，以及從其他大學轉來的 220 名借讀生。雖然設備簡陋，學校大致還差強人意，師生精神極佳，圖書館圖書雖然有限，閱覽室卻經常座無虛席。但是民國 27 年初，也就是南京失陷以後，情形可不同了。日本飛機把長沙作為轟炸目標之一。在長沙久留是很危險的，結果臨時大學在第一學期結束後，經政府核准於 27 年 2 月底向西南遷往昆明。

從長沙西遷昆明是分為兩批進行的，一批包括 300 名左右男生和少數教授，他們組織了一個徒步旅行團，從湖南長沙穿越多山的貴州省一直步行到雲南的昆明，全程 3 千 5 百公里，約合 1 千 1 百 60 哩，耗時 2 月零 10 天。另外一批約有 800 人，從長沙搭被炸得瘡痍滿目的粵漢路火車到廣州，由廣州坐船到香港，再由香港轉到海防，然後又從海防搭滇越鐵路到達昆明。他們由火車轉輪船，再由輪船轉火車，全程約耗 10 至 14 天，視候車候船的時日長短而有不同。另有 350 名以上的學生則留在長沙，參加了各種戰時機構。

搬到昆明以後，「長沙臨時大學」即改名「國立西南聯合大學」，簡稱「聯大」。因為在昆明不能立即找到合適的房子容納這許多新客，聯大當局決定把文學院和法商學院設在雲南第二大城蒙自。民國 27 年 5 月初聯大開課時，4 個學院的學生總數約在 1 千 3 百人左右。同年 9 月間，文學院和法商學院由蒙自遷回昆明，因為當地各中學均已遷往鄉間，原有校舍可以出租，房間問題已不如過去那麼嚴重。這時適值聯大奉教育部之令成立師範學院，真是「雙喜臨門」。5 院 26 系的學生人數也增至 2 千人。

民國 28 年 9 月間，聯大規模再度擴充，學生人數已達 3 千人。聯大過去 10 個月來新建造的百幢茅屋剛好容納新增的學生。抗戰結束時，我們共有 5 百左右的教授、助教和職員以及 3 千學生。多數學生是從淪陷區來的。他們往往不止穿越一道火線才能到達自由區，途中受盡艱難險阻，有的甚至在到達大後方以前就喪失了性命。

我的兒子原在上海交通大學讀書，戰事發生後他也趕到昆明來跟我一起住。他在途中就曾遭遇到好幾次意外，有一次，他和一羣朋友坐一條小船，企圖在黑夜中偷渡一座由敵人把守的橋樑，結果被敵人發現而遭射擊。另一次，一羣走在他們前頭的學生被敵人發現，其中一人被捕，日人還砍了他的頭懸掛樹上示眾。

我有一位朋友的兒子從北平逃到昆明，在華北曾數度穿越敵人火線，好幾次都受到敵人射擊。他常常一整天吃不到一點東西，晚上還得在夜色掩護下趕好幾里路。他和他的兄弟一道離開北平，但是他的兄弟卻被車站上的日本衞兵抓走送到集中營去了，因為他身上被搜出了學生身份的證件。他們是化裝商店學徒出走的，但是真正的身份被查出以後，就會遭遇嚴重的處罰。

據說北大文學院的地下室已經變為恐怖的地牢。我無法證實這些傳說，不過後來我碰到一位老學生，在他設法逃出北平到達大後方以前，曾經被捕坐了兩年牢。據他說，他曾被送到北大文學院地下室去受「招待」。那簡直是活地獄。敵人把冷水灌到他鼻子裏，終至使他暈過去。他醒過來時，日本憲兵上村告訴他，北大應該對這場使日本蒙受重大損害的戰爭負責，所以他理應吃到這種苦頭。上村怒不可遏地說：「沒有甚麼客氣的，犯甚麼罪就該受甚麼懲罰！」他曾經連續三次受到這種「招待」，每次都被灌得死去活來，他在那個地牢裏還看到過其他的酷刑，殘酷的程度簡直不忍形諸筆墨。女孩子的尖叫和男孩子的呻吟，已使中國歷史最久的學府變為撒旦統治的地獄了。

留在北平的學生在敵人的酷刑下呻吟呼號，在昆明上課的聯大則受到敵機的無情轟炸。轟炸行為顯然是故意的，因為聯大的校址在城外，而且附近根本沒有軍事目標。校內許多建築都被炸毀了，其中包括總圖書館的書庫和若干科學實驗室。聯大的校舍約有三分之一被炸毀，必須盡速再建。但是敵機的轟炸並沒有影響學生的求學精神，他們都能在艱苦的環境下刻苦用功，雖然食物粗劣，生活環境也簡陋不堪。

學術機構從沿海遷到內地，對中國內地的未來發展有很大的影響，大羣知識分子來到內地各城市以後，對內地人民的觀念思想自然發生潛移默化的作用。在另一方面，一向生活在沿海的教員和學生，對國家的了解原來只限於居住的地域，現在也有機會親自接觸內地的實際情況，使他們對幅員遼闊的整個國家的情形有較真切的了解。

大學遷移內地，加上公私營工業和熟練工人、工程師、專家和經理人員的內移，的確具有劃時代的意義。在戰後的一段時期裏，西方影響一向無法到達的內地省份，經過這一次民族的大遷徙，未來開發的機會已遠較以前為佳。🕮

第三十一章
戰時之昆明

　　北大等校內遷以後，我也隨着遷居滇緬路的終點昆明。珍珠港事變爆發以前，我曾一度去過緬甸，並曾數度赴法屬印度支那及香港。當時以上數地與昆明之間均有飛機可通。法國對德投降以後，日本不戰而下法屬印度支那，因此我們就築了滇緬路與仰光銜接。珍珠港事變以後，緬甸亦陷敵手，我國與法屬印度支那的海防以及緬甸的仰光，陸上交通均告斷絕，昆明亦陷於孤立狀態。租借法案下運華的軍火，只好由空運飛越隔絕中印兩國的喜馬拉雅山的「駝峰」，才免於中斷。

　　抗戰期間，我曾數度坐飛機去重慶，也曾一度去過四川省會成都。重慶是戰時的首都，位於嘉陵江與長江匯合之處。嘉陵江在北，長江在南，重慶就建在兩江合抱的狹長山地上，看起來很像一個半島。房子多半是依山勢高下而建的，同時利用屋後或屋基下的花崗岩山地挖出防空洞，躲避空襲。日本飛機經年累月，日以繼夜地濫炸這個毫無抵抗力的山城，但是重慶卻始終屹立無恙。成千累萬的房屋被燒毀又重建起來，但是生命損失卻不算太大。敵人企圖以轟炸壓迫戰時政府遷出重慶，但是陪都卻像金字塔樣始終雄踞揚子江頭，它曾經受過千百年的磨練考驗，自然也能再經千百年的考驗。重慶可以充分代表中國抵抗日本侵略的堅忍卓絕的精神。

　　重慶之西約半小時航程處是平坦的成都市。成都和北平差不多一樣廣大，街道寬闊，整個氣氛也和故都北平相似。成都西北的灌縣有兩千年前建設的水利系統，至今灌溉着成都平原百萬畝以上的肥沃土地。嚴重的水災或旱災幾乎從來沒有發生過。這塊廣大豐饒的平原使四川成為「天府之國」，使重慶人民以及駐防省境和附近地區的軍隊，糧食得以供應無缺。

學校初遷昆明之時，我們原以為可經法屬印度支那從歐美輸入書籍和科學儀器，但是廣州失陷以後，軍火供應的幹線被切斷，軍火都改經滇越線運入。滇越鐵路軍運頻繁，非軍用品根本無法擠上火車。我們運到越南的圖書儀器，只有極少一部分獲準載運入滇。

這時候，長江沿岸城市已相繼陷入敵手，日軍溯江直達宜昌，離長江三峽只是咫尺之遙。最後三峽天險也無法阻遏敵人的侵略狂潮而遭到鐵騎的蹂躪。

每當戰局逆轉，昆明也必同時受到災殃。影響人民日常生活最大的莫過於物價的不斷上漲。抗戰第 2 年我們初到昆明時，米才賣法幣 6 塊錢一擔（約 80 公斤）。後來一擔米慢慢漲到 40 元，當時我們的一位經濟學教授預言幾個月之內必定會漲到 70 元，大家都笑他胡說八道，但是後來 1 擔米卻真的漲到 70 元。法屬安南投降和緬甸失陷都嚴重地影響了物價。

物價初次顯著上漲，發生在敵機首次轟炸昆明以後，鄉下人不敢進城，菜場中的蔬菜和魚肉隨之減少。店家擔心存貨的安全，於是提高價格以圖彌補可能的損失。若干洋貨的禁止進口也影響了同類貨物以及有連帶關係的土貨的價格。煤油禁止進口以後，菜油的價格也隨之提高。菜油漲價，豬油也跟著上漲。豬油一漲，豬肉就急起直追。一樣東西漲了，別的東西也跟著漲。物價不斷上漲，自然而然就出現了許多囤積居奇的商人。囤積的結果，物價問題也變得愈加嚴重。鐘擺的一邊盪得愈高，運動量使另一邊也擺得更高。

控制物價本來應該從戰事剛開始時做起，等到物價已成脫韁野馬之後，再來管制就太晚了。一位英國朋友告訴我，英國農人在第一次世界大戰時曾經大發其財，但是第二次大戰一開始，農產品就馬上受到管制了。這次戰爭在中國還是第一次大規模的現代戰爭，所以她對這類問題尚無經驗足資借鑒。

昆明的氣候非常理想，它位於半熱帶，海拔約 6000，整個城有點像避暑勝地。但是因為它的面積大，居民並不認為它是避暑勝地。昆明四季如春，夏季多雨，陣雨剛好沖散夏日的炎暑。其他季節多半有溫煦的陽光照耀着農作密茂的田野。

在這樣的氣候之下，自然是花卉遍地，瓜果滿園。甜瓜、茄子和香橼都大得出奇。老百姓不必怎麼辛勤工作，就可以謀生糊口；因此他們的生活非常悠閒自得。初從沿海省份來的人，常常會為當地居民慢吞吞的樣子而生氣，但是這些生客不久之後也就被悠閒的風氣同化了。

昆明人對於從沿海省份湧到的千萬難民感到相當頭痛。許多人帶了大筆錢來，而且揮霍無度，本地人都說物價就是這批人抬高的，昆明城內到處是從沿海來的摩登小姐和衣飾入時的仕女。入夜以後他們在昆明街頭與本地人一齊熙來攘往，相互摩肩接踵而過。房租迅速上漲，旅館到處客滿，新建築像雨後春筍一樣出現。被飛機炸毀的舊房子，迅速修復，但是新建的房子究竟還是趕不上人口增加的速度。

8 年抗戰，昆明已變得面目全非。昔日寧靜的昆明城，現已滿街是卡車司機，發國難財的商人，以及營造商、工程師和製造廠商。軍火卡車在城郊穿梭往返。

自然環境和名勝古跡卻依然如昔。昆明湖的湖水仍像過去一樣平滑如鏡，依舊靜靜地流入長江，隨着江水奔騰 2000 里而入黃海。魚兒和鵝鴨仍像往昔一樣遨遊在湖中。古木圍繞的古寺雄踞山頭，俯瞰着微波蕩漾的遼闊湖面。和尚還是像幾百年前的僧人一樣唸經誦佛。遙望天邊水際，我常常會想入非非：如果把一封信封在瓶子裏投入湖中，它會不會隨湖水流入長江，順流經過重慶、宜昌、漢口、九江、安慶、南京而漂到吳淞江口呢？說不定還會有漁人撿起藏着信件的瓶子而轉到浙江我的故鄉呢！自然，這只是遠適異地的思鄉客的一種夢想而已。

縱橫的溝渠把湖水引導到附近田野，灌溉了千萬畝肥沃的土地。溝渠兩旁是平行的堤岸，寬可縱馬馳驅；我們可以悠閒地放馬暢遊，沿着漫長的堤防跑進松香撲鼻的樹林，穿越蒼翠欲滴的田野。

城裏有一個石碑，立碑處據說是明朝最後的一位流亡皇帝被縊身死的故址。石碑立在山坡上，似乎無限哀怨地凝視着路過的行人。這可憐的皇帝曾經逃到緬甸，結果卻被叛將吳三桂劫持押回中國。吳三桂原來奉命防守長城抗禦清兵，據傳說他是為了從闖王李自成手中援救陳圓圓，終於倒戈降清。他為了鎮壓西南的反抗被派到雲南，已經成為他階下囚的永曆帝被帶到他的面前受審。

「你還有甚麼話要說沒有？」據說吳三桂這樣問。

「沒有，」明代的末朝皇帝回答說，「唯一我想知道的事是你為甚麼背叛我的祖上？你受明室的恩澤不能不算深厚吧？」

吳三桂聞言之下，真是心驚膽戰，他馬上下令絞死這位皇帝。後人在那裏立了紀念碑，上刻：「明永曆帝殉國處。」

離城約十公里處有個黑龍潭。春天裏，澄澈的潭水從潭底徐徐滲出，流入小溪淺澗。黑龍潭周圍還有許多古寺和長滿青苔的大樹。明朝末年曾有一位學者和他的家人住在這裏。崇禎帝殉國和明朝滅亡的消息傳來以後，他就投身潭中自殺了。他的家屬和僕人也都跟着跳入潭中，全家人都以身殉國，後來一齊葬在黑龍潭岸旁。西洋人是很難了解這件事的，但是根據中國的哲學，如果你別無辦法拯救國家，那末避免良心譴責的唯一方法就是以死殉國。抗戰期間，中國軍人以血肉之軀抵抗敵人的彈雨火海，視死如歸；他們的精神武裝就是這種人生哲學。

這個多少依年分先後記述的故事到此暫告段落。後面幾章將討論中國文化上的若干問題，包括過去的、現在的和未來的；同時我們將討論若干始終未能解決的全國性問題，這些問題在未來的年月裏也將繼續存在。

從 1842 年香港割讓到 1941 年珍珠港事變，恰恰是一世紀。《西潮》所講的故事，主要就是這一段時期內的事情。英國人用大炮轟開了中國南方的門戶，開始向中國輸入鴉片和洋貨，但同時也帶來了西方的思想和科學的種子，終於轉變了中國人對人生和宇宙的看法。中國曾經抵抗、掙扎，但是最後還是吸收了西方文化，與一千幾百年前吸收印度文化的過程如出一轍。英國是命運之神的工具，她帶領中國踏入國際社會。

中國所走的路途相當迂迴，正像曲折的長江，但是她前進的方向卻始終未變，正像向東奔流的長江，雖然中途迂迴曲折，但是終於經歷 2000 多里流入黃海。它日以繼夜、經年累月地向東奔流，在未來的無窮歲月中也將同樣地奔騰前進。不屈不撓的長江就是中國生活和文化的象徵。❀

現代世界中的中國

第三十二章

中國與日本 —— 談敵我之短長

　　日本在培利上將抵達以前，只是中國大陸文化的一支而且是很單純的一支。自從這位海軍上將來過以後，日本就變為中西文化的混合體了。除非你能同時了解中國和西方，否則你就無法了解日本。

　　但是單單了解日本的中西兩種文化的來源是不夠的。分支可能與它們的主體相似，但是並不完全相同。把相似的東西看成完全相同而遽下斷語，很可能差以毫釐而謬以千里。同時，兩種文化的混合，還可能使原來文化變質。

　　中國大陸文化在日本的支流導源於唐朝（618—905 年）。唐代文化中許多可貴的成分，其中包括從西域輸入的印度文化與從伊蘭民族間接輸入的希臘文化，在中國因千餘年來歷經異族侵略，已逐漸衰落，但在日本卻被保留下來了。唐代的舞蹈、音樂、美術、習俗、語音和尚武精神，都還留在日本。如果你想了解一點唐代文化，你最好還是到日本去一趟。日本以唐代文化為基礎，其中包括儒家思想並唐代所吸收的佛教文化及其他外來文化。又在南宋時代（日本鐮倉時代）輸入宋儒朱子之學，蓋隨禪僧而俱來者。因此造成在日本儒佛一致之思想。尋至明末之際，德川氏本其向來保護禪僧研究儒學之素志，於開府江戶（東京古名）時，廣招儒者講學刻書，極一時之盛。並藉新政權之威力，使儒家之學為此後日本興國之張本，而為日本發展了道德、政治、經濟、史學、數學與夫流入民間之教育。日本雖於晉初從朝鮮人王仁得《論語》、《千字文》，而在明末又輸入了陽明之學，但經世之學的中心則在朱子之學。到了咸、同之間，明治維新，以儒家經世之學與西洋近世社會科學、自然科學相接引，遂在短短數十年裏成為史無前例的東西兩洋文化的大結合，而致日本於盛強之境。並予文化祖國的中國以極大的鼓勵與興奮。在我幼年時代，我們一輩青年，都奉日本為師，希望日本反哺文化之母鳥而幫助中國復興。惜乎日本秉國的軍閥，知盡忠於己，而不知施恕於人。知義而不知仁，見小而不見大，識近而不識遠。致使中國近 60 年之歷史成為中日關係之慘痛史，終至鷸蚌相爭，漁翁得利，真是歷史上很大的一幕悲劇。

我們此後應把中國文化廣稱為大陸文化，作為中國、日本、韓國、越南共有之文化，亦猶希羅文化 (希臘羅馬合流之文化) 之為歐美各國共同之文化。若在文化方面抱狹義之國家主義，則反將文化之價值減低了。

實際言之，唐代文化所包含外來因素既廣且多，在當時已成為國際文化，因其來甚漸，故國人不自覺耳。日本於吸收唐代文化時，亦於不知不覺中吸收了當時的國際文化，此亦日本之大幸也。

日本善於效法。她效法唐宋的文化而定立國之基礎；她效法英國建立海軍；效法德國訓練陸軍；效法美國發展工業。她效法 19 世紀的西方建立殖民帝國 —— 只可惜晚了一步。她效法德國閃電戰術而發動珍珠港的突擊 —— 只可惜太遠了一點。

我很欽佩日本的善於模仿，這是中國所做不到的，因為她在這方面似乎有點笨腳。但中國創造能力彌補了這一缺憾，她創造又創造，一直到唐代衰亡。此後千餘年歷經異族侵略、飢饉、疾病等災禍，終至精疲力竭。

美國的情形和日本很相似，美國文化是歐洲文化的一支，所不同的是從英國來的早期殖民者是帶愛好自由的種子而俱來的。因此美國創造又創造，直到她成為世界上最工業化的國家，同時也是最重理想和人道的國家。美國的偉大就在於這兩種矛盾因素的溶而為一。

日本在國際舞台上的空前成就，應該完全歸功於依循西方路線所進行的改革。這些改革是在世襲的統治階級領導下完成的。他們孕育於尚武精神之中，效法他國並使之適應本國，對於領袖和祖國更是精忠不貳。他們統治下的老百姓，最大的美德就是擁護領袖，服從命令。因此從明治初年開始的日本改革運動，始終是堅定不移地朝着固定目標前進。

回頭看看我們自己：中國的改革卻必須從基層開始，也就是由下而上的。我們沒有世襲的統治階層，除了相當於貴族的士大夫階級之外，也沒有貴族階級，要使這遼闊的國度裏的人民萬眾一心，必須仰仗老百姓之間的學者領袖來驅策督導。因此改革的過程必然很緩慢，而且迂迴曲折。政治領袖像孫中山先生，學者領袖像章太炎、梁任公、蔡孑民諸先生，都是來自民間的學者。他們來自民間，又帶着能根據他們的社會理想和知識上的遠見而深入民間。

現代日本是統治階級建立起來的，現代中國係平民百姓所締造。因此，在日本當一個領袖要容易得多，他可以任意獨裁，他要人民做甚麼，人民就會做甚麼；在中國當一個領袖的卻必須教育人民，而且真正地領導人民——這是一種遠為困難的才能，也必須具備超人的才智創造能力。

中國在採取改革措施方面每較遲緩，但是她一旦決心改革，她總希望能夠做得比較徹底。在過去的 100 年中，她從製造炮彈着手，進而從事政治改革、社會改革，乃至介紹西方思想。她揚棄了舊的信仰，另行建立新的，直至這些信仰成為她生活中不可分的一部分為止。她是一位學者，一位道德哲學家，也是一位藝術家。她的文化是從她的生活發展而來的，她不會輕易滿足於西方的思想觀念，除非她能夠把這些觀念徹底同化而納之於她的生活之中。因此與日本比起來，中國的思想是現代化的，但是她的社會和工業建設卻仍舊落在日本之後。這是這位哲學家兼夢想家的天性使然。

中國胸襟寬大，生活民主，而且能自力創造，但是她缺乏組織、紀律和尚武精神。她是學者之國，最受尊敬的是學問，最受珍視的是文化。但是保衛國土的武力則尚待建立。中國的優點正是她的弱點所在。

日本的情形也是優劣互見，日本人是位鬥士，也是位很幹練的行政人員。日本所吸收的西方文明只是軍事方面的上層結構，並未觸及人民較深一層的生活和思想，她的上層結構固然現代化了，她的精神和觀念卻仍然是中世紀的。對這種情形，讀者自然不會感到驚奇，因為封建制度廢除的時間甚短，故封建精神在明治時代仍然存在，中國則在西曆紀元以前就已經廢除了。

日本對同化中國文化和西方文化都只有部分的成功。例如日本對忠和恕這兩個重要的道德觀念只學到忠，卻無法了解恕。這或許受政治與地理環境之影響而使然，然而日本人之不能以恕道待人，卻是事實。忠和恕是中國生活的兩大指導原則，忠在封建國家或黷武國家是必不可少的品德，恕則是學者的美德。日本一向堅執己見，不肯考慮別人的觀點。日本人胸襟狹窄，連他們自己都有此自覺，這種褊狹的心理使他們無法具備建立洲際殖民帝國所必需的領導能力。他們有野心，有武力，但是缺乏政治家風度。所以他們藉武力而建立的「東亞共榮圈」，只如空中樓閣，頃刻幻滅。忠和恕在中國卻是攜手同行的。她不但忠貞，而且處處為人設想。中國並不覺得忠於她自己的思想觀念就應該排斥他人的觀點。她常常設身處地考慮別人的觀點，這就是所謂恕。日本人對恕的觀念很薄弱，所以不克了解中國。

日本的行為很像一個身體健壯的頑童。他抓住了公羊的兩隻角不許它動，公羊急得亂叫亂跳，用角來撞他，結果他不是被迫放手，就是被撞倒地上。他想不通這只公羊為甚麼這樣不聽話。可憐的孩子！他應該想想如果有人抓住他的兩隻耳朵，他的反應又如何？他應該設身處地想一想，這樣他就會了解中國了。

使日本人變為好戰民族的另一重要因素，是他們的一種錯誤信念，他們認為日本是個神聖的國家，係神所締造，而且應該根據神的意志行事，並且征服世界。這種心理是由軍閥御用的歷史家歪曲史實所造成的。為西洋人或中國人所不易了解，但是日本人卻的確如此深信不疑。中國人也相信神佛，但是他們把神佛當作道德的監護者，而不是戰爭的呵護者。日本人卻認為日本稱霸是神的意旨。

從悠遠的年代以來，日本的統治階級一直相信神佛在戰時總是站在大日本這一邊的。元朝不克征服她時，他們就認為那是神佛以無邊的法力保護了她。他們認為吹毀忽必烈汗蒙古艦隊的颱風就是神佛的意旨。我修改本稿時，已在戰後 10 多年了，還在日本箱根遇見一位老尼。她說人們應該信佛，日本打敗蒙古人，就靠佛的法力的。日本人一直相信歷代天皇都是神的嫡親後裔。直到戰後，日本歷史家得到言論自由，才用科學方法，把那些凝結在教科書裏的神話，一口氣吹散了。

中國某大學的一位教授，原是東京帝大的畢業生，他曾作過一件發人深省的歷史研究工作，說明了這種宗教性的愛國熱狂如何發展為日本帝國主義。這種宗教性的愛國熱狂表現於軍人日常生活者更是屢見不鮮。中日戰爭期間，幾乎所有日本士兵身上都帶着佛教或神道的護身符。我曾經見過許多由中國士兵從戰場撿回來的這種護身符。中國士兵因為見得多了，就把這些護身符看作敵人裝備中必備的一部分，除了偶而拿它們開開玩笑之外，並不拿它們當回事。

其次美國空軍與日本入侵飛機發生空戰之後，我曾經權充嚮導，領了一羣美國官兵，乘吉普車經過好幾里崎嶇的山路，去看一架被擊落墜毀的日本轟炸機殘骸。我們從飛行員的屍身上和口袋裏發現常見的佛教和神道的護身符，符上滿是血跡，且已為槍彈所洞穿。一位美軍上尉從日本飛行員屍體上撿出一塊布符，問我那是甚麼。我告訴他那是符。

「那是做甚麼用的？」上尉問道。

「求神佛保佑。」我回答說。

「不過，佛好像並沒有保佑他 —— 」他翻過布符，想看看上面無法辨認的符號究竟說些甚麼，說了一聲「我真不懂」，接着隨手把布符往地上一丟，就立刻把它忘了。中國人也像這位美國軍官一樣，對於這種刀槍不入的表徵始終一笑置之。世界各地人士也是如此。

那次空戰時，我曾經看到 7 架敵機冒着白煙迴旋下墜。其他的搜索隊也從敵機殘骸中撿回許多類似的符，以及彈藥、地圖和科學圖表。這是中世紀迷信和現代科學一種奇怪的混合，但是日本人絕不以為那是迷信；一種存在於冥冥之中的神聖力量驅策着他們為國家奮鬥，神佛則隨時隨地在呵護他們，護符只是那種神聖力量的象徵而已。

香港陷落以後，有一對我很熟識的黃氏夫婦住在香港，他們很了解日本人的心理，當一位日本士兵進他們房子盤查時，他們就送了一尊佛像給他。這位日本兵由香港赴九龍時，所乘小船不意覆沒，船上乘客除他之外全體沒頂。他後來回來向黃氏夫婦道謝，因為他相信是那尊佛像救了他的命。但是按照中國人的想法，他之沒有被淹死，不過是運氣而已。

世界人士對於日本人在戰時的宗教狂熱所知不多，因為日本人自己在他們的宣傳中很少提到它。但是在中國，現代科學卻已削弱了舊的信仰，而且成為使舊信仰解體的一個因素。在日本，現代科學反而成為神的一種有力武器，使日本在侵略戰爭中團結一致。這種由強烈的宗教性愛國心所形成的心理背景，終使日本軍閥無可理喻，使日本兵難於制服，使日本本身成為世界的一個威脅；這就是宗教狂熱與現代科學結合的結果。

任何國家有這一位瘋狂的鄰居都會頭痛。在過去 60 年的動亂時代裏，日本又豈僅使我國頭痛而已！

講到這裏，我們不得不責備從明治以來至戰事結束這一時代之日本歷史家，他們仰軍閥鼻息，無古太史之風。其中雖偶有若干史家，敢批軍閥逆鱗，但在環境逼迫之下，亦屬孤掌難鳴，遂使日本歷史成為神權迷信軍權崇拜之護符。我就在碰見那老尼的同一天，在箱根的一家理髮店理髮。店主自稱其祖若父，曾在封建時代為將軍武士們束髮整容。幼時曾聽人們說，天皇的祖宗是中國人，從中國來的，這些話現在大家敢說了。以前沒有人敢說，說了要殺頭的。可見這些天皇非神說，早在武士階級及民間流傳。他還有幾句有趣的話，我們可以在此作一插曲。他好蓄古錢，在他的小小搜集裏，倒點綴了宋、元、明、清四朝的銅錢，及相當時代的日本錢，他說日本錢是用日本銅在中國鑄的。最有趣味的是，把大正、昭和兩代的硬幣排列成行。中日戰爭開始以後，硬幣步步縮小，戰事愈久，錢縮得愈小，在最後一兩年間，縮小了几等於鵝眼。他很幽默的指着說，這是代表「東亞共榮圈」的。從民間流傳的關於天皇源流故事看來，可以推想到日本歷史雖受軍閥之統制，而民間仍保存着乃祖若宗世代相傳之口史，為軍閥所不能毀滅者。

戰後因思想言論自由，近年來新出版的日本史是值得我們一讀的。昔韓宣子適魯，見易象與魯春秋，曰周禮盡在魯矣。讀日本最近出版之日本歷史並各種學術的書籍，幾乎使我與宣子有同樣的感歎！

六、七十年來，我國與日本所定的國策，同為富國強兵。日本所走的路線為資本主義與軍國主義。用資本主義所產生的財富來養兵，軍閥與財閥聯合操縱軍政大權。他們的權力超越一切黨派與學派。軍國主義與資本主義的日本，一戰而勝中國，再戰而勝帝俄，三戰橫衝直撞而轟炸到珍珠港。

我國為何想富國而國不富，想強兵而兵不強呢？

第一，內政問題。日本倒幕尊皇，政權統一已數十年。我國初則保皇革命，國是未定。繼則軍閥割據，全國擾攘。等到國民革命軍統一全國的時候，內則戰亂頻仍，外則日本侵略，內憂外患接踵而起。那裏還談得到富國強兵呢？

第二，經濟思想問題。我國儒家「不患寡而患不均」的經濟思想，先天上已有不贊成資本主義的色彩，數十年來一般士大夫復頗有仰慕王安石統制經濟之傾向，故對西洋資本主義，雖不一定反對，卻不熱心擁護。這個事實，是誰也不能否定的。只以此而論，就可知道建設一個資本主義的社會是怎樣的不容易了。

第三，門戶開放問題。中國明清兩代均採鎖國主義。日本在德川時代亦採鎖國主義。19 世紀之資本主義逼開了兩國之門。在中國稱之為通商，日本稱之為開國。然日本之開國發之於統一之政府，故全國一致而收實效。中國則此開彼閉，前迎後拒，步驟極不一致。故開國之實效未顯，而瓜分之禍兆已見。

以上對於中國與日本的比較，和對日本之批評，大部分是抗戰期間我在重慶所想到而記下來的。當全國被日軍蹂躪，千千萬萬人民在日軍鐵蹄下犧牲生命財產的期間，我這記錄似乎相當客觀和公平。這是出於儒家忠恕平衡的傳統觀念，而日本卻缺少一個恕字。對日和約，我國主張維持日本皇室，放棄賠款要求，遣送全體俘虜返國，凡此種種，雖出於政治遠見，根本思想還是出於恕道。我國人民知道「不念舊惡」為維持和平的要道，所以這種和約，為全國人民所擁護。

停戰以後，我視察了好多日本俘虜營（湘西、漢口、南京等址）；我未曾看見當地民眾對日俘有嘲笑或侮辱的舉動，使我感覺到中國人民度量的寬宏。

日本戰敗後十餘年，其國內思想頗有變動，有些地方和我們在戰前所見和戰時所論的頗有不同。如民主主義之抬頭，思想和言論之充分自由，神道迷信之漸趨薄弱，歷史之重史實而放棄傳統的虛偽，工業化之加速與產品的進步，學術研究之加速的發達。凡此種種，影響日本本身之將來與東亞之局勢者必甚大。

東歐之西德與遠東之日本，已居冷戰中重要地位。西德則站在西方民主陣線而為其重要的一環。日本則表面似傾向西方，而其內心則猶站在三岔路中，游移未定。親西方乎？中立乎？抑或傾向共產主義集團乎？現在日本各種不同之政見，歸納起來，不外乎此三點。這是日本的內心煩惱，亦是她本身的課題，而亦為西方民主集團的課題。⬤

第三十三章
敵機轟炸中談中國文化

　　東方與西方不同，因為它們的文化不同。但是你仍舊可以找出東西文化之間的相似之點。無論兩種文化如何相似，不可能完全相同，每一文化的特點也必有異於他種文化。就西方而論，不同的文化特徵使德國人異於英國人，同時也使法國人不同於荷蘭人。但是他們之間仍有共通的特徵，這些特徵使西方國家在文化上結為一體，泛稱「西方文化」。這些特徵又使他們與東方各國顯出不同。因此，文化上的異同，不應該由表面上的類似之點來判斷，而應該由各別的基本特徵來論定。

　　在這一章裏，我們將從三方面來討論中國文化的特徵：(一) 中國文化之吸收力。(二) 道德與理智。(三) 中國人的人情。

(一) 中國文化之吸收力

　　大約 50 年前，當我還在學校唸書的時候，外國人和前進的中國人都常常說，中國很像一塊絕少吸收能力，甚至毫無吸收能力的岩石，那也就是說中國文化已經停滯不前，而且成為化石，因此中國已經變得無可救藥地保守。她一直我行我素，誰也不能使這位「支那人」改變分毫。

　　這種說法表面上似乎言之成理，但是結果卻證明完全錯誤。從五口通商開始，至 1894 年中日戰爭為止，中國似乎一直在抗拒西方影響。但是在以前的幾百年內，她曾經吸收了許多先後侵入她生活之中的外來東西。

　　在音樂方面，現在所謂的「國樂」，實際上多半是用起源於外國的樂器來彈奏的。胡琴、笛和七弦琴，都是幾百年前從土耳其斯坦傳入的。我們現在仍舊保留着中國的古琴，但是只有極少數人能夠欣賞，至於能彈古琴的人就更少了。

　　從外國介紹到中國的食品更不計其數：西瓜、黃瓜、葡萄和胡椒是好幾百年前傳入中國的；甘薯、落花生、玉蜀黍則是最近幾百年傳入的；在最近的幾十年中，洋山芋、番茄、花菜、白菜和蓳菜也傳入中國了。切成小塊，用醬油紅燒的西方牛排，也已經變為一道中國菜。鍋巴蝦仁加番茄汁更是一種新花樣。中菜筵席有時也要加上冰淇淋、咖啡和金山柳丁。柑橘原是中國的土產，後來出洋赴美，在加利福尼亞經過園藝試驗家褒朋克改良後，帶着新的頭銜又回到了本鄉，與中國留學生從美國大學帶着碩士、博士的頭銜學成歸國的情形差不多。中國柑橘還在很久很久以前傳到德國，想不到柑橘到了德國卻變成了蘋果，因為德國人把柑橘叫做「中國蘋果」。

　　凡是值得吸收的精神食糧或知識養分，不論來自何方，中國總是隨時準備歡迎的。明朝時，耶穌會教士把天文、數學和聖經傳到中國。大學士徐光啟，不但從他們學習天算，而且還信仰了天主，把他在上海徐家匯的住宅作為天主教活動中心，我們從耶穌會教士學到西方的天文學，有些人因此而成為天主教徒。五口通商以後，徐家匯天文台一直是沿海航行的指針。

　　明末清初有位學者黃梨洲，他非常佩服耶穌會教士傳入的天文學。他曾說過這樣一句話，中國有許多學問因自己沒有好好地保存，所以有不少已經流到外國去了。他有一次告訴一位朋友說：「就天文學而論，我們與西方學者比起來，實在幼稚得很。」可見中國學者是如何虛懷若谷！

　　事實上正因為她有偉大的吸收能力，中國才能在幾千年的歷史過程中歷經滄桑而屹立不墜。世界上沒有任何文化能夠不隨時吸收外國因素而可維繫不墜。我想這是不必歷史家來證明的。西方各國文化間的相互依存關係和相互影響，彰彰在人耳目，無庸爭辯。但是東方文化與西方文化間的相互作用卻比較不太明顯。劍橋大學的尼鄧教授曾告訴我，火藥的膨脹性導致蒸汽機的發明，而儒家的性善學說則影響了法國大光明時代學派的思想。許多東西曾經悄無聲息地從東方流傳到西方。至於這些東西究竟是甚麼，我想還是讓西洋人自己來告訴我們罷。

但是我們除了音樂、食物之類以外，並沒有經由西面和北面陸上邊界吸收其他的東西。這些區域裏的民族，所能提供的精神食糧事實上很少，因此我們轉而求諸印度。在藝術方面，我國的繪畫和建築都有佛教的影響，佛教思想在中國哲學方面更佔着重要的地位，佛教經典甚至影響了中國文學的風格和辭藻。

　　在耶穌會教士到達中國之前好幾百年，中國人已經吸收了佛教的道德觀念，但是對佛教的超世哲學卻未加理睬。佛教傳入中國雖已有千百年的歷史，而且千千萬萬的佛教寺廟也佔據着城市和山區的最好位置，但是佛教的基本哲學和宗教在中國人的思想裏仍然是陌生的。學者們對佛教保持友善或容忍的態度，一般老百姓把它當作中國的諸多宗教之一來崇拜。但是它始終還是外國的東西。在重實用的中國人看起來，佛教的超知識主義並無可用。超知識主義所以能在中國存在，是因為它含有道德教訓，同時遇到苦難的時候，可以作精神上的避風港。中國人只想把外國因素吸收進來充實自己的思想體系；但是他們絕不肯放棄自己的思想體系而完全向外國投降。

　　中國人憑藉容忍的美德，對於無法吸收的任何思想體系都有巧妙的應付辦法。他們先吸收一部分，讓餘留的部分與本國產物和平共存。因此億萬人口中的一部分就接納了外國的思想文化，成為佛教徒、回教徒，或基督教徒，大家和睦相處，互不干擾。

　　中國歷史上最有趣味的兩件事，一件是關於道家思想的。我們把它劈成兩半。一半為老莊哲學，以此立身，為任自然而無為；以此治國，為無為而治。另一半成為道教，起於東漢張道陵之五斗米道。流入特殊社會而成幫會，二千年來，揭竿而起，改朝換代，都是與幫會有關係的。流入通俗社會則成道教。既拜神也拜佛，台灣之「拜拜」即此。通俗所迷信之閻羅王，本為印度婆羅門教冥府之司獄吏，由佛教於無意中傳來中國而入了道教。至輪迴之説，入了道教而亦忘其來源矣。

　　第二件是把佛教也劈成兩半。宗教部分入了道教，哲學部分則合道家而入了儒家。老子之無為主義，湊合了佛家之無為主義，使佛學在中國思想系統裏生了根。故宋儒常把老佛並稱。

自宋以來之儒家，可以說沒有不涉獵道家哲學與佛學的。儒家之灑脫思想，實因受其影響而來。

中國之學人，以儒立身，以道處世，近年以來加上了一項以科學處事。美國本年6月份「幸福」雜誌，以幽默的口氣，謂台灣有人對美國人說，台灣的建設靠三子。一孔子，二老子，三鬼子。問甚麼叫鬼子，則笑謂洋鬼子。

現在讓我們再回頭看一看過去50年間西方文化傳入中國的情形。在衣着方面過去30年間西化的趨勢最為顯著。呢帽和草帽已經取代舊式的帽子和頭巾；昔日電影中所看到的辮子已失去了蹤跡。女人都已燙了頭髮，短裙、絲襪和尼龍襪已使中國婦女有機會顯示她們的玉腿。女人的足更已經歷一次重大的革命，西式鞋子使她們放棄了幾千年來的纏足惡習，結果使她們的健康大為改善。健康的母親生育健康的子女，天足運動對於下一代的影響至為明顯。現代的兒童不但比從前的兒童健康，而且遠較活潑，不但行動比較迅速，心智也遠較敏銳。

在社交方面，男女可以自由交際，與過去授受不親的習俗適成強烈的對照。民法中規定，婚姻不必再由父母安排；青年男女成年以後，有權自行選擇對象。男女同校已經成為通例，男女分校倒成了例外。

在住的方面，一向左右屋基選擇的風水迷信已經漸為現代的建築理論所替代。在若干實例中，古代的藝術風格固然因其華麗或雄偉而保留了下來，但是大家首先考慮的還是陽光、空氣、便利、舒適、衛生等要件。現代房屋已經裝置抽水馬桶、洋瓷浴盆和暖氣設備。硬背椅子和硬板床已經漸為沙發及彈簧牀墊所取代。

中國菜餚花樣繁多，因為我們隨時願意吸收外國成分。西菜比較簡單，我想主要是因為不大願意採用外國材料的緣故。不錯，茶是好幾世紀以前從中國傳入歐洲的。香料也是由東方傳去。哥倫布就是為了找尋到印度的通商捷徑而無意中發現新大陸的。有人告訴我，渥斯特郡辣醬油也是從中國醬油發展而來的。但是除此以外，西菜始終很少受東方的影響。美國的「雜碎」店固然數以萬計，而且美國人也很喜歡「雜碎」，但是除此以外，他們就很少知道別的中國菜了。

中國卻一直不斷地在吸收外國東西，有時候經過審慎選擇，有時候則不分皂白，亂學一氣——不但食物方面如此，就是衣着、建築、思想、風俗習慣等等也是如此。吸收的過程多半是不自覺的，很像一棵樹通過樹根從土壤吸收養分。吸收養分是成長中樹木的本能，否則它就不會再長大。

中國由新疆輸入外國文化並加吸收的過程很緩慢，千餘年來隻點點滴滴地傳入了少許外國東西。因此她是逐步接受這些東西，有時間慢慢加以消化。大體上這是一種不自覺的過程，因此並未改變中國文化的主流，很像磁石吸收鐵屑。鐵屑聚集在磁石上，但是磁石的位置並未改變。

由華東沿海輸入的西方文化，卻是如潮湧至，奔騰澎湃，聲勢懾人；而且是在短短 50 年之內湧到的。西方文化在法國革命和工業革命之後正是盛極一時，要想吸收這種文化，真像一頓飯要吃下好幾天的食物。如果説中國還不至於脹得胃痛難熬，至少已有點感覺不舒服。因此中國一度非常討厭西方文化，她懼怕它，詛咒它，甚至踢翻飯桌，懊喪萬分地離席而去，結果發現飯菜仍從四面八方向她塞過來。中國對西方文化的反感，正像一個人吃得過飽而鬧胃痛以後對食物的反感。1898 年的康梁維新運動，只是吃得過量的毛病；1900 年的「義和團之亂」，則是一次嚴重而複雜的消化不良症，結果中國硬被拖上手術台，由西醫來開刀，這些西醫就是八國聯軍。這次醫藥費相當可觀，共計 4 億 5 千萬兩銀子，而且她幾乎在這次手術中喪命。

張之洞「中學為體，西學為用」的主張，事實上也不過是説：健全的胃比它所接受的食物對健康更重要。因此中國很想穩步前進，不敢放步飛奔。但是西方文化的潮流卻不肯等她。西潮衝擊着她的東海岸，泛濫了富庶的珠江流域和長江流域，並且很快彌漫到黃河流域。雖然她最近鬧了一場嚴重的胃病，她也不得不再吃一點比較重要的食物。

到了 1902 年，胃口最佳的學生已為時代精神所沾染，革命成為新生的一代的口頭禪。他們革命的對象包括教育上的、政治上的、道德上的，以及知識上的各種傳統觀念和制度，過去遺留下來的一切，在這班青年人看起來不過是舊日文化的骸骨，毫無值得迷戀之處。他們如飢如渴地追求西方觀念，想藉此抵消傳統的各種影響。

五口通商後不久，中國即已建立兵工廠、碼頭、機器廠和外語學校，翻譯了基本科學的書籍，而且派學生留學美國。因為她在抵抗西方列強的保衛戰中屢遭敗北，於是決定先行建立一支海軍。一支小型的海軍倒是真的建立起來了，結果卻在 1894 年被日本所毀滅。日本是無法容忍中國有海軍的。

海軍既然建不成，中國就進一步進行政治、陸軍和教育上的改革。北京的滿清政府開始準備採取西方的立憲政制；它建立了新的教育制度，組織了現代化的軍隊和警察，並且派遣了大批學生出洋留學。這可算是中國文化有史以來首次自覺地大規模吸收外國文明，其結果對往後國民生活發生了非常深遠的影響。

最重要的是教育上的改革，因為這些改革的計劃最完善，眼光最遠大，而且是針對新興一代而發的，傳統觀念對這班年輕人的影響最小。後來這班年齡相若的學生逐漸成長而在政府中掌握大權，他們又採取了更多的西洋方法，使較年輕的一代有更佳的機會吸收新的觀念思想。這年輕的一代接着握權以後，他們又進一步從事西化工作，更多的新措施也隨之介紹到政府、軍隊和學校等部門。因此新興的每一代都比前一代更現代化。

民國 8 年 (1919 年) 北京的學生運動，北大教授所強調的科學和現代民主觀念，以及胡適教授所提倡的文學革命，只是自覺地致力吸收西方思想的開端，這種努力在過去只限於工業和政治方面。這次自覺的努力比較更接近中國文化的中心，同時中國文化史也隨之轉入新頁。因為中國正想藉此追上世界潮流。中國文化把羅盤指向西方以後，逐漸調整航線，以期適應西方文化的主流。在今後 50 年內，它在保持本身特點的同時，亦必將駛進世界未來文化共同的航道而前進。

到目前為止，中國已經從西化運動中獲得很多好處。婦女與男子享受同等的社會地位，享受結婚和再嫁的自由，並且解放纏足，這就是受到西方尊重婦女的影響而來的。西方醫藥也已阻遏了猖獗的時疫，麻醉藥的應用已使千萬病人在施行手術時免除痛苦。機器和發明已經改進了生產技術，對於人民的生活提供了重大的貢獻。現代作戰武器增加了殺傷的能力，因而也招致了更大的生命損失。現代科學已經拓寬了知識範圍；中國的歷史、哲學和文學的研究工作已採用了科學方法。大家一向信守不疑的迷信，也因科學真理的啟示而漸漸失勢。我們吸收西方思想的能力愈強，我國的文化亦將愈見豐富。中國的現代化工作愈廣泛徹底，則與中國國民生活結着不解緣的貧困和疾病兩大禍患亦將隨之逐漸消滅。在這一方面，我認為現代化運動和西化運動，即使並非完全相同，也是不可分的，因為現代化運動肇始於西化，而且已經毫無間斷地向前邁進。中國無法取此而捨彼。

西方被迫現代化，多少有點像中國之被迫西化。現代發明浪潮所經之處，隨即改變了生產的方式，招致分配和控制的問題，並進而引起其他新的問題。人類必須適應日新月異的環境，進步就是由環境的不斷改變和人類適應新的環境產生的。你不妨看一看法國革命以後的歐洲情形，你或許會發現自從羅馬帝國以來，歐洲大陸在表面上幾無多大改變。但是你如果再仔細看看工業革命以後 50 年來的歐洲情形，你一定會發現許多顯著的變化。再隔 50 年之後，你又會發現整個歐洲大陸和美洲都已經遍佈了鐵路網，一列列的火車則像千萬條蜈蚣爬行在鐵路上。煙囪高聳入雲的工廠像蜂房一樣集中在工業大城裏。裝載工業成品的輪船在港口穿梭進出，準備把工廠產品運送到世界的每一角落。

半世紀以前，這些輪船曾經把自來火、時辰鐘、洋油燈、玩具，以及其他實用和巧妙的外國貨帶到中國。我童年時代在安寧的鄉村裏就曾經玩過這些洋貨。我們天真而不自覺地吸收這些新鮮的玩藝兒，實際上正是一次大轉變的開端，這次轉變結果使中國步上現代化之途，同時也經歷了相伴而生的苦難、擾攘、危險，以及舊中國恬靜生活的迅速消逝。

中國在此以前所吸收的外國東西，不論是自覺的或是不自覺的，都曾使人民生活更見充實豐富，而且並未導致任何紛擾。但是自從西方工業製品和思想制度傳入以後，麻煩就來了。正像現代的磺胺藥品，它們固然可以治病，但是有時候也會引起嚴重的副作用，甚至致人於死。中國所面臨的問題就是如何吸收西方文化而避免嚴重的副作用。此項工作有賴於實驗與科學研究，因為實驗和科學研究是推動心理、社會、工業各項建設的基本工具。不過這些工具仍然是西方的產物。

(二) 道德與理智

我在加州大學倫理學班上初次讀到希臘哲學家的著作時，我開始覺得中國古代思想家始終囿於道德範圍之內，希臘哲學家則有敏銳深刻的理智。後來我讀了更多有關希臘生活和文化的書籍以後，更使我深信古代中國思想和古希臘思想之間，的確存在著這種鮮明的對照，同時我相信就是東西文化分道揚鑣的主要原因。這種說法也許過於武斷，但是據我後來的經驗來說，我並未發現有予以修正的必要，而且我至今仍如此深信不疑。

我從美國留學回來以後，曾不斷努力使國人了解發展理智的重要，無論是上課或寫作，我總是經常提到蘇格拉底、柏拉圖和亞里斯多德等名字，以致若干上海小報譏諷我是「滿口柏拉圖、亞里斯多德的人」。我發現並沒有多少人聽我這一套，結果只好自認失敗而放棄了這項工作，同時改變策略轉而鼓吹自然科學的研究。事實上這是一種先後倒置的辦法，我不再堅持讓大家先去看源頭，反而引大家先去看看水流。他們看到水流以後，自然而然會探本窮源。

有人曾經請教一位著名的中國科學家，為甚麼中國未曾發展自然科學。他提出四個理由：第一，中國學者相信陰陽是宇宙中相輔相成的兩大原則。第二，他們相信金、木、水、火、土，五行是構成宇宙的五大要素，並把這種對物質世界的分析應用到人類生活以及醫藥方面。第三，中國人的粗枝大葉，不求甚解。這是精確計算的大敵。第四，中國學者不肯用手，鄙夷體力勞動。

這些很可能都是自然科學發展的障礙，但是即使沒有這些障礙，我也不相信自然科學就能發展起來，因為我們根本就沒有注意到這方面的工作。

我們中國人最感興趣的是實用東西。我在美國時常常發現，如果有人拿東西給美國人看，他們多半會說：「這很有趣呀！」碰到同樣情形時，中國人的反應卻多半是：「這有甚麼用處？」這真是中國俗語所謂智者見智，仁者見仁。心理狀態的不同，所表現的興趣也就不同了。我們中國對一種東西的用途，比對這種東西的本身更感興趣。

中國思想對一切事物的觀察都以這些事物對人的關係為基礎，看它們有無道德上的應用價值，有無藝術價值，是否富於詩意，是否切合實用。古希臘的科學思想源於埃及與巴比倫。巴比倫的天文學和埃及的幾何學，和中國天文數學一樣，都以實際應用為目的。但是希臘學者具有重理智的特性，他們概括並簡化各種科學原則，希望由此求出這些科學的通理。這種追求通理的過程為天然律的發現鋪平了道路。

對希臘人而言，一共有兩個世界：即官覺世界與理性世界。官覺有時會弄玄虛；所以哲學家不能信賴他的官覺的印象，而必須發展他的理性。柏拉圖堅主研究幾何學，並不是為了幾何學的實際用途，而是想發展思想的抽象力，並訓練心智使之能正確而活潑地思考。柏拉圖把思想的抽象力和正確的思考能力應用在倫理與政治上，結果奠定了西方社會哲學的基礎；亞里斯多德把它們應用在研究具體事物的真實性上，結果奠定了物質科學的基礎。

亞里斯多德相信由官覺所得知識的真實性。他並有驚人的分析的理智力，他的這種理智力幾乎在任何學問上都留有痕跡。他認為正確的知識不但需要正確地運用理性，同時也牽涉到官覺的正確運用；科學的進步則同時仰賴推理能力和觀察能力的發展。亞里斯多德從應用數學演繹出若干通則，研究與探討這些原則是一種心智的鍛煉，他便由此訓練出一種有力而深刻的理智力。憑着這種訓練有素的理智力以及官覺的正確運用，他創造了一套成為現代化科學基礎的知識系統。使西方思想系統化的邏輯和知識理論也同是這種理智鍛煉的產物。

中國思想集中於倫理關係的發展上。我們之對天然律發生興趣，只是因為它們有時可以作為行為的準則。《四書》之一的「大學」曾經提出一套知識系統，告訴我們應該先從格物着手，然後才能致知。知識是心智發展的動力。

到此為止，我們所談的還是屬於知識方面的。討論再進一步以後，道德的意味就加強了。心智發展是修身的一部分，修身則是齊家的基礎。齊家而後方能治國，國治而後方能平天下。從格物致知到平天下恰恰形成一個完整的、非常實際的、道德上的理想體系。在中國人看起來，世界和平絕非夢想，而是實際的道德體系。因為國家的安定必然是與國際和平密切關聯的。離開此目標的任何知識都是次要的或無關痛癢的。

在這種學問態度之下，查問地球究竟繞日而行，抑或太陽繞地球而運行，原是無關痛癢的事。

再說，我們何苦為沸水的膨脹而傷腦筋？瓦特實在太傻了！我們中國人倒是對沸水的嘶嘶聲更感興趣，因為這種聲音可以使我們聯想到煮茗待客的情調。那該多麼富於詩意！

蘋果落地是自然的道理，中國人可以在這件事情上找出道德意義。他們會說，一樣東西成熟了自然就掉下來。因此，你如果好好地做一件事情，自然就會得到應有的結果，為此多傷腦筋毫無好處。如果你家花園裏的蘋果不是往地下落，而是往天上飛，那倒可能使中國人惴惴不安，認為老百姓即將遭逢劫難。彗星出現，或者其他習見情形失常，中國人就是如此解釋的。只有牛頓這種人才會從蘋果落地想到地心吸力上面去。

我一度鼓吹發展理智，結果徒勞無功，原因不言而喻。這些古希臘人物和他們的學說對中國有甚麼用？在我們中國人的眼光裏，自然科學的價值只是因為它們能夠產生實際的用途。希臘哲學家離現代自然科學太遠了，他們還有些甚麼實際用途呢？我們中國人對科學的用途是欣賞的，但是對為科學而科學的觀念卻不願領教。中國學者的座右銘就是「學以致用」。

在這樣的心理狀態之下，中國未能發展純粹科學是毫不足奇的，因為純粹科學是知識興趣的表現，而非實際應用的產物。我們曾經建造長城和運河，也曾建設偉大的水利工程；我國建築式樣的宏麗，我們的宮殿和廟宇，都曾獲得舉世人士的激賞。這些工程足與世界上最偉大的工程成就相提並論。但是它們並不是純粹科學的基礎上發展而來的。因此它們無論如何偉大，也沒有進一步發展的可能，直到現代工程技術輸入以後，才見轉機。如果沒有純粹科學，現代工程科學根本無法達到目前的巔峰狀態。中國人所發明的指南針和火藥曾使全世界普受其利，但是發現火藥爆炸的膨脹原理，把這原理應用於沸水，並進而發明蒸汽機的，結果還是西洋人。

在中國，發明通常止於直接的實際用途。我們不像希臘人那樣肯在原理、原則上探討；也不像現代歐洲人那樣設法從個別的發現中歸納出普遍的定律。現代歐洲人的這種習性是從古希臘繼承而來的，不過較諸希臘時代更進步而已。中國人一旦達到一件新發明的實用目的，就會馬上止步不前；因此中國科學的發展是孤立無援的，也沒有科學思想足為導向的明燈。科學發展在中國停滯不進，就是因為我們太重實際。

我並不是說中國人不根據邏輯思考，而是說他們的思想沒有受到精密的系統的訓練。這缺點已經反映在中國哲學、政治組織、社會組織，以及日常生活之中。世界其餘各地的人民普遍享受現代科學的光明和工業社會的福利以後，這種缺點在中國已經更見顯著。

除了重實際之外，我們中國人還充滿著強烈的道德觀念。也可以說正因為我們注重道德，我們才重實際。因為道德係指行為而言，行為則必然要憑實際結果來判斷。希臘人在物理學和形而上學方面曾有離奇的幻想和推測，但是我們對行為卻不可能有同樣的幻想和推測。

有時候我們也可能闖出重實際、重道德的思想常規，但是我們一旦發覺離開倫理範圍太遠時，我們馬上就會收回心靈的觸角。宋代的朱子就曾有一次超越道德的範圍。他從山頂上發現的貝殼而推斷到山脈的成因。他認為山勢的起伏顯示千萬年以前的山脈一定是一種流體，山頂上的貝殼正可以說明，目前的山峰一度曾是深淵之底。至於這種流體何時凝結為山脈，如何凝結為山脈，以及海底如何突出水面而成高峰等等問題，他卻無法解答了。

他的推斷也就到此為止，深恐冒險前進要栽筋斗。在朱子之前以及朱子之後都曾有過同樣的觀察自然的例子，但是中國思想家在理論方面的探討一向是謹慎的，唯恐遠離倫理關係的範圍。

中國人當然不是缺乏理智的民族；但是他們的理智活動卻局限於道德與實用的範圍。他們像蠶一樣作繭自縛，自立智識活動的界限。他們深愛他們的道德之繭，而且安居不出。中國人的生活就是一種樂天知命的生活。中國哲學的目標是安定。求進步？算了吧──進步勢將招致對現狀的不滿，不滿現狀則會破壞安定，中國人很滿意現實世界，從來不想對大自然作深入的探討。中國未曾發展自然科學，只是因為她根本無意於此。

希臘人卻大不相同。亞里斯多德的思想可以上天入地，無遠弗屆。整個宇宙都是希臘理智活動的範圍。希臘人覺得運用理智，本身就是一種快樂。他們不管它是否切合實際，也不管它與道德倫理有沒有關係。據說古希臘數學家歐幾裏得的一位學生曾經這樣問過老師：「我學這些東西能得到些甚麼呢？」歐幾裏得吩咐他的僕人說：「既然他一定要從所學的裏面得到些東西，你就給他六個銅板讓他走吧。」希臘人甚至對道德也發展了一套倫理學，以理智的研究來檢討道德的正確性。蘇格拉底就是因此而招致了麻煩，被控以危險的研究毒害青年的心靈。

自然科學之能發展到目前的階段，首先歸功於希臘人對大自然的觀念以及對有系統的智力訓練的愛好，中間經過文藝復興、宗教革命、法國革命，後來又受到工業革命的大刺激。工業革命使工具和技術逐漸改進。西歐在自然科學的後期發展中，從未忽視科學的實際用途。不斷的發現和發明更進一步刺激了科學研究。理論科學和應用科學齊頭並進，而相輔相成。

五口通商以後，現代科學開始涓涓滴滴地流傳到中國時，引起中國學者注意的還是科學的實用價值。他們建立了兵工廠和輪船碼頭。他們附帶翻譯了基本科學的書籍。究竟是太陽繞地球運行或者是地球繞太陽運行，他們仍未感覺興趣。在他們看起來，那是無足輕重的，因為無論誰繞誰轉，對人都沒有實際的影響。三百多年前耶穌會教士把天文數學傳到中國時，學者們馬上發生興趣，因為這些科學可以糾正當時中國日曆上的許多錯誤。不但計算日子、月份、年份缺不得日曆，就是播種收穫，日曆也是不可或缺的。

20世紀初葉，進化論傳入中國。我國學者馬上發現它的實用的道德價值。應用「物競天擇，適者生存」這項天然律，他們得到一項結論，知道世界各國正在互相競爭以求生存，而且經過天擇之後只有適者才能生存。中國會不會是適者？她會不會生存呢？她必須競爭，為生存而競爭！進化論如需證據，只要看街頭大狗和小狗打架，小狗會被大狗咬死，小蟲碰到大蟲，小蟲會被大蟲吃掉的事實。俗語說：「大蟲吃小蟲，小蟲吃眯眯蟲。」這已經足夠證明「物競天擇，適者生存」的正確性了，又何必向達爾文討證據呢？他們就這樣輕易地為達爾文的科學研究披上了一件道德的外衣。下面就是他們道德化的結果，他們說：「弱肉強食。」中國既然是弱國，那就得當心被虎視眈眈的列強吃掉才行。

進化論的另一面則被應用於歷史上，照中國過去學者的歷史觀，世運是循環的。受了達爾文學說影響以後，他們相信世運是依直線進行的，不進則退，或者停住不動。這種歷史觀的轉變，對中國學者有關進步這一觀念產生了重大的影響。

陰陽和五行等觀念顯然是從直接觀察大自然得來，拿這些觀念來理性化宇宙的變幻和人類的行為已經綽有餘裕。我們不必作精密的計算，更不必動手。我猜想，中國學者如果有興趣從事體力勞動，他們寧願去製作實用的東西，或者美麗的藝術品，而不願在科學實驗室裏從事試驗。大家仍舊只根據自己的興趣去思想，去行動。磁鍼永遠是指向磁極的。

這樣的心理狀態自然不是純粹科學的園地。不過中國已在慢慢地、不斷地改變她的態度，她已經從運用科學進而研究純粹科學，從純粹科學進而接觸到新的思想方法，最後終於切實修正了她的心理狀態。我們已經在道德宇宙的牆上開了一扇窗子，憑窗可以眺望長滿科學與發明果實的理智的宇宙。

這種心理狀態的改變已經使大自然有了新的價值，從此以後，大自然不再僅僅是道德家或詩人心目中的大自然，而且是純粹科學家心目中的大自然。對現代中國人而言，宇宙不僅是我國先賢聖哲心目中的道德宇宙，而且是古希臘人心目中的理智宇宙。

道德家觀察大自然的目的在於發現有利倫理道德的自然法則。科學家觀察大自然則是為了發現自然法則，滿足知識上的興趣，也就是為知識而求知識。中國所吸收的現代科學已經穿越她那道德宇宙的藩籬，近代中國學人正深入各處探求真理。他們的思想愈來愈大膽，像一隻小舟在浩瀚的海洋上揚帆前進搜尋秘密的寶藏。這種知識上的解放已經使年輕的一代對某些傳統觀念採取了批評的態度，對道德、政治和社會習俗予以嚴厲的檢討，其影響至為深遠。年紀較大的一代憂慮寧靜的道德樂園將被毀滅，惋嘆太平盛世漸成過去，年輕的一代則為建築新的知識之宮而竟日忙碌。

我想這就是西方對中國的最大貢獻。

在相反的一方面，把中國的學問加以整理研究，也可能對現代科學世界提供重大的貢獻，希臘人研究巴比倫和埃及科學的結果就是如此。近年來對中國建築、醫學和實用植物學的初步科學研究已經有了可喜的成績。

世界各國的文化奠基於不同的宇宙觀。中國人所想的是一個道德的宇宙，並以此為基礎而發展了他們的文化。希臘人所想的是一個理智的宇宙，也以此為基礎發展了他們的文化。今日歐洲人的道德觀念導源於基督教教義——一個上帝所啟示的道德的宇宙。但中國人的道德宇宙是自然法則所啟示的。基督徒努力想在地球上建立一個天國，中國人卻只想建立一個和平安定的王國。

中國道德觀念本諸自然，基督的道德觀念則本諸神權；在中國人看起來，神只是大自然的一部分，在基督徒看起來，大自然卻是上帝所創造的。由此可見基督教教條與科學之間的矛盾必然是很嚴重的，西方歷史已經一再證明如此；科學與中國的道德觀念之間的矛盾卻比較緩和，因為二者的出發點都是大自然，所不同的只是發展的方向。

有人說過，基督教思想是天國的或神國的，中國思想是為人世的，希臘思想是不為人世的，換言之，即越出人世以外的。引導人類發現自然法則的就是這種超越人世的思想。自然法則是現代科學的基礎。有了現代科學，然後才有現代發明。這種不為人世的思想在科學上應用的結果，如果說未為世界帶來和平與安定，至少也已為世界帶來繁榮。

據我個人的看法，歐洲文化的發展過程就是基督教的道德宇宙與希臘的理智宇宙之間的一部鬥爭史。文藝復興、宗教革命和法國革命，都不過是長久淹沒在道德宇宙下的理智宇宙的重現而已，這些運動事實上只是同一潮流中的不同階段。最後工業革命爆發，理智宇宙經過幾百年的不斷發展，終於湧出水面，奔騰澎湃，橫掃全球。工業革命狂潮的前鋒，在我童年時代前後已經突然沖到中國；它沖破了我們的道德宇宙，破壞了我們的安定生活；《西潮》所講的正是這些故事。

道德宇宙不可能產生理智宇宙的果實，理智宇宙也不可能產生道德宇宙的果實。科學之果只能在理智之園成長，在基督教教條或中國的道德觀念之下，不可能產生任何科學。不錯，我們發現古時的墨子也有過科學思想，但是那只是他哲學體系中無關緊要的一部分，這些科學思想只是行星的衛星，墨子的哲學體系基本上仍舊是屬於道德方面的。

科學的發展有賴於人們全力以赴，需要對超越人世以外的真理持有夢寐以求的熱忱；並且有賴於不屈不撓、無休無止的思維和不偏不倚的精神去探索真理；無論身心，均須不辭勞瘁，愈挫愈奮。換一句話說，科學是人的整個靈魂從事知識活動的結果。僅憑玩票的態度，或者偶而探討大自然的奧秘，或者意態闌珊，不求甚解，絕不可能使人類榮獲科學的桂冠。

在現代科學影響之下，中國正在建立起一個新的道德體系。揚棄了迷信和那些對大自然似是而非的推斷，經過理智探究的考驗，並受到社會科學結論的支援，這些結論是根據對社會的實地調查而獲得的。

在另一方面，我們絕不可忘記中國舊的道德體系，這個舊體系是經過千百年長期的經驗和歷代不斷的努力而建立起來的，建立過程中所運用的方法或工具包括四書五經、一般文學、雕刻、音樂、家庭、戲劇、神佛、廟宇，甚至玩具，這個道德體系曾使中國人誠實可靠，使中國社會安定平靜，並使中國文化歷久不衰。道德觀念如忠、孝、仁、義、誠、信、中庸、謙沖、誠實等等都曾對中國人的心情個性有過重大貢獻。現代科學所導致的知識上的忠實態度，自將使幾千年來道德教訓所產生的這些美德，更為發揚光大。

一片新的知識園地將與新的道德觀念同時建立起來，以供新中國富於創造能力天才的發展。我們將在儒家知識系統的本幹上移接西方的科學知識。儒家的知識系統從探究事物或大自然出發，而以人與人的關係為歸趨；西方的科學知識系統也同樣從探究事物或大自然出發，但以事物本身之間的相互關係為歸趨，發展的方向稍有不同。

道德宇宙與理智宇宙將和在西方一樣在中國平行並存，一個保持安定，一個促成進步。問題在於我們是否能覓得中庸之道。

(三) 中國人的人情

我們說，學以致用，那末所謂「用」又是甚麼呢？這裏有兩大原則：第一是有益於世道人心，第二是有益於國計民生。這是為世俗所熟知的，亦即《左傳》裏所說的「正德利用厚生」。這兩大原則是先賢聖哲幾千年來訓誨的總結，他們所說所論，最後總是歸結到這兩點。學者們從先賢學到這些原則，然後又把所學傳播給老百姓。老百姓在這種影響之下已逐漸而不自覺地形成一種重常識與重人情的心理。他們根據上述兩大原則，隨時要問這樣東西有甚麼用，那樣東西有甚麼用。

輪船火車傳到中國時，大家都很願意搭乘，因為它們走得比較快。他們採用洋油燈，因為洋油燈比較亮。電話電報使消息傳遞更為便利，而且不像郵寄或者專差送遞那樣遲緩。有了鐘錶以後，可以不必看太陽就知道正確的時刻。大家購買西方貨品，因為它們能夠滿足日常生活中的實際需要。

傳教士到了中國以後，到處設立學校和醫院。中國人異口同聲地說：這些人真了不起啊，他們為患病者診療，又使貧窮的子弟受教育。當中國人上禮拜堂聽福音時，許多人的眼睛卻瞅在醫院和學校上面。他們的手裏雖然拿着《聖經》，眼睛卻偷偷地瞅着牧師從西方故鄉帶來的實用貨品。我父親與當地的一位牧師交了朋友，因為這位牧師替我們修好了抽水機，並且還送給我們咳嗽糖和金雞納霜。他非常誠實，而且對鄰居很客氣。最後一點非常重要，因為中國人不但實際，而且最重道德。那末，他們所宣揚的宗教怎麼樣？哦，那是一個好宗教，它是勸人為善的。那末，他們的上帝呢？哦，當然，當然。你說他們的上帝嗎？他是個好上帝呀。我們要把它與其他好神佛一齊供奉在廟宇裏。我們應崇拜它，在它的面前點起香燭。但是它不肯與你們的偶像並供在廟宇裏又怎麼辦呢？那末，我們就給它也塑個偶像吧！不行，那怎麼可以？它是無所不能，無所不在的。上帝就在你身上，而不是在偶像上。哦，是的，是的。不過它不在我身上時，也許喜歡託身在偶像上呢。不，它住在天堂。是，是，我知道，其它神佛不也都是住在天上嗎？不過，他也許願意到下界來玩玩，拿廟宇作旅館暫住，那時候我們就可以在廟宇裏祭拜它了。不行，它是獨一無二的神 —— 你崇拜它，就不能崇拜其他的神佛。

這可使中國人頗費躊躇了。最後他們說，好吧，你們崇拜你們的上帝，我們還是崇拜我們的神佛算了。「信者有，不信者無。」中國對宗教的包容並蓄，其故在此。

西方人所了解的現代法律觀念在中國尚未充分發展。中國人以為最好是不打官司。不必訴諸法律就能解決糾紛不是很好嗎？還是妥協算了！讓我們喝杯茶，請朋友評個理，事情不就完了？這樣可以不必費那麼多錢，不必那麼麻煩，而且也公平得多。打官司有甚麼用？你常常可以在縣城附近的大路旁邊看到一些石碑，上面刻着「莫打官司」四個大字。

這或許就是中國人不重法律的原因。但是現代工商業發達以後，社會也跟着變得複雜了，處理複雜的社會關係的法律也成為必需的東西，法律成為必需時，通達人情的中國人自將設法發展法律觀念。但是，如果能憑飲杯茶，評個理就解決事端，法院的負擔不是可以減輕了嗎？

己所不欲，勿施於人。批評家說這是消極的，「己之所欲，施之於人」

才算積極。不錯，這說法很正確。但是中國人基於實際的考慮，還是寧願採取消極的作風。你也許喜歡大蒜，於是你就想強迫別人也吃大蒜，那是積極的作法。我也許覺得大蒜味道好，別人卻未必有同樣的感覺；他們也許像太太小姐怕老鼠一樣怕大蒜。如果你不愛好臭味沖天的大蒜，難道你會高興別人硬塞給你吃嗎？不，當然不。那末，你又何必硬塞給別人呢？這是消極的，可是很聰明。因為堅持積極的辦法很可能惹出麻煩，消極的作風則可避免麻煩。

以直報怨，以德報德。自然，更高的理想應該是愛敵如己。但是歷史上究竟有多少人能愛敵如己呢？這似乎要把你的馬車趕上天邊的一顆星星，事實上，那是達不到的。以直報怨則是比較實際的想法。所以中國人寧捨理想而求實際。

音樂有沒有用處？當然很有用。它可以陶冶性情，可以移風易俗。

藝術有沒有用處？當然很有用。藝術可以培養人民的高尚情操，有益於世道人心。花卉草木、宮殿廟宇、山水名畫、詩詞歌賦、陶瓷鐘鼎、雕塑篆刻等等都足以啟發人的高尚情操。

一個人為甚麼必須誠實呢？因為你如果不誠實，不可靠，人們就不會相信你，你在事業上和社交上也會因此失敗，不誠實是不合算的。誠實不但是美德，它的實際效果對人與人之間的關係也有很大的價值。中國人愛好幽默。為甚麼？因為幽默的話不會得罪人；而且你可從幽默中覓得無限的樂趣。你如果常常提些無傷大雅而有趣的建議，你一定可以與大家處得更好。幽默使朋友聚晤更覺融洽，使人生更富樂趣。

有恆為成功之本。只要有恆心，鐵杵磨成針。

有一個夏天下午，杜威教授、胡適之先生和我三個人在北平西山看到一隻屎蜣螂正在推着一個小小的泥團上山坡。它先用前腿來推，然後又用後腿，接着又改用邊腿。泥團一點一點往上滾，後來不知怎麼一來，泥團忽然滾回原地，屎蜣螂則緊攀在泥團上翻滾下坡。它又從頭做起，重新推着泥團上坡，但結果仍舊遭遇同樣的挫敗。它一次接一次地嘗試，但是一次接一次地失敗。適之先生和我都說，它的恆心毅力實在可佩。杜威教授卻說，它的毅力固然可嘉，它的愚蠢卻實在可憐。這真是智者見智，仁者見仁。同一東西卻有不同的兩面。這位傑出的哲學家是道地的西方子弟，他的兩位學生卻是道地的東方子弟。西方惋嘆屎蜣螂之缺乏智慧，東方則讚賞它之富於毅力。

中國人多半樂天知命。中國人如有粗茶淡飯足以果腹，有簡陋的房屋足以安身，有足夠的衣服可以禦寒，他就心滿意足了。這種安於儉樸生活的態度使中國億萬人民滿足而快樂，但是阻滯了中國的進步。除非中國能夠工業化，她無法使人民達到高度的物質繁榮。或許在今後的一段長時間內，她的億萬人民仍須安貧樂道。

中國人深愛大自然，這不是指探求自然法則方面的努力，而是指培養自然愛好者的詩意、美感或道德意識。月下徘徊，松下閒坐，靜聽溪水細語低吟，可以使人心神舒坦。觀春花之怒放感覺宇宙充滿了蓬勃的精神；見落葉之飄零則感覺衰景的淒涼。

中國人從大自然領悟到了人性的崇高。北京有一個天壇，是用白色大理石建造的，這個天壇就是昔日皇帝祭天之所。一個秋天的夜晚，萬里無雲，皓月當空，銀色的月光傾瀉在大理石的台階上，同時也彌漫了我四周的廣大空間。我站在天壇的中央，忽然之間我覺得自己已與天地融而為一。

這次突然昇華的經驗使我了解中國人為甚麼把天、地、人視為不可分的一體。他們因相信天、地、人三位一體，使日常生活中藐不足道的人升入莊嚴崇高的精神境界。茫無邊際的空間、燦爛的太陽、澄明的月亮、浩繁的星辰、蔥翠的樹木、時序的代謝、滋潤五穀的甘霖時雨、灌溉田地的江河溪澗、奔騰澎湃的海浪江潮、高接雲霄的重巒疊嶂，這一切的一切，都培養了人的崇高精神。人生於自然，亦養於自然；他從大自然學到好好做人的道德。自然與人是二而為一的。

大自然這樣善良、仁慈、誠摯，而且慷慨，人既然是大自然不可分的一部分，人的本性必然也是善良、仁慈、誠摯，而且慷慨的。中國人的性善的信念就是由此而來。邪惡只是善良的本性墮落的結果。中國偉大的教育家和政治家始終信賴人的善良本性，就是這個緣故。偉大政治家如孫中山先生，偉大教育家如蔡孑民先生，把任何人都看成好人，不管他是張三、李四，除非張三或李四確實證明是邪惡的。他們隨時準備饒恕別人的過錯，忘記別人的罪惡。他們的偉大和開明就在這裏。所以我國俗語說：「宰相腹內可撐船」，又用虛懷若谷來形容學者的氣度。

大自然是中國的國師。她的道德觀念和她的一切文物都建築於大自然之上。中國文化既不足以控制自然，她只好追隨自然。中西之不同亦即在此。道德家和詩人的責任是追隨自然；科學家的責任則是控制自然。中國年輕一代在西方文明影響之下，已開始轉變——從詩意的道德的自然欣賞轉變到科學的自然研究。中國此後將不單憑感覺和常識的觀察來了解自然，而且要憑理智的與科學的探討來了解自然。中國將會更真切地認識自然，更有效地控制自然，使國家臻於富強，使人民改善生活。

有人以為科學會破壞自然的美感，其實未必如此。我現在一面握筆屬稿，一面抬頭眺望窗外，欣賞着花園中在雨後顯得特別清新的松樹和竹叢。在竹叢的外邊，我還可以看到長江平靜徐緩地在重慶山城旁邊流過。大自然的美感使我心曠神怡。但是我如果以植物學觀點來觀察樹木，我會想到它們細胞的生長，樹液的循環，但是這種想法並不至於破壞我的美感。如果我以地理學的觀點來看長江，我可能想到挾帶污泥的江水之下的河床，億萬年之前，這河床或許只是一塊乾燥的陸地，也可能是深海之底。這些思想雖然在我腦海掠過，但是長江優美的印象卻始終保留在我心裏，甚至使我產生更豐富的聯想。如果說對於細胞作用的知識足以破壞一個人對松樹或竹叢的美感，那是不可想像的。我覺得科學的了解只有使大自然顯得更奇妙、更美麗。

中國人因為熱愛大自然的美麗，同時感覺大自然力量之不可抗拒，心裏慢慢就形成了一種強烈的宿命論。無論人類如何努力，大自然不會改變它的途徑。因此，洪水和旱災都不是人力所能控制的，人們不得不聽任命運的擺佈。既然命中注定如此，他們也就不妨把它看得輕鬆點。天命不可違，何必庸人自擾？我們發現中國的許多苦力也笑容滿面，原因在此。苦難是命中注定的，何不逆來順受？

抗戰期間，中國人民表現了無比的忍受艱難困苦的能力，秘密就在此。盡力而為之，其餘的聽天由命就是了。你最好樂天知命。秋天的明月、六月的微風、春天的花朵、冬天的白雪，一切等待你去欣賞，不論你是貧是富。🏵

第三十四章
二次大戰期間看現代文化

　　現代文化肇始於歐洲；美國文化不過是歐洲文化的一支而已。中國文化是中華民族自己發展出來的，歷史悠久，而且品級很高。現代思潮從歐美湧到後，中國才開始現代化。在過去 50 年內，她已經逐漸蛻變而追上時代潮流，在蛻變過程中曾經遭受許多無可避免的苦難。中國已經身不由主地被西潮沖到現代世界之中了。

　　「現代文化」是個籠統的名詞。它可以給人許多不同的印象。它可以指更多更優良的作戰武器，使人類互相殘殺，直至大家死光為止。它也可以指更優越的生產方法，使更多的人能夠享受安適和奢華，達到更高的生活水準。現代文化也可以指同時促成現代戰爭和高級生活水準的科學和發明。它可以代表人類追求客觀真理，控制自然的慾望，也可以指動員資源和財富的交通建設和組織制度。對民主國家而言，它可以代表民主政治，對極權國家而言，它又可以代表極權政治。

　　這一切的一切，或者其中的任何一項，都可以叫現代文化 —— 至於究竟甚麼最重要，或者甚麼最標準，似乎沒有任何兩個人的意見會完全相同。那末，在過去多災多難的 50 年中，中國究竟在做些甚麼呢？她可以說一直在黑暗中摸索，有時候，她似乎已掉進陷阱，正像一隻蒼蠅被蜜糖引誘到滅亡之路。有時候，她又似乎是被一羣武裝強盜所包圍，非逼她屈服不可。她自然不甘屈服，於是就設法弄到武器來自衞。總而言之，她一直在掙扎，在暗中摸索，最後發現了「西方文化」的亮光，這亮光裏有善也有惡，有禍也有福。

　　哪些是她應該努力吸收的善因，哪些又是她必須拒斥的禍根呢？這問題似乎沒有一致的結論，個人之間與團體之間都是如此。她所遭遇的禍患，也可能在後來證明竟是福祉。鴉片是列強用槍炮硬加到她身上的禍害，但是她卻因此而獲得現代科學的種子。在另一方面，她接納的福祉在後來卻又可能夾帶着意想不到的禍患。例如我們因為過分相信制度和組織，竟然忘記了人格和責任感的重要。因缺乏對這些品德的強調而使新制度、新組織無法收效的例子已經屢見不鮮。

少數以剝削他人為生的人，生活水準確是提高了。汽車進口了，但是他們從來不設法自己製造。事實上要靠成千的農夫，每人生產幾百擔穀子，才能夠賺換一輛進口汽車的外匯。現代都市裏的電燈、無線電、抽水馬桶等等現代物質享受，也必須千千萬萬農夫的血汗來償付。我們以入超來提高生活水準，結果使國家愈來愈貧困。但是生活水準是必須提高的，因此而產生的禍害只有靠增加生產來補救。為了增加生產，我們必須利用科學耕種、農業機械和水利系統。

這種工作勢將引起其他新的問題。我們吃足了現代文化的苦頭，然而我們又必須接受更多的現代文化。我們如果一次吃得太多，結果就會完全吐出來。1900 年的義和團之亂就是一個例子；如果我們吃得太少，卻又不夠營養。現代文化在中國所產生的影響就是這樣。無論如何，中國還是不得不跟着世界各國摸索前進。

西方在過去一百年中，每一發明總是導致另一發明，一種思想必定引發另一種思想，一次進步之後接着必有另一次進步，一次繁榮必定導致另一次繁榮，一次戰爭之後必有另一次戰爭。唯有和平不會導致和平，繼和平而來的必是戰爭。這就是這個世界在現代文化下前進的情形。中國是否必須追隨世界其餘各國亦步亦趨呢？

大家都在擔憂發生第三次世界大戰，如果另一次大戰爭真的發生的話，很可能仍像第一次大戰一樣爆發於東歐和中歐，也可能像第二次大戰一樣爆發於中國的東三省。中歐的人民想在別處找個生存空間，至於中國的東北，則是別國人民想在那裏找生存空間。中歐是個人口稠密的區域，境內的紛擾很容易蔓延到其他區域；東三省則是遼闊的真空地帶，很容易招惹外來的紛擾。二者都可能是戰爭的導火線，戰爭如果真的發生，勢將再度牽涉整個世界，未來浩劫實不堪設想。

確保東方導火線不著火的責任，自然要落在中國的肩膀上。因此今後2、30年間，中國在政治、社會、經濟和工業各方面的發展，對於世界和平自將發生決定性的影響。一個強盛興旺的中國與西方列強合作之下，即使不能完全消弭戰爭的危機，至少也可以使戰爭危機大為減低。西方列強如能與中國合作，不但同盟國家均蒙其利，即對整個世界的和平亦大有裨益。西方國家在今後5、60年內至少應該協助中國發展天然資源，在今後20年內尤其需要協助中國進行經濟復員和社會重建的工作。

在西方潮流侵入中國以前，幾百年來的禍患可說完全導源於滿洲和蒙古。甲午中日戰爭之後，日本一躍而為世界強國，遂即與帝俄搶奪滿洲的控制權，終至觸發日俄之戰。日本處心積慮，想利用東三省作為征服全中國的跳板，結果發生 9．18 事變。如果唐朝滅亡以後的歷史發展能夠給我們一點教訓的話，我們就很有理由相信，東三省今後仍係中國的亂源，除非中國成為強大富足的國家，並且填補好滿洲的真空狀態。

在建立現代民主政治和工業的工作上，中國需要時間和有利的條件從事試驗。這些條件就是和平和安全。國內和平有賴於國家的統一。國家安全則有賴於國際間的了解。只有在東北成為和平中心時，中國才有安全可言。

我們必須從頭做起，設法把廣大的東北領土從戰亂之源轉化為和平的重鎮。在這件艱巨的工作上，我希望全世界 —— 尤其是美國、英國和蘇俄 —— 能夠與中國合作。如果她們肯合作，這件工作自然會成功，那不但是中國之福，也是全世界之福。

民國 10 年（1921 年），我承上海市商會及各教育團體的推選，並受廣州中山先生所領導的國民黨政府的支持，曾以非官方觀察員身份列席華盛頓會議。翌年我又到歐洲訪問現代文化的發祥地。那時剛是第一次世界大戰結束後不久，歐洲各國正忙於戰後復員，主要的戰勝國則忙於確保永久和平。

但是當時似乎沒有一個國家意識到，實際上他們正在幫着散佈下一次大戰的種子。

法國已經精疲力竭，渴望能有永久和平。她目不轉睛地監視着萊茵河彼岸，因為威脅她國家生存的危機就是從那裏來的。法國的防禦心理後來表現在馬奇諾防線上，她認為有了這道防線，就可以高枕無憂，不至於再受德國攻擊了。秦始皇（公元前246—前207年）築長城以禦韃靼，法國則築馬奇諾防線以抵禦德國的侵略。但是中國的禍患結果並非來自長城以外，而是發於長城之內，法國及其「固若金湯」的防線，命運亦復如是。

英國忙於歐洲的經濟復興，並在設法維持歐陸的均勢。戰敗的德國正在休養將息。帝俄已經覆亡。一種新的政治實驗正在地廣人眾的蘇俄進行。這就是第一次世界大戰後的歐洲政治情勢。

美國因為不願捲入歐洲紛擾的漩渦，已經從多事的歐陸撤退而召開華盛頓會議；九國公約就是在這次會議中簽訂的。此項公約取代了英日同盟，所謂山東問題，經過會外磋商後，亦告解決，日本對華的二十一條要求終於靜悄悄地被放進墳墓。巴黎和會中曾決定把青島贈送給日本，所謂山東問題就是因此而起的。中國人民對巴黎和會的憤慨終於觸發了學生運動，在中日關係上發生了深遠的影響，同時在此後20年間，對中國政治和文化上的發展也有莫大的影響。巴黎和會的決定使同情中國的美國政界人士也大傷腦筋，終至演化為棘手的政治問題。共和黨和民主黨都以打抱不平自任，承諾為中國申雪因凡爾賽和約而遭受的冤抑。因此，美國固然從歐洲脫身，卻又捲入了太平洋的漩渦。20年後的珍珠港事變即種因於此。

美國雖然是國際聯盟的宣導者，結果卻並未參加國聯的實際活動；法國唯一的願望是避免糾紛，防禦心理彌漫全國；英國的注意力集中在維持歐陸均勢上面；結果國際聯盟形同虛設。它只會喑喑狂吠卻從來不會咬人。但是會員本身無法解決的問題，還是一古腦兒往國際聯盟推，結果國聯就成了國際難題的垃圾堆。中國無法應付東北問題的困難時，也把這些難題推到國聯身上，因為日本是國聯的會員國。法國對瀋陽事變得漠不關心，英國所關切的只是歐洲大陸的均勢，唯恐捲入遠東糾紛，因此國聯連向日本吠幾聲的膽量都沒有。結果只懶洋洋地打了幾個呵欠，如果說那是默認既成事實，未始不可。

國聯雖然一事無成，卻是一個很有價值的教訓。世界人士可以從它的失敗中，學習如何策劃未來的和平。國聯誕生於美國之理想，結果因會員國間利益之衝突，以及列強間的野心而夭折。

凡爾賽和約訂立後約 20 年間，世局演變大致如此。由凡爾賽和約播下的戰爭種子在世界每一角落裏像野草一樣蔓生滋長，這些野草終於着火燃燒，火勢遍及全球。但是政治究竟只是過眼雲煙，轉瞬即成歷史陳跡。恆久存在的根本問題是文化。我們無法否認歐洲已經發展了現代科學和民主制度，為人類帶來了許多幸福。

在我看起來，德國是個遍地是望遠鏡、顯微鏡和試驗管的國家。她的發明日新月異，突飛猛進。上海人甚至把高級舶來品統稱為「茄門貨」（德國貨）。德國人在物質發明上的確稱得起能手，但是在人事關係上卻碌碌無能。我想，這或許就是他們無法與其他國家和睦相處的原因。他們透過望遠鏡或顯微鏡看人，目光焦點不是太遠就是太近，因而無法了解人類的行為和情感。他們不可能把國際關係或人類情緒放到試管裏去觀察它們的反應。在人類活動的廣大領域裏，德國人常常抓不到人性的要點或缺點。他們已經發展了其他民族望塵莫及的特殊才智，但是欠缺常識。他們的特長使他們在科學上窮根究底，對世界提供了許多特殊的貢獻；但是他們在常識方面的欠缺，卻使德國和其他國家同受其害。

英國人剛剛與德國人相反。他們是個常識豐富的民族，也是應付人事關係的能手。他們對國際事務的看法以及有關的政策富於彈性和適應性。他們從來不讓繩子拉緊到要斷的程度。如果拉着繩子另一端的力量比較強，英國人就會放鬆一點免得繩子拉斷。如果拉着另一端的力量比較弱，英國人就會得寸進尺地把繩子拉過來，直至人家脫手為止。但是他們絕不會放棄自己拿着的這一端 —— 他們會堅持到底，不顧後果。在國際關係和殖民政策上，英國人的這種特性隨處可見。

英國人的特性中，除了彈性和適應性之外，同時還有容忍、中庸、體諒、公平以及妥協的精神。他們的見解從來不走極端，而且始終在努力了解別人的觀點，希望自己能因此遷就別人，或者使別人來接受他們自己的觀點。他們愛好言論自由和思想自由，憎惡無法適應不同情況的刻板規律。

英國的拘謹矜持幾乎到了冷酷的程度，這是英國人最受其他民族討厭的一種特性，而且常常因此引起猜疑誤會。這種特性使英國人喪失了許多朋友。但是當你對他們有較深的認識時，或者說當他們對你了解較深時，你就會願意與他們交朋友了。

這許多特性湊合在一起時，英國的民主政治才成為可能。因為民主不是抽象的東西，也不是天上掉下來的，民主政治包含着民主先進國家的所有特長。翻開英國的憲政史，你會發現其中充滿了偏執、迫害、腐敗和殘忍的史實。許多生命，包括一位君主，曾經為民主犧牲。英國實行民主的經驗的確值得我們好好研究。

不過，我們必須記住一項事實：英國的民主政治在聯合王國達成統一之後才迅速發展，美國民主政治也是在南北戰爭之後才突飛猛進。歷史告訴我們：只有統一與安全同時並進時，有組織的民主政治才能實現。英國幸而是小島組成的王國，四圍有海洋保護着。在古代，外國侵入英國是不容易的，因此英國人得以永久安全，有足夠的時間從事民主實驗。在民主的孕育和實驗期間，英國的生存始終未受外來侵略的威脅。

美國的情形也很相似。北美大陸本身就是一個大島，周圍的海洋使它不受外來的侵略。從英國來的早期殖民者帶來愛好自由的種子，這些種子遂即滋長為自由大樹，海洋則保護了這些大樹，免受外來侵略者的斧斤之擾。經過約一百年的發榮滋長，美國的民主已經根深蒂固，不但人事方面普遍進行實驗，即在物質方面也是如此，換一句話說，科學研究之風已吹遍美洲的每一角落。美國的民主固然由英國模型發展而來，美國的科學卻受德國之惠不淺。

美國的高等教育制度是英國學院和德國大學的混合體；打個比喻，美國的學術服裝是由一件英國袍子和一頂德國帽子湊合而成的。美國大學裏男女學生的友好相處與交際自由，建立了自由研究的基礎。知識不受嚴格的管制；人與人的關係是經由學生團體的自由接觸而學到的；年輕一代的目光並未受到望遠鏡、顯微鏡或試驗管的局限；凡是有興趣的人都可以接受一種普遍文化的陶冶。

　　在大學部和研究院裏，美國學生普遍接受研究方法的訓練。德國學者的徹底精神普受讚許與提倡，但是這種徹底精神直到我進大學的時代才充分發揮。第一次世界大戰期間，中國舊國旗中的紅黃藍白黑五色一度只剩下黑白兩色。理由是德國顏料因戰事關係已無法再輸入中國。紐約一位美國化學家告訴我，在德國，通常是好幾位專家共同研究一種顏料，在美國卻是一位化學家同時研究好幾種顏料。這是 20 多年前的事了，目前的情況已經有了改變，因為在過去 2、30 年間，美國人民已經深獲德國徹底精神的訣竅。

　　英國民主和德國精神在美國攜手並進，相得益彰。美國以其豐富的天然資源，強大的組織能力，以及對大規模建設的熱誠，已經一躍而登民主國家的首座。有一天，重慶的美國大使館舉行酒會，會中一位英國外交官對我說：「英國美國化了，俄國美國化了，中國也美國化了。」

　　「英國在哪一方面美國化了呢？」我問道。

　　「好萊塢電影就是一個例子。」他回答說。

　　「那末俄國呢 —— 你是不是指大工業？」

　　「是的。」

　　這使我聯想到中國的政治制度、教育制度、社會改革和工業發展，這一切都帶着濃厚的美國色彩。但是我並沒有忘記：中國也已使沖激着她海岸的汪洋染上了她自己的色彩。

　　這位英國外交官用手指着綴有 48 顆星星的美國國旗，帶點幽默地轉身問站在他身邊的一位美國高級將領說：「這上面是 6 行星星，每行 8 顆。如果你們增加一個新的州時，你們預備怎麼安排？」

「呃，我想它們排成 7 行，每行 7 顆星就成了。但是你問這個幹甚麼？你心裏所想的是哪一個新的州？」

「英格蘭。」這位外交官回答說。我們大家都笑了。這當然只是一個笑話，但是從笑話裏，我們可以看出時代的潮流。

昔日西方在東方爭取殖民地時，西方列強除了美國之外都曾或先或後地侵略過中國。甚至連葡萄牙也從廣東省咬走一小塊土地 —— 澳門。美國取自中國的唯一東西是治外法權，但是美國所施於中國者實遠較其所取者為多。這些人人皆知的事實，用不到我浪費筆墨。現在美國與英國都已放棄了在華的治外法權，英國雖然仍舊保持香港，卻已交還了所有的租界。全世界雖然歷經戰爭慘禍，國際烏雲之中已經透露出一線曙光了。希望這一線曙光，在大戰勝利之後，能夠漸漸擴大而成為光芒萬丈的霽日。

美國已經決意參加未來的國際和平組織，她已經英勇地參加戰鬥，為永久和平而戰鬥。歷史上的一個新時代正在形成中。中、美、英、蘇俄如能合力謀求和平，再由一個有效的世界組織來維護和平，永久和平並非不可能的。

就中國而論，在未來 20 年或者 30 年裏，她尤須加倍努力，從事建設和復興。今後 2、30 年將是中國的興衰關頭。我們的努力能否成功，要看我們有無遠大眼光，有無領導人才，以及盟國與我們合作的程度而定。盟國與我們合作的程度，又要看我們國內的政治發展以及我們對國際投資所採取的政策而定。戰爭的破壞，敵騎的蹂躪，更使我們的復興工作倍形困難。

在另一方面，中國必須完成雙重的任務。第一是使她自己富強。第二是協力確保世界和平。在儒家的政治哲學裏，世界和平是最終的目的。中山先生根據儒家哲學，也把世界和平定為他的三民主義的目標。

我們如果能夠度過這二、三十年的難關，自然就可以駕輕就熟，繼續進行更遠大的改革和建設，為中國創造輝煌的將來，到那時候，中國自然就有資格協助世界確保永久的和平了。

有許多地方，中國仍得向西方學習。自從唐朝覆亡以後，中國曾經一再被來自附近亞洲地區的異族所征服。唐亡以後中國文化的衰退，就是蠻夷戎狄不斷蹂躪中國的結果。異族一再入寇中原，加上饑饉、疾病和內亂，終使中國元氣衰竭，人民創造能力大為削弱。西方影響開始侵入中國時，正是中國文化陷於最低潮的時候。

現在我們中國人一提到唐朝文化，不禁眉飛色舞，心嚮往之，滿望能恢復舊日的光榮。唐朝的文化比起後來宋朝禁欲主義的文化要近人情得多。如果我們能從唐朝文化得到些靈感與鼓舞，也未始不是一件好事。從唐人的繪畫裏，我們深深讚歎唐人體格的強健。唐朝的音樂、舞蹈、詩歌、繪畫和書法都有登峰造極的成就，後代少能望其項背。

但中國要想回到歷史上的這個輝煌時代是不可能的。千百年來我們一直在努力恢復過去的光榮，但是我們的文化卻始終在走下坡。因為環境已經改變了。唐代文化賴以滋長的肥沃土壤，已經被歷代禍亂的浪潮沖刷殆盡，但是我們如果能避免重蹈唐代滅亡的覆轍，轉向在藝術、科學、軍事、政治、衛生、財富各方面均有高度成就的現代文明國家如美國等學習，我們或許會發現唐代的光榮將有重臨的一日。在維護和平的工作上，中國的職責將是相當重大的。中國的歷史上曾經有過不少次的戰爭，但是這些戰爭多半屬於國內革命的性質。對外的比較少，國內戰爭多半是被壓迫的農民和苦難人民反抗腐敗的政府所引起。至於對外戰爭，性質上也是防禦多於攻擊。中國受外國侵略者多，侵略外國者少，從築萬里長城的秦始皇開始，中國就一直希望能閉關自守，長城本身就是防禦心理的象徵。

孔子的忠孝、仁愛、信義、和平的教訓和孟子的民主觀念，都使中國適於做一個不願欺凌其他民族的現代民主國家。中國在戰後必須強調的是現代科學和民主政治；科學方面應注重生產方法的應用，民主方面應強調國家的統一。科學和民主是現代進步國家的孿生工具，也是達成強盛、繁榮和持久和平的關鍵。

中國人民深通人情，特別注重待人接物的修養，生活思想習於民主，這一切都使中國具備現代民主國家的堅強基礎。我們在前面已經提到，中國的民主社會組織相當鬆泛。中國人對於個人自由的強烈愛好並未能與現代社會意識齊頭並進。強烈的家族觀念已經阻滯了使個人結合為廣大團體的過程。不過這種褊狹的觀念正在迅速衰退；現代社團已經在大城市裏相繼出現；進一步工業化之後，家族關係自將愈來愈鬆弛，個人社會化的程度也將愈來愈深。

在知識方面，中國人看待事物的態度使他深通人情，但是也使他忽視概括與抽象的重要。他以詩人、藝術家和道德家的心情熱愛自然，因而胸懷寬大，心平氣和。但是這種對自然的愛好尚未推展到對自然法則的研究，人類要控制自然，必須靠這些法則作武器。以中國文化同化能力之強，她必定能慢慢地吸收西方在科學上的貢獻；以中國天然資源之富，人民智慧之高，科學的發展將使她前途呈現無限光明。物質文明發展之後，她的道德和藝術更將發揚光大；她的文學和哲學也將在現代邏輯方法和科學思想影響下更見突出而有系統。

在這個初步的和平與繁榮的新基礎上，中國將可建立新的防衛力量來維護和平。只有戰鬥中的夥伴才有資格成為和平時期的夥伴。中國 8 年抗戰對世界和平的貢獻，已使舉世人士刮目相看。

現代科學，特別是發明和工業上的成就，將與中國的藝術寶藏和完美道德交織交融。一種新的文化正在形成，這種新文化對世界進步一定會提供重大的貢獻。

TIDES FROM THE WEST
A
CHINESE AUTOBIOGRAPHY
BY
CHIANG MONLIN

PART I

IN AN OLD EMPIRE

Chapter 1
How East and West Met

Centuries ago certain wise men from the East, following a star, traveled to the land where a religion was born destined in centuries to come to play a great part in the life of Western nations. A religion based upon meekness was adopted in the course of time by these peoples of extreme vigor. This religion of meekness, which teaches "whosoever shall smite thee on the right cheek, turn to him the other also," won its way through the West slowly but persistently by braving Roman lions and enduring hardships, suffering, and persecution. A few centuries later it began to trickle into China with the same meekness.

The Nestorians came to China during the Tang Dynasty (618-905 A.D.) , and the Tang emperors built churches for them. But they did not find China a fertile soil for their religion. Another few centuries passed; the Jesuits found their way into the court of the Ming Dynasty (1368-1643 A.D.) . They brought with them Western astronomy, which caught the fancy of the Ming emperors.

The Western peoples, meanwhile, with vigorous blood in their veins, not only absorbed the new religion but also created science and made inventions which led to an industrial revolution in recent centuries. As a result they amassed an immense amount of capital, which had to find an outlet in other countries not as yet industrialized. It flowed to the East, first in a trickle, then in torrents, and finally in tides which flooded the Orient and almost swept China off her feet.

China had no trouble with Christianity, nor with any other religion. Only when it was coupled with commercialism supported by gunboats in the middle of the nineteenth century was the religion of meekness seen through Chinese eyes as that of an aggressor. For a religion seen arm in arm with force changes its color, and the Chinese were unable to dissociate the two. This naturally gave rise to the impression that while Buddha came to China on white elephants, Christ was borne on cannon balls.

Since we were knocked out by cannon balls, naturally we became interested in them, thinking that by learning to make them we could strike back. We could forget for the time being in whose name they had come, since for us common mortals to save our lives was more important than to save our souls.

But history seems to move through very curious ways. From studying cannon balls we came to mechanical inventions, which in turn led us to political reforms; from political reforms we began to see political theories, which led us again to the philosophies of the West. On the other hand, through mechanical inventions we saw science, from which we came to understand scientific method and the scientific mind. Step by step we were led farther and farther away from the cannon ball—yet we came nearer and nearer to it.

The story is a long one, but it all happened in the short span of a hundred years, the dramatic part of it in not more than half a century. I say a hundred years because in 1942 Hong Kong was to celebrate its centenary as a British possession, and it was a coincidence that Japan, Britain's former ally, had snatched it from British hands in the previous year by lightning attack. I mention Hong Kong without the least intention of rubbing an old sore, only because it will serve as a convenient landmark for the earlier part of China's westernization. As everyone will remember, this group of hilly islands—situated in the south sea not far from Canton, and nests for pirates a century ago—was ceded to Britain in 1842 at China's defeat in the so-called "Opium War." What actually happened was that China, having forbidden the importation of opium, Britain's principal export from India to that country, burned British opium at Canton. Britain retaliated with cannon balls and China lost the war.

Torrents of Western manufactures began to pour in through the subsequent opening, also stipulated under the treaty, of five coastal cities as commercial ports. These cities lay scattered at fairly regular intervals along the coast of the prosperous southern half of the country. Thus new frontiers were formed; China's frontiers had lain hitherto solely inland, to the north and northwest. This change in China's map was the turning point in her history.

These five seaports—Canton, Amoy , Foochow, Ningpo, and Shanghai—running from south to north in a chain, served as depots for Western manufactured goods which flowed thence into the richest and most populous parts of the country, the Pearl and Yangtze Valleys. Supported by gunboats the Western merchants squatted like octopuses in the ports, sending their tentacles into the interior of the rich provinces. China, an enormous country larger than the United States, was herself unaware of the penetration and blind to what was bound to happen later on. The life of her millions went its leisurely and contented way from the cradle to the grave without making the least effort toward modernization, while a section of the people began casually to pick up foreign manufactures, whether for use, for pleasure, or out of curiosity.

The gunboat policy of the Western Powers, however, carried with it not only manufactured goods and opium but also the healthy seeds of Western science and culture, which we did not see at the time but which were to germinate years later to the benefit of China—one of the ironies of history.

Meanwhile the westernization of Japan went on by leaps and bounds. Again, China was unaware of it. Half a century later, by 1894, the little Island Empire suddenly loomed large over the horizon of the China Sea, sprang a surprise attack upon the sleeping giant, and bit off a mouthful. The next to go after Hong Kong was Formosa , an island province near the east coast hundreds of times larger than Hong Kong. China now began to feel the pinch and rub her eyes in wonder. What was it that was disturbing her sweet dreams?

My original plan was just to write out what I know and feel about my own country. As I have let these mental pictures run their course, one after another, they have developed into a volume something like autobiography, something like reminiscences or contemporary history. Whatever it may be, it is all from the indelible images that unrolled in my mind as clearly and vividly as if they had been printed there only yesterday. In the rapid march of events I felt myself a tiny cog on the vast whirling wheel. ◉

Chapter 2
Village Life

I came into the world as the youngest of five children, four boys and a girl, in a well-to-do family in a small village. The night before I was born my father dreamed of a bear coming to our house, the sign of a male baby. The next day the good omen came true: the spirits of our forefathers in heaven presented another son to the family.

Before my eldest brother was born, Father had dreamed of receiving a bouquet of orchids. So the child was named Orchid. My second brother was named Peach for the same reason. Naturally I was called Bear. As for my sister and third brother, Father had no dreams. My name was afterward changed from Bear to Unicorn when I registered at Chekiang College, because of events in the schools.

I was born a war baby, for the year in which I came into the world saw Britain cut off Burma from Chinese control; and the Sino-French War had just ended the previous year, by which China lost her suzerainty over Indo-China to France. The peeling of dependencies off China was a prelude to further invasion by foreign Powers. For China kept dependencies to serve as buffer states, not for exploitation. She never interfered with their internal administration.

When the peel was gone, germs began to make inroads into the orange. However, people in China were not aware of it. These wars on the southwest frontiers were far away and mere ripples on her vast ocean. The villagers were the least concerned—in their profound isolation they gave less attention to such news than they would to ghost stories. Yet China drew a part of her defense forces from among just such villages, not interested in war.

When I came to know the little world around me I noticed that people spoke more realistically of the Taiping Rebellion, which had destroyed a part of the village some thirty years before. The chief of the elders of the Chiang clan, a carpenter by trade, had once joined the rebels. He told us many stories of pillage and atrocities committed by the Taipings, of which he himself had been guilty. To listen to these horrors often made a chill run all over my body. Yet of the international wars of recent years people talked only casually, utterly unconcerned. There were fabulous stories of victory—simply amusing, in a sense tragic, as one thinks of them in after years. For the fact was that while Chinese troops made a good showing in some engagements, the conclusion was complete defeat.

The spearhead of modern invention had not yet penetrated to the villages and they lay there, secret, primitive, and calm, as our ancestors had founded them some five hundred years before. Yet the people were not idle. The farmers had to plow, sow, and reap; the fishermen to cast their nets in the canals; the women to spin, weave, sew; the traders to buy and sell; the craftsmen to make their beautiful articles; the scholars to read aloud, memorize the Confucian classics, and take civil examinations.

There were hundreds of thousands of such villages in China, varying only in size and mode of life according to topographical and climatic differences. The traditions, family ties, and trades which held them together were more or less the same. A common written language, common ideals of life, a common culture and system of civil examinations bound the whole country into a single nation known as the Chinese Empire.

Together with the large cities and centers of trade, these hundreds of thousands of villages in China kept the country supplied with food, goods, scholars, soldiers, and the rank and file of officials of the government. So long as they remained untouched by modernization, China would remain the same; if she could have built fences round the treaty ports they might have remained the same for centuries to come. But the tide of westernization refused to be contained within the treaty ports. It made itself felt in the immediate surroundings, extending gradually along waterways and highways. Villages and towns near the five invaded cities or along communication lines were the first to succumb. Like transplanted trees feeding on China's rich soil, branching off and multiplying fast, the modern influence extended in the course of some fifty years far into the interior.

The village of the Chiangs was one among many spread—with intervening spaces of one or two miles of luxuriant rice fields—over the alluvial plain formed by the Chien-tang River. This is well known for its scenery, both in the upper part and in the lower section near the mouth where the famous bores of Chien-tang make their impressive seasonal sweep in from the sea. The high, abrupt front of the tidal bore is of a grandeur to over-shadow Niagara Falls. Down the valley, through the centuries, the river slowly laid its rich earth, building its shores farther and farther into Hangchow Bay. On the newly formed shores people erected temporary enclosures to hold the brine from which common salt is made. A large quantity of salt was produced every year, supplying the needs of many millions.

After a number of years, as the shores were further extended, the salt would begin to exhaust itself and dikes would be built along the drying land at some distance from the water. The embanked land was now ready for pasturing. After a long period it was capable of growing cotton to feed the domestic looms, or mulberry trees to nourish silkworms. It was probably still another half century before it could be turned into rice fields. For plenty of water is needed for growing rice, and it takes time to build reservoirs and a network of canals for irrigation. And the land takes time to mature.

The village of the Chiangs, by the time I came to it, was situated about twenty miles from Hangchow Bay. Around it were endless chains of villages, large and small, running in all directions—southward to the mountains, northward to the sea, and east and west to towns and cities all connected by miles of footways or canals. The genealogy of the Chiangs tells us that our first ancestors immigrated to the Yuyao district from Hueichow, a mountainous region where the famous river finds its source. They came presumably to reclaim the then newly formed land. In my own time an ancient embankment was still visible in front of our clan temple, the Temple of the Four No's, popularly known as the "Temple Facing the Embankment."

Perhaps the reader would like to know what is meant by the "Four No's." They mean to see no evil, hear no evil, speak no evil, do no evil. The sets of three monkeys with hands covering their eyes, ears, and mouth, respectively, that one finds in Oriental bazaars exemplify them—the fourth being left out for obvious reasons. These moral precepts came from the Confucian classics. Moral ideas were driven into the people by every possible means— temples, theatres, homes, toys, proverbs, schools, history, and stories—until they became habits in daily life. This was one of the ways by which China attained social stability: governing the life of the people by moral bonds.

During the long centuries of history the population of China had expanded from its northern beginnings to the south, first to the Yangtze Valley, then to the Pearl River Valley, and finally to the mountainous regions of the southwest. The fertile soil of the south and the devastation caused by flood from the incorrigible Yellow River, as well as by invasions of warlike tribes from outside the Great Wall, together with the natural expansion of the race, all contributed to cause repeated southward movements of the Chinese people. It was following in the wake of such a movement that my ancestors came to stay here on the shores of Hang-chow Bay.

Our family tree owes its existence to a sprout of a royal family planted in consequence of a feud somewhere in the lower Yellow River Valley some three thousand years ago. That tract of land was called "Chiang," the ancient name for a species of aquatic grass (Hydropyrum Latifolium). The modern name of this plant is Chiao-pei; used as a vegetable it tastes somewhat like bamboo shoots. The country was probably so called because of the luxuriant growth of the plant in those regions. My first ancestor in the Chiang line was made the first feudal lord to rule over that land toward the end of the twelfth century B.C. He was Pei-ling, third son of Prince Regent Chow-kung of the Chow Dynasty, and his descendants took Chiang as their family name.

In the third century A.D., during the period of the Three Kingdoms, one of our ancestors appears in history. His name was Chiang Wen and he lived in the Yangtze Valley. This shows that the Chiangs living south of the Yangtze had already migrated from the Yellow River region by the third century. From our first ancestor down to the present day all the names in the direct line have been recorded in our genealogy. How authentic they are I cannot tell, for their lives were so obscure that verification is not easy, but this much we can say: all the Chiangs settled in the areas south of the Yangtze are of the same origin. How far we can trace back accurately to this origin we don't know, but it is certain that all the Chiangs living in the province of Chekiang find their common ancestral tree in Hueichow.

I am of the seventeenth generation in the ancestral line. The first settlement of our village by the Chiangs, more than five hundred years ago, came toward the end of the Yuan or Mongol Dynasty. During these five centuries, under two foreign dynastiesand one Chinese, the Chiangs saw the fall of the Mongols, the rise and fall of the Mings and the Manchus, and the Taiping Rebellion which almost overthrew the latter. During these changes they lived, worked, and retired to their graves in the same manner and in the same village. Dynasties came and went, but the village of the Chiangs remained the same.

During the Taiping Rebellion a few houses were burned by the rebels. The people ran into the mountains, but as soon as peace was restored they all came home like bees to the hive. In my childhood some of the ruins still stood to tell the story of the war.

When the Ming Dynasty fell at the hands of the Manchus, I was told by the villagers, people were not aware of it until the edicts of the new regime reached the villages. There was a play going on in one of the near-by village theatres when they were informed that they lived under a new dynasty. Perhaps the only forcible change in the life of my clansmen was the edict ordering the people to wear a queue and forbidding the male population to dress in the Ming style. Resentment was so great that men wore the Ming costume, to their graves; it was a common saying of our clan that "men surrendered but women did not; the living did, but the dead did not." The practice persisted in some cases until the downfall of the Manchu Dynasty in 1911, when the Republic was established—a period of two centuries and a half.

Our village consisted of only some sixty households, with a population of about three hundred. It was one of the smallest among many villages, surrounded by a canal on three sides. On the south side a footway paved with granite slabs ran along it, leading across bridges to neighboring villages and towns. The canal was but part of a network connecting with large rivers which in turn led to such far-flung cities as Hangchow, Soochow, and Shanghai.

Although the village was small, it commanded easy communication by both land and water. Bridges spanned the canals and weeping willows grew luxuriantly on the banks. Fish, shrimps, eels, and turtles were abundant. Here and there one would find anglers taking their ease in the shade of the willows. Oxen could be seen walking in leisurely fashion round the water wheels to propel the chain of paddles which brought fresh water through a long trough to the fields. Miles of wheat fields in the spring and rice fields in summer gave one the feeling of living in a land of perpetual verdure.Swallows shuttled back and forth in the blue sky above a sea of rippling green, while eagles floated high above, circling around the village in search of little chicks.

Such was the background of my childhood and the environment of my clansmen. They lived there for more than five centuries with little change in life. Nature was kind to them. The land was fertile. Floods and droughts were not frequent. Rebellions or wars in the country at large did not disturb them more than once or twice during those long centuries; they lived in peace and contentment in a world by themselves, with little distinction between the very rich and the very poor. Sufficient rice, cotton, silk, fish, meat, bamboo shoots, and vegetables kept the people warm and well fed.

Morals, beliefs, and customs remained unchanged in Chinese villages through centuries of dynastic changes, in peace or war. For the villagers the world was good enough and no improvement was needed. Life alone was unstable, but consolation could be found in the transmigration of the soul. At death the soul was said to leave the body and enter that of a baby then being born. Indeed, in my own time I have seen convicts on the way to execution who shouted to the spectators that after eighteen years they would be young men again. What a consolation!

Our villagers said that a bad or sinful man's soul would be degraded to become a poor man, a horse, or a pig, or even split into minute parts to be insects or worms, according to the degrees of sins he had committed. The soul of a good or virtuous man would be promoted to a higher station in the next life.

What was sinful or virtuous had of course its accepted standards. The highest of all virtues was filial piety; the greatest of all sins was adultery. Filial piety kept the Chinese family intact and chastity kept the Chinese race pure. Respect for the elders, faithfulness to friends, loyalty to the sovereign, honesty in word and deed; kindliness and sympathy to the poor, the infirm or sick, all were regarded as virtuous behavior. Usury, treachery, lying, cheating, and the like were among sinful acts. Denunciation of a person whose conduct one disapproved often took the form of telling him that he would become a dog or a pig in his next life.

In business dealings verbal promises were as good as gold. On the whole, people were honest and trustworthy. Any person found to cheat would be surely tabooed by the whole community.

Marriages were not the business of the parties concerned; the parents of both parties made the match. As a rule, men married at twenty and women at eighteen. The men usually remarried if their wives died, while women of well-to-do families generally remained widows if they survived their husbands. These unfortunates were regarded as most virtuous—Imperial posthumous honors were conferred upon them.

The local government of the village was a fully self-governing body without outside interference. It was a government by elders of the clan with the Ancestral Hall as its seat. "Elders" does not mean elderly men. They might be young but represented the oldest living generations in the ancestral line. They were obligated to see that the ceremonies of ancestral worship were properly performed and were entrusted with the duties of arbitration in case of dispute among the clansmen. No one was allowed to go to law without first going through arbitration. To "open the gate of the Ancestral Hall" meant to summon an arbitration court of the elders. Anyone in the village could go there to observe the proceedings. Candles and incense burned before the tablets of the ancestors and everyone felt that their spirits watched invisibly from the ethereal realm. Before these ancestral spirits the parties concerned must speak the truth, nothing but the truth. Generally they did.

For the arbitrators, fairness was the motto. Public opinion in the village was also a very important factor, of which all parties concerned were conscious, and there was also the public opinion of neighboring villages. No elders would dare to defame the Ancestral Hall with unfair judgments. Thus disputes were usually fairly settled in this way. No lawsuit was necessary.

There were, in fact, few cases of dispute which needed arbitration by "opening the gate of the Ancestral Hall," for people regarded this as a matter of weight, to be resorted to only in a case of grave importance. Disputes were usually settled by informal arbitration before the gate of the hall.

Scholars and the gentry had a strong voice in the local government. They also participated in cases of arbitration and the making of rules and regulations for the village. They formed inter-village committees to settle disputes and look after the common welfare of neighboring villages.

Land taxes were brought by owners of land to the district or hsien treasury, about twenty miles from the village. No tax collectors ever visited us. People never felt the influence of the state—it was a common saying that "Heaven is high above and the Emperor is far away."

Public worship other than ancestral, such as worship in Buddhist temples or temples of deified persons, national heroes, or local gods that had grown out of legends, was a matter of individual concern. Anyone might worship in any or all of these places; there was no religious restriction or persecution. Your gods are as good as mine. If the Christians had allowed their Christ to sit beside Chinese gods in Chinese temples, I am sure that the villagers would have worshiped Him just as reverently as they did other gods.

Superstition grows out of the credulity of simple folk—it rolls like a snowball growing as it rolls along. Thus it is that superstitions gather through centuries of accumulation.

As I have said, the villagers believed in the transmigration of the soul. This does not seem to reconcile with the idea that there are spirits traveling about with lightning speed in the ethereal realm. Soul and spirit, however, were two different things: the soul transmigrated, but the spirit remained in space. The spirit of a great man lives eternally in the invisible realm, while that of a common man evaporates and dwindles, disappearing entirely with the course of time, or rather when it is entirely forgotten. The spirit moves with instant speed anywhere it wills. It may live in the Ancestral Hall or in its grave as it chooses. This is perhaps one reason why the Chinese are always willing to spend large sums on elaborate tombs and palatial ancestral halls.

My people always see things in relation to man. If spirits and gods wandered about in an unseen world without relation to, or contact with, living man, people would not see any use for them and would hardly believe they existed. Yes, they have images and tablets sitting in the shrines. But these sacred things, however awe-inspiring, do not step down and talk to them except in dreams. There must be something more active or lively. This was found in mediums, in automatic writing, or in the interpreting of dreams.

If someone was thinking of a departed friend or a dead relative, he could invoke the spirit to come to him through a medium, who was always a woman from some far-distant place. When the spirit called for approached, she would contract her ears three times as the signal of arrival of the invisible guest. This contraction of the involuntary muscles of the ear was something ordinary people could not do and this made them believe in the medium much more. She usually spoke through her throat like a cat's purr, so that the words uttered could be interpreted to suit the wishes of the listeners.When she had traced out something more definite in the course of conversation, she would purr more distinctly, to the amazement of the audience.

False or true, it served as a comfort to the hearts of living relatives. I still remember how thrilling it was when my dead mother conversed with me through a medium half a century ago.

Automatic writing is of a higher order. It was generally practiced by the educated class. Two persons were needed to hold the ends of a horizontal bar with a long wooden pin attached at the middle, which wrote on a tray of sand. A god or the spirit of some famous personage, it was believed, could be invoked to write. The device—not unlike a Ouija board—could be asked to predict future events. It might foretell a bumper crop in the coming year, or an impending famine, or peace, or war. One could ask almost any question. Poems were written by operators who did not know how to compose a poem; names of persons present unknown to the writers might be written out on the sand. It was all done through the subconscious as any person who knows about psychology can explain.

Mediums invoked only spirits of departed relatives or friends; automatic writing might invoke the gods as well. In dreams both might come voluntarily, uninvited. I heard numerous interpretations of dreams which I do not remember now, except for one instance. One of my great-granduncles went to Hangchow to take the civil examinations for the second degree. In his examination cell (where candidates remained for many hours) he saw in a dream a hand of enormous size stretch into the room through the window. This was interpreted to mean that, since it was the greatest hand he had ever seen, he was to head the list of successful candidates. And the good omen came true when the results of the examination were made known.

Gods, dead friends, relatives, or spirits might enter one's dreams to convey their wishes, requests, or warnings. A dead mother might request her son to repair her tomb. A dead father might demand paper money from his son. A good imitation of paper money was always burned at funerals; it was supposed to accompany the dead for use in the world to which they go.

A tragic coincidence happened in our village about which people talked for years after. Ah Yi, a young farmer, was to take his rice by boat to a neighboring town. Early in the morning he was found sitting on a bench in a somber mood, very rare for a farmer. To inquiry he replied that in his dreams the previous night his dead mother had warned him not to go near water. What could it mean? He was a good swimmer.

At dusk he brought his junk home and shoved the boat toward the landing with his bamboo pole. He joked with his friends on the bank that his danger was over, and laughed heartily. Suddenly his feet slipped and he plunged into the canal, where he struggled for a moment but went under. Friends dived for him but could not find him. After half an hour he was pulled out, cold and stiff, from the entangling roots of an aged willow tree that grew by the water.

People said it was the water ghost that hid him there. Perhaps it was a water monkey that nested in the roots. Several good swimmers drowned near that spot. Often the villagers saw the "water ghost" sitting on the bridge near by in the moonlight, staring at the moon. It plunged into the water as soon as it saw people approaching.

Illusions, hallucinations, dreams, nightmares, imaginings, wishful thinking, coincidence, rumors—every kind of inexplicable phenomenon of mind or nature, all contributed to swell the snowball. And time kept it rolling.

Medicine in the village was, of course, primitive. We had to go miles to see herb doctors in the bigger towns. For ordinary illness or certain more serious cases Chinese medicine is very effective. But in many serious ailments the old medicine is useless or even dangerous.

I myself have been twice at the point of death and was in each case saved by herb medicine, without which I would not be here writing these chapters. On one occasion I had been ill for many months and was reduced to emaciation. A famous herb doctor specializing in children's diseases saved me. On another occasion I contracted diphtheria and was treated by a Chinese throat specialist. He pricked my throat with a needle all over the affected part and then sprayed it with some kind of white powder. I do not know what it was, but my throat felt cool and soothed as after smoking a mentholated cigarette.

That part of my throat was relieved, but the case developed other complications. My tonsils swelled to the size of goose eggs, my cheeks puffed up like a balloon, and I could hardly swallow even liquid food. My nose kept bleeding as if I should bleed to death. Finally I could barely breathe and only a faint hope was left. While my life hung by a thread my father said that he would try to "treat a dead horse like a live one." This was a Chinese proverb meaning that if the horse is ready to die anyway, it is worth trying the most extreme methods to save it. He dug into old medicine books, in which he found a prescription for a case showing similar symptoms. Several heavy doses were taken. The first brought immediate relief; in an hour or two I felt much better. By the next morning my tonsils had dwindled, and after a week or so I could take regular meals.

I have seen with my own eyes broken legs healed by ancient methods, while colds, sore eyes, coughs, and rheumatism were effectively cured by herbs.

Chinese doctors discovered long ago an antismallpox "vaccine" taken from the human body. They used a kind of herb that had once been inserted into the nostrils of an affected child. Putting it into the nose of a normal child gave the latter what was usually a very much milder form of the disease. There were some cases of mortality among the hundreds thus "vaccinated," for I often heard of a death here and there. My father preferred modern vaccination to the old Chinese method. All the children in our family and many of our relatives were vaccinated by the modern method without a mishap.

We did not know how to cure malaria in our village. We let it run for some weeks or even months until it stopped of itself. There were no malignant cases in our locality and while it might sap the energy of the affected person it was not fatal. When quinine powder was brought in by missionaries or merchants from Shanghai, people found great relief in Western medicine.

Some of our clansmen believed in the healing power of the supernatural. They prayed in a temple and took a pinch of ashes from the incense burner as a panacea for all diseases. It was a sort of psychological treatment and did cure in some cases where psychology could play its part.

In the gardens of our house each month of the year was presided over by the chief flower of that month. Camellias were for the First Moon—first month of the year in the lunar calendar, corresponding approximately to the Western late January and early February. In the Second Moon almond blossoms took over the reins of government in the flowery kingdom. Peach blossoms were for the Third Moon, roses for the Fourth, pomegranates for the Fifth, lotus for the Sixth, Feng-hsian (Impatiens balsamina) for the Seventh, Kwei-hua (Osmanthus fragrans) for the Eighth, chrysanthemums for the Ninth, Fu-yung (Hibiscus mutabilis) for the Tenth, Shuei-hsian (Narcissus tazetta) for the Eleventh, and La-mei (Chimonanthus fragrans) for the Twelfth, the last month of the year. Each plant was represented by a particular goddess whom we all loved dearly.

The most popular seasonal flowers were the peach blossoms of spring, lotus in the summer, and osmanthus and chrysanthemums in autumn. In season, the villagers all joined in admiring these beauties of nature.

Festivals brought much enjoyment to both children and grownups alike. The most important was the New Year Festival which began near the end of the old year—on the twenty-third of the Twelfth Moon—when the Kitchen God took leave and went to heaven to report to the Supreme God the year's happenings in the household.

The Chinese believed in polytheism. But above all deities was the Supreme God who controlled them all. It was an anthropomorphic idea that He reigned over the ethereal realm like the Emperor of China. Other gods were his ministers, governors, and magistrates.

The Kitchen God was entrusted by the Supreme God with charge of the household. Naturally he had to report to Him at the end of the year. The Kitchen God was a vegetarian and was therefore treated with a vegetarian dinner before leaving for heaven. Everybody had to be very careful during the year in word and deed, since bad as well as good things were reported. Both the sending-off and the welcome-home ceremonies consisted of dinners for the family, burning of paper money, and firecrackers.

New Year's Eve was celebrated by a family banquet in which every member must participate. If some member was absent, he or she would be assigned a seat in absentia. Candles burned all night until the next morning and most of the grownups sat up through the night to watch the coming of the New Year. Next morning, on the first day of the year, the family worshiped Heaven and Earth. Candles, incense, paper money, and firecrackers were necessary parts of the ceremony.

The Lantern Festival, part of the New Year celebration, began on the thirteenth and ended on the eighteenth of the First Moon, which was also the end of the New Year Festival. Artistic lanterns—horses, rabbits, butterflies, dragonflies, mantis, cicada, lotus, anything one could think of—adorned the houses and the streets of the towns. We used to go to large towns to see the lantern parade; their streets were thronged with merrymakers.

There were other important festivals, such as the Dragon Festival in the Fifth Moon, the Moon Festival in the Eighth Moon, and the like. The Dragon Festival was celebrated by a boat race with all the boats decorated to look like dragons. The Moon Festival was enjoyed quietly and poetically—after a banquet we took a walk in the bright night and looked at the rabbit on the full, silvery autumn moon in a starless, moonlit sky.

Parades were popular, with hundreds of people participating and thousands watching. They were always religious in character: some god was to make an inspection trip around the villages. An image of the deity was carried in a carved, artistically decorated sedan chain, preceded by pennants, flags, floats, bands of music, monster dragons, men on stilts, and so forth.

Dragon dances were performed in the public squares of every village as the parade passed by. The men on stilts danced in theatrical roles in the crowded streets. Monstrous flags with fantastic designs of the dragon, tiger, or lion, each carried by dozens of people and supported by lines of rope in front and rear, were indeed a great sight. They moved up the highway among the fields like the sails of the Spanish Armada on a sea of rippling green. It was said that the idea originated during the old days when pirates from the Japan Sea wrought havoc among the people.

Traveling theatres made visits to the villages during festivals or birthday celebrations of deities, or on other important occasions. Each performance started about three o'clock in the afternoon and continued until the next morning with an intermission for supper. A frantic sounding of the gong served as a prelude to let country folk know that the play was starting. Plays were mostly based on historical episodes; the people learned history from the theatre. At the end of each play the moral lesson was invariably brought out. So it served a triple purpose: to teach history and morals as well as to entertain.

The roles of women were played by men, as in Shakespearean times in England. The actors painted their faces in fantastic designs of various colors to differentiate symbolically among virtuous and vile, honest and sneaky, the great and the mean, the stern and the kind. Thus one whose nose was painted white was either treacherous, cunning, mean, or clownish. In daily life we referred to such a person as "white-nosed." A red face suggested a character which was candid or virtuous in some way, but always kind. The "black face" was generally severe and stern. We often called a man who behaved sternly "black-faced," while "red-faced" meant a man who acted kindly or generously. The tradition of symbolic face painting still persists to the present day in Chinese classical dramas.

Such was the world of my childhood. It has been passing rapidly into history. The intrusion of foreign manufactures began the process; invasion from the West, whether by ideas or gunboats, hastened it; modern science, invention, and industry are to give the finishing touch. ●

Chapter 3
Early Schooling

Education was a family affair. Boys were prepared for the Imperial civil examinations, or for business, in the family school. Girls were tutored separately. Children of poorer families which could not support a teacher were destined to be illiterate.

There was generally one teacher to a dozen pupils, taught individually. There were no blackboards or classes in the school. The teacher was usually serene, sitting the whole day at his desk from early in the morning to sunset. The pupils did likewise. As clocks were very rare then, there was none in the school. In winter, when the day was short, lessons after dark were given by the dim light of a vegetable-oil lamp. Time was measured by a sun dial. On a cloudy or rainy day you had to guess your time. Often you missed the mark by an hour or two, but it did not matter much, for the lessons were given individually.

I was sent to school at the age of six, the traditional school age. But my actual years were only five and a month or so, since with us your age is called "one"—that is, you are in your first year—when you are born. The ordinary desk was a bit too high for me, so that my chair had to be raised by a wooden stand to bring me level with the desk. My tiny feet were thus left dangling from the seat.

I was given a textbook: San-tze-ching, or the "Classics of Three Characters." It is so named because each sentence contains three words, and it was rhymed so as to be easier for children to remember. After fifty-odd years I am still able to recite a great part of it. It starts with the following passage—I give a literal translation:

Man is originally endowed with a nature which is all good.

And therefore by nature people are all alike.

It is practice that makes the divergence.

If they are not properly taught,

Their nature will be thwarted.

The all-good in human nature is the starting point of the Confucian philosophy of life and education, which exercised a strong influence upon the

French Encyclopedists of the eighteenth century.

I understand what it means now, but of course I didn't then.

I must tell how I hated the school! After a short time, noticing that the attention of the teacher was not on me, I climbed down quickly from the chair and ran like a dog that has broken from its chain back home to my mother's lap.

"Why do you come home, my child?" asked my mother in surprise.

"The school is no good, the teacher is no good, and the book is no good," I replied.

"Aren't you afraid of your teacher? He may come and get you," said my mother kindly.

"I'll kill the teacher! I'll burn theschool!"

My mother didn't send me back to school that day, nor did the teacher come.

Early the next morning my nurse woke me, spoke many kind words to me, and persuaded me to go to school again. From childhood I responded to kind words only; no coercion ever did any good. It was the gentle reasonableness of my nurse that made me go back voluntarily.

I took to school my own rattan chair, which was very light. A servant followed me and put it on the stand to match the height of the desk. The teacher made no remark and acted as if nothing had happened, but I noticed several schoolmates making faces at me. I hated them but pretended not to see them. I climbed up on the chair and sat there without resting place for my poor feet. More lessons were given, in the same book. I read very loud, as was required in the old type of school, repeating the meaningless text again and again till every word was learned by heart. When the sun shone directly above our heads it was midday. The teacher ordered me to go home for lunch. Immediately after lunch I went back to school and kept on learning the same thing till sunset.

Day in and day out, there was no change in the curriculum. When I finished one textbook another meaningless one came in turn. It was memory and patience that we were training.

We were taught the "three P's" in reading: presence of mind, presence of eye, and the presence of lips. The first means concentration, a requisite for doing any work well. The second is important because by it one gets a clear impression of the ideographic letters, with the various arrangements of fine and intricate strokes in each letter. The third is attained by reading a passage aloud several hundred times; the words then fall from the lips fluently, thus relieving the burden of the memory. We were warned not to commit words to memory by artificial means, because then we would not retain them. If we stumbled in reciting a passage we were ordered to read it over again one or two hundred times more—if the teacher was not in a good humor you would probably receive in addition, without warning, a crack on the skull. Often when the day was over some boys left school with lumps on their scalps.

Discipline and obedience were aimed at without regard for the interest of the pupil. Sundays were unknown. We had half holidays in the afternoon on the first and fifteenth day of each lunar month. In addition, we had during the year several full holidays on festival days, such as the Dragon Festival and the Moon Festival. A comparatively long vacation came about New Year's time. It started on the twentieth day of the Twelfth Moon and lasted till the same day of the First Moon of the new year, and was called the New Year vacation.

As several years went by, I grew older and learned by heart quite a number of characters. My teacher then began to explain the meaning of the text and studying grew to be less drudgery. From the Confucian classics I began to understand a little of the way to be a righteous man. It began with the culture of the person, then went on to the fulfillment of duties to the family, to the state, and finally the world. I did not appreciate its full significance until much later.

In the earliest years school was indeed a prison to me. The difference was that in a real prison the inmates have little hope, while in school the pupils had hopes for a bright future. Had not all the famous scholars and statesmen gone through years of suffering in schools? It was through suffering that men became great, we were told to believe. The path was difficult but it was the only road to success.

"If you have tasted the bitterest of the bitter you will become the greatest of the great."

"The Son of Heaven honors the scholar."

"While everything else is of a lower order,
learning is the highest of all."

"Do not envy others who possess the sword;
you have a pen that is mightier."

These common sayings spurred me on the road of learning as the odors of an early spring in the air spur a sluggish horse to green pastures. Otherwise I should have dropped my schooling and taken to business in Shanghai. Ideals, hopes, and will power are the most important factors in shaping one's life. If education fails in these, the emphasis in modern methods upon the interest of the pupil is but a trifling thing. Interest is an important factor in education only when it is subordinated to inculcation of ideals.

It seemed tedious and foolish in the old Chinese schools to commit the classics to memory. But there was the advantage that in later years one could go to memory to find ready references for the conduct of life. In a static society where the world moved very slowly and the rules of conduct would need little modification, it seems to me that the old Chinese method of teaching and learning was quite adequate for the needs it filled. Only, in a country school like mine it ran to the extreme, giving unnecessary hardship to the pupils. I wonder how many promising boys were scared away before they began to realize the importance of learning.

There were no sports or physical exercises in any form in my school. The boys were forbidden to run fast; they must walk slowly and be dignified. Right after lunch we were required to practise calligraphy. Young life seemed to be practically squeezed out of us.

Nevertheless, the boys found their own way to satisfy their play instincts. When the teacher was absent we would take over control of the school. Sometimes desks were taken to form a platform on which a play could be staged. Chairs and stools would be used as stage properties. Sometimes we played blindman's buff. On one occasion, while I was serving as the "blind," the teacher returned and all the others slipped away. As I caught an easy prey I felt something strange—it was the teacher. The shock was so terrifying that as I write it reels in my senses as vividly as if it had happened yesterday.

In the spring, when school was over in the afternoon, we flew kites. We made our own. Some took the form of a monster centipede, others a gigantic butterfly. At night we would send into the sky along the kite string a chain of lanterns, numbering usually five, seven, or nine. The smaller boys played with smaller kites, generally in the shape of a dragonfly, a swallow, or an eagle. The "swallows" were the most ingenious; they usually went by pairs, tied to the two ends of a slip of bamboo balanced on the kite string, and danced up and down in the currents of air like a pair of feathered playmates. Once I saw several swallows darting around such a pair, seeking their company.

In summer we played with other boys in the village during the starry evenings. The fireflies in the air looked like moving stars. Some of us preferred to listen to the stories told by some elder of the village. With a big palm-leaf fan in his hands to chase away annoying mosquitoes, and a teapot by his side, the elder would give his account of historical personages, dynastic changes, and past happenings in the village.

About two hundred and fifty years ago [he would begin], when the Ming Dynasty was overthrown by the Manchus, the whole country was in turmoil, but our forefathers living in this village still enjoyed peace. Later on, the Imperial Edict reached our village ordering all male persons to cut their hair according to the Tartar fashion and to wear a queue. Men were terrified and women wept. Barbers came to the village to enforce the order. They had Imperial sanction, if anyone should disobey, to punish the culprit by cutting off his head instead of his hair. No one preferred his hair to his head. Since a man could not retain both his head and his hair, he would stretch his head and let the barber do his job of haircutting and queue braiding. We have got used to it now, but my! it must have looked funny then...

This was a bit of history we learned outside of school. Again, a bit of local anthropology:

Tens of thousands of years ago our far-distant ancestors had tails like the monkey. The man-monkey's tail gradually turned yellow as he grew older. When nine out of the ten segments of his tail had turned yellow, he knew he was about to die. Then he would crawl into his cave and die there. As years went by, his tail dropped. This is why we have no tails now. But you can find at the end of your backbone where it was broken off.

Here is a story about pugilism:

In front of a rice shop a small boy was stationed to sell rice. He amused himself by picking up pinches of it and throwing them swiftly back into the basket. On one occasion a monk came to beg for rice. Instead of giving him some, the boy threw a few grains of it right in his face. To his surprise he saw that the grains had pierced the man's skin. The monk made a polite bow with his hands pressed together palm to palm, saying "Namo Amita Buddha" [Hail, Great Buddha!], and went his way.

Seven days later a pugilist came to the town. By now the boy was looking rather pale. "What's the matter with you, my boy?" asked the pugilist. When he was told the story of the monk he said, "Ah, that monk is the most famous pugilist of our time. You have insulted him. You have received from his bow the terrible internal wounds which will bring you to death in forty-nine days. I have medicine for your cure, but you must run away and not meet him again. He will come again after forty-nine days. Get a coffin, put some bricks in it, and pretend that you have died."

The monk did come, and asked for the boy. When he was told of his death, he sighed and said, "What a pity!" At his request he was led to see the coffin. Running his fingers over the top of it, he muttered, "Namo Amita Buddha." After he had gone the coffin was opened and it was found that all the bricks in it were cracked.

We boys pricked up our ears and listened attentively to these stories; they were one of the sources of my extracurricular education. I could retell many like them if space would allow.

I had several teachers, one after another, in my school. One of them was a kindly rustic scholar who had failed to pass the Imperial civil examinations for the First Degree, despite many attempts, and had to content himself with teaching in a family school. He had a round, moonlike face, was short and stout, and his bespectacled eyes looked habitually over the heavy brass rims of his glasses. His grey mustache hung bristling from his upper lip and he wore no beard. After he had taken egg soup at dinner, yellow particles would be seen adhering to the tips of his unclipped mustache. He was an encyclopedia of endless stories. But his literary style was rather poor; this is why, I presume, he failed repeatedly in the examinations; though he was an endless fountain of witticism. I think his memory in certain respects must have been bad, for he always forgot to carry with him either his umbrella or towel or fan when going back to the school after paying a visit to his friends. Necessity taught him finally to make an inventory of the articles he brought with him: pipe, umbrella, towel, and fan. When about to leave he would repeat, "Pipe, umbrella, towel, and fan." Even in winter, when no fan was needed, he would continue to mention it in his list, sometimes realizing that he had brought no fan with him, but at other times trying to find it, to the great amusement of both friends and pupils.

My mental scope was thus limited to what I learned from the Confucian classics and what the teachers and elders told me. I memorized quite a few of the classics and also had a rich store of stories. My early education, therefore, consisted chiefly of memory work. Yet I was fortunate to have been born and to live in the country, where nature offered plenty of instruction. Once I noticed that some beetles which lived on a large soap tree—so named because we used its nuts for soap—had on their heads horns like those of a deer. These looked exactly like the thorns that grew at the tips of the twigs of the tree. The beetles, I was told, were born of the tree and therefore looked like their mother. Somehow I felt suspicious. I reasoned that if a tree was capable of giving birth to beetles, they would in turn be capable of laying eggs that would be the seeds for the tree. That not being the case, I felt there must be some other reason for the remarkable likeness. I found it when I saw a bird feeding on insects in the tree without noticing the deer-horned beetles near by. The horns were therefore imitations of the thorns of the tree, for protection from the birds.

On the banks of the canal there grew candle trees, so called because the oil from the nuts is good for making candles. In the winter months the farmer would tie a few straws around the trunk of the tree, which he took off in the spring and burned. It was a common belief that by virtue of this act a magic force would kill the parasites. The fact was that if you tied enough straw around the trunk the parasites laid their eggs in the straw, and by burning it youdestroyed the eggs, thus preventing them from propagating. It was no magic.

There were many such instances of naïve nature study in my childhood. The two above mentioned are, I think, enough for illustration.

Thus there were three sources of the education I received in my childhood. The first was the study in school of the Confucian classics, which served as guidance to moral conduct as well as a foundation to the future study of modern social sciences. The second was the storytelling which was to prepare the way for an appreciation of modern literature. The last was the innocent nature study which later served as a stem on which the buds of modern science could be grafted. Had I been born in a crowded city, resembling—on a smaller scale, minus electricity and wide streets—the East Side of New York or London, I would have missed the all-important training of nature. The whole course of my life might have been different. For thenatural endowment of sense perception, observation, curiosity, and reasoning that are in every child and indispensable to life in a modern world might have been altogether smothered by the all-memory traditional training of my early youth.

I must confess that I did not apply myself to study as earnestly as some of my schoolmates, for I did not like to memorize but to see, touch, and reason. My teachers took this as a misfortune or curse of my disposition.

I loved to play and listen to storytelling. I liked to inquire into things to a degree disgusting to the elders. I took delight in watching frogs catch locusts in the rice fields and geese and ducks swimming in the canal. I enjoyed seeing the bamboos grow and flowers blooming, and loved to make kites and fly them. All these propensities were regarded by my teachers as a curse and I myself believed it must be so. But it is an irony of fate that the curse happened to turn out a blessing to me in later years, and the blessings my teachers bestowed upon some of my schoolmates have turned out to be curses. For some have died of consumption and others became bookish scholars, incapable of adjusting themselves to a changing environment when the tides of westernization swept over China. ◉

Chapter 4
Family Influence

During the plastic years of childhood and adolescence, family influence upon youth is indeed formative. Bad as well as good habits acquired during this period are difficult to eradicate in later years. On the whole the influence exercised upon me by my family was good and wholesome.

My father was a small landowner and a shareholder in some native banks in Shanghai. My grandfather had left him fairly well off and his mode of living was always simple so that the family never had uneasiness about financial matters. Father was an honest and generous man, respected by the people of the village in particular and surrounding districts generally. He was frugal in private life but very generous toward public affairs, contributing liberally to benevolent organizations.

He would not say anything with intent to deceive and his words were accordingly trusted by those who came in contact with him. He believed in feng-shui, the spirits of wind and water, and in fortunetelling and therefore—with a sort of fatalism—that a man's life was predetermined by supernatural forces. However, he also believed that by virtuous conduct and clean thinking one could make these forces respond by bestowing blessings upon oneself as well as one's family; thus the predetermined course of life would gradually shift its ground to a better course. His moral influence upon me was really great. The only regret I have is that I have fallen far short of his good example.

My mother was a cultured and beautiful woman. My childhood memories of her have become somewhat vague. I recall that she could play the harp and sing to it—one of the songs she loved most still lives in my memory. It was about a buried harp whose owner had deserted her. Clink, clink, clink, the harp sang to herself that her lover had not yet kept his promises to come back to her. She waited and waited in vain. She remembered how happy they had been when they sang together. Now she was buried on the shady side of crumbling walls. The autumn wind was blowing, the grass fading, and the white clouds deepening. A near-by stream flowed under a broken bridge and no one ever passed by that place. Only gloom and loneliness reigned.

Someone remarked that it was an ill omen that such a beautiful young lady as my mother should like to sing such a sad song.

The drawing room where she played her harp looked out under a giant camphor tree. A canal wound its way around the other side of the bamboo grove which served as a fence. A crêpe myrtle, an osmanthus, and an orange tree struggled for such sunlight as the wide spread of the aged camphor could spare. There she could hear birds singing and fish splashing. At sunset the level beams pierced through the grove and cast the shadows of bamboo leaves dancing on the window screens. The walls were hung with landscape paintings and works of well-known calligraphers. Her lacquered harp, inlaid with jade, lay on a long redwood stand with legs carved in the phoenix motif.

The drawing room was kept as it was for many years after her death. A painted likeness of her hung in the middle of the wall. But Mother was no more! The harp, veiled in dark satin velvet, lay alone on the same stand in the same room. How could I help feeling that I was like that buried harp whose song she used to teach me to sing?

My mother died young. I saw her in her coffin in a beautiful embroidered jacket and skirt, wrapped in a long scarlet satin cape down to her feet. There was a hood attached to the cape. Her face alone was exposed. A large pearl shone on her forehead against the red background of the hood.

My stepmother was a very able woman and she was kind to people, but my relation with her was rather unhappy. She did not live long, and Father never married again.

My grandfather had been the manager of a Shanghai bank. During the time of the Taiping Rebellion (1851-1864) he put up a money stand in the native city of Shanghai. This grew later into a small money exchange shop which in turn developed into a native bank—a concern with unlimited liability, making loans on credit. When Mexican silver dollars were introduced into China as auxiliary currency to taels, the foreign money gained popularity among the people. Counterfeit pesos increased in proportion to the widening circulation of the money. By clinking two dollars on their fingers the bankers could tell the bad from the good. But Grandfather beat them all; he could tell by merely glancing at them.

Unfortunately in the prime of life he suffered a leg injury; the leg had to be amputated and he died of blood poisoning. To my father, at the age of twelve or thereabouts, he left some seven thousand taels, at that time considered a big fortune. This helpless orphan was looked after by his future father-in-law, who was a local scholar. By sound investment and careful economy the property grew, in the course of some thirty years, to the value of seventy thousand taels.

This bit of family history will show the reader that some Western influence must in early days have crept into the family.

Father had an inventive mind. He loved to make plans or designs and direct carpenters, blacksmiths, coppersmiths, farmers and basket makers to carry them out according to specifications. He built houses, made experiments in raising silkworms and planting mulberry trees, manufactured guns (of a type already obsolete in the West), and made many other things according to his fancy. Finally he conceived the bright idea of building a "steamboat" without steam. Father occasionally went to Shanghai to look over his business. He took a rowboat from the village to Ningpo, where he boarded a paddle-wheeled steamer for Shanghai. "It took us three days and two nights to Ningpo in a rowboat," he would say, "and only one night from there to Shanghai by the steamer, while the distance is ten times farther." So he made a sketch of how a miniature paddle-wheel boat might be made.

Carpenters and boatbuilders came. The carpenters were instructed to make paddle wheels, the boatbuilders to build a boat according to my father's plan. A month passed and the boat began to take shape. On the day when the tiny "steamer" was to be launched many visitors came and their mouths gaped in admiration for the wonderful invention. Now the boat was on the canal near our house. Two husky fellows were employed to turn the wheels by a wooden handle. The watching crowd stirred with excitement as the boat started to plow slowly through the water. Presently it began to gather momentum and went faster. When it reached approximately the speed of a rowboat, it refused to accelerate further despite the efforts of the crew. The passengers gesticulated as if helping the boat to go faster. Some even lent their arms to the handle and helped to turn the wheels. But the boat was very stubborn and held to the same speed.

Father made several modifications in the paddle wheels, hoping to increase the speed. All attempts failed. The worst of it was that when the boat went for some distance, weeds and water plants gathered on the wheels and at length even the handle refused to pump. "We have to give all credit to the foreigners who made steamboats," said Father with a sigh.

The "steamer" finally reverted to a rowboat. But it was too heavy to row. Years after, we found it rotting on the banks of the canal, the green moss growing thick on its hull. Even when it failed, however, Father never gave up the idea of making a further attempt until he was told the story of Watt and his boiling kettle. Then he began to see that there was something deeper than appeared in the thing itself. From that time on he was heart and soul for giving his boys a modern education which would some day enable them to learn the foreigners' "tricks" in making wonderful things.

This is an example of how China began to venture on the road to westernization. However, in human relations Father never seriously advocated the foreigners' ways. "The foreigners are as honest, reasonable, and hard working as we Chinese," he would say. He never saw anything beyond that. Neither did he see any objection to his boys learning their ways and manners.

My teacher, on the other hand, was opposed to Father's ideas. "The artifice in making clever things," he would say, "would have a degrading influence on morals. Haven't our sages told us so?" He believed that good morals could only be kept on a high level by living a simple life. Uncle King, my mother's brother, held the same view. He wrote his ideals of life on a piece of red paper which he posted on the wall near his desk: "Burn a stick of incense early in the morning. Be thankful to Heaven, Earth, the Sun, the Moon, and Stars. There shall be no traitors to usurp the power of the ruling dynasty, nor disobedient sons to worry their parents. Everywhere there shall be bumper crops of rice. Then why shall I worry even if I am poor?"

Uncle King was an old scholar. He had passed the civil examinations for the First Degree in his early years. He always carried a long pipe, longer than a walking stick, and one heard him constantly knocking its brass bowl on the brick floor. There were no wrinkles on his forehead in his old age, an indication of peace, health, and contentment. He was so gentle that I never saw him in a temper. He spoke slowly but distinctly and never let unkind words cross his lips. ●

Chapter 5
Trouble Brewing

It was customary during the New Year days for vendors to come to the village to sell pictures, some depicting important or thrilling happenings in the country, others showing theatrical performances. During one New Year vacation the attention of the children was drawn to a set of pictures which were rather novel to them. The multicolored scenes showed the Sino-Japanese War of 1894. One was of a naval battle in the north China Sea. One of the Japanese battleships had struck several large pottery jugs filled with gunpowder, which exploded and set the ship on fire, and it was sinking. There were in the picture hundreds of such jugs floating on the sea. In another picture Japanese prisoners of war were seen locked in chains, and some kept in cages. A great victory for China! It existed only on paper, but we children believed it. As I grew older I began to understand that China had been defeated, that we had lost Formosa, that our navy had been destroyed by the Japanese, and Korea torn away. Within a short span of nine years China had lost three dependencies: first Indo-China, then Burma, and now Korea.

One summer day as the sun was setting a farm helper was seen running breathlessly out of my father's study. He had heard a bell ring there without seeing anyone to cause the sound. To him it must be a ghost. But it was the clock striking seven in the evening.

From time immemorial the villagers had been getting their fire by striking a steel blade on flint. Someone brought a few boxes of matches from Shanghai. The grownups were delighted with this easy method. The children loved the firefly glow obtained by scratching a match on the palm in dark corners. It was called "self-coming light" or "ocean light" because it came from across the sea.

Clocks were unnecessary—for what is the use of keeping exact time in a village? What difference would it make to be two or three hours too late or too early? The country folk counted their time in days and months, not in minutes or hours. Matches were a luxury—had we not got along nicely with our steel blades and flints? But when we came to kerosene it was a different proposition. This made night as brilliant as day. There was a world of difference between this and the dim light of a vegetable-oil lamp.

The Standard Oil Company, known as Meifoo, was the torchbearer that was leading China out of the "dark ages" to modernization. People kept matches and clocks as curiosities but kerosene as a necessity. But if kerosene was a necessity, wasn't the telegraph a necessity to take the place of a foot messenger, and steamboats to take the place of rowboats or sailboats? And so it went.

Few could grasp the significance of one tiny segment of the vast circle. While we played innocently with clocks and matches and enjoyed our kerosene lamps, we never realized that we were toying with a fire that would some day set all China aflame. These were the signs of an impending volcanic eruption which destroyed peace and order first in my village and others like it and eventually in the whole country.

Christian missionaries played their part in introducing foreign manufactures into the interior. Braving hardship, disease, and personal danger, they went to almost every hamlet in the land to save the souls of the heathen Chinese. As a matter of course they took kerosene, cloth, clocks, soap, etc., with them into the interior. People in general were more interested in these things than in the gospel; they opened up a new horizon of wants for the Chinese people. A market for foreign goods was thus created unintentionally by missionaries whose real purpose was to preach the gospel of Christ.

I do not mean that the missionaries were chiefly responsible for the growth of modern commercialism in China. But they played their part—a considerable part, for they penetrated the vast country to every corner. The major role, of course, was played by the merchant ships and gunboats of the Western Powers. It was the Christian missions coupled with gunboats that forced the old literary and agricultural China on the road to modern industrial and commercial life.

With my own eyes I saw the growth of a new class of compradors— middlemen between the Chinese and foreign merchants—and their satellites, and the dying of the old class of literati which I was about to join and from which I eventually sneaked away. The foreign merchants brought their goods to seaports such as Shanghai, Tientsin, and others. Through Chinese compradors they were distributed to cities in the interior and from there to the towns and villages. People were attracted by the easier and larger sums of money they could make. The more enterprising and fortunate entered the new business of dealing directly or indirectly in foreign goods. Some became very rich and many others well to do.

The less fortunate were left behind, to go on tilling their land or to remain in their old trades. As the land was less remunerative and the old trades fast deteriorating in the face of foreign competition, the old economic structure began rapidly to break down. Naturally a number of people were thrown out of economic gear. These unfortunates, jealous of the newly rich and either dissatisfied with their old occupations or deprived of them, became desperate. The flood was surging against the water gate—the autumn flood, symbolic of the turmoil that was to banish peace from my village.

One autumn afternoon as I was running in the fields I heard the frantic sounding of a gong. As the crier approached our village, I heard his cry that the dike had broken through and the flood was coming. I ran back home as fast as I could and told everyone I met on the way.

Everyone got busy at once. We got ready boats, wooden bathtubs, or anything that would float, waiting for the calamity to arrive. Some even chose tall trees for their future abode. None of us slept well that night. The next morning the flood entered our gate and the spearhead of water glided like a giant serpent into our courtyard. By noon, children had begun to row in bathtubs in the hall.

The dike was repaired with sandbags and the Tsao-ao River ceased to overflow. The flood stayed in our village and surrounding districts for about a week, then gradually emptied into the lower lands and disappeared through the rivers into the sea, and all the crops with it.

After a week or so, late in the afternoon a large boat was seen plying toward our village with many people aboard. It docked near our house and they began to disembark. As a precaution we closed our gates. They stormed the main gate with heavy granite slabs and finally it crashed down like an avalanche. The crowd forced their way in. The leader, muscular and heavy built, with his queue round the top of his head, came into the courtyard with his followers after him. He shouted, "We are hungry and want to borrow rice." The crowd joined in chorus. They searched the barn but did not touch it; they wanted to "borrow." Finally, through the mediation of a neighboring farmer, several bushels of rice were "loaned" to them and they embarked with it and sailed away. This was the first intimation of troubles to come.

One incident after another of the same kind but of more serious nature happened in neighboring villages. It started with "borrowing" but ended in robbing. It spread like fire and the scant government forces in the country could not stop it. Moreover, robbery of foodstuffs was not liable to capital punishment and only capital punishment could have checked it, at least temporarily.

The thing dragged on till winter and then the first robbery of a felonious nature took place in the village of the Suns. The victim was a Mr. Sun who owned a prosperous lumber business in Shanghai. His father had amassed a fortune in that port by doing construction work for foreign "hongs" or companies.

It was a cold winter night and everybody had gone to bed early to keep warm. Someone noticed through the window against the background of darkness a column of torchlights moving along the highway toward the village of the Suns. As the lights came near the village a volley of shots was heard. It was bandits. They forced open the gates of Mr. Sun's house and seized all the treasure they could carry—valuable fur coats, silver pieces, jewels, etc. They took Mr. Sun, tied him to the end of a long bamboo pole, and thrust him into the canal. People found him the next morning by pulling up the pole.

Waves of robbery spread through the villages. Overnight the peace and tranquility that the villagers had been enjoying for centuries vanished. Night after night we could not sleep in peace. My father bought revolvers and outmoded guns from Shanghai. All of us, including children, began to practise shooting. Even the birds had no peace, for we took them as our living targets. We went to bed by turns, some keeping a night watch. When we heard dogs barking we fired a few shots in the air as a warning to bandits, real or imaginary; to save ammunition we often mixed firecrackers with gunshots.

This sort of thing could not go on indefinitely. Reluctantly my father gathered together the members of his family and moved to Shanghai.

Meanwhile, during the two years previous to our move I had continued my education at a neighboring provincial city. When I was still studying at the family school, my father asked me one day whether I would like to enter business as a career or prepare for government service. My two elder brothers had both decided for the latter. Father said he would like me to think it over carefully before coming to a decision.

The honor of service to the state had attracted young people for generations. It was only natural that I should be strongly inclined to it. On the other hand, the life of the newly rich, who could enjoy the luxury of the many new and ingenious imported manufactures, was also a temptation. The choice between honor and wealth was more or less contingent upon the ideas and ideals already instilled into one's mind.

I had been told that the people of China fell into four classes. The highest and governing class was the scholars. Next in order came the farmers, who supplied the people with food. The artisans—the third class—manufactured goods for the use of the people. The last were the traders, who transported goods from where there was plenty to where there was a scarcity. Each class had its function to perform in society, but the scholars were the governors of all. So, theoretically speaking, if philosophers were not to be kings, they were at least to be ministers of the state. As there was no hereditary aristocracy in China, the scholars were aristocrats not by birth but by personal endeavor. It was proverbial that a Hsiu-tsai, or person possessing the First Degree by having passed the Imperial civil examinations for that initial degree, was an embryo prime minister to the Imperial Court. Then why should I go into business, which later in life would exclude me from the class of the learned aristocracy?

Thus my mind was set to learning. Of course I understood only vaguely what it meant; to me it was only a steppingstone to something higher up. There were many farmers in our village. There were also a number of businessmen who traded in Shanghai and brought back many interesting things: penknives, whistles, rubber balls, dolls, popguns, watches, and the like. As regarded the artisans, an elder of our clan was a carpenter, as also were his sons. A distant uncle was a silversmith who made rings, bracelets, and trinkets to adorn the ladies of the villages. Of the scholars, another uncle—my mother's brother—was one. He had passed the First Degree but stopped short of the other two. There were carved panels with golden inscriptions hanging high in our Ancestral Hall and tall flagpoles standing before it in honor of clansmen who had been successful in the examinations. I remember that one day the magistrate of our hsien came to a neighboring village to probe a murder case. Did I not see the golden button at the top of his red-tasseled hat, and the string of beads round his neck? Did I not see how his sedan chair was lined with green felt and borne by four persons—each wearing a tall black cone-shaped hat, like a gigantic ice-cream cone, with a feather tilting from the pointed top; and how, as he proceeded in his chair, a pair of gongs kept sounding to announce the presence of His Excellency and that the people must show respect? He was the governor of our district and had, as it were, power over our lives and fortunes. What stuff was he made of? A scholar.

Yes, I knew what a scholar was and the advantage of being one. He might climb up, rung by rung, to the top of the ladder and some day become a very high official, sipping Imperial tea in the majestic palace at Peking. Can the reader blame a village boy like me, whose steps had never carried him more than a few miles from his own village, for aspiring to be a scholar? My childish mind pondered the

Imperial honors which were the scholar's due. I imagined myself growing larger and larger in importance year by year, passing one examination after another from the lowest to the highest, till one day I should be made a high official—much higher than the magistrate—attired in an embroidered gown with a red button on my hat, a long string of beads, and all the other Imperial honors imaginable, coming back home before the eyes of the awe-inspired folk of the village. How wonderful! All these pictures unrolled enticingly. What a bright future lay before me—but only if I applied myself to the study of the classics.

Again, my early schooling, although distasteful to me, had instilled into my mind somewhat vaguely the importance of learning above everything else. Officials of the state were selected through civil examinations and only people who possessed learning could expect to pass them. Officials were honored because learning itself was honored in China.

My own decision was finally to acquire more learning in preparation for the civil examination, to which my father readily agreed. As our family school was inadequate for my further education, I was sent to an advanced school in Shaoshing, the prefectural capital, about forty miles from the village. My two elder brothers had gone there the year before. We went in a small, slender boat, propelled by a long oar pushed by foot power on one side and a short one held by hand as a helm on the other. Along the way I saw on the river banks many pailous standing in rows—pillared arches erected in memory of virtuous widows. River towns appeared at almost regular intervals with their busy traffic on both land and water. We started early in the morning and arrived at the prefectural capital next day in the afternoon after stopping for the night at a large town.

The Sino-Occidental School, as its name implied, offered not only Chinese studies but also courses in Occidental subjects. This was a new departure in Chinese education. Here my mind began to come into contact with Western knowledge, however poorly explained and superficial. My acquaintance with the West had been limited to imported manufactured articles. A mind filled with gods, goddesses, ghosts, fairies, and timeworn traditions was now setting forth to meet some mental imports from the West.

The first and most surprising thing I learned in this school was that the earth is round like a ball. To me it was decidedly flat. I was dumfounded on being further told that lightning is created by electricity and is not the reflection from the mirror of a goddess; that thunder is a by-product of the same electricity and not the beating of a drum by the god of thunder. In elementary physics I learned how rain is formed. It made me give up the idea that a gigantic dragon showers it from his mouth like a fountain high above in the clouds. To understand the meaning of combustion was to banish the idea of fire gods from my mind. One after another, the gods worshiped by my people melted away in my mind like snowmen under the sun. It was the beginning of what little science I know and the end of animism in me. The habit I had formed in my simple nature study in the village, of observing and reasoning without knowing the significance of it, was carried over into the school. As before, I was quite good in reasoning but deficient in memory, and therefore always ready to give up what I had in memory for new ideas that seemed reasonable.

The major part of the curriculum, however, still consisted of literary studies: Chinese literature, classics, and history. There was a considerable amount of memory work to do. As I was not good at it, my name always appeared in the lower middle of the school examination list. I was mediocre in the school, falling far short of brilliance; this was the opinion of my teachers and so it was my own opinion of myself.

Foreign languages were divided into three sections: English, French, and Japanese. I took English and later also Japanese. My Japanese teacher was a Mr. Nakagawa, from whom I learned a correct pronunciation, English was taught us by a Chinese teacher, and his pronunciation of the language was so incorrect that in later years I had to spend much painful time unlearning it. He started us off wrong at the very beginning, even mispronouncing the alphabet. An extreme example is the letter Z, which he called "ütsai."

In the school, in 1898, I heard that Kang Yu-wei and Liang Chi-chao, two liberals from south China who had become unofficial advisers to Emperor Kwanghsü, had succeeded in persuading the Emperor to abolish the civil examinations and establish instead schools along Western lines throughout China. The old scholars were shocked by the news. But the reform was short lived. The Empress Dowager came back into power; Kang Yu-wei and Liang Chi-chao fled to Japan. China was to go on along the old line. When I came home for the vacation I saw the Imperial Edict, printed in bold letters in both the Chinese and Manchu languages on a large yellow paper, posted on the walls in a busy street, ordering the arrest of the two scholar- statesmen. It looked as if the reform were buried forever.

Shaoshing is a city full of historical interest. It was the capital of the ancient kingdom of Yueh (2068-334 B.C.). In 494 B.C., during the reign of King Kou-chien, Yueh was defeated by the kingdom of Wu with its capital at Soochow. The king of Yueh adopted a "twenty-year plan" by which, within ten years, he made his country prosperous and populous and in another ten succeeded in training his people in the arts of war. Meantime he discarded all the comforts that belong to a king, taking very coarse food and sleeping on a rough bed while the king of Wu reveled in luxuries. At the end of twenty years, in 473 B.C., King Kou-chien delivered a deathblow at Wu.

This historical episode has been proverbial ever since, serving as an example for all who hope to rise again after a defeat, whether in private enterprise or national affairs. It illustrates patience, courage, endurance, self-denial, and careful planning. I absorbed this lesson in history right on the spot, and no one could help being impressed by it.

Here also the South Sung emperors (1127-1276 A.D.) made their sojourn when the Tartars had overrun north China and the capital had to be moved to Hangchow. Their Imperial mausoleums could be seen not far from the prefectural capital.

This district, with Shaoshing as its center, supplied lawyers for the whole country. In every yamen or government office throughout the country, large or small, no business could be carried on without a Shaoshing lawyer. And Shaoshing wines were the best in China. Famous scholars, philosophers, poets, and calligraphers who made history in their respective fields were born and lived in the prefecture of Shaoshing. It contained six districts, of which my own, Yuyao, was one.

Shaoshing was also famous for its beautiful scenery. Winding creeks, bridge-spanned canals, rivers, mirrored lakes, and gentle hills together formed a landscape which scholars and philosophers found congenial.

I studied in Shaoshing for two years. My mental horizon rapidly widened. I was made to understand the significance of the Sino-Japanese War of 1894: Japan's victory over China was due to the former's adoption of Western learning. Emperor Kwang-hsü's reforms were inspired by Japan's success in the war. China was to make her erstwhile enemy her teacher. This was why the school offered a course in the Japanese language.

At the end of two years, when bandits made life in the village untenable, my father took me to Shanghai with the rest of the family. My eldest brother had died a year earlier. Here I was put temporarily in a Catholic school to continue my English study. The instruction was given by a French Brother. The pupils were told to call him "Bladda." As he was a foreigner his pronunciation of the language, I imagined, must be good; it was obviously different from that of the Chinese teacher. For instance, he taught us to say "dat" instead of "zat" and "bladda" instead of "bloder." The reader can imagine what curious English we acquired. But I did not stay long in the school. As there was no suitable school in Shanghai for me to go to, Father sent my brother to learn English from an American lady and made me study under him. He thus acted as a comprador of English teaching. I was much dissatisfied with the arrangement, but my father thought it a very clever scheme because it would save money.

Shanghai by 1899 was a small city with a few thousand arrogant foreigners. But the city was well governed, with clean, wide streets and electric or gas lights. I thought the foreigners were wonderful. They knew the secret of electricity. They had invented the steam engine and built steamboats. They took the place of my old gods, who had melted away in the face of my instruction in science, and occupied my mind as new ones. At the same time they served as new devils, too, for their arrogance coupled with the clubs of the policemen, frightened me. In the list of regulations displayed at the entrance of a park on the banks of the Huang-pu River, Chinese as well as dogs were forbidden admission. This said much. The foreigner appeared to my mind half divine and half devilish, double-faced and many-handed like Vishnu, holding an electric light, a steamboat, and a pretty doll in one set of hands, and a policeman's club, revolver, and handful of opium in the other. When one looked at his bright side he was an angel; on the dark side he was a demon.

Western civilization, as viewed by the Chinese in China's recent history, has been either one way or the other at different periods or among different groups of individuals. Li Hung-chang saw the importance of the dark and devilish side and built a navy to beat the devil by his own weapons. Emperor Kwang-hsü saw the importance of the bright and godly side and tried to establish a new school system. The Empress Dowager and the Boxers saw the curse of the devilish side and tried to oust the devils with China's own obsolete arms. The trouble was that the god was strong for the very reason that at times he could be devilish; the devil was powerful because at times he could be godly. He was one and indivisible—you had either to take him as awhole or not at all. Was not Japan the example? Make your erstwhile enemy your teacher!

We lived in Shanghai for about two years, and this home, too, we left hurriedly one night when we were informed that the Empress Dowager had sent instructions to viceroys throughout the country to put all foreigners to death. It was 1900 and the beginning of the Boxer War in North China. The "Boxers" were a fanatical cult claiming magical powers; gymnastics formed a part of their program—hence the name by which they became known. They meant to destroy all foreign manufactured goods and kill every person found in possession of them. They wanted to kill all the foreigners who brought in these terrible things and destroyed their trade. Churches, schools, missionaries, and Christians were all guilty of introducing these poisonous manufactures into China. Get rid of these people by killing them, with swords, knives, magic! Destroy foreign properties by setting them on fire.

The Imperial Court for its own part wanted to destroy all the crazy ideas of foreign origin introduced by Kang Yu-wei and Liang Chi-chao, so that nothing like the reforms of 1898 could happen again. Thus the Boxers wanted to get rid of the manufactured goods and the Empress Dowager and her court wanted to get rid of foreign mental goods; both came from one source—the foreigners. Kill them all! In the beginning of the industrial revolution in England people smashed the machines which destroyed their livelihood. The Boxers went a bit too far. They destroyed the human "machinery" too.

In the south people looked at the foreigner in a different light. They welcomed foreign manufactures but did not understand that it was this very thing that caused the banditry. They put the blame on the obnoxious taxes of the Imperial government and the corruption and incompetence of its officials. So they wanted a revolution.

The people and the Imperial Court in the north were right in holding the foreigners responsible for destroying their trades, but found a wrong solution in smashing the "human machinery." The people of the south had a wrong reason in holding the Imperial government responsible for their plight, but did the right thing in starting a revolution. History seems to consist of a series of accidents, illogical reasoning, and unexpected results, in which the great men appearing on the scene are but the instruments of Fate.

Foreigners cursed banditry in China, but did not know that their own manufactures had caused it in the beginning. In my childhood days we all feared tigers, ghosts, and bandits, but all were imaginary; we only saw them in picture books. Then suddenly the bandit appeared in real life—as if a tiger should dash into your house or a ghost chase you. Finally we dreaded the bandits and forgot about tigers and ghosts. ◉

Chapter 6
Further Education

Thus at the age of fifteen I was brought back home by my father. We were afraid that the Boxer War might extend to Shanghai and so returned to the village; but after a short stay, as the bandits became worse, we moved to Yuyao, the district capital, to live. There I was sent to a local school to study English and arithmetic, and studied Chinese under a private tutor.

After a year or so I went to Hangchow, capital of the province of Chekiang. This was the center of the silk industry in China and also one center of the tea trade. Hangchow silk and tea were famous all over the country.

Hangchow is well known for its scenic beauty. To one side of the city the Chien-tang tides rush up from Hangchow Bay. On the other is the West Lake, mirrored against a blue sky with reflections of temples and villas perched on the surrounding hills. The city was known as a paradise on earth. This was the city that Marco Polo adored in his travels, and it was the ancient capital of King Chien-liao, who kept his domain in peace through long years of incessant invasions and wars in China. Here the South Sungs made their capital for a hundred and fifty years, and here famous poets and men of letters lived. It is a city rich in historical records and monuments. The Imperial Library was filled with valuable books. It was the right place for young scholars to nurse themselves to grow.

In this city of learning I stumbled accidentally into a backward school, a local Christian academy run by an American missionary. Here I hoped that at least I might learn English well. The atmosphere was far from congenial. The principal was a carpenter by trade; this pious American had been carried to China by his religious zeal. He had done some missionary work in my prefecture before being given charge of the academy. As he taught nothing except the Bible, I did not know how much he knew, and since learning was honored in China the carpenter-teacher evoked secret contempt in the hearts of his pupils. My English teacher was a man of vulgar manners, a new convert whose soul may have been saved but whose tongue remained distinctly heathen. I had tramped from this school to that trying to find a really good English teacher, but to my great disappointment I was still simply chasing after shadows.

It was compulsory in the academy to attend exercises in the chapel every morning. We sang hymns in Chinese. Sometimes the clever pupils saw fit to render them in paraphrases which gained more popularity among us than the hymns. In spite of Sunday schools and morning exercises my mind was closed tight as a clam against any spiritual foreign elements. Having got rid of its spirits, ghosts, and gods, it was reluctant to admit any new elements of similar nature. And indeed, ever since that time I have remained an agnostic, trying to find immortality rather in this world than in the next. This conforms with the basic teachings of Confucius.

The only respectable buildings on the campus of the academy were the chapel and the residence of the principal. The students lived in cell-like mud sheds, and classes were held there or in the shabby dining hall.

Out of curiosity some pupils liked to loiter around the principal's house. These unwelcome guests were often told to keep away. Usually they obeyed and walked off, but on one occasion a student rebelled and got into a quarrel with a teacher who happened by.

A crowd began to gather. The student accused the teacher of slapping his face and wept to draw the ready sympathy of the mob. The commotion spread like fire and within a few minutes the majority of the student body had joined in demanding the immediate dismissal of the teacher. The demand being refused by the principal, the crowd became enraged and emotions soared to the highest pitch. The principal told them bluntly that if they did not like the school they could leave. In about two hours the whole school walked out.

This marked the end of my education in a missionary school and I had no regret. The sooner I left the better.

One may ask why such a thing should happen, all of a sudden. It was not a mere outburst of ugliness on the part of unruly students. The slap was only a trigger pulled on a loaded gun; the explosive charge is not to be identified with a little missionary academy. This was part of a country-wide student rebellion against school authority. Even a backward missionary school in Hangchow was not exempt.

The rebellion had started in Nanyang College in Shanghai during the previous year. A student had left an inkstand on his professor's chair and the professor had sat on it. His clothes being stained, he got very angry; it was reported to the president and a few suspects were dismissed. There followed a clash between the college authorities and the student body, the latter supported by a number of faculty members. Eventually all the students walked out.

The younger generation was changing, and it was a change from submission to rebellion. Dismayed at the encroachment of foreign powers upon China, people blamed the Imperial Court for it. The students, inflamed and aroused by Dr. Sun Yat-sen's revolutionary propaganda, were ready to strike whenever there might be opportunity and at anything they could get hold of. They delivered their first blows at the school authorities who were handiest to them.

The Provincial College of Chekiang followed suit. A minor fracas between a student and a sedan chair bearer of the Imperial governor who was visiting the college set off the incident. All the students went on strike in consequence and left the college in a body. Many incidents of like nature occurred in other schools, with eventual disruption of a number of institutions of new learning. It spread throughout the country.

The new elements in the country sympathized with the strikes and blamed the authorities for their despotism; the old elements condemned the students in no uncertain terms and sympathized with the school authorities. Whatever one's opinion, few realized that this was the eve of a revolution. From the time of these early student rebellions to the Revolution of 1911 which marked the birth of the Republic of China was only eight short years.

It was the rebellion of the coming intelligentsia against the class of old literati who controlled China, intellectually and socially as well as politically. With the introduction of the theory of evolution—with special reference to the struggle for existence and the survival of the fittest—and other scientific ideas, the mental attitude of the young generation was undergoing a radical change in social and political philosophy. Eighteenth-century concepts of individual freedom encountered the nineteenth-century industrial revolution: freedom in the form of rebellion against established authority, and industrial revolution in the form of imported products which doomed the old trades to decay. China's old structure was crumbling and the new one was yet to be built.

There was a general unrest throughout the country. Poverty, bandits, famine, plague, official corruption, ignorance of world affairs, and the pinch of foreign aggressions—all were contributing factors. The students, the young blood, merely took the lead. It was not an insignificant inkstand, nor the slapped face of a pupil in a missionary school, nor any altercation between a student and a chair bearer that set educational institutions ablaze throughout China.

After leaving the academy our youthful student body organized a school for themselves—the "School of Reforms and Progress." The name was suggested by Chang Pin-ling, one of the famous revolutionary scholars of our time. Our ambition was to make the school as great one day as Oxford or Cambridge. Pretty soon, as was natural, we found ourselves disillusioned. The student body dwindled in the course of half a year to a few elected officers. When these few found no one to re-elect them, they also departed to seek educations elsewhere.

For my part, I registered at Chekiang College, under a new name lest the college authorities find me persona non grata. I took the entrance examination, passed it, and was admitted. The college had just been reorganized after the strike and was the highest institution of learning in the Province of Scholars, as our province was known. Its forerunner had been Chiou Shih Shu-yuan, or the "School for Seeking What Is Right." It is the proper frame of mind for a scholar to seek what is right, and this was the attitude of Chinese scholars of former generations. This had been a school similar to the Sino-Occidental School of Shaoshing, an old-style Chinese school whose curriculum included some foreign languages and science teaching. As the new subjects grew in importance and were allotted more time it developed into a new type of school and was renamed Chekiang College.

Situated in the provincial capital and maintained by the government, the college served as a center of cultural movements in the province. The curriculum was very similar to that of the Sino-Occidental School, but the courses were more advanced, more various, and better taught, with less sheer memory work. It was a modern school in the making.

I had been trotting along in the dark since entering the school in Shaoshing. My mind always rushed for the place where I caught a glimpse of bewitching light and groped in some other direction when it elusively disappeared. By this time, however, I saw things in much clearer perspective. I had begun to study world history in English. At first it seemed as difficult to understand the doings of other peoples as when one tries to understand the behavior of the masses, but gradually I began to see, albeit dimly, the development of Western civilization. This was of course only in a very general and vague way. But my interest in Western history was aroused and a foundation laid for further study.

Here I was in the midst of intellectual activities. Through reading, lectures, and conversation, my information about China and the world was accumulating. I grew familiar with some forty centuries of China's history, with a fair understanding of the causes, as given by the great historians, of the rise and fall of many dynasties.

This served as the basis for a comparative study of Western history later on.

In the field of contemporary history there was plenty of material. The Sino-Japanese War of 1894, of which I had learned from the misleading colored pictures in my childhood; the short-lived reforms of Kang Yu-wei and Liang Chi-chao in 1898, which had taken place during my stay in the Sino-Occidental School, the Boxer War of 1900, news of which I learned at such close range in Shanghai; and the Russo-Japanese War of 1904 which was even then raging (with China's overwhelming sympathy for Japan)—each and all furnished rich materials for thought and study.

One might study history backward, too: there was the Sino-French War in 1885 in which China lost Indo-China; the Taiping Rebellion (1851-1864) and the ever-victorious army of Generals Gordon and Ward; the Opium War of 1840, as a result of which China lost Hong Kong; and if one went farther back there was the coming of the Jesuits during the later Ming and early Ching periods, and the travels of Marco Polo during the Yuan or Mongol Dynasty; still farther back China had relations with the Roman Empire.

Liang Chi-chao's Young China, an encyclopedic monthly published in Tokyo, furnished a great variety of materials ranging from short stories to metaphysics and including elementary science, history, politics, biographies, literature, etc. His lucid pen was capable of making people understand almost any subject new or difficult to the reader. This was very important at a time when there was a need to introduce Western ideas into China. His style was clear, persuasive, and easy to follow and therefore very profitable reading for students. I was one among thousands who came under his influence. I think this great scholar did more than anyone else in his time to popularize modern knowledge among the rising generation. His was the fountain of wisdom from which every young man drew to quench his thirst for the new learning.

Politically he stood for constitutional reforms under the reigning dynasty. Meanwhile the revolutionaries were publishing a number of periodicals to sponsor Dr. Sun Yat-sen's radical idea that for China a republican form of government was better than a monarchy and that China must be governed by the Chinese and not by the corrupt and degenerate Manchus. That published by the Chekiang students in Tokyo was a monthly: Tides of Chien-tang. This magazine attacked the reigning dynasty so fiercely that it was barred from the mails, among other like periodicals, by the postal authorities. But the movement had the sympathy of the Tokyo government and the tabooed periodicals therefore flowed continuously from Japan, where they were published, into the International Settlement of Shanghai where Chinese jurisdiction reached only partially. So Shanghai became a clearinghouse for revolutionary ideas, and from there the literature was smuggled into other cities by sympathizers as well as profit makers.

Chekiang College itself was deluged with pamphlets, magazines, and books of revolutionary propaganda; some depicting the atrocities committed by the Manchus during their invasion of China , others describing their misrule and the unequal treatment of Manchus and Chinese under the existing regime. The students devoured them voluptuously. No power on earth could stop them.

Moreover, concrete examples of Manchu misrule and incompetence could be found just outside the college gate. Within the city walls of Hangchow was a walled city for the Manchus who were stationed there as a garrison to watch over the Chinese. I was warned not to enter it; anyone did so at his own risk. More than two hundred years earlier this city within a city had been set aside exclusively as barracks for the Manchu soldiers in Hangchow. After them their children's children had lived there, nominally as soldiers, for generations until they were killed by the Taipings during the siege of the capital. Intermarriage between Chinese and Manchus was in general forbidden, but Manchus were allowed to marry Chinese women if they preferred, although such marriages were rare. When the civil war was over, a part of the garrison stationed at Chingchow in Hupeh Province was moved to Hangchow to fill the vacancy. Some of these were still living and spoke Hupeh dialect; most of them had died, but their children lived there and still clung to the dialect of their fathers. Thus they were easily detected by the natives of Hangchow. But the third generation had begun to speak the local Hangchow tongue.

They sent ten of their boys to study at the college. These youths behaved wisely toward the revolutionary movement in the college by pretending not to know of it. One of them, of Mongol origin, actually told me he was in favor of a revolution against the Manchu Dynasty as he was a non-Manchu in spite of being a Manchu "soldier."

These so-called Manchu soldiers were no soldiers at all; they were just the same as civilians. They had families and reared children in the so-called barracks and knew nothing of the arts of war. The only difference was that they lived on government rations and had no occupation. Theirs was a sort of parasitic life, and they degenerated physically, mentally, and morally. They haunted the teahouses on the West Lake, some of them in the fashionable manner carrying a bird in its cage, and people generally kept away from them. They would slap anyone who offended them. These living examples of degeneration, corruption, and arrogance woke hatred and contempt in the hearts of the young students. It was just as effective as revolutionary propaganda, if not more so.

While we got our mental food from Liang Chi-chao, we drew our emotional nourishment from Dr. Sun Yat-sen and his sympathizers. Generally speaking, it is emotion that leads to action when a decisive hour comes; when that hour came in China Dr. Sun, both dreamer and man of action, won a decisive victory over the new literati who stood for constitutionalism.

Such was the general atmosphere of Chekiang College. Similar conditions also prevailed in other institutions. I was interested in all these activities. I liked to get hold of information and to think with the materials thus secured, and also to feel and to act. But nothing carried me away entirely. To play safe I still planned to take the Imperial civil examination, still the only road to a government position except by way of revolution, which seemed long and difficult to me. I was at times timid and shy, at others bold and reckless, and therefore did not trust my own temperament. So I often acted cautiously, feeling my way before making a definite move. Especially at any crossroads, I would consider again and again before coming to a decision. In case of doubt I was apt instead to sit by the roadside and indulge in daydreams. But once a decision was made I would stick to the end. I made mistakes in life, but never so fatally as to be swept away by the advancing tides. ◉

Chapter 7
Imperial Civil Examination

Early one morning, as the time for the civil examination drew near, I started for Shaoshing where the examination was to be held for our district. The luggage man slung his bamboo pole over his shoulder with my suitcase and bamboo basket roped to one end and bedding outfits balancing the other. I followed on his heels. As my luggage swung out of the college gate a teacher who happened to see me smiled and wished me good luck.

After passing through many granite-paved streets and zigzag narrow Hangchow alleys, we came to the banks of the Chien-tang River. I measured my steps along a gangway of narrow, frail planks a quarter of a mile long, with the tides flowing underneath, leading to the waiting ferryboat. The boat was plied by several heavy oars, with the occasional help of sails. It glided along in leisurely fashion. As it could only be controlled by heading against the tide, the slow speed was further reduced and it took us two hours to cross. None of us imagined then that within some thirty years a long steel bridge   would span the river, with trains and cars passing over it.

I then took a sedan chair through miles of mulberry groves to a busy trading city, where I embarked for Shaoshing, arriving next morning after a night on the boat, which was packed with passengers like sardines. One had to lie flat and straight; if you tried to move your legs you found your allotted space gone; if you tried to turn on your side there was no space left to lie flat again.

In Shaoshing I got a room with board in a fan maker's family. The place was small and dark and filled with strange odors from certain vegetable oils used to make fans. In the evening I studied by a vegetable-oil lamp which did not give enough light to read small letters without straining one's eyes. We refrained from using kerosene because of the inflammable materials that filled the place. In the dark we could not walk without stumbling over some sort of stuff for making fans.

The examination began with roll call at the entrance of the Examination Hall at about four o'clock in the morning. The early autumn morning was chilly. A large crowd of literati, several thousand strong and each wearing a red-tasseled hat—without a button—and carrying a lantern gathered around the spacious courtyard. At the entrance to the hall the Prefect sat in stately dignity at a long desk. He wore a red-tasseled hat with a blue crystal button at the top, a black jacket over a deep blue gown, and a chain of beads around his neck. This was his full official attire. With a vermilion pen in his hand he began to call the roll. As he went down the list a man standing by him called out in long-drawn tones the name of each candidate, who promptly sang out at the top of his voice, "Here! So-and-so, the guarantor." Immediately the guarantor sang his own name in acknowledgment of the sponsorship. The Prefect then glanced about quickly to see if anything was wrong and made a red dot above the name with his vermilion pen.

The candidate was then let in. His hat and clothes were searched to see that he carried no notes with him. Anything found written on paper would be confiscated.

The candidates moved on in files to their respective seats, which were numbered, each finding his place accordingly. The names on the examination papers were written on detachable s lips to be torn off before the papers were handed in. Each paper was also numbered in a sealed corner, which was not opened until the papers were marked and the successful candidates selected, so as to prevent any possible favoritism. Toward the end of the Manchu Dynasty, when corruption ran rampant in many branches of government office, the Imperial examination system remained independent and free alike of external interference and internal corruption. This was one reason why the degrees conferred were so much honored in China.

Questions were limited to the Confucian classics and this was why a candidate must commit to memory all the texts in the classics. This I had done through years of laborious conning in my country school and the Sino-Occidental School in Shaoshing. Questions were shown to the candidates by means of cubic lanterns, on the screens of which the questions were written; they were lighted with candles so that the black letters on the white screens could be seen distinctly at a distance. Bearers raised the lanterns high above their heads and carried them up and down the aisles several times, so that none could miss them.

About noon officials went around to check on how far the candidates had gone with their essays and set on each paper a seal at the spot to which the lines had run. At about four in the afternoon cannon began to roar, marking the first call for the collection of papers. The gates were flung open and the band began to play. Candidates who were able to answer the first call handed in their papers and made their way out slowly through the gates with music playing and an anxious crowd waiting. After everyone had made his exit the gates were closed again. The second call was made about an hour later with the same ceremony. The third or final call was made about six, with both cannon and band remaining silent.

We had about a week or ten days to wait for the results of the examination. In the interim there was plenty of time for amusement. Bookstores, large and small, were found everywhere near the Examination Hall. There were chess stands, temporary restaurants with famous Shaoshing wines and delicious dishes at moderate prices, and traveling theatres where we could go and enjoy ourselves.

On the day when the results were to be made public a large crowd waited anxiously in front of a high, spacious wall opposite the entrance of the Examination Hall. Cannon and band announced the moment when the list of names, or rather numbers, of the successful candidates was issued. The numbers were set down in a circular formation instead of in a column, so as to avoid having a top and bottom to the list.

I was pleasantly surprised to find my own number in big black letters among the others in the circle on the enormous oblong paper posted on the wall. To make sure I rubbed my eyes and looked at it several times. When I was sure they had not deceived me, I elbowed through the packed crowd and hastened back to my lodging house. As I made my way out I noticed a man with an open umbrella which caught on a railing. When he jerked it off the umbrella went upward, looking like a giant artichoke, but in his excitement he kept on running and paid no attention to it.

The second session of the examination came within a few days. Everyone who had passed the first had reason to worry, since some would be eliminated. I was lucky in the second trial. In the list of names which was posted on the wall I found mine somewhere in the middle rows.

The third and final session was merely perfunctory. In addition to an essay we were supposed to write down from memory a section of the "Imperial Instructions in Morals"; in reality each of us had with us a copy of the text, which we were allowed to carry into the Examination Hall and which we copied outright. The Imperial Examiner appeared in person to supervise the final examination. His official title I learned from the inscription on two identical pennants about fifteen feet long which streamed in the air from flagpoles standing symmetrically at either side of the e ntrance. It read: "The Imperial Vice-Minister of Rites and Concurrently Imperial Examiner of Public Instruction for the Province of Chekiang, etc."

Early in the morning, some days later, I was awakened from slumber by the rapid beating of a tom-tom outside my window. It was an official reporter coming to announce the award of the First Degree—Wu-shen, popularly known as Hsiu-tsai. The official announcement, which was printed in bold block prints on a piece of red paper about six feet by four, read as follows:

His Majesty's Imperial Vice-Minister of Rites and Concurrently Imperial Examiner of Public Instruction for the Province of Chekiang, etc., wishes to announce that your honorable person, Chiang Monlin, is awarded the Degree of Wu-shen and entitled to enjoy the privilege of entering the District Government School as a government scholar.

The "district school" was an empty Confucian temple with one official in charge who acted as the "government teacher" but in fact never taught anyone or anything. One found, actually, neither school nor teacher; what was called a school was only symbolic. Yet I had to pay the traditional entrance fee of $100—which I paid only partially, through bargaining.

After the examination the pendulum of life swung back once again to my new education. In a few days I went back to Chekiang College. In leaving, I learned from my landlord that one of my fellow lodgers had complained to him in a rage that the Imperial Examiner was so blind as to pass a man almost illiterate, like me, and neglect him, who possessed great literary merits. Such are the hazards of examinations!

Back at the college I plunged at once into studies again and found myself in the midst of algebra, physics, zoölogy, history, and so on. By way of extracurricular activity I indulged in reading revolutionary literature and discussed contemporary politics with my fellow students. Imperial examination days and Chekiang College were worlds apart! It seemed a transformation overnight from misty, immutable medievalism to the whirlpool of a new revolutionary world. I felt as if what had happened had been a dream.

After two months it was time for the winter vacation. I was called back home by my father to receive congratulations from relatives and friends upon my success. I was now nineteen. My close relatives saw a bright future for me; if the feng-shui of my ancestral tombs were favorable I would go right along, passing the two remaining examinations to receive the highest degree, to the glory of family, relatives, and above all, our ancestors whose spirits were in heaven. My second brother had passed his civil examination a few years before me; he was now a student at the Imperial University of Peking, of which I was to be Chancellor after some fifteen years—unpredictable chance.

An announcement printed on a big piece of red paper like the one I had received in Shaoshing was presented by official reporters, to the beating of a tom-tom, to my relatives and family friends. On the day of celebration I dressed in a blue satin gown and wore a red-tasseled hat with a silver button on top. Several hundred relatives and friends, including women and children, came to feast for two days. The spacious guesthall was decorated with artistic red lanterns and an orchestra played Chinese tunes. The happiest man there was my father, who cherished the hope that some day his son might become a grand minister at His Majesty's Imperial Court. For my part, I was puzzled. I was torn between two opposing forces, one pulling toward the old and the other toward the new. "What shall I do? What shall I do?" a voice cried out within me.

After three weeks the college reopened for the new session. Once more I swung back again to my studies in the new learning. I stayed for about half a year, leaving before the summer vacation. All the conflicting ideas, as between new and old, constitutional reforms and revolution, buzzing around in this topsy-turvy world of mine, were more than an immature mind could endure. I became restless and often had a fantasy in which, by a sort of somersault, I rocketed high into the air and then whirled down rapidly to the ground, where I burst to bits and was gone forever.

Being born in a family which had a few cases of insanity among my close relatives, I wondered sometimes whether I, too, had inherited a faint streak of instability which might occasionally tip the scale a little in my otherwise well-balanced temperament. I had been told, moreover, by my father and my granduncle that my ideas and actions during childhood had been quite different from those of the rest of the children. I still remember how my granduncle scolded me one day, remarking that when I grew up I would become either a wise man or a rascal; to which, not knowing the meaning quite clearly, I secretly replied to myself that I wanted to be a wise man.

Was I crazy in this crazy world? At least one problem always remained clear in my mind: how to save China from dismemberment by the foreign Powers. Revolutionary ideas were now fast gaining ground in the minds of students throughout the country. As more and more of them joined the movement, the influence of Dr. Sun Yat-sen grew wider and wider. The days of the reigning dynasty were numbered.

On my part, I longed for a better and more westernized school. For by this time I could see that the wind blew in the direction of westernization, irrespective of whether China had constitutional reforms or revolution. One morning as I passed unintentionally by a passageway where students were forbidden, I met the proctor, who asked me what I was doing there. On the spur of the moment I improvised the story that my mother was ill and had written me to come home.

"That's too bad," he said. "You had better go right away."

I went back to my dormitory, packed up everything, and left the college that same morning. I took a small steamboat, chugging along the Grand Canal, down to Shanghai. There I took the entrance examination for Nanyang College and passed it. This was the year 1904, when the Russo-Japanese War was raging in all intensity for the control of Manchuria. ●

Chapter 8
Westernization

China was now definitely on the track of westernization, whatever her struggles between old and new, between constitutionalism and revolution. The victory of Japan over Tsarist Russia gave further impetus to her reforms along new or Western lines. By this time about fifty thousand Chinese students had gathered about Tokyo, a center of the new knowledge. In the meantime the government had begun a series of reforms; new educational, military, and police systems were adopted, all copied after the Japanese models. Many believed that the Western systems and institutions which had been assimilated by the Japanese and adapted to Japanese life were more suitable to Chinese conditions than purely foreign forms. That is to say, China was to receive Western civilization via Japan. There were others, however, who held that if she must introduce Western civilization for her rejuvenation, why should she not go direct to the West for it?

I was one of those who believed in the direct route. In spite of the persuasions of friends studying in Japan, I stuck stubbornly to my belief. I entered Nanyang College with a view to preparing myself for American universities. As all the textbooks on Western subjects were in English, it suited me splendidly.

The college had been organized with the advice of Dr. John C. Ferguson, a former American missionary who only recently died in New York, and its preparatory department was run along the lines of an American high school. So it was most convenient as the final step to an American college. There were several American teachers who taught us modern subjects. After two years there I could read English fairly well, although I was still quite deficient in speaking. The language was not taught by phonetic methods and I found my tongue too stiff to follow.

The curriculum was divided into two groups, one of Chinese and the other of Western subjects. I always stood high in both, once winning honors in the two examinations simultaneously. The principal summoned me and paid me high compliments, to my great satisfaction.

The college was laid out and built according to Western plan; the main building had in its center a clock tower which could be seen several miles away. In front of a row of buildings was a vast football field, green and well kept. Football and baseball were encouraged by the college authorities and games and sports, generally indulged in by the students. Intercollegiate track and field games were held twice a year, with thousands of spectators.

Born physically frail, I began to realize that a healthy body was necessary for a healthy mind. Besides daily exercise and some sports of the lighter kind, I adopted a course of physical culture for myself. Every morning at about six I practised with dumbbells for half an hour, and again for fifteen minutes in the evening before going to bed. I kept this up for three years without interruption and after that time found myself in good health and always in a cheerful mood.

Spender's principles of education—consisting of three elements: the intellectual, moral, and physical—had by now been introduced into China. So to make up my moral education I reviewed some of the Confucian classics and studied the Sung and Ming philosophers and biographies of great men in history, both Chinese and Western, with a view to imitating their conduct. I entered selected parts of their savings and doings in my diary as I came across those that struck me. Then I did some careful thinking about them, tried to act on them, and watched the results, which were also entered into the diary for further examination.

It was exciting whenever I discovered that Chinese and Western ideas regarding certain matters were similar or almost identical. When they were I knew that in acting in accordance with them I would be guided by a universal truth. When discrepancies occurred I studied them and tried to find out the reasons for them. In this way I unconsciously made a comparative study of morals, or rules of conduct, of East and West. The most important result was that I learned to differentiate essentials from nonessentials and the fundamental from the superficial in moral ideas.

Henceforth I began to be more positive, more d efinite, more self-confident in steering my life on troubled waters. For moral ideas are the charts by means of which a life of action is directed.

I began to see the oneness of East and West and appreciate the dictum of Lu Hsiang-shan, a Sung philosopher, that "the sages born of the Eastern sea will have the same mind and therefore the same reason as the sages of the Western sea." I also began to see unity in chaos, for I came to realize that essentials are but few, while to know the similarities, differences, or contrasts among them is to clarify each and all of them. It was the buzzing of trifling things that made you dizzy. So I followed the teachings o f Mencius and Lu Hsiang-shan that in learning we must grasp the essentials and neglect the trifles and make our own reasoning power the sole arbiter. Thus I began to establish myself on the solid rock of reasoning instead of traditional beliefs. I felt as if I had stripped off clothes that were altogether too tight and stepped forth naked and free.

However, reason does not exist in a vacuum. I indulged in too much thinking, which led to nothing but disappointment. But the way to right thinking had to start from thinking itself, and learning to think by experience. You cannot teach a person how to think if he does not think at all. My belief here was reinforced in later years in America by reading John Dewey's How We Think, to which I owed much.

It is the teaching of the Confucian school that mental culture is the starting point of personal culture, which in turn will serve as the foundation for statecraft. Therefore, in order to save China, save yourself first. So I devoted myself to study and thinking, to physical exercise and to proper conduct. This was, as I understood it, the way to personal culture which would some day serve as the foundation for rendering service to the state.

While I was still at Nanyang College the Imperial Court took a definite step in educational reform by abolishing—in 1905—the agelong system of civil examinations; by this act the door to the past was closed to the younger generation once and for all. The decree was prompted by the victory of Japan over Russia. To replace the old, a new educational system was inaugurated, modeled after the Japanese, which in turn had been introduced to Japan from the West. China was now surely on the road to westernization.

For some time past Shanghai had been the center of a fugitive cultural movement in China. Harbored in the International Settlement and the French Concession, where Chinese jurisdiction reached to only a very limited extent or so far as international or French authorities might agree, Chinese intellectual and revo lutionary leaders made their homes and enjoyed freedom of speech and publication. Here political fugitives and men of radical thought, or those so considered at the time, gathered to discuss, elucidate, and publish their ideas. Life here was comparable to that in one of the old Greek city-states—thinking was free and active.

For my own part, in addition to my training at Nanyang I joined in various activities as a junior member, more by way of learning than active participation. On Saturdays and Sundays I frequented especially Chi-fang, a teashop on Foochow

Road where all the students of Shanghai sipped their tea and indulged in lively discussions. No student of those days can forget the unique figure of the king of rogues, or "King Hsu," who was an inseparable part of the teahouse, selling revolutionary literature to the students. He was dressed in shabby Western clothes with a grey greasy cap on his head, his queue being cut. Among his revolutionary wares he included a pamphlet, A New Treatise on Sex Problems, which he explained was to catch the attention of the reading public. Nobody ever knew his name or where he lived. Any book on revolution nominally tabooed by the municipal authorities by request of the Chinese government could be secured through him.

In the same year that civil examinations were abolished the Tung Men Huei— the "Revolutionary Union," predecessor of the Kuomintang—was organized by Dr. Sun Yat-sen in Tokyo with several hundred students joining, and Dr. Sun was elected president. This was the year of the Portsmouth Treaty, signed by Japan and Russia to end the Russo-Japanese War. After this victory over one of the Western Powers Japan was now ready to launch aggression on China. This was a bare ten years before she delivered her famous Twenty-One Demands, and only sixteen years before the Mukden Incident which led to full-fledged war in 1937.

In Shanghai a boycott movement against American goods was proceeding in all intensity as a protest against the passing of the Chinese Exclusion Act by the American Congress. Students and merchants joined in calling from door to door on Chinese shopkeepers, urging them not to sell American merchandise. The shopkeepers tried to get rid of their boycotted goods as fast as possible at very moderate prices and a number of people were happy to buy them at the back door. Mass meetings were held in which fierce speeches against the exclusion act were made. At one of them the speaker stamped on the platform so hard that the sole of his shoe fell off and was flung into the audience while waves of laughter rang through the hall.

Another important incident, in the following year, was the agitation by the gentry of Chekiang and Kiangsu Provinces and the students and merchants of Shanghai against construction of the Soochow-Hangchow-Ningpo Railway by British capital. There were public demonstrations in the form of mass meetings, circular telegrams, and soapbox orations, and subscriptions were opened for shares in the railway with a view to building it with Chinese capital. The line was changed to run via Shanghai, Hangchow, and Ningpo; Shanghai being substituted for Soochow by the curious reasoning that the latter, an inland city, would thus be spared foreign influence, which was bound to increase with a railway. The British gave in as to the route, though the agitation was unsuccessful in obtaining Chinese capital ownership, and the railway was begun the next year.

Students all over China remained quiet in the schools during those years, partly because of their wider interests in activities outside school and partly because they themselves had wearied of the meaningless troubles they gave the school authorities. Nevertheless, they now turned their attention to the school cooks who prepared food for them. Each student paid six dollars a month for his food in Shanghai; in the interior, three dollars. One could not,therefore, expect very much from the cook, but the students were dissatisfied with what they got. They complained of the coarse rice and the poor quality of meat and vegetables, often demanding additional dishes—generally fried eggs, which were easy to prepare. Eggs were cheap in China then, about fifty or sixty for a dollar. Sometimes the students smashed the plates or bowls or beat up the cooks. No school was free from "strikes in the dining hall" as they were called.

In 1907 a short-lived revolution broke out in Anking, provincial capital of Anhwei. The leader was Hsu Shih-ling, police taotai (chief of police) of that province. He had been a teacher in the Sino-Occidental School in Shaoshing, where I received my early education in Western learning—where I first learned that the earth is round. He was a Chu-jen, the Second Degree awarded through the Imperial civil examinations; had taught in the school for a few years and then gone to Japan to study. Returning to China, he bought the office of taotai with fifty thousand dollars borrowed from friends and was appointed for the province of Anking. With the police under his control, he shot the governor with his own hand and started a coup d'état in the provincial capital. With two personal followers and the police force he occupied the arsenal, training its several cannon on the entrance. Not being adepts in military art, they were unable to make the guns work and soldiers rushed in and arrested him. One of his followers, Chen, was killed in action while the other, Ma, was arrested later.

Ma had been a schoolmate of mine at Chekiang College in Hang-chow, and on their way from Japan to Anking he a nd Chen had stopped in Shanghai, where they came to see me almost every day. They talked at length about the revolutionary movement, which they believed was the only course for China's salvation, and asked me to go to Anking with them; but a cousin of mine, the manager of a native bank, advised me rather to take a trip to Japan. During summer vacation I took the opportunity of going with a friend to Tokyo, where an exposition was being held.

Ma and Chen and I dined in farewell at the I-tse-hsiang Restaurant the evening before my departure, and they also left the next day for Anking, aboard a Yangtze steamer which took them up the river to their fatal destination.

My first experience on an ocean-going steamer was rather thrilling. Everything was novel to me. The flush toilet was a wonder. The Japanese boysans (cabin boys) were courteous. We reached Nagasaki the next morning and were impressed with the beautiful scenery in that port. In the afternoon we passed Shimonoseki, well known in China for Li Hung-chang's visit to it and for the peace treaty concluded in 1895 and known by that name. We landed at Kobe and from there took a train to Tokyo, getting off at Shimbashi Station. A friend of mine who was studying in Tokyo took me to a small hotel, the Kimigayokan in the Koishikawa district. The street was unpaved and muddy on that rainy day.

I visited the exposition in Ueno Park dozens of times and was impressed with the industrial development of Japan. In a war museum where prizes of war were shown I was very much ashamed to see the Chinese flags, uniforms, and weapons seized in the Sino-Japanese War and I tried vainly to dodge the eyes that stared at me. In the evening the park was illuminated with thousands of electric lights and the happy populace of Tokyo paraded on the grounds with myriad lanterns in their hands, shouting Banzai! They were intoxicated with the victory over Russia two years earlier and still went wild about it. On my part, I stood alone at the top of an imitation hill and watched the parade passing. I was so much moved that tears rolled down my cheeks.

Early one morning, within a week or so of my arrival, the neisan or chambermaid brought me a Japanese paper from which I learned of Hsu Shih-ling's revolution in Anking and its failure. I would have been killed if I had gone there with my two friends.

The general impression I had of Japan was very favorable. The whole country was a garden. The people were well dressed, their cities clean. They were perhaps inwardly conceited, but courteous to strangers. Compulsory education made the general level of the people much higher than in China, and this was perhaps the secret of Japan's becoming a world Power. These were the impressions I carried home after a month's stay.

Pretty soon I began to work hard again at the college. The following year, during the summer vacation, I went to Hangchow to take the Chekiang provincial examination for scholarships to study in America. Having failed, I got a few thousand dollars from my father and prepared to go to California for further study. ●

PART II

AMERICAN YEARS

Chapter 9
Further "West"

With part of the money my father gave me I bought hats, shoes, clothes, and other necessary things, and a first-class ticket to San Francisco. The rest I converted into American gold dollars at the rate of two Mexican to one. My queue I got rid of at a barbershop. When the barber applied a pair of long scissors to my hair I felt as if I were on the guillotine—a chill stole all over me. With two quick, heavy cuts my queue fell off and I felt as if my head had gone with it. It was given back to me wrapped in paper and I threw it into the ocean on my way to America.

I acquired a doctor's certificate and a passport, based on Section 6 of the immigration law admitting students, and went to the American Consulate General in Shanghai for a visa. This done, I secured my ticket and boarded an American Mail liner for San Francisco. It was late August, 1908. There were about a dozen Chinese students on the same boat. Leaving the shores of my country seemed to cut away the last link that connected me with my earlier life. I was lucky in being a good sailor and was never sick during the twenty-four long days aboard ship. Perhaps this was due to the practice I had had in swinging for several weeks before embarking. I was good at it, for swinging is a Chinese garden pastime.

The liner was much larger and more luxurious than the Japanese steamer I had taken to Kobe the previous year. The most striking thing to me on board was the dancing. Brought up in a society where men and women did not mix freely, I could not at once reconcile myself to it. But after watching it several times I began to appreciate the beauty of it.

On the day of our arrival at San Francisco a port doctor came on board and carefully examined the eyes of Chinese students to see whether any of us had any trace of trachoma.

The first thing I had felt on landing was the power of the state through the instrumentality of the immigration officials and police. I began to wonder why the people of a republic enjoyed less individual freedom than did the people of China , which was an absolute monarchy. In China we scarcely felt the influence of the state. "Heaven is high above and the Emperor is far away."

We stopped over in San Francisco for a few hours to visit Chinatown. Then two of us who were bound for the University of California were taken to Berkeley by the president of the Chinese Students' Alliance there. In the evening we dined at a restaurant in Berkeley, the Sky Light, on Shattuck Avenue, each paying twenty-five cents for a dinner which consisted of soup, beef stew, and a piece of pie, with bread and butter and a cup of coffee. I took a room at Mrs. Coole's house on Bancroft Way. She was a talkative, elderly lady, very kind to the Chinese students. She told me that I must turn off the light before going out and shut off the water after washing; that I must not throw peanuts into the flush toilet or leave my money on the table; that in leaving the room I needn't lock the door, but if I preferred I might leave the key under the mat. "If you want anything," she said, "you just tell me. I know how a stranger must feel in a foreign country. Make yourself at home." Then she bade me good night and left the room.

As I had arrived in San Francisco too late to enter the fall session of the university, I had to wait for the next term. Meantime I got a coed of the university to coach me in English at fifty cents an hour. I spent all my time studying English; I read the San Francisco Chronicle regularly every morning and subscribed to a weekly magazine, The Outlook, for more serious study. By the aid of Webster's Collegiate Dictionary, which was always at hand and to which every doubtful word was referred, my vocabulary increased day by day and at the end of four months I could read papers and magazines quite freely.

In the beginning I found myself partially blind, deaf, and dumb so far as the English language was concerned. These difficulties had to be surmounted before I could hope to get along well in the university. By concentration and perseverance the first obstacle was largely overcome in the first four months and it was only a matter of time to reduce it completely. The second had to be removed gradually by listening to conversations and lectures. It was easier to understand lectures because they were in the form of organized thought and were slower and more distinct in delivery. Conversations were generally wider in range and carried on in a rapid succession of varied or disconnected groups of ideas in which one had difficulty in following the thread of thought. To listen to a play at the theatre was midway between the two.

It was most difficult, however, to overcome the dumbness. First of all, I had been started off wrong from the very beginning in China. The wrong habits were deeply rooted and it took time to dislodge them. In the second place, as I was ignorant of phonetic methods the mere effort to imitate a word did not necessarily lead to a correct pronunc iation. For there are wide gaps between the tone uttered and the ear that hears it, and between ear and tongue—the ear does not necessarily catch the right tone, nor does the tongue always follow the ear in reproducing it. Moreover, California was not so hospitable a land socially for the Chinese as to make one feel congenial or at ease; I was always overconscious of this, slow to mingle with others and shy when others tried to approach me. Thus many available social connections were cut off, and as language improves only with intercourse, the improvement in the spoken language was indeed very, very slow. This hampered my participation in discussions, both in the classroom and out of it, when I later entered the university. As a rule I remained mute in class and when a question was put to me responded only by a blush. My professors were very considerate and on no occasion tried to exact an answer. Perhaps they realized my social plight, or excused me simply because I was a foreigner. At any rate, from my examination papers—in most cases above "B" grade—they knew I did my classwork conscientiously in spite of muteness.

Time flew—it was soon Christmas. On Christmas Eve I dined alone at a restaurant with better food than on the first occasion, and a larger bill. After dinner I strolled about the streets watching the happy family gatherings through the windows where curtains were not drawn. Christmas trees, some lighted with tiny electric lights and some with candles, were everywhere.

With a few Chinese friends on New Year's Eve I went across the bay to San Francisco. From the ferry we could see at a distance, on the other side of the bay, the Clock Tower bejeweled with hundreds of lights. Moving through the crowd to the exit on landing, one heard the player pianos going full tilt for their nickel's worth. As I followed the packed crowd streaming slowly along the main street, flooded with lights, my ears were deafened by toy bugles and rattles. People took particular pleasure in blowing and rattling at the ears of pretty ladies, who returned the compliment good-naturedly with smiles at the merrymakers. Paper streamers floated in the air and were strung around people's necks. Confetti showered on the crowd like many- colored snow. I branched off to Chinatown, where I found throngs admiring the window decorations with their Oriental touch. Firecrackers made you feel that you were celebrating New Year's Eve in China.

When the clock struck midnight people began to shout "Happy New Year!" at the tops of their voices, and to blow horns and shake rattles. More confetti and more streamers. This was my first New Year in America and I was impressed with the good-naturedness of the American crowd and the spontaneous play spirit of the grownups. They were a young race in their merrymaking.

I got back home quite late and pleasantly tired, went to bed, and slept soundly until late in the morning. After breakfast I took a walk in the residential section of Berkeley. The houses on the gentle slopes of the Berkeley hills were surrounded with flower beds and green lawns. Roses were in full bloom in the mild California winter, for Berkeley, like Kunming in China, is blessed with perennial spring.

After the New Year I looked forward to the beginning of the second term of the university in February. With new hopes and vigor I worked hard at my language study. When the term drew near I applied for admission on credits from Nanyang College in Shanghai and was entered in the College of Agriculture, with Chinese as a substitute for Latin.

Here I must explain why I turned to agriculture when my preparation was along literary lines. This was not a happy-go-lucky move as it might have been with many a young student; it had been carefully considered and decided upon in all seriousness. Since China was mainly agricultural, the improvement of agriculture, as I saw it, would bring happiness and prosperity to the largest number of people in China; moreover, I had always taken delight in plants and animals since my early years in the village, where farming was the main current of life. For national as well as personal reasons, therefore, agriculture seemed the most appropriate study to pursue. Another minor consideration was that as I was born a delicate child my health could be improved by having plenty of fresh air in the country.

I took botany, zoölogy, hygiene, English, German, and physical culture for the term—a period of three hours a week for each course except the last, which took six hours. We were told to buy textbooks at a bookstore on College Avenue, so I went to the store and asked, among other things, for so-and- so's Bo'tany, with the accent on the second syllable.

"What is it you want?" the sales clerk demanded. I repeated the word with the same accent. He shook his head. "Sorry, haven't got it." I pointed to the book on the shelf. He smiled and said, "Oh, excuse me, you mean bo'tany."

I was glad to have the book and also to learn the right pronunciation of the word. Again, we were told to observe certain plants in the botanical garden. Failing to locate the place, I asked a janitor where the bo'tanical garden was—with the accent on the first syllable.

"What?" he said. I repeated.

"Oh, oh—you mean the botan'ical garden," he responded after a moment, enlightened.

I would have liked to swear in good American slang if I had learned any. Years after, when I related the incident to an American friend in Peking, he told me the story of a Frenchman who was asked what difficulties he found in speaking English. The Frenchman replied with characteristic gesture, "Oh, English is easy— but the abominable accent!" pronouncing the last words in French. Indeed, the abominable accent has discouraged many a student who has tried to learn English and found himself caught in an intricate maze.Of course there are rules by which one can somewhat steer his way. But there are too many exceptions; often the exceptions are the rule, so that one has to consider each case and acquire them all gradually and with great pains.

I studied botany and zoölogy with great interest. I still remember the jocular remarks of the professor of botany as we were being taught to use the microscope, "Don't think you 're going to see through the microscope a fly as big as an elephant. No—you can't see even a section of the fly's leg."

My interest in the observation of nature had its roots in the naïve nature study which, during my school days in China, I carried on outside of school as a sort of diversion after the day's tiresome classical study. My improvised observations years before and my interest in botany and zoölogy now all proceeded from a common source—curiosity. The one great difference lay in the tool used. The microscope is an extension of the eye and enables you to see minute particles which the naked eye can never hope to reach. Use of this tool has led to the discovery of microbes, whose limitless numbers are comparable to the stars—which in turn are studied by another extension of the eye, the telescope. I longed to make a pilgrimage to Lick Observatory to see the world's largest telescope, but for some reason or other did not go. Instead I paid twenty-five cents to look into a telescope on the streets to see the planets and was thrilled to behold silvery Saturn in its shining ring, sailing in the blue sky as I had seen it on a celestial map in school.

I stayed in the College of Agriculture for half a year. One of my friends had meanwhile been urging me to take up some branch of social science instead of a practical science like agriculture. He argued that though agriculture was very important, there were other studies more vital for China; unless we could solve our political and social problems in the light of modern developments in the West we could not very well solve the agricultural ones. Moreover, my world outlook would be limited, in agriculture, to a practical science and would not embrace anything beyond the narrow scope of that special field.

As I had studied Chinese history as well as the general outlines of Western history, and was familiar with the general development of national strength in various countries at various times, I could very well appreciate my friend's advice. It set me thinking, for I was again at the crossroads and must sooner or later make a final decision. As I have mentioned, I was always careful in making any decision as to a new field which would determine my future course of life.

Early one morning, on my way to a barn to watch the milking, I met a number of fresh-looking youngsters—pretty girls and lively boys—on their way to school. Suddenly an idea struck me: I am here to study how to raise animals and plants; why not study how to raise men? Instead of going to the barn I went up into the Berkeley hills and sat under an old oak tree overlooking beautiful sunlit San Francisco Bay and the Golden Gate. As I gazed into the bay, thoughts on the rise and decline of the successive dynasties in China presented themselves one after another. All of a sudden I saw as if in a vision children emerging like water nymphs from the waters of the bay and asking me to give them schools. I decided to take education as my major, in the College of Social Science.

It was already late in the morning when I rushed down from the hills, went directly to the Recorder's Office to see Mr. Sutton, and asked to be transferred from the College of Agriculture to that of Social Science. After some argument the transfer was granted. In the fall of 1909 I began to take courses in logic, ethics, psychology, and English history, and was thus launched on what became my real college career.

My student life moved along in an atmosphere of intellectual activity. Days and months rolled on smoothly and pleasantly. As the sands of time gathered, so grew my knowledge.

In logic I learned that thinking has its method—that is to say, we must think logically. There is a difference between inductive and deductive thinking. Observation is very important in inductive thinking, so I wanted to practice it. I began to observe the many things I came across on campus or near the university. Why were cows belled? Why do the leaves of the eucalyptus hang vertical? Why are all California poppies yellow?

One morning as I was walking along the slopes of the Berkeley hills I noticed a pipe from which water was flowing. Where did the water come from? I followed up the pipe line, which led me to the source, and rejoiced over the discovery. Quite high on the hills I began to wonder what was on the other side of them. I climbed over one hill after another and found that there were endless hills, higher and higher as I went farther and farther. Finally I gave up and took a path which led down to a number of farmhouses, finding by the way creeks and woods which I enjoyed immensely.

Of course the endless chain of observation running merely from one thing to another could lead only to disappointment. Finally I learned that observation must have a definite object and a definite purpose, not ramble aimlessly. The astronomer observes the stars, the botanist the growth of plants. Later I came to know that there is another kind of observation, a sort of controlled observation called experiment, by means of which scientific discoveries are made.

In the field of ethics I learned that there is a difference between ethical principles and rules of conduct. The principles tell you why certain accepted rules are desirable at certain stages of civilization, while the rules themselves merely exact observance without inquiry into the underlying principles and their relation to modern society.

As life in China was governed by accepted rules of conduct, the inquiry into their underlying principles created storms in my mind. The old moral foundations which we had taken as final truths began to rock as in an earthquake. Moreover my professor, Harry Overstreet, was not the kind of traditional teacher who simply believed in accepted truths and expected his students to do likewise; his searching mind led me to peer into every crevice in the foundation stones of moral principle. In class there were lively discussions, which I refrained from joining partly because of my deficiency in the spoken language and partly owing to shyness, which grew in me out of a sense of inferiority. For around the year 1909 China was in the darkest period of her recent history and we had very little self-confidence about her future. But I pricked up my ears and listened like an intelligent dog to its master, understanding the meaning but unable to talk.

We were required to read Plato, Aristotle, the Gospel of St. John, and Marcus Aurelius, among other sources. I was impressed with the all-searching mind of the Greeks as revealed through the two Greek philosophers; I felt that while the Confucian classics were richly tinged with moral sense, the Greek philosophers were permeated by all-piercing intellect. This led me later on to a study of Greek history and a comparative study of ancient Greek and Chinese thought. It also led me to understand what an important part Greek thought has played in modern European civilization, and why Greek has been regarded as an indispensable part of a liberal education.

With St. John I began to appreciate the meaning of love as preached by Jesus, stripped of creed and church. It is indeed the highest ideal to "love your enemy." If one could really love one's enemy there would be no enemy.

"Can you love your enemy?" the professor asked the class. There was no answer.

"I can't," the attentive dog yelped.

"You can't?" he smiled.

I quoted Confucius, "Love those who love you, but be fair to your enemy." Upon this he commented, "It's quite sensible, isn't it?" The class made no response. As we dispersed a young American boy came up to me and patted me on the shoulder. "Love your enemy! Tommyrot, eh?"

Marcus Aurelius talked like a Sung philosopher. He meditated and discovered reason as the measure of all conduct. Translated and put among the Sung philosophers, he could easily have passed for one of them.

Things European or American I always measured with a Chinese yardstick. This is the way that leads from the known to the unknown. To gain new experience based upon and constructed out of past experiences is the way to new knowledge. For example, a child who has not seen an airplane can be made to understand it by reference to the flying bird and a "boat with wings." A child who has not seen a bird or a boat cannot easily be made to understand an airplane. A Chinese student learns to understand Western civilization only in the light of what he knows of his own. The more he knows of his own culture, the better able he will be to understand that of the West. Thus arguing in my mind, I felt that my midnight lucubrations on the Chinese classics, history, and philosophy in school in China were not labor lost. Only because of those studies was I now in a position to absorb and digest Western ideas. My work hereafter, I thought, is to find out what China lacks and take what she needs from the West. And in the course of time we will catch up with the West. With these views I grew more self-confident, less self-conscious, and more hopeful for the future.

My interests among the fields of knowledge were indeed rather broad. I took ancient history, English history, the history of philosophy, political science, and even Russian literature in English translation. Tolstoy absorbed me, especially his Anna Karenina and War and Peace. I attended many public lectures given by prominent scholars and statesmen and thus heard Santayana, Tagore, David Starr Jordan, Woodrow Wilson—then president of Princeton—and many other scholars. Science, literature, the arts, politics, and philosophy all interested me equally. I heard Taft and Roosevelt. "I took the Panama Canal and let Congress debate about it," said the latter in one of his lectures in the Greek theatre. His emphasis and characteristic gestures still stand out clearly in my memory.

Traditional education in China seemed narrow, but within its walls one found a diversity of subjects almost encyclopedic. This apparently narrow education, it is not paradoxical to say, furnished the basis for a broad view of knowledge. My diversity of interests probably derived from my past training in that traditional body of thought. The ancient classics contain many branches of knowledge: history, philosophy, literature, political economy, government , war, diplomacy, and the like. They have never been narrow. After the classics, scholars were initiated into even such practical arts as agriculture, irrigation, astronomy, and mathematics. Thus the traditional Chinese scholar was no narrow specialist but had a broad foundation for learning. Moreover, an open-minded search for truth was the aim of Confucian scholars. Their deficiencies seemed to lie in the fact that their knowledge was rather limited to books. Book knowledge can be narrow in another sense.

In school I remember I was given a rhymed book which contained a great varie ty of subjects, starting with astronomy and geography and going on down to vegetables and insects, including between them such topics as cities, commerce, farming, travel, inventions, philosophy, government, and so on. Rhymes are easier to learn by heart and even at the moment of writing I am still able to recite a great part of that rhymed encyclopedia.

The Berkeley hills with their moss-green oaks and scent-laden eucalyptus, their fields of golden poppies and gardens of crimson roses bathed in smiling California sunshine, served as an ideal nursery for the native sons of the Golden West. I felt ever-grateful to share in the care and protection of my Western Alma Mater, in whose lap her foster son from the ancient Eastern empire was nursed to grow.

In this climate in which there was no very cold winter nor any very hot summer, it was indeed pleasant to live in a sort of perpetual spring for four long, enjoyable years. There was no rain to interrupt outdoor life except for winter showers which turned the grass on the hills green again and washed the roses in the gardens clear as with morning dew. Otherwise no inclement weather interrupted the performances in the Greek theatre, surrounded by its forest of eucalyptus. Shakespearean plays, Greek dramas, Sunday concerts, and public lectures were given in the open air. Not far away were the athletic fields in which intercollegiate games and track meets took place. Young Apollos strove hard for the fame of their alma mater. Beauty, health, and intellect were cultivated at the same time. Mens sana in corpore sano—was this ancient Greece re-enacted?

Almost in the center of the campus stood the campanile towering high above the other buildings. At the main entrance leading to College Avenue was Sather Gate with nude carvings standing out in vivid relief which invoked protests from parents who had daughters at the university. "Let girls see more of these nude figures of boys and they will be cured of their false decency," remarked my professor of ethics. We had Venus and other goddesses of the ancient Greeks in our reading rooms in the old library (later torn down when the new Doe Library was built), but there was no criticism from the parents of boys. When I saw these Greek figures for the first time I wondered why the authorities should put such "indecent" things at the fountain of wisdom. But later I assumed that they were meant to teach the idea of mens sana—sometimes translated as "a beautiful mind in a beautiful body." For with the Greeks beauty, health, and wisdom are one and indivisible.

The performance of A Midsummer Night's Dream among the oak groves on campus was really a masterpiece of beauty. Youth, love, beauty, and joy of life are all vividly portrayed in the pleasant masquerade.

Greek-letter fraternity and sorority houses were numerous on the campus. I was told what a wonderful life the members enjoyed together, but I had not visited any until on one occasion I was invited on a bargain—I was to vote for members of that fraternity for class president and other officers. They canvassed the whole class from a list; when they came to a classmate who was likely to vote for their opponents they would say "No good!" and mark the name "NG."

I was received with such cordiality as one would remember a lifetime. The vote was cast next day and I kept faithfully to my promise, for a "Chinaman's" word is as good as gold. I was glad to have made friends with quite a few fellow students during the campaign.

A few days after the election, for some occasion which I don't remember now, a bonfire was made. The glow of the flames lit up the happy faces of the young people. Boys and girls sang, ending each song with college yells. The crackling of the burning logs, the giggles of the girls and the shouts of the boys still echo in my ears. There in the light I came across a fellow student for whom I had cast my vote. To my great surprise his cordiality toward me had already turned to indifference. This is how things go in the world! His kindness to me had been paid for by my vote; the bills being paid, the account was squared—neither owed anything to the other. Thereafter I exchanged no more votes for cordialities and never again voted in college elections.

In the basement of North Hall was a student "co-op," at the entrance of which was a sign which read, "In God we trust, all others pay cash." The most prosperous business in the co-op was the sale of hot dogs at five cents apiece (cash). They tasted fine.

One memorable character on the campus—probably forgotten by my contemporaries but not by me—was the aged janitor of the philosophy building. He was tall and spare, with a very straight carriage. His eyes were deep-sunk in their sockets and his grey eyebrows grew very long, almost covering his eyes, like a Pekingese toy dog. From under his brows one could see him twinkling with friendliness and warmth of heart. We took a mutual liking to each other. After classes and sometimes on Sundays I was a frequent visitor to the basement where he had lived from the time when the university was a small college.

He had been a soldier and fought many battles under the Union flag in the Civil War. He lived in memories of the past and related to me many stories of the war and of his childhood. From him I learned that conditions in America in older days—it is almost a century now—were not very much better than in China then; in some respects worse. He told me that there had existed in his youth many kinds of money: English pounds, French francs, and Dutch guldens. I heard Lyman Abbott speak of this several years later in New York. Modern sanitation seemed to him nonsense. Once he showed me a roll of toilet paper and said, "Nowadays people die young with these sanitary things. We didn't have any sanitation or what you call modern medicine. Look at me, how healthy I am at my age!" He stood erect like a soldier at attention for me to look at him.

West Point was also a joke to him. "You think they can fight? No! They're puffed up by uniforms and sure know how to dress in a parade. But fighting— no. I can teach 'em. In one battle I killed a whole lot of rebels singlehanded. If they want to learn to fight, let 'em come to me!"

He still harbored a grudge in his heart against the Confederates after these long years. He said he once found a rebel lying wounded after a battle was over and tried to help him. "You know what that crittur did? He fired right at me." He leveled his angry eyes at me steadily as if I had been the culprit. "What did you do?" I ventured. "I shot the beast dead right on the spot," was the reply.

To me this old soldier-janitor was an inseparable part of the university. He thought himself so, too, for he had seen the place grow. ◉

Chapter 10
China in America

Before the end of October of my first year in America an important change had taken place in China. This was the death, in rapid succession, of the Emperor Kwang-hsü and the Empress Dowager. There were two versions to the story; one was that she died first, whereupon he was murdered by her followers in the fear that he would come back into power. The other was that, near death, she sent a eunuch to Yun Tai—the island palace in the Imperial Chung Hai Park where this strong-willed woman had kept her Imperial consort imprisoned ever since the short-lived reforms of 1898—who informed the Emperor, always in poor health, that Her Majesty the Illustrious Buddha, as she was called, wished him as a favor to take the medicine she sent. According to this version the poor imprisoned Emperor understood the message and obeyed, succumbing to the poison in a short time. The fact was made known to her before she died and she ordered the issue of an Imperial Edict by which the death of the Emperor was announced and his nephew, little Pu-yi, made successor to the throne.

Whatever the truth of it, the unanimous opinion of the Chinese students in Berkeley was that with the death of the "old woman," as the Empress Dowager was disrespectfully called, there would be plenty of trouble in China. It proved to be so. For with a baby Emperor on the throne and his inexperienced father, Tsai Hsun, as Prince Regent, the authority of the Manchu Dynasty fell into meteoric decline until its last vestige was swept away three years later by the Revolution of 1911.

In 1909 I had joined as an editorial writer the Chinese Free Press, Dr. Sun Yat-sen's revolutionary organ in San Francisco. One evening in the fall of that year, with my co-editor Liu Chun-yu, I called for the first time on Dr. Sun Yat-sen at a hotel on Stockton Street on the outskirts of Chinatown. My heart throbbed with excitement as we entered. Dr. Sun received us cordially in his room. It was a small room with a couch, several chairs, and a small desk. There was a wash basin by the window. The curtains were drawn.

Mr. Liu introduced me to the esteemed leader of China's revolutionary movement. His magnetic personality was such as to win the confidence of any who had a chance to meet him. Dr. Sun's ample and majestic forehead and strong dark brows gave signs of a forceful intellect and indomitable will. His clear, inviting eyes revealed his candor of thought and warmth of heart, while his compressed lips and set jaw made people readily understand that he was a man of courage and decision. His general build was muscular and sturdy, giving the impression of strong nerves and steady emotions. In conversation his line of argument was clear and convincing, whether you agreed with him or not; unless you wished to discontinue he would keep on untiringly expounding his theories to you. He spoke slowly but distinctly and one felt behind his words a deep sincerity. He also listened easily yet was not slow to catch essential points.

Later I found him to be an ardent reader of a variety of books, both Chinese and English. He saved all the money he could to buy books. He was a slow reader but had an extraordinary retentive power. Dr. Sun's wide reading gave him a clear understanding of the development of both Chinese and Western civilizations.

He enjoyed jokes—though he seldom jested—laughing heartily when a good one was recounted to him.

He liked fish and vegetables for his meals, but seldom touched meat and preferred Chinese to Western cooking. "Chinese food is the best in the world," he would say.

Dr. Sun was a real democrat. He lectured in the streets of China-town in San Francisco. With banners of the Nationalist party streaming in the air, he would stand on the sidewalk and talk to the crowd gathering around him. He understood the psychology of the man in the street and could reduce his own language to the simplest terms. "What is revolution?" he would ask rhetorically. "Down with the rule of the Manchus!" The crowd understood and joined in in chorus. Then he would go on explaining in very simple language why the Manchus must be done away with and what he would do when a republican form of government was established in China—how many benefits the people would reap from a new regime.

He would often size up an audience to which he was about to speak, choose an appropriate subject, and improvise a suitable discourse, expressing himself with great eloquence. He usually carried the audience with him to the very end. He was always ready to speak for he possessed a remarkable ability to carry it with him.

Dr. Sun's deep understanding of human nature, his intense love of his country and people, and his insight into what China needed in building up her new nationhood gave him unquestioned leadership in the development of young China. Between travels in the southern and eastern states and in Europe he came back every so often to San Francisco, where Liu Chun-yu and I had the pleasure of seeing him whenever he came.

On October 8, 1911, at about eight o'clock in the evening, Dr. Sun came into the editorial room of the Chinese Free Press wearing a dark overcoat and a derby hat. He appeared happy, though not in the least excited, as he said calmly that from news he had received through certain sources things seemed to be turning out well— the group of people who had laid plans for revolution in Hankow and Wuchang were ready for action. Two days later news reached San Francisco that revolution had broken out in Wuchang. This was the revolution of October 10, 1911, which eventually overthrew the Manchu Dynasty. On that day the Republic of China was born.

Urgent cablegrams advised Dr. Sun to come back to lead the revolution. He left San Francisco and returned to China by way of Europe. On January 1, 1912, he was inaugurated at Nanking as Provisional President of the Republic, and China entered on a new life.

Under Dr. Sun's guidance, for three consecutive years Liu Chun-yu and I wrote editorials for the Chinese Free Press, each of us at first writing one every other day. We supplied these articles to the paper while studying at the university, often burning midnight oil to finish a piece for the next morning's issue. The university work was by no means light and we felt—especially myself—the burden of this extra labor. After the successful revolution Liu went back to China and I had to bear the brunt of the daily editorial war. Though I felt deeply for the future of my country, the constant practice of writing against my will ultimately killed in me all interest in writing. In the unremitting pressure and rush under which I labored, the quality of production deteriorated and I formed the habit of loose and hurried thinking and careless choice of words. Sometimes my thought flowed reluctantly as water through a clogged pipe, but the words still rushed from my pen like a swarm of aimless wanderers. I was rather exasperated at these unwelcome guests. I would, however, let them go since they filled up the columns.

When I first took the job I found a real pleasure in writing, fitting words to thoughts like coins into a slot machine. Only when I tried to jam all the coins into the slots at once, the machine got clogged and refused to take in the superfluous ones, which spilled all around the floor, so to speak. This is how meaningless words fill space when you are forced to write in a rush.

After my graduation in 1912 I gave up the job and felt a great release. Thereafter I feared writing as a schoolboy would Latin composition. When labor is drudgery and done in a hurry as well, no good work will come of it. The bad habits thus formed were difficult to eradicate for years after.

On the Pacific coast during my college days about fifty thousand Chinese immigrants clustered around the centers in the various cities—Sacramento, San Francisco, Oakland, San José, Los Angeles, and others—with isolated small groups or individuals dotting the smaller towns and villages. These centers were called Chinatowns. Chinatown in San Francisco was the largest of all, with a Chinese population of more than twenty thousand. The main street was originally Dupont Street, but its name was afterward changed to Grant Avenue, for what reason I do not know. Grant Avenue was a very prosperous street. Oriental bazaars, Chinese restaurants known as "chop suey houses," fortunetelling stands, gambling houses in the guise of social or literary clubs, and temples for worship of Chinese gods—called "joss houses"—attracted the attention of tourists, sight-seers, and pleasure-seekers.

Once a pretty young American told me that she had seen a wonderful thing in an Oriental bazaar— a Buddha sitting in an artichoke; and had eaten bird's nest soup, sharks' fins, and chop suey in a Chinese restaurant. She was much excited over it. Her younger sisters listened with wondering eyes and gaping mouths. "I declare!" said the grandmother, looking over her spectacles while her hands were busy with her knitting.

"How do you eat soup with chopsticks?" a younger sister asked curiously.

"As you do with your soda straws, my young lady," said I. All joined in the laughter.

In small towns my countrymen kept laundry establishments. Day in and day out they washed and washed from dawn till dusk and often late into the night. The reason many American families liked to send their laundry to the Chinese was because hand wash did not wear out the materials as easily as machines. These hard-working sons of the Celestial Empire saved every bit of their earnings by living a frugal life; they slung silver or gold pieces into the savings bags hidden under their beds and made liberal contributions to the cause of Dr. Sun's revolutionary movement or sent money home to support their families and relatives in Canton, thus helping to enrich the villages of their province.

Kwangtung was the richest province of China, not only because the people did prosperous business in Hong Kong and elsewhere but because it was the reservoir into which gold trickled from all parts of the world where there were Chinese colonies—Malaya, the Dutch East Indies , the Philippine Islands, North and South America, etc. It was from this province that most of the émigrés from China originally came.

The Chinese working and living in foreign lands, numbering in the millions, were not there to exploit. Rather, their labor has been exploited. They had no capital other than the flesh and blood they were given in their mothers' wombs. With hard work, frugality, and endurance, they labored like bees carrying their tiny specks of Sweetness from distant flowers to build up honeycombs in China. There was no political power to back them up, and they carried no guns. They helped to build railroads, open mines, raise rubber; in return for their labor they received a few dollars or shillings or rupees or guldens for a day's hard work. Some, to be sure, especially in Singapore and the Dutch East Indies, became rich and owned palatial mansions and villas, living like maharajahs. A number rose to the level of the middle class and owned property. But the rich and well to do were in the minority; the rank and file had to work hard, and only by hard work managed to make a living and put by some savings.

Among the Chinese in America there were neither very rich nor very poor. Most of them were honest, hard-working people. Almost all had some savings to contribute to that great reservoir, the province of Kwangtung. Their mode of life was mainly Chinese. Taking a boat along the Sacramento River, one would see Chinese towns or villages perched on the banks with bold Chinese signboards in front of the shops. One felt as if he were sailing on the Yangtze River or the Grand Canal in China.

I landed once at one of these Sacramento River Chinatowns and stayed with the owner of an asparagus plantation, Tin San, a friend of Dr. Sun Yat-sen. He treated me to tender asparagus, fat and juicy. Thereafter, whenever I had asparagus for dinner I thought of him. He had a cannery for this delicious vegetable, under American brand names. So I often think that some of the American canned asparagus may have been raised and canned by the Chinese. His way of making money was really good and ingenious. He kept places of amusement for his men, arguing that they must have some diversion after the day's work and if he had not established these houses they would go to other places run by his neighbors. He wanted the water to flow into his own gardens, so to speak, to feed his own plants. His plants—or rather dollars—did indeed grow from the voluntary contributions of his men to these amusement places.

The Chinese immigrants in America as well as elsewhere were truly loyal sons and daughters of that Flowery Kingdom. The men wore queues and some of the women even practised foot-binding. In the streets of Chinatown in San Francisco one could find fortunetellers. One such man who was telling a white man's fortune said to him, "Good luck. By and by, plenty of money." A Negro standing by wanted to have his fortune told and was very much pleased to hear the same words repeated to him. Everything would have been all right if the prophet had stopped there. But he went on to say, "By and by, no more black. Like him—"pointing with his index finger at the white man. The Negro instead of being pleased got mad and kicked over the fortuneteller's stand. This was a case where compliments, overdone, become insults.

There were grocery stores selling salt fish, eels, edible snakes, bean sauce, sharks' fins, birds' nests, dried abalones, and other Cantonese stuff brought to America from Canton or Hong Kong. Once I went to one of the groceries and tried to buy something. Failing to make the man understand my poor Cantonese dialect, I wrote on paper what I wanted. An old woman standing by saw my writing and being ignorant of the fact that China has only one written language for the whole country, despite her many dialects was surprised and asked, if this Chinese cannot speak Chinese (meaning Cantonese), how can he write it? A group of curious people gathered around me. One who could speak enough mandarin to make me understand asked, "Have you ever been in the provincial capital of Canton?" "No," I replied. "Then where did you do your shopping?" "Shanghai," I laughed, and went away with a bottle of bean sauce and a package under my arm.

Schools in Chinatown still stuck to the old curriculum. Pupils were taught to read aloud the old books just as I had been taught in China. The American schools not far away had no influence on them.

These were the times before the revolution. After that date Chinatown began to change, for China herself was changing—changing rapidly. In the course of a few years the fortunetellers disappeared. The number of queues fast decreased until they were gone. The young girls stopped their foot-binding. The schools were reformed and adopted a modern curriculum; more children were sent to near-by American schools. Chinatown resisted the influence of its American neighbors but followed in the footsteps of the mother country in reforms and mode of living. These loyal sons and daughters of China! ●

Chatper 11
New York

As the years went on my mental horizon extended and I became more and more self-confident. In 1912 I was graduated with honors in education and went to Columbia University in New York City for my postgraduate work.

Here I learned the method and acquired the spirit of scientific research as applied to social phenomena. Among the professors who taught me untiringly, from whom I drew my inspiration and to whom I am greatly indebted, there is one I wish to mention particularly because of his connection with Peking University. He is Professor John Dewey, who taught Dr. Hu Shih and myself at Columbia, and later through his writings, lectures, and personal contacts with contemporary thinkers in China, during his two-year sojourn as visiting professor at the National University of Peking, influenced Chinese educational theories and practice to a great extent. His pragmatism finds its counterpart in the practical Chinese mentality. But he warned us that "if a thing is too practical it becomes impractical."

Of the years at Columbia I shall not speak in detail. They were most enriching. I was now acclimated to America and to the language and could absorb what came within my orbit with less overwhelming effort of adaptation.

In New York I was impressed by the skyscrapers, the rapid circulation of subways and elevated trains, the dazzling lights of moving advertisements on the tops of tall buildings; the theatres, night clubs, hotels, and restaurants; fashionable Fifth Avenue, Greenwich Village, the East Side slums, and so on.

On the social side one found Yankees, Irish, Poles, Italians, Greeks, Jews, all living side by side in a neighborly way, and a few thousand of my own countrymen clustered around Chinatown. In my time there were in the great metropolis five hundred Chinese restaurants catering to the public. The agglomerated cosmopolitan mass of the city population, with its politicians, gangsters, scholars, artists, financiers, industrialists, multimillionaires, slum-dwellers, and many others, was fundamentally an American product. There is nothing further from the truth than to say, "When you get into New York, you get out of America." America alone is capable of producing such a great, highly industrialized city and vast melting pot. There was little racial friction. For in New York anyone can do anything he likes if he knows how to stay inside the law. Everyone is permitted to go his own way if he observes a certain degree of public decency. Anyone can expound his theories of society and government if he can find an audience.

Liberty within the orbit of the law and freedom of thought and speech within the domain of reason had free play. Great industries, international banking and big business, and the utilization of invention, engineering, and material resources to the fullest extent, all showed the spirit and application of Americanism. In New York one found it in concentrated form. In the midst of this concentration the eye of the observer is easily dazzled by the glaring lights, thus losing sight of Americanism in its normal state as one would see it elsewhere in America.

During the summer vacations I would go to the Adirondacks. One summer, with a few Chinese friends, I went to Rainbow Lake and camped on one of its hilly islets. In the daytime we went boating and fishing on near-by lakes. Our catches were quite rich—pike weighing over ten pounds were among our prizes for a day's work and pleasure. Big fat frogs were found a-plenty around the island on which we camped. I had learned to catch frogs in my village childhood in China and carried the art over to America. A rod, a string, and a hook rounded out of a good-sized needle with a piece of red cloth attached to it were sufficient for frog fishing; the improvised outfit worked wonders. Usually we could catch two dozen of them in an hour. This was more than enough for two delicious meals a day. The people living around the lake had never eaten frogs—they admired our art of frog fishing but at the bottom of their hearts must have thought, "The heathen Chinese is peculiar."

In the evenings we often joined their barn dances to the tune of the fiddle played by the host. One of the songs they all sang, a part of which still lurks in my recollection, runs something like this:

All the hinges are rusty
And the doors are falling down,
The roof lets in sunshine and rain—
And the only friend I have
Is the little yellow dog
On the trail behind the bush.

This reflects the loneliness of a solitary hermitage in the mountain region, but to the city-dwellers it depicted a charming, quiet life.

Sometimes we penetrated into virgin forests where the luxuriant leaves veiled the sky like thick clouds. The junipers growing along the trail gave out their aromatic scent, and we picked fragrant evergreen branches to make pillows which would bring nature to our beds and send out floating odors to sweeten our gentle sleep.

Sometimes we lost our way back in the dense woods. We would listen then for the whistle of a train to lead us to the railroad tracks. Experience taught me later to take a compass when going into the woods.

To go back to city life after staying in the country for some time is really a pleasure. The city looks refreshed when you come back to it; the country seems doubly enchanting if you go there from the city. It is all because of the change, the contrast. When foreigners go to China they are often charmed with the complacent Chinese life and with the scenery. A Chinese in a foreign land is often delighted with its city life. So you frequently find a Westerner more enthusiastic about things Chinese than the Chinese themselves, and vice versa. It is a change, a contrast, which breaks monotony and refreshes the mind. But the intrinsic values of things are not altered by these changes of mental approach.

During my student days in New York Sino-Japanese relations took a turn which left the two countries at loggerheads later on. After some fifty years of reforms, Japan showed her strength in 1894 by delivering a blow at China. Instead of resentment and enmity, China returned good for evil. The unfriendly act, contrary to expectations, invoked rather the admiration and gratitude of the Chinese people—admiration for Japan's great reforms, accomplished in the short span of fifty years, and gratitude for thus awakening China to her future possibilities. It rekindled the dying flame of hope in China's heart. For some time thereafter she lived under inspiration drawn from Japanese example.

Students went to Japan by thousands every year to study. China's new military, police, and school systems were developed and headed by students returned from Japan. Through Japan, China began to see the significance of Western civilization. The Russo-Japanese War gave further impetus to China's reforms—Japan was held in the hearts of the Chinese as an idol.China absorbed Western civilization gradually through her neighbor, but soon realized that the currents flowing in Japan, from which she drank the waters of modern wisdom, had their source in Europe or America. It was a happy coincidence that America returned the Boxer indemnity; China used it to send more students to the United States than she had done before. Students had previously been sent to Europe and America on government scholarships or by private means, but the number was small. Those who returned direct from the West now grew in numbers and began to occupy some of the key positions in government, industry, commercial enterprise, and educational fields. Missionaries, especially American, helped to educate the youth of the country through mission schools.

Thus, culturally speaking, China began to drift away from Japan. The Japanese idol dwindled in Chinese hearts. And the Japanese were not aware of it.

Taking advantage of the first World War, in 1915 Japan suddenly delivered to Yuan Shih-kai's government the famous Twenty-One Demands, enforcement of which would have reduced China to a Japanese protectorate. This rash act grew out of the upset of the balance of power in the Far East, owing to the preoccupation of the Western Powers with the war and the rapid decline of the military might of Tsarist Russia. It turned China's face once and for all toward the West, and the consequent parting of the ways of the two countries was to change the course of international politics in the years to come. Had Japan been farsighted enough to lend a helping hand to her neighbor in her period of distress, China would have remained a friend. What would have been the effect of this union upon World War II?

While I was in New York the substance of the Twenty-One Demands was allowed to leak out by the Chinese Legation at Washington. It created consternation in all the capitals of the Western Powers. A boycott of Japanese goods spread like wildfire throughout China as a feeble protest, but the Japanese navy was concentrated at important Chinese ports and her armed forces mobilized in south Manchuria and Shantung. On May 7, 1915, four months after the presentation of the demands, Japan sent an ultimatum to Yuan Shih-kai and two days later it was accepted.

By force of circumstances the demands in the course of time dwindled to virtually nothing. But the admiration and gratitude of China were thus turned into fear and suspicion which were to grow in the hearts of her millions. Thereafter, whatever Japan had to say China received with suspicion; whatever she did China watched with fear. The more she professed sincerity, the more China suspected a sinister design behind it.

"Why don't you love us as we love you?" our neighbor would ask. "How can we love you when you make love with the bayonet?" we would reply. "Why should China play off the Western Powers against Japan?" a Japanese general asked me one day, a few years before the Mukden Incident.

"To maintain the balance of power and thus save China from being swallowed up by you," I replied frankly.

"Japan swallow up China! How could we? It's silly."

"It is not silly, General. Didn't Japan deliver us her Twenty-One Demands during the last war, when the Powers were preoccupied? If those demands had been carried into effect, Japan would be in a position to gobble up all China."

"So, so—?" said the general, as if in surprise.

"Yes, yes," I replied briefly. ❶

PART III

THE NEW CHINA

Chapter 12
Rapid Changes

In the midst of American mobilization for a European war for the first time in her history, in June, 1917, I left for home with mixed feelings. The last night I spent in Hartley Hall at Columbia my mind was too much occupied to sleep and I lay the whole night in meditation. The hours ebbed away until the early, summer dawn came in at the window through the creeping vines. The morning air was mild and the petals of the roses were dew-laden. Near by, on the granite steps of the library, the Alma Mater was smiling her grave smile as if wishing her foster son Godspeed. As I stood at the window looking out on the familiar scene that had meant so much to me those five years, tears began to well up in my eyes. Was I to be torn away once and for all from the fountain of wisdom, leaving my friends behind? But it was my duty to go home, just as it had been my privilege to come.

In the afternoon I boarded a train at Grand Central for a city in Ohio. As the train crawled out of the station I kept looking back at the waving hands of my American friends, boys and girls, until they were lost to sight.

One friend accompanied me to Ohio to visit with friends of his there, and we were welcomed to the family by its charming hostess. The host had some sort of business in that city. There was no son in the family; the girl was the sunshine in the house. She was an attractive brunette with an oval face, and the warmth that poured from her young heart would endear her to anyone who met her.

We stayed for about two weeks. It was in the midst of registration and draft; the first groups gathered, marched on the streets, and were sent off for training. The sidewalks were thronged with people. Mothers, sweethearts, and friends bade good-by to their soldiers with kisses, tears, and throbbing hearts.

We formed rowing parties on moonlit ponds dotted with islets of gold and silvery lilies. Fireflies twinkled like moving stars. Fish splashed. The girls sang together—I still remember one of the songs they loved to sing:

The June air is warm and tender.

Why do you hold your petals to display?

Are you afraid someone will

Come and steal your heart away?

The frogs echoed with their ungainly chorus. The girls sang and sang until the breezes of late evening brought a chilly warning. Then we would all go ashore and walk home over the dew-laden grass under the slanting moon.

Time flew and soon the two enjoyable weeks came to an end. I said good-by to my friends and took a train for San Francisco. When the ocean liner steamed gently out of the Golden Gate I stood on the deck facing east thinking of my friends in New York. Good-by, my friends! Good-by, America!

It was still summer in Shanghai. The city had changed much during my absence of nine years. Many streets were wider and better paved. New roads had been built beyond the limits of the Foreign Settlement. Department stores, fashionable hotels, roof gardens, amusement parks, and cabarets had multiplied. Shanghai had caught up with the spirit of New York.

The number of schools had increased manyfold in the city during the years of my absence; all but a few, however, were supported by private or Chinese government sources—these few had been established years before by the international municipal government. I suppose the revenues of the Settlement must have increased a hundred times since these few outmoded schools had been founded decades earlier. But let the Chinese remain ignorant—they would be easier to control and exploit.

The young girls had bobbed their hair and wore short skirts up to their knees in the fashion of the day. No—excuse me—I mean they wore gowns down to their knees, For the dress of the modern Chinese girl was very sensible. It consisted of a straight piece of silk hanging from the shoulders, longer or shorter according to fashion. This had been originally the Manchu gown, and Chinese girls had adopted it after the downfall of the dynasty some six years earlier.

Here, there, and everywhere on the streets high-heeled shoes adorned the dainty feet of young women. When one heard quick heels tapping the sidewalks one felt at once that the rising generation were radically different from their mother. The old modesty had disappeared. They were also better-developed physically, however, thanks to the modern shoes. In the old days women had practiced foot-binding. The movement to free women's feet, as a part of China's reform program, began around the time of the Russo-Japanese War and went on rather slowly until after the Revolution of 1911. I think the high heels helped to accelerate it, for women were surely more ready to give up the practice of squeezing their little daughters' feet into tiny slippers when they saw others wearing dainty high heels.

Men had dropped their queues but still clung to the long gown. It was funny to see a long gown without a queue. But before long I found myself one of the multitude, for Chinese clothing is more convenient and comfortable. No one can resist the temptation of being comfortable and convenient at the same time—it is a matter of practical common sense.

There were still a few individuals who wore queues, especially among the old men. They did not see any sense in getting rid of it; the queue had grown on Chinese heads for more than two centuries and it would do no harm to have it for a few centuries more. There are always die-hards in any movement.

In America I had measured things American by the Chinese yardstick. Now I reversed the process, measuring things Chinese with the American yardstick, or most likely with a sort of hybrid stick, neither Chinese nor American but something of both, or vacillating between the two.

I pitied the rickshaw coolies who ran for a few coppers, out of breath, their sweating tanned backs turned toward you in the hot summer sun. It was something inhuman, my American yardstick would say. Once in a while I came across some of the beastly foreigners who kicked them like dogs—but no, in America I never saw a man kick a dog. Blood rushed to my head and I often wanted to kick back at the human beasts, but refrained from venting my noble sentiments when I saw extraterritoriality looming large behind them. Then I reverted to my ancestral patience. "Coward!" the American yardstick would say. "Patience," returned the Chinese stick of my forefathers. Stop using these rickshaws and have more buses and tramways. But what were the poor coolies to do to eke out their meager subsistence? Return to the farms? No, they were surplus farmers. Three ways were open to them: to turn bandit with the strong, petty thieves with the weak, or beggars with the still weaker. Well then, let them pull the rickshaws. Here you are in a vicious circle.

Build up industry, it will give them employment. But industry is impossible without a stable government. A stable government is hardly possible when there are so many surplus farmers in the country, always ready to join mercenary armies and fight for the warlords who pay them or who let them loose to plunder the people. Here is another vicious circle, difficult to break.

There was an improvement in the notice boards of the Settlement public parks. The list of regulations forbidding the entrance of Chinese as well as dogs now displayed the modified clause: "Respectable Chinese only are admitted." At last even the arrogant foreigners had begun to be aware that there was something to be respected rising in China.

So much for Shanghai.

The great eastern seaport and trading center was now connected by rail with Soochow to the west and Hangchow to the south, cities both regarded as paradises on earth. The line ran from Soochow farther west to Nanking, connected by a ferry across the Yangtze River; and north through Tientsin to Peking, then capital of the Republic. The southern branch stopped at Hangchow and remained as yet to be connected with Ningpo.

My home was not very far from Ningpo, native city of Generalissimo Chiang Kai-shek. It is one of the five treaty ports but has never come into any considerable importance as a port, for the rapid growth of Shanghai as one of the great ports of the world overshadowed it. Three lines had ships running between Shanghai and Ningpo nightly, both incoming and outgoing; two of these were British companies and the third the China Merchants Navigation Company. These ships were the models for the steamless paddle-wheel "steamboat" my father had built so many years earlier and failed to make go. My brother and I took a second-class cabin on one of these boats.

There was not much change in the life of the passengers in twenty years. The gangways and decks were packed with human sardines and one could hardly set foot on the floor without stepping on somebody. We went on board about five in the afternoon to occupy our berths. Hawkers came by in great numbers, selling every kind of goods that a household might need, mostly imported manufactures. Fruit sellers brought bananas, apples, and pears on board. My brother and I had an argument. He wanted to buy the partly rotten fruit because it was much cheaper. "No," I argued, "you will pay much more for the doctor's bill."

"Ha, ha! I have been eating rotten pears and apples for years," he said. "They taste better. I have no trouble from them." He picked up a big, partly decayed red apple, bit off the bad parts and ate the rest. I shuddered. He laughed.

Before dawn we passed the fortresses of Ningpo Harbor, which fired a cannon ball that hit and killed a French admiral in the Sino-French War of 1885.

Day dawned. Clamorous voices from the dock rose to my ears. Streams of porters rushed up, fighting for luggage. The slightest negligence would find your possessions removed without permission. My brother and I elbowed down through the packed crowd, closely following our porters lest they walk off with our belongings.

Ningpo was practically the same as it had been nine years earlier. The air was laden with the smell of salt fish. I felt at home with this smell, for salt fish had been a staple food since childhood. Ningpo is a fishing town and large quantities of salt are produced not far away. We followed our porters to the station and found a train waiting to depart for Yuyao, our home city. Along the railroad I saw miles of well-cultivated fields cushioned with rippling rice that flowered in the autumn morning sun, unfolding like a never-ending scroll of landscape painting before the windows of the moving train. The morning air was stimulating and laden with the scent of flowering rice. Oh—this is my homeland!

As the train pulled into the Yuyao station my heart throbbed with excitement. We crossed the river by a long stone bridge built centuries ago. The ebb tide was racing down the river; through the arches of the bridge anglers could be seen casting their lines in the flowing water. The bridge was called Wu-shen, meaning "brave and victorious," because at the bridgeheads some four centuries ago people fought from time to time to defend the city against the invasions of pirates of uncertain origin from the Japan Sea. The Chinese believed they were Japanese, but Japanese historians deny it.

It was late in the morning when we hurried into the courtyard steeped in brilliant autumn sun. My father stood on the granite steps leading to the spacious hall. He was somewhat aged, his hair turning grey; otherwise in good health and splendid spirits. His kind eyes and smiling lips glowed with the tender emotions that flow from the heart of a loving parent. Before him my brother and I bowed three times in respect; the old way of kowtowing on one's knees had, among certain sections of the people, passed into history with the vanished dynasty.

Father had given up his queue but still wore Chinese slippers. He did not say much: silence conveyed much more than words on such an occasion. Then we all entered the hall. Stiff-backed chairs arranged symmetrically along the walls showed little sign of change in his way of living. The couplet panels inlaid with mother-of-pearl shone on the back walls. On the right side one read: "Fishes have greater freedom in the vastness of the sea," and on the left: "Birds take broader liberty in the wide span of the sky." Between the two panels was a painting of bamboo shadows which seemed to bend in an autumn breeze, all the leaves pointing with the wind. These things all speak of a contented, quiet, and unchanging life.

Behind the hall was a narrow strip of back yard. Miniature mountain scenes set in large rectangular pots brought landscape within the high walls. Tiny temples and pagodas perched on the miniature mountains, and dwarf trees that looked centuries old grew around them. Little monkeys with still smaller babies sitting innocently by their side sat here and there in the quiet recesses of the mountains. They all looked so cute that I wished some of them could grow life sized and jump into my lap. There was a tiny bamboo grove flourishing around a toy pavilion. Goldfish snapping at the air and shrimps stretching out their claws for food all enjoyed undisturbed life in the imitation ponds. All of this led one's mind to nature.

On hearing of my return old Mr. Liu came to call in the afternoon. He had told me stories in my childhood. How we children loved him! That day he recounted many amusing things. He described how the people acted on learning of the successful revolution. All the queues in the city vanished overnight. Young people bought foreign clothes and looked like monkeys in them. And how the short skirts and bobbed hair invaded the city later on! But for him the cutting of the queue that had grown on his head for more than seventy years was sufficient support of the revolution and the Republic. At first he wondered how the world could go on without an emperor sitting upon the dragon throne in Peking, but after some time he was sure that a republic with a president had the same power of maintaining peace and order in the country. At any rate, he said, "Heaven is high above and the Emperor is far away." It was up to the local authorities to do their job of maintaining peace, and they did it well.

When the Taipings had invaded the city some half century before, he said, heads went off shoulders with the queues. Now we lost only our queues and retained our heads. Talking thus, he touched his grey head with his bony fingers in such a comical way that it made everybody laugh. At dusk, after an early supper, in taking his leave he happened to slip on the steps leading to the courtyard. Someone rescued him, holding him up by the arms. He shook his head and joked, "Three thousand years ago Grandfather Chiang at the age of eighty met King Wen and helped him to build a new kingdom. Now Grandfather Liu at the same age may meet King Nian of the other world and help him to govern his invisible realm." He laughed heartily and went away in good spirits.

Several days later word came that "Grandfather" Liu had passed into the invisible realm. For me, I lost my childhood friend and old companion, and there were no more stories from his endless fountain of wit.

A school which my sister and I had established some fifteen years earlier had been turned into a district government school for girls. A hundred girls or so were studying there. They ran and laughed in the playgrounds and rode high in the air on the swing. A new generation of womanhood was in the making. They played

Western tunes on a portable organ; "Swanee River" and "Tipperary" and popular Chinese tunes were wafted through the doors and over the walls.

I stayed at home about a week and then went to the country to pay a visit to the village of the Chiangs. There the children of my childhood had grown to maturity. The grownups of older days had come to old age, their hair turning grey. The old people of days gone by had retired to their graves, except for a few who were still alert, witnessing the turns of fortune in the village.

The village did not look as bad as I anticipated. The banditry of early days had subsided, for people had now adjusted themselves to new trades and many had gone to Shanghai, which was able to accommodate larger numbers as commerce and industry expanded. Change, like birth, gives pain, but after the delivery the mother comes back to her normal state and feels happy with the newly born. Change that China had once hated had come to stay, ever deepening and widening, until she was constantly on the onward march—whither and for what purpose her teeming millions knew not.

My aunt whom I called the Great Mother had been bedridden for months. She was very happy on seeing me, made me sit by her side and stretched out her feeble hands to touch mine. She told me all about the births, marriages, and deaths which had occurred in the village in the last sixteen years. The world was not the same as before, she said. So many changes and so many new things had come in. Women did not weave and spin any more because foreign cloth was much cheaper, and better too. They had not much to do now; some spent their time in quarrels with their neighbors and others devoted themselves to Buddha. The younger ones went to school. Girls made hair nets and crocheted napkins to be exported to America. There was good money in it, she said. The boys were sent as apprentices to factories and machine shops in Shanghai. They took to new trades and made more money. There was now a dearth of farm hands in the village, but there were no more bandits. Tranquility and peace had come to stay. When dogs barked at night people did not have to be anxious for their safety as they had ten years before.

But something very bad she noticed in the girls and boys who had been in schools. They called the worship of gods a superstition. They said that the burning of paper money before our ancestors was silly. To them there were no kitchen gods. All the images of gods in the temples were only blocks of wood and lumps of clay. They thought these images ought to be flung into the river, so as to banish superstition along with them. They said girls had the same rights as boys. The girls said they had the right to marry by their own choice, and to remarry after a divorce or the death of their husbands. The foot-binding of old days was a cruel and inhuman practice, they said. Foreign pills were much better than Chinese herbs. They said there was no such thing as ghosts or transmigration of the soul. Nothing would be left after death but a heap of chemical compounds. They said the only immortality was to render services to the people and the country.

She shook her head and sighed. "Do they teach these things in America?" she asked. I smiled. Apparently she did not like my smile. Perhaps she suspected that the crazy Americans were responsible for teaching Chinese boys and girls these silly notions, for she told me that an American missionary lady had come some time earlier to tell her not to worship idols.

A fat black cat leapt up on her bed and began purring around her pillows. "Are there cats in America?" she asked feebly. I said yes, and saw that she was already asleep. I left her with the purring cat whose soft paws rested upon her pillows and touched her cheek.

My niece, who had been listening all the time, ran out after me. She put her tongue between her teeth for a moment and said mischievously, "Grandma is too old for the change." After a month or so the old lady left this crazy, changing world.

I went to visit with another aunt of mine, whom I called Third Mother. She was a strong elderly lady. Her husband, my "Third Father," owned large farms. There were chickens, ducks, geese, and pigs in abundance. My aunt told me the tragedy of a childhood friend of mine who had speculated in gold in Shanghai and incurred heavy losses. He had lost his job and retired to his home village. The year before, he had committed suicide by taking a big dose of opium. His widow and children were destitute and one of the children had drowned in the canal while fishing for shrimp under the big soap tree.

My aunt snatched a big fat capon which struggled and screamed in her hands and dressed it herself. Later a delicious chicken dinner was served, with fish and shrimp in addition.

My uncle told me that people had used chemical fertilizers for cabbages the year before, and these grew to such enormous size that they thought the abnormal growth must contain poison. So they pulled them up and threw them away. But he kept his, bought them cheap from others, and salted them. They were tender and delicious. A wise old man he was.

An old woman who had held me in her arms when I was a baby came to the village to see me. She must have been over ninety and was partially deaf, yet had walked from her own village some four miles away. She examined me from top to toe and was satisfied to find nothing strange about me. This big boy was once a small, skinny child, she said, and very naughty. He bit his own brother on the knee and left purple marks on it. Then he cried and blamed his brother's knee for having hurt his teeth.

"Do you remember the two brothers who divided their father's property into equal parts when he died?" she asked. They had each got a wing of their father's house and had set a bamboo partition in the middle of the hall, which was thus evenly divided so that each could get an exactly equal portion. One kept a cow in his part and the other retaliated by making his a piggery. They even sawed the boat in two equal halves. The wicked brothers—may the gods curse them! Then there came a fire and turned their house into ashes. Heaven must have eyes.

They sold the lot and a big house of foreign style was later built on it. It belonged to a rich merchant who was in business in Shanghai. When the house was completed she paid a visit to it and got into such a labyrinth of passageways and stairs and doors that she was confused and could not find her way out. She tried the soft chairs and spring beds and was frightened when she sank deep into them. The most curious thing to her was the machine which the owner of the house had brought from Shanghai. When the wheels turned swiftly it lit up bulbs all over the house. The night was as brilliant as day.

The boy who took charge of the machine was the son of her neighbors. He had learned to operate it in Shanghai. She would never have thought that stupid boy could manipulate such an intricate piece of machinery. She stood far away from the swiftly turning wheels lest she be caught and turned into sausage or tough meat balls.

Another curious thing she noticed was that there was no Kitchen God in the kitchen. And the family worshiped no ancestors. The kitchen gods she did not mind so much, but how could a family have no ancestors? The master of the house believed a sort of religion which precluded the worship of other gods. She would not like to belong to that religion, because she wanted to go to any temple she chose and worship any gods she wanted to. She wondered how a god could be so jealous as to forbid people to worship other gods. She was willing to worship that god, for the man in his temple gave her quinine pills which cured her malaria last summer; but she wanted to bend her stiff knees to other gods also to ask for blessings.

She said she had scarcely enough to eat and often went hungry. My father gave her a monthly allowance in rice as a charity, but since her orphaned granddaughter had come to live with her the small girl ate a portion of it. I pulled out a twenty dollar bill and squeezed it into her hands. She scurried away happily, muttering, "From his childhood I know he is a kind-hearted boy, a kind-hearted boy."

Late one afternoon I made a visit to my mother's tomb. A pair of candles and a bunch of incense sticks were displayed before it. The air was still and streaks of smoke from the incense went straight up in the air. Instinctively I bent my knees to the ground and kowtowed. My childhood memories revived. Everything seemed to have happened only yesterday. I felt as if I were still a child paying respects to my mother. I wished her spirit could welcome me with open arms and caress me. I wished I could curl up on her lap and listen to her soothing lullabies. All my thoughts and feelings reverted to childhood days. My mother had died when I was only seven, so I had not much experience in mother love. Perhaps an imaginary mother was even tenderer and sweeter than a real one. A dead mother could not spank you and would not get cross with you when you were naughty.

From the village I walked some three miles through the rice fields to the railway station, on the banks of a placid lake, the reservoir that irrigated thousands of acres of land. It is surrounded on three sides by mountains famous for berries and bamboo shoots. Here I took a train to the bank of the Tsao-ao River. The railway bridge was uncompleted, for the materials ordered from Germany had been held up by the war. Construction of the railroad to Hangchow had also been suspended. A steamship line supplied the missing link. Most travelers took steamships and left the small boats struggling for existence.

I arrived at the Chien-tang River late in the afternoon and crossed it in twenty minutes by a steam ferry. The rowed ferryboats of my high-school days had disappeared.

By sunset I found myself in Hangchow, comfortably settled in a hotel overlooking the West Lake. The sun was sinking behind the thunder peaks, casting red, golden, and purple beams up into the sky. On one side the needle-sharp Pao Su Pagoda stood clear on the mountaintop in the evening light, while directly opposite, in the valley across the lake, the squat Thunder Peak Pagoda was silhouetted against the distant shady blue mountains. Tiny pleasure boats dotted the rippling lake. Fish splashed in the water. Birds flew homeward. Villas and temples perched on the mountainside were gradually enveloped by a thin veil of evening mist, leaving only the streams of smoke from their chimneys standing motionless in the still air. An utter peacefulness stole over me. Despite all modernism, the West Lake retained its enchantment as of old.

But things had changed. My reverie was soon broken by the tapping of the high heels which adorned the short-skirted, bobbed-haired young women of fashion parading the lake boulevard. This new section of the city had been during my school days the seat of the Tartar or Manchu garrison. The Revolution of 1911 had razed it to the ground and upon its ruins a new town had been built, with wide streets and ugly-looking buildings in semi-foreign style. In place of medieval barracks, restaurants, theatres, wine-shops, and tea pavilions had sprung up, and an amusement park, all catering to weekend tourists who came by railway from Shanghai. Hangchow had become a tourist center.

Chekiang College, which I had attended years before, was closed and the buildings had been turned into offices for the new governor. The once-palatial yamen of the Imperial governor had burned during the revolution, leaving a vast rectangular space in the heart of the city overgrown with wild plants and grass.

Revolution had come to Hangchow without shedding a drop of blood. The commanders of the new army met and sent a few pieces of light artillery into the streets in the dark of night. Without firing a shot they forced the Imperial governor of the province to surrender. The army then set his yamen on fire as a symbol of the revolution and the city was lit up with its flames. The Manchu garrison entrenched itself in its own walled city but surrendered after negotiations in which it was promised that no one would be molested. Mr. Kwei Han-hsiang, a Manchu leader, accepted the terms on behalf of the garrison. He was, however, seized by his personal enemies and shot, on the false charge that he was plotting a revolt. It was a case of sheer murder.

The newly elected governor, Tang Shuo-chien, a famous old litterateur, was indignant over this cowardly act and threatened to resign, but the matter was patched up until he was called to Nanking to take up the portfolio of Minister of Communications under the presidency of Dr. Sun Yat-sen.

Northeast of the modern town which had replaced the Manchu city, rows of shacks, totaling five hundred rooms, had been erected to house the families of the former garrison. Some had already melted away into the vast ocean of China's multitudes and left their houses vacant. In the course of a few years all the remnants of the once-conquering race had vanished into the common stream of life of the once-conquered. The Manchus were gone forever. Pictures of their lives still linger in my memory, but the stories about them have sunk into folklore. It is left to history alone to tell the rise, decline, and fall of the Manchu Dynasty.

The quaint old teahouses at which I used to sip my tea quietly with the lake view filling the windows had disappeared in the face of the diabolic modernization; only one or two lingered to recall the memories of the good old days. This was the kind of time-mellowed teahouse I still loved to frequent. I would go there and read Tang poems over a cup of Hangchow tea. It took one back to the dear old days.

I have said that the city was the center of the silk industry. Some factories had introduced textile machines, but many of the smaller establishments still retained the hand looms. A college of engineering had been established in which practical courses in textiles were given. Graduates who had taken courses in mechanical engineering set up small machine shops in the city, with machines run by electricity. The city now had electric light and a telephone system. Hangchow seemed on the eve of industrialization.

I stayed for about a week, visiting many historical sites to refresh my boyhood memories. As I wandered away from the center of commercial activity I found the old life less affected by modernization. The charm of old days still remained intact in the mountain regions and out-of-the-way villages. The monasteries surrounded by tall trees and bamboo groves stood as calmly as they had centuries ago. The life of the monks had undergone little change; they chanted their Buddhist hymns as before. The villagers raised their tea and mulberry leaves as their forefathers had done. A few imported articles were to be seen here and there, but the quantity was negligible. However, the spearhead of future modernization had already reached them—in the schools, where modern textbooks were in use. The mental attitude of the coming generation was changing, under the influence of modern education, in spite of unchanged ways of living. Seeds of new ideas sown in the minds of the young were bound to sprout in the course of time. ❶

Chapter 13
Warlords

In my youthful days I noticed that civil ranks came invariably above the military. Imperial officers wore buttons of different colors at the tops of their red-tasseled hats. The red button was highest in rank; next came the pink, then dark blue, brilliant blue, white, and finally golden, the lowest. Often my wondering eyes watched a military pink-button, though higher in rank, bowing before a blue-button civil official. It was explained to me that the Imperial system had chosen to put the military under control of the civil in order to eliminate the evils of military dictatorship in the country. Through centuries of history we had learned that when the country came under the control of warlords it was divided into spheres of influence; the authority of the Imperial Court became a mere shadow and peace and order vanished like a bubble. We learned this lesson from the later Tangs. Thus there was a popular saying that "good iron is not to be beaten into nails, and good men are not to be made into soldiers." We were taught to look down upon soldiers. I remember that a man of questionable character in one of our neighboring villages joined the army, and when he came home on leave we used to avoid him like a plague. It was borne in upon us that soldiers were a bad lot, something to be despised, feared, and detested.

On the other hand, when a country sank into military impotence it lost all power of resistance before the onslaught of powerful invaders; thus it was that the Sungs fell into the hands of the Mongols and the Mings into the hands of the Tartars. So we were between the devil and the deep sea. What should be our choice?

China must be saved—saved from powerful invaders by land on the north and by sea from the east and south. What, then, was to be done? Build up a modern army in which modern weapons of war would be employed and soldiers well trained and imbued with patriotism. How could we look down upon soldiers? They were the defenders of the land, the saviors of China from partition by the Western Powers. Despise them? By no means—we must elevate and honor them, even worship them. Or who would join the army?

Our people began to argue in their minds. As necessity is the mother of invention, we organized a modern army with imported weapons, modern uniforms, and military bands. Once I saw such an army on the march, bugles blowing, drums beating. It was inspiring. I imagined myself grown up and joining them in the march—marching to victory! Meanwhile I found my real self standing among the silent crowd and watching, overwhelmed with joy. It was my first glimpse of a modern army. Yes—we must honor the soldiers and the commanding officers. Hereafter only good men should be made into soldiers. We must depend upon them to regain the past glories of China. In the old armies of yesterday the soldiers wore jackets and carried bows and arrows, or in some cases obsolete guns discarded and sold to China by European countries. How different from the modern army of today!

While I was studying at Chekiang College in Hangchow I saw a former student who had just come back from a military academy in Tokyo on a visit to the college. He was in military uniform, spick and span, carrying a sword in its shining sheath. A future great general of the Chinese army—how our hearts rushed out to him!

There were a number of embryo generals of that kind who came back from Japan and were entrusted with the duty of organizing new armies. In the course of a few years army units had been organized and stationed at various strategic centers in the country. China was armed, armed to defend herself.

Then came the Revolution of 1911. The revolutionary armies were perhaps not so well trained as the government armies, but commanders and men were full of patriotism and ready to sacrifice their lives for their country. The new armies of the government went over, one after another, to Dr. Sun Yat-sen. Within a few months the agelong Imperial regime had vanished like a ghost at the least rustle of leaves into the dark night. Waves of enthusiasm spread far and wide over the country. China was reborn with little regret for the past and great hopes for the future. Let the Manchus lament their mistake in forming a new army, and let the people be overjoyed by the splendid actions of these modern-trained generals.

But the hour of triumph passed. The candle flickered out in dark streaks of smoke. The generals of the new army had little pity for the Manchus and less love for the revolution; they had tasted power and resolved to keep it. As appetite grows with eating, they longed for larger and higher power, and so fought among themselves for it.

Dr. Sun Yat-sen had returned to China in 1912. After negotiations between the revolutionaries and the Peking government the dynasty agreed to abdicate and the Republic was established. Little Pu-yi was allowed by agreement to retain residence in the Forbidden City, ancient palace of the emperors of China. A constitution was to be drafted, providing for a President and a National Assembly; meanwhile the Provisional Assembly elected Dr. Sun Yat-sen Provisional President of the Republic.

After a short time he resigned in favor of Yuan Shih-kai, who was later elected President by the National Assembly, more or less through coercion and intrigue. Political power again slipped into the hands of the reactionaries. Yuan was a mandarin of the monarchical regime who had begun the training of a modern army. He had fallen into disfavor with the Imperial Court but had been recalled to Peking when the revolution broke out.

Dr. Sun believed that the most important service he could render China was to build railroads; he was content to be at the head of China's national railways and let Yuan Shih-kai hold the reins of government. But he was soon to be disillusioned. When Yuan came into power he knew very well that his strength lay in the army under his control. The National Assembly he regarded as a mere necessary evil; so long as he controlled the army it could prove at worst no more than a nuisance to him. With strong armies behind him the new head of the state usurped all sorts of powers that did not properly belong to the President. He employed methods of intimidation and resorted to the dastardly means of assassination. Politically, he knew the trick of "divide and rule" and fostered dissension in Dr. Sun's Nationalist, or Kuomintang, camp. He went further and encouraged political parties to multiply, so that the influence of the Nationalist party would be further reduced.

Then he took steps to remove its military power. He first assassinated its political leader, Mr. Sung Chiao-ren, on his way to Peking from Shanghai. Then he removed all the Nationalist military governors of the southern provinces by a stroke of the pen, thus provoking those provinces in order to crush them. Dr. Sun Yat-sen attempted a second revolution, but failed. Yuan Shih-kai had by this time almost the whole country under his military control and took steps to disqualify the Kuomintang members of the National Assembly on account of the "rebellion." With the south crushed his appetite grew; he longed for more power and glory. In 1915, as he was about to proclaim himself Emperor of a new Chinese Empire, the provinces revolted, whereupon he abandoned his monarchical scheme and soon died, broken-hearted.

In 1917 Dr. Sun Yat-sen finally entrenched himself in Canton, hoping to form a nucleus of an army in preparation for a new revolution to dethrone the warlords, only to find himself overthrown in 1929 by the warlord of Canton, Chen Chun-ming. In the next year, however, he succeeded in organizing a new Kuomintang government there, in a reinvigorated Nationalist movement to which the Russians gave some assistance after an agreement between himself and an unofficial Russian adviser. But this was only a beginning. After the death of the ambitious and unscrupulous Yuan Shih-kai the country as a whole remained divided among the warring provinces and political turmoil continued for twelve long years until Generalissimo Chiang Kai-shek unified it in 1928, after the triumph of the Nationalist movement.

For sixteen years after the founding of the Republic China was in the grip of warlords. One civil war after another, often supported by foreign interests, devastated the country, bringing innumerable hardships to the people and paving the way for Japanese aggression. The cause of revolution seemed to be doomed. Victorious generals, elated, reached for more and more power. Wounded lions and tigers fell in ignominy and with their tails between their legs limped into the foreign concessions or settlements of Tientsin or Shanghai to lick their wounds and wait for opportunities to come back. When opportunity came they sneaked out, entered the arena again, and caused more suffering to the people.

The soldier, who had been once despised and then honored, was now again despised. ●

Chapter 14
Intellectual Awakening

From Hangchow I went to Shanghai, where I entered the Commercial Press—the largest publishing company in China—as one of its editors. Board and lodging were accorded me at the headquarters of the Kiangsu Provincial Education Association, in return for which I served as a member of the executive committee. But I was not yet old enough to be pinned down to a desk and resigned at the end of a year. My financial arrangements with the publishing company were cleared within another year.

Together with friends I began to issue a monthly, The New Education, published under the auspices of the National University of Peking and the Kiangsu Education Association. I was editor-in-chief. Six months after its inception the magazine had reached a circulation of ten thousand. Its chief aim was to "develop individuality and attain social progress." Encouragement of liberal ideas as against purely traditional thought was what the monthly stood for.

These were the times immediately after the European war when liberalism and democracy were in vogue all over the world and Wilsonian ideals had caught the imagination of the thinking minds of China. Chinese youth was imbued with the new ideas that came in torrents from postwar Europe and America. Newspapers and magazines devoted large sections to international news and developments. China was beginning to think with the world.

La Jeunesse, a radical magazine launched by Chen Tu-hsiu some years before and then taken up by a group of professors in the University of Peking, was advocating democracy and modern science for the rejuvenation of China. In introducing new elements of thought it was quite natural that they should fiercely attack the old beliefs and traditions. Some contributors even went so far as to cry "Down with the Confucian shops!" While all this evoked strong antagonism from the reading public, the youth of the country caught the spirit of the intellectual revolt.

In 1918 Dr. Sun Yat-sen came to reside in Shanghai. As we have seen, the government of the young Republic was having its ups and downs and had come partially under the sway of independent warlords. The Kuomintang, or Nationalist, party of Dr. Sun was strongest in the south and here, in 1917, a government was set up, separate from the Peking regime, to maintain the principles for which the revolutionaries had labored and re-established them throughout the country. Now, however, the veteran leader left his southern government in Canton under the control of a Directorate. The political views of its members did not go beyond their noses, a brevity of outlook to which Dr. Sun could not subscribe. So he settled down in Shanghai to work on his plan for the industrial development of China.

His vision carried him far beyond the political squabbles of the time and his plan, if successfully carried into effect, was one which would relieve the poverty of the people, bring prosperity to the country, and put China on the level of modern industrialized nations of the world. According to Dr. Sun, China's industrial reconstruction fell into four categories: clothing, food, shelter, and transportation, All are necessary for the livelihood of the people and with these elements in view he planned the industrial development of the country.

He worked out a system of railroads and highways to cover all important commercial and military routes in the vast territory of China. He planned ports and harbors through which China's future commerce could flow abundantly. He outlined a project for river conservation, irrigation, and reclamation which would feed millions more in the country. He worked out a scheme for the development of natural resources and for the building up of both heavy and light industries. Seeing China far on the road of deforestation, he made plans to reforest great areas of central and north China.

He laid down two principles or categories under which industry was to be developed: (1) that which could be maintained as private enterprise was to be under private ownership, while (2) that which was beyond the capacities of individual citizens to undertake, or tended to create monopoly, was to be under state ownership. The government was to encourage private enterprise and to protect it by law. Obnoxious taxes must be abolished, the currency system must be improved and unified. Official interference and obstacles must be removed and communications developed to insure an easy flow of trade.

Railroads and highways, river conservation, irrigation, and reclamation, ports and harbors and the like, were to come under state control. The government was also to develop coal and iron resources in Shansi, and establish iron and steel works on a large scale. Foreign capital was to be welcomed and foreign experts employed.

Dr. Sun Yat-sen was the first Chinese statesman to have modern scientific training. His knowledge of scientific data and his mathematical accuracy were amazing. In planning China's industrial development he himself drew up maps and charts and collected his data and checked them carefully. He was familiar with such details as the depths and gradations of the riverbeds and harbors which came under his plan. Once I gave him a map of the Huai-ho Conservancy; he at once spread it on the floor and began to study it seriously. Later it was seen hanging on the walls of his study.

After a careful investigation of the various phases of industrial reconstruction and how they might be dealt with, he wrote it all out in English. Madame Sun Yat-sen did all his typing, while David Yui and I were entrusted to go over the manuscripts carefully. Data were checked over and suggestions gladly considered. Any project that Dr. Sun worked on, political, philosophical, scientific, or whatever, was carried out with great enthusiasm. His broad-mindedness echoed every suggestion or criticism that was offered him.

Because in his views and plans he was ahead of his time he was often exasperated at the shortsightedness of his contemporaries, who frequently dismissed his projects with the proverbial saying, "It is easy to know but difficult to do." From the beginning of his revolutionary movement some forty years earlier he had met with the same stubborn obstacle. So he wrote an essay on "Psychological Reconstruction for China" in which he advanced the theory that it is difficult to know but easy to do. Here he brought out a significant difference between Chinese and Western thought. The practical-mindedness of his own people often unduly emphasized the difficulties—imaginary or real—that lay in the way of practice, at the cost of neglecting the principles underlying the practice. A mind used to handling abstractions and generalizations and familiar with the process of seeking out the basic principles involved in any problem would find it easy to understand what Dr. Sun Yat-sen had in view. For minds, on the other hand, habitually intent on short-range practical results and impatient of deeper effort it was difficult to appreciate what he stood for. In China, during the declining days of the Imperial regime, men of strong will and determination to carry out reforms were not lacking, but those who perceived underlying causes and could lay plans which would strike at the root of things were rare. Dr. Sun, who possessed a clear understanding of the development of Western civilization as well as vision for the future development of China, could not but appreciate the importance of the kind of knowledge which implies foresight, or seeing beyond immediate needs, and a clear understanding of problems.

Once knowledge of this fundamental sort is secured there is no inherent difficulty in carrying it into effect. The real difficulties lie in discovering it. Indeed, even lacking essential knowledge, if one is willing to follow the direction of those who know, as masons and carpenters follow the architect, he may have no difficulty in executing a complex plan. Thus it is very plain in the field of medicine that to diagnose a case is often more difficult than to apply the cure. A medical student knows well that he must have a grasp of biological sciences such as physiology and anatomy before he is in a position to study medical science, and he has had to learn even more general science, such as physics and chemistry, before studying biological sciences. And each science is the result of centuries of research by men who have loved knowledge. Therefore it is very clear that the process of learning medical science is more laborious than the practice of medicine.

Dr. Sun's practical-minded contemporaries wanted to get things done without taking much interest in studying the underlying causes of conditions in China in the light of knowledge gained from history, sociology, psychology, science, or the like; or making plans for the country accordingly. They branded his plans as visionary and impractical. Unaware of the problems which lay beyond their "practical" mental horizon, they did not realize that their own difficulties usually arose from lack of knowledge, or an insufficient or superficial knowledge of problems—certainly, in any case, not alone from lack of practical ability. What they thought they knew was often limited to immediate personal experience or empirical reasoning. Such knowledge is not only easy to obtain but dangerous as a basis for practice.

To the Western mind these are mere philosophical squabbles of theory and practice, or knowledge and conduct—and what have they to do with revolution and reconstruction in China? Yet Dr. Sun Yat-sen was very serious about it, considering psychological reconstruction the first step to successful reconstruction in other realms, whether political, industrial, or social. "Overpractical becomes impracticable," Professor Dewey said to him. "No one in the West would think that 'to know' is an easy matter."

Amid the revolutionary atmosphere of the intellectual world and my own inspiring contact with Dr. Sun, The New Education stood pedagogically for initiative, the needs of children, and much that John Dewey stands for in his Democracy and Education. As regarded Chinese principles of education, it stood for Mencius' ideas on human nature: that it is good. Hence education means a proper development of what there is in the child. As a matter of fact, in its main current Chinese education had followed since Confucius the principle that human nature is all-good. The trouble was that as the centuries accumulated, what is good in human nature came to mean certain moral precepts shrouded in age-worn tradition. Thus while in theory it was very modern, in practice it might lead miles away from original principles. "Development of nature" may in fact come to mean mere conformity to traditional morals, and this is what happened in China.

With the introduction into Chinese thought of Rousseau, Pestalozzi, Froebel, and later Dewey, the Mencian principles came into better perspective and shed a more living light. Children of China were to be set free of hard and fast rules of conduct and traditional moral ideas incongruous to modern society. Thus children must be led to think for themselves and helped to solve their own problems in accordance with their needs and not those of grownups, They should be led to an interest in nature and in their environment. In accordance with the principles of child psychology, a child must be treated as such; he is not a little man and must not be stuffed with knowledge only, much less with books. Education should help a child to grow— mentally, physically, and socially.

Such were the lines of thought that guided the policies of The New Education. As the reader will easily see, it fell in line with the current revolutionary thought of the country. The intellectual ties between The New Education, and the professors and students of Peking University, the whirlpool of intellectual revolt, drew me the next year to that mu ch-troubled institution as professor of education and Acting Chancellor. ❶

Chapter 15
Peking University and the Student Revolt

If you throw a stone into a body of still water, rings of waves begin to rise and travel farther and farther, ever widening and extending away from the center. In Peking, capital of China during five dynasties and more than ten centuries— the seat of conservatism where the Empress Dowager ruled the country from her dragon throne—stood the oldest modern institution of learning in the country, known as the National University of Peking. It was the only landmark left by Emperor Kwang-hsü's short-lived reforms of 1898. The brief tide of reform had ebbed and vanished into history; only a few scattered shells remained, witness to the vicissitudes of fortune in that placid ancient capital. But the university, in which were clustered the living shells that contained pearls, was destined to make valuable contributions to culture and thought within the short span of one generation.

The man who threw the stone of intellectual revolt into that placid water was Dr. Tsai Yuan-pei, who in 1916 became Chancellor of the university. Dr. Tsai was an eminent scholar of China's ancient culture, but imbued with the spirit of Western scholarship and especially the spirit of free inquiry which prevailed in the Hellenic world. His belief in "knowledge for knowledge' sake," in contrast to the "learning for its practical use" of Chinese thought, had its foundation in a thorough knowledge of ancient Greek culture. His views on knowledge were essentially the same as those of Dr. Sun, but the latter had acquired his outlook from the natural sciences, Dr. Tsai his from a study of Greek philosophy.

This renowned scholar preferred the appreciation of beauty to belief in religion. Here we find an interesting blending of Greek and Chinese culture. The traditional love of nature of the Chinese scholar and the Greek sense of beauty working together in Dr. Tsai's mind resulted in a love for Western sculpture and Chinese carvings; Chinese landscape painting and Western portraits; both Chinese and Western architecture, and Chinese and Western music. His views on religion were essentially Chinese: religion is but part of morality. He wanted to elevate the moral sense of youth to a higher level by love of beauty. It was an ancient Chinese belief that there is no greater moral force than that of music. Good morals had their foundation in well- balanced emotions, which could only be brought about by the fine arts and music or poetry, which is closely allied to music.

Dr. Tsai had great faith in natural science. He not only trusted it to yield inventions, engineering, and other benefits, but believed it would foster the mental habits of methodical thinking and research which led to the discovery of general truths, the foundation of all true knowledge.

In his younger days his brilliance was less veiled in modesty. When he was principal of the Sino-Occidental School at Shaoshing which I attended in my boyhood, one evening at a banquet, after a few cups of Shaoshing wine, he stood up and announced at the top of his voice that the reforms of Kang Yu- wei and Liang Chi-chao were too superficial, since they retained the Manchu court to lead them. "I, Tsai Yuan-pei, will not do that. Unless you overthrow the Manchus no reforms will be possible!" He shouted it out, raising his right arm over his head.

Dr. Tsai in his early years wrote essays full of brilliant and stimulating ideas contrary to the common practice of writing in the days of civil examinations. My uncle King told me of a strange essay of his which began, "In sex, food, and drinking human desires lie." He handed in his paper to the Imperial examiners after the time limit. The night was getting on to the small hours and the eyes of the examiners were heavy with sleep. His paper was accepted and he passed the examination for the Second Degree—Chu-jen, or the Promoted Scholar. In the following years he achieved the Third or highest degree—Chin-shih, or Advanced Scholar—when still under thirty. He subsequently entered Hanlin Academy, composed of the highest ranking scholars, which has since ceased to exist.

In his later years he was the personification of what is best in a Chinese scholar, with a broad mind open to Western ideas. His eyes, looking over his spectacles, were alert but calm; his speech easy, clear, fluent, and sincere, though often drowned in a monotone. He never let harsh words cross his thin lips, but when he was indignant his utterance was quick, weighty, and concise—as clearly to the point as a judge rendering judgment or a dagger popping out from under soft velvet cotton.

He was of a light build but his movements were steady. His artistic fingers would run deftly through the pages as he read, as if he read by paragraphs, even by pages, his quick sight grasping essential points and his retentive memory keeping knowledge in store. His love of nature and the arts made his emotions tranquil, thoughts lofty, tastes refined, manners sincere and modest, and ways of living simple and retired. His broad-mindedness was as responsive to every shade of opinion, criticism, or suggestion "as a hollow in the mountains that echoes with every vibration of sound."

In such a scholar the government of Li Yuan-hung, then President of the Republic, found a chancellor for the university. Under his administration the institution underwent a radical change. Science was put on an equal footing with literature, which had reigned in the realm of knowledge in China from time immemorial. History, philosophy, and the classics were studied in the light of modern scientific method. The spirit of knowledge for its own sake was encouraged. Scholars of old conservative schools, new schools, and radical schools were all given an equal chance. Old literati with queues hanging down their backs who still retained faith in a monarchical regime sat shoulder to shoulder with men of radical thought, discussing problems, joking and laughing at the same dinner table. Free inquiry into problems, of knowledge, culture, family, social relations, and political systems was found in the classrooms, seminars, and social gatherings.

It was the intellectual life of ancient China of the pre-Ching period or ancient Greece of the times of Socrates and Aristotle re-enacted. Dr. Tsai was the old, wise Socrates of China, and would have suffered the same fate had he not had sympathizers on a nationwide scale, especially among the Kuomintang members who had a strong hold in Canton. Yet by conservative Chinese and foreigners alike the university was accused of advocating "A- three-ism"—no religion, no government, and no family—just as Socrates was accused by the ancient Greeks of corrupting the souls of young men. No argument could dispel these unfounded suspicions. History alone would disprove them, as it has absolved Socrates.

I have said that Dr. Tsai advocated esthetics as a substitute for religion, and free inquiry as a means of approach to truths. Mr. Chen Tu-hsiu, Dean of the College of Literature, advocated science and democracy as the twin weapons to modernize China. Free inquiry led to freedom of thought. Science sapped the old beliefs. Democracy meant the assertion of popular rights. Meanwhile Dr. Hu Shih, professor of philosophy, worked for a literary revolution by which the language in common use by the people was to replace the classical language as a medium of thought and expression. The colloquial, or common written language, is nearer to the Chinese spoken language and therefore easier to learn, to write, and to understand. It is a better and easier medium for the expression of thought. Its use was to popularize knowledge, hitherto a monopoly of classical scholars.

The movement developed a host of young writers throughout the country. After a few years the Ministry of Education made compulsory the use of the vulgate as a medium of instruction in all elementary schools.

The university was an oasis in the intellectual desert of Peking. But the seeds of intellectual revolt grew in that small green spot with remarkable rapidity. Within three years the whole institution was filled with it.

In that vigorous atmosphere of intellectual activity a mental and moral unrest developed among the students. I have related earlier how, under the influence of French eighteenth-century political idealism with its catchwords of Liberty, Equality, and Fraternity, and as a revolt against established authority which the youth of the nation believed responsible for retarding China's progress and thus inviting the encroachment of foreign Powers, students had gone on strike against their school authorities upon the slightest pretext. This first happened in Shanghai in 1902. The first student revolt had spent itself in the course of a few years and degenerated into strikes against the school cooks. In the end the authorities outwitted the students by handing the management of the kitchens over to the student body. Isolated cases of strikes still persisted for some years. In one instance this ended in tragedy when a dozen students in the provincial high school at Hangchow died of arsenic poisoning which the cooks put in their rice as a revenge. I went to the school after the outrage and found a large number of youths moaning in their beds, while a dozen caskets stood in the open-air gymnasium waiting for relatives to take them for burial.

While the spirit of revolt in the form of school strikes was gradually spending itself, its force turned inward into revolutionary ideas which gained much wider ground outside the schools in the form of a political revolution, resulting ultimately in the downfall of the Manchus in 1911.

The second student revolt burst out suddenly in Peking on May 4, 1919, the eighth year of the Republic. What happened was this. From the peace conference in Paris news reached China that Tsingtao in the Shantung Peninsula, a German-leased port taken from German hands during the war by the Japanese, had been awarded to Japan by the victorious Powers. As China had declared war against Germany, the leased territory should in all justice have been returned to China. The whole nation was indignant over the news. Students in Peking, under the leadership of the National University group, demonstrated against the signing of the Versailles Treaty. Three thousand students held mass meetings and paraded in the streets demonstrating against acceptance of the terms, shouting "Return

Tsingtao to China!" "Boycott Japanese goods!" "Down with the traitors!" Banners streamed in the air bearing the same slogans.

The Peking government, despite the efforts of Dr. Sun Yat-sen's Kuomintang or Nationalist party in Canton and its adherents elsewhere, was still under the thumb of military men and ruled China with a mere semblance of the democracy and parliamentary procedure which the revolution had labored so earnestly to establish. Among its influential high officials were three members of a notoriously pro-Japanese group. Their sympathies were well known. These men—Tsao Ru-lin, Minister of Communication; Chang Chung-hsiang, Chinese Minister of Tokyo; and Lu Chung-yu, another minister—now became the targets of student wrath. The crowd streamed to the residence of Tsao, where secret meetings were supposed to have been going on; they broke in, and combed the house for the three "traitors." Tsao and Lu escaped by the back door; Chang was caught by the mob and badly beaten. Leaving him for dead, the students dispersed, in their retreat smashing everything in sight and setting the place on fire.

Meanwhile, the armed police and gendarmery had thrown a cordon around the house. They arrested some sixty students and sent them to headquarters. The rest—about a thousand strong—followed after, each claiming individually to have been responsible for the outbreak and asking to be arrested. Finally all were put under heavy military guard in the compounds of the Law College of the university.

News concerning the demonstration was strictly censored. Some students outwitted the government, however, by sending a cable through a foreign agency in one of the foreign concessions of Tientsin, and this cable was the sole source of the news that appeared in Shanghai papers on the morning of the fifth.

I was at breakfast on May 5 when the newspapers reached me. On their front pages appeared in bold letters a news item something as follows:

Students in Peking demonstrated against the signing of the Versailles Treaty. Three pro-Japanese high officials—Tsao, Lu, and Chang—were beaten by the students. The residence of Tsao Ru-lin was burned. Several thousand have been detained under heavy armed guard in the Law College of the National University of Peking. Ringleaders were arrested and their state is unknown.

There were no further details.

The whole city was excited by the news. In the afternoon public organizations such as educational associations, chambers of commerce, and provincial and local guilds sent telegrams to the Peking government demanding the dismissal of the three high officials and the release of the students arrested or detained. Through the following day all Shanghai waited anxiously for a reply from the government but there was none. Then the students of the city went on strike, making the same demands as the public organizations, and went forth lecturing on the streets.

Next morning schoolboys and girls went by hundreds from door to door on Nanking Road, the main street of Shanghai, begging the shopkeepers to go on strike. Some in sympathy and others out of fear closed their doors. Many followed suit in imitation of their neighbors. In about an hour's time all the Nanking Road shops were closed as tight as clams. Police interfered but to no avail.

The shop strike spread like fire. By noon all Shanghai was shut. Thousands of people wandered about the streets and traffic was almost blocked. Settlement police became powerless. Boy and girl scouts went out as police to keep order and direct traffic. To see order maintained in the crowded streets by bobbed-haired girl scouts was something novel in the International Settlement of Shanghai. Both Chinese and foreigners wondered why the crowd willingly obeyed the orders of young boys and girls while showing such an ugly temper toward the police.

Within a few days the student strike had grown into a nationwide movement. Shops and commercial houses closed in all the cities near Shanghai. As Shanghai was the center of commerce in the lower Yangtze Valley, these cities were paralyzed when the heart of the great metropolis ceased to beat, and suspended their affairs, not necessarily out of sympathy for the students.

Settlement authorities were alarmed when employees of the water works and the electric company wanted to join the strike. Through the mediation of the chamber of commerce and student representatives they were persuaded to stick to their jobs. The pressure continued for more than a week and the Peking government finally gave in. The three pro-Japanese officials resigned and all the students were set free.

With country-wide sympathy behind them, students everywhere were intoxicated by their success. Thereafter there was no peace for institutions of learning, or for the government. The students of Peking, having won their victory, continued to agitate against corruption in the government and the old traditions which, they thought, enslaved the minds of young people. They had won over the government because they had national sentiment behind them. Everybody in China would have liked to join the demonstrations and parades against the signing of the Versailles Treaty. The students, who were better organized, more articulate, more impulsive and less hesitant, took the lead and thus plucked at the heartstrings of the nation.

When the pro-Japanese officials had resigned and the students had been released by the government—when the general strike had been called off in Shanghai and elsewhere—the incident was considered closed, for the time being at least. But the university itself became a problem. Chancellor Tsai Yuan-pei, apparently shocked by the violence, had resigned and quietly left Peking. He went first to Tientsin, then to Shanghai, and finally slipped into Hangchow, where he lived in a friend's house on the historic West Lake, surrounded by gentle hills, enjoying nature as a traditional scholar of the old days. Despite repeated persuasions he declined to go back to the university. He said that he had never intended to incite the students to revolt, but that in demonstrating against acceptance of the Shantung clause of the Versailles Treaty they had acted on patriotic impulses which could hardly be condemned. As regarded the university, he thought that thenceforth it would be difficult to maintain discipline, as the students were likely to be intoxicated with the cup of success. Once they tasted power there would be no end to their appetite. This was the stand he took in regard to the student movement. The belief that he was always ready to encourage a student revolt was far from the truth.

Finally he approved my going to Peking to take charge of the university for him. I consented rather reluctantly. With the heavy responsibilities thus thrust upon me, I went to Peking in July with one of the student delegates. The student body convened in a mass meeting of welcome, and this was the gist of my first speech to them:

Your patriotic motives in the recent demonstrations are to be highly commended. But if you keep on doing this your valuable time will be wasted and the existence of the institution where you drink at the fountain of wisdom will be endangered. A new nation is not made in one day, and certainly not by demonstrations alone. The demonstrations are trifles in comparison with the work you have to do in classrooms, in the library, in laboratories, and in seminars...

After the storm the clouds began to disperse and a clear day emerged. Dr. Tsai returned to his office in September.

The university was again reorganized, on a sounder basis. The office of dean of administration was created to take charge of the business side of the university. Existing offices were modified and systematized into an organic whole. The dean of faculties was responsible for academic affairs. The Academic Council, members of which were elected by the professors with the deans as ex officio members, was the highest legislative body, empowered to pass on university regulations, grant degrees, and enforce discipline among the students. Various executive committees were set up to perform administrative functions. The university was put on a basis of faculty control. Academic freedom, faculty control, and a fearless spirit of searching for truth were the guiding principles in administration. Student self-government was encouraged as a step to democracy.

For seven long years, in spite of intermittent strikes and demonstrations, the university sailed along under full canvas on the rough sea of political turmoil, with men of courage and foresight at the helm. The number of volumes in the library was vastly increased, laboratory equipment much improved. Scholars of international fame such as John Dewey and Bertrand Russell were invited to join the university as visiting professors.

The two Western philosophers contributed their part to the great intellectual movement in China. Dewey directed the young minds of China to the study of educational and social problems in accordance with the needs of the individual and society. It is true that the very act of thinking of problems in this way led naturally to the creation of other problems which caused trouble in such a static society as that of China in those days. Hu Han-min, a Kuomintang leader, once told me that it was Dewey's teaching that caused unrest in the schools. But he ignored the fact that there were many student strikes under the Imperial regime during prerevolutionary days; as well as the fact that Dewey's teaching, which interested the students in social problems, thus helped the movement against the warlords later on.

It was due to Russell that young minds began to get interested in principles of social reconstruction, which roused them against both religion and imperialism. To the missionaries and members of the British Legation he was an unwelcome guest. He lived in a Chinese hotel and refused to see officials of his own legation. I heard one of them express the view that his coming to China was a matter for regret. In Peking Mr. Russell contracted a serious case of pneumonia and at one time the doctors gave up hope. On his recovery I heard a missionary lady say, "That's too bad." I repeated it to Mr. Russell, who laughed heartily.

During those days of freedom of thought in China just after the first World War, thinking about either social problems or social principles created storms in the thinking mind and waves of emotion in the feeling heart. This prepared the way for the further introduction of Western ideas from postwar Europe. All the "isms" had full play in China. While the intellectuals on the whole moved along the line of Western democracy, a section of them, inspired by the success of the Russian revolution of 1917, were attracted to the ideology of Marxism.Chen Tu-hsiu, editor of La Jeunesse, resigning from his deanship at the University of Peking, became the leader of a Chinese Communist movement. The anti-imperialist movement against Japan also prepared the ground for general sympathy among intellectuals for the Russian Revolution. In 1923 the Third International sent Mr. Joffe to Peking to make contact with Chinese intellectuals, and one evening at a dinner given in his honor at the Chih-ying Restaurant in Peking, Dr. Tsai made a speech of welcome in which he said, "The Russian Revolution has given great inspiration to the revolutionary movement in China."

Russia had repeatedly announced that she was ready to give back to China the Chinese Eastern Railway in north Manchuria, and wished China success in getting rid of both the warlords and the imperialistic Powers that had a grip on the country. This good will of Soviet Russia toward China was welcomed by all the intellectuals as well as by the people as a whole. Among other things, it paved the way for the growth of Communism in China.

Meanwhile, eminent scientists from European and American universities came to guide students in scientific research. A number of periodicals were issued by the faculties as well as by the students. Music and art clubs, athletic associations, library and science associations sprang up in abundance. A society for the study of Marxian theories was established under the leadership of Professor Li Ta-chao. The student army corps, organized some time earlier to give military training to the students, was growing in size. The university gates were flung open to girls— Peking University was the first institution of higher learning in the history of education in China to accept women on an equal footing with men. Faculty and students, immersed in an atmosphere of academic freedom and free inquiry, worked in unison, happy and contented.

The influence of the university was far-reaching. From every intellectual pebble thrown into the waters of ancient Peking waves traveled to every corner of the land. Even the middle schools of the country—the equivalent of American high schools—copied its organization, introducing freedom of thought and opening their doors to girls. Progressive newspapers, magazines, and political parties echoed every movement of the university. In this atmosphere the influence of the Kuomintang revolution extended far and wide, while at the same time the Communist party began to take shape.

The conflicts of the warlords meanwhile roared intermittently around the ancient capital. In one of these internecine wars the gates of Peking were all closed for almost a week. Fighting was going on some ten miles outside the city. It usually began at nightfall and lasted until dawn. Once we went to watch the artillery fire from the top of Peking Hotel. It was like watching a fire on the other side of a river; you got the entertainment of a bonfire at the expense of others without incurring the risk of being licked by the flames. A crossfire of tracers spanned the earth in the dark night like multitudes of rainbows crossing each other. The roar of cannon set the roof trembling as if in a mild earthquake. From dusk till dawn there was no pause in the fighting. When I went home to bed I could not turn my ears to the pillow, for the thundering of the cannon seemed much louder that way. So I lay flat in bed with my eyes toward the ceiling and noticed that the beautifully painted shades of the electric lights were swinging slightly. Glasses rattled. Wolfy, my German police dog, kept moaning, unable to enjoy her usual peaceful slumber on the floor. As soon as she laid her ear to the floor, she would start, get up, groan, dart for the door, and scratch it violently, thinking that these abominable sounds came from beneath the floor of my bedroom. The next morning I scolded her for being naughty the previous night. She stared at me with guilty eyes. From the breakfast table I called to her but she did not respond. I never saw her again. Presumably she wandered away in search of a land of peace where no mocking devils would pound the ground at night and she could sleep well. But I am afraid she was sorely disappointed.

On one of those days in the besieged city I took a walk with a friend along Shun-ching-men Street. People went about their business as usual, without a trace of excitement. As usual, people were pulling or being pulled in rickshaws. We turned at Hsi-tan Pailou into Hsi-ching-an-chieh and then into Central Park. The yellow enamel tiles of the imposing towers on the Wu Gate of the palace glittered in the slanting autumn sun against the cloudless blue. We chose a spot under the spreading branches of one of the ancient spruces planted there in rows and squares by early Manchu emperors centuries ago. The air was laden with their fragrance and light winds brushed our faces with the soothing odor. We sat at a table listening to the gossip at neighboring tables. People all talked about the war and wondered which side was going to win and who was going to have Peking as a spoil of war; all seemed to be utterly unconcerned. What is the use of worrying? Peking had seen many wars and vicissitudes of fortune but remained the same, as the towers of the Wu Gate bore silent witness.

"Let's order a fish for dinner and see whether we get it, with the city gates all closed," said my friend.

A waiter came with a fish wriggling in his hand. "How would you like to have it?"

"Two ways. Split it in half—one half fried with sweet-and-sour gravy spread on top; the other half cooked with bean sauce." The fish came. One of the two halves tasted stale.

"Why, one half of the fish was from a dead one," said my friend to the waiter, who bowed and smiled.

"Oh, I see. The fish sailed in over the city wall. The side that hit the ground was dead, while the other was still alive," I said. When the waiter came back again my friend snatched one of the empty wine jars on the table and showed it to him. "What! You have given us an empty jar."

"Sorry." The waiter was smiling. "The liquor has evaporated." He immediately brought us a new one. Of course both were charged to our account.

We went back home at dusk. That night the fighting ceased. I thought of Wolfy. She must have slept in peace somewhere in the city. The next morning we found the government had changed hands. The palace remained the same. The people went about as usual. The city was undisturbed. The gates were flung open, and thousands of people from the country streamed in with vegetables, meat, eggs, and fish. Donkeys, mules, and camels followed in the wake of the pedestrians. Children gathered empty cannon shells and shrapnel from the battleground and sold them in the streets for a few dollars. Out of these shells we made flower vases.

Many people outside the city lost their property, a number of them lost their lives. I lost my Wolfy.

On the whole the losses to property and life in the various war areas during those long, distressing years were negligible. It was the unsettled state of mind, the disruption of communications, the ruined finances, the disturbances of order and upset of administrative machinery of the government— above all, the obstruction of the tranquil flow of blood in the veins of national life—that reduced China to such a paralyzed state that she became an easy prey to the aggressor neighbor. The division of the country made any nationwide constructive plan for the country well-nigh impossible. Unification was what China needed.

I acted for the second time for Chancellor Tsai when he went for a visit to Europe. At this time a letter from Dr. Sun Yat-sen lauded the movements in the university and ended in the following words: "Lead the three thousand disciples to help the cause of revolution."

Dr. Sun did not live to see his hopes come true, but only a few years later his successor, General Chiang Kai-shek, led the Nationalist army sweeping down from

Canton to the Yangtze Valley, then to the Yellow River Valley, and finally to Peking, treading the path psychologically prepared for the new Nationalist victory by the revolutionary movements which had started in Peking and permeated the minds of all classes of people in the country. ❂

Chapter 16
Years of Troubles

The students after their May 4 victory were indeed intoxicated with the cup of success as Chancellor Tsai, Dr. Hu Shih, and others had predicted. It was beyond their power or any other power in the country to stop, for the root of discontent lay deep in the political, social, and intellectual soil of China. In the schools the students usurped the right of the authorities to engage or dismiss a teacher. Failing to meet their demands, the administration invariably faced a strike. The students struck against teachers who required a severe examination or stood for sterner discipline. They demanded subsidies from the schools for their traveling expenses during spring vacation, or money for student activities. They demanded free copies of the lecture notes (a kind of course syllabus). It was a matter of trying to get as much as possible out of the school in every conceivable way, never thinking of their duties toward it. They were intoxicated with power; their selfishness ran wild. The mere word "discipline" found them with rolling eyes, lips curled, and teeth bared, ready to fall upon you in packs.

Once the senate of the University of Peking passed a regulation that all students must pay for the copies of lecture notes provided by the university. This touched their private pocket. A crowd of several hundred demonstrated against the rule. Chancellor Tsai arrived on the scene and told them that they must obey the university regulations. His words fell upon deaf ears. The mob streamed into the classrooms and offices to find those responsible for the "obnoxious" rule. The Chancellor told them that he alone was responsible.

"You cowards!" he shouted indignantly, rolling his sleeves up to his elbows and shaking his fists in the air. "I'll fight a duel with any one of you who dares. If anyone dares to touch his teachers, I'll knock him down."

The crowd stood in a semicircle in front of him. As the Chancellor moved toward them they stepped back, always keeping at a safe distance. This quiet scholar, tame as a lamb in daily life, was suddenly transformed into a moral lion.

The crowd dwindled; he walked to his office. About fifty students still waited outside the door demanding the abrogation of the rule. The corridor was packed with spectators curiously looking on. The thing came to a deadlock. The Dean of Faculties, Ku Men-yu, brought about a settlement by promising to see that the assessment of lecture note fees was postponed—indefinitely, of course.

Among the worst agitators, who usually took cover behind the crowd to shout their shrill accusations, I noticed a tall young man, too tall to be hidden by the crowd. I did not know him—he was not among those whose names were later struck from the university register. But a number of years afterward, when I saw him as a puffed-up official, I recognized him at once. His countenance was unmistakable; his shouts still rang in my ears. He had developed into a skillful politician and unscrupulous grafter, and died a rich man a few years after the war.

In another demonstration several years later against myself for refusal to listen to their demands, a number of students closed the gates of the compound and thus shut me in my office. Dr. Hu Shih telephoned to ask whether I would like police to break the siege, but I replied in the negative. The gates were closed for two hours. Those who wanted to leave after their classes clamored from inside, while others who wanted to come in to attend courses echoed without. At length the ringleaders, no longer able to withstand the protests of their fellow students, opened the gates. As I came out of my office a score or two of them followed, vociferously denouncing me. Turning my head, I saw a few at close range. The university senate decided to dismiss those whose names I could remember or afterward ascertained.

Several years later as I was walking on the campus of the Central Aviation School, transferred from Hangchow to Kunming during the war, a fine-looking young officer stepped forward and after a military salute told me that he was a student dismissed from the National University of Peking. At once I recognized his honest-looking face and fine, strong physique. The ugliness I had seen in his face as he dogged my steps that day of demonstration was all transformed into shining happy eyes and smiling lips. We were happy to see each other. The president of the school told me later that he was one of the best flyers and instructors they had.

These instances are indicative of the fact that the student demonstrations contained all elements. Those who honestly believed in their cause, rightly or wrongly, and were willing to be responsible for what they had done, often turned out to be good citizens, while the sneaky fellows often proved undesirable elements in society.

The students usually took as their target some international problem which the government was not in a position to solve, or had failed to solve to the satisfaction of the people. Thus they always carried with them the sympathy of the country; herein lay their power. As "incidents" grew in number between China and Japan, their demonstrations were naturally interpreted by the Japanese as an anti-Japanese movement. The root of the trouble lay in the Twenty-One Demands and in the Shantung question created by the Versailles Treaty. After the balance of power in the Far East was upset, Japan enjoyed almost exclusive privileges in strangling China. The policy of partitioning China had given way to the Open Door policy, which was fundamentally dependent upon a balance of power; once this balance was kicked over, China had only two alternatives—to submit to the domination of Japan or fight it out alone every step of the way.

So the students fought, first with demonstrations, strikes, and boycotts against Japanese goods, then turning their attack on the government at Peking, which they believed responsible for all evils. When they found nothing internationally or nationally important to fight, they fought the school authorities. The cause lay in the psychological unrest of youth. Once they were aroused to act, it tended to express itself; to repress emotions that ran so high would have been difficult.

A number of student groups, among them the young Communists, turned their attention to the labor movement and the labor unrest which was then brewing in the treaty ports. Railway and factory workers began to show activity and agitation, which spread like patches of oil. Soon they joined the students in mass meetings and parades. The labor movement was no negligible weapon. With it the Kuomintang government in Canton once devastated Hong Kong with a general strike, reducing the British island colony to a commercial and industrial desert, as it were, for eighteen months.

Nationwide anti-British feeling had been provoked in Shanghai on May 30, 1925, when International Settlement authorities gave orders to shoot into a crowd of sympathizers with the labor movement there, gathered on Nanking Road. A few were killed and many wounded. Under the leadership of both the Kuomintang and the Communists a general strike of laborers, merchants, and students followed. Once more Shanghai was a dead city. On June 23 students, workmen, merchants, and soldiers in Canton demonstrated in sympathy against the British. As the crowd passed through the outskirts of the Foreign Settlement the British garrison fired on them. As a result of the firing Hong Kong went on a general strike which rendered the British colony a dead city. At the instigation of the students Chinese employees of the British Legation at Peking also went on a sympathetic strike, which left these diplomatic officials without cooks or boys for some time.

After the workers had joined the student movement, the number of demonstrators was increased by thousands. Often one would see a vast motley crowd in the mass meetings or parading on the streets of Peking, shouting slogans and waving banners. In one of these meetings a White Russian, shuddering, remarked that he had seen many such mass meetings in Russia—the sure signs of an impending revolution—and he wondered whether it was safe for him to stay in China.

The workers, like the students, when there was no more important demonstration to make, turned their hostility against their employers. There was little peace for the factories. However, it was much easier for the central or local government to deal with striking workmen than with students. In many instances they stopped the strikes by force of arms, in some cases simply firing on the strikers with machine guns.

Supposing that this would be an effective way to stop all strikes, the government under Tuan Chi-jui gave orders to train machine guns on a crowd of students gathering around the executive mansion. I had previously been informed that the government had given the order to fire if the students besieged the building, and I warned them of the danger and tried to prevent them from participating; but they formed in lines on the campus, ready to march, and refused to listen to me. No sooner had they approached the entrance of the mansion than bullets rained upon them.

About four o'clock in the afternoon news reached me of the tragedy. At once I rushed to the scene. The open space in front of the official residence of Tuan Chi-jui was literally covered with bodies of young boys and girls. It was difficult to distinguish the dead from the dying. Ambulances came and picked up all who showed any sign of life. About two dozen remained lifeless on the ground. A number died on the way to hospitals and still more lost their young lives on the operating table. We checked with the various hospitals and found that the casualties ran up over a hundred. This did not include those who left after receiving first aid.

This dastardly action of the Tuan Chi-jui government drew a wave of protest from the whole country, and its resultant unpopularity was among the reasons for its later downfall.

Besides the factors I have mentioned, the most important element in making the students so powerful and uncontrollable at this period was the fact that most of them were the sons and daughters of the ruling classes of China. A revolt of students meant, so to speak, a revolt of sons and daughters against their fathers. The most knotty problem a parent had to face was that of a rebellious son or daughter, especially when his children's actions enjoyed the popular support of his neighbors. Workmen were a different proposition; neither their parents nor relatives held any power in the government or in society. So it was their lot to submit to the whips of policemen or the bayonets of armed forces. Only when they were under the guidance of, or in co-operation with, the students was their power strongly felt.

The student movement was further fortified by the sympathy of teachers within the schools and Kuomintang members and Communists outside of them. Other political forces were also involved. So the movement grew in complexity and magnitude. There were always teachers behind it, from its beginning in 1919. Even during the first student revolt under the Imperial regime there had been teachers behind the movement.

A strike of teachers, to support their demands for payment of arrears of salary owed them by the government at Peking, caused further complications. The poor teachers in the university and in seven other government colleges were very irregularly paid. Often they received only half a month's salary in two or three months. When they demonstrated they could usually squeeze out from a half to one month's salary from the Ministry of Education.

Once several hundred teachers, supported by a still larger number of students, occupied the premises of the Ministry demanding payment of their arrears. The presidents of the eight government institutions went to act as intermediaries. Teachers and students coerced the vice-minister and all the presidents into marching to the presidential mansion to demand their pay. At the exit of the Ministry the vice-minister refused to go any farther on the pretext that it was raining. A student walking beside him opened his umbrella and handed it over, saying brusquely, "Here is an umbrella," and the vice- minister took it from him and marched on reluctantly. The presidents followed grudgingly after. As the crowd approached the entrance of the mansion the gendarmery and police closed the gates. Teachers and students clamored for admittance. Suddenly the gates were flung open and swarms of armed police and gendarmes streamed out with bayonets and rifle butts, stabbing and beating at random. Aged teachers and young girls alike fell into the ditches with hands muddy and faces bleeding, screaming and crying. The president of the College of Law lay on the ground as if dead. A professor of political science argued with the soldiers as to why they should be so unsympathetic as to insult the hungry teachers. A professor of Chinese literature with a big lump on his forehead, his nose bleeding, shouted at them, "You fight your own people. Why don't you fight the Japanese?"

This professor was taken to the French Hospital, where a former provincial governor was sent by the government to offer its apology. The professor's aged mother was sitting by.

"This boy is my only son. The government almost killed him. I demand the reason why?"

To this the former governor replied, "Never mind, Aunty, I am a good fortuneteller. By looking at my cousin's countenance I can see he has a great future before him. Don't worry, dear Aunt, the government is sorry for the misbehavior of the ignorant soldiers. Aunt, I apologize to you."

The old lady was humored into calmness, while everyone in the room repressed his laughter. The faces of the teachers in their hospital beds all lighted up at this humor in the midst of tragedy.

Thus it went. On another occasion the teachers streamed into the Ministry of Finance, demanding their arrears of salary. All the members of the Ministry sneaked out the back doors, leaving the buildings empty behind them. Once the students, in disapproval of government policy toward a certain foreign Power, forced themselves into the Ministry of Foreign Affairs and smashed the big looking glass and quite a few nice chairs. Students, teachers, and workers all joined in strikes against the government in Peking and the aggressor Powers that encroached upon the rights of China. In bad years not a month passed without strikes of some sort.

To be president of a university in those days was really more than a headache. Funds came from the government only occasionally—usually a year or two in arrears. While students demanded more freedom of action, the government desired order and discipline. For whatever happened, in or out of the school, the president was responsible. In demonstrations, parades, and riots, he was called upon either to stop one party or to help another. Every time the telephone rang his heart beat against his ribs, and he was rewarded for untiring work only by the grey hair that grew rapidly on his head.

The writer does not speak idly. After setting down the events in these pages he again spent a night of nightmare, seeing at one moment young boys and girls lying dead on the streets of Peking, at another the gendarmery besieging the university and demanding the surrender of ringleaders. Nor, when he started and woke, and lay sleepless with his head upon the pillows, could he shut out by closing his eyes the unfolding pictures of that tragic record.

Sipping tea under a scent-laden spruce in Peking's Central Park, an old scholar made a remark to me which was, I think, typical of those bad days of the strikes.

"Strikes here, there, and everywhere—strikes yesterday, today, tomorrow and every day. Mr. Chancellor, what are you going to do about them? When is the thing going to end? Someone has said that the new spirit is born, but I say the old tranquil spirit is dead!" ●

PART IV

UNIFICATION

Chapter 17
An Experiment in Constitutionalism

During the warlord regime one evening the Soviet Ambassador at Peking gave a banquet at the Embassy to leading men of the city. About sixty people were present. When the roast suckling pigs were passed round the table some of the guests looked at the steaming roast and burst into subdued giggles, while out of the corners of their eyes they glanced at the President and Vice-President of the National Assembly, who were among the guests. The contagious giggles spread until the whole table caught them except the two officials, who pulled long faces but remained calm. Finally I saw somebody whisper in the ear of the Soviet Ambassador and he, too, succumbed to the contagion.

The story was this. In the old days when the Dutch Indies needed labor, owners of rubber plantations and mines resorted to getting laborers from China by fraudulent means. By painting a rosy picture of the prospects and offering a sum of money, labor agencies in China enticed workers to cross the sea to the islands and there sold them to the development companies with or without the knowledge of the human goods. These unfortunate people were called "pigs" because they had been sold for money like the meanest livestock.

During the early years of the Republic the irregular practices of certain members of the National Assembly became so notorious and contemptible that people reminiscently called them "pigs," since they were willing to sell themselves to the highest bidder. The great majority of members were upright men, but they were unorganized and therefore powerless to check their fellow members. They, too, were so unfortunate as to be tagged with the epithet. When bad men combine the good must associate; if they do not, it is their own fault and they have only themselves to blame.

The idea of a written constitution for China had been introduced from America. The Constitution of the United States was an embodiment of ideas and beliefs of the American people and grew out of the life of the people. The Constitution of China was a copy of imported ideas, adopted according to the fancy of those who drafted the document and alien to the habits and ideas of the Chinese.

During the Imperial regime, in the last few years before the revolution, the provincial assemblies representing the gentry class achieved creditable results because their main interests were more or less the same and there was leadership in that class. The Imperial governor of the province had enough prestige to serve as a check to the assembly. Little or no political squabbling went on in the assembly to obscure the larger issues. The bills passed were generally for the welfare of the people of the province. Little or no corruption was known.

In 1912, when Dr. Sun Yat-sen was Provisional President of the Republic at Nanking, the National Assembly showed healthy signs of becoming a modern parliament, for its members represented revolutionary interests and there were revolutionary leaders to guide it. Dr. Sun's prestige as Chief Executive was high. But when the Assembly came under Yuan Shih-kai, trouble began to brew. This autocratic and reactionary President was hated by the revolutionary leaders and the President hated them in turn. With a strong army in his hands he resorted to intimidation, thus setting a very bad precedent for future development of the legislative body. To illustrate the ludicrously bad effect of this technique on the morale of the members, I may relate here an incident which occurred during Yuan's election to the presidency. Photographers covered the event. In those days indoor picture-taking involved the use of flashlight powder, which exploded noisily with a dazzling light. On this occasion, taking it for a bomb explosion, people ran wildly for safety. One member ducked under a table, shouting, "I voted for Yuan Shih-kai!" Quite a few lost their slippers (Chinese masculine footgear is comfortably loose) and were obliged to look for them after the scare was over. The episode ended with the impeachment of the secretary-general for allowing photographers to frighten the Assembly by a "bomb."

Under Yuan's presidency the activity of the half dozen political parties degenerated into mere political squabbling. Party and personal feelings ran high. The Assembly, discredited in the eyes of the people, was finally washed away in the tides of Yuan's maneuvers for a monarchy and the restoration movement of Chang Hsun. These movements failed, however, and the National Assembly was restored. Political power was now divided among the military governors of the provinces, the shadowy central government in Peking having neither prestige nor power to control the Assembly. Through corruption Tsao Kun, a northern warlord, got himself elected President, and the prestige of the national legislative body sank rapidly as subsequent developments led ever downward to new lows of political integrity.

Quite a number of representatives were elected through corruption. Ku Hung-min, a well-known cynical scholar of international fame, told me that during an election he got eight hundred dollars from a man who bought his vote. He took the money but did not go to the polls. Instead he went to Tientsin and spent all the money there. Later, at an international party in the Grand Hôtel de Pékin, Ku got hold of the man and pointing to him said to the gathering, "This man wanted to buy me for eight hundred dollars. Gentlemen, do you think Ku Hung-min is so cheap?"

When undesirable elements came into the Assembly in this manner, even though the number was not large they naturally made it look like an auction house, representation being sold to the highest bidder.

The students of Peking now directed their attack upon the "House of Corruptions." One afternoon several thousand boys and girls surrounded the Assembly and demanded that a certain bill concerning educational measures be deleted from the agenda. There was a clash between the police on duty there and the student body. Some of the students became so incensed that a few days later they smuggled in three bombs from Tientsin intended for the Assembly. They were persuaded not to carry out this violence and the bombs were taken outside the city and thrown into a river. A few weeks later a fisherman caught one of them and shook it in his hands to find out what was inside. Bang! The bomb went off and carried with it the hands and head of the inquisitive fisherman. Police assumed that it had been dropped there in the days of the revolution and no investigation was made.

Conflicts between the Assembly, and the students continued. The Assembly members tried at first to assert their right as representatives of the people. The students retorted, calling them by their now familiar contemptible name. The Assembly tried to impeach the Chancellor of the National University of Peking; the students retaliated by staging mass demonstrations in which flags bearing the likeness of a pig streamed in the air amid threats to smash the Assembly. Finally the Assembly, conscious of its weakness, declared a truce by letting the universities and students alone. Ku Hung-min, whose cynical views made him contemptuous of students and representatives alike, said to me one day, "You believe in democracy. But to me it is demo-crazy."

If an institution is hated by the public it may still have some grounds to exist;

but when it is sniffed and mocked at, even though for the acts of a mere minority, the whole suffers from the inadequacy of the part and goes down together like a sinking boat. So it was with the Assembly in the early phases of constitutional government in China. At length some of the warlords snatched the opportunity to brush it aside as a scrap of paper.

The story of constitutionalism in the days of the warlords had, of course, two sides to it. On the one hand, the warlords wrecked it by intimidation through force and by corruption with money. They had no prestige, no principle, and no policy by which to guide a democratic body. After Yuan Shih-kai, the power of the central government was a political shadow, the real power being divided among the provinces by the warring rulers who set themselves above the law. What they knew was the military strength of their feudal armies. The central government was not in a position to have any principle or policy; fundamentally it was worthy neither of support nor of opposition.

On the other side, most members of the Assembly were little concerned with national interests. Their preoccupations were either provincial or local, or still worse, personal. National interests they conceived only vaguely, and they themselves were therefore not in a position to have any coherent guiding principles or policy on national issues. Consequently no leadership was possible except in matters of local or personal interest. The Chinese people love freedom but were inexperienced in organized democracy—in other words, in constitutionalism. They did not see the importance of it. For China to follow the constitutional pattern of the West without its background was to hitch China's wagon to the Western star. It was small wonder that the experiment failed miserably.

With this failure before his eyes Dr. Sun Yat-sen devised a system of tutelary government as a steppingstone to constitutional government in his plan for an organized democracy for China. According to this scheme the period of national unification was to be followed by what might be called government in a state of tutelage—i.e., government by the Kuomintang—as a transition to the full-fledged constitutional form. And when the Kuomintang came to power in 1927 the tutelary government at Nanking was indeed meant to offset the bad effects of the corrupt National Assembly, which had become a headache to the entire country. During the next ten years the Nationalist party, under the leadership of Generalissimo Chiang Kai-shek, dislodged many a local warlord from the provinces and achieved to a large extent the unification of the country. The danger to national existence brought upon China by the Japanese militarists further intensified the unification.

Unification of the country was a necessary condition to constitutionalism. With respect for the law on the part of governing and governed alike—with the principles laid down by Dr. Sun Yat-sen, and with efficient leadership both in the government and in the National Assembly—China will be on the road to successful constitutionalism and organized democracy. ◉

Chapter 18
The Death of Dr. Sun Yat-sen

Death calls before Victory descends upon my country.

Patriots that come after me will forever think of the tragedy in tears.

The above lines are from a poem by a famous general who was sent to defend China against an invasion of the Tartars in the twelfth century. They apply only too truly to the death of Dr. Sun Yat-sen. The great leader had struggled in the cause of revolution for forty long and strenuous years, and death snatched him away when the nation needed him for its regeneration.

In the spring of 1925 he had been for some months in poor health as a result of his untiring work for the country. Having admitted the Communists to the Kuomintang he went one step further. Seeing China still a divided house and knowing that strength lay in union, in response to an invitation of the northern generals he came from Canton to Peking to discuss a plan to unify the country. On his way north he made a trip to Japan in an effort to convince the Japanese people that a strong and unified China would be beneficial to that country. When he arrived at Tientsin he fell sick. He was carried from that port to the capital, accompanied by Madam Sun Yat-sen. But he was too ill to discuss plans and could only lie in bed. The doctors of the Peking Union Medical College were at their wits' end. Dr. Hu Shih recommended a Chinese herb doctor. Dr. Sun declined to take the Chinese medicine. He said that as a physician himself he knew that an herb doctor might sometimes cure a disease where scientific medicine failed. "A ship without a compass may reach its destination," he said, "while that which has one may not come to port. But I prefer to sail with that scientific instrument." However, he was persistently advised to take the Chinese medicine, and to meet the wishes of his friends he at length consented. But the ship without a compass did not reach port.

Dr. Sun was presently transferred from the Medical College to the home of Dr. Wellington Koo. This magnificent house, built in the seventeenth century, had once belonged to a famous beauty, Chen Yuan-yuan, wife of General Wu San-kwei of the Ming Dynasty, who surrendered to the Manchus and conducted them inside the Great Wall, so the story goes, in order to rescue the lady from the hands of the bandit leader Li Shih-chung.

On the morning of March 12, 1925, a telephone call from Ma Soo informed me that Dr. Sun was nearing his end. I hastened to his temporary residence. When I entered the chamber Dr. Sun Yat-sen was beyond speech. A moment earlier he had muttered, "Peace, struggle, save China..." These were his last words. We retired to the reception hall and looked at each other in silence. "Is there any chance for the Doctor to recover?" whispered an aged Kuomintang member. All shook their heads, stifling the word upon their lips.

Silence gathered and deepened until one could hear it. Minute melted insensibly into minute. Some leaned against the wall, staring blankly at the painted ceiling. Others sank into the comfortable sofas and closed their eyes. A few tiptoed to the chamber and back without a word.

Suddenly everybody in the hall was alert, listening to sobs barely audible from the bedroom. The faint sounds gave way to a chorus of loud cries—the great leader had passed into history. As we entered the death chamber I saw that Dr. Sun's countenance was serene, as if he were asleep. His son, Sun Fo, was sitting on a bench at the bedside staring into space like a man of stone. Madam Sun bent over the edge of the bed with her face buried in the soft mattress, shaking with sobs that would break one's heart. Wang Chung-huei, standing at the end of the bed, was rocking convulsively, wailing and wiping away his tears with a handkerchief. The elder statesman Wu Chi-huei stood with his hands clasped behind him and tears welling up in his eyes.

As Dr. Sun's body was carried out of the hall covered with a big national flag, Mr. Borodin, the Soviet adviser, said to me sadly that if he could have lived a few years or even a few months longer things would have been very different.

An autopsy made at the Medical College proved that cancer of the liver had caused his death.

Dr. Sun's body lay in state in one of the former palace halls in Central Park. Every day for a week at least twenty to thirty thousand people came to pay their last respects to their leader. The funeral procession, four or five miles long, was joined by all the students from elementary schools up to colleges, and by teachers, government officials, tradesmen, workers, and farmers, a hundred thousand strong.

The casket was placed temporarily in a stone pagoda in Pi-yun Ssu, the Purple Cloud Temple in the Western Hills, about fifteen miles from Peking. This picturesque pagoda was built centuries ago under Tibetan influence, of white marble with a pointed top of gilded bronze. It perches majestically on the south side of Purple Cloud Mountain, surrounded by tall pine trees, and overlooking a sea of whispering pines which sound like waves in the spring breeze and scent the air with their fragrance. The sky was serene. Streams wound their way among the moss-grown rocks. The bells in the eaves of the temple chimed melodiously in the wind.

Dr. Sun, who had lived a life of science and struggle, now rested in peace amid the beauty of art and nature.

While the leader of China's revolution lay in peace, trouble began to brew in his history. A group of leading members of the Kuomintang, who had come to Peking to take part in his funeral, gathered aroung his temporary tomb in the Western Hills discussing ways to circumscribe the growing influence of the Communists in the Kuomintang. The Communists and pro-communists in the party rushed to the scense and broke up the meeting. From that moment the cleavage between the regular members of the party and the Communists grew wider and wider until two years later, in 1927, the latter were purged from the party when the Nationalist armies occupied Nanking. ◐

Chapter 19
The Anti-warlord Campaign

Years of student demonstrations and strikes coupled with internecine wars had sapped the strength of the government in Peking. In the provinces the warlords ruled like maharajahs. The power of the overlord in Peking at any one time depended upon the good will and support of the provinces which had easy access to the city. As its roots in the provinces weakened, the tree of power in Peking grew shaky. No sooner had one warlord entered the capital to take over the reins of government—either himself or through a puppet of his creation—than another would conspire to overthrow him and come to power in turn; when public sentiment as revealed in student demonstrations ran high against the regime in power, some other provincial general was always ready to take advantage of it. Through intrigue, civil war, coups d'état, or reshuffled combinations of power, the government changed hands constantly. During my first nine years in Peking I witnessed so many changes that the rapid shift of scene left in my memory only a jumble of disconnected, though vivid, pictures of the tragicomedy. I could imagine myself a pyramid sitting in the Egyptian desert, watching utterly unconcerned the constant coming and going of caravans and listening to the camel bells chiming their sad tunes.

Financial stringency was acute for the Peking government. National revenues were detained by the warlords in the provinces and spent in maintaining their private armies or to enrich their own coffers. A portion of the money that came to the central government, usually through loans from banks at exorbitant interest, had to go to military expenditure to placate the insatiable warlords who supported the government. Salaries, not only of teachers, as we have seen, but also of government employees and of diplomatic officials stationed in foreign lands, were left unpaid for months at a time or even years.

"What is the future of the Peking government?" asked an American diplomat one day.

"It will dry up like a clam and only the shell will remain," I replied.

The situation grew worse year after year until the last vestige of the public respect due to a government was gone. The students helped to destroy its prestige and the warlords buried it in the Peking dust.

In the meantime the Kuomintang movement in Canton grew in strength by leaps and bounds. It had enjoyed public faith for some time, especially among intellectuals and students, and even won the sympathy of certain enlightened generals of the north—for among the warring northern generals enlightened ones were not lacking. In the basket of rotten oranges it was possible to find a few good ones.

Even after the death of Dr. Sun Yat-sen the spirit of the Nationalist party of China remained undaunted. Dr. Sun's nucleus of an army kept on growing at Huang-pu Military Academy near Canton, of which General Chiang Kai-shek was the president. In the course of a few years General Chiang's newly trained Nationalist troops were ready to deliver a deathblow to the warlords of the north. In 1927 this army of the Nationalist government of the Kuomintang swept northward at lightning speed through the heart of the country to Hankow, and another wing moved along the coast to Hangchow. In a pincer movement the two converged on Nanking, which was made capital of the Nationalist government when the victorious armies entered the city.

That same year, at about the time the Nationalist army started its northern expedition, a notorious warlord, Chang Chung-chang, entered Peking. This renowned leader had the physique of an elephant, the brain of a pig, and the temperament of a tiger. His powerful paws were always ready to snatch at any person he disliked or at any good-looking woman he coveted. I saw him several times in a peace-preserving committee of which I was a member, and felt that he was dangerous even to look at. When I was informed by Sun Pao-chi, ex-premier of the Peking government, that I was on the blacklist, and news reached me in the evening of the execution of Shao Piao-ping, editor of the newspaper Ching Pao, I began to see the shadows of those powerful claws. Without hesitating I got into the car of Dr. Wang Chung-huei, who happened to call on me, and went directly to the Legation Quarter, where I got a room in the Hôtel des Wagons Lits. Here I stayed for three months and passed my time in studying calligraphy.

There were several others in similar plight; Dr. Chu Chia-hua, professor of geology and now director of the Academia Sinica, was one. Quite a few friends ran in from time to time to visit us. But spending three months in even a de luxe prison was no fun at all. We plotted escape and at length, when the situation was somewhat eased, sneaked out one after another. A very able young lady, the wife of a friend of mine, planned my escape. Acting as my wife she escorted me to the East Station without our being noticed by the police. Every casual look from a stranger startled me, though I remained outwardly calm. Following a stream of passengers I boarded a train to Tientsin and from there went by British merchant liner to Shanghai.

On the boat I met Dr. Chu Chia-hua, who from Shanghai was to proceed to Canton, where he later became president of the Sun Yat-sen University. For my part, I went to Hangchow. As the railway from Shanghai had been cut I reached the city by a roundabout way. At this time, before the Nationalist army commanded by General Ho Yin-chin reached the province, the governor appointed by Peking was attempting to revolt against the northern government and go over to the southern side. I called on him, and he revealed to me his plan for joining the southern camp. He told me that he had sent about a thousand men along the railway to the Kiangsu border, where the line was already cut.

I thought privately that he must be intoxicated with the cup of other people's success, or he would not attempt to fight an enemy at least ten times stronger than himself. I left Hangchow again the next morning by the roundabout route back to Shanghai. Within a few weeks his army was utterly routed by northern forces. When they entered Hangchow he was captured and executed.

Then the tables were turned on the northern warlords and Nationalist forces entered the city. Again I went there. Hangchow welcomed the Nationalist army with open arms. Thousands of spectators lined up along the streets with smiling faces to see the victorious modern-equipped troops march through the city. I stood watching in the crowd with my heart thumping against my ribs in ecstasy. After some sixteen years the good name of a modern army in China was once more established.

In about a year's time, in 1928, General Chiang Kai-shek was ready to launch his northern expedition. The army under his command crossed the Yangtze River and moved along the Tientsin-Pukow Railway with Peking as its objective. When it reached the outskirts of Tsinanfu, capital of Shantung Province, the Japanese—fearing a unified China—moved troops from Tsingtao down along the Tsingtao-Tsinan Railway to that capital under the pretext of protecting their vested interests and the lives and properties of the Mikado's subjects. This was intended to frustrate the unification plan by provoking an "incident," i.e., an open clash between China and Japan. The Japanese army murdered the Commissioner of Foreign Affairs and his staff in Tsinanfu, hoping that China would retaliate.

With foresight and forbearance and a sound strategy, the General saved his army and his hopes of unification by turning the spearhead of his forces away from Shantung, quickly crossing the Yellow River, and marching right on to Peking. The Japanese were thus outwitted and left to fight shadows.

Peking fell when the Nationalist army arrived. The giant of hollow papier-ma^ché toppled over before the merest breath of wind from the south.

When the Nationalist army entered Hangchow the year before, I had been appointed a member of the provincial government and Commissioner of Education. Thus in Hangchow, capital of Chekiang Province and city of my boyhood days, my experience in government administration began. The provincial government was formed with a council in charge. Before the national government in Nanking was organized, all the members of the council, with its chairman, were appointed by the supreme commander of the Nationalist army, General Chiang Kai-shek.

Five members of the council acted concurrently as Commissioners of Civil Affairs, Finance, Military Affairs, Reconstruction, and Education. Above the provincial council was a branch council of the central political council of the Kuomintang, of which I was appointed secretary-general. This council was in charge of general policy for the province and gave orders to the provincial government to execute. It was later abolished as conditions in the province gradually settled down.

The provincial government was imbued with the same spirit of reform and reconstruction as the national government of Nanking, whose broader program we shall take up in the next chapter. The provincial reconstruction plan was rather ambitious, but after a revolution it was necessarily handicapped by lack of funds. So it concentrated on building more roads. Within a few years many roads were built—in the capital itself the provincial council ran a pencil through the map of the city and ordered roads to be built accordingly. After two years Hangchow was blessed with many wide streets within the city and roads running along the shores and on the dikes across the West Lake, leading to scenic spots in the Western Hills. A highway linked the city with Shanghai, and this brought many week-end motorists. In the short span of three years everyone noticed how the city had changed. New buildings shot up like mushrooms in the city, around the lake, and in the mountains. The population increased and business prospered.

Many electric plants were set up in local areas. In some rural districts gas pumps were installed to irrigate the rice fields. As Chekiang was the center of silk production, scientific sericulture was started by the government: silkworm eggs were raised scientifically and distributed to the silk producers at cost. The first year strong objections were raised to the new eggs, for the silk producers became suspicious of them under the influence of egg producers who followed traditional methods. But results speak louder than false propaganda; the second year there was more demand for new eggs than the government could supply.

In order to reform the land tax system a general survey was made of agricultural land in the province, and this continued for many years following. In contrast to the drastic methods adopted by the Communists in their dealing with agrarian problems, these were tackled in Chekiang by the mild means of a general 25 per cent reduction of the land rent paid by the tillers to the owners. As a rule the tenant farmers paid about 25 per cent of their main crop as rent; the reduction lowered this figure to 18.75 per cent. As the rates of land rent had existed through centuries and the method and basis of calculation varied in different localities, the tenant farmers of some localities were much benefited, while elsewhere the rule for reduction caused great friction between owners and tenants. Lawsuits streamed in to the Land Rent Reduction Commission. There was so much confusion throughout the province that after some years the scheme was finally abandoned. Shen, the moving spirit in rent reduction, was assassinated for causes still undetermined.

Later, a campaign against illiteracy was launched. After some six or seven years the number of short-term schools to teach the reading and writing of the more commonly used characters had increased by thousands alongside the regular elementary schools.

A new experiment was made in the educational system of the province. The National University of Chekiang was organized with the writer as president. The university was not only to take charge of higher education but also to control the public school system in the province. The office of commissioner of education was abolished and the president of the university was made a member of the provincial government. Two other provinces followed suit with their respective university and school systems. After two years of trial, internal troubles and political complications grew in the other provinces, and the whole system was accordingly abolished in 1929 during my term of office as national Minister of Education. Thus the person by whose hands it was sent to the grave was the one who had nursed it to grow with much work and thought.

I stayed a full year in Hangchow and the next year went back forth between Hangchow and Nanking, where I was appointed Minister of Education of the national government while concurrently holding the presidency of the University of Chekiang. In 1929 I gave up the latter post and stayed in Nanking for another year, when I was forced to resign from the Ministry of Education as a result of disagreement with some of the elder statesmen regarding a question of educational policy. ●

Chapter 20
The Rise of the Kuomintang to Power

After the fall of Peking the country was once more a political whole. The capital of all China was moved to Nanking and remained there. Peking, meaning "North Capital," was changed to Peiping, "Peace in the North," an old name of the city before it was known to the world.

Peking had been the capital of five dynasties—the Liao, King, Yuan (Mongol), Ming, and Ching (Manchu)—over a period of more than a thousand years, and now ceased to be the capital. But it still remained the center of culture and art. The official dialect or language spoken by many of the educated classes in China in addition to their local dialects, used in broadcasting stations and taught in schools, had its home in Peking.

There were two main reasons why Nationalist China shifted the capital from the Yellow River Valley in the north to the Yangtze Valley in the south. The first was that the revolutionary spirit had permeated the latter area, which was therefore fertile soil where it was easier for the new spirit to take firm root, while the Yellow River Valley was the home of the reactionary warlords. Secondly, the Yangtze Valley was the seat of China's financial power, which could provide the government with necessary funds.

Nanking had been the capital for the Taipings, from 1851 to 1864. When they were dislodged from their last stronghold the city was devastated, and has never recovered its past glories. There were more ruins, wheat fields, vegetable gardens, and orchards than streets with buildings in that walled enclosure. The streets were narrow, rough, and filthy, the electric light no better than vegetable-oil lamps. A foot messenger was often speedier than a telephone call.

In the earlier periods of history this city on the bank of the Yangtze was a center of culture and refinement, especially in the time of the southern dynasties. Its life of wine, women, and song dwelt in the memories of generations of literary men, poets, and artists. The Ching-huai Canal, connecting lakes of luxuriant lilies, traversed the city crowded with singing houseboats lit up by painted lanterns and lavishly decorated with articles of art. On either bank of the canal, as a boat sailed leisurely by, there unrolled before one's eyes endless rows of restaurants, and rooms elaborately furnished with painted columns and bamboo screens for literary, artistic, or musical entertainments. The air was laden with enchanting tunes and soothing scents that flowed out from behind the bamboo screens.

Such was the city in days of old. But Nanking was of strategic military importance. In every major war in the country this city was destined to suffer devastation. After every conflict its glories passed into memory, and from memory it was rebuilt upon its ruins when peace came. And from the memory of the past, as it was recorded, I have depicted a part of the old life of Nanking.

Since the Taipings, however, it has never recovered its ancient beauty. It is as if the successive restorations were only copies, done by some vulgar artist, of the original picture; after repeated copying the color of the original was lost and only vulgarity remained. From time to time, in periods after the Southern Sungs (1127-1276), scholars of puritanic bent or stoic leanings objected to the type of effeminate refinement which grew up along the Ching-huai, now but an empty name with pleasant associations. But we must aver that the wrong lay not in enjoying the refinements of life but in the neglect of work and duty which should go with enjoyment. If there were only work and no play, Jack would be a dull boy. The stoic ways of living which came into vogue with the philosophers of the Sung Dynasty bequeathed to China generations of dull Jacks who knew neither play nor the right sort of work. They killed art, and with art, life. They attacked bad morals, but countenanced that abominable and most immoral institution, the foot-binding of women. Compare with this life in the Tang Dynasty (618-905), when work and play went hand in hand and a healthy civilization shone like the brilliant sun upon all its neighbor nations! Think of the Tang dances (mind you, there was no foot-binding then), music, sports, poetry, painting, and calligraphy; and then of its great generals and their glorious armies. During the Tang period Chinese civilization reached its zenith. After the Tangs came declining days. In the time of the Northern Sungs art persisted but the martial spirit waned, until finally the philosophers of the South Sungs with their asceticism and moral speculation killed the arts both of peace and of war.

The Ching-huai Canal still ran through the city of Nanking. The houseboats and the apartments were there, too. But the forms, the quality, and the content were all changed. The refinement of life had disappeared with the flowing waters of the Yangtze, into the Yellow Sea.

When the Nationalist army entered Nanking a new spirit was born—a spirit of reform and reconstruction. Modern science was to revitalize the arts of days past. Upon the debris of the partly ruined city a modern town was built with asphalt roads traversing all sections. Trees were planted and parks designed and developed. Automatic telephones, light, and water were installed. An aerial map was made from the seaplanes of the American gunboats stationed at Nanking. On the basis of this map a new city was planned. The Commission of City Planning, of which the writer was a member in his capacity as Minister of Education, worked for more than a year with an American architect of wide experience in Chinese architectural design in the enchanted city of Peking. The commission planned to retain as far as possible the grandeur and beauty of Chinese architecture together with the convenience and hygienic installations of a modern city.

Old, dilapidated buildings were torn down to make way for new roads and houses. Commerce began to prosper. Modern theatres multiplied to accommodate the growing population. The canal and the lakes were dredged and old temples and other public buildings repaired.

The Central Museum was built to house a part of the treasures from the Palace Museum of Peking, and an underground safety vault constructed for them, of reinforced concrete, in a hill which would be immune to air bombing. For the directors foresaw the impending Japanese aggressions against the new capital. As the situation in the north grew worse and war clouds hung thick over this side of the Great Wall, the more valuable treasures of Peking were moved by hundreds of trainloads to Nanking, and before the fall of the new capital to the Japanese all had been transported for safekeeping to caves in the mountains of the interior.

The gigantic steel gate of the museum vault, with its intricate combination locks, was a piece of American ingenuity which humbled the Japanese. As reported from the occupied city, they worked on the locks for several days and finally gave up.

The buildings of the Ministries of Communications and of Railways were of reinforced concrete with modern lighting system ventilation, and conveniences. But their architectural design was altogether Chinese, with enamel tiles, painted columns, artistic windows, and other exterior decoration. These two imposing buildings stood opposite each other on Chung-shan Road, the main artery of traffic in the new metropolis, as monuments to China's old glory adapted to modern needs. Other buildings were planned and designed, but on account of the war they all had to be postponed.

The Sun Yat-sen Mausoleum, with blue enamel tiles and white marble columns, stood on the Purple Mountains outside the city overlooking the hilly valley and the winding Yangtze. Flights of granite steps led up to the tomb of the father of the Chinese Republic. The mountains were reforested with trees from various parts of China. Flowering plants and fruit trees decorated the gentle slopes. An athletic field and stadium with a swimming pool were built at the foot of the mountain.

A new model village was built in the rolling valley. A general plan was first laid out by the government, with roads, drainage, telephone and lighting systems, and school buildings. In the short space of a few years new houses sprang up like mushrooms, with ample space around them for Oriental gardens. Trees grew and plants flowered; the birds sang and streams flowed. Old ways of living gave place to a new life in which science and art, work and pleasure, nature and human endeavor, went hand in hand.

Such was the nucleus which, it was hoped, would grow and some day transform every corner of the land. It was a modest beginning but had already borne fruit. For the new village movement had within a few years reached a number of cities and their surrounding areas. It was only a matter of time and further economic development for the new villages to change the mode of living of young China.

We could not very well expect that all trouble from the warlords would end with the downfall of Peking. Their seat of government was gone, but their real power was entrenched in the provinces. The country was vast and communications poor. These conditions and the unsettled state of mind in the country afforded them good opportunities to nurse their ambitions. At any favorable moment they were always ready to snatch more power; they lurked in the provinces like germs in the blood, ready to attack when the body weakened. In ten years, from the time his victorious army entered Peking to the eve of the Sino-Japanese War, Generalissimo Chiang Kai-shek had not a day's rest in his effort to unify the country.

Like the Roman generals who bound their ancient empire together by roads, he was not unmindful of the need to build more roads and railways and air lines. With Nanking as a center, highways, railways and airways were made to radiate from the capital to the provinces. A part of the communication system had existed before the Nationalist government came to power; with this as a basis it built new roads to make connections and extensions. Air lines were established to distant cities. From the new capital one could fly to Peking, Kaifeng, Sian, and Lanchow in the north; to Fuchow, Canton, and Kunming in the south; in the west to Hankow, Chungking, and Chengtu.

New railways were built to connect Hankow with Canton and Kowloon, just opposite Hong Kong. If the Japanese had not at this time started trouble in Manchuria, a continuous journey would have been possible in 1931 from either Hong Kong or Shanghai to Paris by rail. A through train ran from Shanghai via Nanking, Tsinan, and Tientsin outside the Great Wall, and via Mukden to Tsitsihar in north Manchuria, by Chinese railroads built parallel to the Japanese-owned South Manchurian Railway . A branch line from Tsitsihar connected with the Trans-Siberian Railway. The progress of unification in China and the building of these parallel lines prompted the Japanese to try to take Manchuria, or the "Three Eastern Provinces," at a stroke—which became known to the world as the "Mukden Incident" of September 18, 1931.

Along the coast the gap between the Chien-tang and Tsao-ao rivers on the Shanghai-Hangchow-Ningpo line was filled, but the laying of track was suspended when war broke out. The new line between Soochow and Hangchow, however, was completed before hostilities began. Another new line from Hangchow running west to Kiangsi was finished just before the war and during the war was prolonged farther west to Hunan, where it connected with the Canton-Hankow Railway. The line was also further extended to Kweilin, capital of the southwest province of Kwangsi.

Highways were extended more rapidly. The Nanking-Hangchow highway was built during my sojourn in Nanking and I had the pleasure of going through it before it was opened to traffic. It traversed the richest sections of Chekiang and Kiangsu Provinces. As the car wound its way along Tai Lake one felt like stopping for a few days to sit under the pine trees and watch the sails rise or vanish over the horizon in the sunset. The fishermen cast their nets and drew up shining carp from the water. Tai is one of the five largest lakes in China, irrigating millions of acres of fertile land in the two most populous and cultured provinces of the country.

This highway also passed through a bandit-infested region, but the bandits disappeared when the road was opened because troops could be rushed to the spot.

Local troubles sometimes brewed as fast as construction progressed. At times the railway and highway lines had to run a race with disturbance in areas without modern roads. The rebellion in Fukien Province a year before the war was frustrated by central troops rushed down through the then newly built Hangchow-

Kiangsan Railway and along the roads also newly built, from Hangchow to that province. More roads meant less rebellion and less banditry, aside from the easy flow of products from one locality to another.

Communication is the key to modernization and reforms and to the discovery of possibilities of future development of the country. Thus the Nationalist government began its reconstruction program with the building of roads and railways. This was also the way to secure the unification of the country; any local rebellion could be put down easily if good roads were available. Again, better and more communication means more travel and quicker exchange of ideas. Beautiful scenery hitherto hidden in inaccessible parts of the country suddenly opened to the appreciative eyes of scholars, painters, poets, and lovers of nature.

Under the influence of the Nationalistic government the provinces themselves began to build more roads. Existing roads were fast extended after the Kuomintang came to power. During the war, troops were freely shifted on these roads from one province to another. A year or two before the war a motor trip was made from Nanking to Kunming—that is, from the east coast to the southwest frontier city, the starting point of the Burma Road.

In the field of administration an attempt was made to increase the efficiency of official business. New filing systems for official documents were devised and put into trial use. The form of language in official documents was simplified.

A civil examination system was again inaugurated, but to the disappointment of those who had seen the old Imperial days, without the pomp and honors that had greeted the successful candidates.

A new code of civil law was drafted. The status of women was raised to the same level as that of men. Daughters were to inherit property of their parents as hitherto only sons had done. Freedom of marriage was granted to the parties concerned when they came to legal age. A mutual agreement of the parties concerned is sufficient for legal divorce.

The school curriculum was standardized and the proportion of science teaching increased. Physical training was emphasized. New laws were promulgated governing the universities, and the Central Research Institute, Academia Sinica, etc., were established to carry on research in science, history, economics, and engineering.

The obnoxious internal customs system of likin, which we shall see more of in the next chapter, was abolished. Government finance was put on a sounder basis. National currency was standardized, government banks reorganized. The circulation of silver was later suspended and only government bank notes allowed to circulate; during the war we began to realize the importance of this move, for if we had had to rely upon bulky silver as the medium of exchange it would have been well-nigh impossible to carry on the long years of war, while if the shift had been made in wartime it would have caused great confusion.

From 1927, when the capital was established at Nanking, to 1937, when the Japanese army fired its first shots at the Marco Polo Bridge, only ten short years were allowed to the Nationalist government to do its job. During these ten years intermittent rebellions and other obstacles retarded the progress of reforms and reconstruction, yet in this brief time 7,300 kilometers of railway were constructed, in contrast to 8,300 kilometers during the last fifty years. More than 100,000 kilometers of highway were built, and 33,000 kilometers of new telegraph lines were added to those already in existence. Yet naturally there could be only a moderate beginning in each phase of construction in so short an interval, and so it must be considered.

After the Kuomintang came to power the struggle with the Communists continued. While they lost control in the cities, their influence spread in the country districts and worked among the peasants. From 1928 to 1934 agrarian uprising occurred in more than two hundred hsien, scattered among eighteen provinces, where landowners were "liquidated" and the land distributed among the peasants by the same drastic methods witnessed in the early days of the Russian Revlution.

The stronghold of the Communitsts was in the provinces of Kiangsi, where they occupied fifty-nine districts. After several years of fighting between Nationalist forces and Communists in that province, the latter withdraw to the northwest corner of the country and later established their capital in Yenan. There they gave up their more violent measures and as an expedient adopted a moderate policy of agrarian reform—a modified form of the Kuomintang program of land rent reduction which we have seen.

Meanwhile the popularity of Generalissimo Chiang Kai-shek among the people became very great—so great that warlords and others on occasion were forced by popular sentiment to submit to his moral force as the national leader.

One extreme and dramatic example was the Sian affair, In this instance the Generalissimo flew to Loyang and then to Sian on an inspection trip. Many political and military leaders went there later to discus national problems with him and get orders form him. Then something undreamed-of happened. In the stillness of night shots were heard near his quarters. Armed soliders pressed in, searching for him. As a man who had gone through many battles, he was always alert and got away from the place, but he was found and delivered into the hands of General Chang Hsueh-liang, on whom he had lavished much time and kindness, helping him to develop. The incident reflected, through in distortion, the desire for national unification in order to resist Japanese encroachments.

When the startling news was broadcast to the whole country, people were distraught and worried, and women and children wept. Telegrams came from every part of the country to Sian urging the young general to use his better judgment. Madam Chiang Kai-shek and Dr.T.V. soong risked putting more prizes in the hands of the crazy young general and flew direct to Sian. In the face of strong public opinion the young man faltered and finally sent the Generalissimo and his lady safely to Loyang.

Before his safety became known there had been a dancing party held inf the barracks of the U.S. Marine Guards at the American Embassy, at which members of the various embassies and legations were present and I also was a guest. A Tass correspondent asked me why I did not dance. I told him that I was worring about the safety of our national leader. He said calmly, "Don't worry. He'll come out pretty soon. Nothing will happen to him." I looked at him in a high state of expectation and said,"I hope your prophecy will come true."

The next evening about dinnertime my telephone rang. "Hello, this is the Central News Agency. Generalissimo Chiang Kai-shek arrived safely at Loyang and flew to Nanking." The news seemed too good to be true—I could not believe my own ears. I telephoned Dr. Hu Shih who was at dinner with a party. Cheers reached me across the wire.

In the Chih-hsiang Theatre at the Tung-an Market, where the extras first circulated, waves of applause swept the audience, to were unaware of the happy tidings. In about half an hour the stillness of the gloomy winter evening in Peking was suddenly broken by the gay sound of the firecrackers, while stars of firworks splashed joyously in the dark sky.

A friend of mine, on a train from Nanking to Shanghai, wondered at the noise of the firecrackers as the train approached Soochow. At the station the happy news reached the passengers, who flet like setting off a few themselves to let out their pent-up emotions; none were to be had at the station, so the schoolgirls on the train began to sing instead.

The warlords had wrought havoc in the country for a quarter of a century, and people longed for some national leader to rise and sweep away these obstacles to national unity. They had found him in the person of Generalissimo Chiang Kai-shek. His difficulties were enhanced by the double task of dislodging the remnants of the snarling "tigers" from their lairs in the provinces, on the one hand, and building up adequate forces to resist Japanese invasion on the other. But public opinion was solidly behind him in carrying out his great task. ◉

PART V

SOME ASPECTS OF CHINESE LIFE

Chapter 21
The "Leakage" System

Foreigners coming to China for the first time used often to meet with the annoying practice of petty "squeeze" among their servants and cooks and naturally felt that something must be wrong with China. But they would presently be informed by old China hands, familiar with the China of Imperial days and the later regimes of the warlords, that the practice of "squeeze" was not only to be found in servant circles but also among those higher up. "Squeeze is a national system," they would say and cite concrete examples to illustrate their point.

This reference to happenings of bygone days that lingered in their memories would focus the eyes of the newcomers on remnants of the dark side of Chinese life which are fast passing, and the effect has been to throw a veil over unprejudiced minds in their effort to see the living, new China of today. This is very unfortunate for foreign observers who have tried to understand China, and unfair to both this and the last generation of Chinese leaders, who endured hardships and sacrificed their lives for reforms in China's national life.

I propose now to paint a dark, vivid, and real picture of Chinese economic life in the past, without exaggerating or minimizing—which I hope I can do even better than the old China hands.

Anyone who witnessed the downfall of the Imperial regime must be aware that one of the main factors which caused the Manchu government to lose control of the country was its decrepit system of public finance. Large numbers of public servants were paid only nominal salaries and left to finance themselves by Lou-kwei, or the "leakage" system. This practice deprived them of any sense of public morality and caused them to countenance corruption as a matter of course. The Imperial government connived at the irregular gains of its officials, and the officials in turn connived at those of their subordinates. The poisonous sap circulated in the whole tree of state, reaching to every twig of every branch and every leaf on each twig. It flowed through all the roots of the tree and every rootlet.

From the government offices through which public revenues passed, the government required only certain fixed amounts to be forwarded to the national treasury. The officials in charge of the revenues could, by various means and all sorts of excuses and plausible reasons, attach a variety of fees to the regular taxes. In this way, for every tael of silver that flowed into the government treasury at least the same amount or even more would be diverted to "leakage" funds. In the later years of the Imperial regime more wine leaked into private cups than remained in the public barrel. The government, finding itself parched as a fish in a dry pond, pressed hard for more money—whence still more "leakage" for public servants and heavier burdens for the people.

Failing to realize funds by taxation or other means, such as offering public offices for sale, the Imperial government resorted to borrowing from foreign sources by awarding them concessions for building railroads or opening mines. This was to quench thirst by drinking poison. It may be remembered that the nationalization of railways in Szechuan Province, as a preliminary step to awarding the building rights to foreign concerns, pulled the trigger for the Revolution of 1911.

But as to the "leakage" system and how it worked. China was then divided into some twenty-two provinces, comprising about two thousand hsien. The chief executive of the hsien was the magistrate, who took charge of all financial matters and concurrently filled the role of administrator of justice in his district. His salary—not more than a few taels a month—was nominal. All expenses incurred by the holder of the office had to be paid out of "leakage" funds. When higher officials of the Imperial government passed through his district he had to entertain them and secure for them all the "necessities" required for their travel. To the entourage of any higher official he had to offer "presents," usually in the form of money.

On the banks of the Yaokiang River just outside the city wall of my native Yuyao stood a welcome pavilion at which the magistrate welcomed passing officials of higher rank. One sunny afternoon some forty years ago I noticed crowds gathering at a distance, near the pavilion. I joined them and watched the landing of the Imperial Examiner and his entourage, on their way to Ningpo to hold civil examinations in that prefecture. On the previous day the magistrate had "caught," or requisitioned, many houseboats from the people and the one set aside for the Imperial Examiner was loaded with sealed cases, their contents known only to those who had prepared them.

I watched the party change boats. The Imperial Examiner stepped into the most prominent; the sails were set and the little flotilla with the officials and "leakage" gifts on board floated downriver with the ebbing tide to the seaport city of Ningpo. Under that inspiration I said to myself that from now on I must study hard, so that some day I myself might be an Imperial Examiner blessed with such mysterious gifts as lay hidden in those cases.

Regular "gifts" had to be presented to the secretaries of the civil governor (fantai) of the province. Failing that, a magistrate could not expect them to speak kind words for him to the governor and would find them faultfinding in his official relations with the governor's office. Added together, the amount required for plain sailing in his career was by no means small. Human nature also made him not unmindful of the necessity to provide for a rainy day. And he had his family and followers to support.

Candidates for magistracy who had pull were covetous of the districts with large revenues. I remember that in the hsien in which we lived during my school days no magistrate had ever held office for more than a year. The regular term of office was three years, in which a magistrate could realize approximately a hundred thousand dollars. In those times this sum was considered very great. So the governor appointed acting magistrates, whose term was usually one year. In this way there would be more chances for expectant magistrates to share the profit.

When a magistrate retired from office after the expiration of his term and paid an official call on the governor, he was usually asked by his superior whether his district had been a good one, meaning how much he had got out of the "leakage" funds. His friends and relatives also asked him the same question by way of starting a conversation.

The higher the rank of the official through whose hands the government revenues passed, the more "leakage" flowed into his private coffer. The taotai of Shanghai was known to reap a profit of some 100,000 taels a year. Governors and viceroys of rich provinces and the powerful princes and grand ministers in Peking usually enjoyed large yearly incomes.

The system was upheld even by the great statesman and scholar, General Tseng Kuo-fan, who put down the Taiping Rebellion for the Manchu Dynasty. In one of his letters he argued that "leakage" was indispensable to the smooth running of the government; the expenses incurred by an official were great and he had a family and relatives to provide for. The system was countenanced by scholars as well. In his diary a famous scholar-official who lived in Peking during the Hsien-feng and Tung-chi period complains that Viceroy Chang Chi-tung presented him with only a small "gift." A later entry reads something like this: "Went to Tao Ren Pavilion in the afternoon to sip tea. Chang Chi-tung entered. I pretended not to see him and left the place." This may be safely interpreted to mean that the famous viceroy had offended the prominent scholar by presenting him with too small a gift from his "leakage" funds.

During the Imperial regime promising candidates could keep servants with very little pay or none at all. The servants would stick to their masters through thick and thin for years, hoping that some day when luck fell into the laps of their masters they too could share the "leakage" with their lords. When luck did come master and servant alike would strive to make it still leakier, so that each and all could have cupfuls of this wine to their hearts' content. If luck failed to appear they would keep on waiting until the last ray of hope was gone. Under pressure of starvation some unfortunate masters found relief in the rope, with which they ended their lives. In Hangchow during my school days the news circulated by word of mouth that an expectant magistrate, idle for years, had hanged himself on a New Year's Eve when his creditors pressed him hard for the money he owed them.

The poisonous sap penetrated even to the households of the well to do. The cook would poke "holes" in his vegetable and meat baskets in order to make them "leak." Servants got something from the purchases they made for the household—especially in Peking the shops always added a certain percentage to the price for the servants who made the purchase.

The practice of "leakage" even went abroad and found its way into the household of Napoleon. Napoleon had a Chinese cook who served his master very faithfully. On his deathbed this great French general remembered his faithful servant, saying, "Treat him well because his country will be one of the greatest in time to come. But the Chinese love money. Give him five hundred francs." On the other hand, the Dean Lung Professorship of Chinese Literature in Columbia University was established in memory of a Chinese laundryman with the money earned by a lifetime of washing. Before his death Dean Lung handed over a bag of gold to his master and asked him to do something good for China. The master, adding a sum to it, established the chair in memory of the patriotic laundryman.

The practice of "leakage" permeated the entire system of likin. And likin, like a gigantic octopus with tentacles reaching to every communication line in the country, sucked the blood out of the trade and commerce of the nation. It had been installed during the Taiping Rebellion to raise war funds for the support of the Imperial army. The Taipings were gone, but the obnoxious system was there to stay.

It worked this way. Anyone who knew how to "squeeze" the people would bid—say two hundred thousand dollars a year—to government agents for the right to run the likin at a certain station or a number of stations established at points on the highway where merchandise passed from one city to another. The person who won the bid would become likin commissioner at that station or group of stations and had the right to assess duties on the goods passing through. If he could realize a sum of three hundred thousand dollars within the year, he would turn over two hundred thousand to the government and keep the remainder for himself and his partners. So he would make most goods dutiable in order to swell his private fortune.

Once I saw a boat loaded with watermelons passing under the bridge at a station. It was stopped by a long bamboo hook from shore and several inspectors jumped down and began to thrust iron rods into the melons. The owner begged them to desist and promised to pay any amount they demanded. The "duties" were paid; the poor farmer sailed on.

I remember how small traders and farmers hated likin. Everybody would have liked to smash the stations to pieces. Once a group of young scholars going by boat to take an Imperial examination passed by a likin station, ignoring the order to stop. The inspectors detained the boat and began to search their belongings. The scholars leaped ashore, entered the station, and smashed everything they could lay their hands on. Only the flag, emblem of the authority of the Imperial government, was left drooping in the air with its inscription: "To Collect Likin by His Majesty's Orders." Triumphantly the scholars departed under the gaze of the admiring crowd.

After the Revolution of 1911 the "leakage" system was gradually suppressed, and the system of likin was abolished later on. Higher salaries were paid to officials. But cases of corruption were still frequent. The practice persists among servants in the form of petty "squeeze." A lady once scolded her cook for being too greedy in getting his "squeeze," and got into a quarrel with him. Someone remarked that he was as greedy as a hungry wolf, to which he replied, "If one were not greedy, he would not become a cook."

In one of the embassies in Peking the ambassador's cook charged ten cents for an egg, while his secretary's cook charged his master five cents. "Why should I have to pay more for an egg than the wife of our secretary?" asked the ambassador's wife. "Madam, the ambassador receives a higher salary than the secretary," was the reply. Owners of cars often found their gas tanks "leaky," because the drivers helped themselves to cupfuls of gasoline.Unwarranted repairs made bills for maintenance mount up.

Since the Nationalist government came to power in 1927 China has been endeavoring to check the occasional corruption in the government. Severe punishment has been meted out to offenders. However, the legacy from centuries of the "leakage" system, which existed even before the Manchus, is difficult to discard totally within a few years or even a generation. Under the leadership of Generalissimo Chiang Kai-shek official corruption has been reduced to a few isolated cases. With the introduction of a modern financial system and the gradual enlightenment of public conscience, China has done much in checking these malpractices. As the technique of government improves with time, she will attain the level of a modern, well-organized country in which more efficient methods of taxation and effective control of public finance will be devised.

The Chinese have always trusted in the intrinsic good of human nature, believing that evils arise only from perversion of that good through negligence or lack of proper education. It was the decrepit system of public finance that caused China's trouble in this respect, not lack of a sense of moral responsibility. But the system had such a demoralizing influence on public practice that we still suffer from its effects.

Concrete examples have shown us that the remedy lies in building up a good system to supersede the bad ones. It is not sufficient merely to abolish the bad. The customs administration organized by the British for China was free of the bad influence of "leakage." Employees were properly trained and adequately paid. Ample pensions were given them after retirement. Patronage was little known. The control of this important branch of national revenue by foreign governments as a guarantee for the payment of indemnities and foreign debts has been humiliating and extremely dangerous to national integrity, but the adequate system of revenue built up as a by-product is an unintended blessing to China.

The postal administration was organized under the Western system. It has been running efficiently since its inception—even long years of civil war did not disrupt its work. Ever since the Japanese aggression started it has been marvelous to see letters circulating in the occupied areas as freely as in Free China. Mail carriers have constantly crossed the firing lines to deliver the mails entrusted to them.

The salt administration is another example. Even during the long years of Japanese aggression the people have been adequately supplied with this daily necessity.

The Huang-ho Commission was well known formerly for its "leakage" system; indeed, the famous Shantung and Honan cuisines were the product of the rich appetites and well-lined coffers of the gluttonous commissioners of the Huang-ho works. In the same way, Yangchow cooking became renowned through the epicurean salt merchants of Yangchow.

With the formation of a Huang-ho Conservancy Board with modern trained engineers in charge of the conservation work, the "leakage" system itself was cast into the river and flowed down into the Yellow Sea. The gluttons disappeared with their system; only the art of cooking remains. Yangchow delicacies, too, are still admired by men of good taste, while the innovators who introduced them are gone and forgotten since the introduction of the salt gabelle, a modern, well-organized system of salt administration.

With well-organized administration, a well-trained and well-paid personnel, tenure of office ensured and adequate pensions provided after retirement, the good that is in human nature has full play.

It may be said that these successes have depended on foreign assistance. But let me ask: Are they due alone to the good morals of the foreigners—or rather to the good system they have introduced into China? Without personal integrity no such system would work, yet could we depend on foreign morals alone to obtain the desired results? Could a handful of foreign experts on top be powerful enough to check the irregular practices of hundreds and thousands of Chinese personnel? It is through the co-operation of the rank and file of Chinese employees under a good system that the customs, salt, and postal administrations have been successful. This is what Mencius, disciple of Confucius, has said: "Good morals alone will not make a good administration; systems alone will not carry the work to the desired ends."

The modern banking system and railway administration in China are also commendable examples. The banks and railways on the whole run efficiently and are free of gross maladministration of funds.

Modern universities in China are further examples of honest administration of funds, aside from their stand for intellectual honesty. Teachers have worked hard, through privations on account of the abnormally high cost of living during the war, to maintain their standards of scholarship. The majority of students coming under the good influence of the teachers and the university organization cannot but form healthy ideas and correct habits as regards honest and efficient administration of public funds, along with the modern training they have received. And we must remember that in their hands the future of China lies.

Above all, the attitude toward the administration of public funds has basically changed. In the old days the "leakage" system was connived at or even admired.

At present it is disliked and reviled by all intelligent people. This change of public sentiment will have an important bearing, given modern methods, upon the future handling of funds in all spheres of public administration.

It is more difficult to eradicate the practice of "squeeze" among servants, cooks, and chauffeurs. Perhaps it will take a generation or two to alleviate the economic status of these people; until that is done, we cannot very well expect that they will drop their bits of "sweets." Perhaps by then it will be difficult in any case to find people to work as household servants. Yet in my six years of sojourn in Kunming during the war I have met with one cook, one man servant, one maid, and one chauffeur in our employ who never "squeezed." Our present cook and man servant have a spotless record as regards money matters.

Let the reader turn the leaves of a textbook of European history to the period just before the French Revolution; let him glance through the constitutional development of England or the history of India in the times of Warren Hastings; he will readily agree with the writer that the "leakage" system of China was but a mild form of corruption. Yet, along with other forces, it did gradually sap the vitality of a reigning dynasty, once very powerful, and render it in the end financially anemic and politically impotent. Finally the Manchu Empire crumbled like a house of cards before the moral force of Dr. Sun Yat-sen. ❶

Chapter 22
Social Structure and Social Progress

It has been a common belief that China's four hundred million people were as loosely connected as the sands of the sea. It would be nearer the truth to say that her great population is—or was—segmented into many small self-governing units. Chinese democracy has consisted of tens of thousands of such units, loosely knit together by a common language, a common culture, and common ideals of life achieved through centuries of cumulative effort. These units, large or small, developed on a basis of family, trade, and tradition. Individuals were bound by these common ties to each self-governing group and so were more intimate with the members of their own group than with a broader society. They understood local problems better than national ones. This was the fundamental reason the constitutional National Assembly failed to work, and this was why the people allowed themselves to be governed by warlords. It was the frame of mind that gave birth to the nationwide idea in Imperial days, often quoted here, that "Heaven is high above and the Emperor is far away."

Individuals, unless they broke with society in some way, were always part of the unit, but the units were not well cemented by any effective national organization. This was a strong point as well as a weakness in China's national life—a strength because it made China democratic and enduring through ages of war and invasion, and a weakness because it made her central authority impotent and rendered her vulnerable to the attack of invaders.

The existence of these units in Chinese life has its historical background. They came into being by the slow work of centuries. As the Chinese gradually moved into the less populated or unpopulated areas, they went in groups to form separate colonies which grew into self-governing villages or communities. The vast Chinese Empire was built up by centuries of peaceful colonization of outlying territory by just such social clusters. In recent years, by a study of the dialects of China, we have been able to trace the path of this development. The Cantonese dialect is found to be closely related to the spoken language of the Tang Dynasty.

We may reasonably infer that the predominant part of the population of Canton are descendants of the Tangs. Later arrivals, forming their own distinct groups, spoke a quite different dialect known as Hak-ka, which shows the language characteristics of recent centuries. Even along the Yangtze Valley the slight difference in dialect in various localities affords a subtle record of the stages of colonization.

The migration of the Chinese population to the south was hastened in the tenth century by the downfall of the Tangs when north China was devastated by invaders from outside the Great Wall. The southern provinces, especially Kwangtung, Hunan, and Chekiang, which were not vulnerable to the successive invasions and were less affected by intermittent wars, became reservoirs of Chinese culture destined to irrigate the vast territory of New China in the last fifty years.

If a reform was to be truly effective in the direction of national unity and coherence, it had to touch the age-old local units by effecting some sort of change in the family, the trades, and tradition. And inversely, since these units were knit together by a common language and culture and common ideals of life, any modification of culture and ideals through the common language would be bound to affect the life of these social clusters and consequently of the country.

China was first set on the road to change when foreign manufactures began to affect the trades. Thus one of the three strands that bound her society was loosened. That was the early stage of change when she first came under modern influence, and the process was unconscious. Then the introduction of modern ideas through books and newspapers and the school system further weakened the already slipping knot by loosening the strand of tradition. The last remaining element, that of family ties, had finally to give way with the other two.

The loosening of these three ties which bound people to their local units caused years of disturbance. Individuals groping for new effective bonds created trouble of many sorts. The students were the first to be affected by the new ideas and it was they who started the trouble; workers in the new industries lost their old trade bonds and they, too, joined the students in troublemaking, as we have seen. The internecine wars of the warlords, the failure of constitutionalism, and the existence of the demoralizing "leakage" system neither prevented the disintegration of the old social organizations nor retarded social progress to any great extent. The troubles caused by the warlords were but ripples on China's vast social sea. The undercurrent went on swirling under the surface, with or without them, or the debased National Assembly, or the "leakage" system. These were evils in the superstructure merely; the self-governing units themselves remained temperamentally peaceful and morally clean.

In the long course of history, especially since the latter days of the Tang Dynasty, China has been weak in national defense because her invaders have all been organized on a war footing while she was organized on a basis of peace. Defense forces have had to be drawn from peaceful communities and maintained by a central authority which was a mere superstructure above a peace-loving society.

The Chinese under the leadership of the Mings overthrew the Yuans or Mongols not so much through their own military might as because of the failing strength of the Mongols. Through long years of wars on two continents the military force of the descendants of Genghis Khan had spent itself. Under Chung Chu, second emperor of the Ming Dynasty, China succeeded in organizing a strong army which conquered a great part of Manchuria during his reign; but this military power gradually weakened after his death. When the warlike Manchus rose outside the Great Wall the Mings were helpless in the face of Tartar invasion, and the Ming Dynasty gave way to the Ching or Manchu Dynasty without much effective fighting. After more than a century in China the Manchus in turn were contaminated by the peaceful spirit of the Chinese, and when the Western Powers attacked China with gunboats she was again helpless.

Studying the past, Japan assumed that history would repeat itself and on this assumption began her continental campaign against China in 1894. Up to that year she was right. But Chinese history then began to shift its course as China learned the "tricks" of Western civilization. Japan was either unaware of this change or tried to nip it in the bud. In either case she did not hesitate to launch a new continental campaign some thirty years later, and was surprised to find that a stumbling block had risen in her way.

This was China's social progress. Japan had seen at the top the weak and corrupt Imperial Peking government whose financial strength had been sapped by the "leakage" system; later she saw on the surface the warring warlords; but she was blind to the undercurrents which had slowly but persistently moved in China's immense ocean during the last fifty years.

In the old days organized national ties had existed in secret societies. The members lived outside the village units, gathering around large cities and along commercial routes. Their main purpose was mutual protection against oppression, but this sometimes degenerated into illicit trade. They were powerful in time of internal rebellion but not of much use against foreign aggression. They lacked new ideas and the notion of social progress was alien to them.

But now, on the fringes of the many thousands of self-governing units in the country there had gathered people imbued with national ideas as against local prejudices and newly learned patriotism as against family loyalty. These individuals hummed like honeybees round a hive and gradually gathered in clusters along the edges. More and more individuals sneaked out to join those outside. As the clusters grew in size, they began to make intrusions into the hive and affected the life of the whole colony. At the same time they began to organize themselves into a national union, so to speak, and took China as their common hive.

Such was the growth of China's modern national institutions. The process was hastened by the rapid extension of communication: steam navigation, highways, railroads, and airways. Educational associations, chambers of commerce, labor unions—scientific, engineering, and political science societies and other bodies—all were organized on a national basis. Political parties, whether the Kuomintang or those whose views were opposed to it, all led the people to think along national lines. The universities took members of the family and molded them into leaders of the nation. Schools instilled national consciousness and patriotism into the formative minds of the new generation.

In spite of continuous civil wars, even before the unification of the country the number of public schools had multiplied in all the provinces. Private citizens established private schools as a way of expressing their patriotism. These millions of elementary school graduates, entering thousands of local self-governing communities, spread ideas of patriotism even to the humble hamlets of the interior.

Once, traveling in the interior during the fight along the Great Wall, I saw a solitary small boy playing soldier. He took a tree for his imaginary enemy and stabbed it with his dagger. Then he imagined that his enemy struck back. He made gestures of defending himself, then fell to the ground with his eyes closed and whispered to himself, "I die for my country." Evidently he was defending the country against the Japanese invasion. During the later war, after a few of the Chungking people had deserted to the Japanese, way back in the hinterland I saw a little boy digging a small grave with a spade. When the work was done he put a sign on the grave: "The Traitor." In one mountainous region, where the nearest school was miles away, a mining engineer saw small boys writing on the walls of their village: "Long live the Three People's Principles of Dr. Sun Yat-sen." These instances show the growth of the national bonds that were taking the place of local ones.

Under the influence of the new education, organized into a national school system, children all over the country now made paper airplanes and sailed them in the air. They made toy water pumps and built toy automobiles. They began to be mechanically minded—a good groundwork for future industrialization of the country.

The growth of light industries in recent years has drawn more and more individuals from the local units and they have begun to associate into a national body instead of local guilds. Radio has brought new ideas to the people through the air. Customs, superstitions, dialects, folksongs, religions, domestic industries, and the economic condition of the tottering local trades and of the suffering farmers have been investigated and studied scientifically from data gathered by institutions of higher learning and learned societies. China has begun to know herself through scientific research.

The turmoils of half a century had set the people thinking. Their attitudes toward life began to change. They tried to create a new stability out of chaos by forming effective national bonds to hold China together in the face of invasion and by working for the progress of the country. This new social and national consciousness was not yet strong enough to face modern warfare with full force. But it was formidable enough to offer stubborn resistance, with indomitable will. ●

Chapter 23
Enchanted City of Peking

As Paris has inherited the spirit of the ancient Roman Empire, Peking has inherited that of the Chinese Empire of the old glorious days. Paris is the city of cities in the West, Peking in the East. Of Paris you feel that it is not only a city of Frenchmen but also your own; so Peking is not the city of the Chinese alone but universal. In both Paris and Peking one says, "This is my city, where I would like to live."

I lived in Peking for fifteen years until the Evil One dislodged me in 1937. As I look back to the old days there even the annoying dust of Peking is rich in pleasant associations. I miss it and long for it. In the early morning when the rising sun cast its beams upon the paper windows, with shadows of creeping vines dancing upon them, you would see a thin layer of dust sprayed evenly upon your mahogany desk from the night before. It was a pleasure to dust it off carefully with a feather duster. Then you would dust the brush-holder carved with landscapes, and the carved ink stone once owned by famous scholars of past centuries who dusted and washed it centuries before you. And you would do the same for the porcelains of Chien-lung, the bronzes of the Chow Dynasty, the oracle bones of the Shang period—used for divination four thousand years ago—and other timeworn treasures. Even the books, printed long before the West knew anything of the art and lying peacefully on your shelves, did not escape your attention. Let your fingers touch the covers; you would find that the dust did not grudge its favor.

Then you felt that you had done well your morning's preliminary work. The sunlit windows with their dancing shadows now smiled before you. The spotless desk with its ageless pieces of art displayed before your eyes beckoned you on. With a tranquil mind and contented heart you set to your day's work.

In such an atmosphere of antiquity you might read of the period when Confucius taught his disciples; or when the Nestorians came to the glorious empire of the Tangs; or the Jesuits made their astronomical instruments at the Ming court; or Buddha preached his doctrine of eternity; or Napoleon carried his campaign into Russia and drank oil from the street lights; or Genghis Khan sent his invincible armies to the Danube basin, founded an empire on two continents, and made Peking the capital of one of his sons. In Peking one could read history in its true perspective. For this city was as grand as nature itself and as old as history. As a capital it has witnessed the rise and fall of five dynasties—dynasties came and were gone, but Peking remained.

The palace buildings were all rectangular and symmetrically arranged like an armchair, with a vast rectangular courtyard in the middle in which stood proudly the giant incense burners of gilded bronze whose smoke, when incense was burning, streamed to the sky. Bronze deer stood in rows and pairs of crouching lions of stone or bronze guarded the entrances. Over a hundred of these courtyards with imposing buildings on three sides were fitted together like the squares of a chessboard in the Forbidden City, which was shut in by rectangular yellow walls with yellow-roofed towers standing out against the sky at the four corners. The Mongols began it, the Mings rebuilt it, and the Manchus improved it to its present form.

The yellow enamel tiles of the roofs shone under the brilliant sun in a speckless blue sky. At dusk or before dawn the triumphal towers of Wu Men—the main entrance of the Forbidden City—silhouetted against the pale sky, looked like castles in the air. On a cloudless moonlit night they made one feel that he was near some fairy palace of the moon which he might admire but not reach.

Before the little Emperor Pu-yi, who reigned over this city within the city of Peking, was ousted from the Forbidden City by General Fung Yu-hsiang in 1926, semimonthly audiences were granted to the remnants of Manchu officialdom. Attired in the quaint old Manchu costumes the officials clustered around the back doors of his toy empire seeking admittance.

A few days after the coup d'état I went into the palace to witness a government committee sealing, house by house, the doors of the halls. A few of the eunuchs were still retained, from whom I got quite a bit of information about life in the palace and stories of the doings of emperors and empresses, princes and princesses, of bygone days.

One story was about the large looking glass which ran from the ceiling to the bottom of the wall. The Empress Dowager loved to sit opposite it so that she could see for herself how stately she was. One day the governor of Shensi was granted an audience by Her Majesty. As he entered the door he saw her in the mirror and bent his knees before the image, kowtowing.

"What did the Empress Dowager do? I suppose she was angry," I said.

"No, no. She smiled and said to him kindly, 'You are seeing me in the mirror.'"

I met some of the eunuchs who attended the princes at the palace school for princes and found them to be all illiterate. Imperial household regulations forbade them to have an education, so that they would remain ignorant of what was taught in the school.

Perched on frames hanging in the veranda, red, yellow, and blue parrots talked the language of the princesses who had spent much time in teaching them. "Please come in. Guests coming. Bring tea..." said the blue one to me, and the red and yellow ones echoed, "Bring tea! Bring tea!" This was the first time I ever saw a blue parrot. Goldfish—black, white, red, and gold varieties—many of them almost a foot long, darted in the palace ponds, their periscope eyes looking skyward while their multiple fan-shaped silken tails waved gracefully in the water.

The living quarters of Pu-yi looked vulgar. A cheap-looking long foreign table stood in the middle of the hall with a few ugly chairs at either side. A pair of pink glass vases decorated the table. It was more like a second-rate country inn in America than the residence of an emperor of China. All the fine furniture and art treasures had been pushed aside and bundled up in the background. The vulgar Western civilization of the treaty ports had invaded the palace; nothing could be more out of place. Cheap magazines were scattered about. Half an apple, freshly cut, and a newly opened box of biscuits lay on the table. Apparently the Emperor had been taken by surprise and left the place as it was at the moment.

When the sealed doors were subsequently opened for a methodical checking over of the art treasures, the variety of beautiful objects was amazing. There were watermelons carved out of jade which looked like real ones, porcelains the color of "blue skies after a shower," bronzes that had witnessed thirty centuries of peace and war, and Imperial seals of jade which had set their mark on many an important document.

Among the famous paintings of the Tang, Sung, Yuan, Ming, and Ching periods were landscapes depicting the beauty and harmony of nature which invited you to step in and enjoy a tranquil life; horses that looked ready to trot out from the picture; fish that seemed to be swimming in water; geese hissing and honking as if painted in sound; bamboo shadows that appeared to bend in the autumn breeze; lotus leaves fresh with morning dew; orchids that seemed to pour forth their mild scent into the air. Great painting in China meant to render not the likeness alone but the motion, sound, color, characteristics—all that would stir the imagination and evoke feeling. In other words, it tried to paint the spirit of the subject.

For two years the committee, with a staff of over a hundred persons, ransacked every recess of the vast palace for treasures of art and checked many hundreds of thousands of articles accumulated through generations of emperors. Some of the storerooms were sealed with spider webs and others had dust ankle deep, a sure sign that they had been a no-man's-land for a century or more. Some treasures had lain there unnoticed for many, many years, no one knew how long.

At long last the palace was thrown open to view and the Palace Museum established to exhibit its treasures. The public, especially the younger generation, opened their eyes at the riches and wonderful achievements of Chinese art through the centuries. Peking was already a center of art; connoisseurs were many and artists not lacking, and with the opening of the Palace Museum the city was much enriched. Things heretofore secluded in the depths of the palace were now revealed for anyone to see—things previously accessible only to the royal family were now open to the common people.

As science is the expression of the mind in knowing and searching for the laws of nature, art is the expression of the heart in feeling their reality. Art is an expression of the life of the people who create it, and makes life richer and more enjoyable. Science is the product of the activity of the mind in satisfying its intellectual interest, and creates material prosperity. In modern civilization the two must join hands to make life complete.

There was a chain of three lakes—the South, Middle, and North "Seas"—to the left of the Forbidden City, with camel-back bridges spanning the creeks between them, trees centuries old along the shores, lilies growing luxuriantly in the water, and pavilions perched on the surrounding heights with golden enamel tiles, vermilion columns, and artistically painted beams. A fish caught some time ago in the lake, so the story has it, bore a gold plate with the sign of "Yung-lo" of the Ming Dynasty (1368-1643).

In the Middle Sea was Yun Tai, an islet surrounded by lotus where the Emperor Kwang-hsü was imprisoned by the Empress Dowager after the unsuccessful reforms of 1898 and where he died broken-hearted in 1909 . On the island was a group of palace buildings with spacious courtyards. Moss-grown trees stood high above the yellow tiles of an intricate system of halls, pavilions linked together with winding corridors of vermilion beams and columns. Miniature hills with rocks and caves brought mountain scenes into the Imperial gardens. How much the unfortunate Emperor enjoyed life in his beautiful prison only Kwang-hsü and those who were with him could tell. During the long days of his lonely existence he was perpetually tortured by ailments of mind and body until death relieved him.

Water was formerly conducted into the lakes through stone conduits connected with springs in the Western Hills. Parts of these pipes still lay along the highways. The drainage system in Peking was a great engineering feat of the old days. Underground aqueducts resembling modern subway tunnels were constructed to drain the sewage from the city. During the latter part of the Manchu Dynasty they were all choked, but the system of yearly inspection of the drainage was still retained to the last days of the regime. In the early days inspectors were ordered to walk through the tunnels to see whether any section needed repair. Later, when passage was obstructed by deposits of dirt, they deceived the eyes of their superiors by a cunning method of cheating: two inspectors in uniform climbed down at one end of the aqueduct and stayed there, while another pair in identical uniforms, hidden at the other end, appeared as the inspector general rode by on his horse. The example illustrates how the spirit of the system had evaporated through years of stagnation while the system still remained as a symbol. This happened in many departments of the Imperial government in the later years. It was small wonder that the government of Imperial China had become a mere symbol.

Peking was a city of trees. In the spacious courtyards and gardens of private residences were moss-grown trees which shot heavenward with a wide spread of branches and luxuriant leaves. If you stood on Coal Hill or some other height, the city seemed to be built in a forest. Wide streets running parallel and crosswise like the lines in a checkerboard traversed the "Bois de Boulogne" of Peking. By an old Imperial rule trees might be planted but never cut down in the capital. With the years people forgot about the rule but had acquired the good habit of loving trees—an instance in which the spirit got into the veins of the people while the system was forgotten. Here lies a secret of China's regeneration.

Few of those who have lived in Peking will fail to retain the pleasant memory of its palaces and other public buildings with their gleaming tiles under the cloudless blue. Imperial parks and gardens were blessed with junipers planted in rows and squares centuries ago and filling the air with soothing scent. Restaurants with exquisitecuisine were always ready to satisfy the wants of the epicure. Curio shops displayed antiques and jades, catering to connoisseurs. Public and private libraries preserved centuries of wisdom on their shelves and in archives. Most remote of all were the oracle bones which threw light on that misty era of Chinese history, the Shang Dynasty (1766-1122 B.C.) . And there was the awe-inspiring

Altar of Heaven, which made one feel the grandeur of nature and the sublimity of the spirit of man.

Only yesterday, comparatively speaking—in 1898—the modern National University of Peking was founded as a direct successor to the centuries-old Imperial Academy, Kuo-tse-chien, in an atmosphere of centuries of accumulated culture. This institution served both as a center of the old culture and a fountain of new wisdom. Scholars, artists, musicians, writers, and scientists came to Peking to develop their minds and enrich their hearts in the congenial atmosphere of the ancient city. There the inspiration of the past, the influence of contemporary thought, and hope for the future flowed into one inseparable stream of wisdom, and the youth of the country came and drank at its fountain. ●

Chapter 24
Life in the Four Cities

Hangchow was the city of natural beauty; Shanghai that of foreign manufactures; Nanking, of revolutionary spirit; Peking, of the golden age—of art and leisure. In my childhood I was reared in a small village in Chekiang, lived among the farmers and craftsmen and played with their children. During my boyhood I was educated in the city of Hangchow and later in Shanghai. When I returned from America my work required that I live, first in Shanghai, then in Peking, then in Nanking and Hangchow, and finally again in Peking until the beginning of the war.

As to their geography, Peking stands in the northern plain not far from the seaport of Tientsin, in the Huang-ho (Yellow River) Valley. It is a northern city, while the other three are southern cities of the Yangtze basin. Hangchow is situated on the banks of the river Chien-tang, where Hangchow Bay begins to spread its broad waters out to the ocean. In the old days Hangchow and Peking were connected by the Grand Canal, 2,074 kilometers long, which crosses both the Yangtze and the Yellow River. The Canal is still partly navigable to the present day.

Northeast of Hangchow, Shanghai perches on the banks of the Whangpoo River, which empties near the mouth of the Yangtze into the Yellow Sea—a body of water which is an integral part of the Pacific, different only in name. Nanking lies a little inland, farther north and west of the other two, along the southern bank of the Yangtze. Not far down the river from it the Grand Canal crosses the Yangtze at Yangchow, where Marco Polo resided as magistrate under the Mongol Dynasty. The four cities are all connected now by railways. Generally speaking, they all border on the Pacific.

The southern cities of the lower Yangtze Valley have approximately the same climate. Spring and autumn days are very pleasant. Sprouting willows are signs of the coming of spring—joyous spring seekers pluck the budding branches and bring them home to decorate their doors as symbols of welcome. When the leaves turn red they tell the coming of fall, and the crimson leaves in the setting autumn sun lend inspiration to poets. The damp season falls in spring, when there is plenty of rain; during the other seasons sunshine and rain are about evenly distributed. Summer and winter are not severe.

The soil is fertile. Rice is the chief product. Sericulture is a family industry. Fish, shrimps, crabs, eels, pork, mutton, beef, vegetables, and fruits abound. Out of these materials the famous Yangchow cuisine was created.

Shanghai was the financial center of the Yangtze Valley. It owed its growth to the commercial and industrial activities of the foreigner. Foreign capital was the foundation of its economic structure and foreign merchants and capitalists its aristocrats, before whom all the Chinese living in the city bowed their heads. These foreigners lived a life by themselves. Even if they had been there for several decades, China remained to many of them a terra incognita. They lived in beautiful mansions with spacious gardens and were served like lords by obedient Chinese servants. The masters got rich by exploitation and the servants got their modest share of profit by petty "squeeze." Their clubs excluded the Chinese worth knowing; their libraries excluded the books that were worth reading. Their minds were full of arrogance, ignorance, bigotry, and racial prejudice, but were closed like clams to such science and art as the great masters of their own people had created and were creating, and to the new ideas and new movements that were growing in China or in their own countries. Their life had no higher ideal than the amassing of money.

Second in rank to these foreigners, the Chinese compradors shared their masters' ignorance and their money. Compradors of foreign banks and concerns were held in high esteem by the Chinese merchants. When they looked up to their masters and opened their mouths for a bone, their compatriots wagged their tails sympathetically, their mouths watering. The compradors, like alchemists, spent their time turning coppers into silver, while their foreign masters transformed silver into gold. They spent a part of their silver in getting concubines; their masters were much smarter and spent only gold on their "friends."

The third class of people in Shanghai were the merchants and shopkeepers. They waited on the doorsteps of the compradors to buy foreign manufactured goods. When they made money they sent it back home to buy land. Occasional visits to their families, who as a rule lived in their native villages, towns, or cities, brought "inspiration" to the provincial folk, and thus more relatives came back to Shanghai to share their business.

I can speak of these things that existed in Shanghai with intimacy and without exaggeration, for many of my relatives were merchants and some were compradors in that city. I know well their mode of life and their ways of thinking; I also knew quite a few foreigners there and have heard many stories about them. Enlightened foreigners, especially the Americans whom I knew well, shook their heads with knit brows when we talked about Shanghai.

The fourth class were the factory workers. They were surplus farmers or those who had given up farming to come to the great city to make more money. They were slum-dwellers.

The fifth and last were the rickshaw coolies, who came from the poor districts north of the Yangtze. These human animals pulled and ran like horses on their two hind legs, with small carriages rolling after them. This cheaper and handier means of communication kept Shanghai constantly in motion—the coolies kept the blood circulating in the city's business veins.

These five classes of people together formed what came to be called the "Settlement mind"—the mentality which grew in the Foreign Settlement of Shanghai. It is a mind which worships power and admires superficialities. Power, whether financial, military, extraterritorial, or in any other form, superficiality bordering on vulgarity in painting, calligraphy, singing, music, and every phase of life. These reigned supreme in Shanghai. Hai-pai, or the "Shanghai School," was the epithet invented for this kind of mentality; the opposite is Ching-pai, or the "Peking School," which admires the arts in their deeper meaning and strives for perfection. Shanghai was a financial sea but an intellectual desert.

People were all busy as ants at their hoarding. The more they piled up, the more they were admired. In Shanghai both Western and Chinese civilizations were at their worst. The Chinese misinterpreted the West and foreigners misunderstood the Chinese; the Chinese hated the foreigners, who in turn despised the Chinese, both with reason. But they had one thing in common—their equally deculturated state; and one mutual understanding—hoarding. These two elements welded Chinese and foreigners together in a common brotherhood of money. "You exploit me, I squeeze you."

There were oases in the desert, and in them lay the redeeming feature of Shanghai. In the first decade of the century extraterritoriality here afforded a refuge and clearinghouse for revolutionary ideas and literature. The seeds of the theory of evolution and the ideas of democracy were first sown in these oases and blown far and wide to the intellectual centers of China. While in other parts of China they grew into giant trees, in international Shanghai they remained dwarfs. In the 'twenties a rapid growth of Chinese industry took place in and around the Settlement, protected from the exploitation of warlords by the same extraterritoriality. When returned students came into financial and industrial power, the Chinese began to put into use foreign tricks of management and production, learned, however, more often directly from Europe and America than from the foreigners of Shanghai.

The life of Peking must be painted in other colors, as we have already seen. Aside from beautiful palaces and Imperial gardens, one's first impression was that there seemed to be only two classes of people in the city: those who pulled rickshaws and those who were pulled in them. But when you lived there longer you discovered that there were various classes among those who rode. It would be difficult to find any "top" classes; there were simply people of various professions coexisting side by side in a good, neighborly way. In the old days the Manchus were born aristocrats, but these had now vanished into the multitude. All men were born equal and their differences were of their own making. The only aristocracy was that of learning—the painters, the calligraphers, the poets, the philosophers, the historians, the literary men, and in recent times also the scientists and engineers.

The connoisseurs of art who could put their finger on the genuine amid the counterfeit; the craftsmen who made a thousand and one articles of art; the booksellers who were living bibliographies and the seal carvers who could make you feel your name worth preserving in artistic seals; the rug designers who beautified your floors and brightened up your living quarters—all lived side by side in the enjoyment of knowing or making things for the enjoyment of others. Knowledge and crafts were the keynote of life in Peking.

All could find some leisure in the day to enjoy beautiful things in many different ways. You might drop into an old, dingy-looking bookstore, converse with the man in charge and glance over the books on the shelf; you would feel that your mind was being led into the treasure of knowledge of the past and of the present. You might spend two or three hours there if you liked—when you left you would be invited courteously to come again. You need not buy unless you wanted to.

You might go into a curio shop if you felt like it, to look over all the beautiful things, both genuine and cle ver imitations, and enjoy them to your heart's content. You would be always welcome whether you bought or not at the time. But once you became interested you would very likely spend the last dollar you had counted on for supper.

You might go to a theatre and hear the singing of some of the great actors. It was perfect in every detail, touching the strings of your heart, which vibrated with every note. Or you could go to the Palace Museum and admire the treasures of art created by geniuses of the past. In this atmosphere of arts that always strive after perfection and the deeper meaning of life there grew up the mentality I have just mentioned which came to be called Ching-pai.

If you preferred you might go to the Imperial Gardens and sit under the moss-grown trees sipping tea, or upon the ancient rocks on one of the artful little miniature hills, watching the geese swimming in the pond. On holidays one could go by donkey, rickshaw, or automobile to the Western Hills to see historic spots and breathe air laden with the fragrance of hoary pines.

In seeking wholesome pleasures scholars, artists, craftsmen, scientists, and engineers all united in their enjoyment of old Peking. At work, they carried on their activities in widely diverse fields. The scientists worked in their laboratories to make contributions to the stock of human knowledge, the engineers went back to their slide rules and drawing tools, the scholars buried themselves in books to reconstruct from the past ideas and ideals for the future. The craftsmen produced more beautiful goods; the artists, having drawn inspiration from nature and from the past, cast their mental images on paper or in other materials with their deft fingers.

Years of trouble and war had left Peking undisturbed. Governments had come and gone but the fine old city remained the same. As we have seen, the name was changed to Peiping when the capital of China was removed to Nanking. Peiping, however, still remained Peking and has a good chance to be the capital again in the future. With the shift of the capital a portion of Peking went to the new seat of government—some of the scholars and artists, the architectural design and treasures of art—but the atmosphere and flavor of Peking remained unchanged. Railways and airplanes kept the blood of the two cities interflowing to mutual advantage.

Nanking is different. It is a city that had to be built upon ruins. In the new capital there reigned a spirit of building up the new structure and tearing down old remains. In Peking, people were nurtured on old glories while they cast their minds into the future. But Nanking had no past to rely upon except memories; everything had to be built anew. Therefore in the collective mind all was thinking, planning, and work, and life kept pace with these activities. Everybody was busy attending meetings and carrying out orders. The atmosphere was always tense. The leisurely spirit of Peking could not have flowered in Nanking.

On the streets pedestrians hustled, rickshaw coolies dashed by; even the inert donkeys fell in with the rapid flow of traffic with hurried steps. Every month new streets shot through old blocks and new houses sprang up like mushrooms. Everywhere was growth—rapid growth.

Even pleasure had to be secured through hard work. Restaurants served delicious food in congested corners, waiting for new quarters under construction. People planned gardens and waited impatiently for the trees to grow. Things you wanted had to be improvised. Without constant constructive activity you fell out of line and were left behind; you had to keep up with the spirit of the time. After some six or seven years of hard work Nanking became a new and prosperous city. Old ruins were fast disappearing while the spirit of thinking, planning, and work was constantly growing, and it radiated to other cities in the provinces and into the future of the country.

Your mind ran ahead into the future to catch up with the spirit of progress in the world. But your steps were necessarily slower—too slow to keep pace with your mind. You can plant trees but you cannot make them shoot skyward overnight; railways and highways must be laid yard by yard; policies of reform have to be carried out day by day. Then, you would think, what is all this hustle and bustle for?

What people sometimes felt about their effort may be summed up in words current and typical in those times: "Discussions ended with no decisions, decisions ended with no actions, and actions ended with no results." It was not really as bad as that. But one thing was certain: people felt their work did not measure up to the efforts made. And that was the spirit of progress.

Hangchow had something of all three of the other cities, yet it was different from them all. It was like Peking in its old culture, for it is the capital of a province of scholars; yet it lacked the grandeur of the former capital of China. Like Shanghai it was tinged with commercialism, yet more lightly, while the absence of foreign overlords left the city freedom for self-expression. It was something like Nanking in its spirit of reforms and reconstruction. But it was provincial-minded, as Peking and Nanking were national-minded. Hangchow is the city of a province in China, while the others are cities of China.

The great asset of the city is the West Lake, which not only supplied the richness of nature but retained the pleasant associations of generations of poets and scholars who once lived there. Hangchow's shortcomings also lie in its historic scene. For its people so treasured the lake that they could not look beyond its horizons; they fooled themselves into thinking it greater than the Pacific Ocean and as alluring as the veriest Paradise on earth. They were, in fact, hypnotized into believing the proverbial saying: "In the heavens you have Paradise and on earth you have Soochow and Hangchow." Just forget Soochow, they would think; Hangchow is here and Paradise is with us.

So Hangchow is West-Lake-minded. If you stayed there too long you were in danger of being engulfed, like the lovers of the South Seas; you would grow and wither there, and become complacent in life.

But the spirit of reforms and reconstruction emanating from Nanking awakened Hangchow from its slumber. Rubbing its eyes, it began to see the possibilities of future development of the province and the part it was to play in the rebuilding of China.

Peking, too, had its broad and tranquil water view. Outside the walled city, from the tops of the Western Hills, one had a bird's-eye panorama of the valley with the river Yunting winding its gentle way through vast tracts of cultivated land. The pagodas in the city were visible to the east. To the west the Marco Polo Bridge spanned the river where it lay like a sleeping dragon undisturbed through peace and war. Under this long, historical bridge the muddy, loess-laden water flowed steadily, day and night, month after month and year by year.

The name "Yunting" means "perpetual stability" or "everlasting peace." Was peace everlasting? The Chinese cherished that hope, and so we gave the river its name and then did little to make the peace secure. Finally it slipped from our hands and vanished into the flowing water under that very bridge. For at that bridge, on July 7, 1937, the first shots were fired by the Japanese army in the undeclared war which ultimately set all China aflame. Japan had become intoxicated with the cup of seeming success. And in the Japanese magic box the flames of China were transformed into a streak of lightning that blasted Pearl Harbor on December 7, 1941. ●

PART VI

WAR

Chapter 25
Manchuria and Korea

In the summer of 1918, some nineteen years before the outbreak of actual war between Japan and China, I made a trip with a friend, Huang Yen-pei, to Manchuria. As this is the area where Japanese aggression in China began, it will not be inappropriate to describe how it appeared in those early years.

We took a train from Shanghai to Nanking, and thence, from across the Yangtze at Pukow, went by the Tientsin-Pukow Railway to Peking. From Pukow north, for two days and a night, the train traversed a vast plain. The dry dust, the arid yellow soil, and the cornfields in this enormous plain of the northern section of the country, which I was visiting for the first time, contrasted greatly with the humid black earth, winding creeks, rice fields, and hilly valleys of the south in which I was born and reared.

I wondered whether the difference in geographical surroundings between north and south had much to do with the difference in physical and mental make-up of their respective peoples. The eastern coastal provinces of Chekiang and Kiangsu, where my ancestors had lived for generations and indeed for many centuries, were the regions in China which, down the long avenue of history, had produced great numbers of scholars, artists, and statesmen.But northern Kiangsu, together with that part of northern Anhuei through which we now traveled, struck me as the poorest part of the country, where deforestation was extreme and the frequent floods of the Huai River played havoc among the population.

Then we came to the Yellow River Valley—to Shantung, the northern coastal province where people were tall, muscular, and hard working, but much crowded through overpopulation—and finally to Peking. From the capital, of whose parks and palaces, museums and gardens, I then had my first glimpse, we continued to Mukden by the Peking-Mukden Railway, passing through Shanhaikwan Pass, the coastal terminal of the world-famous Great Wall of China which, like a gigantic dragon, runs hundreds of miles from Kansu to the coast, separating China proper from Manchuria and Mongolia. Before the train went through the pass we heard cicadas singing in chorus on the leaves of summer trees, just as noisily as in every other part of China. But as soon as we crossed the pass, all the trees were silent, without those singing homopterous insects. They lived and sang only inside the Great Wall!

We came at night into Mukden station, in the Japanese settlement of the city. The streets were dotted with Japanese shops and looked like a small city in Japan. Penetration of the Japanese in Manchuria was already a fact—nothing short of victorious war could stop it. Historically Manchuria, together with that vast territory to the west called Mongolia, had been the center of China's troubles. From time to time the peoples of these great areas—the Huns, the Mongols, and the Tartars—made inroads inside the Great Wall and wrought havoc there. The Japanese were to be modern Tartars after entrenching themselves in Manchuria.

We saw a number of officials working under General Chang Tso-lin, the local warlord in power, and learned much about Manchuria from them. We wanted to interview the general but were advised by friends not to do so. Mukden, former capital of the Manchus before they conquered China some three hundred years ago, was the capital of Fengtien Province, over which Chang Tso-lin ruled. We visited the Imperial Manchu mausoleums near the city, where Manchu emperors were buried before they came inside the Great Wall.

From Mukden we traveled by the South Manchurian Railway, owned and operated by the Japanese, to Kuan-cheng-tse, which was later—after the Mukden Incident of 1931—renamed Shinching, or Seijo, and made capital of the Japanese-made puppet empire of Manchukuo. Here the penetration was very evident. Japanese shops were everywhere to be seen.

On both sides of the railroad endless miles of luxuriant wheat nourished in the virgin soil of Manchuria bore witness that this tremendous area of north China beyond the Great Wall was the richest portion of China and could well support the tens of thousands of immigrants that flowed yearly from Shantung and Hopei Provinces into this northernmost part of the Chinese Republic. To cut off Manchuria from China was to deprive her of lebensraum and suffocate the provinces in the Yellow River Valley.

Kuan-cheng-tse was the terminal of the Japanese-owned South Manchurian Railway and the starting point of the Chinese Eastern Railway, formerly owned and operated by Tsarist Russia. This company had inherited a legacy of corruption from the tsarist regime and the line was operated by a gang of corrupt White Russian employees. People who bought tickets had to fight for a seat on the train, while free riders occupied comfortable compartments. Theft was rampant. One passenger who slept with his shoes on in an upper berth next morning found one of them gone. He stared at his shoeless foot and wondered how the shoe could have been stripped off without his knowing it; and I wondered what was the earthly use of stealing one shoe without the other. All passengers kept a watch on their belongings after this strange incident. As a precaution my companion hid his supply of rubles in the pockets of his underwear and slept with his Chinese gown on. The next morning the rubles were gone. On our return trip, at Harbin station as I was talking to a Chinese customs official—an American—through a window of the train, I felt somebody meddling with my hip pocket. Before I could turn around my own rubles were gone.

The dilapidated city of Harbin, international metropolis of the extreme north, was a meeting place of East and West. Poor Chinese and Russian children in rags played together in the streets and intermarriages were frequent. Children spoke a sort of hybrid language, part Chinese and part Russian. The free mixing of the poorer classes of inhabitants of Harbin was something novel to me. The bigoted foreigners of Shanghai looked down upon the poorer classes of Chinese as something that would contaminate them. Perhaps this was because few poverty-stricken Europeans ever came to stay in Shanghai.

The streets of Harbin, once well paved, had gone unrepaired for years. The carriages in which we rode bounced up and down on the rough ground so badly that comfort was a negligible factor—we had constantly to grasp at something to avoid being thrown out. The sewers were choked up. After a shower the streets turned into rivers in which the water often came up to one's knees. We met a number of people from south China who were in trade there. All the merchants did prosperous business in that frontier city by speculating in wheat, soy beans, and minerals. So long as their business was good they had no time to worry about the dilapidated state of the Russian-developed city.

We went to Kirin, capital of Kirin Province—one of the three provinces of Manchuria—and were impressed with its beautiful scenery. The city is situated on the banks of the Sungari River. Climbing to the temple on the hill in the city and looking down over the widest part of the river, one saw that it was like a lake, and I was reminded of West Lake at Hangchow. The river was rich in fish. The best fish I ever tasted was whitefish from the Sungari. In old Imperial days this delicious fish found its way only to the tables of the Imperial Court and the princesses and grand ministers. Ginseng, the life- sustaining drug that China treasured, was also indigenous to the province; large quantities found their way every year inside the Great Wall to all the provinces.

We paid a short visit to Tsitsihar, capital of the province of Heilungkiang. There we experienced an abrupt turn of summer to winter. Overnight we noticed that the green leaves began to wither and drop from their branches. This was the northernmost city within Chinese boundaries; we could go no farther unless we went on to Siberia by the branch line which connected with the Trans-Siberian Railway.

Returning to Harbin, we chartered a steamboat and sailed down the gentle Sungari to Fuchin Hsien. For two days and a night we enjoyed the mountain scenery on both sides, while mountain islands wreathed in virgin forest appeared here and there in the winding river. The evening was blessed with a brilliant moon in a clear sky, the air crisp in the northern summer night. The moon was reflected from the water, which broke into ripples of silver as our boat plowed calmly through. Often the Sungari itself appeared to have ended in a lake, with dark forested mountains rising ahead of us against the moonlit sky. But as we drew near the river suddenly opened to left or right, and as our boat changed its course and curved gradually around the mountains, the river seemed to straighten out and roll down ahead beyond the horizon.

Fukchin, or Fuchin Hsien, was a city of granaries. The wheat and soy beans produced in the surrounding hundreds of square miles all were brought to this frontier city. In the winter it was defended against possible attacks of bandits— the "Red Beards"—by walls built round it with bricks of ice which melted away in summer when the defense was less necessary. Everyone carried a gun and knew how to use it. The new stock of Chinese in the frontier provinces was primitive, full of fighting spirit, and not burdened with the overrefinements of old culture. What a contrast with the overcivilized stock inside the Great Wall! Before the war we drew our best fighters in the Chinese Air Forces from this strong stock from the virgin soil of Manchuria.

Our final destination was Lu-pu Hsien and the plantation of a friend of ours. This district was situated at the sharp end of that spearhead of land where the Sungari and Amur rivers meet and flow concurrently into the Huen-tung—the lower part of the Amur. We went by small boat down the river, arriving at dusk, and were put up for the night in a small lonely hut with thatched roof. A section of the broad brick bed was already occupied by an old woman and a cat, the remainder being set aside to accommodate us. Two pigs lay comfortably on the mud floor, snoring occasionally. Mosquitoes and bedbugs annoyed us the whole night.

Long before dawn we set out for the plantation. A party of four, we trotted on horseback in single file through miles of woods and wheat fields. Before we reached our destination the sun had begun to come up over the horizon. Mountains were barely visible in shady outlines on the Russian side of the Amur Valley. Horseflies began to gather and the animals bled profusely; I was riding a white horse, whose coat showed streaks of blood running down. We did our best to chase away the flies with a horsetail duster. At about six in the morning we came to a plantation run by a Dane. We were told that a band of Red Beards had visited the place a week before. The walls were riddled with bullets.

We arrived at our destination at about eight. The plantation yielded fairly good profits for the first few years of cultivation in that virgin soil, but bandits were the real problem. A few months earlier the "Little White Dragon" and his band had paid them a visit and carried away a large portion of the cattle and poultry. The bandits were on friendly terms with the people on the plantation, apparently, and exchanged their bad guns for good ones. "After all," said the manager, "the bandits are really not so bad, but if the Japanese should get control of this part of the country it would be the end of us all."

This was the final point of our northern journey. At the southern tip of the Manchurian mainland we also visited Dairenand Port Arthur , both Japanese-leased territories. Dairen was a commercial port through which soy beans were exported in immense quantities. Port Arthur was a naval base, the key to Manchuria, over which the Japanese fought the Russians in 1904. The defeat of Tsarist Russia had resulted in a transfer of the lease to Japanese hands. With railways starting from Port Arthur and Korea and running through south Manchuria, the Japanese had already got control of the heart and veins of the Chinese Three Eastern Provinces.

We wandered about the naval base for a day and climbed many hills trying to get a bird's-eye view. Finally, on top of one of them, in the slanting sun we came across a stone monument inscribed with the famous lines of the Tartar general who conquered the Sungs in 1276: "March an army of a million men to the West Lake and mount, on horseback, the first peak of the Wu Mountains." At Hangchow, overlooking the lake, the Sungs had established their capital in 1127. To follow in the Tartar's steps was the dream of Admiral Togo and his people after the Russo-Japanese War. And after some thirty years the dream came true, when a Japanese army entered Hangchow after the fall of Shanghai.

Korea was the springboard by means of which Japanese imperialism leapt to the mainland of Asia. It was over Korea that China and Japan clashed in 1894. The Sino-Japanese War for control of that ancient kingdom was the starting point of Japan's aggression on the continent. It opened a new chapter of China's history— the chapter which was to see China's reforms, revolutions, wars, sufferings, humiliation, and eventual westernization and modernization.

After our trip to Manchuria we turned off to Korea. Crossing the Yalu River which forms the boundary line between China and her erstwhile protectorate, we arrived by train at Chemulpo. From there we proceeded to Seoul, capital of the country.

The Japanese governor general of Korea resided in the capital. His imposing, Western-style office building was located right in front of the royal palace, as if put there purposely to insult the Korean kings. The kings were gone, but the palace remained to endure the humiliation of being put back into the background.

The royal palace looked exactly like the Chinese Imperial Palace in Peking, but on a very much smaller scale, rather like a toy palace. In the old times, when the Chinese Imperial ambassador condescended to call, the king had to descend from the granite steps to meet the honored guest in the courtyard. If the ambassador had an Imperial Edict to deliver, His Majesty had to bend his knees in receiving the Imperial favor.

At the back of the palace was a Chinese pavilion in which the princesses performed the ancient Chinese dances of the Tang Dynasty. In Korea as well as Japan, ancient Chinese customs still prevailed. Their pronunciation of Chinese words, their customs, dances, music, and ways of living could all be traced back to influences of the Tang era. As I stood in the pavilion gazing up at the mist-mantled hills of Seoul, my mind reverted to the glorious times of that dynasty (618-905) when Chinese civilization shone as brilliant as the sun in a clear sky, casting its beams far beyond the horizon upon such lands as Japan, Korea, and Indo-China. The offshoots of Chinese civilization grew, were preserved and later rejuvenated in Japan, whereas in Korea and Indo- China they grew and withered. The mother country of this glorious civilization had changed its manners, customs, and ways of life as the waves of invasion swept over it. Japan, which succeeded in building up a new civilization in the last century by the introduction of Western civilization upon a foundation of Chinese Tang culture, had gobbled up Korea, and as appetite grew with eating, was on the way to swallow up China, her teacher and benefactor. But Japan taught China a lesson in her turn: how to build a strong new nation upon a foundation of old civilization. Hence China's reforms, revolutions, westernization, and modernization.

While I mused thus over the past and the future, sunshine was peeping through the clouds and the mist was fast fading from the Seoul hills. The Korean who had taken me there, an old Chinese scholar, was standing by in silence but now called my attention to a dinner engagement. We left the pavilion and passed the spot where the Princess Ming was assassinated, presumably by the Japanese for her sympathy toward China. "I know what you have been thinking," said the old scholar. "It is too late for my country now. Our kings preferred dances to the affairs of state. But China, which is your country and may be regarded as mine, has a bright future. I am old now. Brother, you are young. Do your best for China."

The dinner was ready at the Chinese Consulate General, formerly the residence of China's special ambassador. What had happened behind the doors of this historic mansion during the quadrangular love affairs of China, Tsarist Russia, and Japan in courtship of the Korean lady, only those who participated knew. History gives bare outlines only; personal records, if any, remain yet unpublished. Matters have had to be left to the imagination of posterity.

Life in Seoul was being fast engulfed in Japanization. Japanese bazaars, banks, shops, and restaurants occupied prominent sections of the streets. Managers of big business, government officials, and teachers of the more important schools were all Japanese. The life of the vanquished people was fast receding into the background, like their palace. Here and there you would see Koreans squatting complacently on the sidewalks with long stick-like pipes in their mouths, puffing to their heart's content, and women walking leisurely by with heavy loads on their heads. Some of the old type of school, in which Confucian classics were taught, had been left to struggle for existence. I went into such a school, which had one old scholar of the classics as teacher and a dozen pupils squatting around him on the matting. The Koreans and Japanese still kept the ancient Chinese way of squatting on their heels on the floor. It was slightly heated from beneath even in summer and was kept as clean as a bed. The pupils had to learn the Chinese classics by heart as I had done in childhood. Although they used the same textbooks they pronounced the words quite differently. Like the Japanese and the Indo- Chinese, they had been influenced by the Tang pronunciation.

All the people wore padded cotton stockings even in summer. I asked the reason and was informed that the earth was cold in the northern country. Yet they all wore white linen gowns which were quite cool.

The Koreans as well as the Japanese and Indo-Chinese loved Chinese landscape painting, calligraphy, and poetry. But each of the three peoples retained their own individual characteristics. As it was with their arts, so it was with their lives. Korea and Indo-China had come more under the Ming influence in later centuries while Japan, beyond the sea, escaped it. Moreover, the seafaring people of Japan were highly adventurous and therefore kept the martial spirit of ancient China, while the Koreans and Indo-Chinese were touched more deeply with that complacency that tinged Chinese life in later centuries. The system of civil examinations which conferred so much honor upon scholars in China found its way to Korea and Indo-China, but stopped at the gates of Japan.

In its relation to China the younger generation in Korea was undergoing a change under the pressure of Japanese-controlled modern schools, in which the sacred person of the Mikado was worshiped, the virtues of the Japanese exalted to the skies, and the vices of the Chinese amplified to monstrous proportions. If the attitude of young Koreans toward Japan was hatred, toward China it was contempt. While the older generation lamented the passing of the good old ways of Chinese culture, the young people were made to think that they were now the blessed subjects of the Mikado's glorious empire. ◉

Chapter 26
War Clouds Deepening

In October, 1930, after my resignation from the office of Minister of Education in the national government, I had gone back to Peking—now called Peiping. Again I was entrusted by Generalissimo Chiang Kai-shek, then President of the Executive Yuan (the title of the executive branch of government), with charge of the National University of Peking.

The number of student demonstrations was very much reduced. When the capital was moved to the south the focus of political activities went with it. There was not much left for students to demonstrate against except for occasional outbursts provoked by Japanese aggression, which had started in Manchuria and was now fast extending inside the Great Wall.

On the morning of September 19, 1931, as I was sitting at my desk in the Chancellor's office of the university, a telephone call brought me the fatal news of the previous day. Japan had delivered a blow at Mukden and the Chinese troops had evacuated the city to avoid a clash.

I have tried to show, little by little, some of the steps in this movement from the beginning; to put its futher development in a nutshell, let me sum up in the following story:

After the Sino-Japanese War of 1894, China began to adore Japan. She daubed her face and rouged her lips, ready for Japan to make advances. But her hero returned her love with contemptuous smiles. As a small boy I once wrote a little essay in which I said, "China and Japan are of one race and one language." My Japanese teacher, Mr. Nakagawa, scrawled along the margin: "No, no. These two countries are not of one race. Poor China is to be sliced like a melon by the Powers. What a pity it will be!" This rebuke thrust like a knift into my little heart. I remember how I wept that night for the future of my country.

If she could not win the love of her hero, China still hoped that japan would at least remain a friend. But her hero suddenly turned a dagger on her in the form of the Twenty-One Demands. It barely missed her. Then she began to realize that this hero was, after all, but a villain in the disguise of Bushido, or the spirit of chivalry. When he came in turn to make love to her, she was always in defiant mood. For by now she knew very well that what he was after was her rich dowry of natural resources.

Then the act of strangulation began. The villan put a rope of economic "co-operation" round her neck and tried to make her believe it was a necklace. On the fatal night of September 18, 1931, when everyone else was asleep, all of a sudden he tightened the rope.

She woke from slumber in dismay and ran away as fast as she could. But the cord around her neck was an endless nightmare rope which grew longer and longer as she ran, yet remained always in the grip of the villan-sorcerer at the other end. She was frightened and screamed. The American Secretary of States, Mr. Henry Stimson, called on Great Britain to join the United States in a forceful note to Japan. Sir John Simon, speaking for his country, refused. Stimson thus stood alone and Japan was left free to pursue the policy of strangulation.

China's lukewarm friends under the leadership of Lord Lytton came halfheartedly to the rescue. They visited Mukden, the spot where the crime was committed, and pronounced the villain guilty. But thery would not untie the rope. The Italian Commissioner of the Chinese Post Office at Mukden, Mr. Poletti, in his memorandum to Lord Lytton intimated that if the Powers did not stop Japan right in Manchuria, he was sure that his own country, Italy, would poke her fingers into Ethiopia. But what weight could be attached to the words of an insignificant postal commissioner?

"Sorry, my young lady," said the neighbors. "We can do no more than declare our sympathy with you."

Sympathy she got, but help there was none.

A few months later I made the trip back to the south. The afternoon of January 28, 1932, I went to Shanghai station to take the train back to Peiping. As I entered a sense of utter strangeness stole over me—the station looked as quiet as a deserted village. A station guard told me that there was no outgoing train. "It looks as if the Japanese are ready for a blow," he said. "You had better leave here right away. Something may happen any minute."

That night I was suddenly wakened by the roar of cannon, followed by the rat-tat-tat of machine guns. I jumped from my bed and followed the stream of guests to the roof of the hotel. The sky was red with the glow of fires that leapt out here and there from the vicinity of the station. Japanese aggression seemed to have followed on my very heels from north to south. The next morning I went up again to the roof and my heart ached with the sight of the Commercial Press Library on fire. Several Japanese bombers kept on bombing the building of the Commercial Press. The dark smoke rose heavenward, carrying with it scraps of scorched paper which floated in the sky and sailed idly over the roofs. The print still visible on some of the fragments read dearly "The Commercial Press."

The Japanese had opened an attack on Shanghai. It resulted in the bitterest fighting before 1937, but China was finally forced to accept terms under which Japanese troops were permitted to remain in the city.

For seven years, from 1930 to 1937, I was at the helm of the university, endeavoring to steer that ship of learning through the rough seas of Sino- Japanese conflict. With the aid of many friends—particularly Dr. Hu Shih, Mr. V. K. Ting, and Mr. Fu Shih-nian—the university sailed smoothly with only an occasional trimming of her canvas.

The standard of science teaching and research was raised. A serious study was made of Chinese history and literature. The faculty had ample time for research and the students were led to direct their attention to study; the whirlpool of revolutionary activity and student demonstration was gradually transformed into a center of learning. During all these years there was only one demonstration worth recording, As the Japanese forces drove rapidly inside the Great Wall the students in Nanking and Shanghai clamored for war. Demonstrations on a large scale were frequent in the capital and the students in Peiping wanted to join the movement. One day a crowd of students tried to take a south-bound train at the East Station. Being refused entrance to the train itself, the boys and girls lay on the track day and night to prevent it from leaving the station. At length a few hundred were allowed to go and join their comrades in Nanking.

Seeing that war clouds hung thick over our heads, during the next years we tried to gain time by sailing along the shallows of caution, not venturing on those high seas where we would be bound to clash full-force with the Japanese tidal wave. But our caution was not timidity. When Japanese scholars, fifth columnists in disguise, came to pay "respects" to the "center of culture" (which really meant to them the center of the anti-Japanese movement), we talked frankly with them. One, I remember, spoke at length about cultural relations with our professors and was told that we did not see any cultural relations between the two countries but only the military ambition of Japan. "Give up your military ambition and China and Japan will co-operate well."

These men—geologists, economists, biologists, and other scholars—came to us from time to time seeking the "friendship" of the university. They all complained about our anti-Japanese movement. We told them that anti-Japanese we were not, but anti-Japanese-militarism we were. Their minds, however, were set on the strangulation of China; nothing short of a complete surrender could change their course.

Meanwhile the Japanese Kwantung army stationed in Manchuria made rapid inroads inside the Great Wall. The Chinese army fought against the intruders along the Wall, then in the northern part of Hopei Province, and finally withdrew to Peiping and its vicinity. Wounded soldiers streamed in and all the hospitals were filled. A hospital was established supported by faculty members. Wives and young co-eds acted as nurses. Here I came into close contact with the fighting forces and learned their psychology. In conversations at their bedsides the soldiers showed no sign of weakness toward the Japanese. They attributed their defeat to the lack of modern weapons, especially guns, which permitted the enemy to break through the Chinese wall of human flesh.

I wish to remind the reader that this undaunted spirit of the Chinese army built a wall of flesh and blood for the defense of their country against the steel and fire of the enemy. It enabled China to fight on and on for eight long, suffering years, with millions of dead and wounded, without a murmur. China lost many battles but was still winning the war.

When the fighting was going on along the Great Wall, General Ho Yin-chin, Minister of War, came to Peiping to direct the operations. He and I wanted to effect a truce in order to gain time. I went to call on Sir Miles Lampson, the British Ambassador, to sound out his feelings as to acting as mediator. He said that Mr. Suma of the Japanese Embassy had intimated to him that the Japanese, too, desired a truce. Cables were sent to London and the reply permitted Sir Miles to act as mediator. Washington was informed through the good offices of Mr. Nelson Johnson, the American Ambassador. But the plan fell through when the Foreign Minister, Lo Wen-kan, told the British Embassy in Nanking that no one was authorized to deal with a foreign country but himself.

Then the Japanese forces broke through the defense lines along the Great Wall and swept down toward Peiping. The city was about to be evacuated.

As I was laid up in the Peking Union Medical College after an appendix operation, I was not informed. But early in the morning I heard Japanese planes droning over our heads and smelt something wrong. I got permission from the doctor in charge to leave the hospital and limped to the residence of General Ho Yin-chin, who was surprised to see me still in the city and informed me that the Japanese were about to attack. I made plans to leave the next day.

Next morning at dawn my telephone rang. It was the general. "A truce has been arranged—you don't have to leave the city." At once I telephoned Dr. Hu Shih.

"Why, the Japanese planes are droning over our heads," he said.

"I have just received a message from General Ho Yin-chin to that effect," was all I could say. But the Tangku Agreement had been signed for China at midnight by Huang Fu, by the terms of which the Japanese forces were to halt after occupying the northern part of Hopei.

The Japanese, having occupied this area and established a puppet "autonomous government" there, urged the Chinese commander of the remaining Hopei forces to co-operate by establishing an autonomous government in Peiping. Rumors circulated widely in the city that the commander, General Sung Chieh-yuan, would give in to the Japanese. In this momentary crisis the university professors issued a statement that they were unconditionally opposed to the so-called auton omous movement in north China. The general, in point of fact, did not comply.

One afternoon a month or two later a Japanese gendarme called on me in the university. "The Japanese garrison in the Legation Quarter invites you to go there and talk over some matters which they wish to understand and which need explanation," he announced. I promised to go in an hour, and he left.

Before dark I went alone to the Japanese barracks in the Legation Quarter, after informing my family and some of my friends. As I entered the offices of General Kawabe I heard the click of the key which meant that the door was locked behind me. A Japanese colonel stood up and said, "Please be seated." I took the seat and out of the tail of my eye saw a soldier standing by the door with a drawn revolver.

"Our commanding general invites you to come here and wishes to know why you carry on an extensive propaganda against Japan." He offered me a cigarette as he spoke.

"What do you mean? I carry on anti-Japanese propaganda—? Nothing of the sort," I replied, accepting the cigarette.

"Then did you sign that statement opposing the autonomous movement?"

"Yes, I did. It is our internal problem. It has nothing to do with an anti-Japanese movement."

"You wrote a book in which you attacked Japan."

"Show me the book."

"Then you are a friend of Japan?"

"Not exactly. I am a friend of the Japanese people, but an enemy to Japanese militarism, just as I am an enemy to Chinese militarism."

"Well, you know, there is some misunderstanding about it in the Kwantung army. Would you go there and have a talk with General Itagaki at Dairen?" The telephone rang and the colonel answered, then turned to me. "A special coach has been prepared for you. Would you go to Dairen tonight?"

"No, I will not."

"Don't be afraid. The Japanese gendarmes will go with you for your protection."

"I am not afraid. If I had been I would not have come here alone. If you want to use force, go ahead—I am in your hands. But I advise you not to. You will become a laughing stock when the world, including Tokyo, is informed that the Japanese army has abducted the Chancellor of Peking University."

His face changed color and he looked as if I were now a problem to him. "Please don't be afraid," he said casually.

"Afraid? No, no. Confucius has told me as well as you to remain calm in the face of danger. You believe in Bushido. Bushido would not harm a defenseless person." I puffed the cigarette calmly.

The telephone rang again, and again he turned to me. "Well, Chancellor Chiang, the general wanted me to thank you for your visit. You may wish to go to Dairen some other time—whenever you like. Thank you. Good-by." The key clicked again. The colonel helped me with my overcoat, accompanied me to my car, and opened the car door. Darkness had already fallen.

The following afternoon General Sung Chieh-yuan sent a major general to advise me to leave Peking lest he should be unable to protect me. I thanked his representative and said that I would remain on my own responsibility.

I stayed on, but nothing happened to me. Occasionally some Koreans came to the university and acted very queer—these incidents were reported to me but I did not pay much attention to them. Then the tactics of the Japanese changed. General Matsumoro was sent to Peiping as special agent of the Japanese army. He made friends with me and came to my house often. He denounced the Japanese general for grilling me at the Legation barracks, and for about half a year we were very friendly. At the end of his term of office he came in full military uniform to say good-by. He told me that he was being sent to Hailar, on the border between

Manchuria and Siberia, to command a cavalry division, and said that he was afraid the war clouds were deepening and that a clash between China and Japan would be very unfortunate. "If the war should come," he said, "the Japanese army would go as far as Hankow."

"Yes, General, I agree with you. If our two countries should be so unfortunate as to come to an open clash, international complications might arise and all the Japanese navy be sent to the bottom of the sea, and the Island Empire might be reduced to a few tiny dots on the map of the Pacific Ocean."

He sighed and said, "That may be. But Japan would still be an independent nation, while China will be destroyed by the Western Powers."

"It may be so. Next time we meet I hope we shall not embrace each other, weeping for what we have done so foolishly. No matter what happens in the future, General, let us remain friends." We parted with heavy hearts.

General Imai succeeded him. He called on me and I returned his call. We talked quite frankly along the same lines as I had talked with his predecessor. Once two members of the Japanese House of Peers called. One had formerly been governor of Formosa. After looking around to see whether anyone was within hearing he inquired in a whisper who had been the person responsible for detaining me in the Japanese barracks. I told him it was Takahashi. He shook his head and said, "Ridiculous."

The Japanese had found out by now that the University had no immediate desire to start an anti-Japanese movement and they hoped to win it to the Japanese side by making friends with leading members of the faculty. Both sides were cautious in dealing with each other and the tension between the university and the Japanese army was somewhat eased.

General Tashiro came to Tientsin as commander of the army there. The Japanese had treaty rights, with other Powers, to station troops in that city. The general came to Peiping and gave a banquet, to leading Chinese and Japanese officials, military as well as civil. In a speech at the banquet he advocated economic co-operation between China and Japan. Some of the Chinese officials responded but spoke rather equivocally. On the score of economic co-operation I remained as silent as a sphinx except for occasional jokes at the table. To my great surprise a telegram came to me in code from Nanking a few days later, informing me that the Japanese Embassy had intimated to the Ministry of Foreign Affairs that the Chancellor of Peking University supported Sino-Japanese co-operation.

This was how the Japanese worked on China. The procedure seemed to be:

first sweet words, then political intrigue, then intimidation, again sweet words, and finally blitzkrieg. The order might vary somewhat, but they never deviated from their fundamental course—the subjugation of China. This was also the way the Japanese went about dealing with America before Pearl Harbor. ●

Chapter 27
War

When Peiping was Peking, the city was a center of intellectual activities and the student movement. When it became Peiping it turned into the center of Sino-Japanese conflict. During the early months of 1937 one incident after another happened in the vicinity. The arrow was drawn and must in time fly. With lightning speed it went off at the Marco Polo Bridge. On the night of July 7 the Japanese army under cover of darkness suddenly shelled the outskirts of the city from their side of the bridge, and the Chinese army stationed in the city returned fire.

I was at Kuling, a summer resort on the middle Yangtze, when the war god descended upon Peiping. Generalissimo Chiang Kai-shek had summoned a group of intellectuals for discussion of national problems in the cool Kuling mountains during those hot summer days. The sky was clear and patches of shade from the trees made lacelike patterns on the green lawns. One day after lunch, as I was resting in a one-room cottage, one of a group of houses the Generalissimo had set aside for his guests, and was looking through the window into a tall shady tree and listening to the singing of the cicadas, Chen Tsang-po, editor of the Central Daily News, broke the quiet of the noon hour by knocking at the door with the news that the Japanese had struck at Marco Polo Bridge the previous night. I leapt from the bed and inquired for further details. There were none.

We discussed the possibilities. As I was fresh from Peiping he asked my opinion from what I knew of conditions in the city. I told him that from my impression of the Japanese commanding generals there and their conservative views, the thing looked like another local incident. The Japanese plan seemed to be to bite off the Chinese cheese piece by piece, and I was not inclined to think they were ready to swallow the whole chunk. But by this policy of slow motion—gnawing off a bit from time to time and slowly accumulating, day after day—in a few years they would have entrenched themselves firmly in north China and it would be difficult to dislodge them. The Yangtze Valley would be at their mercy. Japan had swallowed up Manchuria by a slow process and had then come to north

China. What Manchuria was to north China, so north China was to the south. The same method and the same process. That seemed to be the policy of the Japanese vis-â-vis China.

There was desultory fighting for some days. Twelve days later, as skirmishing went on outside the city, Generalissimo Chiang Kai-shek, in an address to several thousand officers from various armies in the country who were under training in the Kuling Training Center, expressed the view that the Japanese were about to launch a general war against China and we must get ready to defend the country at any cost. "But if such a general war should start," he said, "we must be ready to sacrifice... It will be a long war and the longer it drags on, the more we shall suffer."

It was the first time I had heard him speak in such unequivocal terms of the Japanese question. General Chen Chun, General Hu Chung-nan, and other commanding generals of the Chinese armies who later distinguished themselves at the various fronts were among the listeners. A few days after this speech Generalissimo Chiang Kai-shek returned to Nanking by air and the commanding generals rejoined their respective armies. With some of my friends I flew to the capital and tried to get back to Peiping, but northbound trains were all suspended.

In about two weeks the war was spreading like a flood in the vicinity of Peiping. General Sung Chieh-yuan fought gallantly as casualties mounted. The commander of the Japanese army, Tashiro, with whose conservative views regarding China problems I was well acquainted, fell ill and the radical younger officers got control of the Japanese forces. After a few days General Tashiro died. Was it illness, suicide, or assassination? Rumors were rampant but nobody could find out the truth. General Sung Chieh-yuan still clung to the idea of localizing the incident and urged the central government troops, which were being rushed northward, to stop at Paoting. And at Paoting, accordingly, they made a halt.

But the Japanese army, now under the direction of young officers, did not stop; Sung's forces were attacked by the enemy right and left and on all sides. One of the commanding generals died in action. Finally General Sung withdrew from Peiping and the Japanese entered the city without firing a shot.

Now the Japanese had control of Peiping. Would north China suffer the same fate as Manchuria after they occupied Mukden some six years earlier? Would Japan stop at north China for the moment, wait a few years more, and use that base for a further attack on south China? Or was she tired of waiting—would she strike at south China with a single blow and get the thing done, once and for all? Either way seemed possible. The plan of slow motion seemed on the whole more dangerous to

China. All the ranking officers in Nanking and the military leaders in the provinces favored a country-wide resistance to the aggression. All China—officials, generals, and the people—stood up as one man to face the greatest calamity in history to fall upon the country.

Meanwhile Japan began to dispatch troops to Shanghai from across the sea. China at the same time rushed her own troops down the Yangtze to the same port. In that small area, face to face, were massed tens of thousands of men. A tiny spark would set off a terrific explosion in the powder magazine. It was immaterial which side should strike it first—whether by the accidental discharge of a gun by a careless soldier without orders, or by the policy of men high up in power.

The Japanese army knew very well that the men responsible for the Mukden Incident, such as Generals Honjo and Doihara, had received the highest rewards and honors for their meritorious acts. Those responsible for the Marco Polo Bridge Incident were to receive like honors, there was no doubt. Who could blame the commanding generals from across the sea for aspiring to similar rewards?

All of us in Nanking knew that the thick war clouds hanging over the whole country were bound to break into a storm. I left for Hangchow by motorcar to stay with a friend in a villa on the historic West Lake. In the serene quiet of the place I had a chance to muse over the past and think of the future. Every day, and every succeeding night, we expected a clash between the two opposing forces in that tightly congested area of Shanghai. Every now and then my friend, Wang Wen-po, telephoned to Shanghai to inquire about the situation. On August 12 the voice at the other end replied abruptly, "No news. Tomorrow at ten, at ten. That's all." The receiver was hung up.

Next morning the fatal hour struck. Smoke rose sky-high. Bombers from both sides blasted the lines of the opposing forces. A full-scale war had begun. There would be no more local incidents, no more piecemeal ways. Japan must either gobble up all China or give it up. But gobble she could not—quite, and give up she would not. It was bound to be a long-drawn-out war.

Two days later, on a cloudy afternoon, I was sitting under a willow tree watching the fish shuttling back and forth in the shallows of the lake. Peals of thunder were audible over the other side of the city. The telephone rang for me. "Hello—do you hear that?" More thunder. "Yes, it's thundering."

"No—the enemy is bombing our airfield."

Seven bombers had flown over from Formosa without escort. They were met by Chinese fighters stationed at Hangchow and five were shot down on the spot. The remaining two flew for their lives and were forced to land at some distance. The pilots were captured, and we learned that they had been told by their commanding officers that there were no fighter planes in China.

Next day the Japanese bombed Nanking. In the beginning of the war the enemy dropped only one bomb at any one place, so that all their bombs were scattered. This caused much less damage than concentrated bombing, which they learned a year later from the Russians at Changkaofen, a border town between Manchuria and Siberia where they had a clash with Soviet forces.

My friend Wang Wen-po was a member of the Chekiang provincial government and Commissioner of Reconstruction. He had to get busy. Hundreds of trucks were taken over from the bus lines and munitions shipped to the front in them. Once a fleet of some twenty such trucks was sent to the front. It ran into the rear of the enemy and was fired upon. One truck driver got out of his car and hid in the fields; under cover of darkness he crawled on his stomach through the enemy lines and came back to Hangchow. A few days later he found another truck and dashed off again for the front.

Refugees from Shanghai poured into Hangchow. The temples were filled with women and children. Humble huts in the mountains were turned into temporary homes for fashionable young ladies. They talked and laughed as if nothing had happened to them. The Chinese were always in good humor even in time of danger.

A friend of mine, formerly a cotton magnate, came to Hangchow with his daughters and young children and lived in a temple up in the mountains. He told me that he would like to build a house for his family.

"What for?" I asked.

"I should like to stay in Hangchow during the war in Shanghai," he said.

I was surprised at his idea of the war. I told him that he had better move into the interior as the war would surely spread to Hangchow and all coastal cities and perhaps up the Yangtze as far as Hankow. He was stunned and could not believe my words. Five years later I met him in Chungking, where he told me that he and his family had left Hangchow before war descended upon the West Lake.

In Nanking a plan was afoot for the evacuation of three of the northern universities: Peking and Tsinghua Universities in Peiping and Nankai University in Tientsin. These three institutions were to combine into a union university at Changsha; an inland city on the upper Yangtze. Hu Shih telephoned from the capital and asked me to go back to Nanking to put the scheme into effect. I did not welcome the idea but was finally forced to accept the plan. There are things in the world which you do not want to do but must do in the end, willy-nilly. Like war itself: when war comes, you find yourself fighting whether you like it or not. This was my attitude toward the associated university.

Knowing that I would be unable to see my father's home again before the end of the war and that the hazards of war are difficult to foresee, I borrowed a Buick from a friend and drove home. My father, now very old, was all smiles. When I left again for Nanking I told him that China would be reborn through fire and blood.

"What do you mean?" he asked, giving me a steady look from his twinkling eyes.

"The thing is this. The war will be a long war. Hundreds and thousands of houses will be burned and thousands and millions of lives will be lost. This is what I mean by fire and blood. And in the end China will emerge victorious."

When I left him I had the feeling that most probably I would not see my beloved father again, to whom I owed so much and had returned so little. When bombs visited the native city of my boyhood days, he moved into the mountains and there enjoyed his trees, flowers, and birds. After two years of war he got up early one morning as usual and felt dizzy. He went back to bed and there his spirit fled, at the age of nearly eighty. He was but one of many indirect casualties of war. War is rather hard on old people.

I stayed at Nanking for several days and then boarded a steamer sailing upriver for Hankow. Near the docks wooden boxes containing government archives, books of the Central University library, and art treasures from the Palace Museum were piled high along the banks of the Yangtze, ready for shipment. And on the way to Hankow we met boat after boat packed with troops steaming down the river to reinforce Shanghai.

From Hankow I took the Canton-Hankow Railway to Changsha. On the way we met trainloads of troops crowded in open cars, coming up to Hankow from Canton and Kwangsi. The war was now really on a national footing, not a mere local war as heretofore. The spirit of the fighting men was high. I asked where they were going.

"Fight the Japs!" they replied with zest. ●

Chapter 28
Life in Changsha

Changsha is an inland city. For the first time in my life I lived far away from the sea. Even in America I had stayed first in California for four years and then in New York for another five, always on the seacoast. Living in an inland city I felt a kind of dryness in spite of the damp climate and Tung-ting Lake not far away. My ideal of a place to live was in the mountains near a vast plain or on the plain near the mountains, in either case not far from the sea. Away from the sea, the sense of space in my mind seemed to fill up with solid earth. I began to feel somewhat uncomfortable.

When I arrived at Changsha Mei Yi-chi, President of Tsinghua University, was already there. To run a university in troubled times is something of a headache. To do it during a war, in conjunction with two other institutions not lacking in the diverse personalities and idiosyncrasies common to university professors, was worse. With the worries of war and anxiety as to my family and friends in the war zones or occupied areas, it was more than nay health could endure. "Headache" is a figurative term, but real stomach trouble saps one's spirit and physical vigor. In spite of frequent stomachaches I had to exert myself to help my colleagues steer our precarious craft with its mixed crew over a rough sea.

Teachers and students of the three component institutions flocked to Changsha. Some came by sea from Tientsin, taking a British steamer to Hong Kong and then a plane or the Canton-Hankow Railway; others took the Peiping-Hankow Railway to Hankow and then the Canton-Hankow line to Changsha. Within a few weeks some two hundred professors and over a thousand students had gathered around the Changsha Bible School, which the Union University rented as its temporary home. Books and laboratory apparatus were bought and shipped in from Hong Kong. In less than two months the university was in full swing.

Owing to lack of space in the city the College of Literature moved to the sacred mountains of Nan-yu. I made two trips there, and these are among my pleasantest recollections of this part of the country. On one of them I wandered with friends deep into the mountains on a three-day jaunt, crossing on our way the road by which a fugitive Ming emperor passed to the southwest almost three centuries ago to avoid capture by t he Manchus. A stone tablet in his memory stands there to this day, with the names of all the officials who followed him inscribed upon it. Oddly, at one of the temples we visited, a tree planted by the fleeing emperor had grown into a crooked shape looking like an old, old man taking a rest after a very long journey. We were now treading the same path, standing in the same temple. For what reason? Foreign invasion from the north, which had troubled China through ten centuries.

The first night we stopped at the Fang-kwang Temple. Here a famous Ming scholar passed the remainder of his life after the fall of the Ming Dynasty. It was a clear night—the full moon sailed low over the mountains in the empty sky. I had never seen the moon look so low and so near, as if one could poke one's fingers in its smiling face.

The second night we stopped at a monastery near the highest peak of the sacred mountains. A spring gushes from the very top of the peak, and a temple is perched there. This is the house of the Fire God and a symbol of the ancient practical wisdom that water should always be ready near fire, which may thus be controlled.

Near this temple we saw the sun come up next morning, a wonderful sight. It rose out of a sea of clouds, first sending up violet, golden, pink, and blue tints through the cloud bank and then emerging to lie like a golden ostrich egg on a white velvet cushion. All of a sudden it split into four brilliant oranges, then in the flash of a few seconds merged again into one great ball. For some moments it seemed to change color with every fraction of a second, as if with the turning of a moving-picture color camera. Then it stopped, glowed mellow gold for a few instants, and finally became a great ball of fire from which we had to turn our eyes. The icebergs of cloud disappeared and the still waves vanished. Only a thin layer of mist veiled the valleys down below. Through it one could see chimneys sending up their smoke in the mild morning sun.

Pilgrims came by thousands to the sacred mountains. Many walked from several hundred miles away. Old and young, rich and poor, all joined in common worship of the Buddha.

Changsha is the capital of Hunan Province, a center of rich rice production feeding many millions of people outside its boundaries. Fish, shrimp, eels, and turtles from the river Hsiang were abundant, oranges and persimmons bountiful.

Pork was tender and full of flavor. The bean curd, China's national food for rich and poor alike, was as pure and smooth as thickened milk. The only drawback was the high humidity—there were far more rainy or cloudy days in a year than sunny ones.

Every time I went up by airplane from the city, as I sometimes had to do, I thought of the crystal palace deep in the sea where the king of dragons lives, as we all learned in Chinese fairy tales. There would still be clouds above my head, while down below mist enveloped the city like the white around the yolk of an egg. Farther up, there would be another ceiling of cloud without a streak of sun.

The people were healthy, independent, and hard working. They loved to fight. The slightest provocation would find them ready for combat, whether vocal or by fists. At highway stations one often saw signs: DO NOT QUARREL and DO NOT FIGHT. Rickshaw coolies sauntered along the streets and refused to run. If you told a coolie to run faster he would invariably say, "You pull the rickshaw—I'd like to see you run." While the temper of the people was quick, their movements were slow. Here was a case where temper and tempo did not go together.

They were frank and sincere, not easily influenced by other people's opinions. They would be either your friends or your enemies, with no halfway between. They are good soldiers. "No Hunanese, no army." It was by his Hunan army that Tseng Kuo-fang defeated the Taipings in 1864. Even now no Chinese army is found without some soldiers from Hunan. It is the Sparta of China.

The Japanese invaded Changsha three times in the course of the war, and three times suffered defeat there. The people co-operated with the national army wholeheartedly, through blood and fire.

In Changsha we had news of the war in Shanghai. For three long months Chinese troops of flesh and blood held at bay the Japanese army of fire and steel. Finally the Chinese army withdrew to save further futile sacrifice. Now the enemy converged on Nanking. An exodus of the population from the capital began— thousands of people streamed along the highway to Changsha. Trains of trucks and cars miles long poured into the city. Suddenly it was congested with refugees. Some ministries of the government moved to Changsha, others to Hankow.

Before long the Japanese army entered Nanking, where animal instincts ran wild in the Japanese soldier. Women were raped to death and fleeing people were machine-gunned at random. Military trucks ran through streams of people on the streets. The atrocities committed by the Japanese will remain forever a black spot in human history.

At the turn of the new year the Japanese army headed upriver toward Nanchang. It seemed to be approaching Changsha, while the Chinese army was concentrated around Hankow. The capital of Hunan Province was now vulnerable to enemy attack. I flew to Hankow to sound out the Generalissimo as to the removal of the Union University still farther inland. I interviewed first the Minister of Education, Chen Li-fu, who advised me to see the Commander in Chief. So I went to call on him. He agreed that the university ought to move farther west, and I suggested that we move to Kunming, which had access to the sea through the Yunnan-Indo-China Railway. He readily agreed and suggested that some-one go there first to select a site for the university.

The month of January, 1938, passed in preparation for the removal. Books and scientific apparatus were packed and trucks and gasoline bought. In February, as the preparations were almost complete, I flew to Hong Kong, where I took a French liner to Haiphong in French Indo-China. Thence I went by train to Hanoi, capital of the French colonial government, and from there to Kunming by the Yunnan-Indo-China Railway through one of the most mountainous regions of China. ●

Chapter 29
Indo-China and Burma

Just as, some twenty years earlier, I had found the ancient Chinese ways of life still persisting in Korea, so now, taking the opportunity of going to Kunming by way of Indo-China, I found there the same ancient Chinese ways. Like the Koreans, they wore a dress similar to that of the Ming Dynasty. Their pronunciation of Chinese words stemmed from that of the Tang Dynasty; villages, cities, and administrative districts bear Chinese names pronounced somewhat after the Tang fashion.

The French preferred for general use a romanization of the Annamese language, which is itself a modified form of Chinese. I must admit that it is much easier for the common people to learn. But this romanized Annamese will further widen the gap between China and Indo-China.

The capital of Annam, where the titular emperor, Pao-dai, lived, was very much like the palace of the former Korean kings and, again, like the Imperial Palace in Peking on a much smaller scale. Indeed, the court of Annam looked like a living branch of the Imperial Ming Court. The French had preserved it as a sort of living museum, while the Japanese preferred to transport the Korean king to Tokyo and make a Japanese out of him.

I was told that the first ancestor of the emperor of Annam was buried on a hill in Kunming. For he was Chinese. One afternoon, later, I tried to locate the grave but failed to find it.

While Hanoi, capital of the French colonial government, had become a French city with wide streets and imposing public buildings, the peasants lived in miserable villages which seemed to be sinking down into the earth. Liberty, Equality, and Fraternity! Colonial governments are an anachronism and bad as a system, for the governors are there for exploitation and not interested in the welfare of the governed, which is contrary to modern theory of government.

Here I wish to make one exception: the colonial government of the Philippine Islands. The Americans had an ideal—to raise the people to a higher level of civilization. The American colonial government in the Philippines established a system of public schools not inferior to American schools. I went to the Philippines in 1931. Everywhere I saw schools in which history, literature, science, and democratic ideals were taught. The United States endeavored to make the Philippine Islands a republic in the image of her own.

Britain had to depend on her colonies for her national existence; France had to be fed with riches from her colonies. Each was interested in the welfare of the governed peoples only in the sense that the geese should be kept alive to lay more golden eggs. In Korea and Formosa Japan was pressing the geese flat in order to squeeze the eggs out of them. Before the war Japan had amassed a great fortune from trade with China. But she was not satisfied; she wanted to make China a vast colony so as to be completely free to squeeze that giant goose.

The British way of keeping the geese alive was rather ingenious. They controlled the key industries and let the natives live on what was left. Let the geese feed on the corn and fish they can catch in the pond. So the geese were happy with their corn and small fish and the owners were happy with their golden eggs. The British never interfered with the customs, manners, superstitions, or beliefs of the governed peoples, and the natives could enjoy their life undisturbed except in matters affecting public health. For public health concerns alike both governors and the governed; you cannot segregate contagious disease or pestilence. Roads, too, were built and maintained, for peace and order and commerce depend upon good roads.

Defense was built up only to the extent required to put down rebellions within the colony; to defend it against attacks from some other Power was left to the prestige of the British Empire, and when that prestige weakened the colony was at the mercy of a powerful neighbor. This was how Hong Kong and Burma were temporarily lost, and this was why Britain was so jealous for her prestige, especially in the Far East.

Burma borders on the southwest corner of Yunnan. I went there as leader of a goodwill mission just about a year before Pearl Harbor. The British way of governing colonies was clearly evident. I saw the oil refineries, lumber mills, and rice mills—these were key industries and were under British control. Other things were left to the Burmese. Sacred cows roamed the streets in Rangoon without interference from the police. Here, there, and everywhere were temples with their gilt pagodas and monks respected by both the governors and the governed. The Burmese enjoyed an undisturbed life under British rule; the geese, swimming in their pond, were satisfied with their fish and corn, and as far as I could see showed no sign of unrest. And the owners got their golden eggs.

But the light that shone brilliantly in the homeland of the governors could not be altogether smothered in the colonies. In India Gandhi went unmolested except for imprisonment in times of crisis. Such instances would be dealt with underhandedly in the colonies of certain other European nations. But Great Britain, that land of liberty, could not help shedding some of her light through the clouds of a colonial sky. There are signs that Britain is on the road to a more enlightened policy toward her colonies. I hope that these streaks of light will be broadened to strong beams of liberty, illuminating the peoples she is entrusted to lead. British friends, give them more of that light which you have so plentifully in the British Isles. Chuck overboard the anachronisms!

As far as types of civilization are concerned, the former kingdom of Annam, now a part of Indo-China, is Chinese, while Burma is Indian. The palace of the former king of Burma at Mandalay is Indian in architectural design. The names of the cities and towns bear no trace of Chinese origin. The Annamites, like the Chinese, eat with chopsticks; the Burmese, like the Indians, with their fingers. Yet both Annam and Burma, as we have seen earlier, were formerly tributaries of China, and their loss was part of her awakening.

When Burma fell to British hands the royal family escaped into Yunnan and is supported by the provincial government down to this day, although its title is only nominal now. Its children and grandchildren entered Chinese schools and became Chinese. But they are known to the people of Tengtsung in Yunnan as descendants of the Burmese royal family, whose ancestors once reigned over the kingdom of golden pagodas and yellow-robed monks from their peacock throne in the royal palace at Mandalay. ◉

Chapter 30
The Migration of Universities

The migration of universities from the coastal provinces where Chinese institutions of higher learning were originally centered to the hinterland of China was a direct sequel to the outbreak of war. Besides the three I have mentioned, other institutions located nearest to the scene of war and likely to be first affected moved gradually toward the interior. As a result there were toward the end of the war some twenty universities and colleges, with a total enrollment of about sixteen thousand students, boys and girls, newly established in Free China.

These institutions were scattered all over the interior provinces. They were housed either in temples or in the buildings of local schools. Some were able to rent private mansions when no public buildings were available. Still others had to put up temporary shacks. All brought with them such scientific apparatus and books as conditions permitted. The amount was of course negligible, yet even this scanty equipment was not infrequently ruined by the deliberate and merciless bombing of the enemy.

A large number of the students were from the occupied areas. Their support from their parents was naturally cut off; some even lost track of their families in the war zones. It may be noted, also, that some parents in the occupied areas deemed it wise, when questioned, to report as dead sons who were actually studying in Free China. The national government in Chungking consequently allotted large sums of money to care for these helpless students.

As the Japanese invasion began in north China the universities first affected were naturally those located in the areas of Tientsin and Peiping. When the two cities were occupied many students and faculty members, realizing the futility of expecting to have any spiritual freedom at the point of the invader's bayonet, went south or elsewhere to join their universities. Two combined universities were established by order of the national government then at Nanking: one at Changsha as I have related, and the other at Sian in the northwest. The Northwestern Union University consisted of two former national universities and two colleges. It was later moved from Sian to Hanchung and has since been broken up into more or less its original components.

As the war spread to other parts of China, universities which had hitherto been able to remain where they were had now to follow our example. Thus the National Central University was moved from the former capital to the war capital of Chungking; Chekiang University was moved from Hangchow to the interior province of Kweichow; Chungshan University was moved from Canton in south China to Yunnan in the southwest.

I shall describe in some detail the former Union University in Changsha: how it was organized—or associated, to use a better term—and later transplanted from Changsha to Kunming. The story may serve as an example of the handling of other migrating universities.

As I have already related, the Union University at Changsha was formed by the association of three former Peiping and Tientsin universities by order of the Ministry of Education, then at Nanking. They were the National University of Peking, the oldest and the first government-sponsored modern university in China; the National Tsinghua University; and Nankai University at Tientsin. The presidents of these three institutions were made members of the presidium. All their faculty members and students were turned over to the Union University. Classes were resumed at Changsha by November 1, 1937, with an enrollment of approximately 1,250 students from the three universities, and an additional 220 students from other institutions which had also been moved. The latter were admitted as visiting students. The university was in fairly good shape, though equipment and facilities were meager. The spirit among the professors and students was excellent; the reading rooms were, for the most part, packed with students despite the handful of books available. But early in 1938—that is, after the fall of Nanking—things changed. Japanese planes made Changsha one of their bombing objectives. A prolonged stay in the city was perilous, so with the approval of the government, after the completion of a semester's work the Union University moved, at the end of February, 1938, southwest to Kunming.

The migration from Changsha to Kunming was made in two groups: some three hundred male students with a few professors constituted themselves a walking party, hiking from Changsha in Hunan through the mountainous province of Kweichow all the way to the remote city of Kunming in Yunnan—a trek of 3,500 li, or approximately 1,160 miles, accomplished over a period of two months and ten days. The others, numbering about eight hundred, rode from Changsha to Canton on the much-bombed Canton-Hankow Railway, thence by boat to the British colony of Hong Kong, and again by boat to Haiphong. From here they traveled by the French Indo-China Railway to Kunming, their final destination. The rail-boat and boat-rail trip required from ten to fourteen days, depending upon connections. Over three hundred and fifty students remained in Changsha to join the various war organizations.

After its removal to Kunming the title "Union University" was changed to the present name: National Southwest Associated University. As Kunming had no immediately available and suitable buildings to put at the disposal of the newcomers, the university—called "Lienta" from the abbreviation of its Chinese name—decided to locate its College of Arts and College of Law and Commerce at Mengtsz, probably the second largest city in the province, and keep the College of Science and Engineering in Kunming. When classes began in early May, 1938, there were around thirteen hundred students in the total enrollment for these four colleges of Lienta. In September of the same year the two colleges at Mengtsz moved back to Kunming, where the housing problem had become less acute as all the local middle schools had by then been moved to the country and their school buildings could be rented. The "happy-double-union" was celebrated by the founding of a teachers' college by order of the national government at Chungking. Enrollment in the five colleges, comprising twenty-six departments, increased to two thousand.

In September, 1939, Lienta again grew in size. There were by now over three thousand students. The university was fortunate, as its hundred shacks, built in the past ten months, could then be used to accommodate the growing student body. At the close of the war we had about five hundred professors, assistants, and administrative officers and three thousand students. Most of the latter came from the occupied areas and had to cross more than one firing line to reach the free zone; they went through much hardship and suffering, and others lost their lives before they could reach Free China.

My son, a student in Chiao-tung University in Shanghai, on his way to join me at Kunming met with several incidents. Once, on a dark night, with a number of friends he tried to go by small boat under a bridge guarded by the enemy and was shot at. On another occasion the party traveling ahead of his lost one of its members, who was arrested by the enemy and his head was later found by his friends dangling from a tree.

The son of a friend of mine came from Peiping to Kunming, traversing many firing lines in the north, and was shot at by the enemy several times. Often he had nothing to eat during the day and had to walk miles under cover of night. He had left Peiping with his brother, who was arrested by the Japanese guard at the station and sent to a detention camp because something was found in his pocket which identified him as a student. They had disguised themselves as apprentices of a shop. When the identity of such a person was established it was a serious offense.

It was reported that the basement of the College of Literature in the University of Peking had been turned into a dungeon in which terror reigned. I had no way to verify actual conditions there, but later met a former student of mine who had been arrested and imprisoned for two years before he managed to leave Peiping for Free China. He said that he was sent there for a "treat." The place was a living hell. Water was forced into his nose until he lost consciousness. When he came to, a Japanese gendarme by the name of Uyemura told him that he deserved the treatment because his alma mater was responsible for this terrible war in which Japan had suffered so much. "No pity!" said Uyemura in a rage. "Let the punishment fit the crime!" Three times he was thus "treated," fainting each time. In that dungeon he saw other tortures which do not befit my pen to describe. The shrieks of the girls and the groans of the boys turned that seat of learning into an inferno where Satan had his day.

While the students left in Peiping moaned under torture, the university in Kunming was blasted by enemy bombs. The bombing was done deliberately, since the seat of the university was outside the city wall with no military objective near by. Many buildings were destroyed, including the stacks of the main university library and some of the science laboratories. About one third of the university buildings were rendered useless and had to be rebuilt as fast as possible. Despite all this, the spirit of the students was wonderful. As a rule they studied hard in these trying circumstances, with meager food and poor living conditions.

This migration of institutions of learning from the seacoast to the interior has an important bearing on the future development of China's hinterland. The presence of a large number of intellectuals in various localities in the interior will exercise a strong influence upon the mental outlook of people in those localities. Moreover, students as well as teachers who have lived for a long time along the coast with only a local knowledge of the country have now had an opportunity to learn actual conditions in the interior, which has given them a better perspective on conditions in the vast country as a whole.

The migration of universities, combined with the removal of industries, both government and private, and of skilled laborers, engineers, experts, and managers, was indeed epoch-making. In the postwar period ahead of us the development of China in regions far from the coast, hitherto inaccessible to Western influence, will have a better chance than ever before. ●

Chapter 31
At the Terminal City of the Burma Road

With the migration of the universities, I came to stay for the duration of the war at Kunming, terminal city on the Burma Road. Before Pearl Harbor I made one visit to Burma and many to Indo-China and Hong Kong; all were connected with Kunming by air. After the capitulation of France, Indo-China was given over to Japan virtually without a fight. So we built the Burma Road to connect the city with Rangoon. After Pearl Harbor Burma, too, was lost to the enemy. Land communications with Haiphong in Indo-China and Rangoon in Burma were cut. Kunming was now bottled up. Lend-Lease ammunition ceased to flow into the city except by air over the "hump" of the Himalayas which separates China from the land of Buddha.

In the last few years I have visited Chungking by air many times and once also Chengtu, capital of Szechuan Province. The hilly wartime national capital of China is situated on the banks of the Yangtze River within the Yangtze gorges. The city is built on hills. Its narrow strip of land is girdled by the Yangtze on the south and the Kialing River on the north, the two rivers merging into the greater Yangtze at the easternmost point of the narrow strip. Thus Chungking looks like a tiny peninsula. Most of the houses are built upon terraces, and dugouts were made at their back doors or under the buildings through the granite hills. For several years Japanese planes rained explosives on the defenseless city day after day, night after night, month after month. But the capital remained undaunted. Buildings were hit and destroyed and rebuilt by tens of thousands, yet comparatively few lives were lost. The enemy tried to bomb the wartime government out of its capital, but the city still stands like the pyramids, which have endured their many centuries of hardship and will stand many centuries more. Chungking embodies to perfection the spirit of stubborn resistance against the Japanese invaders.

To the west of the hilly capital, about half an hour distant by air, is the flat city of Chengtu. This walled city is as spacious as Peking. The streets are wide. The atmosphere is also somewhat like that of the former capital. The irrigation system at Kwan Hsien, established some twenty centuries ago, waters over a million acres of fertile land in the Chengtu Valley. Serious flood or drought are almost unknown. This immense, rich valley kept the people in Chungking and the army stationed in the province and adjacent districts amply fed.

When we moved our university to Kunming we had in mind the possibility of importing books and scientific instruments from Europe and America through Indo-China. But after the fall of Canton the main line for the supply of munitions was cut and shipments were diverted to the Indo-China- Yunnan route. The congestion on the railway precluded the shipment of nonmilitary cargoes. Only a small fraction of our shipments was allowed to trickle in.

Meanwhile all the cities along the Yangtze River fell one after another into the hands of the enemy, up to I-chang, not far from the Yangtze gorges. Finally that too failed to stem the tide of advancing enemy might and went under the heel of the invader.

Kunming felt the pinch of every adversity of war. What most affected the daily life of the people was the rising cost of living. When we came there, in the second year of war, rice per Chinese bushel (eighty kilograms) cost $6 in Chinese currency. When it had increased by degrees to $40 a bushel one of our professors of economics predicted that after a few months it would rise to $70. People laughed at him. But it did go to $70. The capitulation of Indo- China and the loss of Burma both severely affected the price of commodities.

The first noticeable rise in prices came after the first bombing of the city by enemy planes. The country people were afraid to come in, and fewer vegetables and meats were brought to market. The shopkeepers worried over the safety of their goods and raised prices to cover their possible loss. The embargo on certain imported goods also affected the prices of similar or allied home products. Thus the embargo on kerosene raised the prices of vegetable oils. The rise in price of vegetable oils carried with it an increasing price for lard. When lard went up, pork followed suit. One thing thus led to another. The upward run of prices naturally gave rise to a host of hoarders. Hoarding in turn aggravated the price situation. When the swing of the pendulum went higher on one side, momentum brought it high again on the other.

The thing to have done, of course, was to control prices by controlling commodities from the very beginning of the war; not try to regulate prices after it was too late. I was told by a British friend that British farmers made a good deal of profit out of the First World War, but that farm products were controlled at the beginning of this war. Since this was the first modern war on a large scale in China, she had no past experience of such problems.

The climate of Kunming is really ideal. Situated in the semitropical zone at an altitude of six thousand feet, the city is something like a great summer resort. But because of its size the inhabitants do not think of it as such. It is perpetual spring. The rainy season falls in summer, when, frequent showers cool off the summer days. During the other seasons most of the days are filled with smiling sunshine cast upon the luxuriant growth in the fields from a cloudless blue sky.

Flowers abound in that climate and fruits are plentiful. Melons, eggplant, and citrons grow to enormous sizes. People do not have to work hard to make a living; they enjoy a complacent life and take things in leisurely fashion. Newcomers from the coastal provinces were at first exasperated by the slowness of the inhabitants, but they themselves gradually melted into that sea of tranquility.

The people of Kunming were quite concerned about the flow of thousands of refugees into the city from the coast. Many brought large sums of money and spent it freely. The local people blamed them for the increasing cost of living. The city was crowded with fashionable young ladies and well-dressed folk from the coast. In the evenings they rubbed shoulders with native citizens on the sidewalks of the main streets of Kunming. House rents rose fast. Hotels were all filled to capacity; on arrival people often found no place to stay. New houses shot up like mushrooms. Old houses destroyed by bombs were rapidly restored. Yet the population grew faster than houses could be built to accommodate it.

Within the few years of the war Kunming was transformed. The old tranquil scene was filled with truck drivers, war profiteers, contractors, engineers, and manufacturers. Munitions trucks shuttled through the outskirts of the city.

The natural and historic surroundings, however, remained unchanged. Kunming Lake, which flows into the Yangtze and over two thousand miles into the Yellow Sea, remained as placid as before. Fish and duck enjoyed their watery life as in days of old. Historic temples with quaint trees around them perched on the hills overlooking the wide span of the rippling lake. The Buddhist monks chanted their prayers as others had done centuries ago. Looking over the lake to the horizon I often wondered: If a sealed bottle with letters in it were thrown into the water, might it not be carried by the outgoing current down the Yangtze, passing through Chungking, I-chang, Hankow, Kiu-kiang, Anking, and Nanking to the sea near Shanghai? And perhaps some fisherman might pick it up and forward it to my native land of Chekiang. It was, of course, only the dream of an exile thinking of home.

A network of aqueducts, built between two parallel embankments protected by age-old spruces, conducts water to irrigate tens of thousands of acres of fertile land. The embankments are wide enough to run a horse on; one could trot leisurely along this endless trail for miles in the forest of scent-laden spruce, traversing the luxuriant fields.

In the city a stone tablet marking the spot where the last refugee emperor of the Mings was strangled to death looks tragically down the slope at the passers-by. The much-to-be-pitied emperor fled to Burma, but was taken back to China by General Wu San-kwei, the one who later, while defending the Great Wall against the Manchus, was to go over to the enemy in order to save his lady from the bandit leader. In his campaign against his own people in south China he came to Yunnan, where the captive emperor was brought before him.

"What do you have to say?" asked the general, as the story has it.

"Nothing," replied the last emperor of the Mings. "The only thing I want to know is, why did you rebel against my forefathers, from whom you received so much favor and so many honors?"

Wu San-kwei trembled at these words and ordered the captive emperor strangled at the spot where the stone tablet now stands. It reads: "Here died Emperor Yung-li of the Ming Dynasty for his country."

About ten kilometers from the city is the Black Dragon Pool. Spring water, crystal clear, oozes out from the bottom and overflows into tiny streams. Around it are temples and gigantic moss-grown trees. A scholar and his family lived here toward the end of the Ming Dynasty. When news of the emperor's death and the consequent downfall of the dynasty reached him, he plunged into the pool and committed suicide. His family and servants followed suit. The whole family died for their country by suicide and were all buried there. This is difficult for the Western mind to understand, but Chinese philosophy holds that if you cannot do anything else to save your country, death is the only way to redeem the debt of your conscience. By this philosophy the Chinese soldiers laid down their lives during this war willingly by hundreds of thousands in a battle often of simple flesh and blood against the enemy's steel and fire.

Our more or less chronological story is here ended for the time being. The following chapters will discuss some of the problems of Chinese civilization and culture, past, present, and future, and some of the persistent national problems that will present themselves in China in years to come.

From Hong Kong in 1842 to Pearl Harbor in 1941 is a period of exactly one century; to tell the story of that period this volume has been written. England was instrumental in blasting China's southern gates open to world commerce. With the flow of opium and Western manufactures came the seeds of Western thought and science, which affected China's view toward life and the universe. She resisted, struggled, and finally absorbed Western culture, as she did Indian culture centuries and centuries before. England was the instrument of Fate that brought China into the community of the world.

The course China took was rather roundabout, like the winding of the Yangtze River. But in direction she remained unchanged—like the Yangtze which moves down over its course of more than two thousand miles to color the Yellow Sea, in spite of its many windings. It flows day and night, month after month, year after year, and will flow in the same way for endless centuries to come. The invincible Yangtze is the symbol of China's national life and culture. ●

PART VII

CHINA IN THE MODERN WORLD

Chapter 32
China and Japan—a Comparison

Before the coming of Admiral Perry Japan was an offshoot of Chinese civilization, pure and simple. After that time she became a blend of offshoots of both Chinese and Western civilizations. Unless one understands both China and the West he is not in a position to understand Japan.

Yet there is something more. Offshoots may be similar to their main roots, but they are not identical. To render judgment upon things similar as if they were the same may lead miles away from the truth. Moreover, the blending of two civilizations may change the character of the contributing originals.

The offshoots of Chinese civilization in Japan were of the Tang era (618-905). While many of the precious elements of Tang culture had been worn away in China through centuries of barbaric invasion, they were preserved in Japan. Dancing, music, the arts, ways of living, the pronunciation of Chinese words and China's martial spirit, all of Tang origin, found living embodiment in the Island Empire of the Rising—or hereafter the Setting—Sun. If you want to know something about the Tang civilization, go to Japan. Upon a foundation of Tang culture Japan made herself great by the absorption of Western science.

However, an offshoot is but an offshoot; it has to receive nourishment from the roots of the mother tree. As soon as the mother tree in China withered, the offshoot had to depend for nourishment on the local soil of Japan. Now, Japan had every nourishment in her soil to nurse the Tang offshoots to grow, save one—originality. In this respect she failed miserably, and for lack of this one element Japan remained a dwarf tree.

After Perry's arrival she began to tap the flow of Western civilization to fertilize her land. The tree did shoot up heavenward after receiving new nourishment from this source. But again she failed in respect of that most valuable element of Western civilization—originality.

She copied. She copied the Tangs in her civilization. She copied England in building up her navy. She copied Germany in training her army. She copied

America in developing her industry. She copied the nineteenth-century Western anachronism of building a colonial empire—a bit too late. She copied Germany's blitzkrieg by hitting at Pearl Harbor—a bit too far. Japan is a wonderful copy which is almost as good as the original but falls short in reproducing the spirit behind it, something rather elusive. Her copybook is closed now, I hope, forever. She grew on copying, became strong on copying, and I hope will not commit hara-kiri on copying.

I admire Japan for her genius of exact aping—something China was unable to do, for she was too clumsy for that. But China made up for it by the possession of originality. She created and created until her energy was sapped by centuries of barbarian invasion, famine, and disease after the downfall of the Tangs.

In parallel fashion, America is an offshoot of European civilization. But here the case is different, for the early colonist from England brought with him the seeds of a love of freedom, which is an expression of originality in ideas. So America created and created till she became the most highly industrialized nation in the world: the most materialistic and at the same time the most idealistic and humanitarian. In the combination of these great opposing elements into one unity lies the greatness of America.

The martial spirit of Japan, of which the Japanese are very proud, is embodied in Bushido, the way of chivalry, which she incorporates into what she calls vaguely Yamato, the "spirit of Japan." Bushido as revealed in peace is an intense loyalty to one's country; in war it means to fight to the last man. Japan has forgotten that what she calls Bushido is nothing more than the martial spirit of ancient China. The very word shows the Tang origin. The modern Chinese pronunciation is Wu-shi-tao—in Cantonese, Mu-shi-do, very similar to Tang pronunciation, whence the Japanese Bu-shi-do.

With strict discipline and efficient organization, and with a thorough application of modern science, Bushido became a mighty weapon of war with which Japan won victory in the Sino-Japanese and Russo-Japanese Wars and ultimately hoped to conquer China and the world. Out of it grew a will to power; upon this foundation she built up a military empire which recognized nothing but power.

The secret of the phenomenal success of Japan in world power lies in reforms along Western lines made by hereditary ruling classes nurtured in the martial spirit, with a strong aptitude for copying and an intense loyalty to leaders and to their native land. They had at hand a people whose supreme virtue is to follow their leaders and obey orders. So the reforms of Japan since the beginning of the Meiji period have moved in a constant and unchanging direction.

Reforms in China, on the other hand, have to start from the bottom. There have been no hereditary ruling classes, no aristocracy but the aristocracy of learning. The vast country has to be whipped into unity of purpose by learned leaders from among the common people. Thus the process is necessarily slow and follows a zigzag way. Political leaders such as Sun Yat-sen and intellectual leaders such as Chang Pin-ling, Liang Chi-chao, and Tsai Yuan-pei have all been scholarly men drawn from ordinary backgrounds. From the common people they came and to the common people they went with their great gifts of social and intellectual vision.

Modern Japan has been built up by ruling classes, modern China by the common people. It is therefore much easier to be a leader in Japan, where a leader dictates to the people; in China he has to educate and really lead them—a much more difficult art, which requires a good deal of resourcefulness and originality.

China was comparatively slow in making reforms, but once she made up her mind to it she always tried to find their deeper meaning. In the course of the last hundred years, as we have seen, she began by making cannon balls, from which she was led to political reforms, thence to social reforms and to the introduction of ideas from the West. She wanted to strike at the core of everything. She penetrated deeper and deeper to the heart of Western civilization. She recast her old beliefs and constructed new ones until they became part and parcel of her life. She is a scholar, a moral philosopher, an artist. Her civilization and culture have grown out of her life and she could not be satisfied with Western ideas until they were thoroughly assimilated into that life. In contrast to Japan, therefore, China's thought is modern but her social and industrial structure still lags behind. This is something inherent in the philosopher, the dreamer.

China is broad-minded and democratic and possesses originality but she lacks organization, discipline, and the martial spirit. She is a country of scholars, where learning is most honored and culture most treasured. Yet the military might to defend herself within her own boundaries is something that China has yet to achieve. In China's strong points her weaknesses lie.

So it is with Japan. The Japanese is a warrior and an efficient administrator. The adopted Western civilization has been but a military superstructure which made Japan a militarily potent nation but did not touch the deeper life and thought of the people. While her structure is modern, her spirit and ideas are medieval.

This should not surprise the reader, since the feudal system actually existed in Japan until only yesterday—the beginning of the Meiji period. Its abolition took place almost simultaneously with the introduction of Western civilization, while China abolished feudalism before the Christian era.

By elevating the martial spirit to the highest plane which it is possible to maintain by strict discipline, Japan has sacrificed the creative spirit which, in the long run, is the heart of a culture and the sure foundation of a nation. The creative spirit is something one cannot ape. The more one relies on imitation, the more one is apt to lose his creativeness. The more strict the discipline for war required of a people, the more that people will lose the creative spirit.

In the assimilation of Chinese culture, as with the Western, Japan was only partially successful. For example, of the two important moral precepts which are the guiding principles of life in China—loyalty and considerateness—Japan learned loyalty, an indispensable virtue in a feudal state or a militaristic nation, but failed to understand considerateness, which is the virtue of the scholar. She stuck to her own ideas stubbornly or faithfully but refused to consider other people's viewpoints. The narrow-mindedness of the Japanese, of which even they themselves are conscious, deprived them of the leadership necessary for a continental colonial empire. They had ambition and military might but no statesmanship. The Japanese see things very clearly within certain limits but are blind to major cultural movements of the world. They are bigoted, intolerant, and inflexible under the cover of extreme courtesy.

On the other hand, the two virtues went hand in hand in China. She is faithful and at the same time considerate. China does not feel that faithfulness to her own ideas precludes the existence of other points of view. She always tries to imagine herself in the position of others. That is considerateness, of which Japan was not capable. So she failed to understand China.

Japan has acted like a strong little boy who tries to take a ram by the horns. It snorts, jumps, arches its back, and butts at him until he is forced to let go or is laid flat on his back. Then he wonders why the creature should act that way. Poor boy! Think what you would do if someone took you by the ear try to see yourself in another's position—and you will understand China.

Another important factor that has made the Japanese a war-loving race is the belief that Japan is a divine country, born of gods and living and conquering by divine will. This is not easily understood either by the West or by the Chinese. But it is a fact that the Japanese believe it reverently. The Chinese believe in gods, but they take them as the guardians of morals, not of war. For the Chinese the gods have nothing to do with the rise or downfall of an empire. But to the Japanese the rise of Japan was the will of the gods.

From time immemorial the ruling classes of Japan have believed that in war the gods are always on the side of Dai Nippon. When the Yuans or Mongols failed to conquer her, they thought the gods had protected her with their divine power. The typhoon that destroyed Kublai Khan's Mongol fleet was an act of the gods. The reigning dynasty of the Mikado, the Japanese have believed up to now, is of divine origin and its emperors the direct descendants of gods.

A Chinese graduate of Tokyo Imperial University, later a professor in a Chinese university, has done an illuminating piece of historical research to show how Japanese imperialism grew out of this religious-patriotic fervor. Expressions of it in the everyday life of the soldier are not lacking. During the war Japanese soldiers almost all carried Buddhist or Shinto charms for protection in battle. I saw many such charms brought back from battlegrounds by Chinese soldiers, who finally came to regard them as an indispensable part of enemy military equipment and paid no more attention to them, except to joke about them occasionally.

After one battle between the American Air Force and the Japanese invaders I acted as guide to a party of American officers and soldiers who drove in jeeps over miles of rugged mountain paths to a crashed Japanese bomber. In the pockets and on the bodies of the dead pilots we found the usual Buddhist and Shinto charms; smeared with blood and riddled with bullets. An American captain pulled a cloth charm from the dead pilot and asked me what it was. I told him.

"What's the use of it?" asked the captain.

"For divine protection," I replied.

"No protection, though—" he turned over the cloth and tried to make out the indecipherable signs on it, "—you get me?" And he threw it on the ground casually and forgot about it. Like this American officer, the Chinese had come to dismiss lightly these tokens of invulnerability. So it is with the world.

On the day of that aerial battle I saw seven enemy bombers spinning down from the skies in white smoke. The other search parties brought back from the wrecked planes many similar talismans, besides cartridges, maps, and scientific charts. A curious combination of medieval superstition with modern science. But to the Japanese it is no superstition; there is a living divine force which spurs them on to fight for their country, protected by the gods. The charms are but the symbol of that divine power.

After the fall of Hong Kong a Chinese couple—a Mr. and Mrs. Huang whom I know well and who understand the psychology of the Japanese—presented an image of Buddha to a Japanese soldier who entered their house. Crossing the harbor to Kowloon the little boat he took capsized and all on board were drowned but himself. He came back to them to express his gratitude, for he believed that the image had saved his life. But to the Chinese way of thinking the image had protected the couple from being molested by the enemy, while the escape from drowning was mere luck.

The world does not know much about Japanese religious fanaticism in war because the Japanese themselves have not said much about it in their propaganda. While in China modern science has sapped the old beliefs and is a disintegrating factor in relation to them, in Japan it became merely a powerful weapon of the gods to weld the country together in a war of aggression. This psychological background of intense religious patriotism has made the Japanese warlords unamenable to reason, the Japanese soldier a hard nut to crack, and Japan herself a menace to the world; such is the result of fanaticism combined with modern science.

To have such a fanatical neighbor would be a headache to any country. And Japan has been much more than a headache to China during the last fifty long, troubled years. Only utter defeat and unconditional surrender could make Japan come to her senses. The inevitable fate awaited her, and we must now hope that it will have its bitter but salutary consequence.

When the gods of the Allied nations have fulfilled their mission, Japan—as I can imagine—may be a picturesque and peaceful country, with enchanting mountain scenery, pretty gardens wreathed in sakura blossoms, attractive pavilions with ladies in beautiful kimonos; and an industrious, courteous, and docile people, in whose ears will ring no voices of gods urging them onward to war and to conquest.

Then, and not until then, will peace reign in Japan, in China, in the Far East, and in the world. •

Chapter 33
Characteristics of Chinese Culture

East and West are different because their cultures are different. Yet you will find similarities in both. These parallels, no matter how close, will not make two cultures alike; the peculiar characteristics of each still render one different from the other. In the West varying culture traits make the Germans different from the English and the French from the Dutch. Yet there are characteristics common to all—common ties which hold the Western nations together culturally under the loose name of "Western culture." These again differ from the Eastern nations. Similarities or contrasts of culture, therefore, are not to be judged by outward parallels but by the fundamental character of each.

In this chapter we will examine the characteristics of Chinese culture under three headings: (1) the absorbing power of Chinese civilization, (2) morals and intellect, and (3) the practical wisdom of the Chinese people.

1. The Absorbing Power of Chinese Civilization

Some forty years ago, when I was still in school, we were constantly told by foreigners and progressive Chinese alike that China was like a solid rock which absorbs little or nothing. That is to say, Chinese civilization was stagnant and petrified and China was incurably conservative. She loved and lived by her own ways. Nothing could effect a change in John the Chinaman.

This appeared to be all right but proved all wrong. From the opening of the treaty ports until after the Sino-Japanese War in 1894 China appeared to resist Western influence. However, during previous centuries she had absorbed many of the outlandish things which from time to time made inroads upon her life.

In music, the so-called "national" Chinese music of the present day is played on instruments mostly of foreign origin. Forms of the fiddle, flute, and harp were introduced from Turkestan centuries ago. We also kept the ancient Chinese harp, but only a few understand its music and still fewer can play it.

Various foods have been introduced to the Chinese dinner table from foreign lands: watermelons, cucumbers, grapes, and peppers came hundreds of years ago; sweet potatoes, peanuts, and Indian corn have appeared in recent centuries. In late decades the Irish potato, tomato, cauliflower, cabbage, and lettuce have found their way into Chinese cooking. Tenderloin steaks of the West, chopped very fine and served with bean sauce, have kept delightful company with Chinese dishes. Tomato soup with tender shrimp meat and hot fried rice hissing euphoniously in it was an innovation. Dinner in China is sometimes topped off with ice cream, American coffee, and Sunkist oranges, together with fruits of native production. Oranges grew originally in Chinese soil, traveled to America, received their education in the Luther Burbank school of California, and returned to their native land with a new title—something like the B.A. or Ph.D. brought back by Chinese students from American universities. Chinese oranges also went to Germany many, many years ago, where they turned into apples—for the Germans called orange apfelsine, Chinese apple.

Spiritual or intellectual nourishment from any quarter that was worth the trouble of absorbing China was always ready to welcome. During the Ming Dynasty the Jesuits brought to China astronomy, mathematics, and the Bible. An Imperial minister was converted and his residence in the Siccawei district of Shanghai was made a center of Catholic activities. From the Jesuits the Chinese learned Western astronomy and some became Christians because of it. The Siccawei Observatory has been a guiding star for shipping along that coast ever since the opening of the treaty ports.

Huang Chung-hsi, a great Ming scholar living during the end of the Ming and the beginning of the Ching (Manchu) Dynasty, was one of the admirers of Western astronomy brought by the Jesuits. He said: "Learning has been preserved in foreign lands while China has lost it owing to the lack of proper care." He once told a friend that "so far as astronomy is concerned, we are only babies in comparison with the Western scholar." Which shows how open-minded great Chinese scholars were.

The fact is that China has endured many vicissitudes of fortune in the course of her centuries because of her great capacity for absorption. No civilization in the world could sustain itself without taking in alien elements from time to time in one way or another. I think it needs no historian to prove that point. The interdependence and mutual influences of Western civilizations are so obvious as to require no argument. But the interaction of Eastern and Western civilizations is less apparent. I have been told by Professor Joseph Needham of Cambridge that the expanding properties of gunpowder influenced the discovery of steam power, and that the idea of good in human nature, of the Confucian school, influenced the Encyclopedists in France. A number of things have trickled from time to time into the West from the East. But I would like to leave it to the West to tell us.

We did not absorb more than music, foodstuffs, and things of similar nature through our western and northern frontiers by land because there was not much more to absorb. The races in those regions had little spiritual or mental food to offer. For the latter we turned to India. In the field of arts Chinese painting and architecture were influenced by Buddhism; in Chinese philosophy Buddhist thought played a very important part, and it even affected the style and vocabulary of Chinese literature.

Centuries before the Jesuits the Chinese had assimilated the moral aspects of Buddhism, but they left the system of other-worldly philosophy alone. After centuries of sojourning in China, with tens of thousands of Buddhist temples and monasteries occupying the best sites on mountains as well as in cities, its basic philosophy and religion still remain foreign to the Chinese mind. The scholars befriend or tolerate it and the common people worship it as one of the religions in China. Nevertheless it remains foreign. To the practical-minded Chinese its metaphysical system is not palatable. It exists in China because there are moral teachings in it and in time of distress one could find moral refuge in it. The Chinese only wanted to absorb foreign elements into their own system of thought, to be enriched by them; they would not surrender their own system to an alien one.

Out of their virtue of tolerance the Chinese had an ingenious way of dealing with any system they could not absorb into their own. They would take part of it and leave the rest to co-exist with the indigenous products. Thus a portion of her teeming millions would take in the imported system and become Buddhists, Mohammedans, or Christians, and all lived side by side in a good, neighborly way.

But to go back to the introduction of Western civilization during the last half century. In the matter of clothing the process of westernization in the past thirty years has been still more striking. Felt or straw hats have taken the place of old types of headgear; cut hair has banished the "Chinaman's queue" as you have seen it in old pictures. Women wear bobbed hair with permanent waves. Short skirts and silk and nylon stockings have given Chinese women a chance to show their pretty and well-developed legs. As regards their feet, they have indeed gone through a revolution. Western shoes have relieved the agelong agonies of foot-binding, with subsequent improvement in their bodily health. Healthy mothers bring forth healthy children—the effect upon the coming generation has been remarkable. Our children are not only healthier as compared with children of days gone by, but more active—quicker in movement and keener in mind.

In social affairs both sexes intermingle more freely in contrast with the old customs of segregation. In civil law marriages no longer have to be arranged by parents; young men and women have the right to find their lovers and choose their own mates. Coeducational institutions are rather the rule than the exception.

As regards dwellings the old superstition of feng-shui that affected the choice of sites for buildings has given way to modern theories of architecture. While the old artistic styles are still preserved for their beauty and grandeur in some cases, air, light, convenience, comfort, and hygienic conditions are first considerations. Flush toilets, baths, and a steam heating system are installed in modern houses. Stiff-backed chairs and hard beds have given way to sofas and spring mattresses.

Chinese food is rich in its variety because it is always ready to absorb alien elements. Western food is comparatively simple because it is, I think, not so ready to take in foreign materials. Tea was indeed introduced into Europe from China centuries ago. Spices were introduced from the East, and in search for a shorter trade route to India Columbus happened upon America. Worcestershire sauce, I am told, was developed from Chinese bean sauce. Aside from these, Western food has remained untouched by Eastern influences. Chop suey houses are found by the hundreds in America and Americans are quite fond of chop suey but know few other Chinese dishes.

On the other hand, China keeps on absorbing more and more alien elements, sometimes sensibly and at other times rather indiscriminately—not only food but clothing, shelter, ideas, social customs, and so forth. In most cases the process of absorption is through unconscious rather than conscious action. It is something like the absorption of nutriment from the soil by the roots of a tree: they absorb and cannot do otherwise. It is the nature of a growing tree to absorb, or it would cease to grow.

The introduction and absorption of alien civilization from China's western frontiers were accomplished in the course of many, many centuries, during which foreign elements came into the country only in trickles. Therefore she took them in gradually and slowly digested them. It was for the most part an unconscious process; it did not change the main course of Chinese civilization, but was something like the attraction of a magnet for iron particles. They cluster around it, but the magnet does not change its position.

Western civilization, on the other hand, came to China's eastern frontiers by sea in torrents, in all its fierceness, speed, and magnitude, and in the short span of some fifty years. To try to absorb Western civilization—with all that the French and industrial revolutions had contributed to it—was like gobbling up many days' food supply at one meal. Naturally China suffered some discomfort—not to say unbearable stomachache. Thus Western civilization at one time became so distasteful to China that she feared it, cursed, kicked the table over, and turned from it in despair, only to find more food being pressed on her. The reaction against Western civilization was a reaction against food after a stomachache through much overeating. The abortive reforms of 1898 were but a case of overeating. The Boxer Rebellion of 1900 was a violent case of acute and complicated indigestion. China was forced on the operating table, to be operated on by Western doctors—the allied armies of eight nations. For that she had a handsome bill to pay— 450,000,000 taels—and in the operation almost lost her life.

The doctrine of Chang Chi-tung that "Chinese culture is fundamental and Western civilization is supplementary" is no more than to say that a sound stomach is more important to health than the foods it is to take. So China tried to move cautiously, measuring her steps instead of lengthening them. But the tides of Western civilization would not wait for her. They lashed her eastern shores, overflowed into the rich Pearl and Yangtze Valleys, and rapidly extended to the Yellow River Valley. She had to go on taking more imported food in spite of her recent serious upset.

By 1902 the students, who had the best appetites, caught up with the spirit of the times, and revolution—against established authorities, educational, political, and moral, as well as intellectual—became the catchword of the rising generation. Burdened with a legacy of the past which seemed to them at the time no more than the dead hand of a bygone civilization, the receptive mind of youth took so enthusiastically to Western ideas as to offset the influences of tradition.

Soon after the opening of the five treaty ports, China had established arsenals, dockyards, machine shops, schools of foreign languages; had translated books on elementary sciences and sent students to study in America. Being defeated in various wars of self-defense against Western Powers, she started to build a navy. A small navy was built, indeed, only to be destroyed by Japan in 1894. Japan could not endure to have China have a navy.

Failing this, China went a step further by taking up the reform of government, army, and education. The Inertial government at Peking began to prepare for the adoption of a Western constitutional form of government; it established new systems of education, organized modern armies and police, and sent large numbers of students to study abroad. This may be regarded as the first conscious effort in history to absorb a foreign civilization on a large scale, and it had far-reaching consequences in China's national life.

The reforms in education were the most important, because they were the best planned, with most foresight, and dealt directly with the rising generation whose minds were least fettered by traditional ideas. Later, when the students of one school generation grew up and came into power, they adopted more Western ways and consequently those of the succeeding generation were in a better position to absorb more new ideas. When these came to power in their turn, they went still further in westernization and more new measures were introduced into the government, army, and schools. Thus each new generation was more modernized than the previous one.

The 1919 student movement in Peking, the emphasis upon science and modern democratic ideas by professors of the National University there, and the literary revolution sponsored by Professor Hu Shih, were the beginnings of conscious effort to absorb Western thought, hitherto limited mainly to the industrial and political spheres. This effort came nearer to the heart of Chinese culture and with it a new leaf was turned in the cultural history of China. For by this means China has been trying to catch up with the advancing tides of the world. Chinese civilization, with compass pointing to the West, has gradually shifted its course to meet the main currents of Western civilization, and in the next fifty years, while still retaining its own characteristics, it will flow in the common channels of the coming civilization of the world.

So far China has already received much benefit from westernization. The freedom of women to be on equal terms with men in social activities, to marry and remarry, and to have their feet unbound has been gained through the influence of Western respect for women. Western medicine has prevented plagues which wrought yearly havoc among the teeming millions. Painless operations have relieved the suffering of thousands of people. Machinery and inventions have improved means of production and contributed much to the enjoyment of life. And it goes without saying that modern weapons of war have also helped people to kill more, and to be killed. Modern science has widened the scope of knowledge; scientific methods have been carried into the study of Chinese history, philosophy, and literature. Above all, the old superstitions in which people used to live are giving way to the enlightenment of scientific truths. The greater our capacity to absorb Western ideas, the more our civilization will be enriched. Poverty and disease, twin curses of Chinese national life, will gradually disappear in proportion to the extent and thoroughness of China's modernization. To me, in this respect, modernization and westernization seem inseparable, if not identical, since the process of modernization began in the West and has gone forward without interruption. So China cannot get one without getting the other.

In a way, modernization has been as much imposed upon the West as westernization upon China. Wherever the spearhead of modern invention passes through, it changes the means of production, creates problems of distribution and control, and thus gives rise to new problems. Men must adjust themselves to changing conditions; the constant changes of environment and adjustments of man to them impose a progress on him. Imagine yourself looking down on Europe after the French Revolution; you would see that there had not been much visible change on the surface of that continent since the Roman Empire. But if you took another look half a century after the industrial revolution the changes would be quite noticeable. After still another half century you would find networks of railways covering the surface of all Europe and America, too, with trains crawling on them like thousands of centipedes. Here and there factories with chimneys sticking up would cluster in the large industrial centers like fantastic beehives. Steamboats carrying manufactured goods would be shuttling in and out of harbors, ready to bear the finished products of the factories to all the corners of the earth.

These same steamboats half a century ago brought to China the lucifer matches, clocks, kerosene lamps, toys, and other useful and ingenious foreign articles that I played with in childhood in that tranquil village. The innocent and unconscious absorption of these curious things was the beginning of the great change that was to bring China in line with the trend toward modernization—with all its accompanying sufferings, turmoils, and perils, and with the rapid disappearance of the pleasant, tranquil life of old China.

Heretofore the absorption of foreign elements, conscious or unconscious, had enriched the life of the people and led to no complications. With the absorption of modern Western manufactures and systems or ideas, trouble began to spring up. Like the modern sulfa drugs, they cure diseases but sometimes cause serious reactions, which may prove fatal. To absorb Western civilization with less violence of reaction is the problem China has yet to face. It calls for experiment and scientific research, which again are western products—machine tools to make all modern machinery, mental, social, or industrial.

2. Morals and Intellect

When for the first time I read the Greek philosophers in the ethics class in California I began to feel, as I have said before, that Chinese thinkers in ancient times were enclosed in an atmosphere of morals, while the Greeks possessed the quality of all-piercing intellect. As I read more books on Greek life and culture it became more clear and convincing to me that some such striking contrast did exist between ancient Chinese and Greek thought, and that among other causes this was probably the main one for the divergence in development of Eastern and Western civilizations. Perhaps this assertion will seem rather too sweeping, but as my experience grew with the years I could not see it otherwise, and I still believe it to be so.

After my return from abroad I constantly tried to drive home to the minds of my people the importance of the development of intellect. The names of Socrates, Plato, and Aristotle appeared in my lectures and writings so often that I was caricatured by tabloid papers in Shanghai as "a man with mouthfuls of Plato and Aristotle." Seeing that I was not carrying the public with me, I gave it up as a bad job and changed my tactics to preaching the study of natural science. Instead of leading people to the source of the current I reversed the process by letting them see the current first. Naturally they would go back to the sources later on.

My compatriots, children of ages of practical sense, had rebuked me for forgetting the true nature of my own people.

A prominent Chinese scientist once was asked why China has not developed natural science. He offered four reasons: First, the belief of Chinese scholars in Yin, the negative, and Yang, the positive, as complementary principles of the universe. Second, the belief in the Five Elements—metal, wood, water, fire, and earth—as the constituents of the universe, and the application of this analysis of the material world around us to human life, even to medicine. Third, the Chinese rule-of-thumb ways, which are an enemy to accurate calculations. Fourth, the aversion of scholars to using their hands or doing manual work.

All these may be obstacles to the growth of natural science; but quite aside from them I do not believe that natural science would have grown up. It could not, for our attention was not directed along that line.

My people are most interested in things practical—something useful to them. I often noticed in America that when people were shown something they were apt to say, "That's interesting." The response from my own people in like case would be, "What is the use of it?" This shows the truth of the common Chinese saying that the virtuous see virtue while the wise see wisdom in the things they come in contact with. A difference in mental attitude produces different manifestations of interest. The use of a thing interests my people more than the thing itself.

Chinese thinkers see all things in their relation to man, to moral applications, to artistic or poetic sense, or to practical use. The scientific thought of ancient Greece found its origin in Egypt and Babylon. Babylonian astronomy and Egyptian geometry, like astronomy and mathematics in China, aimed at practical applications. But the intellectual quality of the Hellenic genius was to seek the general truth in these sciences by generalizing and formulating their principles, a process which paved the way for the discovery of natural law.

For the Greeks there were two worlds: the world of the senses and the world of reason. The senses deceive us; therefore the philosopher should not trust his sense impressions but develop his reason. It was not for its practical use that Plato insisted upon the study of geometry, but in order to develop the faculty of abstraction and train the mind to correct and vigorous thinking. Applying these powers to ethics and politics, Plato laid the foundation of Western social philosophy, and by their application in studying the reality of concrete things Aristotle laid the foundation of physical science.

For Aristotle trusted reality as seen through the senses. His was a great systematizing intellect which has left its imprint on nearly every branch of knowledge. For him, to know properly involved a correct use of the senses as well as of the reason; the advance of science depends upon development of both speculation and observation. From applied mathematics Aristotle deduced certain general laws, the study and exploration of which provided a form of mental gymnastics through which he disciplined a powerful and penetrating intellect. And by means of the same well-exercised intellect and right use of the senses, he created a system of knowledge which has been the foundation of modern science. Logic and the theory of knowledge were outgrowths of these same intellectual exercises which systematized Western thought.

Chinese thought is centered upon the development of human relations. We are interested in natural laws only so far as they are capable of serving as guides for human conduct. The Great Learning, one of the Confucian classics, taught us a system of knowledge to which I have alluded in an earlier chapter. It starts with the search for truths in things, from which we gain our knowledge. Knowledge is the power by which the mind is developed.

So far the story is intellectual. But as it goes on the shading of moral sense begins to grow. Mental development is for personal culture, which in turn will serve as the foundation for a well-ordered family life. The latter is the foundation of a well-governed state, which in turn will serve a s a step toward international peace. From the rudiments of knowledge down to international peace this forms a complete scheme of practical moral idealism. To the Chinese, world peace is not something to be dreamed about but a practical moral scheme. For national prosperity is invariably bound up with peace between nations. A type of knowledge which does not lead to this end is but secondary or trifling.

For such an attitude toward learning, to ascertain whether the earth goes round the sun or the sun round the earth is but trivial.

Or again, what is the use of bothering with the expansion of water in a boiling kettle, as Watt did if we are to believe the story? The Chinese would be more interested in the hissing sound, which suggests making tea in preparation for guests. It is poetic.

The drop of an apple to the ground is only natural. The Chinese would moralize it. They would say that when a thing is ripe, it drops. When you do things in a proper way they come to their natural conclusion. There is no use in puzzling about it. Should the apples in your garden shoot up to the sky, it would set the Chinese to fearing that some great calamity might fall upon the people; as would the appearance of a comet, or some other perversion of the familiar order of things. It would take a Newton to think along the line of the attraction of the earth.

Thus with my own effort to preach. What is the use to China of those figures of Greek antiquity or their teachings? In my people's eyes natural science is useful only because practical uses come out of it. The Greek philosophers are remote even from modern natural sciences. What earthly use is there in them? The Chinese are in sympathy with the usefulness of science but recoil from the idea of science for science' sake. "Learning is for the sake of its use," is an accepted dictum among Chinese scholars.

With such a mental attitude it is small wonder that China has not developed pure science, an elaboration of intellectual interest rather than of practical considerations. We built the Great Wall and the Grand Canal and developed a system of irrigation; the grandeur of our architectural design, our palaces and temples, has inspired world-wide admiration. These works are among the greatest engineering feats the world has ever known. But they were not developed from a foundation of pure science and therefore, however remarkable they were, no further development was possible until modern engineering came to the rescue. For without pure science the applied science of modern engineering could not attain its present high plane. The discovery of the compass and gunpowder by the Chinese has served useful purposes in the world. But it was a Western mind that observed the principle of explosive expansion in gunpowder and applied it to boiling water, thus making possible the discovery of steam power.

In China discoveries stopped at their immediate practical use. We did not, like the Greeks, try to venture into generalization; nor, like modern Europeans, did we try to get universal laws from particular discoveries—a trait inherited from the Hellenic world in its improved form. Once the useful purposes of an invention were served, we stopped there; therefore Chinese science traveled unaided and without the guiding light of scientific thought. The development of science in China was arrested because we were too practical-minded.

I do not mean to say that the Chinese do not think logically. But their minds were not aided by systematic mental gymnastics. This defect has been reflected in Chinese philosophy, political and social organization, and daily life. It has become more glaring as the rest of the world came to live under the light of modern science in an industrialized society.

Besides being practical, our people are imbued with a sound moral sense. It may also be said that because we are moral we are practical. For morals refer to conduct, which is necessarily judged by practical results. There will be no such fanciful ideas or speculation about conduct as the Greeks had with physics and metaphysics.

At times we may venture beyond that practical moral way of thinking, but the antennae of our minds recoil as soon as we feel we are getting away from the sphere of human relations, and stop right there. A Sung philosopher of the twelfth century once stepped over the moral bounds by speculating on the formation of mountain ranges and on the finding of seashells on the tops of mountains. He observed that the waves of the mountain ranges indicated the fluidity of the mountains many thousands of years earlier, while the shells bore witness to the fact that their peaks must once have been at the bottom of the sea. But when and how the fluid suddenly coagulated into mountains, and how the bottom of the sea was raised to such a height, he had no means of discovering. There he stopped, fearing shipwreck if he should venture too far. There have been similar instances of observing nature both before and after this philosopher, but Chinese thinkers were always scrupulous, in their mental excursions, not to drift too far away from the camp of human relations.

That the Chinese are not a nonintellectual people needs no proof as it is so evident; but their intellect was exercised within the sphere of morals and practical uses. Thus they set limits to their own intellectual activities. Like silkworms, they wove their moral cocoons with threads drawn from their own minds, as it were, to encase themselves. And they loved their encasement and felt comfortable in it. Chinese life is a life of contentedness. Stability is aimed at in Chinese philosophy. Progress? No—it will create discontent, which will destroy stability. The Chinese is contented with his immediate world and has never wanted to speculate far and deep in nature. China has not produced natural science because she did not want it.

The Greeks were quite a different sort of people. Aristotle's mind ventured high up into the heavens, low down beneath the earth, and far away beyond the corners of the land. The universe was material for the exercise of Greek intellect. To the Greeks the mere use of the intellect was a pleasure. They did not care much about whether it was practical or had anything to do with morals or human relations. "What do I get by learning these things?" asked a pupil of Euclid. "Give him sixpence, since he must make gain out of what he learns," said Euclid to his servant, as the story runs. Even with morals they developed a system of ethics, looking into the validity of moral laws through intellectual inquiry, and this was how Socrates got into trouble, being accused of poisoning the souls of young people with dangerous questionings.

Out of Greek ideas about nature and love of intellectual exercise in systematic thinking—flowing intermittently through the Renaissance, the Reformation, and the French Revolution and receiving great impetus from the industrial revolution, through which it gradually improved its instruments and technique—natural science has grown to its modern stage. The practical considerations of science were never neglected in its later development in Europe. Frequent inventions and discoveries gave further impetus to scientific research. Scientific generalizations and applied science marched shoulder to shoulder. So the influences of pure and applied science react one upon another to their mutual benefit.

When modern science began to trickle into China after the opening of the commercial ports, it was its practical value that attracted the attention of the Chinese scholars. They built arsenals and dockyards. Incidentally they translated books on elementary science. They were not interested in whether the sun goes round the earth or vice versa; it was immaterial to them, since the alternatives had no practical consequence in their relation to man. More than a century earlier, when the Jesuits brought mathematics and astronomy to the court of the Ming emperors, scholars were interested because these sciences would mend the deficiencies then found to exist in the Chinese calendar. For the calendar is indispensable not only for reckoning days, months, and years but also for sowing and harvesting.

Around the beginning of the twentieth century the theory of evolution was brought into China. Chinese scholars at once saw the practical moral significance of it. With the application of a natural law of "struggle for existence," "natural selection," and "survival of the fittest," they came to the conclusion that nations in the world were struggling for existence, and through natural selection only the fittest would survive. Would China be the fittest and would she survive? She must struggle—struggle for existence. As to the validity of the theory, they had no particular interest and no scientific background to start an investigation, anyhow. Right away they threw a moral cushion over the intellectual undertaking of Darwin. At once they moralized it by saying, "The flesh of the weak is the food of the strong." Being a weak nation, China had to worry about her flesh. Countrymen, arise! It is your duty to your country to look out for the "cannibal" nations around us!

Another phase of the theory of evolution was taken up in its application to history. History goes round in a circle, the Chinese scholars believed. Under the influence of Darwinism they recast their old belief into a new faith that history forges ahead, or else recedes, or remains stationary. This change in the conception of history exercised a paramount influence upon the minds of Chinese scholars in regard to progress.

The conceptions of Yin and Yang and the Five Elements undoubtedly grew out of naïve observations of nature. They were good enough for rationalizing the conduct of nature and man. No minute calculations were necessary, much less the use of the hands. I presume that if Chinese scholars were interested in manual work, they would apply it to making useful or beautiful objects of art rather than to experiments in the scientific laboratory. People would still think and do only along the lines where their interests lay. The magnetic needle will only point in the direction of the magnetic pole.

Such an attitude of mind is of course no fertile soil for pure science. However, slowly but steadily China is modifying her attitude—from applied science she has been led to pure science, from pure science to new ways of thinking, and finally to actual modification of her attitude of mind. We have opened windows in the walls of our moral universe and looked into the gardens of a new intellectual universe where the fruits of science and invention abound.

This modification of mental attitude has set a new value upon nature—nature as the pure scientist sees it and not only as the moralist or poet sees it. The universe to the modern Chinese is not only a moral one as the ancient Chinese saw it but also an intellectual one as the Greeks saw it.

The moralist studies nature with a view to finding its laws for the benefit of human relations. The scientist studies it with a view to finding its natural laws for intellectual interest—knowledge for the sake of knowledge. China's absorption of modern science has penetrated through these moral bounds of her universe and the minds of the modern Chinese are reaching further and further out to search for truths. Their thinking has been becoming more adventurous, like a ship sailing in unknown seas, exploring for hidden treasures. In other aspects this intellectual release has caused the minds of the younger generation to adopt a critical attitude toward traditional ideas—make critical inquiries into morals, government, and social customs—with far- reaching consequences. While men of the older generation have been very much alarmed at the possible destruction of their tranquil moral abodes and have lamented the passing of the good old days, the younger generation has busied itself in building a new intellectual edifice.

All that, I think, is one of the most valuable contributions that the West has made to China.

Inversely, as the Greeks found with the Babylonian and Egyptian sciences, a study of Chinese sciences may yield profitable contributions to the modern scientific world. A modest beginning made in recent years in the scientific study of Chinese architecture, medicine, and economic botany has yielded fruitful results.

Civilizations are built around different systems of the universe as men conceive it. The Chinese conceived a moral universe, around which they built their civilization. The Greeks conceived an intellectual universe, around which they built theirs. European morals as they are today have been drawn from Christianity—a moral universe as revealed through God. On the other hand, the Chinese moral universe is as revealed through nature's ways. The Christians have endeavored to build a kingdom of heaven on earth, while the Chinese were content with trying to build a kingdom of peace and stability.

Chinese morals are derived from nature; Christian morals from divine power;

for the Chinese the gods are but part of nature, while to Christians nature is but the creation of God. On these grounds it is plain that the conflicts between Christian dogma and science were bound to be very serious, as Western history has proven in abundance; while the conflicts between science and Chinese moral precepts would be mild since both started from the same ground—nature—only traveling in different directions.

It has been said that Christian thought is heavenly or godly, Chinese thought is worldly, and Greek thought unworldly. It is this unworldly thought that has led men to the discovery of the natural laws which are the foundation of modern science and hence of modern invention. The unworldly thought in the applications of science has brought prosperity to the world, if not peace and stability.

The development of European civilization, as I see it, is a struggle at various times between the Christian moral universe and the Greek intellectual universe. The Renaissance, the Reformation, and the French Revolution were but the bursting out of a submerged intellectual universe under the domination of a moral one—these various movements were only different phases of the same current. Finally came the industrial revolution in which the same intellectual universe, continuously developing through centuries, came to the surface in an overwhelming torrent and swept aside everything in its way. Its spearhead had already taken China unawares before and during the time of my childhood; it pierced our moral universe, burst out later to destroy the stability of Chinese life, and thus furnished the materials for the writing of this volume.

One universe cannot be expected to produce the fruits of another. The fruits of the tree of science ripen in intellectual gardens alone—within the system of Christian dogma or that of Chinese moral precepts no science could have been produced.

Though, indeed, we find much scientific thought in Mencius in ancient times, this is a nonessential part of his philosophical system. Such thoughts are but satellites to a planet; his system is fundamentally moral.

For science grows out of man's whole being, a burning desire for unworldly truths; a fearless, ever-searching intellect with unbiased spirit continuously reaching out for truth, and an indomitable vigor of mind and body; in other words, it grows out of the very soul of man in his intellectual world. No mere side interests or occasional excursions of the mind into nature, or lukewarm desire to understand it, could ever crown man with the glorious garland of science.

In China, under the influence of modern science, there is growing up a new moral edifice stripped of superstition and false analogies to nature; tested through intellectual inquiry and supported by findings of social science based upon methods adapted from physical research to the investigation of society.

On the other hand we must not forget that the old Chinese moral edifice, built up through centuries of vicarious experience and generations of continuous effort, by such various means as the Confucian classics, literature in general, the graphic arts, music, the family, theatre, gods, temples, even toys—this moral structure has made Chinese people trustworthy, their society stable, and their civilization enduring. Such moral precepts as loyalty, honesty, love of parents, truthfulness, benevolence, righteousness, moderation, and broad-mindedness have contributed much toward the moral emotional make-up of the Chinese people. Intellectual honesty that grows out of modern science will reinforce these virtues that have grown out of ages of moral teaching.

Side by side with the new moral universe, a new intellectual edifice will be raised to house the achievements of the creative genius of young China. On the stem of the Confucian system of knowledge, which starts with the investigation of things, or nature, and leads to human relationships, we shall graft the Western system of scientific knowledge, which starts with the same investigation of things or nature but leads the other way round to their interrelationships.

As in the West, the moral universe will co-exist in China with the intellectual, one for stability and the other for progress. Can we strike the happy mean?

3. The Practical Wisdom of the Chinese People

Learning is for the sake of its use. What is this use? It comes under two main principles. First, whatever has to do with the elevation of moral sentiments in the masses and with the cultivation of right moral attitudes in the individual. Second, whatever will contribute to national prosperity and the people's livelihood. These principles are the summary of ages of teachings from the sages and scholars. Whatever they say and teach has come eventually to these. Scholars learned them and diffused their learning to the common people. The common people, under this influence, through ages of accumulated effort have gradually and unconsciously developed a mentality, as the reader will readily see, of common sense and practical wisdom. They have kept on asking what is the use of this or that in the light of these same principles.

When trains and steamboats came to China, people were ready to ride on them because they went much faster. They used kerosene oil because it gave more light. Telephone and telegraph facilities transmit messages without the necessary delay of mail or foot—or even house—messengers. Clocks and watches give exact time without looking at the sun. People bought Western manufactures because they served useful purposes in daily life.

When missionaries came they established schools and hospitals. What wonderful people they are, said the Chinese: they heal the sick and educate the children of the poor. When the Chinese assembled to listen to the preaching of the gospel, the eyes of a number of them were usually directed toward the hospitals or the schools. Through the leaves of the Holy Bible they peeped at the useful things of Western manufacture the preacher had brought to China from his homeland. My father made friends with a local missionary because he repaired our water pumps and gave us cough drops and quinine powder. He was honest and friendly in dealing with his neighbors. The last is important because the Chinese are both practical and moral. What about the religion they taught us? Oh—that is a good religion. It teaches people to be good. What about their God? Oh, yes. Their God? He is a good God. Put him in our temples beside many other good gods. We'll worship him, burn candles and incense before him. But He will not sit in your temples beside your idols. Well, we'll make an idol for him. No, that can't be done. He is omnipotent and omnipresent. God is in you, not in the idol. Yes, yes. When he is not in me, maybe he likes to be in an idol. No, He is in heaven. Yes, I know he is, as all the other gods are. Maybe he wants to take a trip down to earth and use the temples as his hotels. Then we can worship him there. No, He is the only God—when you worship Him you cannot worship other gods.

Then our people would hesitate and say, you worship yours; we will worship ours. "There it is if you believe it so; it is not there if you do not believe it." Herein lies China's wisdom of religious toleration.

Modern legal sense as the West understands it is not developed in China. Avoid the courts if you can. Let us settle our disputes without going to law. Let's compromise. Let's have a cup of tea and sip together with friends and talk things over. It is much less expensive, much less troublesome, and much fairer. What is the use of going to law? You often see stone tablets on the highways near a hsien capital bearing these bold letters: "DO NOT GO TO LAW."

This may be the reason for the nonlegal-mindedness of the Chinese. But as modern industry and commerce grow, society will grow in complexity, and laws for governing the complicated social relations will be necessary. When laws become a necessity, the practical wisdom of the Chinese will see to it that we are more legal-minded. But would it not lessen the burdens of the courts if people should settle their cases by sipping a cup of tea?

Do not do unto others what you would not have others do unto you. Critics say this is negative, while "Do unto others what you would have others do unto you" is positive. Yes, that is true. But the Chinese prefer the negative, from practical sense. You may like onions, so you try to force them upon others. That is positive. Onions may taste good to me, but others may not have the same feeling; they may fear them as ladies do rats. If you were not a lover of this obnoxious vegetable, would you like others to impose it upon you? No, of course not. Then why should you impose it upon others? It's negative, but it's more sensible. For the positive way, if you persist, will lead to trouble, while the negative way will avoid it.

Love your friend, be fair to your enemy. Of course it is a higher ideal to love your enemy. But how many in all history have ever loved their enemy? It looks like hitching your wagon to a star—it is something unattainable. It is practical idealism to be fair to your enemy. So the Chinese prefer it to pure idealism.

Is there any use in music? Yes, it is very useful. It can bring the feelings of an individual to harmony. It can raise the morals of a people to a higher level.

Is there any use in the arts? Yes, they are very useful. They will cultivate the finer sense of the people and thus raise their morals to a higher level. Landscape gardening, splendid palaces and temples, landscape painting, literature, poetry, calligraphy, porcelains, bronzes, skillful carvings, and the like all cultivate this finer sense in man.

Why must a man be honest? Because if you are dishonest and untrustworthy people will not believe and trust you. Then you will fail in business and in dealing with other people. Dishonesty simply does not pay. Not only is honesty a virtue, but its practical results are invaluable to human relations.

The Chinese love humor. Why? Because you can say things without offending people; besides, you can get a lot of innocent pleasure from it. You can get along with people better by innocent and amusing suggestions. Humor makes company more congenial and life more enjoyable.

Perseverance is one of the great virtues necessary to success. If you keep on filing and filing, you will break the steel. If you keep on grinding and grinding, you will shape the precious stone.

In the scenic Western Hills of Peking, one summer afternoon, Professor John Dewey, Dr. Hu Shih, and I watched a Sisyphus beetle pushing a tiny mud ball up the slope. It pushed first with forelegs, then with hind legs, and then with its side legs. The ball rolled up and up until some mishap occurred which set it rolling down to where it started with the diminutive Sisyphus riding on it. He repeated the process but met with the same failure. Again and again he tried. We admire his perseverance, said both Hu Shih and I. Yes, but his lack of intelligence is regrettable, said John Dewey. Thus the virtuous see virtue; the wise see wisdom. There are different aspects in the same thing. The eminent philosopher is truly a loyal son of the West, while his disciples are truly loyal sons of the East. The West pitied Mr. Sisyphus' lack of head, while the East admired his heart.

The Chinese people are contented with their lot. If a Chinese lives on a frugal diet, takes a humble house, and has enough clothes to keep warm, he feels satisfied. This attitude toward a simple way of living keeps China's millions contented and happy, but it precludes progress as the West understands it. Unless China is industrialized, she cannot lift the people to any level of material prosperity. Perhaps for years to come her countless people will have to be content with their lot.

The Chinese people are devoted to nature, not in the sense of finding the natural laws but in the sense of cultivating the poetic, artistic, or moral sense of lovers of nature. To be under pine trees steeped in the moon and listen to streams flowing gently over the rocks gives one a placid mind and a tranquil heart. To see spring flowers in bloom makes one feel the universe filled with the spirit of growth; to observe autumn leaves falling serves as a warning of the approach of declining days.

From nature the Chinese learns the sublime nature of man. In Peking there is the Altar of Heaven, built of white marble somewhat like a great theatre, but terraced upward toward the center, which is raised higher than the surrounding terraces. At this altar the emperors of the past worshiped heaven. On one clear moonlit autumn night, when the sky was blue without a speck of cloud upon it, the full moon shone directly upon my head and the marble terraces were flooded with silver light overflowing into the vast space around me. I stood at the center of the altar and all of a sudden felt as if heaven, earth, and myself merged into one vastness.

This experience of sudden sublimation made me understand why the Chinese regard heaven, earth, and man as one and inseparable. By believing in their unity the Chinese elevate man from the pettiness of daily life to the higher plane of sublime spirit. The vastness of space, the brilliance of the sun, the placidity of the moon, the multitude of stars, the luxuriant growth of plants, the rotation of the seasons, the timely rains that nourish the crops, the winding rivers that irrigate the fields, the dashing tides that reveal the power of nature, the high mountains that touch the sky—each and all furnish rich materials in cultivating man's sublime spirit. Of nature man is born; to nature man owes his life; from nature he learns his ways of good living. Nature and man are one and inseparable.

Nature is so good, so kind, so sincere, and so generous that man in his own very nature—which is but part and parcel of greater nature—must be good, kind, sincere, and generous. Here comes the belief of the Chinese that human nature is all-good. Evils grow only out of the perversion of good. This is why great Chinese teachers and statesmen always trust the good that is in man. Great statesmen like Dr. Sun Yat-sen and great teachers like Dr. Tsai Yuan-pei always take any Tom, Dick, or Harry for a good man until he proves the contrary. And they are always ready to forgive and forget. Herein lies their greatness and broad-mindedness. It is proverbial that a statesman's mind is so broad that you could row a boat in it, while a scholar's heart is as resonant as a hollow in mountain regions that echoes with every vibration of sound.

Nature is China's national teacher. Upon nature she built her moral universe, and thus her culture and civilization. Since Chinese civilization furnishes only inadequate means to control nature, she follows nature. Here lie the differences between East and West. It is the duty of the moralists and poets to follow nature; it is the duty of the scientist to control it. Under the influence of Western civilization the younger generation is changing—changing from a poetic and moral appreciation to a scientific study of nature. Hereafter China will understand nature not only through feelings and empirical observation but through the intellect and scientific research. China will know nature more intimately and control it more effectively to bring prosperity to the nation and better the livelihood of the people.

At the same time, science will not destroy the sense of beauty in nature as some people th ink it may. As I write I look out through the windows and see in the gardens the old pine trees and bamboo groves, flesh after a rain, and over the bamboo trees I see the Yangtze River gracefully winding its tranquil way past the hilly city of Chungking. The sense of the beauty of nature gives me peacefulness of mind and tranquility of heart. But if I think of the plants botanically, I see in them the growth of the cells and the circulation of the sap, which does not lessen my sense of beauty at all. If I look at the river geologically, I see through its silt-carrying waters to its bed, which millions and millions of years ago may have been just dry land or even the bottom of a rough sea. Thinking in this way, the beauty of the gentle Yangtze remains in my mind just the same or even with richer associations. That a knowledge of the working of their cells should destroy one's sense of the beauty of pine trees or bamboo groves is unthinkable. It makes me feel that nature is even more wonderful and beautiful with a scientific outlook.

From love of the beauty in nature and a feeling of her irresistible force, a strong fatalism grew up in the minds of the Chinese people. In spite of all human efforts, nature will stick to its invariable course. Thus flood and drought are beyond human power to control, and people have learned to submit to Fate. Since it is Fate, they may just as well take it good-naturedly. What is the use of making much fuss over Fate? This is why one finds many a toiler in China with a smiling face. Misery is a fate—why not take it in good humor?

Here is one secret of why the Chinese people have had so great a capacity to stand hardship and suffering during the years of war. Do your best, perform your duty, and let Fate take care of the rest. "Enjoy Nature's way and be contented with your lot." The placid autumn moon, the tender June breeze, spring blossoms, winter snows, all are in store for your enjoyment, rich and poor alike. ◉

Chapter 34
Modern Civilization

Modern civilization originated in Europe; American civilization is but its offspring. Chinese civilization, which developed from its own sources and is of a very high order, is regarded as ancient—China began to be modernized only with the influx of modern influences from Europe and America. In the last fifty years she has been going through the metamorphosis of coming up to date, with its accompanying agonies. She has been forced into the modern world step by step, by the tides of westernization, as we have seen in these pages.

"Modern civilization" is an ambiguous term. It yields various impressions. It may mean more and better weapons of war for men to massacre each other with, until it destroys them all. It may mean better means of production, to support more millions in comfort and luxury and create a higher standard of living. Or the term may be used for the science and invention that have made both modern warfare and a high standard of living possible. It may represent the mentality which searches for objective truths in order to enable man to control nature. It may refer to better communication, and better organization in mobilizing resources and wealth. It may signify democracy to the democratic countries or totalitarianism to totalitarian nations.

Part or all of these may be called modern civilization—as to what is most essential or most truly typical no two people seem to agree. Then what has China been doing during these fifty troubled years? She has trodden in the dark. Sometimes she has seemed to be walking into a trap, as a fly will, by licking the sweetness that leads it along the path of doom. At other times she seems to have been cornered by a group of armed gangsters who forced her into submission. This she resented, and afterward tried to get weapons to defend herself. All in all, she has struggled and muddled and finally began to see light in what is called Western civilization, with its good as well as evil, blessings as well as curses.

What are the goods and blessings she should try to absorb, what evils reject? Here, too, there seems to be no agreement, whether among individuals or groups.

The evils she has taken in may later prove to be laden with blessings. Thus from the evil of opium, forced upon China by superior weapons of war, she got the seeds of modern science. The goods she has adopted may prove to be accompanied by unsuspected evils. For example, by relying too much on system and organization we forgot the virtues of individual integrity and responsibility. There are cases where new systems and organizations have failed in their work for lack of due emphasis upon these qualities.

The standard of living was raised for the few who lived upon the exploitation of many. Thus automobiles were imported and used without making an effort to manufacture them. It takes thousands of farmers, each raising hundreds of bushels of rice, to produce the means of exchange for one imported car. Modern conveniences in modern towns, such as electric lights, radios, flush toilets, and other comforts, must be paid for by the sweat of millions of tillers of the land. In lifting our standard of living we are impoverishing the country by an unfavorable trade balance. Yet the standard of living must be raised, and accompanying evils must be remedied by scientific agriculture, farm machinery, and an irrigation system for increased productivity.

These again will give rise to new problems. We have suffered much from modern civilization, yet we still need more of it. If we take too much at a time we vomit it forth again violently as in the case of the Boxer uprising of 1900; if we take too little it is ineffective. This seems to be how modern civilization goes in China. Yet China must muddle along with the world, willy-nilly.

In the West, during the last hundred years, one invention has led to another, one idea to another, one step in progress to another, one prosperity to another, and one war to another. Only peace did not lead to another peace, but to war. This is how the world has forged ahead in the name of modern civilization. Must China fall in line with the rest of the world?

If there should be another war, as the world so much fears, it seems probable that it will start again, like the first World War, in eastern and middle Europe; or like the recent cataclysm, in the Chinese Three Eastern Provinces, known as Manchuria. The people of middle Europe want lebensraum elsewhere, while as to Manchuria, outside peoples want to find their lebensraum there. The former, being a densely populated area, tends to spill its troubles, while the latter—a vast vacuum—sucks trouble in. Either is a potential source of war, in which, if it comes, the whole world must again be involved, to its incalculable disaster.

In safeguarding the powder magazines of the East, responsibility will inevitably rest upon the shoulders of China. Therefore the political, social, economic, and industrial development of China during the next twenty or thirty years will have a determining effect upon the peace situation of the world. A strong and prosperous China, co-operating with the major Powers of the West, could eliminate the danger to a very great extent if not entirely. It is to the mutual interest of the Allied Powers and of world peace in general that the Western Powers should co-operate with China, say for a period of fifty years, in the development of her natural resources; and for the coming twenty years, perhaps, in the work of her economic and social rehabilitation.

Before Western influence made inroads into China, her troubles for many centuries had come solely from Manchuria and the neighboring region known as Mongolia. When Japan became a world Power after the Sino-Japanese War, she contended with Tsarist Russia for control over that vast territory, a conflict which culminated in the Russo-Japanese War. Japan's scheme to use that part of China as a steppingstone to control of the whole country led to the Mukden Incident. If history since the downfall of the Tangs has taught us anything, we may be reasonably sure that the Three Eastern Provinces will still be a trouble center for China and a cause of worry to the world until China herself is strong and prosperous and the vast vacuum of Manchuria is filled.

In building up a modern democracy and industries China needs time and favorable conditions for experiment. These conditions are peace and security. Internal peace depends upon unification of the country. Security depends upon international understanding. China will have security only when Manchuria becomes a center of peace.

We shall have to start anew in creating our future by making that vast territory a focus of peace instead of war. In that important work I hope the world— especially America, Britain, and Soviet Russia—will co-operate with China. With their co-operation the task must be crowned by complete success, a blessing for China in particular and for the world generally.

In 1921 I was elected an unofficial observer to the Washington Conference by the Chamber of Commerce and educational associations in Shanghai, and supported by Dr. Sun Yat-sen's Nationalist government in Canton. In the following year, 1922, I went to Europe for a visit to the source of modern civilization. It was very soon after the first World War. One could see that every country in Europe was busy planning postwar rehabilitation and the major victorious Powers were occupied in trying to make peace more enduring. But no one seemed to realize then that they were all helping to sow the seeds of a next war.

France was tired and longed for a permanent peace. Her eyes looked over the Rhine, whence came the danger to her national existence. Her defensive mood was later embodied in the Maginot Line, which she thought would make her immune to German attack. Like the first emperor of the Chin Dynasty (246-207 B.C.) who built the Great Wall to defend China from the attack of the Tartars, France built the Maginot Line. And as trouble for the empire of the Chins came not from outside but from inside the Great Wall, so it was with the French Republic and her "impregnable" barrier.

England was busy with the economic reconstruction of Europe and endeavoring to maintain the balance of power on the Continent. Germany, defeated, was licking her wounds. Tsarist Russia was utterly ruined and a new political experiment was under way in that gigantic Republic of Soviet Russia.

Such was the political aspect of Europe after World War I.

America, unwilling to pull European chestnuts out of the fire, had withdrawn from that much-troubled continent and summoned the Washington Conference, at which the Nine-Power Treaty was penned, the Anglo-Japanese Alliance superseded, and the Shantung question settled; this, to save Japan's face, was negotiated outside the conference. The Twenty-One Demands, superseded by the new treaty, were thus unostentatiously sent to the grave. Tsingtao, a seaport in the peninsula of Shantung, had been awarded to Japan at Versailles and the complications which grew out of the award were known as the Shantung question. Indignation at this move gave rise in China to the student movement which had such far-reaching repercussions in Sino-Japanese relations, as well as in political and cultural developments in China, during the following twenty years. In America it troubled public men who had sympathy for China and became a knotty political problem. Both the Republican and Democratic parties more or less committed themselves to right the wrongs done to China by the ill-fated Versailles Treaty; thus while America withdrew her fingers from Europe she dipped them deep into Pacific waters. The result, twenty years later, was Pearl Harbor.

Without the active participation of America in the League of Nations of which she was the author; with a defensive psychology on the part of France, whose only desire was to avoid trouble; and with Britain's main interest focused on maintaining the balance of power on the Continent, the League became toothless. It barked a lot but never meant to bite. Yet any problem that member nations could not handle among themselves was handed over to the League. So it became a dumping ground for international difficulties. When China was unable to meet her difficulties vis-à-vis Manchurian problems she, too, dumped them on the League, of which Japan was a member. In the ease of the Mukden Incident France was not interested. Britain was concerned only so far as the balance of power in the Far East was involved, but she was afraid of being drawn in. The League, therefore, had scarcely even the nerve to bark at Japan. Its few mild yelps might indeed be construed as connivance.

The League, however, made an invaluable contribution to our experience. Learning from its failures, the world may profit in planning the coming peace.

Born of American idealism, it died of conflicting interests and the ambitions of member nations, especially the major Powers.

So matters developed in the course of some twenty years after the Versailles Treaty. The seeds of war sown at Versailles grew in every corner of the world like weeds, which eventually caught fire and set the whole world aflame.

But politics are but a passing show destined soon to vanish into history. What will always remain is the fundamental problem of culture. It is undeniable that Europe has produced modern science and organized democracy, which have brought to mankind more blessings than evils.

Germany appeared to me a country of telescopes, microscopes, and test tubes; her inventions and discoveries multiplied by leaps and bounds. In Shanghai foreign manufactures of superlative quality became known as Jahming huo—"German goods." The Germans were masters of material things but fell short in human relations. This, as I see it, is why they often got into trouble in dealing with other nations. Their sight was focused through the microscope or the telescope, which concentrated their view either too near or too far to perceive human behavior or feelings. They could not very well put international relations or human feelings into a test tube to observe their reactions. In the broader realm of human activities the Germans often failed to grasp the essentials or shortcomings of human nature. They had highly developed special senses in which other nations did not excel, but they were short of common sense. Their special endowments gave them the scientific thoroughness which has made so many special contributions to the world, and their lack of common sense brought misery alike to their own country and to others.

The British were just the opposite. They were a nation of common sense and masters of human relations. Their views on world affairs and policies relative to them were flexible and adaptable. They never let the cord stretch to the point of breaking. If a stronger force pulled at the other end of the rope, the British would loosen it a little to save it from snapping. If the other side was weaker they would keep on drawing the cord to themselves until it slipped from their opponents' hands. But the British would never let go their end of the rope—they would stick to the last, irrespective of consequences. In relations with other countries and in colonial policies this trait of the British people was seen everywhere.

Hand in hand with flexibility and adaptability went such other British traits as tolerance, moderation, considerateness, fair play, and an attitude of compromise. They never went to extremes in their views, and were always trying to understand other people's view in order either to bring themselves to it or to bring others to their own. They loved freedom of speech and thought, disliked hard and fast rules which might prove unadjustable to varying conditions.

The British are reserved to the point of brutal coolness, a trait disliked by other peoples and often the cause of suspicion. It has lost the British many a friend among other nations. But when you know them better, or rather when they know you better, you want to make friends with them.

Some or all of these traits together made English democracy possible. For democracy is not something abstract, something that has dropped from the sky. It consists of the best traits there are in the people who have succeeded in it. If you run through the constitutional history of England, you will find that intolerance, persecutions, corruption, and cruelties fill its pages. Quite a number of lives, including that of a king, have been sacrificed to democracy. The experience of English democracy is worth our serious study.

One fact, however, we must bear in mind: that English democracy grew fast after the unification of the United Kingdom, and American democracy, too, developed by leaps and bounds only after the Civil War. History teaches us that unification and security must go hand in hand to make an organized democracy. For England was lucky in that her islands were small and protected by the sea. In the old days invasion was not easy. So the English enjoyed security and therefore had plenty of time for trial and error. Their national existence was not endangered by foreign invasion during the period of incubation and experiment.

A similar situation existed in America. The North American Continent is itself a gigantic island, the seas around it preventing any formidable invasion. The early colonists from England brought with them seeds of the love of freedom which grew into a great tree of liberty, sheltered from the ax of foreign invaders. In the course of a century or so the democracy of America took firm root. Not only was experiment freely made in human relations but also in things material, by which I mean scientific research. While American democracy grew out of the English model, American science owed a great debt to the Germans.

The American system of higher education is a combination of the English college and the German university; the American academic dress is, so to speak, an English gown with a German cap. In the American colleges boys and girls lived in a spirit of comradeship and free association and secured a liberal foundation of learning. Knowledge was not strictly regimented; human relationships were learned through free mingling of the strident body; the sight of the younger generation was not simply narrowed into telescopes, microscopes, or test tubes; a general culture was furnished to all those who cared to absorb it.

In the university proper, or the graduate school, American students were taught methods of research, German thoroughness was admired and encouraged, but its full realization had yet to be achieved at the time of my college days. During the First World War the five colors of the former Chinese flag—red, yellow, blue, white, and black were reduced to two: black and white. The reason was that German dyes were no longer available in China on account of the war. An American chemist in New York told me that in Germany several specialists worked on one color, whereas in America one chemist dealt with many colors. This was some twenty years ago. Conditions have changed by now, since Americans have acquired so much of the German t horoughness during the last two or three decades.

Thus on the American side of the water English democracy and German science have gone hand in hand. With her rich natural resources, her power of organization and love of great projects, America may now easily be ranked as first of the democracies of the world. Just the other day at a party in the American Embassy in Chungking, a British diplomat remarked to me that "England is Americanized, Russia is Americanized, and China is Americanized."

"In what way is England Americanized?" I asked.

"Hollywood, for example," was the reply.

"Russia—in the sense of great industries?"

"Yes."

Meanwhile flashes of pictures passed rapidly through my mind, in which I saw that Chinese political and educational systems, social changes, and industrial developments were richly tinged with Americanization. At the same time I was not unaware of the fact that China colors all the sea that washes her shores.

Pointing at the six rows of eight stars each on the American flag, the same diplomat turned to a high-ranking American military officer standing by and asked with a touch of humor, "What are you going to do when you add one state more?"

"Well, we'll make it seven rows of seven, but what new state do you have in mind?"

"England," replied the diplomat. We all laughed. It was only a joke, but in jokes one may see the temper of the times.

In days of old, when the West fought for colonial empire in the East, all the important Western Powers except America at various times wronged China. Even Portugal bit off a tiny piece of land called Macao, in the province of Kwangtung. The only thing America got from China was extraterritoriality, but what she has done for China is far more and will be remembered for generations to come. As everybody knows this, I need not elaborate here. Now both America and Britain have abolished that system and Britain has returned all the settlements, which were an anachronism—though Hong Kong remains in British hands. In spite of terrible wars all over the world, much encouraging light has shone through the international clouds. Let us hope that, with victory achieved, it may grow into brilliant sunshine in a cloudless sky.

America has definitely joined the coming international peace organization. She has fought the war. She is to fight for an enduring peace. A new epoch in history is in the making. The combined resources of America, Britain, Soviet Russia, and China are so great that if they desire peace, with an effective world organization backed up by an international defense force to enforce it, peace will indeed be enduring.

For China's part, she will have to redouble her effort of reconstruction and regeneration for the coming twenty or probably thirty years. This will be a critical period for China. Success depends upon foresight and leadership, and the extent to which our Allies will co-operate. The extent to which co- operation is given will also depend upon our political developments and how sound a policy we adopt regarding international investments. Our difficulties are enhanced by the devastations of war and wanton destruction in all the once-prosperous provinces where the heel of the enemy has trodden.

On the other hand, China has a double duty to perform. First, it is her duty to herself to become strong and prosperous. Second, it is her duty to the world to help make world peace secure. In the political philosophy of the Confucian school, peace for the world is the ultimate aim. On the basis of the Confucian philosophy

Dr. Sun Yat-sen aimed at world peace in his Three Principles of the People.

If we can bridge over this critical period of twenty or thirty years the momentum thus gathered will carry reforms and reconstruction forward, ever increasing and ever widening, into a glorious future in which China will be in a position to help the world in assuring a more permanent peace.

From the West China has still much to learn. Ever since the downfall of the great dynasty of the Tangs she has been overrun from time to time by peoples from the immense outlying territories of Asia. The decline of Chinese civilization after the fall of that dynasty was due to the invasion of barbarians who at intermittent periods devastated the country and turned it into a stretch of ruins. The successive invasions, together with famine, disease, and internal dissensions, sapped the energy of the Chinese people and thus weakened their creative power. When Western influence began to come into China, therefore, she met it with her civilization at the lowest ebb.

People in China now talk of the Tang civilization as if in hopes of restoring the glories of that era. It is a good thing, so far as we can, to draw inspiration from the Tangs and be stimulated by their more humanistic civilization as contrasted with the ascetic type of the later Sungs. In Tang paintings we admire the strong physique of the people. Music, dancing, poetry, painting, and calligraphy were developed to a very high level, which finds no equal in later days.

But for China to go back to this brilliant period of her history is next to impossible. For centuries we have tried to recover our past glories, yet our civilization slid progressively downward in steady decline. For conditions had changed. The fertile soil in which the Tang civilization grew had been washed away by the tides of long years of devastation. If, however, we can get rid of the cause of the Tang downfall by learning from such modern Tangs as America and other countries where arts, science, political and military organization, health and wealth, are on a very high plane, we shall then perhaps find the glories of the Tangs redescending upon us.

In making the peace China's part will be by no means small. Throughout her history she has had many wars. But they have been wars more in the nature of internal revolution than external aggression—internal conflicts generally caused by the rebellion of oppressed farmers and suffering people against a rotten officialdom. Even her external wars have been more defensive than offensive in nature. China has been oppressed much more than oppressing. Ever since the time of the first emperor of the Chin Dynasty who built the Great Wall—symbol of a defensive mentality—China has wished to be let alone.

Confucius' teaching of proper human relations and world peace, and the democratic ideas of Mencius, will fit China to be a modern democratic state which wishes to do no wrong to other peoples. What China must emphasize after the war is modern science with its applications to means of production; and democracy in its organized form, with emphasis upon unification of the country. Science and democracy, twin instruments of a progressive modern state, is the key to power, prosperity, and a more lasting peace.

With the practical wisdom of her people, in its special emphasis on human relations and democratic ways of living and thinking, China has the solid foundation for a modern democracy. As we have seen, her democracy is loosely organized. Her intense love of individual liberty has not kept step with modern social consciousness. Strong family ties have been partly responsible for retarding the organization of individuals into a broader society. But these ties are rapidly loosening; modern institutions have appeared in the larger cities, and further industrialization will mean a further loosening of family bonds and socialization of individuals.

In the field of knowledge China's way of looking at things has given her a practical wisdom but made her neglect the importance of generalization and abstraction. Her love of nature in poetic, artistic, and moral ways has given her breadth of mind, as exemplified by great scholars and statesmen, and a harmony of feeling, as revealed in the arts and in conduct; it has not extended to the investigation of natural laws, which are the indispensable weapon of man in controlling nature. With the assimilating power of Chinese civilization, the Western contribution of science will be absorbed in due course of time, and with the rich natural resources of the country and high intelligence of her people, the integration of science into her life will open up wonderful opportunities in the future. Chinese morals and arts will prosper in the material wealth thus developed, while Chinese thought and the rich store of literature and philosophy will tend to be clarified and systematized by modern logical and scientific ways of thinking.

On this new basis of initial peace and prosperity, China will be in a position to build up a new defense force to preserve and sustain peace. No country would be a worthy partner for peace that was not a worthy partner for war. The attention of the world has already been drawn to China by the contribution she has made to the world in a war of resistance for eight long years, in spite of weaknesses and shortcomings in some aspects of her national life during the war.

Modern science, with special reference to inventions and industry, will fuse with China's rich treasures of art and sound morals. A new civilization is in the making; perhaps it, too, can contribute to the world's progress.